A

Lydia Maria Child

Reader

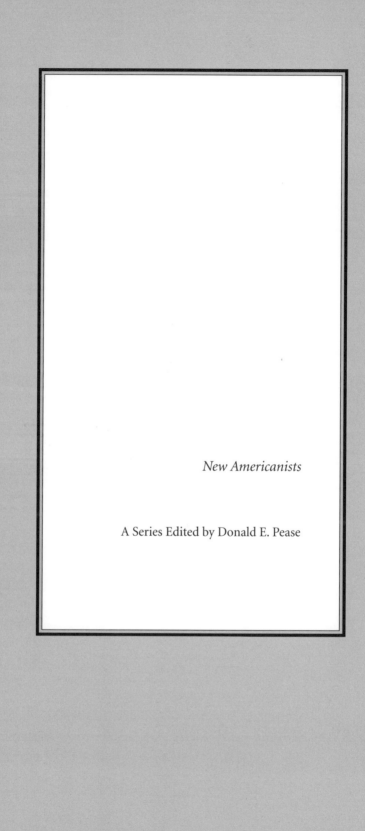

New Americanists

A Series Edited by Donald E. Pease

A
Lydia Maria Child
Reader

Carolyn L. Karcher, Editor

Duke University Press

Durham & London

1997

© 1997 Duke University Press

All rights reserved

Printed in the United States of America on acid-free paper ∞

Typeset in Minion by Keystone Typesetting, Inc.

Library of Congress Cataloging-in-Publication Data appear

on the last printed page of this book.

Contents

To

Martin

Acknowledgments

In dedicating this collection of Lydia Maria Child's writings to my husband, Martin, who has lived with her as long and almost as intensely as I have, I both acknowledge the unstinting support he has always given my work and express admiration for the courage and idealism he has shown in his own work.

H. Bruce Franklin first suggested reprinting Child's writings when I started research on my biography of her in 1982. I am especially grateful for his helpful criticisms of the introductions to the volume as a whole and to part 3, "Slavery, Race, and Reconstruction." The manuscript benefited even further from the rigorous criticisms of Jeannie Pfaelzer, Andrea Kerr, and Thorell Tsomondo, members of my Washington writers' group.

The extraordinary generosity and astute advice of the two scholars who read the manuscript for Duke University Press—Sterling Stuckey and William Cain—proved instrumental in enabling me to choose the selections and present them in the format best suited for classroom use. Both read through more than six hundred pages of proposed texts in addition to the introductory material. Their many invaluable suggestions are reflected in the table of contents and introductions, and William Cain in particular may take credit for the inclusion of the annotations, bibliography, and index.

All scholars working on Child owe a debt to Milton Meltzer and Patricia G. Holland, whose splendid collection of her letters laid the groundwork for future research and made available in microfiche several of the texts reproduced in this volume. Milton Meltzer himself originally contemplated editing a collection of Child's writings and generously shared his prospectus for it with me fourteen years ago.

Without the aid of Clark Evans in the Library of Congress's Rare Book Room; two valiant research assistants at Temple University, Noreen Groover Lape and Clare Cotugno; and a superlative typist, Lydia Maningas, this book would never have made it to press. Clark personally photocopied for me all the texts from the Rare Book Room's holdings. Noreen undertook the onerous task of photocopying all of Child's newspaper articles from microfilm. Clare's imaginative and indefatigable sleuthing tracked down quotations, identified obscure names and titles, saved me from embarrassing errors, and supplied the information that went into at least half the annotations. Lydia retyped the newspaper articles to provide readable text for the printer and assembled enlarged copies of all the documents.

Finally, I thank Reynolds Smith of Duke University Press for giving this project such enthusiastic support.

Introduction

✦ For half a century Lydia Maria Child (1802–80) was a household name in America, as familiar to the public then as her Thanksgiving song, "Over the river, and through the wood,/To grandfather's house we go," remains today. The famous antislavery agitator William Lloyd Garrison hailed Child as "the first woman in the republic." An African American correspondent of Garrison's newspaper, the *Liberator,* proposed enshrining her alongside John Brown in the pantheon of his people's white benefactors. The Radical Republican Senator Charles Sumner credited her with inspiring his career as an advocate of racial equality and sought her advice on Reconstruction policy. A newspaperman ranked her popular weekly column of the 1840s, "Letters from New-York," "almost at the head of journalism in America." The suffragist leader Elizabeth Cady Stanton cited Child's encyclopedic *History of the Condition of Women* (1835) as an invaluable resource for feminists in their battle against patriarchal ideology. Another feminist reformer, who had grown up reading Child's stories for young people, judged her children's magazine, *The Juvenile Miscellany* (1826–34), superior to any of its successors "in simplicity, directness, and moral influence." The transcendentalist theologian Theodore Parker pronounced Child's monumental *Progress of Religious Ideas* (1855) "*the* book of the age; and written by a *woman!*" Edgar Allan Poe praised her novel *Philothea* (1836) as "an honor to our country, and a signal triumph for our country-women." The *National Anti-Slavery Standard* proclaimed her *Romance of the Republic* (1867) "one of the most thrilling books . . . ever written, involving the rights of the colored people—not excepting Uncle Tom's Cabin." And Child's earliest biographer, the abolitionist Thomas Wentworth Higginson, converted by her 1833 *Appeal in Favor of That Class of Americans Called Africans,* paid tribute to it as the "ablest" and most comprehensive antislavery book "ever printed in America." Tracing her "formative influence" on the activists of his generation back to the "intellectual provision" she had furnished them in their youth, he reminisced: "In those days she seemed to supply a sufficient literature for any family through her own unaided pen. Thence came novels for the parlor, cookery books for the kitchen, and the 'Juvenile Miscellany' for the nursery."[1]

---

1. [William Lloyd Garrison], "MRS. CHILD," *Genius of Universal Emancipation,* 20 Nov. 1829, p. 85; Samuel Jackson to LMC, "Letter from a Colored Man in Ohio to L. Maria Child,"

This litany barely begins to suggest the scope of Child's contributions to nineteenth-century American culture. Merely to total up her output—forty-seven books and tracts, enough uncollected fiction and journalism to fill up one or two more volumes, and more than two thousand surviving letters—is to recognize the magnitude of her achievement. Her professional career, which lasted some fifty-five years, spanned one of the most turbulent eras in American history and encompassed nearly all the intellectual and social movements of the time.

In the literary sphere alone, the variety and innovativeness of Child's work identify her as a trailblazer. She helped shape the American historical novel and the short story in the 1820s, just when these genres were emerging, and she specifically oriented them toward envisioning alternatives to racial conflict. Her stories of the 1840s and 1850s, which ranged in mode from science fiction to realism, also exposed the contradictions of the sexual double standard, entertaining the prospect of liberating both sexes from repressive taboos. Child heralded the birth of transcendentalism as well. Expressing the same belief in the reality of visionary experience and the illusoriness of the material world, *Philothea*, the mystical novel so admired by Poe, appeared a few weeks before Emerson's *Nature* (1836), the founding manifesto of transcendentalism. One young votary of transcendentalism, Henry David Thoreau, even copied two pages of extracts from *Philothea* into his notebook while a student at Harvard.[2] Likewise written in a transcendentalist vein,

---

Liberator 23 Dec. 1859; LMC to Charles Sumner, 7 July 1856, in *Lydia Maria Child: Selected Letters, 1817–1880*, ed. Milton Meltzer, Patricia G. Holland, and Francine Krasno (Amherst: U of Massachusetts P, 1982) 286 [hereafter *SL*]; "L. Maria Child," *Springfield Republican*, rpt. *Woman's Journal* 6 Nov. 1880, pp. 354–55; Elizabeth Cady Stanton, Susan B. Anthony, and Matilda Joslyn Gage, *History of Woman Suffrage*, vol. 1: 1848–1861 (1881; New York: Arno P, 1969) 38; Caroline Healey Dall, "Lydia Maria Child and Mary Russell Mitford," *Unitarian Review* 19 (June 1883): 525–26; Theodore Parker to LMC, 3 Nov. 1855, in *The Collected Correspondence of Lydia Maria Child, 1817–1880*, ed. Patricia G. Holland, Milton Meltzer, and Francine Krasno (Millwood, N.Y.: Kraus Microform, 1980) 31/888 [hereafter *CC*; the slash mark divides microfiche card number from letter number]; and LMC to J. Peter Lesley, 1 Jan. 1856 (misdated 1855), *SL* 271; [Edgar Allan Poe], Review of *Philothea*, *Southern Literary Messenger* 2 (Sept. 1836): 659–62; "The Standard," *National Anti-Slavery Standard* 20 June 1868, p. 3; Thomas Wentworth Higginson, "Lydia Maria Child" (1868), *The Writings of Thomas Wentworth Higginson*, vol. 2: *Contemporaries* (Boston: Houghton Mifflin, 1900) 108, 123.

2. Kenneth Cameron, *Philothea, or Plato Against Epicurus: A Novel of the Transcendental Movement in New England*, by Lydia Maria Child. *With an Analysis of Background and Meaning for the Community of Emerson and Thoreau* (Hartford, Conn.: Transcendental Books, 1975) 2–3, 135–36.

though adapted to readers of the *National Anti-Slavery Standard* and the *Boston Courier,* Child's "Letters from New-York" inaugurated a new genre, the journalistic sketch. In this newspaper column, Child publicized the plight of the urban poor; spoke out against capital punishment and the imprisonment of women for prostitution; called for prison reform, including humane treatment, rehabilitation programs, and job placement after release; and argued that only eliminating poverty could solve the problem of crime. In short, Child's fiction and journalism explored territory avoided by such writers as Cooper, Hawthorne, Poe, Emerson, and Thoreau, conjuring up possibilities they refused to acknowledge.

Child's work in a less appreciated department of letters was equally pioneering. She essentially created American children's literature, which she used as a vehicle for combating racial prejudice at a time when her rivals in the field steered clear of controversial topics. She also became a national authority on homemaking by writing the earliest domestic advice books to address the needs of low-income housewives and mothers, and the first to treat all aspects of child rearing, from infancy to adolescence: *The Frugal Housewife* (1829) and *The Mother's Book* (1831). When she returned to the domestic advice genre later in life with an anthology aimed at presenting positive images of old age—*Looking toward Sunset* (1865)—she anticipated the current flood of literature on and for the elderly.

Child further distinguished herself as a scholar who put her impressive research in the service of the reforms she advocated. Again anticipating late twentieth-century trends, her *History of the Condition of Women* covers every known race and ethnic group and devotes extended attention to Africans. Both the book itself and Child's courageous public stand against slavery, in defiance of proprieties barring women from the political sphere, helped inspire agitation for women's rights—a cause she supported for nearly forty years. The goal of counteracting bigotry similarly prompted Child to delve into the subject of comparative religion. *The Progress of Religious Ideas, through Successive Ages,* the massive study that won the accolade of Theodore Parker, highlights the merits of Hinduism and other non-Western religions denigrated as "heathen" and "idolatrous" by most of her contemporaries.

An activist as well as a woman of letters, Child played a key role in the main reform movements of her age. Besides campaigning for woman suffrage, she pushed for justice toward Indians throughout her life. The 1820s found her protesting against Cherokee removal, the 1860s denouncing the genocide of the Plains tribes and launching a new crusade with her impassioned *Appeal for the Indians* (1868). Unlike so many of her contemporaries, she refused to palliate the theft of Indian land and the extermination of Indians themselves with the comforting theory that the aboriginal was "*destined* to disappear before the white man."[3]

It was in the struggle against slavery, however, that Child left her greatest legacy as a writer, scholar, and reformer. No white abolitionist researched African cultures more exhaustively or dedicated her/himself more concertedly to refuting racist myths. Her *Appeal in Favor of That Class of Americans Called Africans* still speaks powerfully to readers today, providing an eloquent response to the pseudoscientists whose obsessive drive to prove the inferiority of the Negro keeps generating tomes of propaganda. Many of Child's other antislavery works remain equally modern in conception, notably the school reader she compiled for ex-slaves, *The Freedmen's Book* (1865), made up entirely of selections by or about people of African descent. The value of Child's legacy can be measured, on the one hand, by the changes she and her fellow abolitionists succeeded in bringing about—the abolition of slavery, the extension of civil and voting rights to African Americans, and the founding of black and integrated educational institutions—and, on the other hand, by the continuing relevance of the issues she tackled.

Child's background sheds little light on what led to her remarkable career. Still, it does point toward factors that positioned her simultaneously as an insider and an outsider in her culture—a position that may account for both the authority she attained as a cultural spokesperson and the critical perspective she brought to bear on her society's ills. Her roots stretched back to the first settlers of Massachusetts, where her forebear, Richard Francis, had arrived in 1636; but the artisan stock from which the Francis family derived did not place her ancestors among New England's ruling elite. Her grandfather, Benjamin Francis, was a weaver, her father, Convers, a baker. Child's Massachusetts heritage also included her grandfather Benjamin's exploits at the Battle of Lexington, where he shot five redcoats. Nevertheless, fighting in the Revolution did not improve the Francis family's fortunes; a hardscrabble existence remained their lot.

Born on 11 February 1802 in Medford, Massachusetts, Lydia Francis (she had herself rebaptized Maria at nineteen because she disliked the name

---

3. *An Appeal for the Indians,* reprinted in this volume, 94; "Letter from L. Maria Child," *National Standard* 27 May 1871, p. 4, *CC* 75/1995a.

Lydia) learned precociously to depend on her own resources. The youngest of five surviving children, she grew up among "hard-working people, who had had small opportunity for culture,"[4] and whose round of daily chores kept them too busy to give her the emotional sustenance she craved. Convers Francis owned a family-operated bakery famous for producing Medford Crackers. Although he and his wife, Susannah Rand Francis, had built it into a thriving business before Lydia's birth, both had known severe poverty in their youth, and they never ceased practicing—or requiring of their children—the hard manual labor and rigid economy that they saw as the cornerstone of their prosperity. Overwork and constant childbearing fatally sapped Susannah's health even before she succumbed to the tuberculosis that killed her at age forty-eight, when Lydia was twelve years old. The emphasis on industriousness, frugality, and plain living remained with Child throughout her adulthood. She also retained other middle-class attitudes and values her parents inculcated: hatred of what she called "aristocracy" (or what we would now call elitism), contempt for the idle rich, determination to avoid debt at all costs, belief in the importance for men and women alike of being self-supporting, and faith in the power of the individual to overcome adversity and poverty if unimpeded by discriminatory laws.[5]

Child's parents transmitted to her as well a sense of obligation toward poorer neighbors and a vision of community that extended the bonds of family beyond blood kin. Every week they sent a Sunday dinner to their children's first teacher, the old, tobacco-chewing spinster Ma'am Betty, who held a "dame school" in her untidy bedroom. And every Thanksgiving eve they invited "all the humble friends of the household—'Ma'am Betty,' the washerwoman, the berry-woman, the wood-sawyer, the journeymen-bakers"—for a festive meal.[6] The example set by her parents influenced Child's concept of her mission as a reformer: "to help in the breaking down of classes, and to make *all* men feel as if they were brethren of the same family, sharing the same rights, the same capabilities, and the same responsibilities."[7]

4. LMC to John Weiss, 15 Apr. 1863, *SL* 425.

5. On the association of these values with the emergent middle class, see Isaac Kramnick, "Children's Literature and Bourgeois Ideology: Observations on Culture and Industrial Capitalism in the Later Eighteenth Century," *Culture and Politics: From Puritanism to the Enlightenment,* ed. Perez Zagorin (Berkeley: U of California P, 1980) 203–40; and Max Weber's classic study, *The Protestant Ethic and the Spirit of Capitalism,* trans. Talcott Parsons (1905, 1920; New York: Scribner's, 1958).

6. Higginson, "Lydia Maria Child" 112.

7. LMC to Lucy Osgood, 4 Feb. 1869, *SL* 484.

"*All* men" for Child included African Americans—a fact that differentiated her sharply from the majority of her contemporaries but once again reflected her parents' values. Convers Francis "detested slavery" and may have participated in the rescue of an escaped slave named Caesar in 1805, which had earned Medford the honor of being the first American town to shield a fugitive against recapture.[8] He and Susannah seem to have told their daughter some of the anecdotes about slavery in Massachusetts that later found their way into her abolitionist tracts. Long afterward Child would describe the class to which her parents belonged—small "farmers and mechanics [artisans], who work[ed] with their *hands*" and owned their own homes—as the backbone of the antislavery movement.[9] She would describe New England's ruling elites, by contrast, as the movement's bitterest enemies outside the South. Child's class position may thus have facilitated her entry into abolitionist ranks and prompted her to envisage an alliance between native-born white working people and slaves (though it also exacerbated her tendency to scapegoat the proletariat made up of Irish immigrants). Neither class origin nor family influence suffices to explain the road Child took, however, for none of her siblings shared her ardent abolitionist sympathies, and many of her closest abolitionist friends came from wealthy mercantile families of the ilk Child despised.

If Child's parents fostered the egalitarian convictions and identification with working people that characterized her as a reformer, they did nothing to cultivate her intellect. The Francis household contained few books, and Mr. Francis actively discouraged his daughter from reading. He continued to harbor a "violent prejudice against literature" and "taste" even after his daughter had earned a name for herself as a novelist.[10]

Child's first intellectual mentor was her brother Convers, six years her senior. Unlike their parents and three elder siblings, the younger Convers and Lydia cherished a "passion for books."[11] Indeed, Child credited her brother with inspiring her literary bent. He passed his schoolbooks on to her and directed her reading of the English literary classics: Shakespeare, Milton,

8. John Weiss, *Discourse Occasioned by the Death of Convers Francis, D.D., Delivered before the First Congregational Society, Watertown, April 19, 1863* (Cambridge, Mass.: Privately printed, 1863) 62–63.

9. See LMC to Sarah Shaw, 25 Aug. 1877, *SL* 544; "Through the Red Sea, into the Wilderness," reprinted in this volume; and *A Romance of the Republic* 293–94, 319–24, 336–39.

10. LMC to Louisa Loring, 19 July 1840 and 17 Feb. 1841, *CC* 8/209, 9/226.

11. LMC to John Weiss, 15 Apr. 1863, *SL* 425–26.

Samuel Johnson, Joseph Addison, Edward Gibbon, and Sir Walter Scott. When she set about writing the historical fiction through which she rose to fame, he procured manuscripts and books for her from libraries barred to women. It was in Convers's study that Child wrote her first novel, *Hobomok, A Tale of Early Times* (1824). While the novel was gestating in her imagination, Convers also introduced her to Ralph Waldo Emerson, with whom he went on to found the Transcendental Club in 1836.

Yet far from setting his sister on the path toward radical reform, Convers, a Unitarian clergyman, exhibited the constitutional timidity of a minister dependent for his salary on his parishioners' approval. He counseled prudence and moderation when Child publicly espoused abolitionism in 1833, and he waited until the cause became respectable before endorsing it. Not Convers's mentorship, but the disparity between the encouragement of his ambitions and the stifling of hers, sparked the rebellion against injustice that would turn her into a fighter for universal equality. Although both children displayed striking intellectual potential, only Convers's gifts won the attention of Medford's notables, the Congregational minister and the town physician, who joined in persuading Mr. Francis to send his son to Harvard. Instead, Lydia's formal education, confined to Medford's public school and a year at its ladies' academy, stopped at age thirteen; "alarmed at her increasing fondness for books,"[12] her father sent the motherless adolescent to her married sister, Mary Francis Preston, in Norridgewock, Maine (then a province of Massachusetts), to be schooled in the domestic arts befitting a woman.

The experience of being denied the education lavished on her brother sowed the seeds of a feminist consciousness in Child, just as it did in two women's rights leaders of the 1830s and 1840s who acknowledged her as a forerunner—Sarah Grimké and Elizabeth Cady Stanton. Equally formative, the experience of being forced to make her own education liberated Child from dependency on the authority of the conservative professors who dominated the universities and vocally opposed the radical reforms she would later promote. As early as age fifteen, she was drawing unorthodox conclusions from the books she read without professorial instruction. "[D]on't you think that Milton asserts the superiority of his own sex in rather too lordly a manner?" she wrote to Convers from Maine in her first surviving letter. For proof, she cited Eve's address to Adam:

12. Quoted in Anna D. Hallowell, "Lydia Maria Child," *Medford Historical Register* 3 (July 1900): 97.

My author and disposer, what thou bid'st
Unargu'd I obey; so God ordained.
God is thy law, thou mine: to know no more
Is woman's happiest knowledge, and her praise.

She did not back down when Convers pronounced her interpretation wrong.[13]

Teaching her to question social practices that privileged men over women, Child's sense of being unfairly relegated to an inferior education because of her sex once again positioned her simultaneously as an insider and an outsider in her culture. Her resentment of such gender discrimination no doubt predisposed her to identify with other victims of injustice, reinforcing whatever lessons she may have learned from her parents about human brotherhood.

Child's six-year sojourn on the Maine frontier (1815–21) added yet another element to the dual identity as insider and outsider that marked her as a writer and reformer. While removing her quite literally to the outskirts of New England society, it also transplanted her to a settlement that lacked the rigid class structure of her hometown—a settlement where she derived her social standing not from her father, the baker, but from her brother-in-law, the lawer and future county probate judge, Warren Preston. At the same time, Norridgewock exposed Child to a culture outside the Anglo-American orbit and aroused her sympathy for Maine's dispossessed and impoverished Indians, the first of the many oppressed peoples she would champion. Named for an Abenaki hamlet razed in a massacre of 1724, Norridgewock had founded its prosperity on genocide. A few Abenaki and Penobscot families still lived in the surrounding hemlock forests, and Child visited their camps often. She listened to their traditional stories, watched them weave and dye baskets, observed some of their ceremonies, admired the "athletic" bodies of the young Penobscot men, and enviously noted how much more physical freedom the "vigorous" Penobscot women seemed to enjoy than their Anglo-American sisters, constrained by "false education and enfeebling habits." She also compared Abenaki accounts of the Norridgewock massacre with the versions she heard from the town's white settlers.[14] Reflected in works as

13. LMC to Convers Francis, 5 June and September 1817, *Letters of Lydia Maria Child with a Biographical Introduction by John G. Whittier and an Appendix by Wendell Phillips*, [ed. Harriet Winslow Sewall] (1882; New York: Negro Universities P, 1969) 1–2 (*Paradise Lost* as quoted by LMC).

14. See Child's reminiscences in "The Indian Boy," *Juvenile Miscellany* 2 (May 1827): 31; "Physical Strength of Women," *The Woman's Journal* 15 Mar. 1873, p. 84; and *Letters from New*

diverse as *Hobomok,* "The Church in the Wilderness," *Juvenile Miscellany's* many Indian tales, *An Appeal for the Indians,* and *The History of the Condition of Women,* Child's contacts with Indians probably contributed more than anything else to firing her literary imagination and developing her cross-cultural perspective as a reformer.

Child left Maine in 1821 after a brief stint as a schoolteacher, and rejoined her brother Convers in Watertown, Massachusetts, where he had taken over the pulpit of the First Unitarian Church. Three years later, at age twenty-two, she found her literary vocation. Leafing through an old volume of the *North American Review* in her brother's study, she came across an article that called on American writers to exploit the resources they had at hand for creating a national literature: the sagas of Puritan pioneers and Indian warriors and the grandeur of the American wilderness. Her ambition sparked, Child "siezed [*sic*] a pen" and wrote the opening chapter of *Hobomok.*[15]

Although it reveals only a rudimentary political awareness, *Hobomok* uncannily predicts Child's career as a reformer and anticipates many of the causes she would espouse: justice for Indians; protest against antimiscegenation laws and other forms of racial discrimination; women's rights; religious toleration. By allowing her Puritan heroine to marry an Indian, live with him for three years, and bear him a son; by reintegrating both mother and son into Puritan society; and by hinting that intermarriage and assimilation would continue in subsequent generations, Child also provided a paradigm of race relations that differed radically from James Fenimore Cooper's. When Cooper rejected interracial marriage in *The Last of the Mohicans* (1826) and *The Wept of Wish-ton-Wish* (1829), he may well have been countering the threat *Hobomok* posed.

Child's reviewers condemned her interracial marriage plot as "unnatural" and "revolting . . . to every feeling of delicacy in man or woman," but they recognized her literary promise.[16] Thanks in part to Convers's ties with the Harvard intelligentsia—ties Child eagerly cultivated—the arbiters of the literary world began inviting Child to their salons. Meanwhile, she followed up

York [*First Series*] (1843; New York: Books for Libraries P, 1970) 29. Child's description of an Indian wedding ceremony in *Hobomok* also appears to be based on personal observation. Both "The Church in the Wilderness," reprinted in this volume, and "The Adventures of a Bell" (*Juvenile Miscellany* 2 [March 1827]: 24–30) contrast Abenaki, French, and English perspectives on the Norridgewock massacre.

15. LMC to Rufus Wilmot Griswold, [October? 1846?], *SL* 232.

16. Review of *Hobomok, North American Review* 19 (July 1824): 263; [Jared Sparks], "Recent American Novels," *North American Review* 21 (July 1825): 87, 90.

her success by publishing a patriotic children's book, *Evenings in New England* (1824), and a second historical novel, *The Rebels, or Boston before the Revolution* (1825). Laced with political rhetoric, including an imaginary speech by the Revolutionary hero James Otis that generations of schoolboys memorized as an authentic example of patriotic oratory, *The Rebels* exhibits the polemical talents later evident in Child's antislavery tracts.

The novel's command of political discourse attracted the attention of its most enthusiastic reviewer, David Lee Child, editor of the *Massachusetts Journal,* a proto-Whig newspaper sponsored by Daniel Webster and John Quincy Adams. "If *James Otis* spoke in this fashion, the wonder is that the Revolution did not begin sooner," he cheered. Introduced to Lydia Maria Francis in December 1824, David seems to have fallen in love with her through her novels. "It has been said that personal beauty is a good letter of recommendation," he wrote in his review of *The Rebels.* "We will add that a work, whose title page discloses the fact that the author has previously written a tale so beautiful as 'Hobomok,' needs no letter of recommendation from anyone."[17]

In many respects the two were ideally matched. David, too, came from a family of plain "farmers and mechanics, who work with their *hands*"[18]—the stock Child identified as the core of the middle class (his father eked out a precarious living on a small farm in West Boylston, Massachusetts). He shared with his future brother-in-law, Convers Francis, the distinction of having earned admission to Harvard purely on the strength of his intellectual gifts. More important, he shared with his future bride a commitment to the egalitarian ideals of the American Revolution, an abhorrence of injustice, a sense of solidarity with people of color, a rare freedom from racial prejudice, and a tendency toward religious iconoclasm. He also respected the rights of women.

Counterbalancing David's high ideals, unfortunately, were character defects that would dog the Childs' marriage: a tendency to flit from one enthusiasm to another, a resistance to completing the projects he undertook, an inability to keep track of money, an addiction to grandiose (and dubious) financial schemes, and a habit of borrowing recklessly and failing to repay his debts. These propensities had already checkered his career: in his early thirties, he was making his third vocational debut and not yet earning a steady

17. "New Historical Novel," *Massachusetts Journal* 3 Jan. 1826: 1. This was the inaugural issue of the paper. I use the term proto-Whig because the party then went by the name National Republican.

18. LMC to Sarah Shaw, 25 Aug. 1877, *SL* 544.

income. Perhaps because his prospects were still uncertain, he did not propose marriage until October 1827.

In the interim, Child[19] assiduously pursued her literary career. Describing the exhilaration of that period, when she was just spreading her wings, she recalled the "fiery charm" of "[r]estless, insatiable ambition," boundless hopes, and gushing creativity. It had then seemed impossible to "*avoid* being intellectually great," impossible to keep from writing: "the mind is a full fountain that *will* overflow—and if the waters sparkle as they fall, it is from their own impetuous abundance."[20]

Conveniently, Child's brimming energies found two new outlets in 1826: annual gift books seeking short fiction, and publishers seeking to start a children's magazine, which the author of *Evenings in New England* seemed ideally qualified to design and edit. She took full advantage of both opportunities. While her stories for *The Token, The Atlantic Souvenir,* and *The Legendary*—among them "The Lone Indian," "The Indian Wife," "The Church in the Wilderness," and "Chocorua's Curse"—enhanced her literary reputation, *The Juvenile Miscellany,* which Child founded in September 1826 and edited for eight years, elevated her to the status of a cultural authority and redoubled her popularity. Reporting to her sister Mary that the *Miscellany*'s subscription list had shot up to 850 names within four months, Child boasted: "It seems as if the public was resolved to give me a flourish of trumpets, let me write what I will. . . . Valuable gifts, jewels, beautiful dresses pour in upon me, invitations beyond acceptance, admiring letters from all parts of the country."[21] As these enthusiastic tributes indicate, the *Miscellany* filled a vital cultural need at just the right moment.

Child quickly turned the magazine into a sophisticated professional enterprise, enlisting a network of contributors that featured such luminaries as Lydia Huntley Sigourney, Sarah Josepha Hale, and Catharine Maria Sedgwick. It was Sedgwick whom Child most prized. The older writer had thrilled Child by sending her an endorsed copy of *Hope Leslie* (1827)—a gesture that implicitly acknowledged Child's *Hobomok* as an inspiration—and Child had praised it extravagantly without being able to say "*half* of what I felt." Sedg-

19. To avoid confusion, I will refer to Lydia Maria Child as Child and to David Lee Child as David.

20. "The First and Last Book," *The Coronal. A Collection of Miscellaneous Pieces, Written at Various Times* (Boston: Carter and Hendee, 1832) 282–83.

21. LMC to Mary Francis Preston, [1826], *CC* 1/22, as quoted in Hallowell, "Lydia Maria Child" 101.

wick offered Child the role model she had long yearned for. "It is one perpetual wish to *think,* and *write,* and *be,* like you. If ever I devote what intellectual faculties I have to a lofty and useful purpose, much, much, my dear Miss Sedgwick, will be owing to your salutary influence," she confided to her idol.[22] She also dedicated her first collection of short stories, *The Coronal* (1831), "To the Author of Hope Leslie," inscribing herself "a sincere admirer of her pure and beautiful writings."

Simultaneously, Child herself was serving as a role model to the teen-aged Margaret Fuller, whom she met in the summer of 1825. "She is a natural person,—a most rare thing in this age of cant and pretension. Her conversation is charming," enthused Fuller, who would eventually become famous for her own "Conversations."[23] A portrait of Child by Francis Alexander, painted in 1826, captures the "glow and enthusiasm" that the dark-haired, dark-eyed author of *Hobomok* exuded. Yet it reveals as well a hint of defiance in the eyes, mouth, and chin that another female acquaintance, Mary Peabody, sister of Sophia Peabody Hawthorne, caught. "I can compare the expression of her face to nothing but a tiger," wrote Peabody.[24] The look of tigerish defiance would deepen with the years, as Child's battles with racist opponents etched lines into her face.

Battles with less worthy foes—the debts David Child accumulated through mismanagement and the libel suits his pugnacious editorial style provoked—began shortly after the couple's marriage in October 1828. It was to meet the first of many financial emergencies that Child published *The Frugal Housewife* in 1829. Its runaway success—six thousand copies sold the first year—no doubt persuaded Child to shift her energies from fiction to domestic advice books.

At the same time, Child was also undergoing an initiation into politics. From the start, David and Maria Child defined their relationship as a political partnership. Each influenced the other—David teaching his wife the craft of journalism and encouraging her to drop the guise of fiction and to address

22. LMC to Catharine Maria Sedgwick, 28 Aug. [1827], Catharine Maria Sedgwick Papers, Part III, Massachusetts Historical Society (not in *CC*). I am indebted to Catherine Tuggle and her splendid exhibition at the Daughters of the American Revolution Museum, Washington, D.C., "Talking Radicalism in a Greenhouse," for bringing this and other letters between Child and Sedgwick to my attention.

23. Margaret Fuller to Susan Prescott, 10 Jan. 1827, *The Letters of Margaret Fuller,* ed. Robert N. Hudspeth, 6 vols. (Ithaca: Cornell UP, 1983–94) 1: 154.

24. LMC to Mary Francis Preston, [1826], *CC* 1/21, as quoted in Hallowell, "Lydia Maria Child" 101; Mary T. Peabody to Miss Rawlins Pickman, 16 Apr. 1826, Massachusetts Historical Society, Horace Mann II Papers. I am grateful to Megan Marshall for sharing this letter with me.

political issues openly, Maria directing her husband's attention to the wrongs done to the Indians. Together they crusaded in 1828–31 against a scheme to remove the Cherokee from their ancestral land. Child's contributions went unnoticed by the Cherokee because they took a traditionally feminine form and were published anonymously: a children's book, *The First Settlers of New-England* (1829), "by a lady of Massachusetts," and a handful of stories about Indians, "by the author of Hobomok." But David's militant editorial championship of Cherokee rights won him a personal letter of thanks from Chief John Ross in 1831.[25]

By late 1830 both Childs were gravitating toward the radical abolitionism of William Lloyd Garrison, who had worked briefly for David as a journeyman printer on the *Massachusetts Journal* in 1828. David not only defended Garrison in the columns of the *Massachusetts Journal* when the young abolitionist editor was imprisoned for libel in 1830; he also expressed his sympathy for the slave rebellion led by Nat Turner in September 1831, which cost the lives of fifty-five slaveholding whites. "[W]e will never swerve from the principle that the oppressed and enslaved of every country, Hayti and Virginia as well as France and Poland, have a right to assert their 'natural and unalienable rights' whenever and wherever they can do it," he declared editorially.[26] His tract *The Despotism of Freedom; or the Tyranny and Cruelty of American Republican Slave-Masters, Shown to be the Worst in the World* (Jan. 1833) provided "the best and fullest exposition" of radical antislavery principles before Maria Child published her more encompassing *Appeal in Favor of That Class of Americans Called Africans* eight months later.[27]

With the *Appeal,* Child eclipsed David as an antislavery propagandist. Reviewers in the abolitionist press hailed the book's "extensive research," "forcible, conclusive reasoning," "flashes of wit," and stylistic elegance. In contrast, they criticized David's style as "not what would be called easy, flowing and elegant."[28] The couple's reversal of roles—which followed the collapse of David's *Massachusetts Journal* in 1832—seems to have undermined David's self-esteem and added to the strains on the Childs' marriage.

The most immediate impact that the *Appeal*'s notoriety had on the cou-

25. J[oh]n Ross to David Lee Child, 11 Feb. 1831, Lydia Maria Child Scrapbook, Schlesinger Library, Cambridge, Mass.

26. "*Insurrection in Virginia,*" *Massachusetts Journal,* rpt. *Liberator* 10 Sept. 1831, pp. 146–47.

27. John Greenleaf Whittier and William Lloyd Garrison to LMC, 23 Sept. and 25 Oct. 1874, CC 83/2180, 2191.

28. "Mrs. Child's 'Appeal,'" *Unionist,* rpt. *Liberator* 14 Dec. 1833: 200; "Speech of David Lee Child, Esq.," *New-England Telegraph,* rpt. *Liberator* 4 Jan. 1834, 1.

ple, however, was to destroy Child's literary career and thus jeopardize the household's only source of income. *The Juvenile Miscellany* folded, *The Mother's Book* went out of print, sales of *The Frugal Housewife* plummeted, and gift book editors turned their backs on Child. Intensifying the shock, the boycott fell just as Child reached the peak of her popularity. In July 1833, a month before the *Appeal* came off the press, the most prestigious journal of American letters, the *North American Review*, had crowned her with its laurels in a twenty-five-page appraisal of her entire oeuvre. "[W]e are not sure that any woman in our country would outrank Mrs. Child," the *Review*'s editors had asserted, pronouncing her "just the woman we want for the mothers and daughters of the present generation."[29] Child had long coveted this literary recognition, and it must have taken enormous moral courage to renounce it—along with her means of livelihood—at a moment when she and David could least afford the sacrifice.

Child's embrace of the abolitionist cause wrecked many of her friendships as well. Few losses could have cost her more dearly than the rupture of her cherished bond with Catharine Sedgwick. After Child sent Sedgwick a copy of the *Appeal* and invited her to contribute to a projected antislavery gift book, *The Oasis*, the older writer noticeably "cooled." In a long-delayed reply, she accepted only on the condition that she be allowed to take a moderate position and to put in a good word for "colonization"—the plan of tying emancipation to the repatriation of blacks to Africa, which abolitionists had rejected as racist. Child refused point-blank. The plan merely diverted "*honest* men and women" into a blind alley, she objected: "I now abhor [colonization] even more than slavery—inasmuch as I dislike hypocrisy more than crime." "Moderation! How *can* you be moderate?" she remonstrated. Neither "the influence of others" nor the impulses of sentimentalism had led her to her conclusions, Child assured Sedgwick, but "an honest patient examination" of the evidence. Moreover, she had "ceased to shed tears" over the plight of the slaves. "The emotions that used to produce them now boil up and create steam to supply my indignation and energy, till they move at the rate of steam cars." Emphasizing that abolition had become a total commitment, she vowed: "To the last hour of my life my voice and my pen shall be given to the work—by the way-side and by the fire-side—at the corners of streets, in the recesses of the counting room—in the publicity of the stage-coach, and

29. "Works of Mrs. Child," *North American Review* 37 (July 1833): 138–64. The quotations are from 138–39.

the solitude of prayer. For this cause I wish to live—for this cause I am willing to die."[30]

Child made good her vow. In the wake of the *Appeal* she published four more antislavery works. Two deserve special mention: *The Oasis* (1834), which includes her superb antislavery story, "Malem-Boo. The Brazilian Slave," as well as several pieces by David; and *Anti-Slavery Catechism* (1836), which disarmingly answers readers' concerns about the possible ill effects of immediate emancipation. Child also threaded protest against slavery and racism into her two other major works of that period, *The History of the Condition of Women, in Various Ages and Nations* (1835) and the novel *Philothea* (1836).

By 1836, David's professional instability and financial entanglements were threatening the couple's marriage and derailing Child's career. First the Childs had to cancel a trip to England as official agents of the American Anti-Slavery Society because David was arrested for debt on the quay, just as they were boarding the ship. Then an ill-advised project of joining a free-labor colony that the Quaker Benjamin Lundy was hoping to establish in Texas fell through after proslavery settlers took over the region from Mexico and declared their independence. Ultimately David decided to grow sugar beets in Northampton, Massachusetts, with the aim of providing a free-labor alternative to cane sugar, one of the slave South's main crops. During the two trying years Child spent as a farm wife (1838–39 and 1840–41, interrupted by a year in Boston), she sank into depression and stopped writing. Only an offer of one thousand dollars a year to edit the *National Anti-Slavery Standard* in New York—an offer Child accepted both to help finance David's failing beet farm and to serve the antislavery cause at a critical juncture—extricated her from the morass. Her departure initiated an eight-year informal separation.

Child's exile in Northampton had coincided with the outbreak of factional disputes between Garrisonian and evangelical abolitionists that had led to a major schism in 1840. As editor of the Garrisonian *National Anti-Slavery Standard*, a position she held from 1841 to 1843, she sought to heal the split between the warring groups, refocus abolitionists on their real enemy—slavery—and reach out to a broader audience. The infighting continued to rage, however, and Child finally resigned from the *Standard* and resumed her literary career.

30. LMC to Catharine Maria Sedgwick, 31 May 1834, Massachusetts Historical Society, Catharine Maria Sedgwick Papers, Part III. See also LMC to Sarah Shaw, 20 May 1872, *SL* 506.

Beginning with the republication of her popular column for the *Standard* as a book, *Letters from New-York* (1843), Child entered a new phase of creativity. The mainstream newspapers and periodicals that had shunned her since her espousal of abolitionism gradually reopened their columns to her, and her contributions started appearing in the *Boston Courier*, the *Broadway Journal*, the *Columbian Lady's and Gentleman's Magazine*, and the *Union Magazine of Literature and Art*. Within five years, she produced a second volume of *Letters from New York* (1845), three volumes of children's stories (*Flowers for Children*, vols. 1, 2, and 3, 1844–1847), and a collection of short stories, *Fact and Fiction* (1846). Restoring to her a measure of her previous fame, they won her many admirers among the New York literati: the poets James Russell Lowell and William Cullen Bryant, Bryant's son-in-law Parke Godwin, and the coeditors of the *Broadway Journal*, Edgar Allan Poe and Charles F. Briggs. In addition, Child renewed her intimacy with Margaret Fuller and cultivated the acquaintance of a large circle of artists and musicians, reviewing their work and securing patronage for them from wealthy benefactors.

One of these musicians was the Norwegian violinist Ole Bull, who inspired several of her "Letters from New-York" and the stories "Thot and Freia" and "Hilda Silfverling." Along with the young Quaker lawyer John Hopper, son of Child's host in New York, Isaac T. Hopper, Bull also inspired a chaste romantic attachment that helped to console Child for her broken marriage. In 1847, Bull's departure for Europe and John Hopper's marriage combined to precipitate an emotional crisis that launched Child on a religious quest. It would bear fruit eight years later in her three-volume comparative study, *The Progress of Religious Ideas, through Successive Ages* (1855). Amid her research for this study, she also reconciled with David, who agreed to relinquish control of the family's finances to her. The two moved back to rural Massachusetts in 1850, eventually settling in Wayland, where Child inherited her father's cottage in 1856.

With the termination of her religious research, Child enjoyed another burst of creativity. She published the best of her books for young folk, *A New Flower for Children* (1856); a fine collection of stories reflecting her evolution from romanticism to realism, *Autumnal Leaves* (1857); a story and a melodrama in the abolitionist gift book *The Liberty Bell* (1856, 1858); and a lushly sensuous story of interracial marriage in the inaugural volume of the *Atlantic Monthly*, "Loo Loo. A Few Scenes in a True History" (May-June 1858).

The proliferation of antislavery tales and her contributions to *The Liberty Bell* also signaled Child's reentry into the abolitionist movement. The thirteen years that had intervened since her resignation from the *Standard* had seen one victory after another by proslavery forces. In 1845 the United States annexed Texas—a step David and other abolitionists had waged a valiant struggle to prevent (David's 1845 tract, *The Taking of Naboth's Vineyard*, compares the theft of Texas from Mexico to the wicked Old Testament King Ahab's seizure of his subject's land). War with Mexico swiftly followed, resulting in the conquest of vast new territories to which slavery seemed destined to spread. In 1850 Congress passed a draconian fugitive slave law obliging northern citizens to act as slave catchers. In 1854 the Kansas-Nebraska Act lifted all remaining restrictions against slavery in the territories, unleashing a civil war in Kansas between pro- and antislavery settlers. The event that rekindled Child's activism, however, was the bludgeoning on the Senate floor of her disciple, Massachusetts Senator Charles Sumner, by South Carolina Congressman Preston Brooks, who sought to punish Sumner for his May 1856 speech, "The Crime against Kansas."

Child responded with a rousing story, "The Kansas Emigrants." Published in the *New York Tribune* just before the November 1856 election and reprinted in *Autumnal Leaves*, it called on antislavery partisans to unite behind the free-soil settlers in Kansas and the Republican presidential candidate, John C. Frémont, who had vowed to oppose the extension of slavery. Meanwhile she organized relief shipments to the beleaguered free-soilers and David stumped for Frémont. The Childs had at last succeeded in reestablishing their political partnership of the 1830s, this time on a footing that no longer sacrificed Maria's needs to David's.

Child's activism intensified as the struggle over slavery reached its climax. In October 1859, John Brown's raid on the federal arsenal at Harpers Ferry, Virginia, elicited her most widely circulated antislavery tract, *Correspondence between Lydia Maria Child and Gov. Wise and Mrs. Mason, of Virginia* (1860), which sold 300,000 copies. Praising Brown's heroism while decrying his "method," it warned Southerners that the time for compromises had passed, and it steeled Northerners to risk civil war rather than yield another inch on slavery. The tract prompted scores of letters from admirers and detractors all over the country, to which Child replied at the rate of twenty or thirty a week. She also raised money for the families of the men slain or hanged at Harpers Ferry and helped Garrison organize a mass meeting to mourn Brown's execution.

Within the year, Child somehow found time to write three more antislavery tracts: *The Right Way the Safe Way*, *The Patriarchal Institution*, and *The*

Duty of Disobedience to the Fugitive Slave Act. Simultaneously, she undertook the task for which she is best known today—editing Harriet Jacobs's *Incidents in the Life of a Slave Girl*. The collaboration initiated a warm friendship between the two women, which they kept up through the late 1860s.

During and after the war, Child agitated ceaselessly for the measures she considered vital to completing the work of emancipation: a black suffrage amendment, education and job training programs for the freedpeople, and the redistribution of the former slaveholders' estates among blacks and poor whites. She crowned her long antislavery career with a reader for the ex-slaves, *The Freedmen's Book* (1865), and a novel holding up interracial marriage as America's destiny, *A Romance of the Republic* (1867).

In her last years, while maintaining her vigilance over the defense of African American rights, Child concentrated on advocating woman suffrage, working for a just Indian policy, and fostering religious tolerance. She and David lived reclusively in Wayland. He died there in September 1874 at age eighty, she in October 1880 at age seventy-eight. Their deaths coincided with a backlash against progressive movements that eliminated much of the Reconstruction legislation for which abolitionists had fought. Child's friends refused to let her legacy be buried with her, however. They published a one-volume selection of her letters, which became a posthumous best-seller and generated a deluge of reviews. Summing up reviewers' accolades, the *New York Times* delivered an encomium rivaling Garrison's salute to Child half a century earlier as "the first woman in the republic": "Here was a most remarkable woman, one who lived a great life, but lived it so simply and with such limited consideration for herself that the more you study it the more it grows to be perhaps the truest life that an American woman has yet lived."[31]

Child underwent another resurrection in 1903 when the African American writer Pauline Hopkins reprinted a generous sampling of her letters in a biographical sketch occupying three issues of the *Colored American Magazine.* "[H]er trenchant pen would do us yeoman's service in the vexed question of disfranchisement and equality for the Afro-American," wrote Hopkins. "If the influence of the lives of such great-hearted Anglo-Saxons as she could radiate through space, and enwrap the Negro youth round about, how different would be the lot of a dependent race!"[32]

Today, as more and more scholars are reprinting, teaching, and studying

31. "Lydia Maria Child," Review of *Letters of Lydia Maria Child, New York Times* 1 Dec. 1882, p. 3.

32. Pauline R. Hopkins, "Reminiscences of the Life and Times of Lydia Maria Child," *Colored American Magazine* 6 (May 1903): 454; 6 (Feb. 1903): 280.

Child's work, she is finally regaining her rightful place in her culture's historical memory. Readers of this anthology—and of the novels, stories, tracts,
and letters that presses are making available in new editions—will now be
able to enjoy the prose and benefit from the insights of a preeminent American writer. Like Pauline Hopkins, Child's twenty-first-century heirs may find
that repossessing themselves of her bequest to posterity will arm them to
carry on the struggle she waged for justice, equality, and human dignity.

Suggestions for Classroom Use and

Explanation of Editorial Policy

This anthology seeks to represent all the major facets of Lydia Maria Child's career. With the goal of facilitating its use in a broad range of courses and helping teachers to identify the readings most pertinent to their fields, the selections have been grouped by topic in six parts: "The Indian Question"; "Children's Literature and Domestic Advice"; "Slavery, Race, and Reconstruction"; "Journalism and Social Critique"; "The Woman Question"; and "Religion." Within each part, works are arranged in chronological order to enable readers to follow the evolution of Child's views. Rather than divide works by genre, I have chosen to respect Child's own practice—and to illustrate her stylistic versatility—by juxtaposing short stories, letters, newspaper and magazine articles, tracts, histories, advice literature, and children's literature. My introductory essays recapitulate the various facets of Child's career and set the readings that follow in historical and literary context. Teachers requiring textual explications of individual readings should consult my full-length study, *The First Woman in the Republic: A Cultural Biography of Lydia Maria Child.*

Although the variety of topics covered in this anthology reflects Child's breadth, the space occupied by her antislavery writings inevitably suggests how central her engagement with America's race problem was to her career and remains to us today. The introductory essay for part 3, "Slavery, Race, and Reconstruction," similarly required more pages than the others to do justice to both the complexity of the issues discussed and the number of selections presented.

Teachers can use the anthology in many ways: to provide students with a window on nineteenth-century American culture; to immerse students in the specifics of the era's principal controversies, as defined by a key participant; to pair Child with writers who took different positions on the same issues; to supplement more traditional literature and history courses; and to furnish interdisciplinary courses with primary documents that themselves cross an array of disciplines.

While capturing the multiplicity of Child's interests, this collection of her writings is far from comprehensive. Space constraints forced a number of difficult choices. A conspicuous omission, for example, is Child's post-Civil War commentary on the labor question, which betrays her artisanal origins

and inadequate understanding of the problems facing the industrial proletariat (see the "Letter from L. Maria Child" of 17 September 1870 and
"Economy and Work"). Several of her best stories, notably "The Kansas
Emigrants" and "Loo Loo," had to be sacrificed on grounds of length. In the
case of two or more stories on analogous themes, only one could be included
(hence the omission of "Thot and Freia" and "The Rival Mechanicians"
from part 5, and of "Malem-Boo," "Mary French and Susan Easton," and
"The Quadroons" from part 3). A few pieces (such as the extracts from *The
Mother's Book, The History of the Condition of Women,* "Woman and Suffrage," and the two-part article "Concerning Women") have been abridged in
the interests of avoiding overlap between selections and retaining texts whose
length would otherwise have ruled them out. To maximize the representation
of new material, this volume sparingly features texts available in other modern editions, and assigns priority to items hitherto buried in newspaper
columns. Many of the selections in this anthology have never before been
reprinted, and some—in particular "Through the Red Sea into the Wilderness," "Women and the Freedmen," and "Homesteads"—have only recently
been unearthed.

Wherever possible, the people, texts, and events mentioned by Child, as
well as her quotations from other sources, have been identified. Those without annotations remain unidentified. Child's own annotations and several
textual notes supplied by Patricia G. Holland in "Prejudices against People of
Color" have been identified with the initials LMC and PGH, respectively.

Texts were taken from the following sources: "The Church in the Wilderness" from *The Legendary;* "Willie Wharton" from the *Atlantic Monthly; An
Appeal for the Indians* from the 1868 pamphlet edition (all three as reprinted
in the Rutgers University Press edition of *HOBOMOK and Other Writings on
Indians*); "Louisa Preston" and "Jumbo and Zairee" from *Juvenile Miscellany;*
"Management during the Teens" from *The Mother's Book,* 1844 edition; "Let-
ter from an Old Woman, on Her Birthday" from *Looking toward Sunset,* 1865
edition; "Prejudices against People of Color" from *An Appeal in Favor of That
Class of Americans Called Africans,* as reprinted in the University of Massa-
chusetts Press edition; "To Abolitionists," "Annette Gray," "The Iron Shroud,"
"Talk about Political Party," "Speaking in the Church," "Letters from New-
York" numbers 12 and 33 and the uncollected and unnumbered "Letter from
New-York" on the Amelia Norman case, "Mrs. L. Maria Child to the Presi-
dent," "Emancipation and Amalgamation," and "Homesteads" from the *Na-
tional Anti-Slavery Standard;* "Education of Children" and "Advice from an
Old Friend" from *The Freedmen's Book,* 1865 edition; "Through the Red Sea

into the Wilderness," "A High-Flying Letter," and "Concerning Women" from the *Independent;* "Woman and Suffrage" from the *Independent,* as reprinted in Milton Meltzer, Patricia G. Holland, and Francine Krasno, *Lydia Maria Child: Selected Letters, 1817–1880* (abbreviated *SL*); "Women and the Freedmen" from *The Woman's Advocate;* "African Women" from *The History of the Condition of Women,* 1854 edition (retitled *Brief History of the Condition of Women*); "Letters from New York" numbers 1, 11, 14, 29, and 34 from the third edition of *Letters from New York [First Series];* "Hilda Silfverling" from *Fact and Fiction;* "The Intermingling of Religions" and "William Lloyd Garrison" from the *Atlantic Monthly.* I have supplied page numbers in the Source Notes for those articles taken directly from newspapers; for newspaper articles taken from the microfiche edition of *The Collected Correspondence of Lydia Maria Child, 1817–1880,* ed. Patricia G. Holland, Milton Meltzer, and Francine Krasno (Millwood, NY: Kraus Microform, 1980), abbreviated *CC,* I have supplied microfiche card number and letter number, divided by a slash mark.

I have not tampered with spelling or punctuation, except to correct obvious misprints. Hence, the texts exhibit the inconsistencies of spelling, hyphenation, and punctuation (including the use of single rather than double quotation marks in a few texts) typical of nineteenth-century publications. Such typographical features as the use of periods after titles have not been reproduced, however.

A word, finally, about the numbering and hyphenation of "Letters from New-York." In collecting her "Letters from New-York" in the *National Anti-Slavery Standard* for publication in book form, Child renumbered the letters. The first edition of the book (1843) retained the hyphenation of New-York in the title; the revised third edition (1845) and its successors dropped the hyphenation. After the appearance in 1845 of the second series of *Letters from New York,* written for the *Boston Courier,* the designations *First Series* and *Second Series* were added to distinguish between the two volumes. I have followed Child's practice of hyphenating the title in the uncollected letters taken from the newspaper column and of dropping the hyphenation in those taken from the third edition of the First Series. In the rare cases where New-York is hyphenated in the book title, I am referring specifically to the 1843 first edition. I have retained the original numbering for uncollected letters, but conformed to the new numbering for letters taken from the book version, indicated by the italicized title *Letters from New York.*

Part One

The Indian Question

Introduction

Engaging Child's imagination as early as age thirteen, the plight of the Indians inspired her first ventures into both literature and social reform. So powerful an impression did her youthful introduction to a wronged people make on Child that she continued to wrestle with the Indian question for the rest of her life. In fiction, journalism, and didactic literature spanning the four decades from the Cherokee removal controversy of 1828–38 to the post–Civil War conquest of the Plains tribes, she protested against Indian dispossession and genocide and sought to dramatize such alternatives as assimilation, cultural blending, and intermarriage.

Soon after moving to Norridgewock, Maine, in 1815, Child stumbled on the town's buried history of Indian-white conflict. That year, traces resurfaced of the 1724 massacre that had razed the Abenaki hamlet of Norridgewock seven miles upriver. When a thunderstorm overturned an ancient oak and disinterred a cracked, corroded bell entangled in its roots, Child learned from "the old inhabitants of Norridgewock" that the bell had once belonged to a Catholic church for Abenaki converts, presided over by the French Jesuit priest Sebastien Rale, and that British troops had burned the church, murdered the priest, and wiped out his Abenaki congregation in a raid conducted while the victims were at worship.[1] She would research the details and retell the story in "The Adventures of a Bell" (March 1827), written for her children's magazine, *The Juvenile Miscellany,* and "The Church in the Wilderness" (1828), featured as the lead selection in Nathaniel P. Willis's gift book, *The Legendary.*

Although driven off their land, a handful of Abenaki and Penobscot Indians still lived in the nearby hemlock forests, and during her six-year stay in Maine, Child "used to go to the woods, and visit the dozen wigwams that stood there, very often."[2] She could not help noticing the poverty to which her Abenaki hosts were reduced, and like the young boy in one of her educational dialogues for children, she must have wondered, "if [Indians] were so very thick when Maine was first settled, where can they all have fled," and "what right had we to take away their lands?"[3] As her Abenaki friends grew to

---

1. "The Adventures of a Bell," *Juvenile Miscellany* 2 (March 1827): 30.
2. "The Indian Boy," *Juvenile Miscellany* 2 (May 1827): 28–31.
3. "Indian Tribes," *Evenings in New England* (Boston: Cummings, Hilliard, 1824) 73–74.

trust her, they may also have told her the stories their parents and grand-parents had passed down to them about the Norridgewock massacre—stories that differed intriguingly from the versions the descendants of the white settlers recounted. Watching Abenaki boys weave baskets, demonstrate their hunting and running skills, and point out "the names and uses of every tree, far and wide," she quickly realized that they possessed knowledge rivaling the kind she derived from books.[4]

She was even more struck by the physical strength and independence the women displayed. One winter while Child was staying with friends in Wins-low, a Penobscot woman from an encampment in the vicinity showed up at the door. "She had waded four miles through very deep and almost unbroken snow, to beg for a salt-fish," being unable to obtain her usual food because of the heavy snowfall. The following day, to the astonishment of Child's hosts, the woman returned "with a new-born babe strapped to her back." She had given birth the preceding evening, and in accordance with Penobscot cus-tom, had washed the baby in the river, after "first cut[ting] a hole in the ice with her hatchet." This time she requested a sack of potatoes, which she "slung . . . over her shoulders, with her baby." As the woman retraced her four-mile hike through the snow "with vigorous strides,"[5] Child stared en-viously. At an age when she herself was chafing against the constraints that nineteenth-century feminine ideals of decorum and delicacy imposed on middle-class white women, she may well have pondered the implications of Indian women's greater stamina and questioned the claim that physical frailty was an innate feminine trait. Her observations of Penobscot and Abenaki women no doubt prompted the cross-cultural perspective on child-rearing practices, sexual mores, and gender roles that would inform her *History of the Condition of Women, in Various Ages and Nations* (1835).

On another occasion Child saw Penobscot women build temporary wig-wams on a white neighbor's timber lots and cut down "his best trees, to make baskets and brooms." When the irate landowner confronted them, the women retorted: "You have wood enough to burn—what for you want more wood? When you die, you no carry wood with you."[6] Their words must have sunk into the well of her consciousness. Years later she would say: "I have almost as strong an aversion to Land-Monopoly, as I have to Slavery."[7]

Of all the Indians Child encountered in Maine, she would remember

---

4. "The Indian Boy," *Juvenile Miscellany* 2 (May 1827): 28–31.
5. "Physical Strength of Women," *Woman's Journal* 15 Mar. 1873, p. 84.
6. "Pol Sosef. The Indian Artist," *Juvenile Miscellany* n.s. 5 (Jan.–Feb. 1831): 278–79.
7. LMC to George W. Julian, 27 March 1864, *SL* 439.

none more vividly than the "majestic" Penobscot chief Etalexis, "a tall, athletic youth, of most graceful proportions." What could have been more romantic than eating "supper with [his] tribe in a hemlock forest, on the shores of the Kennebec"? And how striking the young chief looked "with a broad band of shining brass about his hat, a circle of silver on his breast, tied with scarlet ribbons, and a long belt of curiously-wrought wampum hanging to his feet." Child recalled raising the belt's "heavy tassels" with "girlish curiosity." In after years, whenever the artist Benjamin West's exclamation at the sight of the Apollo Belvidere came to mind—"My God! how like a young Mohawk warrior!"—Child "always used to think of Etalexis."[8] Was she thinking of Etalexis when she described her Indian hero Hobomok's "tall, athletic form," "manly beauty," and "elastic, vigorous elegance of proportion"? Did she ever fantasize, like her heroine, Mary Conant, about eloping with an Indian "whose nature was unwarped by the artifices of civilized life"?[9] We can only speculate.

Still, there is no mistaking the formative influence that coming of age in a frontier community exerted on Child's imagination. In launching her literary career, she turned first to Indian subjects. The pattern set in *Hobomok* (1824), dashed off in a white heat at age twenty-two, continues in her second book, *Evenings in New England* (1824), where Indians personify the conquest of North and South America in the opening selection. The pattern continues as well in the *Juvenile Miscellany,* where "Adventure in the Woods" (Sept. 1826), a story of peaceful interdependency between white settlers and Indians, leads off the inaugural issue. Fiction enabled Child to imagine possible solutions to the "Indian problem"—and to explore its roots in colonial history, as she does in "The Church in the Wilderness"—well before she formulated critiques of U.S. Indian policy in her polemical writings.

When the conflict over Cherokee removal erupted in 1828, however, just as Child was being initiated into political journalism by her newlywed husband, David Lee Child, she felt impelled to seek a more direct means of championing the Indian cause. The Cherokee had adapted to market agriculture, invented an alphabet, founded a bilingual newspaper (the *Cherokee Phoenix*), and written a Constitution modeled on that of the United States, yet the state of Georgia clamored for their expulsion, and President-elect Andrew Jackson had pledged to transport them beyond the Mississippi. The

8. *Letters from New York [First Series]* (1843; rpt. Freeport, N.Y.: Books for Libraries P, 1970) number 4: 29.

9. *HOBOMOK and Other Writings on Indians,* ed. Carolyn L. Karcher (1824; rpt. New Brunswick, N.J.: Rutgers UP, 1986) 16, 36, 121.

crisis spurred Child to write a revisionist history of Indian-white relations, *The First Settlers of New-England: or, Conquest of the Pequods, Narragansets and Pokanokets: As Related by a Mother to Her Children* (1829). In it she pleads for allowing the Cherokee to "retain what is left of their native inheritance." "It is, in my opinion, decidedly wrong, to speak of the removal, or extinction of the Indians as inevitable," she boldly asserts. For the first time, she also openly suggests what her early fiction had hinted: that by "intermixing" racially and culturally with Indians, white Americans could not only eliminate perpetual warfare but regenerate their society. Anticipating objections to mingling the blood of "superior" and "inferior" races, she even cites evidence that Europeans owe their arts and sciences to the dark-complexioned peoples of Asia and Africa.[10]

The First Settlers may have heralded Child's career as a reformer, but it went unnoticed by reviewers, politicians, and the Cherokee themselves. Its hybrid form as a book addressed to mothers and children while aimed at promoting action in the public sphere indicates that Child had not yet made the transition from feminine to masculine discourse, from domestic advice to political advocacy.

Reformers far more seasoned than she also failed to stem the forces that militated against the Cherokee. Despite the support of Christian missionaries, northern Whig politicians, and many activists who would subsequently join the antislavery movement, and despite a Supreme Court decision in their favor by Chief Justice John Marshall in 1832, the U.S. Congress voted for Cherokee removal in 1830, and President Jackson forged ahead with the program. In 1835 a minority Cherokee faction, including Elias Boudinot, the former editor of the *Cherokee Phoenix,* gave up what they perceived to be a fight against hopeless odds and signed the Treaty of New Echota, agreeing to removal. The Cherokee Nation as a whole, led by Chief John Ross, refused to endorse the treaty, but their opposition did not prevent the U.S. Senate from ratifying it. In 1838 U.S. troops herded the tribe on a forced march to the Oklahoma Territory that strewed the ground with corpses. Some four thousand to eight thousand people died during the operation the Cherokee called the Trail of Tears.

10. Published anonymously "By a Lady of Massachusetts" and privately printed for Child by Munroe and Francis of Boston, this work is extremely rare and may never have been distributed. Quotations are from 65–68, 259, 281. For a more extended discussion, see Carolyn L. Karcher, *The First Woman in the Republic: A Cultural Biography of Lydia Maria Child* (Durham, Duke UP, 1994) ch. 4.

The three selections reprinted in this section illustrate the complementary ways in which Child's fiction and political tracts digest the lessons of American history and promote the incorporation of Indians into the U.S. body politic. "The Church in the Wilderness" shows how warfare tragically dooms the alternative models of Indian-white relations—interracial marriage, cultural fusion, and mutually beneficial exchanges of goods and services—embodied by the biracial Otoolpha and Saupoolah; their French Jesuit foster father, Sebastien Rale; and their English benefactor, Mrs. Allan. "Willie Wharton" (1863) envisions the transformation of America into a biracial family enriched by elements of Indian culture. It also dramatizes the tactful and gradual approach toward fostering acculturation that Child would advocate five years later in "An Appeal for the Indians" (1868).

First published in the *National Anti-Slavery Standard* and reissued in pamphlet form later that year,[11] "An Appeal for the Indians" inaugurated a new campaign among the reformers whose long struggle to liberate and enfranchise African Americans had just culminated in the Civil War and Reconstruction. During the war, troop movements and shifting battle lines between Union and Confederate forces had displaced thousands of Indians from their homes, often uprooting tribes that had already been "removed" in the 1830s and 1840s. The accelerating pace of road and railway construction across tribal lands was threatening the buffalo herds on which the Plains Indians depended for food and was causing frequent clashes between them and white settlers. Major Indian wars had broken out in 1862 and 1864–65 among the Minnesota Santee Sioux and the Colorado Teton Sioux and Cheyenne. In the infamous Sand Creek massacre of 1864, U.S. troops had butchered 105 Cheyenne women and children, "mutilated the living and the dead, cut off and displayed as trophies the sexual organs" of their victims, and ripped fetuses out of pregnant women, according to eyewitness testimony presented in Congress.[12] To investigate and end the unrest, Congress had appointed an Indian Peace Commission, which had just issued its report. It recommended confining the Indians to reservations governed by benevolent, but firm, white authorities; weaning them from hunting to "agriculture and manufactures," from collective to individual modes of life; and compelling

11. "A Plea for the Indian," *National Anti-Slavery Standard* 11 Apr. 1868, p. 3 and 18 Apr. 1868, pp. 2–3, retitled *An Appeal for the Indians* (New York: William P. Tomlinson, 1868).

12. Richard Slotkin, *The Fatal Environment: The Myth of the Frontier in the Age of Industrialization, 1800–1890* (1985; Middletown, Conn.: Wesleyan UP, 1986) 401–2; Dee Brown, *Bury My Heart at Wounded Knee: An Indian History of the American West* (New York: Holt, 1970) 87–93.

them to abandon their cultural and tribal identity. A prime objective, stressed the report, must be "to blot out" the differences of language and custom dividing Indians into "distinct nations" and to "fuse them into one homogeneous mass."[13]

Taking issue with these recommendations, Child's "Appeal for the Indians" calls instead for a program of education based on positive incentives rather than force and oriented toward cultivating rather than destroying Indians' pride in their own identity. The bilingual school readers she suggests, containing selections from tribal literature and history, draw on the one she herself designed for emancipated slaves: *The Freedmen's Book* (1865).

Child differed from the commissioners—and from other reformers—mainly in favoring a more humane style of acculturation. Typifying the model she rejected is a communication to the *National Anti-Slavery Standard* by a Quaker missionary. Although the Quakers were the most liberal of the Christian sects working among the Indians, this missionary advised removing Indian children from their families, immuring them in mission boarding schools, cutting off their hair, washing off their "paint and dirt," confiscating their earrings and bracelets, dressing them in "decent" clothes, and forcing them to "drop their lingo, and acquire our language."

If Child subscribed to a broader and more tolerant ideal of assimilation, she nevertheless shared with other progressive thinkers of her day a theory of historical evolution that measured cultures on an ascending scale and described them as rising from savagery through barbarism and pastoralism to civilization. Such a theory necessarily implied that to "advance" toward "civilization," Indians (like the Celtic tribes of Britain with whom Child compared them) must abandon their "primitive" cultures. The reformers of Child's generation could not conceive of culture in pluralist or relativist terms. Nor could the vast majority of Americans, who viewed Indians as irredeemable savages, either doomed to extinction or deserving of extermination. In sum, the proofs Child offered of the Indians' capacity for civilization, the similarities she pointed out between Indians and Europeans, the sensitive methods of acculturation she urged, and the freedom from prejudice she displayed in promoting intermarriage along with assimilation placed her in the vanguard of nineteenth-century white opinion.

13. U.S. Cong., House of Representatives, *Annual Report of the Commissioner of Indian Affairs,* 40th Cong., 3rd Sess.; 1868, "Report to the President by the Indian Peace Commission, January 7, 1868," House Executive Document 1: 486–510, quotation from 504.

The Church in the Wilderness

There stood the Indian hamlet, there the lake
Spread its blue sheet, that flashed with many an oar,
Where the brown otter plunged him from the brake,
And the deer drank—as the light gale blew o'er,
The twinkling maze-field rustled on the shore;
And while that spot, so wild, and lone, and fair,
A look of glad and innocent beauty wore,
And peace was on the earth and in the air,
The warrior lit the pile and bound his captive there.

Not unavenged the foeman from the wood
Beheld the deed, and when the midnight shade
Was stillest, gorged his battle-axe with blood;
All died—the wailing babe—the shrieking maid—
And in the flood of fire, that scathed the glade,
The roofs went down; but deep the silence grew,
When on the dewy woods the day-beam played;
No more the cabin smokes rose wreathed and blue,
And ever by their lake, lay moored the light canoe.
　　　　　—Bryant[1]

There is a solitary spot, in a remote part of Maine, known by the name of Indian Old Point. The landscape has no peculiar beauty, save the little sparkling river, which winds gracefully and silently among the verdant hills, as if deeply contented with its sandy bed; and fields of Indian corn,

---

The Legendary, ed. Nathaniel P. Willis (Boston: Samuel G. Goodrich, 1828) 1–23.

1. From William Cullen Bryant, "The Ages," stanzas 30–31, the opening piece in his first published volume, Poems (Cambridge, Mass.: Hilliard and Metcalf, 1821). According to Bryant's son-in-law Parke Godwin, the editor of his collected Poetical Works, "The Ages" was commissioned by the Phi Beta Kappa Society of Harvard and read before it at the 1821 commencement ceremony, contributing more to securing Bryant's reputation than any of his other early poems, including "Thanatopsis." In a note that appears in all collections of his poems from 1832 on, Bryant writes: "In this poem . . . the author has endeavored, from a survey of past ages of the world, and of the successive advances of mankind in knowledge, virtue, and happiness, to justify and confirm the hopes of the philanthropist for the future destinies of the human race." The stanzas that follow describe a miraculous transformation of the wilderness into fertile agricultural land and populous cities as white colonists replace Indians.

tossing their silken tresses to the winds, as if conscious of rural beauty. Yet there is a charm thrown around this neglected and almost unknown place, by its association with some interesting passages in our earliest history. The soil is fertilized by the blood of a murdered tribe. Even now the spade strikes against wampum belts, which once covered hearts as bold and true, as ever beat beneath a crusader's shield, and gaudy beads are found, which once ornamented bosoms throbbing with as deep and fervent tenderness, as woman ever displayed in the mild courtesies of civilized life.

Here, one hundred years ago, stood the village of the Norridgewocks, one of the many tribes of the scattered Abnakis. These Indians have been less celebrated than many of their brethren; for they had not the fierce valor of the Pequods, the sinewy strength of the Delawares, or the bell-toned language of the Iroquois. They were, however, an influential nation; of consequence on account of their numbers, as well as their subtilty. The Jesuits, too, had long been among them, led by their zeal to fasten the strong girdle of an imposing faith around the habitable globe; and they had gained over the untutored minds of these savages, their usual mysterious and extraordinary power. The long continued state of effervescence, produced by the Reformation, tended to settle this country with rigid, restless, and ambitious spirits. Our broad lands were considered an ample tract of debatable ground, where the nations of the earth might struggle for disputed possession; and terrible indeed was the contest for religious supremacy between France and England, during the early part of the eighteenth century. Of the energy and perseverance displayed in this cause, there are few more striking examples than Sebastian Rallè, the apostle of the Norridgewocks. His rude, cross-crowned church, standing in the heart of the American wilderness, proved the ambition and extent of that tremendous hierarchy, 'whose roots were in another world, and whose far stretching shadow awed our own.'[2] Surrounded by the wigwams of the Abnakis, it seemed like an apostle of Antioch descended among savages, pointing out to them the heaven he had left. Our forefathers indeed thought it wore a different, and most unholy aspect; but to romantic minds, the Catholic church, even in its most degraded state, must ever be an object of interest. The majestic Latin, so lofty in its sound, and yet so soulless now to all save the learned, seems like the fragments of a mighty ruin, which Rome, in her decaying pride, scattered over the nations of the earth; and the innumerable ceremonies, more voiceless than the language in which they are pre-

2. From Bryant's "The Ages," stanza 23 (referring to the Catholic Church).

served, forcibly remind one of the pomp and power rivalled only by atten-
dant corruption. In this point of view only could the humble church of the
Norridgewocks kindle the imagination; for it had little outward proportion,
or inward splendor. It stood in a sheltered spot, between two small, verdant
hills, with one graceful feathery elm at its side, bending forward, at every
signal from the breeze, and half shading the cross, as if both bowed down in
worship.

Various opinions were formed of the priest, who there administered the
rites of a mysterious religion. All agreed that he was a learned man; some said
he was benevolent and kind; while others pronounced him the most subtle
and vindictive of hypocrites. The English settlers, who resided about three
miles from the village of the Abnakis, regarded him with extreme aversion;
but to the Indians he was the representative of the Good Spirit. It is true the
maxims of the Jesuits had given something of sternness and cunning to a
character naturally mild and frank; but he verily thought he was doing God's
service, and he did it with a concentration of power and purpose well worthy
of the respect it inspired. For thirty years he lived in the wilderness, sharing
the dangers and privations incident to savage life. The languages of all the
neighbouring tribes were familiar to him; and his utterance could not have
been distinguished from that of a native, had it not been for a peculiarly
softened cadence, and rapid enunciation. A restless light in his small, hazel
eye, and the close compression of his lips, betokened one, who had, with a
strong hand, thrown up dykes against the overflowing torrent of his own mad
passions. The effort had likewise turned back many a gentle current of affection, which might have soothed and refreshed his heart; but let man do his
worst, there are moments when nature will rebound from all the restraints
imposed on her by pride, prejudice, or superstition.

There were two objects in the secluded residence of the self-denying
Jesuit, on whom he poured forth in fulness the love he could not wholly stifle
within him. When he came to America, he found among the savages the
orphan son of the Baron de Castine,[3] by a beautiful young Abnakis. The child
was remarkably pretty and engaging; and the lonely priest, finding his heart
daily warming toward him, induced the squaw who nursed him, to take up
her abode in his own wigwam. The Indians called him Otoolpha, 'The Son of

3. Jean-Vincent d'Abadie, Baron de St. Castin (spelled Castine by English writers), a French
nobleman who had married an Abenaki woman and left his children in the care of their
mother's people, is mentioned both in Child's sources and in the anonymous story, "Narant-
sauk," in the *Atlantic Souvenir* for 1829.

the Stranger,' and seemed to regard the adopted one with quite as much interest as their own offspring. Not a year after Otoolpha and his nurse were domesticated in the dwelling of the Jesuit, some of the tribe, on their return from Canada, found a nearly famished female infant in the wood. Had not Sebastian Rallè been of the party, its sufferings would, probably, have met a violent end; but at his suggestion, comfortable nourishment, and such care as they could give it were afforded. A nose slightly approaching to aquiline, and a complexion less darkly colored than usual, betrayed an origin half European; but as her parentage and tribe were unknown, they gave her the emphatic name of Saupoolah, 'The Scattered Leaf,' and engrafted her on the tree of Abnakis. From the first dawn of reason she gave indications of an impetuous, fearless, and romantic spirit. The squaw who nursed her, together with the little Otoolpha, tried in vain to curb her roving propensities. At four and five years old, she would frequently be absent several days, accompanied by her foster brother. The duties of the missionary often called him far from home, and it was absolutely impossible for him always to watch over them, either in kindness, or authority. Their long excursions during his absence, at first occasioned many anxious and wretched thoughts; but when he found his wayward protégés invariably returned, and when he saw they could cross streams, leap ditches, and thread their way through the labyrinths of the wilderness, with the boldness and sagacity of young hunters, he ceased to disturb himself on their account.

During the whole of their adventurous childhood but one accident ever happened to them. They had been at the English settlement to beg some beads in exchange for their little baskets, and on their return, they took a fancy to cross the Kennebec, when recent rains had swollen its deep and beautiful waters. Saupoolah's life nearly fell a sacrifice to the rapidity of the current; but her foster brother ran, with the speed of lightning, to call assistance from the village they had just left. A muscular, kind hearted woman, by the name of Allan, lived in a log-house, very near the river. In the midst of his terror, Otoolpha remembered this circumstance, and went there for succor. His frightened looks told his story, even more plainly than his hurried exclamation;—'Ogh! Saupoolah die—the Great Spirit drink her up!' Mrs. Allan saved the Indian child at the risk of her own life, dried her clothes, gave them something warm and comfortable to eat, and conducted them into their homeward path in safety. To this woman and her children Otoolpha and Saupoolah ever after clung with singular intensity of affection. During their childish summers, it was a daily occupation to fill baskets with berries for her little ones, whom they always chose to feed with their own hands, watching every morsel of the fruit as it disappeared between their rosy lips, with the most animated expressions of delight; and when they arrived at maturer years, they used the great influence they had with the tribe, to protect Mrs. Allan from a thousand petty wrongs and insults, with which her white brethren were not unfrequently visited.

Educated by the learned priest, as far as such fetterless souls could be educated, and associating only with savages, these extraordinary young people grew up with a strange mixture of European and aboriginal character. Both had the rapid, elastic tread of Indians; but the outlines of their tall, erect figures possessed something of the pliant gracefulness of France. When indignant, the expression of their eyes was like light from a burning-glass; but in softer moments, they had a melting glance, which belongs only to a civilized and voluptuous land. Saupoolah's hair, though remarkably soft and fine, had the jet black hue of the savage; Otoolpha's was brown, and when moistened by exercise, it sometimes curled slightly around his high, prominent forehead. The same mixture of nations was shown in their costume, as in their personal appearance. Otoolpha usually wore a brown cloth tunic, with tight sleeves, and large buttons, under which appeared a scarlet kilt falling to his knees, in heavy folds, edged with the fur of the silver fox, and fastened at the waist by a broad girdle, richly ornamented with Indian hieroglyphics. A coronet of scarlet dyed fur, to which were fastened four silver bells, gave indication of his noble descent; and from his neck were suspended a cross and rosary of sandal wood, which Sebastian Rallè declared to have been sanctified by the blessed touch of Innocent the Eleventh. Saupoolah's dress was nearly similar. Her tunic was deep yellow; and her scarlet kilt touched the fur edge of her high, closely fitted, and very gaudy moccasins. Her cap was not shaped unlike a bishop's mitre; gaily ornamented with shells and beadwork, and surmounted by the black feathers of three eagles her own arrow had slain. In the chase, she was as eager and keen eyed as Otoolpha. It was a noble sight to see them, equipped for the chase, bounding along through the forest. The healthful and rapid blood, coursing beneath their smooth, brown cheeks, gave a richness and vividness of beauty, which a fair, transparent complexion can never boast; and their motions had that graceful elasticity produced only by activity, unconsciousness, and freedom. Sebastian Rallè had been several years at Rome, in the service of the Pope, and had there acquired a refinement of taste uncommon at that early period. His adopted children sometimes accompanied him on his missionary expeditions to Canada and elsewhere, on which occasions the game they killed served for his support. When he saw them with their dark eyes fixed on a distant bird, arrows ready for flight, their majestic figures slightly bending backward, resting on one knee, with an advancing foot firmly fixed on the ground, displaying, by a natural bend of the limb, outlines most gracefully curved, he gazed upon them with uncontrolled delight; and he could not but acknowledge that the young savages, in their wild and careless beauty, rivalled the Apollos and woodnymphs to which classic imaginations had given birth. Such endowments are rare in Indian women; for the toils imposed upon them, usually weigh down the springs of the soul, till the body refuses to rebound at its feeble impulses; but when it does occur, it is the very perfection of ideal loveliness. Otoolpha would suffer no one to curb Saupoolah in her wildness and inspiration. To him and the Jesuit, she was docile and affectionate; to all others, haughty and impetuous. The Norridgewocks regarded them both with wonder and superstition, and frequently called them by a name, which signified the 'Children of the Prophet.' The distant tribes, who frequently met them in their hunting excursions, were lost in admiration of their swiftness and majesty, and called them, by one consent, the 'Twin Eagles of Abnakis.'

Contemptuously as some think of our red brethren, genius was no rare endowment among them; and seldom have souls been so rich in the wealth of nature, as the two powerful and peculiar beings, whom we have described. Many were the bold and beautiful thoughts which rushed upon their untutored imaginations, as they roamed over a picturesque country, sleeping in clefts where panthers hid themselves, and scaling precipices from which they scared the screaming eagles. Perhaps cultivated intellect never received brighter thoughts from the holy rays of the evening star, or a stormier sense of grandeur from the cataract, than did these children of the wilderness. Their far leaping ideas, clothed in brief, poetic language, were perhaps more pleasant to the secluded priest, than frequent intercourse with his own learned, but crafty order. To him they were indeed as 'diamonds in the desert;' and long and painful were the penances he inflicted upon himself, for an all-absorbing love, which his erring conscience deemed a sin against that God, who bestowed such pure, delicious feelings on his mysterious creatures. The Jesuit was deeply read in human nature, and it needed but little sagacity to foresee that Saupoolah would soon be to her brother 'something than sister dearer.' When Otoolpha was but seventeen, and his companion not quite fifteen, their frank and childish affection had obviously assumed a diffcrent character. Restlessness when separated, and timidity and constraint when they met, betrayed their slavery to a new and despotic power. Sebastian Rallè observed it with joy. Early disappointment and voluntary vows had made the best and most luxurious emotions of our nature a sealed fountain within his own soul; but the old man had not forgotten youthful hopes and feelings, and for these beloved ones he coveted all earth had of happiness. They were married in presence of the whole tribe, with all the pomp and ceremony his limited means afforded. This event made no alteration in the household of the Jesuit. The old squaw, who had taken care of his adopted children from their infancy, performed all the services their half civilized way of life required, and the young hunters led the same wandering and fearless life as before. At the hour of sunset, it was the delight of the lonely priest to watch for their return, from a small opening, which served as a window to his study. It was a time he usually devoted to reflection and prayer; but the good man had virtues, which he called weaknesses and sins, and a spirit of devotion would not always remain with him at such seasons. The vine covered hills of France, his mother's kiss, and a bright, laughing girl, who had won his heart in early youth, would often rise before him with the distinctness of visions. The neglected rosary would fall from his hand, and love, as it first stole over a soul untainted by sensuality or selfishness, was the only heaven of which he dreamed. Such were the feelings with which he awaited the return of Otoolpha and Saupoolah, on the eleventh of December, 1719. Notwithstanding the lateness of the season, the day had been as mild as the first weeks of September. The drowsy sunshine dreaming on the hemlocks, pines, and cedars, had drawn forth an unusual fragrance; the children were at rest in the wigwams; most of the sanups[4] had gone to Moose Head Lake, on a hunting expedition; and the few old men who remained, sat at the doors of their huts smoking their pipes in lazy silence.

Wautoconomese, an aged prophet among them, declared this unnatural warmth to be a prelude of terrible things. He had gained his power of judging by a close observation of electrical phenomena and all the various changes of the weather, and it was no difficult matter to make his tribe mistake experience for inspiration. The women were all in alarm at his predictions; nor is it strange that the learned Jesuit, living as he did in a superstitious age, and believing doctrines highly calculated to excite the imagination, should be more affected by their terrors than he was willing to acknowledge, even to

---

4. sannup, derived from the Abenaki word *senanbe:* a married Indian male.

himself. These feelings naturally embodied themselves in anxiety concerning the two eccentric beings, whose presence was as morning sunshine in his dreary dwelling. The hour at which they usually returned, had long since passed; and strong and vigilant as he knew them to be, fearful thoughts of panthers and wolves crowded on his heart. Waking, he knew the fiercest prowlers of the wilderness would have shunned them; but they might have slept where loup-cerviers[5] were in ambush, and roused too late for safety.

While philosophy was struggling with these harassing ideas, and every moment growing weaker in the contest, he observed in the north a flash more brilliant than ever precedes the rising sun. For a moment it was stationary; then it moved, quivered, hurtled, and flashed, as if there had been 'war in heaven,' and the clouds, rolling themselves up 'as a scroll,' showed the gleaming of javelins, thrown thick and fast along the embattled line.[6] All at once, a vivid stream of light from the south towered up, like Lucifer in his terrific greatness, and rushed onward with a mighty noise. The fiery forces, nearly meeting at the zenith, were separated only by a clear, deep spot of blue, surrounded by a few fleecy clouds. The effect was awful. It seemed as if the All-seeing Eye were looking down upon a sinful world, in mingled wrath and pity. The Catholic bowed his head, and his subdued spirit was mute in worship and fear. His solitude was soon interrupted by Wautoconomese, whose trembling agitation betrayed how little he had foreseen that his pompous prophecies would be thus sublimely fulfilled. Next the aged squaw, who, from fear of interrupting her master in his devotions, had long been crouching in her own corner of the wigwam, more dead than alive, came in, and reverentially crossing herself, implored permission to remain. To these were soon added an accession of almost all the women in the hamlet. Perhaps Sebastian Rallè was hardly aware how much the presence of these rude, uninformed beings relieved his spirit. His explanations to them, mixed with the consolations of religion, nerved his mind with new strength; and he began to look upon the awful appearance in the heavens with a calmness and rationality worthy of him. By degrees the light grew dim, then closed upon the speck of blue sky, which had appeared to keep watch over the souls of superstitious men, and the glorious scene seemed about to end. But suddenly a luminous bow shot from north to south with the rushing sound of a rocket,

5. loup-cervier: lynx.

6. See Rev. 6.14 and 12.7: "And the heaven departed as a scroll when it is rolled together. . . ."; "And there was war in heaven: Michael and his angels fought against the dragon. . . ." See also *Paradise Lost*, Book 1.

and divided the heavens with a broad belt of brightness. The phenomena of that night had been more extraordinary than any the Jesuit had ever witnessed; but until that moment he had known their name and nature; and, with that strange tendency to a belief in supernatural agency, which the greatest and wisest minds have, in a state of high excitement, his cheek now turned pale, and his heart dropped heavily within him, at what he deemed a sure presage of ruin to those he loved. Reason would have indeed told him that it did not comport with the economy of Providence to change the order of creation for so insignificant a thing as man; but who is not more under the influence of feeling than of reason?

Unable to endure the terrific creations of his own fancy, he left the house, followed only by one of the tribe, and entered the path by which the young hunters usually returned. He pursued this route, for nearly a mile, without seeing any traces of the objects of his anxiety. At last he heard a loud 'Willoa.' The source of the clear, ringing sound could not be mistaken; for Saupoolah alone could give the shrillest tones of the human voice such depth and smoothness of melody. The Jesuit, by his long residence with the savages, had acquired their quickness of eye and ear, and a few moments brought him within view of his adopted child. She was standing in a thickly shaded part of the wood, her hand resting on her brow, looking backward, apparently listening with eagerness to the coming footsteps. A slight shade of disappointment passed over her face when she saw Otoolpha was not with her father; but it soon gave place to an affectionate smile, at his enthusiastic demonstrations of joy. From her brief account it appeared they had early in the evening heard distressed noises apparently proceeding from a human voice; that they had separated in search of those from whom it came, and had thus lost each other. As she finished her story, another loud shout sent echoing through the forest, betrayed more anxiety than was common to her fearless nature. Yet even amid her doubt and perplexity, her romantic soul was open to the influence of the sublime scene above her. As they wound along through the forest, ever and anon shouting with their united voices, in hopes the echo would arouse Otoolpha, she occasionally fixed her eye on the bright arch, which still preserved its wavy radiance, though a little softened by light flashes of clouds, through which the stars were distinctly visible. 'The arrows have been flying fast among the tribes of heaven to night,' said she. 'The stars have chased their enemies over the hills. They are returning victorious; and the moon has spread her mantle in their war path.'

When such thoughts as these came over her, Saupoolah's eyes had a brightness totally different from the keenness and outward brilliancy common to fine looking Indians; it was a light that came from within, gleaming up from fires deep, deep down in the soul. It was probably this peculiarity, which had so universally gained for her the title of 'Daughter of a Prophet;' and its effect on the savage, who had attended the Jesuit, was instantly observable; for he devoutly crossed himself, and walked at a great distance from the object of his veneration. Sebastian Rallè, accustomed as he was to the wild freaks, and almost infantile tenderness of his adopted children, had often smiled at their power over the tribe; yet something of pride, almost of deference, mingled with his own love of them. Saupoolah's remark, and the look of inspiration, with which she fixed her eye on the heavens, awakened in his mind the remembrance of many a season, when he had listened to their wild eloquence with wonder and delight. This train of thought betrayed itself in an eagerly affectionate glance at Saupoolah, and a loud shout to Otoolpha, that made the woods ring again. The young wife suddenly assumed the Indian attitude of intense listening; and joy flushed her whole face, like a sunbeam, as she exclaimed, 'It is answered!' Another shout! there could be no mistake. It could not be the reverberation of an echo, for it was repeated louder and louder, at irregular intervals. A rapid and devious walk, guided by sounds which evidently grew nearer, brought Otoolpha in sight. Quick as a young fawn, overflowing with life and frolic, Saupoolah bounded forward, and sprang upon his neck. But the eye of the Jesuit, always rapid and restless in its movements, quickly glanced from his new found treasure to the objects around. A European lady, possessed of much matronly beauty, lay lifeless at his feet; and a fragile looking boy, apparently eight or nine years old, was bending over her, and weeping bitterly. This child, alone in the wilderness with his dead mother, had uttered those cries of distress and terror, which had startled Otoolpha and his companion. The sight of a white man seemed to the desolate boy a pledge of safety. He nestled close to the side of the priest, and looking up in his face imploringly, burst into tears. The heart of the Jesuit was touched. There was something in the boy's voice and the lady's features, that troubled the waters of a long sealed fountain. The Indians exchanged whispers with that air of solemnity, which the presence of the dead always inspires. They read a mixed feeling of agony and doubt in the countenance of Sebastian Rallè, but they did not ask, and they never knew its origin. After a moment's silence, during which he seemed struggling with powerful emotion, he placed his hand gently on the boy's head, and spoke soothing words in French, which the child understood with perfect facility. No sigh, no outward sign of despair escaped him; but there was a marble stillness, which, like the ominous quiet of a volcano, betrayed that raging materials were at work within.

He ordered the corpse to be borne to his wigwam with all possible gentleness; and when the unevenness of the path occasioned the least violence of motion, he would cringe, as if an adder had stung him. It was in vain that Wautoconomese and his frightened companion sought protection from him, on his return. Remarkable electrical appearances, in every variety of form, continued during the whole night; but the miserable man regarded them not. The lifeless mother was placed in his study, and he knelt down beside it with the boy, and spoke not a word. The old squaw brought in her tallest bayberry wax candles, and tried to prolong her stay in the room by a thousand little officious arts; but a gentle signal to withdraw was all she could gain from her heart stricken master. Day dawned, and found him unchanged in countenance or position. The boy, weary with grief and fatigue, had fallen asleep, and lay on the floor in a slumber as deep and peaceful as if unalloyed happiness had been his portion. The sight of his tranquil innocence, as the daylight shone upon his childish features, brought tears to the eyes of the rigid priest. It was a charm that broke the spell of agony which had bound down his spirit. The terribly cold and glassy look departed from him; but never, after that night, was Sebastian Rallè as he had been. Affliction did not soften and subdue him. It deepened the gloom with which he had long looked upon the world, and seemed to justify him in giving up his whole soul to the stern dictates of Jesuitical maxims. Even Otoolpha and Saupoolah met with occasional harshness; and William Ponsonby, the English boy, alone received uniform mildness and affection at his hands. He was a fair and delicate blossom; such a being as the heart would naturally cling to for its very fragility and dependence; but to none on earth, save Sebastian Rallè, was it known that there were other and deeper reasons for his peculiar tenderness.

The lady, whom he had loved in early youth, had been induced by her parents to marry a wealthy Englishman, in preference to the unportioned Frenchman, whom alone she had truly loved. Her husband lost much of his fortune, and joined his countrymen against the French, during the troubled period between 1690 and 1762. He was taken by the Indians, and his wife saw him suffer a horrid and lingering death. By the humanity of one of the savages, she made her escape, with her youngest son, the only one remaining of eight fine boys. She well knew the residence of that devoted lover, whom her weakness of purpose had driven to a life of solitude and self-denial; and to him she resolved to appeal for protection. Worn out with wandering and privation, she died suddenly in the wilderness, when her arduous journey was well nigh completed; and the conscientious priest, even in the anguish of a breaking heart, felt that it was well for him she had died; for to have seen the widowed one depending upon him for protection, when the solemn vows of his order had separated them forever, would have been worse than death to endure. The affection he had borne the mother rested on the child; and in him he found, what he had in vain wished for since his residence in the New World, a docile and intelligent scholar.

The boy was indeed a sort of 'young Edwin;' a sad, imaginative child, fond of his books, and still more fond of rambling far and wide with the wayward Saupoolah. The log-house of good Mrs. Allan was the only place where William spoke in the language of his father; for English was a hateful sound to the ear of the Jesuit. The troubles between the neighbouring villages of English and Abnakis increased daily; and not a few of the latter were induced to revolt against their spiritual ruler. Distrust, jealousy, and weakness characterized all their councils. Their deep, but fluctuating feelings alternately showed themselves in insults to the priest, and acts of violence on their neighbours. Representatives were sent from the English villages on the Kennebec to the government at Boston, who protested against Sebastian Rallè, for constantly using his influence to excite Indian revenge to its utmost rancor; and letters filled with charges of this nature may still be seen in the records of the Historical Society. It is probable that they were, in some measure, well founded; for it was the dangerous creed of the Jesuits, that all human power, good or bad, should be made subservient to one grand end. Yet the Norridgewocks had so much reason to complain of the fraud and falsehood of the English, that it is difficult to decide to whom the greatest share of blame rightfully belongs. Be that as it may, affairs went from bad to worse. Mutual dislike became every day more inveterate; and Mrs. Allan was the only one who had not in some way or other suffered from the powerful arm of the implacable Otoolpha. His French origin, the great influence he had over his tribe, and his entire submission to the will of the Jesuit, procured for him a double portion of hatred. Dislike was returned with all the fierceness and impetuosity of his savage nature; and English mothers often frightened their children into obedience by the use of his terrible name. In the autumn of 1724, these discontents were obviously approaching a fearful crisis. A Council Fire was kindled at the village of the Abnakis; and fierce indeed were the imprecations uttered, and terrible the resolutions taken against the English.

Wautoconomese in his fury said, that the Evil Spirit had governed them ever since William Ponsonby[7] came among them; and he demanded that the boy should at once be sacrificed to an offended Deity. The lip of the venerable priest quivered and turned pale for an instant; but it passed quickly, and so carefully had even the muscles of his face been trained in obedience to the Society of Jesus, that rigid indifference could alone be read there, as he carelessly asked, 'Wherefore should the child die?' The fierce old prophet watched his emotions as the snake fixes her infernal eye on the bird she is charming unto death. 'Because the Great Spirit, who dwells among the windy hills, and covers himself with the snow mantle, has whispered it in the ear of the wise man,' said he proudly. 'Wherefore else did he breathe softly on the wood, for four sleeps, and take his garments from the sun, that it might give warmth to the pale papoose, on his way through the wilderness? I tell you, he sent him to Wautoconomese, that he might sacrifice him instead of the young fawn and the beaver; for he loves not the white face and the double tongue of the Yengees.'

'And the love I bear them is such as the panther gives the stricken deer,' replied the Jesuit. 'Ye are all one! ye are all one!' answered the raging prophet. 'The Yengees say their king has counted more scalps than any other chief; and you say he is but a boy to the great king, who lives where the vines run with oil. Ye both have faces pale as a sick woman. One hisses like a snake, and the other chatters like a mad cat bird; but both hunt the poor Indian like a buffalo to his trap. Wautoconomese was once a very big prophet. The Great Spirit spoke to him loud, and his tribe opened their eyes wide, that they might look on him. What is Wautoconomese now? He speaks the words of the Great Spirit; and ye laugh when ye tell the young men of his tribe that his ears are old, and he cannot hear.'

His stormy eloquence awakened the slumbering pride of his warlike nation; and against the whole race of white men they inwardly breathed a vow of extermination.

The boy was bound for sacrifice, and evil eyes were cast upon the Jesuit. The ingratitude of those for whom he had toiled thirty long years, and the threatened loss of the dearest object which God had left to cheer his lonely pilgrimage, seemed to freeze the faculties of the old man; and that day would

---

7. William Ponsonby: a fourteen-year-old English boy, who had been captured by the Indians six months before the English raid on Norridgewock, was found among the wounded and was said to have been shot and stabbed by Rale himself. None of Child's sources mentions his name. Her account of the boy's parentage is fictitious.

have ended his trials with his life, had not Otoolpha stepped into the centre of the Council Circle, and, with a low bow to Wautoconomese, demanded to be heard. He spoke reverently of the prophet; but, by all the sufferings and kindness of their French Father, he conjured them not to be ungrateful to him in his old age. He begged for the boy's life, and promised to lead his tribe to war against every white man, woman, and child, from Corratwick Falls to the Big Sea, if they would thus reward his victory.

He was a favorite with his tribe, and they listened to him. After much consultation, they determined on midnight marches at the end of three weeks, by which means they intended to surprise and put to death all the English settlers on the Kennebec. If successful in this attempt, William Ponsonby was safe; if not, the innocent child must fall a victim to their savage hatred.

Saupoolah slept little the night after she listened to the Council of her tribe. She thought of Mrs. Allan's kind looks, when she saved her from drowning; and she remembered the happy hours when she used to feed the children from her little berry basket. Could she not save her from the general ruin? She asked Otoolpha if no stratagem could be devised. He told her it would lead to detection, and the life of William and the priest would be forfeited. In her uneasy slumbers she dreamed of the murder of her benefactress; and she started up, declaring she would save Mrs. Allan's life at the peril of her own. Otoolpha resolutely and somewhat harshly forbade her to do it. It was the first time he had ever spoken to her in a tone of authority; and her proud spirit rose against him. 'I have loved him,' thought she, 'but not with the tameness of a household drudge; if such is the service he wants, let him leave Saupoolah, and find a mate among the slaves of Abnakis.' Her manner the next day was cold, suspicious, and constrained towards her husband. She said no more to him of her plans, but sought advice from the priest. The heart broken old man was roused into sudden energy, and solemnly and vehemently forbade her project. Saupoolah's soul struggled in cords to which she had been entirely unaccustomed. She was silent, but determined. That night she left Otoolpha in a sound sleep, and effected her dangerous purpose secretly. She told Mrs. Allan all the plans of the Norridgewocks, beseeching her to make no other use of the knowledge, than to save herself and family. The terrified matron promised she would not. But could, or ought, such a promise to be kept?

Time passed on, and threw no light on the dangerous deed Saupoolah had dared to perform. Fears of its consequences haunted her own soul, like a restless demon; and again and again did she extort from Mrs. Allan a vow never to betray her. More than half of her fault sprang from a kind and generous nature; but she could not forgive herself for the vexation that had mingled with better feelings. Her pride and her buoyancy were both gone; and upon Otoolpha, Sebastian Rallè, and William Ponsonby, she lavished the most anxious fondness.

The old priest cared little whether life or death were his portion; for he was old, and disappointment had ever been the shadow of his hopes. But for the dead mother's sake, his heart yearned for the life of the boy. Saupoolah, ever enthusiastic and self-sacrificing, promised to convey him away secretly, and place him under the protection of a Canadian priest. The time appointed was four days before the intended massacre of the English, when a Council Fire of one of the neighbouring tribes would induce most of the Norridgewocks to be absent. The night preceding his departure was a weary one to Sebastian Rallè. He spent it at William's couch in wakefulness and prayer. Affections, naturally intense, were all centered on this one object; and he had nerved himself to think that he must part with him, and then lay him down and die.

The gray tints of morning rose upon him, showing the whole of his miserable little apartment in cheerless obscurity. The old priest, stern, philosophic, and rigid elsewhere, was in the seclusion of his own apartment, as wayward and affectionate as a child. He stooped down, and parting William's soft hair, imprinted a kiss on his forehead. The boy, half unconscious what he did, fondly nestled his cheek into the hand that rested on him. Sebastian Rallè looked upward with an expression that seemed to say, 'O Father, would that this cup might pass from me.' Just then the church bell, with feeble but sweet tones, announced the hour of early mass. William was on his feet in an instant, and as quickly knelt to his venerable friend to receive his customary benediction. In a few minutes, every living soul in the hamlet was within the walls of the church. Wigwams were all quiet, and canoes were wimpling about in Sandy river. The savages had all bowed down and crossed themselves before the unseen God. The broken voice of the Jesuit was heard loudly beseeching, '*Ora, ora pro nobis,*' when armed men rushed in amid their peaceful worship. The clashing of swords, the groans of the dying, and the yells of the frantic, mingled in one horrid chaos of clamor. Not one escaped; not one. Some called out, 'Save William Ponsonby and the priest!' Others aimed at the breast of the Jesuit, as if he had been the only victim desired. The English boy threw himself forward and received a stab, aimed at the heart of his old friend; and the priest, with one convulsive bound, and one loud shriek of agony, withdrew the sword and plunged it deeply in his own breast.

Saupoolah's noble heart broke with intensity of suffering. She fell lifeless by the side of the murdered William, and a dozen swords at once were pointed at her. Otoolpha cast one hurried glance upon her; and man has no power to speak the mingled rage, despair, and anguish, which that wild glance expressed. With the concentrated strength of fifty savages, he forced his way unhurt to the river side, and sprung into Saupoolah's favorite canoe. The boat filled with water; and he found that even here the treacherous revenge of his enemies would reach his life. With desperate strength he gained the shore, and ran toward the forest. His coronet and belt made him a conspicuous victim; multitudes were in pursuit; and he died covered with wounds. * * * Before the setting of the sun, the pretty hamlet was reduced to ashes; and the Indians slept their last sleep beneath their own possessions. * * * For many years two white crosses marked the place where the Jesuit and his English boy were buried; but they have long since been removed. The white man's corn is nourished by the bones of the Abnakis; and the name of their tribe is well nigh forgotten.

Willie Wharton

Would you like to read a story which is true, and yet not true? The one I am going to tell you is a superstructure of imagination on a basis of facts. I trust you are not curious to ascertain the exact proportion of each. It is sufficient for any reasonable reader to be assured that many of the leading incidents interwoven in the following story actually occurred in one of our Western States, a few years ago.

It was a bright afternoon in the spring-time; the wide, flowery prairie waved in golden sunlight, and distant tree-groups were illuminated by the clear, bright atmosphere. Throughout the whole expanse, only two human dwellings were visible. These were small log-cabins, each with a clump of trees near it, and the rose of the prairies climbing over the roof. In the rustic piazza of one of these cabins a woman was sewing busily, occasionally moving a cradle gently with her foot. On the steps of the piazza was seated a man, who now and then read aloud some paragraph from a newspaper. From time to time, the woman raised her eyes from her work, and, shading them from the sunshine with her hand, looked out wistfully upon the sea of splendor, everywhere waving in flowery ripples to the soft breathings of the balmy air. At length she said,—

"Brother George, I begin to feel a little anxious about Willie. He was told not to go out of sight, and he is generally a good boy to mind; but I should think it was more than ten minutes since I have seen him. I wish you would try the spy-glass."

The man arose, and, after looking abroad for a moment, took a small telescope from the corner of the piazza, and turned it in the direction the boy had taken.

"Ah, now I see the little rogue!" he exclaimed. "I think it must have been that island of high grass that hid him from you. He has not gone very far; and now he is coming this way. But who upon earth is he leading along? I believe the adventurous little chap has been to the land of Nod to get him a wife. I know of no little girl, except my Bessie, for five miles round; and it certainly is not she. The fat little thing has toppled over in the grass, and Willie is picking her up. I believe in my soul she's an Indian."

"An Indian!" exclaimed the mother, starting up suddenly. "Have you heard of any Indians being seen hereabouts? Do blow the horn to hurry him home."

A tin horn was taken from the nail on which it hung, and a loud blast stirred the silent air. Moles stopped their digging, squirrels paused in their gambols, prairie-dogs passed quickly from one to another a signal of alarm, and all the little beasts wondered what could be the meaning of these new sounds which had lately invaded the stillness of their haunts.

George glanced at the anxious countenance of his sister, and said,—

"Don't be frightened, Jenny, if some Indians do happen to call and see us. You know you always agreed with me that they would be as good as Christians, if they were treated justly and kindly. Besides, you see this one is a very small savage, and we shall soon have help enough to defend us from her formidable blows. I made a louder noise with the horn than I need to have done; it has startled your husband, and he is coming from his plough; and there is my wife and Bessie running to see what is the matter over here."

By this time the truant boy and his companion approached the house, and he mounted the steps of the piazza with eager haste, pulling her after him, immediately upon the arrival of his father, Aunt Mary, and Cousin Bessie. Brief explanation was made, that the horn was blown to hurry Willie home; and all exclaimed,—

"Why, Willie! who is this?"

"Found her squatting on the grass, pulling flowers," he replied, almost out of breath. "Don't know her name. She talks lingo."

The whole company laughed. The new-comer was a roly-poly, round enough to roll, with reddish-brown face, and a mop of black hair, cut in a straight line just above the eyes. But *such* eyes! large and lambent, with a foreshadowing of sadness in their expression. They shone in her dark face like moonlit waters in the dusky landscape of evening. Her only garment was a short kirtle of plaited grass, not long enough to conceal her chubby knees. She understood no word of English, and, when spoken to, repeated an Indian phrase, enigmatical to all present. She clung to Willie, as if he were an old friend; and he, quite proud of the manliness of being a protector, stood with his arm across her brown shoulders, half offended at their merriment, saying,—

"She's *my* little girl. *I* found her."

"I *thought* he'd been to the land of Nod to get him a wife," said Uncle George, smiling.

Little Bessie, with clean apron, and flaxen hair nicely tied up with ribbons, was rather shy of the stranger.

"She'th dirty," lisped she, pointing to her feet.

"Well, s'pose she is?" retorted William. "I guess *you*'d be dirty, too, if you'd been running about in the mud, without any shoes. But she's pretty. She's like my black kitten, only she a'n't got a white nose."

Willie's comparison was received with shouts of laughter; for there really was some resemblance to the black kitten in that queer little face. But when the small mouth quivered with a grieved expression, and she clung closer to Willie, as if afraid, kind Uncle George patted her head, and tried to part the short, thick, black hair, which would not stay parted, but insisted upon hanging straight over her eyebrows. Baby Emma had been wakened in her cradle by the noise, and began to rub her eyes with her little fists. Being lifted into her mother's lap, she hid her face for a while; but finally she peeped forth timidly, and fixed a wondering gaze on the new-comer. It seemed that she concluded to like her; for she shook her little dimpled hand to her, and began to crow. The language of children needs no interpreter. The demure little Indian understood the baby-salutation, and smiled.

Aunt Mary brought bread and milk, which she devoured like a hungry animal. While she was eating, the wagon arrived with Willie's older brother, Charley, who had been to the far-off mill with the hired man. The sturdy boy came in, all aglow, calling out,—

"Oh, mother! the boy at the mill has caught a prairie-dog. Such a funny-looking thing!"

He halted suddenly before the small stranger, gave a slight whistle, and exclaimed,—

"Halloo! here's a funny-looking prairie-puss!"

"She a'n't a prairie-puss," cried Willie, pushing him back with doubled fists. "She's a little girl; and she's *my* little girl. I found her."

"She's a great find," retorted the roguish brother, as he went behind her, and pulled the long black hair that fell over her shoulders.

"Now you let her alone!" shouted Willie; and the next moment the two boys were rolling over on the piazza, pommelling each other, half in play, half in earnest. The little savage sat coiled up on the floor, watching them without apparent emotion; but when a hard knock made Willie cry out, she sprang forward with the agility of a kitten, and, repeating some Indian word with strong emphasis, began to beat Charley with all her might. Instinctively, he was about to give blows in return; but his father called out,—

"Hold there, my boy! Never strike a girl!"

"And never harm a wanderer that needs protection," said Uncle George. "It isn't manly, Charley."

Thus rebuked, Charley walked away somewhat crestfallen. But before he disappeared at the other end of the piazza, he turned back to sing,—

"Willie went a-hunting, and caught a pappoose."

"She a'n't a pappoose, she's a little girl," shouted Willie; "and she's *my* little girl. I didn't hunt her; I found her."

Uncle George and his family did not return to their cabin till the warm, yellow tint of the sky had changed to azure-gray. While consultations were held concerning how it was best to dispose of the little wanderer for the night, she nestled into a corner, where, rolled up like a dog, she fell fast asleep. A small bed was improvised for her in the kitchen. But when they attempted to raise her up, she was dreaming of her mother's wigwam, and, waking suddenly to find herself among strangers, she forgot the events of the preceding hours, and became a pitiful image of terror. Willie, who was being undressed in another room, was brought in in his nightgown, and, the sight of him reassured her. She clung to him, and refused to be separated from him; and it was finally concluded that she should sleep with her little protector in his trundle-bed, which every night was rolled out from under the bed of his father and mother. A tub of water was brought, and as Willie jumped into it, and seemed to like to splash about, she was induced to do the same. The necessary ablutions having been performed, and the clean nightgowns put on, the little ones walked to their trundle-bed hand in hand. Charley pulled the long hair once more, as they passed, and began to sing, "Willie went a-hunting"; but the young knight-errant was too sleepy and tired to return to the charge. The older brother soon went to rest also; and all became as still within-doors as it was on the wide, solitary prairie.

The father and mother sat up a little while, one mending a harness, the other repairing a rip in a garment. They talked together in low tones of Willie's singular adventure; and Mrs. Wharton asked her husband whether he supposed this child belonged to the Indians whose tracks their man had seen on his way to the mill. She shared her brother's kindly feeling toward the red men, because they were an injured and oppressed race. But, in her old New-England home, she had heard and read stories that made a painful impression on the imagination of childhood; and though she was now a sensible and courageous woman, the idea of Indians in the vicinity rendered the solitude of the wilderness oppressive. The sudden cry of a night-bird made her start and turn pale.

"Don't be afraid," said her husband, soothingly. "It is as George says. Nothing but justice and kindness is needed to render these wild people firm friends to the whites."

"I believe it," she replied; "but treaties with them have been so wickedly violated, and they are so shamefully cheated by Government-agents, that they naturally look upon all white men as their enemies. How can they know that we are more friendly to them than others?"

"We have been kind to their child," responded Mr. Wharton, "and that will prevent them from injuring us."

"I would have been just as kind to the little thing, if we had an army here to protect us," she rejoined.

"They will know that, Jenny," he said. "Indian instincts are keen. Your gentle eyes and motherly ways are a better defence than armies would be."

The mild blue eyes thanked him with an affectionate glance. His words somewhat calmed her fears; but before retiring to rest, she looked out, far and wide, upon the lonely prairie. It was beautiful, but spectral, in the ghostly veil of moonlight. Every bolt was carefully examined, and the tin horn hung by the bedside. When all preparations were completed, she drew aside the window-curtain to look at the children in their trundle-bed, all bathed with silvery moonshine. They lay with their arms about each other's necks, the dark brow nestled close to the rosy cheek, and the mass of black hair mingled with the light brown locks. The little white boy of six summers and the Indian maiden of four slept there as cozily as two kittens with different fur. The mother gazed on them fondly, as she said,—

"It is a pretty sight. I often think what beautiful significance there is in the Oriental benediction, 'May you sleep tranquilly as a child when his friends are with him!'"

"It is, indeed, a charming picture," rejoined her husband. "This would be a text for George to preach from; and his sermon would be, that confidence is always born of kindness."

The fear of Indians vanished from the happy mother's thoughts, and she fell asleep with a heart full of love for all human kind.

The children were out of their bed by daylight. The little savage padded about with naked feet, apparently feeling much at home, but seriously incommoded by her night-gown, which she pulled at restlessly, from time to time, saying something in her own dialect, which no one could interpret. But they understood her gestures, and showed her the kirtle of plaited grass, still damp with the thorough washing it had had the night before. At sight of it she became quite voluble; but what she said no one knew. "What gibberish you talk!" exclaimed Charley. She would not allow him to come near her. She remembered how he had pulled her hair and tussled with Willie. But two bright buttons on a string made peace between them. He put the mop on his head, and shook it at her, saying, "Moppet, you'd be pretty, if you wore your hair like folks." Willie was satisfied with this concession; and already the whole family began to outgrow the feeling that the little wayfarer belonged to a foreign race.

Early in the afternoon two Indians came across the prairie. Moppet saw them first, and announced the discovery by a shrill shout, which the Indians evidently heard; for they halted instantly, and then walked on faster than before. When the child went to meet them, the woman quickened her pace a little, and took her hand; but no signs of emotion were perceptible. As they approached the cabin, Moppet appeared to be answering their brief questions without any signs of fear. "Poor little thing!" said Mrs. Wharton. "I am glad they are not angry with her. I was afraid they might beat her."

The strangers were received with the utmost friendliness, but their stock of English was so very scanty that little information could be gained from them. The man pointed to the child, and said, "Wik-a-nee, me go way she." And the woman said, "Me tank." No further light was ever thrown upon Willie's adventure in finding a pappoose alone on the prairie. The woman unstrapped from her shoulder a string of baskets, which she laid upon the ground. Moppet said something to her mother, and placed her hand on a small one brightly stained with red and yellow. The basket was given to her, and she immediately presented it to Willie. At the same time the Indian woman offered a large basket to Mrs. Wharton, pointing to the child, and saying, "Wik-a-nee. Me tank." Money was offered her, but she shook her head, and repeated, "Wik-a-nee. Me tank." The man also refused the coin, with a slow motion of his head, saying, "Me tank." They ate of the food that was offered them, and received a salted fish and bread with "Me tank."

"Mother," exclaimed Willie, "I want to give Moppet something. May I give her my Guinea-peas?"

"Certainly, my son, if you wish to," she replied.

He ran into the cabin, and came out with a tin box. When he uncovered it, and showed Moppet the bright scarlet seeds, each with a shining black spot, her dark eyes glowed, and she uttered a joyous "Eugh!" The passive, sad expression of the Indian woman's countenance almost brightened into a smile, as she said, "Wik-a-nee tank."

After resting awhile, she again strapped the baskets on her shoulder, and taking her little one by the hand, they resumed their tramp across the prairie,—no one knowing whence they came, or whither they were going. As far as they could be seen, it was noticed that the child looked back from time to time. She was saying to her mother she wished they could take that little pale-faced boy with them.

"So Moppet is gone," said Charley. "I wonder whether we shall ever see her again." Willie heaved a sigh, and said, "I wish she was my little sister."

Thus met two innocent little beings, unconscious representatives of races widely separated in moral and intellectual culture, but children of the same Heavenly Father, and equally subject to the attractions of great Mother Nature. Blessed childhood, that yields spontaneously to those attractions, ignoring all distinctions of pride or prejudice! Verily, we should lose all companionship with angels, were it not for the ladder of childhood, on which they descend to meet us.

It was a pleasant ripple in the dull stream of their monotonous life, that little adventure of the stray pappoose. At almost every gathering of the household, for several days after, something was recalled of her uncouth, yet interesting looks, and of her wild, yet winning ways. Charley persisted in his opinion that "Moppet would be pretty, if she wore her hair like folks."

"Her father and mother called her Wik-a-nee," said Willie; "and I like that name better than I do Moppet." He took great pains to teach it to his baby sister; and he succeeded so well, that, whenever the red-and-yellow basket was shown to her, she said, "Mik-a-nee,"—the W being beyond her infant capabilities.

Something of tenderness mixed with Mrs. Wharton's recollections of the grotesque little stranger. "I never saw anything so like the light of an astral lamp as those beautiful large eyes of hers," said she. "I began to love the odd little thing; and if she had stayed much longer, I should have been very loath to part with her."

The remembrance of the incident gradually faded; but whenever a far-off neighbor or passing emigrant stopped at the cabin, Willie brought forward his basket, and repeated the story of Wik-a-nee,—seldom forgetting to imitate her strange cry of joy when she saw the scarlet peas. His mother was now obliged to be more watchful than ever to prevent him from wandering out of sight and hearing. He had imbibed an indefinite idea that there was a great realm of adventure out there beyond. If he could only get a little nearer to the horizon, he thought he might perhaps find another pappoose, or catch a prairie-dog and tame it. He had heard his father say that a great many of those animals lived together in houses under ground,—that they placed sentinels at their doors to watch, and held a town-meeting when any danger approached. When Willie was summoned from his exploring excursions, he often remonstrated, saying, "Mother, what makes you blow the horn so *soon?* You never give me time to find a prairie-dog. It would be capital fun to have a dog that knows enough to go to town-meeting." Charley took particular pleasure in increasing his excitement on that subject. He told him he had once seen a prairie-dog standing sentinel at the entrance-hole of their habitations. He made a picture of the creature with charcoal on the shed-door, and proposed to prick a copy of it into Willie's arm with India-ink, which was joyfully agreed to. The likeness, when completed, was very much like a squash upon two sticks, but it was eminently satisfactory to the boys. There was no end to Willie's inquiries. How to find that hole which Charley had seen, to crawl into it, and attend a dogs' town-meeting, was the ruling idea of his life. Unsentimental as it was, considering the juvenile gallantry he had manifested, it was an undeniable fact, that, in the course of a few months, prairie-dogs had chased Wik-a-nee almost beyond the bounds of his memory.

Autumn came, and was passing away. The waving sea of verdure had become brown, and the clumps of trees, dotted about like islands, stood denuded of their foliage. At this season the cattle were missing one day, and were not to be found. A party was formed to go in search of them, consisting of all the men from both homesteads, except Mr. Wharton, who remained to protect the women and children, in case of any unforeseen emergency. Charley obtained his father's permission to go with Uncle George; and Willie began to beg hard to go also. When his mother told him he was too young to be trusted, he did not cry, because he knew it was an invariable rule that he was never to have anything he cried for; but he grasped her gown, and looked beseechingly in her face, and said,—

"Oh, mother, do let me go with Charley, just this once! Maybe we shall catch a prairie-dog."

"No, darling," she replied. "You are not old enough to go so far. When you are a bigger boy, you shall go after the cattle, and go a-hunting with father, too, if you like."

"Oh, dear!" he exclaimed, impatiently, "when *shall* I be a bigger boy? You *never* will let me go far enough to see the prairie-dogs hold a town-meeting!"

The large brown eyes looked up very imploringly.

Mr. Wharton smiled and said,—

"Jenny, you do keep the little fellow tied pretty close to your apron-string. Perhaps you had better let him go this time."

Thus reinforced, the petted boy redoubled his importunities, and finally received permission to go, on condition that he would be very careful not to wander away from his brother. Charley promised not to trust him out of his sight; and the men said, if they were detained till dark, they would be sure to put the boys in a safe path to return home before sunset. Willie was equipped for the excursion, full of joyous anticipations of marvellous adventures and promises to return before sunset and tell his parents about everything he had seen. His mother kissed him, as she drew the little cap over his brown locks, and repeated her injunctions over and over again. He jumped down both steps of the piazza at once, eager to see whether Uncle George and Charley were ready. His mother stood watching him, and he looked up to her with such a joyful smile on his broad, frank face, that she called to him,—

"Come and kiss me again, Willie, before you go; and remember, dear, not to go out of sight of Uncle George and Charley."

He leaped up the steps, gave her a hearty smack, and bounded away.

When the party started, she stood a little while gazing after them. Her husband said,—

"What a pet you make of that boy, Jenny. And it must be confessed he is the brightest one of the lot."

"And a good child, too," she rejoined. "He is so affectionate, and so willing to mind what is said to him! But he is so active, and eager for adventures! How the prairie-dogs do occupy his busy little brain!"

"That comes of living out West," replied Mr. Wharton, smiling. "You know the miller told us, when we first came, that there was nothing like it for making folks know everything about all *natur'*."

They separated to pursue their different avocations, and, being busy, were consequently cheerful,—except that the mother had some occasional misgivings whether she had acted prudently in consenting that her darling should go beyond sound of the horn. She began to look out for the boys early in the afternoon; but the hours passed, and still they came not. The sun had sunk below the horizon, and was sending up regular streaks of gold, like a great glittering crown, when Charley was seen coming alone across the prairie. A pang like the point of a dagger went through the mother's heart. Her first thought was,—

"Oh, my son! my son! some evil beast has devoured him."

Charley walked so slowly and wearily that she could not wait for his coming, but went forth to meet him. As soon as she came within sound of his voice, she called out,—

"Oh, Charley, where's Willie?"

The poor boy trembled in every joint, as he threw himself upon her neck and sobbed out,—

"Oh, mother! mother!"

Her face was very pale, as she asked, in low, hollow tones,—

"Is he dead?"

"No, mother; but we don't know where he is. Oh, mother, do forgive me!" was the despairing answer.

The story was soon told. The cattle had strayed farther than they supposed, and Willie was very tired before they came in sight of them. It was not convenient to spare a man to convey him home, and it was agreed that Charley should take him a short distance from their route to a log-cabin, with whose friendly inmates they were well acquainted. There he was to be left to rest, while his brother returned for a while to help in bringing the cattle together. The men separated, going in various circuitous directions, agreeing to meet at a specified point, and wait for Charley. He had a boy's impatience to be at the place of rendezvous. When he arrived near the cabin, and had led Willie into the straight path to it, he charged him to go into the house, and not leave it till he came for him; and then he ran back with all speed to Uncle George. The transaction seemed to him so safe that it did not occur to his honest mind that he had violated the promise given to his mother. While the sun was yet high in the heavens, his uncle sent him back to the log-cabin for Willie, and sent a man with him to guide them both within sight of home. Great was their alarm when the inmates of the house told them they had not seen the little boy. They searched, in hot haste, in every direction. Diverging from the road to the cabin was a path known as the Indian trail, on which hunters, of various tribes, passed and repassed in their journeys to and from Canada. The prints of Willie's shoes were traced some distance on this path, but disappeared at a wooded knoll not far off. The inmates of the cabin said a party of Indians had passed that way in the forenoon. With great zeal they joined in the search, taking with them horns and dogs. Charley ran hither and thither, in an agony of remorse and terror, screaming, "Willie! Willie!" Horns were blown with all the strength of manly lungs; but there was no answer,—not even the illusion of an echo. All agreed in thinking that the lost boy had been on the Indian trail; but whether he had taken it by mistake, or whether he had been tempted aside from his path by hopes of finding prairie-dogs, was matter of conjecture. Charley was almost exhausted by fatigue and anxiety, when his father's man guided him within sight of home, and told him to go to his mother, while he returned to give the alarm to Uncle

George. This was all the unhappy brother had to tell; and during the recital his voice was often interrupted by sobs, and he exclaimed, with passionate vehemence,—

"Oh, father! oh, mother! do forgive me! I didn't think I was doing wrong,—indeed, I didn't!"

With aching hearts, they tried to soothe him; but he would not be comforted.

Mr. Wharton's first impulse was to rush out in search of his lost child. But the shades of evening were close at hand, and he deemed it unsafe to leave Jenny and Mary and their little girls with no other protector than an overtired boy.

"Oh, why did I advise her to let the dear child go?" was the lamenting cry continually resounding in his heart; and the mother reproached herself bitterly that she had consented against her better judgment.

Neither of them uttered these thoughts; but remorseful sorrow manifested itself in increased tenderness toward each other and the children. When Emma was undressed for the night, the mother's tears fell fast among her ringlets; and when the father took her in his arms to carry her to the trundle-bed, he pressed her to his heart more closely than ever before; while she, all wondering at the strange tearful silence round her, began to grieve, and say,—

"I want Willie to go to bed with me. Why don't Willie come?"

Putting strong constraint upon the agony her words excited, the unhappy parents soothed her with promises until she fell into a peaceful slumber. As they turned to leave the bedroom, both looked at the vacant pillow where that other young head had reposed for years, and they fell into each other's arms and wept.

Charley could not be persuaded to go to bed till Uncle George came; and they forbore to urge it, seeing that he was too nervous and excited to sleep. Stars were winking at the sleepy flowers on the prairie, when the party returned with a portion of the cattle, and no tidings of Willie. Uncle George's mournful face revealed this, before he exclaimed,—

"Oh, my poor sister! I shall never forgive myself for not going with your boys. But the cabin was in plain sight, and the distance so short I thought I could trust Charley."

"Oh, don't, uncle! don't!" exclaimed the poor boy. "My heart will break!"

A silent patting on the head was the only answer; and Uncle George never reproached him afterward.

Neither of the distressed parents could endure the thoughts of discontinuing the search till morning. A wagon was sent for the miller and his men, and, accompanied by them, Mr. Wharton started for the Indian trail. They took with them lanterns, torches, and horns, and a trumpet, to be sounded as a signal that the lost one was found. The wretched mother traversed the piazza slowly, gazing after them, as their torches cast a weird, fantastic light on the leafless trees they passed. She listened to the horns resounding in the distance, till the *tremolo* motion they imparted to the air became faint as the buzz of insects. At last, Charles, who walked silently by her side, was persuaded to go to bed, where, some time after midnight, he cried himself into uneasy, dreamful slumber. But no drowsiness came to the mother's eyelids. All night long she sat watching at the bedroom-window, longing for the gleam of returning torches, and the joyful *fanfare* of the trumpet. But all was dark and still. Only stars, like the eyes of spirits, looked down from the solemn arch of heaven upon the desolate expanse of prairie.

The sun had risen when the exploring party returned, jaded and dispirited, from their fruitless search. Uncle George, who went forth to meet them, dreaded his sister's inquiring look. But her husband laid his hand tenderly on her shoulder, and said,—

"Don't be discouraged, Jenny. I don't believe any harm has happened to him. There are no traces of wild beasts."

"But the Indians," she murmured, faintly.

"I am glad to hear you say that," said Uncle George. "My belief is that he is with the Indians; and for that reason, I think we have great cause to hope. Very likely he saw the Indians, and thought Wik-a-nee was with them, and so went in pursuit of her. If she, or any of her relatives, are with those hunters, they will be sure to bring back our little Willie; for Indians are never ungrateful."

The mother's fainting heart caught eagerly at this suggestion; and Charley felt so much relieved by it that he was on the point of saying he was sure it must have been either Moppet or a dogs' town-meeting that lured Willie from the path he had pointed out to him. But everybody looked too serious for jesting; and memory of his own fault quickly repressed the momentary elasticity.

Countless were the times that the bereaved parents cast wistful glances over the prairie, with a vague hope of descrying Indians returning with their child. The search was kept up for days and weeks. All the neighbors, within a circuit of fifteen miles, entered zealously into the work, and explored prairie and forest far and wide. At last these efforts were given up as useless. Still Uncle George held out the cheerful prospect that the Indians would bring him, when they returned from their long hunting-excursion; and with this the mother tried to sustain her sinking hopes. But month after month she saw the snowy expanse of prairie gleaming in the moonlight, and no little footstep broke its untrodden crust. Spring returned, and the sea of flowers again rippled in waves, as if Flora and her train had sportively taken lessons of the water-nymphs; but no little hands came laden with blossoms to heap in Emma's lap. The birds twittered and warbled, but the responsive whistle of the merry boy was silent; only its echo was left in the melancholy halls of memory. His chair and plate were placed as usual, when the family met at meals. At first this was done with an undefined hope that he might come before they rose from table, and afterward they could not bear to discontinue the custom, because it seemed like acknowledging that he was entirely gone.

Mrs. Wharton changed rapidly. The light of her eyes grew dim, the color faded from her cheeks, and the tones of her once cheerful voice became plaintive as the "Light of Other Days."[1] Always, from the depths of her weary heart, came up the accusing cry, "Oh, why did I let him go?" She never reproached others; but all the more bitterly did Mr. Wharton, Uncle George, and above all poor Charley, reproach themselves. The once peaceful cabins were haunted by a little ghost, and the petted child became an accusing spirit. Alas! who is there that is not chained to some rock of the past, with the vulture of memory tearing at his vitals, screaming forever in the ear of conscience? These unavailing regrets are inexorable as the whip of the Furies.

Four years had passed away, when some fur-traders passed through that region, and told of a white boy they had seen among the Pottawatomie Indians. Everybody had heard the story of Willie's mysterious disappearance, and the tidings were speedily conveyed to the Wharton family. They immediately wrote the United-States Agent among that tribe. After waiting awhile, they all became restless. One day, Uncle George said to his sister,—

"Jenny, I have never forgiven myself for leaving your boys to take care of themselves, that fatal day. I cannot be easy. I must go in search of Willie."

"Heaven bless you!" she replied. "My dear James has just been talking of starting on the same journey. I confess I want some one to go and look for the poor boy; but it seems to me selfish; for it is a long and difficult journey, and may bring fresh misfortunes upon us."

After some friendly altercation between Mr. Wharton and the brother, as

---

1. The "Light of Other Days": apparently an allusion to the line "The light of other days is faded," from *The Maid of Artois* by Alfred Bunn (1796?–1860).

to which should go, it was decided that George should have his way; and brave, unselfish Aunt Mary uttered no word of dissuasion. He started on his arduous journey, cheered by hope, and strong in a generous purpose. It seemed long before a letter was received from him, and when it came, its contents were discouraging. The Indian Agent said he had caused diligent search to be made, and he was convinced there was no white child among the tribes in that region. Uncle George persevered in efforts to obtain some clue to the report which had induced him to travel so far. But after several weeks, he was obliged to return alone, and without tidings.

Mrs. Wharton's hopes had been more excited than she was herself aware of, and she vainly tried to rally from the disappointment. This never-ending uncertainty, this hope forever deferred, was harder to endure than would have been the knowledge that her dear son was dead. She thought it would be a relief, even if fragments of his clothes should be found, showing that he had been torn to pieces by wild beasts; for then she would have the consolation of believing that her darling was with the angels. But when she thought of him hopelessly out of reach, among the Indians, imagination conjured up all manner of painful images. Deeper and deeper depression overshadowed her spirits and seriously impaired her health. She was diligent in her domestic duties, careful and tender of every member of her household, but everything wearied her. Languidly she saw the seasons come and go, and took no pleasure in them. A village was growing up round her; but the new-comers, in whom she would once have felt a lively interest, now flitted by her like the shadows in a magic-lantern. "Poor woman!" said the old settlers to the new ones. "She is not what she was. She is heart-broken."

Eight years more passed away, and Mrs. Wharton, always feeble, but never complaining, continued to perform a share of household work, with a pensive resignation which excited tenderness in her family and inspired even strangers with pitying deference. Her heartstrings had not broken, but they gradually withered and dried up, under the blighting influence of this life-long sorrow. It was mild October weather, when she lay down to rise no more. Emma had outgrown the trundle-bed, and no one occupied it; but it remained in the old place. When they led her into the bedroom for the last time, she asked them to draw it out, that she might look upon Willie's pillow once more. Memories of her fair boy sleeping there in the moonlight came into her soul with the vividness of reality. Her eyes filled with tears, and she seemed to be occupied with inward prayer. At a signal from her, the husband and brother lifted her tenderly, and placed her in the bed, which Aunt Mary had prepared. The New Testament was brought, and Mr. Wharton read the fourteenth chapter of John. As they closed the book, she said faintly, "Sing, 'I'm going home.'" It was a Methodist hymn, learned in her youth, and had always been a favorite with her. The two families had often sung it together on Sabbath days, exciting the wonderment of the birds in the stillness of the prairie. They now sang it with peculiar depth of feeling; and as the clear treble of Aunt Mary's voice, and the sweet childlike tones of Emma, followed and hovered over the clear, strong tenor of Uncle George, and the deep bass of Mr. Wharton, the invalid smiled serenely, while her attenuated hand moved to the measure of the music.

She slept much on that and the following day, and seemed unconscious of all around her. On the third day, her watchful husband noticed that her countenance lighted up suddenly, like a landscape when clouds pass from the sun. This was followed by a smile expressive of deep inward joy. He stooped down and whispered,—

"What is it, dear?"

She looked up, with eyes full of interior light, and said,—

"Our Willie!"

She spoke in tones stronger than they had heard from her for several days; and after a slight pause, she added,—

"Don't you see him? Wik-a-nee is with him, and he is weaving a string of the Guinea-peas in her hair. He wears an Indian blanket; but they look happy, there where yellow leaves are falling and the bright waters are sparkling."

"It is a flood of memory," said Mr. Wharton, in a low tone. "She recalls the time when Wik-a-nee was so pleased with the Guinea-peas that Willie gave her."

"She has wakened from a pleasant dream," said Uncle George, with the same subdued voice. "It still remains with her, and the pictures seem real."

The remarks were not intended for her ear, but she heard them, and murmured,—

"No,—not a dream. Don't you *see* them?"

They were the last words she ever uttered. She soon dozed away into apparent oblivion; but twice afterward, that preternatural smile illumined her whole countenance.

At that same hour, hundreds of miles away, on the side of a wooded hill, mirrored in bright waters below, sat a white lad with a brown lassie beside him, among whose black shining tresses he was weaving strings of scarlet seeds. He was clothed with an Indian blanket, and she with a skirt of woven grass. Above them, from a tree glorious with sunshine, fell a golden shower of autumn leaves. They were talking together in some Indian dialect.

"A-lee-lah," said he, "your mother always told me that I gave you these red seeds when I was a little boy. I wonder where I was then. I wish I knew. I never understood half she told me about the long trail. I don't believe I could ever find my way."

"Don't go!" said his companion, pleadingly. "The sun will shine no more on A-lee-lah's path."

He smiled and was silent for a few minutes, while he twined some of the scarlet seeds on grasses round her wrist. He revealed the tenor of his musings by saying,—

"A-lee-lah, I wish I could see my mother. Your mother told me she had blue eyes and pale hair. I don't remember ever seeing a woman with blue eyes and pale hair."

Suddenly he started.

"What is it?" inquired the young girl, springing to her feet.

"My mother!" he exclaimed. "Don't you see her? She is smiling at me. How beautiful her blue eyes are! Ah, now she is gone!" His whole frame quivered with emotion, as he cried out, in an agony of earnestness, "I want to go to my mother! I *must* go to my mother! Who can tell me where to find my mother?"

"You have looked into the Spirit-Land," replied the Indian maiden, solemnly.

Was the mighty power of love, in that dying mother's heart, a spiritual force, conveying her image to the mind of her child, as electricity transmits the telegram? Love photographs very vividly on the memory; when intensely concentrated, may it not perceive scenes and images unknown to the bodily eye, and, like the sunshine, under favorable circumstances, make the pictures visible? Who can answer such questions? Mysterious beyond comprehension are the laws of our complex being. The mother saw her distant son, and the son beheld his long-forgotten mother. How it was, neither of them knew or thought; but on the soul of each, in their separate spheres of existence, the vision was photographed.[2]

---

2. "the vision was photographed": Child wrote repeatedly about clairvoyant phenomena, notably in her novel *Philothea* (1836), Letters 4 and 22 of *Letters from New York, Second Series* (1845), *The Progress of Religious Ideas* (1855), "The Ancient Clairvoyant" and "Spirit and Matter" in her collection *Autumnal Leaves* (1857), and her article "Spirits," published in the *Atlantic* of May 1862. Her own leaning toward mysticism gave her an intuitive sympathy for the visionary aspect of American Indian culture; see, for example, "She Waits in the Spirit Land," in her collection *Fact and Fiction* (1846).

In the desolated dwelling on the prairie, they were all unconscious of this magnetic transmission of intelligence between the dying mother and her far-off child. As she lay in her coffin, they spoke soothingly to each other, that she had passed away without suffering, dreaming pleasantly of Willie and the little Indian girl. Their memories were excited to fresh activity, and the sayings and doings of Willie and the pappoose were recounted for the thousandth time. Emma had no recollection of her lost brother, and the story of his adventure with Moppet always amused her young imagination. But such reminiscences never brought a smile to Charley's face. When he heard the clods fall on his mother's coffin, heavier and more dismally fell on his heart the remembrance of his broken promise, which had so dried up the fountains of her life.

Four times had the flowers bloomed above that mother's grave, and still, for her dear sake, all the memorials of her absent darling remained as she had liked to have them. The trundle-bed was never removed, the Indian basket remained under the glass in the bedroom, where his own little hands had put it, and his chair retained its place at the table. Out of the family he was nearly forgotten; but parents now and then continued to frighten truant boys by telling them of Willie Wharton, who was carried off by Indians and never heard of after.

The landscape had greatly changed since Mr. Wharton and his brother-in-law built their cabins in the wilderness. Those cabins were now sheds and kitchens appended to larger and more commodious dwellings. A village had grown up around them. On the spire of a new meeting-house a gilded fish sailed round from north to south, to the great admiration of children in the opposite schoolhouse. The wild-flowers of the prairie were supplanted by luxuriant fields of wheat and rye, forever undulating in wave-like motion, as if Nature loved the rhythm of the sea, and breathed it to the inland grasses. Neat little Bessie was a married woman now, and presided over the young Squire's establishment, in a large white house with green blinds. Charley had taken to himself a wife, and had a little Willie in the cradle, in whose infant features grandfather fondly traced some likeness to the lost one.

Such was the state of things, when Charles Wharton returned from the village-store, one day, with some articles wrapped in a newspaper from Indiana. A vague feeling of curiosity led him to glance over it, and his attention was at once arrested by the following paragraph:—

"A good deal of interest has been excited here by the appearance of a young man, who supposes himself to be twenty-three years old, evidently white, but with the manners and dress of an Indian. He says he was carried away from his home by Indians, and they have always told him he was then six years old. He speaks no English, and an Indian interpreter who is with him is so scantily supplied with words that the information we have obtained is very unsatisfactory. But we have learned that the young man is trying to find his mother. Some of our neighbors regard him as an impostor. But he does not ask for money, and there is something in his frank physiognomy calculated to inspire confidence. We therefore believe his statement, and publish it, hoping it may be seen by some bereaved family."

Charles rushed into the field, and exclaimed,—

"Father, I do believe we have at last got some tidings of Willie!"

"Where? What is it?" was the quick response.

The offered newspaper was eagerly seized, and the father's hand trembled visibly while he read the paragraph.

"We must start for Indiana directly," he said; and he walked rapidly toward the house, followed by his son.

Arriving at the gate, he paused and said,—

"But, Charles, he will have altered so much that perhaps we shouldn't know him; and it may be, as the people say, that this youth is an impostor."

The young man replied, unhesitatingly,—

"I can tell whether he is an impostor. I shall know my brother."

His voice quivered a little, as he spoke the last word.

Mr. Wharton, without appearing to notice it, said,—

"You have a great deal of work on hand at this season. Wouldn't it be better for Uncle George and me to go?"

He answered impetuously,—

"If all my property goes to ruin, I will hunt for Willie all over the earth, so long as there is any hope of finding him. I always felt as if mother couldn't forgive me for leaving him that day, though she always tried to make me think she did. And now, if we find him at last, she is not here to"—

His voice became choked.

Mr. Wharton replied, impressively,—

"She will come with him, my son. Wherever he may be, they are not divided now."

The next morning Charles started on his expedition, having made preparations for an absence of some months, if so long a time should prove necessary. The first letters received from him were tantalizing. The young man and his interpreter had gone to Michigan, in consequence of hearing of a family there who had lost a little son many years ago. But those who had seen him in Indiana described him as having brown eyes and hair, and as saying that his mother's eyes were the color of the sky. Charles hastened to Michigan. The wanderer had been there, but had left, because the family he sought were convinced he was not their son. They said he had gone to Canada, with the intention of rejoining the tribe of Indians he had left.

We will not follow the persevering brother through all his travels. Again and again he came close upon the track, and had the disappointment of arriving a little too late. On a chilly day of advanced autumn, he mounted a pony and rode toward a Canadian forest, where he was told some Indians had encamped. He tied his pony at the entrance of the wood, and followed a path through the underbrush. He had walked about a quarter of a mile, when his ears were pierced by a shrill, discordant yell, which sounded neither animal nor human. He stopped abruptly, and listened. All was still, save a slight creaking of boughs in the wind. He pressed forward in the direction whence the sound had come, not altogether free from anxiety, though habitually courageous. He soon came in sight of a cluster of wigwams, outside of which, leaning against trees, or seated on the fallen leaves, were a number of men, women, and children, dressed in all sorts of mats and blankets, some with tufts of feathers in their hair, others with bands and tassels of gaudy-colored wampum. One or two had a regal air, and might have stood for pictures of Arab chiefs or Carthaginian generals; but most of them looked squalid and dejected. None of them manifested any surprise at the entrance of the stranger. All were as grave as owls. They had, in fact, seen him coming through the woods, and had raised their ugly war-whoop, in sport, to see whether it would frighten him. It was their solemn way of enjoying fun. Among them was a youth, tanned by exposure to wind and sun, but obviously of white complexion. His hair was shaggy, and cut straight across his forehead, as Moppet's had been. Charles fixed upon him a gaze so intense that he involuntarily took up a hatchet that lay beside him, as if he thought it might be necessary to defend himself from the intruder.

"Can any of you speak English?" inquired Charles.

"Me speak," replied an elderly man.

Charles explained that he wanted to find a white young man who had been in Indiana and Michigan searching for his mother.

"*Him* pale-face," rejoined the interpreter, pointing to the youth, whose brown eyes glanced from one to the other with a perplexed expression.

Charles made a strong effort to restrain his impatience, while the interpreter slowly explained his errand. The pale-faced youth came toward him.

"Let me examine your right arm," said Charles.

The beaver-skin mantle was raised; and there, in a dotted outline of blue spots, was the likeness of the prairie-dog which in boyish play he had pricked into Willie's arm. With a joyful cry he fell upon his neck, exclaiming, "My brother!" The interpreter repeated the word in the Indian tongue. The youthful stranger uttered no sound; but Charles felt his heart throb, as they stood locked in a close embrace. When their arms unclasped, they looked earnestly into each other's faces. That sad memory of the promise made to their gentle mother, and so thoughtlessly broken, brought tears to the eyes of the elder brother; but the younger stood apparently unmoved. The interpreter, observing this, said,—

"Him sorry-glad; but red man he no cry."

There was much to damp the pleasure of this strange interview. The uncouth costume, and the shaggy hair falling over the forehead, gave Willie such a wild appearance, it was hard for Charles to realize that they were brothers. Inability to understand each other's language created a chilling barrier between them. Charles was in haste to change his brother's dress, and acquire a stock of Indian words. The interpreter was bound farther north; but he agreed to go with them three days' journey, and teach them on the way. They were merely guests at the encampment, and no one claimed a right to control their motions. Charles distributed beads among the women and pipes among the men; and two hours after he had entered the wood, he was again mounted on his pony, with William and the interpreter walking beside him. As he watched his brother's erect figure striding along, with such a bold, free step, he admitted to himself that there were some important compensations for the deficiencies of Indian education.

Languages are learned rapidly, when the heart is a pupil. Before they parted from the interpreter, the brothers were able, by the aid of pantomime, to interchange various skeletons of ideas, which imagination helped to clothe with bodies. At the first post-town, a letter was despatched to their father, containing these words: "I have found him. He is well, and we are coming home. Dear Lucy must teach baby Willie to crow and clap his hands. God bless you all! Charley."

They pressed forward as fast as possible, and at the last stage of their journey travelled all night; for Charles had a special reason for wishing to arrive at the homestead on the following day. The brothers were now dressed alike, and a family-likeness between them was obvious. Willie's shaggy hair had been cut, and the curtain of dark brown locks being turned aside revealed a well-shaped forehead whiter than his cheeks. He had lost something of the freedom of his motions; for the new garments sat uneasily upon him, and he wore them with an air of constraint.

The warm golden light of the sun had changed to silvery brightness, and the air was cool and bracing, when they rode over the prairie so familiar to the eye of Charles, but which had lost nearly all the features that had been impressed on the boyish mind of William. At a little distance from the village they left their horses and walked across the fields to the back-door of their father's house; for they were not expected so soon, and Charles wished to take the family by surprise. It was Thanksgiving day. Wild turkeys were prepared for roasting, and the kitchen was redolent of pies and plum-pudding. When they entered, no one was there but an old woman hired to help on festive occasions. She uttered a little cry when she saw them; but Charles put his finger to his lip, and hurried on to the family sitting-room. All were there,— Father, Emma, Uncle George, Aunt Mary, Bessie and her young Squire, Charles's wife, baby, and all. There was a universal rush, and one simultaneous shout of, "Willie! Willie!" Charles's young wife threw herself into his arms; but all the rest clustered round the young stranger, as the happy father clasped him to his bosom. When the tumult of emotion had subsided a little, Charles introduced each one separately to his brother, explaining their relationship as well as he could in the Indian dialect. Their words were unintelligible to the wanderer, but he understood their warmth of welcome, and said,—

"Me tank. Me no much speak."

Mr. Wharton went into the bedroom and returned with a morocco case, which he opened and placed in the stranger's hand, saying, in a solemn tone,—

"Your mother."

Charles, with a tremor in his voice, repeated the word in the Indian tongue. Willie gazed at the blue eyes of the miniature, touched them, pointed to the sky, and said,—

"Me see she, time ago."

All supposed that he meant the memories of his childhood. But he in fact referred to the vision he had seen four years before, as he explained to them afterward, when he had better command of their language.

The whole family wept as the miniature passed from hand to hand, and, with a sudden outburst of grief, Charles exclaimed,—

"Oh, if *she* were only here with us this happy day!"

"My son, she *is* with us," said his father, impressively.

William was the only one who seemed unmoved. He did not remember his mother, except as he had seen her in that moment of clairvoyance; and it had been part of his Indian training to suppress emotion. But he put his hand on his heart, and said,—

"Me no much speak."

When the little red-and-yellow basket was brought forward, it awakened no recollections in his mind. They pointed to it, and said, "Wik-a-nee, Moppet"; but he made no response.

His father eyed him attentively, and said,—

"It surely *must* be our Willie. I see the resemblance to myself. We cannot be mistaken."

"I *know* he is our Willie," said Charles; and removing his brother's coat, he showed what was intended to be the likeness of a prairie-dog. His father and Uncle George remembered it well; and it was a subject of regret that William could not be made to understand any jokes about his boyish state of mind on that subject. Mr. Wharton pointed to the chair he used to occupy, and said,—

"It seems hardly possible that this tall stranger can be the little Willie who used to sit there. But it *is* our Willie. God be praised!" He paused a moment, and added, "Before we partake of our Thanksgiving dinner, let us all unite in thanks to our Heavenly Father; 'for this my son was dead and is alive again, he was lost and is found.' "[3]

They all rose, and he offered a prayer, to which heart-felt emotion imparted eloquence.

Charles had taken every precaution to have his brother appear as little as possible like a savage, when he restored him to his family; and now, without mentioning that he would like raw meat better than all their dainties, he went to the kitchen to superintend the cooking of some Indian succotash, and buffalo-steak *very* slightly broiled.

For some time, the imperfect means of communicating by speech was a great impediment to confidential intercourse, and a drawback upon their happiness. Emma, whose imagination had been a good deal excited by the prospect of a new brother, was a little disappointed. In her own private mind, she thought she should prefer for a brother a certain Oberlin student, with whom she had danced the last Thanksgiving evening. Bessie, always a stickler

---

3. From the story of the Prodigal Son, Luke 15.24, the words in which the father expresses his joy over the return of his long lost son.

for propriety, ventured to say to her mother that she hoped he would learn to use his knife and fork, like other people. But to older members of the family, who distinctly remembered Willie in his boyhood, these things seemed unimportant. It was enough for them that the lost treasure was found.

The obstacle created by difference of language disappeared with a rapidity that might have seemed miraculous, were it not a well-known fact that one's native tongue forgotten is always easily restored. It seems to remain latent in the memory, and can be brought out by favorable circumstances, as writing with invisible ink reappears under the influence of warmth. Tidings of the young man's restoration to his family spread like fire on the prairie. People for twenty miles round came to see the Willie Wharton of whose story they had heard so much. Children were disappointed to find that he was not a little rosy-cheeked boy, such as had been described to them. Some elderly people, who prided themselves on their sagacity, shook their heads when they observed his rapid improvement in English, and said to each other,—

"It a'n't worth while to disturb neighbor Wharton's confidence; but depend upon it, that fellow's an impostor. As for the mark on his arm that they call a prairie-dog, it looks as much like anything else that has legs."

To the family, however, every week brought some additional confirmation that the stranger was their own Willie. By degrees, he was able to make them understand the outlines of his story. He did not remember anything about parting from his brother on that disastrous day, and of course could not explain what had induced him to turn aside to the Indian trail. He said the Indians had always told him that a squaw, whose pappoose had died, took a fancy to him, and decoyed him away; and that afterward, when he cried to go back, they would not let him go. From them he also learned that he called himself six years old, at the time of his capture; but his name had been gradually forgotten, both by himself and them. He wandered about with that tribe eight summers and winters. Sometimes, when they had but little food, he suffered with hunger; and once he was wounded by a tomahawk, when they had a fight with some hostile tribe; but they treated him as well as they did their own children. He became an expert hunter, thought it excellent sport, and forgot that he was not an Indian. His squaw-mother died, and, not long after, the tribe went a great many miles to collect furs. In the course of this journey they encountered various tribes of Indians. One night they encamped near some hunters who spoke another dialect, which they could partly understand. Among them was a woman, who said she knew him. She told him his mother was a white woman, with eyes blue as the sky, and that she was very good to her little pappoose, when she lost her way on the prairie. She wanted her husband to buy him, that they might carry him back to his mother. He bought him for ten gallons of whiskey, and promised to take him to his parents the next time the tribe travelled in that direction,—because, he said, their little pappoose had liked them very much.

"We remember her very well," said Mr. Wharton. "Her name was Wik-a-nee."

" 'That not *name*," replied William. "Wik-a-nee mean little small thing."

"You were a small boy when you found the pappoose on the prairie," rejoined his father. "You took a great liking to her, and said she was *your* little girl. When she went away, you gave her your box of Guinea-peas."

"Guinea-peas? What that?" inquired the young man.

"They are red seeds with black spots on them," replied his father. "Emma, I believe you have some. Show him one."

The moment he saw it, he exclaimed,—

"Haha! A-lee-lah show me Guinea-peas. Her say me give she."

"Then you know Wik-a-nee?" said his father, in an inquiring tone.

The wanderer had acquired the gravity of the Indians. He never laughed, and rarely smiled. But a broad smile lighted up his frank countenance, as he answered,—

"Me know A-lee-lah very well. She not Wik-a-nee now."

Then he became grave again, and told how he was twining the red seeds in A-lee-lah's hair, when his mother came and looked at him with great blue eyes and smiled. Most of his auditors thought he was telling a dream. But Mr. Wharton said to his oldest son,—

"I told you, Charles, that mother and son were not separated now."

William seemed perplexed by this remark; but he comprehended in part, and said,—

"Me see into Spirit-Land."

When asked why he had not started in search of his mother then, he replied,—

"A-lee-lah's father, mother die. A-lee-lah say not go. Miles big many. Me not know the trail. But Indians go hunt fur. Me go. Me sleep. Me dream mother come, say go home. Me ask where mother? Charles come. Him say brother."

The little basket was again brought forth, and Mr. Wharton said,—

"Wik-a-nee gave you this, when she went away; but when we showed it to you, you did not remember it."

He took it and looked at it, and said,—

"Me not remember"; but when Emma would have put it away, he held it fast; and that night he carried it with him to his chamber.

Some degree of restlessness had been observed in him previously to this conversation. It increased as the weeks passed on. He became moody, and liked to wander off alone, far from the settlement. The neighbors said to each other,—"He will never be contented. He will go back to the Indians." The family feared it also. But Uncle George, who was always prone to look on the bright side of things, said,—

"We shall win him, if we manage right. We mustn't try to constrain him. The greatest mistake we make in our human relations is interfering too much with each other's freedom. We are too apt to think *our* way is the *only* way. It's no such very great matter, after all, that William sometimes uses his fingers instead of a knife and fork, and likes to squat on the floor better than to sit in a chair. We mustn't drive him away by taking too much notice of such things. Let him do just as he likes. We are all creatures of circumstances. If you and I were obliged to dance in tight boots, and make calls in white kid gloves, we should feel like fettered fools."

"And *be* what we felt like," replied Mr. Wharton; "and the worst part of it would be, we shouldn't long have sense enough to *feel* like fools, but should fall to pitying and despising people who were of any use in the world. But really, brother George, to have a son educated by Indians is not exactly what one could wish."

"Undoubtedly not, in many respects; but it has its advantages. William has already taught me much about the habits of animals and the qualities of plants. Did you ever see an eye so sure as his to measure distances, or to send an arrow to the mark? He never studied astronomy, but he knows how to make use of the stars better than we do. Last week, when we got benighted in the woods, he at once took his natural place as our leader; and how quickly his sagacity brought us out of our trouble! He will learn enough of our ways, by degrees. But I declare I would rather have him always remain as he is than to make a city-fop of him. I once saw an old beau at Saratoga,—a forlorn-looking mortal, creeping about in stays and tight boots; and I thought I should rather be the wildest Ojibbeway that ever hunted buffaloes in a ragged blanket."

The rational policy recommended by Uncle George was carefully pursued. Everything was done to attract William to their mode of life, but no remark was made when he gave a preference to Indian customs. Still, he seemed moody, and at times sad. He carried within him a divided heart. One day, when he was sitting on a log, looking absent and dejected, his father put his hand gently upon his shoulder, and said,—

"Are you not happy among us, my son? Don't you like us?"

"Me like very much," was the reply. "Me glad find father, brother. All good."

He paused a moment, and then added,—

"A-lee-lah's father, mother be dead. A-lee-lah alone. A-lee-lah did say not go. Me promise come back soon."

Mr. Wharton was silent. He was thinking what it was best to say. After waiting a little, William said,—

"Father, me not remember what is English for squaw."

"Woman," replied Mr. Wharton.

"Not that," rejoined the young man. "What call Charles's squaw?"

"His wife," was the reply.

"Father, A-lee-lah be my wife. Me like bring A-lee-lah. Me fraid father not like Indian."

Mr. Wharton placed his hand affectionately on his child's head, and said,—

"Bring A-lee-lah, in welcome, my son. Your mother loved her, when she was Wik-a-nee; and we will all love her now. Only be sure and come back to us."

The brown eyes looked up and thanked him, with a glance that well repaid the struggle those words had cost the wise father.

So the uncivilized youth again went forth into the wilderness, saying, as he parted from them, "Me bring A-lee-lah." They sent her a necklace and bracelets of many-colored beads, and bade him tell her that they remembered Wik-a-nee, and had always kept her little basket, and that they would love her when she came among them. Charles travelled some distance with his brother, bought a new Indian blanket for him, and returned with the garments he had worn during his sojourn at home. They felt that they had acted wisely and kindly, but it was like losing Willie again; for they all had great doubts whether he would ever return.

He was incapable of writing a letter, and months passed without any tidings of him. They all began to think that the attractions of a wild life had been strong enough to conquer his newly awakened natural affections. Uncle George said,—

"If it prove so, we shall have the consciousness of having done right. We could not have kept him against his will, even if we had wished to do it. If anything will win him to our side, it will be the influence of love and freedom."

"They are strong agencies, and I have great faith in them," replied Mr. Wharton.

Summer was far advanced, when a young man and woman in Indian costume were seen passing through the village, and people said, "There is William Wharton come back again!" They entered the father's house like strange apparitions. Baby Willie was afraid of them, and toddled behind his mother, to hide his face in the folds of her gown. All the other members of the family had talked over the subject frequently, and had agreed how they would treat Wik-a-nee, if she came among them again. So they kissed them both, as they stood there in their Indian blankets, and said, "Welcome home, brother! Welcome, sister!" A-lee-lah looked at them timidly, with her large moonlight eyes, and said, "Me no speak." Mr. Wharton put his hand gently on her head, and said, "We will love you, my daughter." William translated the phrase to her, heaved a sigh, which seemed a safety-valve for too much happiness, and replied, "Me thank father, brother, sister, all." And A-lee-lah said, "Me tank," as her mother had said, in years long gone by.

All felt desirous to remove from her eyebrows the mass of straight black hair, which she considered extremely becoming, but which they regarded as a great disfigurement to her really handsome face. However, no one expressed such an opinion, by word or look. They had previously agreed not to man-ifest any distaste for Indian fashions.

Mr. Wharton, apart, remarked to Charles,—

"When you were a boy, you said Moppet would be pretty, if she wore her hair like folks. It was true then, and is still more true now."

"Let us have patience, and we shall see her handsome face come out of that cloud by-and-by," rejoined Uncle George. "If we prove that we love her, we shall gain influence over her. Wild-flowers, as well as garden-flowers, grow best in the sunshine."

Emma tried to conform to the wishes of the family in her behavior; but she did not feel quite sure that she should ever be able to love the young Indian. It was not agreeable to have a sister who was clothed in a blanket and wore her hair like a Shetland pony. Cousin Bessie thought stockings, long skirts, and a gown ought to be procured for her immediately. Her father said,—

"Let me tell you, Bessie, it would be far more rational for you to follow *her* fashion about short skirts. I should like to see *you* step off as she does. She couldn't move so like a young deer, if she had long petticoats to trammel her limbs."[4]

But Bessie confidentially remarked to Cousin Emma that she thought her father had some queer notions; to which Emma replied, that, for her part, she thought A-lee-lah ought to dress "like folks," as Charley used to say, when he was a boy. They could not rest till they had made a dress like their own, and had coaxed William to persuade her to wear it. In a tone of patient resignation, she at last said, "Me try." But she was evidently very uncomfortable in her new habiliments. She often wriggled her shoulders, and her limbs were always getting entangled in the folds of her long, full skirts. She finally rebelled openly, and, with an emphatic "Me no like," cast aside the troublesome garments and resumed her blanket.

"I suppose she felt very much as I should feel in tight boots and white kid gloves," said Uncle George. "You will drive them away from us, if you interfere with them so much."

It was agreed that Aunt Mary would understand how to manage them better than the young folks did; and the uncivilized couple were accordingly invited to stay at their uncle's house. Emma cordially approved of this arrangement. She told Bessie that she did hope Aunt Mary would make them more "like folks," before the Oberlin student visited the neighborhood again; for she didn't know what he *would* think of some of their ways. Bessie said,—

"I feel as if I ought to invite William and his wife to dine with us; but if any of my husband's family should come in, I should feel *so* mortified to have them see a woman with a blanket over her shoulders sitting at my table! Besides, they like raw meat, and that is dreadful."

"Certainly it is not pleasant," replied her father; "but I once dined in Boston, at a house of high civilization, where the odor of venison and of Stilton cheese produced much more internal disturbance than I have ever experienced from any of their Indian messes."

This philosophical way of viewing the subject was thought by some of the neighbors to be assumed, as the best mode of concealing wounded pride. They said, in compassionate tones, that they really did pity the Whartons; for, let them say what they would, it must be dreadfully mortifying to have that

4. "long petticoats to trammel her limbs": women's rights advocates—among them Amelia Bloomer, Elizabeth Cady Stanton, and the Grimké sisters—were currently agitating for dress reform, a movement with which Child sympathized. The "hybrid between English and Indian costumes" that A-lee-lah eventually adopts resembles the feminist Bloomer garb.

squaw about. But if such a feeling was ever remotely hinted to Uncle George, he quietly replied,—

"So far from feeling ashamed of A-lee-lah, we are truly grateful to her; and we are deeply thankful that William married her. His love for her safely bridges over the wide chasm between his savage and his civilized life. Without her, he could not feel at home among us; and the probability is that we should not be able to keep him. By help of his Indian wife, I think we shall make him contented, and finally succeed in winning them over to our mode of life. Meanwhile, they are happy in their own way, and we are thankful for it."

The more enlightened portion of the community commended these sentiments as liberal and wise; but some, who were not distinguished either for moral or intellectual culture, said, sneeringly,—

"They talk about his Indian wife! I suppose they jumped over a stick together in some dirty wigwam, and that they call being married!"

Uncle George and Aunt Mary had been so long in the habit of regulating their actions by their own principles, that they scarcely had a passing curiosity to know what such neighbors thought of their proceedings. They never wavered in their faith that persevering kindness and judicious non-interference would gradually produce such transformations as they desired. No changes were proposed, till they and their untutored guests had become familiarly acquainted and mutually attached. At first, the wild young couple were indisposed to stay much in the house. They wandered far off into the woods, and spent most of their time in making mats and baskets. As these were always admired by their civilized relatives, and gratefully accepted, they were happier than millionnaires. They talked to each other altogether in the Indian dialect, which greatly retarded their improvement in English. But it was thus they had talked when they first made love, and it was, moreover, the only way in which their tongues could move unfettered. Her language no longer sounded to William like "lingo," as he had styled it in the boyish days when he found her wandering alone on the prairie. No utterance of the human soul, whether in the form of language or belief, is "lingo," when we stand on the same spiritual plane with the speaker, and thus can rightly understand it.

The first innovation in the habits of the young Indian was brought about by the magical power of two side-combs ornamented with colored glass. At the first sight of them, A-lee-lah manifested admiration almost equal to that which the scarlet peas had excited in her childish mind. Aunt Mary, perceiving this, parted the curtain of raven hair, and fastened it on each side with the gaudy combs. Then she led her to the glass, put her finger on the uncovered brow, and said,—

"A-lee-lah has a pretty forehead. Aunt Mary likes to see it so."

William translated this to his simple wife, who said,—

"Aunt Mary good. Me tank."

Mr. Wharton happened to come in, and he kissed the brown forehead, saying,—

"Father likes to have A-lee-lah wear her hair so."

The conquest was complete. Henceforth, the large, lambent eyes shone in their moonlight beauty without any overhanging cloud.

Thus adroitly, day by day, they were guided into increasing conformity with civilized habits. After a while, it was proposed that they should be married according to the Christian form, as they had previously been by Indian ceremonies. No attempt was made to offer higher inducements than the exhibition of wedding-finery, and the assurance that all William's relatives would be made very happy, if they would conform to the custom of his people. The bride's dress was a becoming hybrid between English and Indian costumes. Loose trousers of emerald-green merino were fastened with scarlet cord and tassels above gaiters of yellow beaver-skin thickly embroidered with beads of many colors. An upper garment of scarlet merino was ornamented with gilded buttons, on each of which was a shining star. The short, full skirt of this garment fell a little below the knee, and the border was embroidered with gold-colored braid. At the waist, it was fastened with a green morocco belt and gilded buckle. The front-hair, now accustomed to be parted, had grown long enough to be becomingly arranged with the jewelled side-combs, which she prized so highly. The long, glossy, black tresses behind were gathered into massive braids, intertwined on one side with narrow scarlet ribbon, and on the other with festoons of the identical Guinea-peas which had so delighted her when she was Wik-a-nee. The braids were fastened by a comb with gilded points, which made her look like a crowned Indian queen. Emma was decidedly struck by her picturesque appearance. She said privately to Cousin Bessie,—

"I should like such a dress myself, if other folks wore it; but don't you tell that I said so."

Charles smiled, as he remarked to his wife,—

"The grub has come out of her blanket a brilliant butterfly. Uncle George and Aunt Mary are working miracles."

After the wedding-ceremony had been performed, Mr. Wharton kissed the bride, and said to the bridegroom,—

"She is handsome as a wild tulip."

"Bright as the torch-flower of the prairies," added Uncle George.

When William made these compliments intelligible to A-lee-lah, she maintained her customary Indian composure of manner, but her brown cheeks glowed like an amber-colored bottle of claret in the sunshine. William, though he deemed it unmanly to give any outward signs of satisfaction, was inwardly proud of his bride's finery, and scarcely less pleased with his own yellow vest, blue coat, and brass buttons; though he preferred above them all the yellow gaiters, which A-lee-lah had skilfully decorated with tassels and bright-colored wampum.

The next politic movement was to build for them a cabin of their own, taking care to preserve an influence over them by frequent visits and kind attentions. They would have been very happy in the freedom of their new home, had it not been for the intrusion of many strangers, who came to look upon them from motives of curiosity. The universal Yankee nation is a self-elected Investigating Committee, which never adjourns its sessions. This is amusing, and perhaps edifying, to their own inquiring minds; but William and A-lee-lah had Indian ideas of natural politeness, which made them regard such invasions as a breach of good manners.

By degrees, however, the young couple became an old story, and were left in comparative peace. The system of attraction continued to work like a charm. As A-lee-lah was never annoyed by any assumption of superiority on the part of her white relatives, she took more and more pains to please them. This was manifested in many childlike ways, which were extremely winning, though they were sometimes well calculated to excite a smile. As years passed on, they both learned to read and write English very well. William worked industriously on his farm, though he never lost his predilection for hunting. A-lee-lah became almost as skilful at her needle as she was at weaving baskets and wampum. Her talk, with its slightly foreign arrangement, was as pretty as the unformed utterance of a little child. Her taste for music improved. She never attained to Italian embroidery of sound, still less to German intonations of intellect; but the rude, monotonous Indian chants gave place to the melodies of Scotland, Ireland, and Ethiopia. Her taste in dress changed also. She ceased to delight in garments of scarlet and yellow, though she retained a liking for bits of bright, warm color. Nature guided her taste correctly in this, for they harmonized admirably with her brown complexion and lustrous black hair. She always wore skirts shorter than others, and garments too loose to impede freedom of motion. Bonnets were her utter aversion, but she consented to wear a woman's riding-hat with a drooping feather. Those outside the family learned to call her Mrs. William Wharton; and strangers who visited the village were generally attracted by her handsome person and the simple dignity of her manners. Her father-in-law regarded her with paternal affection, not unmixed with pride.

"Who, that didn't know it," said he, "could be made to believe this fine-looking woman was once little Moppet, who coiled herself up to sleep on the floor of our log-cabin?"

Uncle George replied,—

"You know I always told you it was the nature of all sorts of flowers to grow, if they had plenty of genial air and sunshine."

As for A-lee-lah's little daughter, Jenny, she is universally admitted to be the prettiest and brightest child in the village. Mr. Wharton says her busy little mind makes him think of his Willie, at her age; and Uncle Charles says he has no fault to find with her, for she has her mother's beautiful eyes, and wears her hair "like folks."

An Appeal for the Indians

❖ *I earnestly desire* to call the attention of humane and thinking people to the recent "Report of the Indian Peace Commission." I know not who wrote this report; but whoever he may be, he is obviously a just and humane man, with opinions concerning the relations of the human race more enlightened and liberal, than is common with public men. Gen. Terry[1] is one of the signers, and I am always ready to believe that any good thing may come from him.

I welcomed this Report almost with tears of joy. "Thank God!" I exclaimed, "we have, at last, an Official Document which manifests something like a right spirit toward the poor Indians! Really, this encourages a hope that the Anglo-Saxon race are capable of civilization?"

That those who have not seen it may judge of its spirit, I will make a few extracts somewhat condensed: "In April, 1864, when the Indians were confessedly at peace, a man named Ripley came into Camp Sanborn and stated that the Indians had taken his stock; he did not know what tribe. Who or what Ripley was, we know not. That he *owned* stock we have *his own* word, and the word of no one else. He asked for troops, and forty men were placed under his guidance, with instructions to disarm the Indians and take possession of Ripley's stock. In the course of the day, Indians were found, and Ripley claimed some of the horses. The Lieutenant ordered the herd to be stopped, and called to the Indians to come and talk with him. As soon as they rode forward, the soldiers were ordered to disarm them. The Indians of course resisted and a fight ensued. . . .

"In May following, Major Downing asked for a force to attack the Indians; for what reason we do not know. Soldiers were given him, and his own account is: 'I captured an Indian and ordered him to go to the village of Cheyenne with us, or I would kill him. We rode all day and night, and about daylight succeeded in surprising the Cheyenne village. We commenced shooting. They lost some twenty-six killed, and thirty wounded. I burnt up their lodges and everything I could get hold of. I took a hundred of their

An Appeal for the Indians (Wm. P. Tomlinson, 1868).

1. General Alfred Howe Terry (1827–90) won fame for capturing Fort Fisher, North Carolina, during the Civil War. Child's high opinion of him is probably based on reports that he treated the black troops in his division well. Ironically, he later played a leading role in the Sioux War of 1876, perhaps bearing some responsibility for Custer's Last Stand.

ponies and distributed them among the boys. That is the usual way in New Mexico.' During the Summer, similar occurrences were frequent. In the Fall, several prominent Chiefs sent word to Major Wynkoop,[2] Commander of Fort Lyon, that war had been *forced* upon them and that they desired peace. The Major accompanied seven of the Chiefs to the house of the Governor of Colorado, to communicate their wishes for peace and protection. The Governor replied, 'I am sorry you brought them here. I have nothing to do with them. They are in the hands of the military authorities. But I don't think it is policy, anyhow, to make peace with them, till they are properly punished; for, if we did, the United States would be acknowledging themselves whipped. In consequence of my representations at Washington, the Third Colorado Regiment was raised to kill Indians, and Indians they *must* kill.' Major Wynkoop then ordered the Indians to move nearer to the Fort, and bring their women and children; promising them military protection. They accordingly encamped near the Fort, to the number of about five hundred. A new commander, who soon after took the place of Major Wynkoop, renewed the promise to protect them. But while they imagined themselves secure under this pledge, the Third Colorado Regiment surrounded their Camp at daylight and commenced indiscriminate slaughter. The heart-rending particulars of this massacre are too well known to need repetition. It is enough to say that it scarcely has its parallel in the records of Indian barbarity. Fleeing women, holding up their hands, and praying for mercy, were brutally shot down; infants were killed and scalped in derision; and men were tortured and mutilated in a manner that would put to shame the ingenuity of savages. No one will be astonished that a war ensued which cost the government thirty millions of dollars, and carried conflagration and death to our border settlements. During the Spring and Summer of 1865, no less than eight thousand troops were withdrawn from the effective force engaged in suppressing the Rebellion, to meet this Indian war. The result of the year's campaign satisfied all reasonable men that war with Indians was useless and expensive. Fifteen or twenty Indians had been killed, at the expense of more than a million dollars apiece, while hundreds of our soldiers had lost their lives, many of our border settlers had been butchered, and much property destroyed. To those who reflected on the subject, *knowing the facts,* the war was something more

---

2. Major Edward W. Wynkoop, special agent to the southern Cheyenne, tried to steer a middle course between his contradictory responsibilities as a military man and as an Indian agent; he later resigned from the Indian Commission to avoid being used against the Indians he was supposed to protect.

than useless and expensive; it was dishonorable to the nation, and disgraceful to those who originated it."

The Report goes on to say: "As soon as Treaties were signed, the war which had been waged for nearly two years instantly ceased. During the Summer and Winter of 1866, General Sherman[3] travelled without escort to the most distant posts of his command, with a feeling of perfect security. To say that no outrages were committed by the Indians, would be claiming for them more than can be justly claimed by the most moral and religious communities. Many bad men are found among the whites, who commit outrages despite all social restraints, and often escape punishment. Is it to be wondered at that Indians are no better than we? . . . If it be said that because they are savages they should be exterminated, we answer that aside from the *humanity* of the suggestion it would prove exceedingly difficult. If money considerations are permitted to weigh, it costs less to civilize than to kill. Among civilized men, war usually springs from a sense of injustice. The best possible way, then, to avoid war is to do no act of injustice. When we learn that the same rule holds good with Indians, the chief difficulty is removed. It is said our wars with them have been almost constant. Have we been uniformly unjust? We answer, unhesitatingly, yes." . . .

"The white and Indian must jointly occupy the country, or one of them must abandon it. If they could have lived together, the Indian would have become civilized, and war prevented. All admit this would have been beneficial to the Indian; and if we grant that it would have proved a little inconvenient as well as detrimental to the white, it is questionable whether the policy that *has* been adopted has not been *more* injurious. What prevented their living together? First, the antipathy of race; second, difference of customs and manners; third, difference of language, which in a great measure prevented a proper understanding of each other's motives and intentions. Now, by educating their children in the English language, these differences would have disappeared, and civilization would have followed. Nothing would then have been left but the antipathy of race; and that, too, is always softened in the beams of a higher civilization." . . .

3. Civil War General William Tecumseh Sherman (1820–91) was famous for his march through Georgia in 1864, which left a trail of destruction and introduced into military history the concept of total war—the attempt to break the will of the enemy by making war on the civilian population. As commander of the Division of the Mississippi after the Civil War, he conducted an equally brutal campaign against the Plains Indians in the fall and winter of 1868. He was one of several military men who served on the Peace Commission.

"Naturally, the Indian has many noble qualities. He is the very embodiment of courage. If he is cruel and revengeful, it is because he is outlawed, and the companion of wild beasts. Let civilized man be his companion, and the association warms into life virtues of the rarest worth. Civilization has driven him away from the home he loved; it has often tortured and killed him; but it could never make him a slave. Considering we have had so little respect for those we did enslave, we ought, for consistency's sake, to admire *this* element of Indian character."

Cordially as I approve of this Report, I dissent from it in a few particulars. It proposes that the tribes should be collected into some Territory, indicated by Congress, and "a man of unquestioned integrity and purity of character should be placed over them as Governor, with salary sufficient to place him above temptation." I would ask what salary *would* place a white Governor of Indians above temptation? I imagine the Treasury of the United States, in its most plethoric condition, would prove insufficient for such a purpose, unless the Governor was subject to a great deal of careful overseeing.

The Report says that schools should be established to instruct the children in English, and "their barbarous dialects should be blotted out." This partakes too much of our haughty Anglo-Saxon ideas of force. I would say, let their books, at first, be printed in Indian, with English translations; and let them contain selections from the best of their own traditionary stories, and records of such things as have been truly honorable in the history of their "braves." Give them pleasant associations with the English language by making it constantly the medium of just principles and kindly feelings. Let proficiency in English, and the habit of speaking it, be rewarded with some peculiar privileges and honors. The Report says, "Let Polygamy be punished." I would rather say let it be discountenanced, and reasoned against, and privileges conferred on those who live with one wife. In this way, the fixed habit of many generations might be weakened, and the way prepared for wise laws on the subject. Indians, like other human beings, are more easily led by the Angel Attraction, than driven by the Demon Penalty. But, alas, Force is the Anglo-Saxon God; and thus we are practically "Devil Worshippers." We have so long indulged in feelings of pride and contempt toward those whom we are pleased to call "the subject races," that we have actually become incapable of judging of them with any tolerable degree of candor and common sense. How *ought* we to view the peoples who are less advanced than ourselves? Simply as younger members of the same great human family, who need to be protected, instructed and encouraged, till they are capable of appreciating and sharing all our advantages.

I know it is an almost universal opinion that Indians are incapable of civilization; but I see no rational ground for such an opinion. Their mode of warfare is certainly barbarous; but, then, all wars are barbarous to a shocking degree. The difference between Indian and civilized warfare is, that we take prisoners, while it is their custom to kill all they conquer. To give no quarter in battle is the international law of their tribes. If this proves incapacity for civilization, the Greeks and Romans were incapable of it; for they did the same. The Lacedemonians slaughtered three thousand Athenians, taken by them at the naval battle of Ægospotami, four hundred years B.C., and all ancient history is full of such examples.

Do we say that their modes of torture indicate irreclaimable barbarism? Let us glance at the record of modern nations, and see whether it proves *our* natures to be essentially different from *theirs*. The Inquisition was in full operation, for centuries, in several Catholic countries. In the course of three hundred years, three hundred and forty-one thousand victims were prosecuted by the Inquisition, *in Spain alone*. Thirty-one thousand nine hundred and twelve of them were burnt alive; and uncounted numbers were subjected to tortures more or less cruel and protracted. The limbs of these poor creatures were stretched by an infernal machine called the rack, till the bones started from their sockets; they were compressed into iron hoops, till the blood gushed from eyes and nostrils, and sometimes from feet and hands; their hands were broken to pieces with thumb-screws and iron gauntlets; and their legs were forced into iron boots, into which wedges were driven, till flesh and bones became a clotted mass; they were confined for days in cages so constructed that they could neither walk, stand, sit, or lie down at full length. I might fill columns with similar monstrosities practiced by nations of the white race. The tortures of the Inquisition were almost entirely for differences of belief concerning theological doctrines; an insanity of cruelty of which Indians were never guilty.

The civil laws of all European countries authorized tortures in various forms. People were legally pinched to death with red hot pincers; they were slowly pressed to death by great weights; they were sawed in pieces alive; they were crucified, head downward; they were torn and devoured by wild beasts; their limbs were pulled asunder by wild horses. Prisoners in the Tower of London had their bones cracked on the rack, and their hands mutilated with thumb-screws. Such things continued to be common during the reign of Elizabeth, called "the Augustan Age of England." By the laws of that country, a person who was proved guilty of high treason was hung by the neck, cut down alive, his entrails taken out and burnt while yet alive, his head cut off, his legs and arms cut off, and exposed in public places. It is little more than two hundred years ago, that the Earl of Montrose was beheaded by the Covenanters for his adherance to the cause of Charles the 1st. His body was dismembered, and his limbs exposed over the gates of various cities, infecting the air with putrefaction, and depraving the moral instincts of mankind. England has ceased to do such things now; but even within a few years she placed Hindoo rebels before the muzzle of cannon, and scattered the blood and brains of the poor wretches in all directions.[4] The English newspapers were ferociously barbarous concerning that rebellion; and Mr. Spurgeon[5] preached a sermon denouncing vengeance against the Hindoos, in terms that seemed less in accordance with the education of a Christian minister than with the savage training of "Black-Hawk," "Pouncing-Eagle," or "Wild-Cat."

We Americans came upon the stage when the world had advanced so far in civilization that our record ought to be much cleaner than it is. The plain truth is, our relations with the red and black members of the human family have been one almost unvaried history of violence and fraud. Our ancestors, whether Catholics or Puritans, were accustomed to regard heathen tribes as Philistines, whom "the Lord's people" were commissioned to exterminate root and branch, or to hold them as bondmen and bondwomen. The early settlers of this country, with the exception of William Penn, treated the native tribes in this spirit. Benevolent individuals tried, from time to time, to ameliorate this state of things; but their efforts availed little, because the spirit of pride and violence pervaded all the laws, all the customs, and all the churches. In 1646, the Apostle Elliot[6] began to labor as a Christian missionary among the Indians in towns around Boston. Very touching is the question they asked him: "The English have been among us twenty-six years. If they thought the knowledge of their God so important, why did they not teach it to us sooner? If they had done so, we might have known much of God by this time, and many sins might have been prevented." The theological teaching of that time must have been bewildering to unsophisticated minds. Mr. Elliot,

---

4. The Indian Mutiny of 1857–59, ignited by a rumor that the rifle cartridges distributed to Indian troops were greased with beef and pork fat (unclean to Hindus and Muslims), spread rapidly across North India and was put down with great severity by the British.

5. Charles Haddon Spurgeon, (1834–92), English Baptist preacher, was famous for his oratorical powers, which made him "the most popular preacher of the day" (*Dictionary of National Biography, DNB*).

6. John Eliot (1604–90), known as the Apostle to the Indians, began preaching to the Indians at Nonantum, near Roxbury, Massachusetts, in 1646. His converts numbered around 3600 at the height of his mission, but diminished rapidly after King Philip's War.

however, succeeded in gathering congregations in various towns, until there were over a thousand styled by him "praying Indians." They reverenced their teacher, and seemed glad to open their minds to such gleams of light as they could receive from the white man's religion. But while a few were engaged in this good work, multitudes were continually abusing and cheating the natives. King Philip,[7] driven to desperation by the continual encroachments of white men, went to war to defend his territories from invaders, just as white monarchs do. This was considered sufficient warrant for a general crusade against Indians. It did not occur to them that a course of strict honesty and impartial justice would have been a safer, cheaper, and better process. There was a camp of "praying Indians," called Wamesits, near the town now called Chelmsford. A barn, filled with corn and hay, was burned in the neighborhood. The Wamesits had nothing to do with it; but the white settlers, filled with the prevailing prejudice against Indians, determined to make them suffer for it. They accordingly went to their encampment and called them out to talk with them. The Wamesits being known as peaceable Christians, and, as they supposed, under the protection of Christians, came forth without hesitation. As soon as they made their appearance, a volley was fired at them. One was killed and seven wounded. Those who could, escaped to the woods, where several of them perished with hunger. The wigwams were set on fire, and seven, who were too old and infirm to get out, were burned alive. Subsequently, some of the fugitives were captured and sold for slaves. Under such circumstances, the teaching of the Apostle Elliot, of course, left no more trace than smoke in the air. How could those simple people believe in a religion whose professors manifested no sense of justice or of mercy toward them?

In consequence of a feud between the French and the English, an Indian village in Norridgewock, Maine, was stealthily attacked by a band of English settlers, in 1724. Men, women and children were all massacred. Their Catholic priest, to whom they were devotedly attached, was shot and scalped, his skull smashed with hatchets, and his limbs broken and mangled in many different ways.

Indians are at least more consistent than white men. They profess to believe in revenge, and practice accordingly; while we profess a religion of love and forgiveness, and do such things as these!

---

7. King Philip (Metacom), sachem of the Wampanoags, led a general uprising of Indian tribes in 1675–76. The bloodiest Indian war in New England's history, it was provoked by the Puritans' execution of three Wampanoag warriors.

The Seminole war, which cost the United States forty or fifty millions of dollars, was caused by the forcible carrying off of the wives and children of Florida Indians, who had intermarried with fugitive slaves, or with the descendants of fugitive slaves. The Indians paid a large sum, by way of compromise, but the Georgia slaveholders, not content with making them pay for their wives and children, demanded and took from the Creeks one hundred and forty-one thousand dollars, as payment for children that the slaves *might* have borne to their masters, if they had not escaped from bondage. Lawless bands were continually going into Florida, capturing whomsoever they pleased, and selling them into slavery, without attempting to establish any claim to them by law; and our government, if it did not connive at these wicked proceedings, neglected to furnish any redress. How can we blame the Indians for fighting, when we ourselves should have fought with half the provocation? Osceola,[8] whose beautiful wife had been torn from him and sold into slavery, fought like a tiger. Is it any wonder that he hated white men? At last, pacified by fair promises, he and other Chiefs agreed to meet the officers of the United States for the purpose of negotiating a treaty of peace. They met *under a flag of truce* and were immediately seized and thrown into prison, where Osceola lingered miserably a while, and died. Such are the methods we take to make the Indians in love with Christianity!

Similar atrocities continue to be perpetrated up to the present time. The record of Fremont's[9] pathfinders in California is enough to fill any humane soul with horror. By their own showing, his band were accustomed to shoot down Indians in mere sport, wherever they came in sight. The gold-hunters in Oregon burn wigwams and shoot the inmates whenever they want to take possession of any spot. They have claimed pay for such barbarities, under the name of military service in subduing the Indians; and they have actually received three millions of dollars from the United States government. If we wish to redeem the American name from everlasting infamy, something must be done to prevent the repetition of such wrongs.

Good Father Beeson,[10] who had lived in the Northwest, bore public testi-

8. The Seminole warrior Osceola led tribal resistance in Florida to the U.S. government's Indian removal policy. His wife was a runaway slave. Child gives accounts of Osceola and the Seminole War in *Selected Letters* (*SL*) 301 and 514–15.

9. John C. Frémont (1813–90), explorer, politician, soldier, made several expeditions to California in 1844–46 with the scout Kit Carson and played a major role in the conquest of California during the Mexican War in 1846–47.

10. John Beeson, Illinois Methodist and abolitionist, settled in Oregon in 1853 and began

mony concerning the outrages committed within his own knowledge. It was painful to hear him tell how thoroughly dejected and hopeless the poor Indians were. I do not suppose the United States government have intended to sanction such proceedings; but they have been unpardonably careless. Rascals and swindlers have often been employed in various departments of Indian service. They have put a great part of the funds intrusted to them into their own pockets. Instead of the good articles stipulated by treaty, the Indians have received moth-eaten blankets, damaged guns, etc., in payment for their lands. Worse than this, soldiers and agents have often treated the Indian women as overseers are accustomed to treat negro slaves; and if an Indian seeks to revenge the violence done to wife or daughter, a hue and cry is raised that the savages are making war upon the whites, troops are called for to put them down, and, without inquiry into the cause of the difficulty, troops are sent.

In view of the facts I have presented, it seems to me that the Indians, even if judged from the most unfavorable side of their character, are no more barbarous than our own ancestors were a few centuries ago; and if *their* descendants have become civilized, why should we consider it impossible for Indians to become so? But are we civilized? When I reflect upon what we *have* done, and *are* doing toward our red brethren, I cannot in conscience answer yes. When I remember how professed Christians, claiming to be the model gentlemen of the nineteenth century have, in the mere wantonness of power, burned negroes alive, hunted them with blood-hounds, seared them with red-hot irons, blistered them with perforated paddles, and lacerated them with wire-pointed whips, I cannot, for very shame, say yes. When I remember how that same "chivalry" stabbed dying soldiers when the battle was over, how they deliberately starved helpless prisoners, and let them perish with cold in sight of acres of forest, from which they begged leave to cut a little fuel;[11] when I remember these things, I cannot say that Indians are the worst savages.

Still, the world has moved, and does move, though it is but slowly. One encouraging fact distinctly proves this. In former ages, the masses of the

---

agitating for Indian rights—an activity that subjected him to harassment by white settlers and night riders. Child may be referring either to his *Plea for the Indians* (New York, 1858) or to his speech at a public meeting in Faneuil Hall on October 9, 1859, in which a number of leading abolitionists also participated.

11. Child is probably referring to the scandal aroused by conditions at the Confederate prison of Andersonville, Georgia, where some 13,000 Union prisoners of war died.

people were utterly ignored; now, the weakest cannot be outraged without finding powerful voices to proclaim their wrongs.

Good Father Beeson tried his utmost to obtain a hearing from the people concerning the wicked oppressions practiced upon our red brethren. But a death-grapple with Slavery was then coming upon the republic, and all felt that one or the other must die. There was too much excitement and anxiety to admit of attention to any other topic. But I think the time has now come when, without intermitting our vigilant watch over the rights of black men, it is our duty to arouse the nation to a sense of its guilt concerning the red men. Legislators are bound to examine, carefully and candidly into the dealings with that much-abused race, and to see that justice is done, for the good fame of the nation, if for no better reason. Lecturers should urge the removal of such a stain on an age of progress. Ministers and missionaries should exert their influence to prevent the name of Christianity from being further disgraced by such diabolical doings. I especially hope that the Quakers will put their hands to the work; for they, better than any others, can "reach the witness" in untutored minds, because they let alone incomprehensible doctrines of theology, and inculcate those great principles of morality, easily understood and recognized by all men. But little can be accomplished either by missionaries or schools, unless government is careful to employ none but honest, just and humane men in their transactions with these poor people. Hitherto, it has been the misfortune and disgrace of the nation that the very offscouring of society have generally been employed in our Indian affairs.

Britain derives its name from an ancient word signifying parti-colored; because the inhabitants painted their bodies with various pigments. None of them cultivated the ground; they all lived by hunting and raising herds of cattle. They wore no other dress than the skins of beasts, and they lived in small huts of wicker-work covered with rushes. How little descriptive is this of Great Britain now.

I have no doubt that every nation and tribe on earth is capable of being softened and refined if brought under the right influences. But the great, the almost insurmountable difficulty in the way of universal civilization has always been that Christian nations, in their transactions with peoples of other religions, have never considered themselves bound by the same moral principles which regulate their conduct toward those of similar faith and equal power. They are more savage toward "heathens" in war, they are more fraudulent with them in trade, and in personal intercourse they treat them with less civility. Their philanthropic labors among them are nearly deprived of efficacy by an assumption of superiority, a pride of condescension, which is so ingrained in their habits that they are unconscious of it. When Moravian Missionaries attempted to convert the Delawares to Christianity, one of the Chiefs said: "There are two ways that lead to God; one is for the white man, the other for the red man; but the red man's path is the straighter and shorter of the two. If the Great Spirit came down into this world, and was treated as you say, I assure you the Indians are not to blame for it, but white men alone. As for your Book, we cannot understand it; it is too difficult for us." To which the Missionary replied, "I will tell you the reason of that. The Devil is the Prince of Darkness. Where *he* reigns all is dark; and he reigns in *you*; therefore, you cannot comprehend anything about God, or his Word." The missionaries were accustomed to repeat this conversation, with entire un-consciousness that such a method of conversion was ill-adapted to gain proselytes.

Contempt, whether expressed or implied, alienates all men; but it operates with peculiar force upon Indians, because they have by nature great pride of independence; a pride capable of producing glorious results, if rightly developed and applied. Nothing keeps down individuals, or races, like the consciousness of being considered inferior by those around them. It is not only mortifying and discouraging in its effects, but it produces a feeling of isolation, that builds up a complete wall of separation. An Indian of the Kennebec tribe, who had gained a high character by uniform good conduct, had a grant of land from the State, in a new township where a number of white families were settled. He applied himself to the cultivation of it, and was orderly and industrious. But his neighbors, though they found no pre-text for molesting him, had the common prejudice against Indians, and they habitually treated him as an outcast. When his only child sickened and died, not one of them went near him. Soon afterward, he said to some of them: "When white man's child die, Indian sorry. He help bury him. When my child die, nobody speak to me. I make his grave all alone. I can no live here." He abandoned his farm, dug up the body of his child, and carried it two hundred miles through the forest, to join a Canadian tribe.

In reading Dr. Livingston's Travels in Africa,[12] the perfect feeling of hu-

12. David Livingstone (1813–73), celebrated Scottish traveler and missionary, discovered the Victoria Falls of the Zambezi. His *Missionary Travels and Researches in South Africa* was published in London in 1857.

man brotherhood which he invariably manifests toward those rude tribes is cheering to my heart. His dealings with them are uniformly just and kind, and his estimate of them always rests as a basis on the thought, "Thus should I do and be, if I had grown up under such circumstances; and they would be as I am, if they had received the same education." This spirit everywhere inspired confidence and attachment. Tribes accustomed to regard (with abundant reason) all white men with suspicion, fear and abhorrence, welcomed Dr. Livingston as a friend, and were zealous to serve him. Speke, the traveller,[13] seems to have been actuated by a different spirit. He was always ready to assert superiority and intimidate by threats; and the natural result was, that the native Chiefs were always wrangling with him and seeking to annoy him.

The native tribes of America are doubtless much more revengeful than those of Africa; but so much has been said of their horrid cruelties, and they have taken such deep hold of the popular mind, that it would be like throwing petroleum on a flaming village for me to repeat them. I will, therefore, pass them by, and endeavor to show that their character has its bright side.

Much as we are accustomed to abhor and despise them, they are in some respects, decidedly superior to white men. Gen. Houston,[14] who lived two years among them, said in the Senate of the United States, "I never knew an Indian to break a promise, or violate a treaty." Mr. Schoolcraft,[15] who was for twenty-five years an agent of the United States among the Chippewas and Ottawas, told Mrs. Jameson,[16] "I have never known an Indian to break a promise or violate a treaty." He regretted his inability to say as much in favor of his own government. At the very time he spoke those words he was troubled by orders to require the Indians to take goods instead of the money

13. John Hanning Speke (1827–64), British explorer. His *Journal of the Discovery of the Source of the Nile* was published in Edinburgh in 1863.

14. Samuel Houston (1793–1863), Mexican War hero and statesman, spent three years among the Cherokee from 1829 on and later served as president of the republic of Texas and governor of that state.

15. Henry Rowe Schoolcraft (1793–1864), explorer, ethnologist, and Indian agent, produced many influential books on Indians, including *Algic Researches* (2 vols. New York, 1839), which was Longfellow's source for *The Song of Hiawatha*. The Mrs. Schoolcraft to whom Child refers is his part-Chippewa wife, whom he married in 1823.

16. Anna Brownell Jameson (1794–1860), prolific English author of travelogues, art books, and literary criticism, took a feminist perspective in her works. Child is quoting from her *Winter Studies and Summer Rambles in Canada* (3 vols. London, 1838), whose feminist commentary also attracted Margaret Fuller's attention.

promised them in exchange for their lands. They needed the money to pay for articles they had obtained on credit, founded on the promise of it. They were indignant at what they justly considered a violation of the treaty; but so little did the United States regard their rights that a contract had actually been made with a trader to supply the goods, and he was there ready to deliver them, before the form was gone through of asking the Indians whether they consented or not. Mrs. Jameson, who was there at the time, says: "The mean petty-trader style in which American officials make and break treaties with the Indians is shameful. I met with no one who attempted to deny or excuse it." In this case, the Indians, after remonstrating in vain, became so exasperated that they killed some of the men who tried to force goods upon them in lieu of the promised money; and, as usual, a general hue and cry was raised about "Indian atrocities," without inquiring into the cause. I pass over the long record of similar facts. The amount of the whole is that the Indians never broke a treaty, and the white man never kept one. William Penn is an exception. His dealings with the natives were uniformly just and kind; and the consequence was that his little Colony lived in the midst of the numerous and warlike Delawares as safely as they could now live in his "City of Brotherly Love." Only one Quaker was ever killed by the Indians, and that was by mistake; his dress, and the gun he carried, having led them to suppose he did not belong to Penn's Colony.

The Indians have one marked trait of character, which is much less universal among the whites. They never return kindness with treachery; their gratitude is as lasting as their revenge. Edwin Corey, once an officer in the United States army, joined the Society of Friends, and was sent by them on a mission to the Indians. After residing among them for some years, he returned to transact some business. People were surprised that he did not bring his wife with him, and inquired anxiously, "Won't she be very much afraid there in the woods without you to protect her?" "O no, she won't be afraid," replied he. "She is perfectly safe. I left nine Indians with her."

Had the views of William Penn been faithfully carried out, we should doubtless see a very different state of things from that which now exists. But emigrants whose opinions and practices were different from the Quakers settled in that region, and his plans for the civilization and comfort of the natives all fell through. The Delawares have been three times removed from their lands, and are now about being removed again from the tract reserved for them in Kansas.

There is another trait in Indian character, which contrasts favorably with the frequent practices of white nations. They never, not even in their wildest moments of revenge, offend the modesty of female captives. Mr. Schoolcraft says: "The whole history of Indian warfare might be challenged in vain for a solitary instance of this kind. They think it would be degrading to a warrior to take dishonorable advantage of female prisoners; that it would render him unfit for manly achievements, and unworthy of them." Compare this with the disgusting details of towns and cities sacked by Christian nations! Compare it with the brutal treatment that Indian women receive from United States soldiers, agents, gold-diggers, fur-traders, and other lawless adventurers!

One would hardly expect to find enlightened views of education among the Indians; but I think one of their maxims on that subject is the wisest I ever read. They never strike children, giving this as a reason for it: "Before a child is old enough to understand, there is no *use* in striking him; and when he is old enough to understand, no one has a *right* to strike him." It is but a short time ago that an orthodox minister in New York whipped to death his child of three years old, to compel it to repeat a prayer. It would have been well for him if he had learned the maxim of the Indians, and practised it. Mrs. Jameson, describing her short sojourn with some of these uncivilized tribes, says: "I never heard the children scolded or threatened, and their mothers told me such language was never used. I saw no evil results from this mild system. The general reverence and affection of the children for their parents was delightful to witness."

Theologians and politicians have been prone to adduce the enslavement of negroes as sufficient proof of their natural inferiority. Judged by this standard, there is no justice in classing Indians among "the subject races." White men have outnumbered them, as a thousand to one, they have tortured and slaughtered them, they have hunted them like wild beasts, they have brutified them with drink, they have heaped enough of discouragement and contempt upon them to crush all manhood out of them; but they could never succeed in making them slaves.

The quiet decorum of Indians imparts a dignity to their deportment rarely met with in the most elegant drawing-rooms. Mrs. Jameson, after describing strange costumes, grotesque finery, rags and dirt, adds, "But in *manners* they are the most perfect gentlemen I ever saw. We are twenty white people, with three thousand seven hundred of these wild creatures around us, and I never in my life felt more security. I never met with people more genuinely polite."

The stoicism of their manners has given rise to the idea that they are deficient in feeling; but in reality their affections are very strong. This is especially indicated by their tender memories of the dead, and their longing to rejoin them. When a delegation from the Chippewas visited Washington, in 1849, a babe that was brought with them sickened and died. The grief of the parents knew no bounds. A person who pitied their distress caused a daguerreotype likeness of the dead child to be taken. The bereaved mother carried it in her bosom, and ever and anon she would take it out, cry over it, kiss it, and offer it to her husband, whose keen black eyes would fill with tears as he kissed it also. Every morning, they bowed their heads solemnly over the little picture, and uttered a brief prayer before they entered upon the duties of the day. Another proof that their natures are emotional is that they are extremely fond of music, which missionaries have found peculiarly useful in arresting their attention and touching their feelings.

Notwithstanding the many discouragements that weigh them down, there have been not a few individuals among them, who have proved, beyond dispute, their capability for moral and intellectual culture. Miss Brandt, daughter of a Mohawk Chief, attracted attention by her intelligence and lady-like manners. The mother of Mrs. Schoolcraft was an unmixed Indian, who married a white trader by the name of Johnson. These intermarriages are by no means rare; and they prove, as plainly as the complexions of mulattoes and quadroons, that the "antipathy of races" is not a *natural* antipathy. Mrs. Johnson was an uncommon woman. Her father, a Chippewa Chief, was celebrated among his tribe for his talent in making allegories and stories. She inherited the gift, and some of her productions are quite poetic. Mrs. Jameson says: "Her habits and manners are those of a genuine Indian squaw, but her talents and domestic virtues command the highest respect. Her two sons-in-law, Mr. MacMurray, and Mr. Schoolcraft, both educated in good society, the one a clergyman, and the other a man of science and literature, look up to this remarkable woman with sentiments of affection and veneration. In her own language she is eloquent, and her voice, like that of her people, is low and musical. Many kind words were exchanged between us, mostly, in French, for she understood English but little. When I said anything that pleased her, she laughed softly, like a little child. I was not well, and she took me in her arms, laid me on a couch, and began to soothe and caress me. She had the strongest marked Indian features, but her countenance was open, benevolent, and intelligent. Her manners were easy and simple, yet with something of motherly dignity. She set before us the best dressed and best served dinner I had seen since I left Toronto, and presided at her table with unembarrassed, unaffected propriety."

It is generally supposed that the Indians knew nothing of agriculture, till they saw it practised by the whites; but this is not true. In our war with the Indians, 1794, Gen. Wayne[17] destroyed many settlements of the Wyandots and Miamis on the shores of Lake Erie. In an official dispatch, he wrote thus: "The very extensive and cultivated fields and gardens show the work of many hands. The margins of the rivers appear like one continued village for miles. I have never beheld such immense fields of corn in any part of America, from Canada to Florida." All this was laid waste by white men. The Cherokee tribe in Georgia, numbering about twenty thousand, resolved to adopt our mode of life. They made good progress in Agriculture and various mechanic arts, and were as orderly as any other citizens. But the State of Georgia coveted their lands, and they were driven off to a Territory beyond Arkansas, by a series of insupportable persecutions, at which the government of the United States winked, if it did nothing worse. How *can* people improve, who are never secure in the possession of their lands? Yet, while we are perpetually robbing them, and driving them "from post to pillar," we go on repeating, with the most impudent coolness, "They are *destined* to disappear before the white man." And we "nail it with Scripture," just as we did our enslavement of the negroes; "Japhet shall be enlarged, and inhabit the tents of Shem, and Canaan shall be his servant." If the white man is Japhet, all I have to say is, he has behaved in a rascally manner toward Shem and Canaan.

Presented from such points of view, how must our religion appear to the Indians, who have always believed in One Great Spirit, the Father of the whole human race? No wonder there has been so little success in attempts to convert them to Christianity. Their ideas of politeness prevent them from ever ridiculing or contradicting the theological opinions of other people; but when missionaries told them of a hell, where sinners were punished to all eternity, perhaps there was some latent sarcasm in their reply, "If there be such a place, it must be for white men only."

17. General Anthony Wayne (1745–96) defeated the Indian tribes of the Ohio region at Fallen Timbers (1794). His victory has been attributed to the Indians' half-starved condition, resulting from the destruction of their crops.

Part Two

Children's Literature and

Domestic Advice

Introduction

Although Child made her reputation as the author of *Hobomok* and won considerable praise for her literary talents, she owed her popularity primarily to her domestic writings for women and children. She turned to these genres mostly for financial reasons—fiction did not pay, and she required a means of supporting herself and her perpetually debt-ridden husband—but she also tapped into cultural needs born of changing socioeconomic conditions. Closely associated with the rise of the middle class, the shift of economic production from home to factory, and the beginnings of industrial capitalism, manuals on housekeeping and childcare and didactic literature for children served to inculcate a new ideology. That ideology glorified women's roles as wives and mothers, assigned unprecedented importance to the moral edification of children, and stressed values crucial to the development of capitalism: hard work, productivity, usefulness, frugality, self-denial, orderliness, and punctuality.

Until the 1820s, British writers supplied Americans with their children's literature and advice books. Recognizing that British works did not suit American circumstances, Child set out to provide her compatriots with a domestic literature of their own. Her earliest effort in this line, *Evenings in New England* (1824), took its cue from a British model, Anna Letitia Barbauld's *Evenings at Home; or, The Juvenile Budget Opened* (1792), but substituted lessons in American history and republican manners for their British equivalents. The enthusiastic reception of *Evenings in New England* gave publishers the idea of asking Child to design and edit a magazine featuring the same mixture of entertaining stories, informative articles, and moral precepts. The result was *The Juvenile Miscellany,* America's first successful magazine for young folk, which Child founded in September 1826 and edited for eight years. It proved so popular that children used to sit on their doorsteps waiting for the delivery of each bimonthly number. Many of its youthful fans remembered their favorite stories for the rest of their lives. Acutely aware of the "fearful responsibility" she bore toward the impressionable readers whose values she sought to mold, Child took her craft very seriously. "Who can calculate how far the influence of a single story may spread throughout the community, and how much it may have to do with closing, or expanding young and ductile minds to the influence of truth in after life," she wrote to

Catharine Sedgwick, one of the many women she enlisted as contributors to the *Miscellany*.[1]

"Louisa Preston" (March 1828) typifies the qualities that account for the *Miscellany*'s broad appeal. Preaching the approved message that hard work, perseverance, and education can enable the poor to achieve middle-class status, the story also encourages the prosperous to hold out a helping hand to deserving members of the working class. Its heroine, with her drive to distinguish herself in her studies and pursue a career as a schoolteacher, offers girls a role model at once liberating and constraining—Louisa earns the right to fulfill her intellectual ambitions, but only after performing her duty by assisting her mother with household chores and nursing her dying sister.

Alongside stories like "Louisa Preston," the *Miscellany* included many selections that taught young readers more subversive values—to respect foreign cultures, repudiate racial prejudice, condemn slavery, and embrace Indians and blacks as their brothers and sisters (see, for example, "Jumbo and Zairee," reprinted in part 3 of this volume). Child's willingness to take controversial stands in her writings for juveniles distinguished her markedly from her rivals in the field.

Editing the *Juvenile Miscellany* earned Child an income of three hundred dollars a year, on which she lived comfortably as a single woman. Shortly after her marriage in October 1828, however, she faced a financial crisis because her husband, David, had borrowed thousands of dollars to keep his newspaper, the *Massachusetts Journal,* afloat and had just lost two libel suits. The exigency impelled her to publish *The Frugal Housewife* (1829), a grab bag of pointers on how to stretch a scant budget by salvaging worn-out goods, doing "Cheap Common Cooking," and manufacturing soap, candles, and other items that wealthier people purchased in shops. Distilled out of her own experience, *The Frugal Housewife* adapted the domestic advice manual, hitherto aimed at upper middle-class wives, to a new group of consumers— poor and "middling" women who could not afford servants. Child gauged her market cannily. The book sold six thousand copies the first year and went through thirty-three editions in the United States, twelve in England and

---

1. L. M. Francis to Catharine M. Sedgwick, 28 August [1827], Catharine Maria Sedgwick Papers, Part III, Massachusetts Historical Society. For reminiscences of the *Miscellany* by readers it influenced, see Caroline Healey Dall, "Lydia Maria Child and Mary Russell Mitford," *Unitarian Review* 19 (June 1883): 525–26, 528; and Thomas Wentworth Higginson, "Lydia Maria Child," *Contemporaries,* vol. 2 of *The Writings of Thomas Wentworth Higginson* (Boston: Houghton Mifflin, 1900) 108, 116.

Scotland, and nine in Germany. Subsequent editions incorporated Child's "Hints to Persons of Moderate Fortune," on such topics as "How to Endure Poverty," "Reasons for Hard Times," and "Education of Daughters," a series of essays originally published in the *Massachusetts Journal*.

Child followed up the success of *The Frugal Housewife* with an even more innovative venture that had no European precedent: *The Mother's Book* (1831), a comprehensive guide to child rearing covering everything from stimulating sensory awareness in infants to furnishing teenaged daughters with sex education. Again oriented toward less privileged sectors of the "middling" class, the book instructs "people of moderate fortune [who] cannot attend exclusively to an infant" on how to combine childcare with other chores (4–5) and emphasizes the importance of teaching girls not only housewifely arts but skills they can use to support themselves. *The Mother's Book* also differs from such comparable texts as Lydia Huntley Sigourney's *Letters to Mothers* (1838) and Catharine Beecher's *Treatise on Domestic Economy* (1841) in omitting homilies on wifehood and motherhood as women's highest vocations. Instead Child stresses middle-class values applicable to both sexes—"habits of order," "usefulness," prudent management of money, and perseverance. Likewise discernible between the lines of *The Mother's Book* are principles Child would soon advocate as an abolitionist: adhering to "the honest convictions of our own hearts" regardless of public opinion (38); being willing to "deny ourselves for the benefit of others" (134); and opening opportunities for education to all, whatever their "station" in life (138–40). Child's boldest departure from the norms of nineteenth-century advice literature is her recommendation that mothers treat curiosity about sex as "natural and innocent," and that they respond to their daughters' questions with "a frank, rational explanation." At the same time, her warnings against the dangers of "pollution" should young girls learn about sex from servants and "vulgar associates" reflect the sharp demarcation between prevailing middle- and working-class attitudes toward sexuality.

Although reviewers pointedly limited their approval to the tips on how to handle infants and young children, *The Mother's Book* sold out in six weeks and ran through five printings in two years. Then, with the publication of her *Appeal in Favor of That Class of Americans Called Africans* (1833), Child abruptly lost her authority as a purveyor of domestic advice. A woman who defied both racial prejudice and taboos against female involvement in politics clearly could not be trusted to dispense moral counsel to mothers and children. *The Mother's Book* promptly went out of print, *The Juvenile Miscellany* foundered as parents canceled subscriptions en masse, and even sales of *The Frugal Housewife* plummeted.

If Child ceased to rely on advice books as a source of income, she did not abandon the domestic field entirely. "Letter from an Old Woman, on Her Birthday," from her anthology for the elderly, *Looking toward Sunset* (1865), and "Education of Children," from her reader for the emancipated slaves, *The Freedmen's Book* (1865), show how Child wove domestic advice into her later writings and adapted it to different constituencies.

Louisa Preston

Louisa Preston was the daughter of a very poor widow, who lived in Devonshire-street. Her father was an Englishman. He came to America because he could not earn his bread in his own country; and though he always found sufficient employment, he continued poor, because he had a large family of children to support, and his wife had very slender health. When Louisa was about ten years old, he died; and his widow was obliged to support herself by taking in washing. At this trying period, Louisa, young as she was, was a great help and consolation to her mother. She would bring in the water, hang out the clothes, wash the hearth, and tend her little baby sister, till it seemed as if her arms would break. Besides all this, she went to school constantly, and was always pronounced the first scholar there. I have heard her mother say that after Louisa had been working hard for her, until eleven o'clock at night, she had often found her, at the very first grey peep of day, with her head out of the window, studying her lessons for school. Yet though Louisa sat up late, rose early, and worked hard, neither her looks nor her health were injured. She was not beautiful, it is true; but she had that interesting face, which goodness of character generally gives. Her mouth expressed energy and resolution; and her large grey eyes were so mild and affectionate, that the very kitten, when her paw was hurt, went to Louisa, as if she knew by instinct that she had the kindest and best heart in the world. As for her infant sister, she loved her so much, that when she was sick, or grieved, her cry always was, "Loolly! Loolly!" and it was seldom her mother could get her to sleep, till her clever little nurse came home to rock her, and tell her stories. It was enough to do one's heart good to see the little chubby Mary tottle to the door, the moment she heard her sister's well known footstep—and then to see her jump up and down so prettily—and throw her arms round Louisa's neck with such an excess of joy!

Poor Louisa had few comforts at home, and many vexations at school; and it seemed as if her heart were more wrapped up in this interesting little one, because she had few other things to love. She often pleased herself with thinking how much she and her brother John, who was about two years younger than herself, would do for Mary and their mother, as soon as they were old enough to support themselves. This excellent girl hoped, and in-

Juvenile Miscellany 4 (March 1828): 56–81.

tended, to fit herself for teaching one of the primary schools; and so anxious was she to help her mother, that she often cried to think she was no older. Sometimes too, she was almost discouraged in trying to learn; for it took so much of her time to assist her mother in washing, to mend her brother's clothes, and to tend the baby, that it seemed to be almost impossible for her to get her lessons. But to the industrious and persevering, nothing is impossible; and Louisa Preston, with all her discouragements, was always the best scholar in school.

Yet even there she had vexations; though her teacher thought highly of her, and her companions generally loved her for her amiability and obliging manners. There were some in the school, who did not like that she should always keep above them in the class; and as their ill-nature could find nothing in her to blame, they would often indulge themselves in laughing at her dress.

"Well, Miss Creak-shoes, I hope you are easy, now you've got up to the head again," said Hannah White.

"I should be ashamed to be at the head, or any where else, if I had to show myself in such a coarse, short, narrow gown, as yours is;" said Harriet May.

"It is the best my mother can afford to give me," answered Louisa, meekly.

"Then I'd stay at home, and help her wash," said Hannah White; and then all the girls set up a shout, as if there had been some disgrace in having a poor, industrious mother.

Louisa blushed like the sinking sun; the loud laugh of her associates went through her heart like a dagger; and she was dreadfully ashamed of being a washwoman's daughter. She turned to Hannah White suddenly, and was very near saying some angry things; but she had learned to govern her temper; and as the flush on her cheek died away, the tears came to her eyes,—but she spoke not a word. Children are naturally kind; and when they do cruel things, they usually do them thoughtlessly. The sight of their school-mate's tears, made the little girls feel sorry.

"I am sure I did not mean to do any harm by laughing," said one. "I should be ashamed, if I were you, Hannah White," said another; "for you know Louisa is always the best girl that ever was." "Don't you cry, Louisa," said a third. "We did not think what we were doing, when we laughed; for we all love you, just as well as if you had on a silk gown."

Louisa was comforted by these expressions; but she could not forget that they had laughed at her gown, and put her in mind that her mother was a washwoman. She was mortified and grieved; and she did not step home so lightly as usual.

When she entered their dark, miserable looking room, she found her mother standing at the wash-tub, looking very pale and tired. "Here is Loolly, dear," said she, speaking to little Mary, who, busied with scrubbing her own baby-rags in a little wooden bowl, did not notice her sister's entrance. "Oh, Loolly! Loolly!" shouted the little one; and her voice sounded as merry as a Christmas bell. Her mother smiled, and looking affectionately at her eldest daughter, she said, "Oh, how should I get along without you, Louisa? You are the best child that ever lived; and God will bless you for your kindness to your poor mother!"

Louisa's heart was full; and she could not endure this. She threw her arms round her mother's neck, and burst into tears.

"What is the matter?" asked her mother.

"Nothing—or, at least, nothing that I can tell," said Louisa.

When her mother urged her to keep none of her troubles secret from her, she replied, "I would tell you, certainly I would, if it were right; but the girls at school said something to me, which hurt my feelings very much; and it is not proper for me to tell you what it was."

Her mother did not urge her,—for she knew Louisa was a girl to be trusted; and she suspected that it was something about their poverty, which, with genuine delicacy, she had forborne to mention.

Louisa persuaded her mother to sit down and dry her feet, while she hung out the clothes, washed the room, put John and Mary to bed, and made a cup of hot tea. While she was busily engaged in performing these kind offices, her mother often looked upon her with an expression of love, which seemed to say she had nothing else in the wide world to lean upon, but her. Louisa understood the language of her face; and it filled her with self-reproach. She asked her own heart, "How could I, for one moment, feel ashamed of that good mother, who has always loved me; who took care of me, when I was a babe; and who has toiled many and many a time, when she was very ill, in order to make me comfortable!"

Her father had always taught her to go to God and pray for forgiveness and strength, when bad feelings were in her mind. Most girls of her age would not have been so much troubled, because they were for a few minutes, ashamed of a poor, hard-working parent; but Louisa had a very tender conscience; and she knew that such pride was wicked in the eyes of her Heavenly Father. Before she went to bed that night, she prayed long and earnestly that such feelings might never again come into her mind; and the sleep of that good girl was more sweet and refreshing for this act of piety.

In the morning, her mother said, "Louisa, I do not like to keep you one moment from school; but Mrs. White's bundle of clothes is too heavy for John,—and I have nobody but you to carry it."

Louisa's face was crimsoned, for a moment. It was but the day before, that Hannah White had ridiculed her for being a washwoman's daughter; and she could not bear to carry her clothes home, when she was very likely to meet her on the way to school; but she remembered how wretched such thoughts had made her, the day before,—and she answered with one of her sweetest smiles, "Oh, I can go just as well as not, mother. I shall get to school in good season, if I walk quick."

Her mother thanked her; and with a large bundle in one hand, and her book and atlas in the other, she left home with an approving conscience, and a light heart. She met several of her companions on the way; and she thought some of them looked as if they pitied her; but she did not let that trouble her. When she reached school, she found her class had just risen to recite. Her heart beat violently,—for she was very anxious to keep at the head, and she had had no time to review her lesson. She could not answer the second question that was asked her—she lost her place four times successively—and when the recitation was finished, Hannah White remained at the head.

Her rival looked a little triumphant,—and poor Louisa found bad feelings were again rising up in her heart. She tried to crowd them back; but overcome with her many temptations and troubles, she burst into tears. The instructer supposed all her grief was occasioned by losing her place; and as he knew there must be some very good reason why she had neglected her lesson, he felt exceedingly sorry for her mortification. He did not, however, say any thing to her,—for he did not like to call upon her the attention of the whole school; but, by way of exciting her hopes, he mentioned that a committee of gentlemen would visit them, in a few days, and that one of them proposed to give a handsome copy of Miss Edgeworth's "Moral Tales,"[1] and one year's education at the best school in the city, to the young lady who should, at the end of eight weeks, evince the most thorough knowledge of ancient and modern geography. All Louisa's class felt sure she would get the prize; and next to being successful themselves, they wished her to be so. Hannah White and Harriet May were the two next best scholars in school, and they resolved in their own minds that they would be victorious, if studying would make

1. *Moral Tales* (1801), by Maria Edgeworth (1767–1849), was a classic of early British children's literature.

them so. Not that they cared about the year's schooling—for their parents were pretty rich—but it was an honour, which they thought well worth trying for. Louisa knew they were the only competitors she had to fear; and she was conscious it would cost her an effort not to be jealous of them. Hannah White was not a bad-hearted girl; but she had very pert, unpleasant manners. During recess that day, she said many sneering things, which made Louisa feel unhappy, in spite of herself; and more than one little girl said, "If I were Louisa Preston, I'd never speak to that Hannah White again." The young lady, who had told Miss White and Miss May that they ought to be ashamed of themselves for laughing at Louisa's short, coarse gown, was named Emily Minot. She now came up to Louisa very kindly, and putting her arm within hers, offered her half the orange she was eating. This Miss Minot was a very kind girl; but wild and thoughtless, and very fond of fun. When they again went into school, she amused herself by cutting figures in paper, and holding them up for the entertainment of her companions. One of these figures was so very ridiculous, that all who saw it burst into an unconstrained laugh. The instructer looked up surprised—but every face was sobered, and intent upon a book. A few minutes elapsed,—and a tittering laugh was again heard throughout the school-room. The teacher became angry, and insisted upon knowing the cause. No one was willing to tell. When his inquiry commenced, Emily Minot knew by his angry tone, that there would be some danger in being discovered; she therefore pushed the papers out of her way, and sat as demure as a quaker. The mischievous papers were found in Hannah White's desk; and as she was very apt to be roguish, the teacher very naturally concluded she was the culprit. He requested her to leave her seat, and stand by the side of his desk, till he had decided what punishment was most appropriate for a young lady, who spent her time in disturbing the school. Hannah White again and again declared that she had not cut the papers, or shewn them; but the teacher was fearful she did not speak the truth,—and as she was not a favourite in school, and Emily Minot was, no one liked to step forward and vindicate her. Trembling and blushing, with her eyes full of tears, she prepared to obey the commands of her instructer, when Louisa Preston rose, and in a modest, but firm tone, said, "Miss White is not to blame, sir; she only laughed,—and we all did that." "Who then has done the mischief?" asked the teacher. Louisa was silent, and hung down her head. Emily Minot had always been so kind to her, and had been always so ready to take her part, when the other girls vexed her, that she could not bear to bring her into trouble, though she knew very well, that she deserved it. The instructer was seriously offended at being thus interrupted. "Very well, Louisa," said he, "if you know who the culprit is, and will not tell, you must take her place yourself." The poor girl was frightened—she had never been disgraced at school, and such was her laudable pride, she would rather have had her soundest tooth drawn, than to have met with such a misfortune. She glanced timidly round the room; but no one dared to look up at her,—for their master, though not a passionate, was a very severe man. Then she remembered how Emily Minot had taken her arm, and given her half an orange that morning,—and with an aching heart she left her seat, and stood beside the instructer's desk. There was a long and awful silence in school—Emily Minot felt grieved and ashamed! but she had not quite courage enough to acknowledge her fault, and take the consequences. She sat trembling and hesitating, until she saw a fool's cap, ornamented with her paper figures, about to be placed on Louisa's head. She could not endure it any longer,—but bursting into tears she said, "It was I."

The instructer was very glad to find so much good and generous feeling in his pupils; and after expressing his unwillingness to punish, and urging upon them the necessity of keeping good order in school, he declared his readiness to forgive an offender, who could not see another punished in her stead. The adventure of that day was long remembered by the parties concerned. Hannah White was touched by Louisa's disinterested vindication; she was conscious that she did not deserve it,—and from that period her character and manners began to change. She was ever kind and polite to her playmates, and particularly so to Louisa.

A day or two after this affair, she whispered to her, as they left school together, "Louisa, my mother wishes you should come and spend the day with me, on Saturday. She particularly wishes it, and you must not fail to come." Louisa and her mother were both very much astonished,—but both of them thought it would be proper and polite to go. Mrs. White gave her visiter a very affectionate reception,—praised her conduct,—and told her that all she had heard from her companions and teacher had made her resolved to be her friend; and she added that she had sent for her that day, on purpose to promise assistance to herself and mother, so long as she continued to behave as she had done. She then gave a mantuamaker orders to take her measure; and the next week, two very plain, neat suits of clothes were sent her. Other ladies, hearing her good character, likewise took an interest in her. Poor Mrs. Preston no longer suffered from extreme poverty. She had constant employment, and many comfortable presents. She was grateful to her Heavenly

Father for having sent her such a daughter; and often, after they had knelt down and prayed together, she would put her emaciated hands affectionately on Louisa's forehead, and say, "I always knew you'd bring down blessings on all you love!" And at such times Louisa felt glad that she was a washwoman's daughter,—since it gave her the means of doing so much good, and conferring so much happiness on her destitute mother.

This was a sunny spot in the good girl's life. She was useful and beloved at home; and at school, she went on improving and gaining friends every day. Her progress in Geography surprised even her teacher, who expected wonders from her; and there seemed to be no doubt that she would win the prize. Little Mary did not know any thing about this good luck. She had loved her sister as well as ever she could before; and she could not love her better now. One day, when Louisa had kissed her, and bade her good bye, just as she was going to school, the little pet took hold of her gown, and said in a most coaxing tone, "Loolly stay wi' Mary! Loolly stay wi' Mary!" "But I can't stay," said Louisa—I must go to school now; but bye and bye, Loolly will come back to see Mary." The little child sighed,—and still kept hold of her gown, and said, in her artless, prattling way, "Mary love Loolly—don't Loolly go." Louisa's heart was so much stirred by these simple demonstrations of infant love, that she could hardly resolve to leave her little favourite; but it was quite school time, and after putting the hair nicely out of her eyes, and kissing her pretty white forehead, she ran away from her; just casting one look back upon her, as she stood peeping out of the door.

With a light and bounding heart, she went to school; and among all the rich and indulged little ladies in town, not one could have been found that day, who was happier than Louisa Preston. She had been there two hours, when a boy came running in, out of breath, and asked for her. She rose up to answer him—"Mary is burned to death!" exclaimed he,—and ran out for the doctor. Louisa turned as pale as ashes; and her limbs trembled so that she could scarcely leave her seat. She ran through the street, like one distracted; yet she hardly knew she had left the school room, till she found herself at her mother's bed. Oh, what a sight was there—it was enough to break one's heart to look upon it! Poor little Mary was not dead; but she was burned so dreadfully, that Louisa could not see anything in the shape of a face, where she had that morning kissed the prettiest features, and the purest skin, that ever adorned a little child. Her tongue which had uttered such sweet sounds when she left her for school, was now useless. She could not speak. The doctor said she never would speak more;—and Louisa knew that she should never see the sweet expression of her eyes again. It was very, very hard to endure; and the affectionate sister's heart ached so that she could not cry. Sometimes indeed, when the little sufferer nestled close up to her cheek,— and when she made a mournful noise, as soon as the supporting arm was withdrawn from her head,—Louisa could weep. For three weeks, Mary lingered on in pain and restlessness. During that time, it was difficult to persuade her to let her sister leave her, for one moment; and it was not until she had said half a dozen times, "Loolly will come back again," that she could get away from the bed-side. The poor little creature could not answer her—she could not even smile, or look her love—but her sister knew very well by the patient manner in which she withdrew and laid down her hand, that she was willing she should go; and when she returned, the eagerness with which she nestled toward her, spoke volumes of love.

At last Louisa's long and painful service ended. Little Mary died, and was buried in the ground. Her gentle, affectionate soul went home to its Heavenly Father, never more to know suffering, or death!

Louisa did not weep bitterly; for she had seen the dear little being in too much agony to wish her to stay longer among them. It was a consolation to her to hear her mother say, "Louisa, what should I have done in this dreadful trial, if it had not been for you, and the friends you have raised up for me?"

Then there was John to love—and he had left his boyish and noisy sports of late, and seemed to pity his good mother and sister with all his little soul. Affliction has a softening effect, even on children; and ever after John saw his little merry sister laid down and covered up in the ground, he became gentle, attentive, and useful.

When Louisa had recovered a little from the grief which her sister's untimely and dreadful end had occasioned, she began to think about school. Her mother was too ill to be left alone, and another fortnight passed away without this industrious girl's finding much time to study the maps she was so very eager to learn; at last with a long drawn and bitter sigh, she gave up all hopes of getting the prize. She did not tell her mother that it made her unhappy; for she knew one might as well be utterly selfish, and make no sacrifices at all to the comfort of others, as to make them, and keep constantly complaining about it. But we always want to tell our troubles to somebody; and though John was as yet quite young, and had heretofore been a remarkably heedless boy, she knew he would be interested in her fears and anxieties,—and often when their mother was asleep, she would talk with him upon the subject of the prize: "I should not have cared about losing the books," said she, "though I do dearly love to read; but I did so hope I could go to a private school for one year. I am sure I could teach school myself, if I could but do that." John took a deep interest in her plans and wishes. It made him feel like a man to have her confide in him; and he resolved to be indolent no longer,—but to rouse up his sleepy faculties, and see if he could not be as famous for learning as his sister had been. In his homely phrase, he used to say, "Now Louisa, I'd give all my old shoes if you could but get that prize. Why wont you go to school, and let me stay at home, and take care of mother." "Oh, I should not like to have her know how much I want to go," replied Louisa; "besides, you could not do the mending mother has taken in[,] you know." "I can carry it home, and tell the folks we can't do it," said John. "But you know mother wants the money, and cannot get it, without I earn it for her." "Mrs. White will give you some money, if you go and tell her that mother is sick," replied the boy. "No, no, John, I will never beg, so long as I can work," said Louisa; and "beside that, you should remember John, rich people will not help us, and ought not to help us, without we try to do for ourselves." "I have heard mother say a hundred times that all the friends which had been raised up for her lately were owing to your being so industrious and discreet. I suppose that is the way to make friends, and keep them too; and now I mean to try what an industrious and discreet boy I can be." Louisa kissed him affectionately, and told him "she meant to earn money enough to put him to a good school; and that she hoped to live to see him a great blessing and support to their good mother, when she was old and infirm." Such kind of conversation sobered the boy, and made him, like Louisa, older in character, than in years.

At the end of a fortnight, Mrs. Preston was able to sit up, and get along very comfortably with John's prompt assistance. Louisa, who had studied every half minute she could find, had still some faint hopes of receiving the prize,—and again took her accustomed seat at school, with a beating heart. Hannah White and Harriet May were a little startled to see her. They had not expected she would be able to come again, before the prize was declared; and they had not, therefore, made their usual exertion. However, Louisa's example had shown them that it was possible to be very ambitious, and yet be amiable and disinterested. It is only bad dispositions that cannot love a rival. A truly generous heart may indeed feel grievously sorry at want of success,— but never dislike a friend because she excels.

The three girls felt willing it should be a fair trial of scholarship and industry. They talked openly about it; and though each one said she hoped to gain the prize herself, they all promised to feel pleasantly toward each other if they lost it. This is the way scholars should do. Emulation is a very good thing; but great care must be taken, that no envy mixes with it. I know by experience that rivals at school are great trials to a little girl's disposition and temper; but the only way to be really good, is in overcoming trials.

It was soon evident that Louisa had well employed what little time she had been able to command, during her mother's and sister's illness; and the instructer thought her chance was at least equal to any of her competitors. At last, the important day arrived. The committee, together with several visiters, came to examine the school. They were well pleased with the young ladies in general; but Louisa's neat appearance, her mild and winning ways, and the facility with which she answered the most difficult questions addressed to her, soon made her judges think they should, at least, be very glad to have it in their power to present her the prize. It was a very equal trial between the three best scholars, whom we have mentioned; and for a long time, it seemed doubtful whether it were possible to decide. Toward the close of the examination, Harriet May missed two questions in succession. She, of course, was thrown out of the list. The scholars now watched Hannah White and Louisa Preston, with anxious eagerness. At length, Louisa found herself unable to answer a question. It was passed to her rival, who gave a very prompt and accurate reply. Louisa's hopes had been very highly excited,—and now, that they were so suddenly disappointed, her heart, all at once, seemed to stop its movement, like a watch when its spring is broken. This painful feeling, however, soon passed away; and she looked up and smiled sweetly in Hannah's face, as if she sincerely wished her joy;—and her good heart was sincere in its congratulation,—for she had made such use of afflictions and temptations, as our Heavenly Parent intends we should;—they had made her wiser and better. Let not my young readers think Louisa was too much of a woman for her years. If little girls would resist the very appearance of bad feeling in their hearts—if they would but adorn their minds, with half the zeal they do their persons—we should often see young ladies, who, like Miss Preston, united the wisdom of womanhood with the simplicity of a child.

Hannah White did not appear triumphant. She bore her victory very meekly; and when the volumes were bestowed upon her, with high praise of her scholarship, she blushed deeply, and said, "I do not think I should have gained the prize, if Louisa Preston had not been obliged to stay at home five weeks, to nurse her sick mother and sister!" The tears came to Louisa's eyes,— and I shall never forget the expression of gratitude and love, which beamed from them, as she looked up and smiled upon her rival.

The gentlemen were highly pleased with this expression of mutual good feeling. "Young ladies," said one of them, "this is more to your credit, than any literary honor you could gain. Your whole conduct meets with our entire approbation; and since your recitations have been so nearly equal, we shall give you both equal prizes."

Hannah White was never so happy in her life as she was that day. She found there was nothing half so pleasant as being good and generous—no victory half so delightful, as a victory over one's own selfishness!

"It was very kind of you to speak so of me," said Louisa, putting her arm round her friend's neck, and kissing her affectionately, as they were about to leave school together.

"If I am good, it is you who have taught me to be so," replied Hannah.

The friendship thus begun, continued through life. The girls afterward went to the same school,—and both obtained a gold medal the day they left it.

When Louisa was sixteen, she began to teach school; and she gained the affection of her pupils as rapidly as she had formerly gained that of her playmates. Miss White and her family assisted her in every way they could; and at the age of nineteen, she had the satisfaction of seeing her mother able to live comfortably, without working any more than she chose, for her own amusement. By her exertions, and the influence of these kind friends, she has likewise placed her brother John at college, where he had a very high reputation both as a scholar, and a man. When his sister affectionately reminded him that she had prophesied he would be a comfort to their aged mother, he smilingly answered, "You, my good Louisa, have made a man of me."

It was true, that he owed all to her; and let this instance teach elder brothers and sisters, that their kindness and energy may be the means of making their whole families prosperous, good, and happy.

There is no Louisa Preston now. She has married Miss White's brother; and it is but recently that I heard her husband say, "No doubt, Louisa was a great blessing to her mother and brother; but she is a greater blessing to me."

Mrs. White has one little daughter, whom she has named Mary Preston. She is a pretty, fat little cherub, as I ever looked upon. She just begins to talk a little. The other day, I saw her look up most bewitchingly in her mother's face, as she lisped out, "Mamy love ma'!" Her mother caught her to her heart, and half smothered her with kisses—then, turning to me, she said, "I wish the dear little creature would learn to say, "Mamy love Loolly."

Management during the Teens

The period from twelve to sixteen years of age is extremely critical in the formation of character, particularly with regard to daughters. The imagination is then all alive, and the affections are in full vigor, while the judgment is unstrengthened by observation, and enthusiasm has never learned moderation of experience. During this important period, a mother cannot be too watchful. As much as possible, she should keep a daughter *under her own eye;* and above all things she should encourage *entire confidence towards herself.* This can be done by a ready sympathy with youthful feelings, and by avoiding all unnecessary restraint and harshness. I believe it is extremely natural to choose a mother in preference to all other friends and confidants; but if a daughter, by harshness, indifference, or an unwillingness to make allowance for youthful feeling, is driven from the holy resting place, which nature has provided for her security, the greatest danger is to be apprehended. Nevertheless, I would not have mothers too indulgent, for fear of weaning the affections of children. This is not the way to gain the perfect love of young people; a judicious parent is always better beloved, and more respected, than a foolishly indulgent one. The real secret is, for a mother never to sanction the slightest error, or imprudence, but at the same time to keep her heart warm and fresh, ready to sympathize with all the innocent gayety and enthusiasm of youth. *Salutary* restraint, but not *unnecessary* restraint, is desirable.

I will now proceed to state what appears to me peculiarly important at the age I have mentioned. . . . I shall first mention the great importance of habits of order, and neatness. The drawers, trunks and work-box of a young lady should be occasionally inspected, for the purpose of correcting any tendency to wastefulness, or sluttishness. Particular care should be taken of the teeth; they should be washed with a clean brush and water at least twice a day; to cleanse them just before retiring to rest promotes sweetness of breath, and tends to preserve them from decay. Buttons off, muslins wrinkled, the petticoat below the edge of the gown, shoestrings broken, and hair loose and straggling, should never pass unnoticed. Serious advice from a father on these subjects does more good than anything else. Smooth, well arranged hair, and feet perfectly neat, give a genteel, tasteful appearance to the whole person. . . .

Nothing tends to produce a love of order so much as the very early habits

The Mother's Book (1831), chapter 10, pp. 129–155.

of observation, and attention to trifles, which I have so particularly urged in various parts of this book. . . . I would take every precaution to conquer the spirit that leads young people to say 'I don't care.' 'No matter how it is done.'—&c. . . .

Habits of order should be carried into expenses. From the time children are twelve years old, they should keep a regular account of what they receive, and what they expend. This will produce habits of care, and make them think whether they employ their money usefully. It is an excellent plan for a father, at the beginning of the year, to state what he is willing each child, older than twelve, should expend per quarter. At first, the greater part might be under a mother's direction, for clothes, and other necessaries; and only a small portion be at the disposal of the child. In this way, a father knows certainly what he expends for each; and domestic discord is not likely to be produced by bills unexpectedly large. When the arrangement is once made, nothing should be added; the idea of being helped out of difficulties brought on by thoughtlessness and extravagance, would defeat the express purpose of an allowance. A mother can generally tell very nearly what it is necessary and proper for a daughter to expend yearly; if you find you really have not allowed enough, make larger provision the next year; but never add to what was originally agreed upon, except under very extraordinary circumstances. At sixteen years of age, or perhaps sooner, where there is great maturity of character, a young lady may be profited by being trusted with the whole of her allowance, to spend at discretion; always, however, rendering an exact account to her parents, at the end of the year.

Some may think such a system could be pursued only by the wealthy; but it is no matter whether the quarterly allowance is fifty dollars, or fifty cents— the principle is the same. The responsibility implied by such trust gives children more self-respect, and self-command; it helps them to remember how much they owe to the generosity of parents; and checks their heedlessness in the expenditure of money. But its most important use is in teaching them to be really benevolent. Children who go to a parent and ask for things to give away, may know what kind *impulses* are, but they know nothing about real benevolence of *principle*. True generosity is a willingness to deny ourselves for the benefit of others—to give up something of our own, that we really like, for the sake of doing good. If a child has a quarter of a dollar a month to expend, and gives half of it to a poor sick neighbor, instead of laying it up to buy a book, or a trinket, he knows more of real benevolence, than could be taught by all the books and maxims in the world. When you know of any such action, let a child see that it increases your affection and respect. Do not let the hurry of business, or the pressure of many cares, keep you from expressing marked approbation. Human nature is weak, and temptation strong. Young people need to be cheered onward in the path of goodness; and they should never be disappointed in the innocent expectation of giving pleasure to a parent. But do not praise them in the presence of others; and do not say much about it, as if it were any great thing—merely treat them with unusual affection and confidence. Do not compensate their benevolence by making them presents. This will lead them into temptation. It will no longer be self-denial in them to give; for they will be sure they shall lose nothing in the end. They should learn to take pleasure in losing their own gratifications for the benefit of others.

One very good effect resulting from keeping an exact account of expenses, had well nigh escaped my memory. Should your daughter ever become a wife, this habit will enable her to conform more easily to her husband's income. A great deal of domestic bitterness has been produced by a wife's not knowing, or not thinking, how much she expends. Every prudent man wishes to form some calculation about the expenses of his family; and this he cannot do, if a wife keeps no accounts, or keeps them irregularly.

In connexion with this subject, I would urge the vast importance of a thorough knowledge of arithmetic among women. It is a study that greatly tends to strengthen the mind, and produce careful habits of thought; and no estate can be settled without it. In England and France, it is no uncommon thing for the wife of a great manufacturer or merchant, to be his head clerk.

An American lady, now residing in Paris, is said to be an invaluable partner to her wealthy husband, on account of her perfect knowledge of his extensive business, and the exact and judicious manner in which she conducts affairs during his absence. I do not wish to see American women taking business out of the hands of men; but I wish they were all *capable* of doing business, or settling an estate, when it is *necessary*. For this purpose, a very thorough knowledge of book-keeping should be attained; both the old and the new system should be learned. Nor should a general knowledge of the *laws* connected with the settlement of estates be neglected. Every young person ought to be well acquainted with the contents of Sullivan's Political Class-Book.[1] Many a widow and orphan has been cheated in consequence of ignorance on these subjects.

---

1. *The Political Class-Book* (1831), by the lawyer William Sullivan (1774–1839), was one of a series of "class books" he published to further the spread of popular education.

Should your daughter never have an estate to settle, or business to transact, her knowledge of arithmetic, book-keeping and penmanship may be valuable to her as a means of support. I do think children should be brought up with a dread of being dependent on the bounty of others. Some young ladies think it a degradation to support themselves; and to avoid it, they are willing to stay with any relation, who will furnish them a home. This is not indulging a right spirit. We ought to be resigned and cheerful in a dependent situation, when we cannot possibly provide for ourselves; but a willingness to burthen others, when we can help it by a little exertion, is not resignation—it is mere pride and indolence. Next to a love of usefulness, knowledge should be valued because it multiplies our resources in case of poverty. This unwillingness to subsist on the bounty of others should not be taught as a matter of pride, but of principle; it should proceed from an unwillingness to take away the earnings of others, without rendering some equivalent, and a reluctance to share what properly belongs to the more unfortunate and needy. There is nothing selfish in this. It springs from a real regard to the good of others.

I would make it an object so to educate children that they could in case of necessity support themselves respectably. For this reason, if a child discovered a decided talent for any accomplishment, I would cultivate it, if my income would possibly allow of it. Everything we add to our knowledge, adds to our means of usefulness. If a girl have a decided taste for drawing, for example, and it is encouraged, it is a pleasant resource which will make her home agreeable, and lessen the desire for company and amusements; if she marry, it will enable her to teach her children without the expense of a master; if she live unmarried, she may gain a livelihood by teaching the art she at first learned as a mere gratification of taste. The same thing may be said of music, and a variety of other things, not generally deemed *necessary* in education. In all cases it is best that what is learned should be learned well. In order to do this, good masters should be preferred to cheap ones. Bad habits once learned, are not easily corrected. It is far better that children should learn one thing thoroughly, than many things superficially. Make up your mind how much you can afford to spend for one particular thing; and when you have decided that, spend it as far as it will go in procuring really good teachers. I believe this to be the best economy in the end. . . .

While speaking of acquirements, I would again urge the great necessity of *persevering* in whatever pursuits are commenced. Time, talent, and money, are often shamefully wasted by learning a variety of things, because they prove more difficult than was at first imagined; and what is worst of all, every individual instance of this kind, strengthens the pernicious habit of being easily discouraged at obstacles. A young lady should be very sure she knows her own mind before she begins any pursuit; but when it is once begun, it should be an unalterable law that she *must* persevere.

Perhaps some parents of moderate fortune will ask if there is no danger of unfitting girls for the duties of their station, and making them discontented with their situation in life, by teaching them accomplishments merely ornamental. For myself, I do not believe that *any* kind of knowledge ever unfitted a person for the discharge of duty, *provided that knowledge was acquired from a right motive.* It is wonderful what different results the same thing will produce, when the motives are different. No matter what is learned, provided it be acquired as a means of pleasing a parent, of becoming useful to others, or of acquiring a necessary support. If you induce children to learn any particular thing for the sake of showing off, or being as grand as their neighbors, then indeed you *will* unfit them for their duties, and make them discontented with their situation. Looking to others for our standard of happiness is the sure way to be miserable. Our business is with our own hearts, and our own motives. . . .

My idea is this—First, be sure that children are familiar with all the duties of their present situation; at the same time, by schools, by reading, by conversation, give them as much *solid* knowledge as you can,—no matter how much, or of what kind,—it will come in use some time or other; and lastly, if your circumstances are easy, and you can afford to indulge your children in any matter of taste, do it fearlessly, without any idea that it will unfit them for more important duties. Neither learning nor accomplishments do any harm to man or woman if the *motive* for acquiring them be a proper one; on the contrary, those who know most, are apt to perform their duties best—provided the heart and the conscience have been educated as well as the understanding. I believe a variety of knowledge (acquired from such views as I have stated) would make a man a better servant, as well as a better president; and make a woman a better wife, as well as a better teacher. A selfish use of riches leads to avarice, pride, and contempt of manual exertion; a selfish use of knowledge leads to pedantry, affectation, unwillingness to conform to others, and indolence in any pursuit not particularly pleasing to ourselves. But the fault is not in the riches, or the knowledge—the difficulty lies in the *selfish use* of these advantages. If both were held in trust, as a means of doing good, how different would be the result! . . .

It is certainly very desirable to fit children for the station they are likely to fill, as far as a parent can judge what that station will be. In this country, it is a difficult point to decide; for half our people are in a totally different situation from what might have been expected in their childhood. However, one maxim is as safe, as it is true—i.e. A well-informed mind is the happiest and the most useful in all situations. Every new acquirement is something added to a solid capital. . . . The same remarks that apply to music, drawing, &c, apply to a variety of things, that may be acquired at little or no expense—such as braiding straw, working muslin, doing rug-work, &c.—I would teach a child to learn every innocent thing, which it was in her power to learn. If it is not wanted immediately, it can be laid by for future use. I have a strong partiality for those old-fashioned employments, marking and rug-work. The formation of the figures, counting the threads, and arranging the colors, require a great deal of care; and the necessity of close attention is extremely salutary to young people.

Important as a love of reading is, there are cases where it ought to be checked. It is mere selfishness and indolence to neglect active duties for the sake of books; we have no right to do it. Children of a languid and lazy temperament are sometimes willing to devote all their time to reading, for the sake of avoiding bodily exertion; such a tendency should be counteracted by endeavoring to interest them in active duties and amusements. 'Particular pains should be taken to induce them to attend to the feelings of others. Whatever services and attentions they exact from others, they should be obliged in their turn to pay.' Out of door exercise, frequent walks, and a lively attention to the beauties of nature, are very beneficial to such dispositions. On the contrary, those who have no love for quiet, mental pleasures, should be attracted by interesting books and entertaining conversation. A mother needs to be something of a philosopher.—In other, and better words, she needs a great deal of practical good sense, and habits of close observation. . . .

With regard to lessons, reading, and work, the attention of children should be kept awake by talking with them, asking questions on the subject, and showing them the best and most convenient methods of doing whatever they are about; but great care should be taken not to help them too much. No more assistance than is absolutely necessary should be given.—Leave them to their own ingenuity. Young people will always be helpless, if they are not obliged to think and do for themselves.

With regard to the kind of books that are read, great precaution should be used. No doubt the destiny of individuals has very often been decided by volumes accidentally picked up and eagerly devoured at a period of life when every new impression is powerful and abiding. For this reason, parents, or some guardian friends, should carefully examine every volume they put into the hands of young people. In doing this, the disposition and character of the child should be considered. If a bold ambitious boy is dazzled by the trappings of war, and you do not wish to indulge his disposition to be a soldier, avoid placing in his way fascinating biographies of military heroes; for the same reason do not strengthen a restless, roving tendency by accounts of remarkable voyages and adventures. I do not mean to speak disparagingly of Voyages and Travels; I consider them the best and most attractive books in the world; I merely suggest a caution against strengthening any dangerous bias of character.

A calm, steady temperament may be safely indulged in reading works of imagination,—nay, perhaps requires such excitement to rouse it sufficiently,—but an excitable romantic disposition should be indulged sparingly in such reading. To forbid all works of fiction cannot do good. There is an age when all mortals, of any sense or feeling, are naturally romantic and imaginative. This state of feeling, instead of being violently wrestled with, should be carefully guided and restrained, by reading only the purest and most eloquent works of fiction. . . .

Never countenance by word or example that silly affected sensibility which leads people to faint or run away at the sight of danger, or distress. If such a habit is formed, try to conquer it by reasoning, and by direct appeals to good feeling. Nothing can be more selfish than to run away from those who are suffering, merely because the sight is painful. True sensibility leads us to overcome our own feelings for the good of others.

Great caution should be used with regard to the habits of talking in a family. Talk of *things* rather than of *persons*, lest your children early imbibe a love of gossipping. Particularly avoid the habit of speaking ill of others. We acquire great quickness of perception in those things to which we give attention in early life; and if we have been in the habit of dwelling on the defects of others, we shall not only be ill-natured in our feelings, but we shall actually have the faculty of perceiving blemishes much more readily than virtues. This tendency always to look on the black side is a very unfortunate habit, and may often be traced to the influences around us in childhood.

Some people fly to the opposite extreme. From the idea of being charitable, they gloss over everything, and make no distinction between vice and virtue. This is false charity. We should not speak well of what we do not believe to be good and true. We may avoid saying anything of persons, unless we can speak well of them; but when we are *obliged* to discuss a subject, we should never in the least degree palliate and excuse what we know to be wrong.

It is a great mistake to think that education is *finished* when young people leave school. Education is never finished. Half the character is formed after we cease to learn lessons from books; and at that active and eager age it is formed with a rapidity and strength absolutely startling to think of. Do you ask what forms it? I answer the every-day conversation they hear, the habits they witness, and the people they are taught to respect. Sentiments thrown out in jest, or carelessness, and perhaps forgotten by the speaker, as soon as uttered, often sink deeply into the youthful mind, and have a powerful influence on future character. This is true in very early childhood; and it is peculiarly true at the period when youth is just ripening into manhood. Employ what teachers we may, the influences at home *will* have the mightiest influences in education. School-masters may cultivate the *intellect;* but the things said and done at home are busy agents in forming the *affections;* and the last have infinitely more important consequences than the first.

A knowledge of domestic duties is beyond all price to a woman. Every one ought to know how to sew, and knit, and mend, and cook, and superintend a household. In every situation of life, high or low, this sort of knowledge is a great advantage. There is no necessity that the gaining of such information should interfere with intellectual acquirement, or even with elegant accomplishments. A well regulated mind can find time to attend to all. When a girl is nine or ten years old, she should be accustomed to take some regular share in household duties, and to feel responsible for the manner in which it is done,—such as doing her own mending and making, washing the cups and putting them in place, cleaning the silver, dusting the parlor, &c. This should not be done occasionally, and neglected whenever she finds it convenient; she should consider it her department. When they are older than twelve, girls should begin to take turns in superintending the household, keeping an account of weekly expenses, cooking puddings, pies, cake, &c. To learn anything effectually, they should actually do these things themselves,—not stand by, and see others do them. It is a great mistake in mothers to make such slaves of themselves, rather than divide their cares with daughters. A variety of employment, and a feeling of trust and responsibility add very much to the real happiness of young people. All who have observed human nature closely will agree that a vast deal depends upon how people deport themselves the first year after their marriage. If any little dissensions arise during that period,—if fretfulness and repining are indulged on one side, indifference and dislike on the other will surely follow,—and when this once takes place, farewell to all hopes of perfect domestic love. People may indeed agree to live peaceably and respectably together,—but the charm is broken—the best and dearest gift God gives to mortals is lost. Nothing can ever supply the place of that spontaneous tenderness, that boundless sympathy of soul, which has been so thoughtlessly destroyed. 'Beware of the first quarrel,' is the best advice that was ever given to married people. Now I would ask any reflecting mother, whether a girl brought up in ignorance of household duties, is not very likely to fret, when she is first obliged to attend to them? Will not her want of practice decidedly interfere with the domestic comfort of her family, and will it not likewise be a very serious trial to her own temper? I have known many instances where young married women have been perplexed, discouraged, and miserable, under a sense of domestic cares, which, being so entirely new to them, seemed absolutely insupportable. The spirit of complaint to which this naturally gives rise is not very complimentary to the husband; and it is not wonderful if he becomes dissatisfied with a wife, whom he cannot render happy. . . .

Many unhappy matches have been the result of placing young people under the influence of . . . sentimental excitement, before they were old enough to know their own minds. Such unions are often dignified with the name of *love*-matches; but love has nothing to do with the business—fancy, vanity, or passion is the agent; and vanity is by far the most busy of the three. To call such thoughtless connexions *love*-matches is a libel upon the deepest, holiest, and most thoughtful of all the passions. . . .

There is one subject, on which I am very anxious to say a great deal; but on which, for obvious reasons, I can say very little. Judging by my own observation, I believe it to be the greatest evil now existing in education. I mean the want of confidence between mothers and daughters on delicate subjects. Children from books, and from their own observation, soon have their curiosity excited on such subjects; this is perfectly natural and innocent, and if frankly met by a mother, it would never do harm. But on these occasions it is customary either to put young people off with lies, or still further to excite their curiosity by mystery and embarrassment. Information being refused them at the only proper source, they immediately have recourse to domestics, or immodest school-companions; and very often their young minds are polluted with filthy anecdotes of vice and vulgarity. This ought not to be. Mothers are the only proper persons to convey such knowledge to a child's mind. They can do it without throwing the slightest stain upon youthful purity; and it is an imperious duty that they should do it. A girl who receives her first ideas on these subjects from the shameless stories and indecent jokes of vulgar associates, has in fact prostituted her mind by familiarity with vice. A diseased curiosity is excited, and undue importance given to subjects, which those she has been taught to respect think it necessary to envelope in so much mystery; she learns to think a great deal about them, and to ask a great many questions. This does not spring from any natural impurity; the same restless curiosity would be excited by any subject treated in the same manner. On the contrary, a well-educated girl of twelve years old, would be perfectly satisfied with a frank, rational explanation from a mother. It would set her mind at rest upon the subject; and instinctive modesty would prevent her recurring to it unnecessarily, or making it a theme of conversation with others. Mothers are strangely averse to encouraging this sort of confidence. I know not why it is, but they are usually the very last persons in the world to whom daughters think of applying in these cases. Many a young lady has fallen a victim to consumption from a mother's bashfulness in imparting necessary precautions; and many, oh, many more, have had their minds corrupted beyond all cure.

I would not by any means be understood to approve of frequent conversations of this kind between parent and child—and least of all, anything like jesting, or double meanings. I never saw but two women, who indulged in such kind of mirth before their daughters; and I never think of them but with unmingled disgust. I do believe that after one modest and rational explanation, the natural purity and timidity of youth would check a disposition to talk much about it.

It is usually thought necessary, even by the very conscientious, to tell falsehoods about such subjects; but I believe it cannot do good, and may do harm. I would say to a young child, 'I cannot tell you now, because you are not old enough to understand it. When you are old enough, I will talk with you; but you must remember not to ask anybody but me. You know I always have a reason for what I say to you; and I tell you it would be very improper to talk with other people about it. I promise you that I will explain it all to you, as soon as you are old enough to understand it.'

This promise ought to be faithfully kept; and if young people meet with anything in books that requires explanation, they should be taught to apply to their mother, and to no one else. Such a course would, I am very sure, prevent a great deal of impurity and imprudence.

It is a bad plan for young girls to sleep with nursery maids, unless you have the utmost confidence in the good principles and modesty of your domestics. There is a strong love among vulgar people of telling secrets, and talking on forbidden subjects. From a large proportion of domestics this danger is so great, that I apprehend a prudent mother will very rarely, under any circumstances, place her daughter in the same sleeping apartment with a domestic, until her character is so much formed, that her own dignity will lead her to reject all improper conversation. A well-principled, amiable elder sister is a great safeguard to a girl's purity of thought and propriety of behaviour. It is extremely important that warm-hearted, imprudent youth, should have a safe and interesting companion. A judicious mother can do a vast deal toward supplying this want; but those who have such a shield as a good sister are doubly blessed. . . .

To have the various members of a family feel a common interest, as if they were all portions of the same body, is extremely desirable. It is a beautiful sight to see sisters willing to devote their talents and industry to the education of brothers, or a brother willing to deny himself selfish gratifications for a sister's improvement, or a parent's comfort. Little respectful attentions to a parent tend very much to produce this delightful domestic sympathy. Nothing is more graceful than children employed in placing a father's armchair and slippers, or busying themselves in making everything look cheerful against his return; and there is something more than mere looks concerned in these becoming attentions—these trifling things lay the foundation of strong and deeply virtuous feelings. The vices and temptations of the world have little danger for those who can recollect beloved parents and a happy home. The holy and purifying influence is carried through life, and descends to bless and encourage succeeding generations. For this reason, too much cannot be done to produce an earnest and confiding friendship between parents and children. Mothers should take every opportunity to excite love, gratitude, and respect, toward a father. His virtues and his kindness should be a favorite theme, when talking with his children. The same rule that applies to a wife, in these respects of course, applies to a husband. It should be the business of each to strengthen the bonds of domestic union. . . .

Letter from an Old Woman, on Her Birthday

You ask me, dear friend, whether it does not make me sad to grow old. I tell you frankly it did make me sad for a while; but that time has long since past. The *name* of being old I never dreaded. I am not aware that there ever was a time when I should have made the slightest objection to having my age proclaimed by the town-crier, if people had had any curiosity to know it. But I suppose every human being sympathizes with the sentiment expressed by Wordsworth:

> "Life's Autumn past, I stand on Winter's verge,
> And daily lose what I desire to keep."[1]

The first white streaks in my hair, and the spectre of a small black spider floating before my eyes, foreboding diminished clearness of vision, certainly did induce melancholy reflections. At that period, it made me nervous to think about the approaches of old age; and when young people thoughtlessly reminded me of it, they cast a shadow over the remainder of the day. It was mournful as the monotonous rasping of crickets, which tells that "the year is wearing from its prime." I dreaded age in the same way that I always dread the coming of winter; because I want to keep the light, the warmth, the flowers, and the growth of summer. But, after all, when winter comes, I soon get used to him, and am obliged to acknowledge that he is a handsome old fellow, and by no means destitute of pleasant qualities. And just so it has proved with old age. Now that it has come upon me, I find it full of friendly compensations for all that it takes away.

The period of sadness and nervous dread on this subject, which I suppose to be a very general experience, is of longer or shorter duration, according to habits previously formed. From observation, I judge that those whose happiness has mainly depended on balls, parties, fashionable intercourse, and attentions flattering to vanity, usually experience a prolonged and querulous sadness, as years advance upon them; because, in the nature of things, such enjoyments pass out of the reach of the old, when it is too late to form a taste

Looking toward Sunset (1865), pp. 212–222.
1. From "The Excursion" (1814), by William Wordsworth (1770–1850), "Book the Fourth, Despondency Corrected," 611–12.

for less transient pleasures. The temporary depression to which I have alluded soon passed from my spirit, and I attribute it largely to the fact that I have always been pleased with very simple and accessible things. I always shudder a little at the approach of winter; yet, when it comes, the trees, dressed in feathery snow, or prismatic icicles, give me far more enjoyment, than I could find in a ball-room full of duchesses, decorated with marabout-feathers,[2] opals, and diamonds. No costly bridal-veil sold in Broadway would interest me so much as the fairy lace-work which frost leaves upon the windows, in an unceasing variety of patterns. The air, filled with minute snow-stars, falling softly, ever falling, to beautify the earth, is to me a far lovelier sight, than would have been Prince Esterhazy,[3] who dropped seed-pearls from his embroidered coat, as he moved in the measured mazes of the dance.

Speaking of the beautiful phenomenon of snow, reminds me how often the question has been asked what snow *is*, and what *makes* it. I have never seen a satisfactory answer; but I happen to know what snow is, because I once saw the process of its formation. I was at the house of a Quaker, whose neat wife washed in an unfinished back-room all winter, that the kitchen might be kept in good order. I passed through the wash-room on the 16th of December, 1835, a day still remembered by many for its remarkable intensity of cold. Clouds of steam, rising from the tubs and boiling kettle, ascended to the ceiling, and fell from thence in the form of a miniature snow-storm. Here was an answer to the question, What *is* snow? This plainly proved it to be frozen *vapor*, as ice is frozen *water*. The particles of water, expanded by heat, and floating in the air, were arrested in their separated state, and congealed in particles. It does not snow when the weather is intensely cold; for the lower part of the atmosphere must have some degree of warmth, if vapor is floating in it. When this vapor ascends, and meets a colder stratum of air, it is congealed, and falls downward in the form of snow.

"The snow! The snow! The beautiful snow!" How handsome do meadows and fields look in their pure, sparkling robe! I do not deny that the winter of the year and the winter of life both have intervals of dreariness. The *miserere* howled by stormy winds is not pleasing to the ear, nor are the cold gray river and the dark brown hills refreshing to the eye. But the reading of Whittier's

2. marabout: a large African stork
3. Prince Esterhazy: Prince Nicholas IV (1765–1833) of Hungary, whose extravagance almost led to the loss of his vast estates.

Psalm[4] drowns the howling of the winds, as "the clear tones of a bell are heard above the carts and drays of a city." Even simple voices of mutual affection, by the fireside, have such musical and pervasive power, that the outside storm often passes by unheard. The absence of colors in the landscape is rather dismal, especially in the latter part of the winter. Shall I tell you what I do when I feel a longing for bright hues? I suspend glass prisms in the windows, and they make the light blossom into rainbows all over the room. Childish! you will say. I grant it. But is childishness the greatest folly? I told you I was satisfied with very simple pleasures; and whether it be wise or not, I consider it great good fortune. It is more fortunate certainly to have home-made rainbows *within*, especially when one is old; but even outward home-made rainbows are not to be despised, when flowers have hidden themselves, and the sun cannot manifest his prismatic glories, for want of mediums appropriate for their transmission.

But Nature does not leave us long to pine for variety. Before the snow-lustre quite passes away, March comes, sombre in dress, but with a cheerful voice of promise:

> "The beechen buds begin to swell,
> And woods the blue-bird's warble know."

Here and there a Lady's Delight peeps forth, smiling at me "right peert," as Westerners say; and the first sight of the bright little thing gladdens my heart, like the crowing of a babe. The phenomena of spring have never yet failed to replenish the fountains of my inward life:

> "Spring still makes spring in the *mind*,
>   When sixty years are told;
> Love wakes anew this throbbing heart,
>   And we are never old."

As the season of Nature's renovation advances, it multiplies within me spiritual photographs, never to be destroyed. Last year I saw a striped squirrel hopping along with a green apple in his paws, hugged up to his pretty little white breast. My mind daguerrotyped him instantaneously. It is there now; and I expect to find a more vivid copy when my soul opens its portfolio of pictures in the other world.

---

4. "My Psalm" (1859), by John Greenleaf Whittier (1807–92), is a poem about coming to terms with advancing age and remaining young at heart: "I mourn no more my vanished years," "But, grateful, take the good I find,/ The best of now and here."

The wonders which summer brings are more and more suggestive of thought as I grow older. What mysterious vitality, what provident care, what lavishness of ornament, does Nature manifest, even in her most common productions! Look at a dry bean-pod, and observe what a delicate little strip of silver tissue is tenderly placed above and below the seed! Examine the clusters of Sweet-Williams, and you will find an endless variety of minute embroidery-patterns, prettily dotted into the petals with diverse shades of colors. The shining black seed they produce look all alike; but scatter them in the ground, and there will spring forth new combinations of form and color, exceeding the multiform changes of a kaleidoscope. I never can be sufficiently thankful that I early formed the habit of working in the garden with loving good-will. It has contributed more than anything else to promote healthiness of mind and body.

Before one has time to observe a thousandth part of the miracles of summer, winter appears again, in ermine and diamonds, lavishly scattering his pearls. My birthday comes at this season, and so I accept his jewels as a princely largess peculiarly bestowed upon myself. The day is kept as a festival. That is such a high-sounding expression, that it may perhaps suggest to you reception-parties, complimentary verses, and quantities of presents. Very far from it. Not more than half a dozen people in the world know when the day occurs, and they do not all remember it. As I arrive at the new milestone on my pilgrimage, I generally find that a few friends have placed garlands upon it. My last anniversary was distinguished by a beautiful novelty. An offering came from people who never knew me personally, but who were gracious enough to say they took an interest in me on account of my writings. That was a kindness that carried me over into my new year on fairy wings! I always know that the flowers in such garlands are genuine; for those who deal in artificial roses are not in the habit of presenting them to secluded old people, without wealth or power. I have heard of a Parisian lady, who preferred Nattier's manufactured roses to those produced by Nature, because they were, as she said, "more like what a rose *ought* to be." But I never prefer artificial things to natural, even if they *are* more like what they *ought* to be. So I rejoice over the genuineness of the offerings which I find on the milestone, and often give preference to the simplest of them all. I thankfully add them to my decorations for the annual festival, which is kept in the private apartments of my own soul, where six angel-guests present themselves unbidden,—Use and Beauty, Love and Memory, Humility and Gratitude. The first suggests to me to consecrate the advent of a new year in my life by some acts of kindness toward the sad, the oppressed, or the needy. Another tells me to collect all the books, engravings, vases, &c., bestowed by friendly hands on the preceding birthdays of my life. Their beauties of thought, of form, and of color, excite my imagination, and fill me with contemplations of the scenes they represent, or the genius that produced them. Other angels bring back the looks and tones of the givers, and pleasant incidents, and happy meetings, in bygone years. Sometimes, Memory looks into my eyes too sadly, and I answer the look with tears. But I say to her, Nay, my friend, do not fix upon me that melancholy gaze! Give me some of thy flowers! Then, with a tender, moonlight smile, she brings me a handful of fragrant roses, pale, but beautiful. The other angels bid me remember who bestowed the innumerable blessings of Nature and Art, of friendship, and capacity for culture, and how unworthy I am of all His goodness. They move my heart to earnest prayer that former faults may be forgiven, and that I may be enabled to live more worthily during the year on which I am entering. But I do not try to recall the faults of the past, lest such meditations should tend to make me weak for the future. I have learned that self-consciousness is not a healthy state of mind, on whatever theme it employs itself. Therefore, I pray the all-loving Father to enable me to forget *myself;* not to occupy my thoughts with my own merits, or my own defects, my successes, or my disappointments; but to devote my energies to the benefit of others, as a humble instrument of his goodness, in whatever way He may see fit to point out.

On this particular birthday, I have been thinking more than ever of the many compensations which age brings for its undeniable losses. I count it something to know, that, though the flowers offered me are *few,* they are undoubtedly *genuine.* I never conformed much to the world's ways, but, now that I am an old woman, I feel more free to ignore its conventional forms, and neglect its fleeting fashions. That also is a privilege. Another compensation of years is, that, having outlived expectations, I am free from disappointments. I deem it a great blessing, also, that the desire for knowledge grows more active, as the time for acquiring it diminishes, and as, I realize more fully how much there is to be learned. It is true that in this pursuit one is always coming up against walls of limitation. All sorts of flying and creeping things excite questions in my mind to which I obtain no answers. I want to know what every bird and insect is doing, and what it is done for; but I do not understand their language, and no interpreter between us is to be found. They go on, busily managing their own little affairs, far more skilfully than we humans could teach them, with all our boasted superiority of intellect. I peep and pry into their operations with more and more interest, the older I grow; but they keep their own secrets so well, that I discover very little. What I do find out, however, confirms my belief, that "the hand which made them is divine"; and that is better than any acquisitions of science. Looking upon the world as a mere spectacle of beauty, I find its attractions increasing. I notice more than I ever did the gorgeous phantasmagoria of sunsets, the magical changes of clouds, the endless varieties of form and color in the flowers of garden and field, and the shell-flowers of the sea. Something of tenderness mingles with the admiration excited by all this fair array of earth, like the lingering, farewell gaze we bestow on scenes from which we are soon to part.

But the most valuable compensations of age are those of a spiritual character. I have committed so many faults myself, that I have become more tolerant of the faults of others than I was when I was young. My own strength has so often failed me when I trusted to it, that I have learned to look more humbly for aid from on high. I have formerly been too apt to murmur that I was not endowed with gifts and opportunities, which it appeared to me would have been highly advantageous. But I now see the wisdom and goodness of our Heavenly Father, even more in what He has denied, than in what He has bestowed. The rugged paths through which I have passed, the sharp regrets I have experienced, seem smoother and softer in the distance behind me. Even my wrong-doings and short-comings have often been mercifully transmuted into blessings. They have helped me to descend into the Valley of Humility,[5] through which it is necessary to pass on our way to the Beautiful City. My restless aspirations are quieted. They are now all concentrated in this one prayer:

> "Help me, this and every day,
> To live more nearly as I pray."

Having arrived at this state of peacefulness and submission, I find the last few years the happiest of my life.

To you, my dear friend, who are so much younger, I would say, Travel cheerfully toward the sunset! It will pass gently into a twilight, which has its own peculiar beauties, though differing from the morning; and you will find that the night also is cheered by friendly glances of the stars.

---

5. In *The Pilgrim's Progress* (1678, 1684), an allegory by John Bunyan (1628–88), the Valley of Humiliation is one of the many way stations through which Christian passes while traveling from the City of Destruction to the Celestial City.

Education of Children

People of all colors and conditions love their offspring; but very few consider sufficiently how much the future character and happiness of their children depend on their own daily language and habits. It does very little good to teach children to be honest if the person who teaches them is not scrupulous about taking other people's property or using it without leave. It does very little good to tell them they ought to be modest, if they are accustomed to hear their elders use unclean words or tell indecent stories. Primers and catechisms may teach them to reverence God, but the lesson will lose half its effect if they habitually hear their parents curse and swear. Some two hundred years ago a very learned astronomer named Sir Isaac Newton lived in England. He was so devout that he always took off his hat when the name of God was mentioned. By that act of reverence he taught a religious lesson to every child who witnessed it. Young souls are fed by what they see and hear, just as their bodies are fed with daily food. No parents who knew what they were doing would give their little ones poisonous food, that would produce fevers, ulcers, and death. It is of far more consequence not to poison their souls; for the body passes away, but the soul is immortal.

When a traveller pointed to a stunted and crooked tree and asked what made it grow so, a child replied, "I suppose somebody trod on it when it was little." It is hard for children born in Slavery to grow up spiritually straight and healthy, because they are trodden on when they are little. Being constantly treated unjustly, they cannot learn to be just. Their parents have no power to protect them from evil influences. They cannot prevent their continually seeing cruel and indecent actions, and hearing profane and dirty words. Heretofore, you could not educate your children, either morally or intellectually. But now that you are freemen, responsibility rests upon you. You will be answerable before God for the influence you exert over the young souls intrusted to your care. You may be too ignorant to teach them much of book-learning, and you may be too poor to spend much money for their education, but you can set them a pure and good example by your conduct and conversation. This you should try your utmost to do, and should pray to the Heavenly Father to help you; for it is a very solemn duty, this rearing of young souls for eternity. That you yourselves have had a stunted growth,

The Freedmen's Book (1865), pp. 221–25.

from being trodden upon when you were little, will doubtless make you more careful not to tread upon them.

It is necessary that children should be made obedient to their elders, because they are not old enough to know what is good for themselves; but obedience should always be obtained by the gentlest means possible. Violence excites anger and hatred, without doing any good to counterbalance the evil. When it is necessary to punish a child, it should be done in such a calm and reasonable manner as to convince him that you do it for his good, and not because you are in a rage.

Slaves, all the world over, are generally much addicted to lying. The reason is, that if they have done any mischief by carelessness or accident, they dare not tell the truth about it for fear of a cruel flogging. Violent and tyrannical treatment always produces that effect. Wherever children are abused, whether they are white or black, they become very cunning and deceitful; for when the weak are tortured by the strong, they have no other way to save themselves from suffering. Such treatment does not cure faults; it only makes people lie to conceal their faults. If a child does anything wrong, and confesses it frankly, his punishment ought to be slight, in order to encourage him in habits of truthfulness, which is one of the noblest attributes of manhood. If he commits the same fault a second time, even if he confesses it, he ought not to be let off so easily, because it is necessary to teach him that confession, though a very good thing, will not supply the place of repentance. When children are naughty, it is better to deprive them of some pleasant thing that they want to eat or drink or do, than it is to kick and cuff them. It is better to attract them toward what is right than to drive them from what is wrong. Thus if a boy is lazy, it is wiser to promise him reward in proportion to his industry, than it is to cuff and scold him, which will only make him shirk work as soon as you are out of sight. Whereas, if you tell him, "You shall have six cents if you dig one bushel of potatoes, and six cents more if you dig two," he will have a motive that will stimulate him when you are not looking after him. If he is too lazy to be stimulated by such offers, he must be told that he who digs no potatoes must have none to eat.

The moral education which you are all the time giving your children, by what they hear you say and see you do, is of more consequence to them than reading and writing and ciphering. But the education they get at school is also very important; and it will be wise and kind in you to buy such books as they need, and encourage them in every way to become good scholars, as well as good men. By so doing you will not only benefit them, but you will help all your race. Every colored man or woman who is virtuous and intelligent takes away something of prejudice against colored men and women in general; and it likewise encourages all their brethren and sisters, by showing what colored people are capable of doing.

The system of Slavery was all penalty and no attraction; in other words, it punished men if they did *not* do, but it did not reward them for *doing*. In the management of your children you should do exactly the opposite of this. You should appeal to their manhood, not to their fears. After emancipation in the West Indies,[1] planters who had been violent slaveholders, if they saw a freedman leaning on his hoe, would say, "Work, you black rascal, or I'll flog you"; and the freedman would lean all the longer on his hoe. Planters of a more wise and moderate character, if they saw the emancipated laborers idling away their time, would say, "We expect better things of free men"; and that appeal to their manhood made the hoes fly fast.

Old men and women have been treated with neglect and contempt in Slavery, because they were no longer able to work for the profit of their masters. But respect and tenderness are peculiarly due to the aged. They have done much and suffered much. They are no longer able to help themselves; and we should help them, as they helped us in the feebleness of our infancy, and as we may again need to be helped in the feebleness of age. Any want of kindness or civility toward the old ought to be very seriously rebuked in children; and affectionate attentions should be spoken of as praiseworthy.

Slavery in every way fosters violence. Slave-children, being in the habit of seeing a great deal of beating, early form the habit of kicking and banging each other when they are angry, and of abusing poor helpless animals intrusted to their care. On all such occasions parents should say to them: "Those are the ways of Slavery. We expect better things of free children."

1. Great Britain emancipated the slaves in her West Indies colonies on 1 August 1834 after a protracted struggle led by British abolitionists. The British example exerted a great influence on American abolitionists. Child devotes a long chapter in *The Freedmen's Book* to "The Beginning and Progress of Emancipation in the British West Indies."

Part Three

Slavery, Race, and

Reconstruction

Introduction

Child's coming of age coincided with the eruption of the conflict over slavery that had lain dormant since the ratification of the Constitution. In the wake of the Revolution, slavery appeared to be dying out. All the northern states passed gradual emancipation laws, and most opponents of slavery assumed that the southern states would follow suit, especially after the law banning the African slave trade went into effect in 1808. Meanwhile, humanitarian white reformers channeled their energies into what seemed the most practical scheme for phasing out slavery: "colonization," or the repatriation of free blacks to Africa. Events had not taken the course humanitarians expected, however. The 1793 invention of the cotton gin combined with the Industrial Revolution to reinvigorate the slave system, generating enormous profits both for the cotton plantations of the South and for the burgeoning textile factories of Britain and New England. The Louisiana Purchase of 1803 opened up a vast expanse of fertile land to cotton and sugar production, and slavery was penetrating the Northwest Territory as well, despite a 1787 prohibition. For their part, African Americans were vehemently rejecting colonization and agitating for equal rights in the country their labor had helped to build—a stand they would soon persuade their white sympathizers to adopt.

As Child neared the end of her stay in Norridgewock, Maine's bid for statehood was being held hostage to Missouri's admission as a slave state, in violation of the Northwest Ordinance. The sectional crisis ended with the Missouri Compromise of 1820, which maintained the numerical balance between free and slave states and readjusted the limit on the growth of slave territory. Nevertheless, the crisis had struck what Jefferson called "a firebell in the night."

Child began pondering the vexed question of slavery as early as her first year of authorship. Her children's book *Evenings in New England* (1824) features a story whose endorsement of gradual voluntary emancipation and relocation barely contains the strong antislavery sentiments impelling her toward radicalism: "The Little Master and His Little Slave." Its young hero "cannot bear the idea of keeping slaves" and eagerly embraces the solution his aunt offers—educating the slaves and sending them to Haiti, where they can be "as free and happy as I am" (146–47). If Child did not yet envisage a biracial republic, she went well beyond prevailing white opinion in favoring

Haiti (a republic established by slave revolutionaries and not recognized by the U.S. government until the Civil War) over Liberia (the puppet state for emancipated slaves established by the slaveholder-dominated American Colonization Society).

Child started rethinking her stance on slavery around June 1830, after meeting the fiery young abolitionist William Lloyd Garrison, who sought to recruit her because he admired her writings. Then coeditor of the *Genius of Universal Emancipation,* an antislavery newspaper founded by the Quaker Benjamin Lundy, Garrison had already begun advocating immediate emancipation and airing African American protests against colonization in the *Genius's* columns. When he launched his own newspaper, *The Liberator,* on New Year's Day 1831, he publicly "repudiate[d] all colonization schemes" in one of his earliest editorials (22 Jan. 1831).[1] Child moved step by step in the same direction. Her new commitment to agitating against slavery first became visible in her children's magazine, the *Juvenile Miscellany;* nearly every number from September 1830 on carries some item aimed at countering antiblack prejudice. "Jumbo and Zairee" (January 1831) reflects Child's evolution away from the gradualism of "The Little Master and His Little Slave" and toward greater militancy. The story's graphic depiction of white cruelty, its outspoken denunciation of slavery and the slave trade, its sympathetic depiction of African culture, and its implication that once masters recognize slavery as "wrong in the sight of God," they ought to free their slaves en masse, represent significant departures from colonizationist rhetoric, even though the ending restores the protagonists to their African homeland.

Simultaneously, Child was collecting the facts and arguments she would use in her *Appeal in Favor of That Class of Americans Called Africans* (1833), whose very title defines blacks as Americans, not Africans, and categorizes them as an assimilable class, not a biologically separate race. The most comprehensive indictment of slavery ever written by a white abolitionist, the *Appeal* was the first American book to call for immediate emancipation, an end to all forms of racial discrimination, and the integration of African Americans as equal citizens. While owing many debts to the African American abolitionist David Walker's *Appeal to the Colored Citizens of the World* (1829), as well as to Garrison's *Liberator* and its African American correspondents, Child synthesizes her predecessors' contributions into an ambitious, meticulously documented compendium. Her eight chapters survey the his-

---

1. See Garrison's editorial "Removal to Texas," *Liberator* 22 Jan. 1831, p. 13.

tory of slavery and the African slave trade (chap. 1); compare the United States with other slave societies, ancient and modern, and describe American slave law as the harshest in the world (chap. 2); demonstrate the possibility of safe emancipation and the greater profitability of free labor over slave labor (chap. 3); examine the ways in which the Constitution allows slaveholding states to dominate Congress and govern national policy (chap. 4); expose the racism of the American Colonization Society and its resettlement scheme (chap. 5); refute claims that Africans are intellectually inferior (chap. 6) and morally debased (chap. 7); and condemn racial prejudice in the North (chap. 8, reprinted here). The *Appeal*'s chief originality, distinguishing it from all other antislavery tracts by white Americans, lies in its thorough dismantling of racist ideology and its respectful and detailed treatment of African cultures. Indeed, the historian Sterling Stuckey credits Child with displaying a fund of knowledge about Africa matched only by Martin Delany among her African American contemporaries and by Mary Lowell Putnam and Herman Melville among whites.[2]

The *Appeal* propelled Child to the forefront of the abolitionist movement, elevating her to a position of unparalleled political influence for a woman. It also converted many future leaders to the antislavery cause, among them the orator Wendell Phillips, the Unitarian ministers William Ellery Channing and Thomas Wentworth Higginson, and the Radical Republican Senator Charles Sumner. Child's hitherto adoring public greeted the *Appeal* with outrage, however, reacting with special venom against her critique of racism. Former patrons ostracized her, the Boston Athenaeum canceled her free library privileges, a prominent Massachusetts politician hurled the *Appeal* out of his window with a pair of tongs, and readers boycotted her writings.

As this virulent response indicates, the elites who benefited from ties with the South—merchants, manufacturers, bankers, politicians, newspaper editors, and clergymen—went to extraordinary lengths to prevent any discussion of slavery. In the North, churches and municipal halls barred abolitionist speakers, and rioters led by "gentlemen of property and standing" disrupted abolitionist meetings, threatened abolitionist leaders with lynching, destroyed abolitionist printing presses, and, in a particularly notori-

2. Sterling Stuckey, reader's report to Duke University Press, 4 March 1996. See in particular Martin Delany's novel *Blake; or, the Huts of America*, ed. Floyd J. Miller (1859; Boston: Beacon P, 1970); Mary Lowell Putnam's *Record of an Obscure Man* (Boston, 1861); and Melville's "Benito Cereno" (1855).

ous instance, killed the abolitionist newspaper editor Elijah Lovejoy.[3] Riots against African Americans were even more vicious, sometimes leveling whole neighborhoods. In the South, people merely suspected of abolitionist tendencies were hounded out of town and sometimes publicly whipped. A campaign to reach white Southerners through the mails fared no better than attempts to speak to them in person—mobs ransacked post offices for antislavery literature and fed the "offensive documents" into bonfires. The U.S. Congress simply refused to hear antislavery petitions, instead passing a "gagrule" that automatically tabled them without debate or mention in the written record.

Antiabolitionists typically justified their high-handed proceedings by accusing their foes of inciting slave insurrections and endangering the Union—charges to which the outbreak of the Nat Turner rebellion in September 1831, nine months after Garrison started publishing the *Liberator,* and the frequency of southern states' threats to secede if their "peculiar institution" were not protected lent a semblance of plausibility. Yet, according to historians Leonard L. Richards and James Brewer Stewart, the best explanation for the ferocity of the antiabolitionist backlash lies in the rapid proliferation of antislavery societies.[4] Beginning with the New England Anti-Slavery Society in January 1832, forty-seven associations pledged to fight for immediate abolition sprang up in ten states within less than two years.

In December 1833, abolitionists formed a centralized national organization, the American Anti-Slavery Society, with headquarters in New York. Symbolizing their intention to complete the work of the Founding Fathers by fulfilling the promise of liberty and equality set forth in the Declaration of Independence, abolitionists chose Philadelphia as the site of their national convention and issued a Declaration of Sentiments that spelled out the relationship between their enterprise and their Revolutionary forebears':

Their principles led them to wage war against their oppressors, and to spill human blood like water, in order to be free. Ours forbid the doing of evil that good may come, and lead us to reject, and to entreat the oppressed to reject, the use of all

3. See Child's "Letters from New-York," number 33, which gives a vivid account of how Child and other women helped the British antislavery lecturer George Thompson escape from one of these antiabolitionist mobs. She mentions the murder of Lovejoy and other incidents of mob violence in "To Abolitionists" and "The Iron Shroud."

4. See Leonard L. Richards, *"Gentlemen of Property and Standing": Anti-Abolition Mobs in Jacksonian America* (New York: Oxford UP, 1970), chap. 2; and James Brewer Stewart, *Holy Warriors: The Abolitionists and American Slavery* (New York: Hill and Wang, 1976) 65.

carnal weapons for deliverance from bondage; relying solely upon those which are spiritual. . . .

Their measures were physical resistance. . . . Ours shall be such only as the opposition of moral purity to moral corruption—the destruction of error by the potency of truth—the overthrow of prejudice by the power of love—and the abolition of slavery by the spirit of repentance.[5]

The plan to convert the country to antislavery through "moral suasion" could not withstand the violent and systematic suppression of public debate, however. By 1838, stymied in their original approach, abolitionists were exploring new strategies. This process ignited disputes between Garrisonian radicals and conservative evangelical abolitionists over such matters as whether to allow women equal participation in the movement, whether to form an antislavery political party, and whether to break with churches and ministers who refused to condemn slavery. The bitter infighting climaxed in 1840 with a major schism as the evangelicals walked out of the American Anti-Slavery Society and founded their own organization, the American and Foreign Anti-Slavery Society, which excluded women, supported the idea of an abolitionist political party, and sought to conciliate the clergy. African Americans, disillusioned by their white allies' internecine quarrels and failure to integrate them into the movement's leadership, resumed the independent struggle for self-determination they had waged prior to the emergence of Garrisonian immediatism. Besides reviving forums for defining their own agenda without white interference—among them "Colored Conventions," the first of which had been held in 1830—African American leaders such as Henry Highland Garnet and Martin Delany started developing more militant tactics: defending their communities through vigilance committees that mobilized against kidnappers, advocating slave rebellion, and promoting emigration (though not under the aegis of the American Colonization Society).

To help heal the movement's splits and redirect abolitionists from attacking each other to combating slavery, Child was asked to take over the editorship of the *National Anti-Slavery Standard,* the official organ of the pro-Garrison American Anti-Slavery Society, based in New York. She occupied the post—a milestone for a woman—from May 1841 until May 1843. During her tenure she conducted a courteous dialogue with African Americans (un-

5. The American Anti-Slavery Society's 1833 Declaration of Sentiments, authored by Garrison, is reprinted in William E. Cain, ed. *William Lloyd Garrison and the Fight against Slavery* (New York: Bedford Books of St. Martin's P, 1995) 90–94.

like the *Standard*'s previous editors, who had editorialized against colored conventions and other forms of black separatist action). Reprinting articles from African American newspapers and speeches by Frederick Douglass, William C. Nell, and others, she seconded their rebukes of racism in abolitionist ranks. She treated evangelical and political abolitionists with equal courtesy. Instead of impugning her rivals' motives and trading insults, as antislavery editors had been doing for the past year, she sought merely to persuade them to reconsider policies she found shortsighted. Above all, she expanded the paper's outreach by gearing the *Standard* toward the general public rather than toward readers already committed to abolition.

The editorials "To Abolitionists," "Annette Gray," "The Iron Shroud," and "Talk about Political Party" exemplify Child's journalistic style and show how she combined Garrisonian ideology with attempts to transcend factionalism and appeal to a broader audience.[6] "To Abolitionists" (20 May 1841), her inaugural message, looks back nostalgically to the period before the schism of 1840 and compares sectarianism among abolitionists with its precedents in Christian history. While taking a philosophical view of the disagreements between radicals and conservatives, Child urges each to honor the other's motives and to concentrate on fighting slavery. Illustrating Child's efforts to turn abolitionists back to their original objectives, "Annette Gray" (22 July 1841) is one of several editorials Child devoted to telling the stories of fugitive slaves. It exhibits parallels with her fictional tale "Slavery's Pleasant Homes" (1843), as well as with *Incidents in the Life of a Slave Girl* (1861), the narrative she edited for Harriet Jacobs. In this editorial Child defends the character of slave women coerced into unwanted sexual relations with their masters and drives home the message that slave law governs the citizens of the "free" states by preventing them from sheltering fugitives.

Wider in scope, "The Iron Shroud" (3 March 1842) comments on the progress the antislavery cause has made in recent years and interprets both the growth of northern opposition to slavery and the heightening of southern intransigence as signs that the institution's demise is inevitable. Mob violence and unconstitutional abridgements of free speech have ultimately won more adherents to abolitionism, Child argues, pointing to the surprising public sympathy for the blacks who revolted on the slave-trading ships *Amistad* and *Creole* in 1839 and 1841. Once again seeking to promote unity in antislavery ranks, Child pays tribute not only to Garrison but to members of

6. See also "Speaking in the Church," reprinted in part 5 of this volume.

the opposing faction who likewise deserve credit for the movement's successes: the evangelical businessman Arthur Tappan, who bailed Garrison out of prison in 1830 by paying his fine; and the former students of the Lane Theological Seminary in Cincinnati, Ohio, numbering among them several Southerners, who converted to abolitionism in 1834 after an eighteen-day debate and left the college en masse when its trustees and president, Lyman Beecher, forbade their antislavery activities. Child also hails the nonabolitionist Massachusetts congressman John Quincy Adams for his lonely campaign against the gag rule.

By contrast, "Talk about Political Party" takes a staunchly Garrisonian position, even as it displays Child's ability to engage adversaries in a respectful dialogue about strategy and principles. Child corrects the misconceptions that Garrisonians oppose any participation in politics and that all Garrisonians are "non-resistants." (Non-resistants rejected human governments as coercive and corrupt, recognizing only the government of God as legitimate.) She then explains why she and her fellow Garrisonians view the establishment of an abolitionist political party (the Liberty party) as a tactical mistake tending to reduce the leverage of antislavery voters, and why they prefer to act outside the system as a moral pressure group, influencing rather than playing the role of politicians.

Although most of Child's antislavery writings took the form of polemical tracts and articles, she continued to use fiction, as she had in "Jumbo and Zairee," to promote empathic identification with slaves. Indeed, she pioneered the genre of antislavery fiction that Harriet Beecher Stowe would later popularize. "The Black Saxons" (1841) and "Slavery's Pleasant Homes" (1843), both written for the abolitionist gift book *The Liberty Bell,* articulate the rage of slaves who, like the rebels on board the *Amistad* and the *Creole,* choose to end their oppression through violence. "The Black Saxons" reminds white readers that their vaunted Anglo-Saxon ancestors were once slaves to the Normans who conquered England in 1066 A.D., hence that all races react alike to tyranny, submitting when they must and rebelling when they can—a point Child develops at greater length in her editorial "Our Anglo-Saxon Ancestry" (28 April 1842). "Slavery's Pleasant Homes," one of Child's most trenchant stories, fictionalizes cases of rape, murder, slave revenge, and heroic self-sacrifice reported in antislavery newspapers.

However adept at repackaging the antislavery message for multiple audiences, Child proved unequal to the task of quelling the infighting among abolitionists. Garrisonian radicals objected to her policy of keeping personal attacks on their rivals out of the *Standard* and insisted that she endorse their new strategy of "come-outism," which called on abolitionists to "come out of" churches and political parties open to slaveholding members. Worn out by the perpetual dissension, Child resigned from the *Standard* and the American Anti-Slavery Society in May 1843 and resumed her literary career. For the next thirteen years, she confined her antislavery work to helping fugitive slaves and reprinting her less radical abolitionist writings for a commercial audience.

During Child's period of withdrawal from activism, prospects for ending slavery dimmed. The territory conquered in the Mexican War of 1846–48, which abolitionists had vainly tried to prevent, threatened to expand the South's slave empire as far as the Pacific coast. The Compromise of 1850 staved off another sectional crisis with further concessions to the South, chief among them a draconian fugitive slave law. This law not only prohibited any court, judge, magistrate, or private citizen in the free states from obstructing the recapture of runaway slaves, but also denied blacks seized as fugitives the right to testify in their own defense. Slave catchers now roamed the streets of northern cities, often kidnapping free blacks with impunity; northern judges acted as agents of the slave system by sending fugitives back to their masters; and African Americans fled in droves to Canada. Then, in 1854, the Kansas-Nebraska Act decreed that all new territories could decide by "popular sovereignty" whether to allow slavery within their borders—a provision that nullified the 1820 Missouri Compromise's restrictions against slavery north of the 36°30′ line. Pro- and antislavery immigrants to Kansas consequently raced for electoral dominance. As the vastly outnumbered proslavery settlers attempted to achieve through terrorism what they could not win at the polls, civil war broke out between the two groups in December 1855.

The event that galvanized Child back into action was the brutal beating on the Senate floor of her disciple, Massachusetts Senator Charles Sumner, by South Carolina Congressman Preston Brooks, in retaliation for Sumner's May 1856 speech denouncing the "rape" of Kansas by proslavery settlers and their congressional allies. Child responded with a powerful story, "The Kansas Emigrants," which was serialized in the daily and weekly editions of the *New York Tribune* just in time for the 1856 presidential election.[7] Through it, she sought to unify antislavery partisans behind the two groups mounting

---

7. Child reprinted "The Kansas Emigrants" in *Autumnal Leaves: Tales and Sketches in Prose and Rhyme* (New York: C. S. Francis, 1857) 302–63.

the most effective challenges to southern dominance: the settlers fighting to make Kansas a free state, and the Republican party, pledged to oppose the extension of slavery. Supporting armed struggle and party politics represented new departures for Child, but the preconditions she had stipulated in her editorials "To Abolitionists" and "Talk about Political Party" had come to pass: peaceful means of abolishing slavery had been tried in vain, and the broadening of the former Liberty party into a coalition including antislavery Whigs and Free-Soil Democrats had produced a party with a realistic chance of furthering an antislavery agenda in Congress.

Still, Child remained distrustful of politicians (always excepting Sumner) and highly ambivalent about violence. "I honor those who conscientiously fight for justice, truth, or freedom; but I revere those who will *die* to advance great principles, though they will not *kill*," she wrote to Sumner of the men engaged in the war for a free Kansas.[8] One of those men was John Brown, whom Child would embrace with similar ambivalence, recoiling from his "method" but lauding the heroism with which he sacrificed his life to free the slaves. Brown first won the admiration of abolitionists for his reprisals against proslavery atrocities in Kansas and his daring trek across slave territory with a band of fugitives whom he piloted to Canada. When he sought backing for a secret mission that would strike a major blow against slavery, six wealthy men agreed to finance him, among them Child's nephew-in-law, George Luther Stearns, and her friend Thomas Wentworth Higginson. None knew the precise details of Brown's plan, however. He had merely intimated that it would involve swooping down on a plantation community in Virginia, liberating a large number of slaves, and organizing them into guerrilla bands that would operate out of camps in the mountains and make periodic forays into slave territory for recruits and supplies. Thus Brown's raid of 16 October 1859 on the federal arsenal at Harpers Ferry, Virginia, conducted with a small force of sixteen white and five black followers, took everyone by surprise.

Brown's actual intentions remain unclear. Most historians believe that he hoped to spark a large-scale slave rebellion, yet Brown repeatedly denied that such had been his purpose, and a leading historian of African American slave revolts, Herbert Aptheker, finds this denial credible.[9] The united testimony of Brown's confidants (of whom Frederick Douglass is the best known) points

8. LMC to Charles Sumner, 7 July 1856, *SL* 285.
9. Herbert Aptheker, *Abolitionism: A Revolutionary Movement* (Boston: Twayne, 1989) 132–33. For an opposing view, see Stephen B. Oates, *To Purge This Land with Blood: A Biography of John Brown*, 2nd ed. (Amherst: U of Massachusetts P, 1984).

to his having designed the Harpers Ferry raid as a spectacular hit-and-run operation serving to recruit slaves into a mobile guerrilla force that would wage a prolonged war of attrition against planters.[10] At the same time, some of Brown's correspondence with his supporters suggests that he may have been contemplating a heroic suicide mission aimed at inspiring a national crusade to destroy slavery once and for all. Perhaps he never quite decided between these two irreconcilable goals. Whatever Brown's intent, the raid ultimately took the form of a suicide mission rather than a guerrilla operation. The qualms that doomed Brown as a revolutionary canonized him as a martyr. Therein lay the secret of Child's profound identification with him.

As a military maneuver, the raid failed dismally. True, Brown easily captured the town and the arsenal, but instead of retreating to the mountains with his hostages, he lingered until the next morning. By noon on 17 October, Virginia and Maryland militia had surrounded Brown's band, and on the eighteenth federal marines under Colonel Robert E. Lee captured him and his surviving men. Though Brown was denounced as a monster who had aimed to unleash a servile insurrection and whet "knives of butchery" for innocent " 'Mothers, sisters,' daughters, 'and babes' " (in the words of Virginia's governor, Henry Wise),[11] his own guerrilla army suffered most of the casualties at Harpers Ferry. Ten out of twenty-two were killed, including two of Brown's sons; in comparison, four Harpers Ferry residents and one marine lost their lives, and Brown's hostages sustained no injuries. Of the twelve raiders who lived through the battle, the seven captured were swiftly tried and hanged. Only five succeeded in escaping, most notably Osborne Anderson, who would publish the sole eyewitness account of the raid by an African American participant, *A Voice from Harpers Ferry* (1861).

Albeit militarily defeated, Brown wrested the laurels from his captors in the widely publicized interview he gave the day after the debacle. Speaking from his bloodstained pallet on the floor of the armory, he turned the interrogation into one of the most potent antislavery sermons the nation had ever heard. "I respect the rights of the poorest and weakest of colored people,

10. See Frederick Douglass, *Life and Times of Frederick Douglass* (1892; New York: Collier, 1962) 314–15, 319; Thomas Wentworth Higginson, *Cheerful Yesterdays* (1898; New York: Arno P, 1968) 216–34; and Franklin B. Sanborn, ed., *The Life and Letters of John Brown, Liberator of Kansas, and Martyr of Virginia* (Boston: Roberts Brothers, 1891) 425, 434–36, 438–40, 444, 450, 541–42. For a more extensive analysis, see Karcher, *The First Woman in the Republic: A Cultural Biography of Lydia Maria Child* (Durham: Duke UP, 1994) chap. 17.

11. Henry Wise to LMC, 29 Oct. 1859, *CC* 41/1127.

oppressed by the slave system, just as much as I do those of the most wealthy and powerful," Brown proclaimed. "I pity the poor in bondage that have none to help them: that is why I am here; not to gratify any personal animosity, revenge, or vindictive spirit."[12]

These words, spoken by a man who had proved himself ready to die for the slaves and to lay his sons' lives on the same altar, moved Child so deeply that she offered to nurse Brown in prison, thus initiating a famous exchange of letters with Brown and his Virginian detractors, Governor Henry Wise and Mrs. Margaretta Mason, wife of Senator James M. Mason. When Brown replied that she could do him more good by staying home and launching a fund-raising drive for his bereaved family, Child accepted the charge and plunged into a whirl of activism and tractwriting that fueled the militancy Brown had triggered. Of her myriad enterprises in the wake of Harpers Ferry, none surpassed her *Correspondence between Lydia Maria Child and Gov. Wise and Mrs. Mason, of Virginia* (1860). First published in the newspapers on Wise's initiative as part of a propaganda war for American public opinion, and later reprinted as a tract, it features Child's and Brown's letters to each other, Child's official request for permission to nurse Brown, the retorts by Wise and Mrs. Mason accusing Child of fanaticism and hypocrisy, and Child's answers debunking their proslavery arguments. The tract sold 300,000 copies—a record figure—and exerted an enormous influence. In her own way, Child had joined Brown in mobilizing the North for a war against slavery.

The year and a half that intervened before war actually broke out crackled with tension. The southern states threatened to secede if the Republican presidential candidate, Abraham Lincoln, won the 1860 election. Mob violence again swept the North as the same elites responsible for fomenting the riots of the 1830s sought to conciliate the South by suppressing antislavery demonstrations. After Lincoln's victory Republicans themselves scrambled to avert secession with more compromises. Yet secession proceeded, beginning with South Carolina in December 1860. Finally, in April 1861, Confederate batteries bombarded Fort Sumter—the opening round of the Civil War.

Child and her fellow abolitionists defined the goals of the war very differently from Lincoln, as her passionate letter of 22 August 1862, "Mrs. L. Maria

12. Originally published in the *New York Herald,* this interview was reprinted in newspapers across the country, including the *Liberator,* and in most early biographies of Brown. See, for example, Sanborn, *Life and Letters of John Brown* 562–69, 584.

Child to the President of the United States," indicates. Whereas Lincoln wished to save the Union, abolitionists like Child, Garrison, and Frederick Douglass wished to destroy slavery and reconstruct the nation on a basis of racial equality. Indeed, the slogan "No Union with Slavery" had stood at the masthead of Garrison's *Liberator* for the past twenty years. The problem was that three border slave states—Delaware, Maryland, and Kentucky (Lincoln's birthplace and his wife's home state)—had opted to stay in the Union, and Lincoln was anxious to retain their loyalty. He also hoped to woo moderates in the Confederate states by showing that the Union government was abiding by its constitutional obligation not to interfere with slavery. Thus, when slaves started fleeing to Union army camps, Lincoln instructed officers to return them to their masters—a policy that infuriated abolitionists.

Despite Child's strong disagreement with Lincoln, she realized that the majority of the northern public shared his commitment to restoring the Union. The role of abolitionists, as she saw it, was to help build grassroots support for an emancipation proclamation. Meanwhile, she worked to per-suade unionists that it was "absurd *policy* . . . [t]o send back those [fugitive slaves] who want to *serve* us" when they would be "employed by the rebels to help them in *shooting* us."[13] This argument soon occurred to military and political leaders as well. In May 1861 General Benjamin Butler landed on the solution of treating slaves who sought refuge from Confederate masters as "contraband of war"—"goods . . . directly auxiliary to military operations" and therefore properly subject to confiscation.[14] His camp at Fort Monroe, Virginia (referred to in Child's letter to Lincoln), became a haven for "con-trabands" and a laboratory for testing methods of educating the future freedpeople.

Yet it took until March 1862 for Congress to pass an article of war forbid-ding army officers to hand fugitive slaves back to their masters, and even then, as Child complained to Lincoln, some officers ignored the law. The same month, Lincoln appealed to border state unionists to back a resolution of Congress offering financial aid to states that adopted gradual emancipa-tion plans—an appeal they rejected. (Almost simultaneously, Child was mak-ing her own appeal to border state unionists. Her tract *The Right Way the Safe*

13. The quotation is from LMC to Henrietta Sargent, 26 July, *CC* 49/1321. Child publicly advanced this position in a pseudonymous article in the *New York Weekly Tribune* 17 Aug. 1861, p. 5, titled "What is to be done with the Contrabands?" and published under the name "Straight Line."

14. See James M. McPherson, *The Struggle for Equality: Abolitionists and the Negro in the Civil War and Reconstruction* (Princeton: Princeton UP, 1964) 69–70.

Way, Proved by Emancipation in the British West Indies, and Elsewhere [2d ed., 1862], which she mailed to all Maryland and Delaware legislators, attempted to convince southern moderates that they could best serve their economic interests by voting to abolish slavery.) To Child's disgust, while Lincoln let the border states dally and refused to discipline officers who disobeyed laws protecting fugitives, he acted against the abolitionist generals David Hunter and John Phelps. He countermanded Hunter's military decree proclaiming the emancipation of all slaves in South Carolina, Georgia, and Florida; and he allowed Phelps to be forced out of his command for enlisting "contrabands" as soldiers.

By the time Child wrote to Lincoln, public opinion had come around to favoring emancipation as a military necessity. Her letter was one of many pleas to Lincoln for an emancipation proclamation in the summer of 1862, including *New York Tribune* editor Horace Greeley's "Prayer of Twenty Millions" (20 Aug.) and Harriet Beecher Stowe's "Prayer" (*Independent* 28 Aug.). Reinforcing these pleas, moreover, were 400,000 signatures collected by Elizabeth Cady Stanton and the National Woman's Loyal League. What Child and other spokespersons did not know was that Lincoln himself had decided to issue an emancipation proclamation and was only waiting for a battlefield victory to give him a propitious occasion. He announced the decision on 22 September 1862, after the Union army repelled Lee's attempted invasion of Maryland at Antietam.

Child could not rest content with an abolition decree based merely on military expediency, however. Fearing that "everything *must* go wrong, if there is no heart or conscience on the subject,"[15] she continued her efforts to promote a change in racial attitudes. Her article "Emancipation and Amalgamation" (3 Sept. 1862) counters the phobia of interracial marriage that the Democrats were exploiting in the 1862 congressional election campaign as a means of forestalling emancipation. Three weeks earlier, Lincoln had responded to Democratic race baiting by reviving the long-discredited colonization scheme of inducing African Americans to emigrate—a scheme he abandoned only in 1864, after the costly failure of a resettlement attempt on an unhealthy Caribbean island. In contrast, Child exposes the sophistry of polemics against race mixing and subtly conjures up the vision of a regenerated society in which prejudice has disappeared and public opinion accepts intermarriage as natural.

Emancipation was only the first of the goals Child and other abolitionists

15. LMC to Gerrit Smith, 7 Jan. 1862, *CC* 50/1364.

sought to achieve. The second was to give African Americans, slave and free, the right to fight for their own liberty by joining the Union army—a right that such leaders as Frederick Douglass and Martin Delany had been insistently demanding. In her letter to Lincoln, Child answers the contradictory arguments commonly urged against arming blacks—that they would degenerate into savagery or dissolve into cowardice. By November 1862 she enjoyed the satisfaction of seeing enacted the measure she had advocated since the start of the war. Her friend Thomas Wentworth Higginson led the first regiment of slaves officially mustered into the Union army. A few months later, young Robert Gould Shaw, the son of even closer white abolitionist friends, headed the first regiment of free African Americans, the Fifty-fourth Massachusetts, recruited by Frederick Douglass, whose sons marched in its ranks.

These pioneer black soldiers confronted the challenge of proving the bravery of their race to a skeptical nation. Such was the cruel imperative that drove Shaw and his men in July 1863 when they (like the Harpers Ferry raiders before them) undertook what amounted to a suicide mission—an assault on impregnable Fort Wagner, which guarded Charleston Harbor. Despite a barrage of cannon fire that mowed them down right and left, the men advanced steadily across the beach and up the slope to the fort, not retreating until half of the six hundred soldiers and seven of the ten officers, including Shaw, were killed, wounded, or missing in action. Shaw's body was rifled and thrown into a mass grave along with his men's. "Our darling son, our hero, has received at the hands of the rebels the most fitting burial possible . . . with his brave, devoted followers, who fell dead over him and around him," wrote his parents in a letter Child quoted for readers of the *National Anti-Slavery Standard* (22 Aug. 1863). By paying tribute to the self-sacrificing courage that the Shaw family and the men of the Fifty-fourth had alike displayed, Child held up to the nation a model of interracial solidarity for the future. She was also commenting indirectly on the vicious New York draft riots, which coincided by a tragic irony with the martyrdom of the Fifty-fourth. To Child, the rampaging mobs of Irish workers who protested their conscription into a rich man's (and black man's) war by torching black neighborhoods, lynching and murdering "any unfortunate black man, woman, or child" found in their path, and looting the homes of antislavery whites seemed to represent the horrific alternative the country would face if it rejected the abolitionist ideal.[16]

16. "Parts of Two Private Letters," *National Anti-Slavery Standard* 22 Aug. 1863, CC 56/1499. On the riots, see "The Draft. Riot in the City of New-York" and "The Riot," *New York Weekly*

The war finally ended with Lee's surrender to Grant at Appomatox on 9 April 1865, having taken an unparalleled toll in bloodshed. But peace did not bring the fulfillment of abolitionists' remaining goals. On 14 April, three days after delivering a speech cautiously endorsing limited black suffrage, Lincoln succumbed to the bullet of proslavery actor John Wilkes Booth. By then, Child had concluded that she had earlier "underrated the qualities of both his head and his heart," as she admitted in a letter to the New York *Independent:* "One rarely sees such honest unselfishness of purpose combined with so much shrewdness in dealing with men for the accomplishment of purposes. . . . It is not easy to think of another man who possessed such a combination of qualities as would enable him to hold steadily in leash so many refractory forces, and to guide them at last to the desired result."[17]

Lincoln's successor, Andrew Johnson, a former Tennessee slaveholder of poor white origins, conspicuously lacked those qualities. A far wider political gap separated him from abolitionists than had been the case with Lincoln. Soon after his accession he began granting wholesale pardons to ex-Confederates and restoring their property rights in plantations confiscated during the war. Many of the confiscated plantations had been farmed by ex-slaves in the interim, and Child, along with other white and black abolitionists, had been lobbying Congress to reward their labor with ownership of the land they had been tilling. By dividing the former slaveholders' estates into forty-acre homesteads and allocating them to freedmen, Union soldiers of both races, and poor whites, Child argued, the U.S. government could break the back of the planter aristocracy and lay the foundation for an egalitarian new South. Johnson, of course, subscribed to an entirely different plan for rehabilitating the South. He indicated his willingness to readmit the former Confederate states into the Union with minimal changes in their proslavery constitutions and without provisions for black suffrage—another target abolitionists had set. Such a procedure would result in a Congress even more dominated by the South than before the war, for unlike slaves, who each had counted as three-fifths of a person in the census determining state representation, each free black would now count as one person. Disfranchised themselves but used to increase their former masters' voting power in Congress, the freedpeople would be completely at the mercy of a class bent on

---

Tribune 18 July 1863, pp. 3–5; and Iver Bernstein, *The New York City Draft Riots: Their Significance for American Society and Politics in the Age of the Civil War* (New York: Oxford UP, 1990).

17. "Letter from Mrs. L. M. Child" to Theodore Tilton, editor of the *Independent,* 6 May 1865, *Independent* 11 May, CC 62/1659.

keeping them in a condition of quasi slavery. Within months, several of the ex–Confederate states, emboldened by Johnson's leniency, passed draconian Black Codes reinstituting slavery in all but name. Meanwhile, antiblack violence reached epidemic proportions as terrorist groups like the Ku Klux Klan proliferated. Yet Johnson responded by rapidly demobilizing the Union army, withdrawing the garrisons stationed in the South, and replacing commanders sympathetic to the freedpeople with prosouthern bigots.

What gave Johnson a free hand during the critical period right after the war was the eight-month recess of Congress, which lasted until December 1865. Once Congress reconvened, however, Johnson's course set him at loggerheads not only with Radical Republicans such as Child's friends, Massachusetts senators Charles Sumner and Henry Wilson and Indiana congressman George Julian, but even with moderates. His vetoes of two bills in particular—the first extending the life of the Freedmen's Bureau, established in March 1865 to protect the emancipated slaves, the second a Civil Rights act defining African Americans as U.S. citizens and invalidating discriminatory state codes—made clear to everyone that Johnson was determined to reverse the outcome of the war. Congress overrode Johnson's veto of the Civil Rights bill and seized the initiative in formulating Reconstruction policy, but for the remainder of his presidency, every piece of legislative reform had to muster a veto-proof two-thirds majority. Johnson's efforts to sabotage the Reconstruction acts passed by Congress ultimately led to his impeachment, though his conviction failed by one vote. Still, the battles with Johnson and the excesses committed by former Confederates probably swung many moderates over to supporting black suffrage as a means of retaining Republican control of the South. The culmination of the antislavery crusade, the Fifteenth Amendment granting voting rights to all (male) U.S. citizens regardless of "race, color, or previous condition of servitude," would be ratified in 1870.

Commenting directly and indirectly on these events, Child's reader for the emancipated slaves, *The Freedmen's Book* (1865), and her articles for the *Independent* and the *National Anti-Slavery Standard*, "Through the Red Sea into the Wilderness" (21 Dec. 1865) and "Homesteads" (20 March 1869), assess the gains of the Civil War, address the problems posed by Johnson's Reconstruction policy, and point toward long-range objectives. While the two articles summon abolitionists and Radical Republicans to complete their work, *The Freedmen's Book* seeks to empower the ex-slaves themselves by offering them the education they need to defend their own rights.

Child conceived the project of compiling a reader for the freedmen during the war, when she realized how unsuited the educational materials she was sending to the "contrabands" at Fort Monroe were to the needs of a newly emancipated people. Primer, anthology, history text, and self-help manual rolled into one, *The Freedmen's Book* anticipates twentieth-century educators in conceptualizing the teaching of literacy as a process that starts with the cultivation of students' pride in their own identity. Accordingly, all the selections relate to African peoples' struggle to liberate themselves from slavery and racial proscription in the New World. Biographical sketches offer a variety of black role models for the freedpeople to emulate, and historical articles on the Santo Domingo revolution and emancipation in the British West Indies distill the lessons to be learned from other societies that have undergone the transition from slavery to freedom. Child also makes a point of including a number of "colored authors," whom she identifies with an asterisk. Rounding out the volume are four essays proffering political, moral, and domestic advice. Of these, "Advice from an Old Friend" is reprinted here, and "Education of Children" is in part 2. Both invite comparison with the counsels Child furnishes to white parents in *The Mother's Book.* "Advice from an Old Friend" additionally reflects Child's awareness that the freedpeople's employers had formed cabals to keep them in subjection and that local magistrates belonged to those cabals. Yet the inadequate recourses she recommends—quitting exploitative employers, appealing to regional authorities for protection, petitioning Radical Republicans in Congress—testify starkly to how little the freedpeople could rely on the remedies the political system provided.

Like *The Freedmen's Book,* "Through the Red Sea into the Wilderness" appeared just as Congress was reconvening. Clearly aimed at fortifying Republicans against "the old chronic disease of Congress—weakness of the spine," it encourages firmness by simultaneously tallying the achievements of the long struggle against slavery and highlighting the challenges that remain. Child credits the heroism that African Americans displayed in the war as soldiers and guides with having played a key role in conquering racial prejudice. The country owes them a debt that Congress must ensure is justly repaid, she implies.

Written more than three years later, after the inauguration of the next Republican president, General Ulysses S. Grant, "Homesteads" appeals to the new president and Congress to right the wrongs of the Johnson administration by enacting land reform. Child uses the example of the hardworking freedman, Moses Fisher, to win sympathy for the idea of enabling poor blacks and whites to purchase small farms of their own "at moderate prices." Land for this purpose can still be obtained through "confiscation, fines, or sale for taxes" of the former slaveholders' large estates, she suggests.

The land redistribution policy Child advocated was never seriously considered by Congress. Instead, elected officials looked the other way as the Klan's reign of terror continued, targeting local black leaders, white Republicans, black schools and churches, educators of both races serving the freedpeople, black landowners and entrepreneurs, and any who availed themselves of Reconstruction laws designed to safeguard them against exploitation. The situation required a prolonged military occupation of the South, but the northern public had neither the political will to impose such an occupation nor the financial altruism to fund it through taxes. Thus whites rapidly lost interest in Reconstruction. The catastrophic depression of 1873 and the corruption scandals of the Grant administration precipitated the abandonment of the freedpeople, finalized in 1877 when Grant's successor, Rutherford B. Hayes, withdrew the last federal troops from the South.

No event better symbolized the end of an era than the death of the abolitionist William Lloyd Garrison in May 1879. Fittingly, it occurred in the midst of a crisis dramatizing the nation's betrayal of its responsibility to the slaves who had helped win the Civil War—the mass exodus to Kansas of desperate freedpeople determined to escape de facto reenslavement. Just as fittingly, Garrison spent his last days writing rousing calls for a resumption of the "battle of liberty and equal rights"—calls that could no longer enlist an abolitionist army ready to wage a forty-year struggle.[18]

Yet affirmation rather than mourning characterizes Child's tribute to the man who brought her into the antislavery movement. Her eulogy of Garrison in the *Atlantic Monthly* (August 1879) celebrates the values for which he stood, enumerates the signs of progress showing his crusade has not been in vain, and draws the lesson future generations should learn from his life—that a person whose entire being "revolve[s] round a centre of fixed principle" can revolutionize the world. A plea for hope in a dark time and for moral courage in an age of cowardly truckling, this article was Child's last word to the public before her own death in October 1880.

18. See Garrison's letters to Robert Morris and George T. Downing, 22 Apr. 1879, *The Letters of William Lloyd Garrison*, vol. 6: *To Rouse the Slumbering Land, 1868–1879*, ed. Walter M. Merrill and Louis Ruchames (Cambridge: Belknap P of Harvard UP, 1981) 578–81.

Jumbo and Zairee

Little Jumbo and his sister Zairee were two pretty negro children. Their father was a prince; and he lived near the coast of Guinea. Ships from Europe and America, often go there for gold dust and ivory; and I am very sorry to say the Americans have sometimes stolen the negroes, and sold them for slaves.

It happened that an English vessel was once wrecked not far from where Jumbo lived. Every body on board perished, except one gentleman, who clung to a mast, and was thrown upon the sand. Jumbo's father took this unfortunate stranger to his house, and warmed and fed him, as if he had been his own son. He lived several months with the negro prince; during which time he enjoyed himself very much in hunting, fishing, and riding: the English king could not have treated a guest with more kindness and generosity. The two children, Jumbo and Zairee, were very much attached to the white man. They would listen to his stories by the hour together; their yams and calabashes of milk were always brought for him to share; and many a crying time they had, because their mother made them go to bed, before he came home from hunting. They often teased Mr. Harris, for that was the gentleman's name, to live always in Africa, with them; but this he would not promise—for though he felt very grateful to his benefactor's family, and even loved them dearly, he could not conceal that his heart longed for white faces, and his native language.

The children would sigh deeply, when they heard him say that he must go back to England, and would ask, "May Jumbo and Zairee go, too?" Their mother would say, "What! and leave me all alone!" This always made the affectionate little creatures very sorry; and they would look up in her face very sorrowfully, as they replied, "Oh, no—Mother would be very sick, if Jumbo and Zairee went away."

At last, a British vessel brought letters and money for Mr. Harris, and he made preparations to return home. He earnestly entreated to take the children with him; promising to send them back after they had been a few years at school. The prince was willing to have them go; for he said they would then be able to teach their people a great many new things: but the mother grieved, as if she would break her heart. When Mr. Harris saw how much she was

Juvenile Miscellany, n.s. 5 (Jan. 1831): 285–99.

troubled, he would not consent to take the children; but he did every thing he could to show his gratitude.

He gave the prince a beautiful sword, a pair of pistols, and a hunting horn; which he had ordered to be brought from England, on purpose for him; to his wife he gave a large scarlet shawl, an amber necklace, and gold bracelets; Jumbo had a drum and fife; and Zairee a doll almost as big as herself, that could move its eyes, and open its mouth. At first, it frightened her very much to look at it; for she had never seen such a thing before, and she thought it would bite her. However, she got accustomed to it in a few hours; and then she was so delighted with it, that she talked like a parrot the whole time.

The children were very anxious to go on board the English vessel, the day Mr. Harris was to sail; but as they had been several times, and as their father was absent hunting, they were strictly forbidden to go near the sea-shore. Mr. Harris did not tell them what hour the vessel was to sail, because he knew how they would cry, if they thought they should see him no more. He was far away, almost out of sight of the African coast, before Jumbo and Zairee knew anything of the matter. At first, they cried bitterly; and when they had dried their tears a little, it popped into their heads to run off in search of the vessel. They ran along the sea-shore hand in hand, for nearly a mile, without seeing anything of the ship. At last they grew weary, and sat down on the beach, and picked up the prettiest shells they could find. While they were thus employed, they saw a boat at a distance; as it came nearer, they perceived it to be filled with white men. The foolish little creatures were overjoyed; for they had never seen any white man, but Mr. Harris, and the crew of the vessel in which he sailed, and they were now quite sure they should hear of their friend. They forgot how often their careful mother had told them that cruel white men came to steal away little negro children.

The boat came nearer, and at length the white men leaped on the beach, spoke very kindly to the children, and offered to give them some beads for their shells. Jumbo and Zairee, in broken English, asked where Mr. Harris was, for they wanted to see him. The men told them that he was in a vessel a little ways off, and that if they would jump into the boat, they should go and see him. Jumbo was for going directly; but Zairee wanted to go back and tell her mother; because she said her mother would cry if she could not find them. The sailors promised her that they should be carried back to their mother in a very little while; and the poor little creatures were tempted to go in the boat. They were cruelly deceived. The vessel on board which they were carried was an American slave ship! and Jumbo and Zairee were tied together, and put in a dark hole with a great many other wretched negroes. Oh, then how bitterly they wept to think they had disobeyed their good mother, by running away! She, poor woman! was almost crazy when she found they were gone. All the country round was searched in vain. At first, she thought they had wandered on the sea-shore, and had been eaten up by crocodiles. Crocodiles abound in Africa. They are very large ugly creatures, with a monstrous mouth, and a back covered with shell, so hard that it is said to be bullet-proof. They often seize upon people and devour them. And this was thought to be the fate of poor Jumbo and his sister, until a huntsman brought in word that he had seen a ship off the coast, and white men prowling about on shore.

This almost broke the mother's heart; for several days she would not taste any food. She feared that her husband would be very angry with her, for allowing the children to be out of her sight. And then she said she had rather, a thousand times over, that they had been swallowed by crocodiles, than to be carried off, and made slaves by the white men. She hated the sound of a white man's name. She would not allow even Mr. Harris to be mentioned before her; for she could not help sometimes suspecting that he had returned and stolen her treasures from her.

When Jumbo's father returned, he was very angry—not with his wife,— for she was so sick and broken-hearted, that he could not be angry with her; but he vowed revenge against all the white men. Never again, he said, would he save one from death; if they were shipwrecked on his shores, they should perish. Many a white man was afterwards murdered by the prince and his tribe. Was it not melancholy that the cruelty of white men, should thus turn the kindness of a savage heart into gall and bitterness?

As for Jumbo and Zairee, they had a wretched voyage. The bread that was given them was mouldy and hard, and even of that they seldom had as much as they wanted. The want of pure air made them ill; and for many days Jumbo thought poor little Zairee would die. Five of the negroes did die, and were thrown overboard during the voyage. The hard-hearted captain did not seem to pity his miserable captives in the least; he was only angry to have them die, because he thought he should not get quite so much money. You will ask me if this man was an American? One of our own countrymen, who make it their boast that men are born free and equal? I am sorry to say that he was an American. Let us hope there are but few such.

After a long and wearisome voyage, the vessel arrived in the port of Savannah, the capital of Georgia. The negroes were tied in pairs, and driven to the market-place to be sold. In this hour of distress, it was a great consolation to Jumbo and Zairee that they were not separated from each other. They were put up at auction together, and the same planter bought them both. For the first two or three years, they did not find slavery so bad a thing as they had feared. It is true, they were kept at work all the time; but they were comfortably clothed and fed, and nobody abused them.[1] But, at the end of that time, a new overseer was appointed, who was a very cruel man. Their master was a kind-hearted man; but he was too indolent to take much trouble; and he let the overseer of the slaves do pretty much as he pleased. Almost every day, some one or other of the slaves had a severe whipping, by order of this wicked tyrant; and he made them work harder than Kamschatkadale dogs.[2] Jumbo bore his fate with patience and fortitude; but many a time, when his work was done, did he and Zairee weep to think of their beloved Africa, and of the pleasant times they used to have, sitting under the cocoa trees, eating yams and milk for supper.

Jumbo had borne several cruel beatings himself without complaint; but one day, when the overseer ordered Zairee to be tied to a post, and receive twenty lashes, merely because she had broken an earthen pitcher, he could endure it no longer. He ran to the post, seized hold of his sister, and tried to prevent her being tied. This did no good. The poor creature was forced away; and Zairee was ordered to receive forty lashes, and her brother seventy-five.

After this dreadful whipping, it was many days before Jumbo could creep out of his miserable bed. His heart was full of fury towards the white men. Alas! can we blame the poor creature for it? Even a Christian would have found it very hard to forgive such injuries; and Jumbo had never been taught to read his Bible.

Not long after his recovery, he was accused of wounding the overseer in the back, with an intent to kill him; but the thing could not be proved; and, as all the negroes hated him, it was as likely to be one as another. Jumbo escaped punishment; but as suspicion rested pretty strongly upon him, he was offered for sale. Zairee begged hard to be sold with him; but her request was denied. Jumbo was sold to a cotton planter, who lived about twenty miles distant. The parting of brother and sister was painful indeed. The only consolation they had had in their misery was the liberty of being together. Zairee could not eat any food the day that Jumbo left her; and when the overseer heard of this, he

1. We believe this is generally the case with slaves at the south; but the *principle* is wrong, even if there are nine hundred and ninety nine good masters out of a thousand. [LMC's note]

2. Kamschatkadale dogs: In Kamchatka, a peninsula in eastern Siberia whose inhabitants were called Kamchadales, dogs were used to pull sleds.

ordered her to be whipped. "The next thing I shall hear," said he, "will be that she is ill and unable to work. I shall not allow of any such nonsense."

A plate full of food was placed before Zairee, and a man stood over her with a whip, to beat her, if she did not eat every mouthful. This was in the United States of America, which boasts of being the only true republic in the world! the asylum of the distressed! the only land of perfect freedom and equality! "Shame on my country—everlasting shame." History blushes as she writes the page of American slavery, and Europe points her finger at it in derision.

It was so ordered, by divine Providence, that what threatened to be the greatest calamity to the unhappy Zairee, turned out in the end to be a blessing.

Among Jumbo's new companions in slavery, was one very dignified middle-aged negro, who attracted his particular attention. He was very melancholy and said but little; but when he did speak, he betrayed intelligence unusual among people of his color, who have so few advantages of education. He and Jumbo soon became very much attached to each other. One evening, as they sat in their hut making brooms, the elder negro said, in imperfect English, "I believe one reason I like you so well Jumbo, is on account of your name. They call me Pompey; but I am prince Yoloo." Jumbo dropped his broom and looked up eagerly—the name sounded like something he had known and forgotten. "I had a son named Jumbo," continued the black prince; "but the accursed white man stole him from me when he was only nine years old."

Jumbo sprang on his feet and uttered a shriek of joy. He had found his father! A long and earnest conversation followed, in the course of which Jumbo discovered that the Ashantees,[3] a neighboring tribe, had made war upon his father, had taken him prisoner, and sold him to an American captain.

Yoloo wept like a child when he found that both Jumbo and Zairee were alive and well. The most wonderful thing he had to tell was that Mr. Harris had bought a plantation in America, and actually lived within five miles of them. "I did not know it," said Yoloo, "till about six weeks ago, when master sent me to his house of an errand. It made my blood very hot, when I saw the

3. The Ashanti, or Asante, people of southern Ghana built a powerful empire in the eighteenth and early nineteenth centuries. Through wars against neighboring peoples, they obtained captives to sell to British and Dutch slave traders in exchange for firearms, which in turn enabled them to maintain their dominance.

white man, whom I had treated with so much kindness in my own country; for I thought he had stolen away my children; and I have ever since been thinking how I could find an opportunity to kill him."

Jumbo was glad his father had not killed him; for he said he felt sure he was good and kind, though he was a white man.

Yoloo now felt very anxious to see Mr. Harris; for he thought he would buy him and his children, if he once knew who they were; and every body said he was the kindest master in the world; that he visited his slaves every day, listened to their complaints, relieved their wants, and never allowed the overseer to punish them without his knowledge.

Yoloo and Jumbo talked a great deal about making themselves known to Mr. Harris. But they did not dare to talk in the presence of the overseer; for they were obliged to speak English, because Jumbo had forgotten his native tongue. When Yoloo repeated a song, with which his mother used to lull him to sleep, it sounded pleasant to his ears, and he smiled as a baby smiles, when he hears music; but he did not understand one word of all that was said.

One day as they were busily at work, picking cotton, a gentleman on horseback stopped and spoke to Yoloo. "You seem to be a very industrious fellow," said he; "What is your name?" "My name is Yoloo," replied the slave; "they call me Pompey"—as he spoke, he looked very expressively at Jumbo.— "Yoloo!" exclaimed the stranger—"and were you a prince in Africa?" "I was." "Do you remember Mr. Harris the white man?" "He lived with me many months." "God be praised!" exclaimed the stranger—and forgetting black and white, master and slave, he fell into Yoloo's arms, and clasped him warmly to his bosom.

Mr. Harris immediately expressed his wish to buy Yoloo and Jumbo. Their master, finding him eager for the purchase, demanded eight hundred dollars a piece for them.

The next day, Mr. Harris paid the money, and took the two negroes home with him. He then went in search of poor Zairee. The news had got abroad that Mr. Harris owed a debt of gratitude to this family, and would pay any price for them. Zairee's master took advantage of this. He first asked eight hundred dollars for her; and when he found Mr. Harris was willing to pay it, he demanded a thousand—then twelve hundred—then fifteen hundred. "Promise me in writing that I shall have the slave if I pay down fifteen hundred dollars," said Mr. Harris. The master, fearing he should never make one half so good a bargain, complied. Zairee was purchased; and in a few hours the affectionate girl was in the arms of her father and brother.

Yoloo and his children expected to be employed as slaves on the plantation of their kind friend. But Mr. Harris said, "Prince Yoloo, who treated me like a king in his own country, shall never labor for me. You shall all return to Africa; and with you shall go every slave in my household. I have tried to show my gratitude to the negroes by being a kind master; but I am satisfied this is not all I ought to do. They ought to be free. What is wrong in the sight of God, cannot be made right by the laws of man." When Yoloo heard these blessed words, he knelt and kissed his benefactor's feet. Mr. Harris did as he promised. He bought a ship, and gave his slaves free liberty to return in it to their native country. Two old negroes preferred remaining with him. The others returned with Yoloo.

Jumbo and Zairee found their mother still alive. The great doll, which Mr. Harris had given them, remained in just the same dress it wore, when they ran away. Zairee, although she was now a woman, kissed it and wept over it; she would hardly let any one touch it, so great was her reverence and gratitude for Mr. Harris.

Often, as they sat together, under the pleasant shade of their native cocoas, did they repeat to their neighbors, the story of the good white man.

Prejudices against People of Color, and Our Duties in Relation to This Subject

"A negro has a *soul,* an' please your honor," said the Corporal, (*doubtingly.*)

"I am not much versed, Corporal," quoth my Uncle Toby, "in things of that kind; but I suppose God would not leave him without one, any more than thee or me."

"It would be putting one sadly over the head of the other," quoth the Corporal.

"It would so," said my Uncle Toby.

"Why then, an' please your honor, is a black man to be used worse than a white one?"

"I can give no reason," said my Uncle Toby.

"Only," cried the Corporal, shaking his head, "because he has no one to stand up for him."

"It is that very thing, Trim," quoth my Uncle Toby, "which recommends him to protection."[1]

While we bestow our earnest disapprobation on the system of slavery, let us not flatter ourselves that we are in reality any better than our brethren of the South. Thanks to our soil and climate, and the early exertions of the Quakers, the *form* of slavery does not exist among us; but the very *spirit* of the hateful and mischievous thing is here in all its strength. The manner in which we use what power we have, gives us ample reason to be grateful that the nature of our institutions does not intrust us with more. Our prejudice against colored people is even more inveterate than it is at the South. The planter is often attached to his negroes, and lavishes caresses and kind words upon them, as he would on a favorite hound: but our cold-hearted, ignoble prejudice admits of no exception—no intermission.

The Southerners have long continued habit, apparent interest and dreaded danger, to palliate the wrong they do; but we stand without excuse. They tell us that Northern ships and Northern capital have been engaged in this wicked

An Appeal in Favor of That Class of Americans Called Africans (1833).

1. From *The Life and Opinions of Tristram Shandy, Gentleman* (1759–67), vol. 9, chap. 6, by Laurence Sterne (1713–68). In chapter 6 of the *Appeal,* "Intellect of Negroes," Child quotes a letter Sterne wrote to the African Ignatius Sancho, "in which he tells him that varieties in nature do not sunder the bands of brotherhood; and expresses his indignation that certain men wish to class their equals among the brutes, in order to treat them as such with impunity."

business; and the reproach is true. Several fortunes in this city have been made by the sale of negro blood. If these criminal transactions are still carried on, they are done in silence and secrecy, because public opinion has made them disgraceful. But if the free States wished to cherish the system of slavery forever, they could not take a more direct course than they now do. Those who are kind and liberal on all other subjects, unite with the selfish and the proud in their unrelenting efforts to keep the colored population in the lowest state of degradation; and the influence they unconsciously exert over children early infuses into their innocent minds the same strong feelings of contempt.

The intelligent and well informed have the least share of this prejudice; and when their minds can be brought to reflect upon it, I have generally observed that they soon cease to have any at all. But such a general apathy prevails and the subject is so seldom brought into view, that few are really aware how oppressively the influence of society is made to bear upon this injured class of the community. When I have related facts, that came under my own observation, I have often been listened to with surprise, which gradually increased to indignation. In order that my readers may not be ignorant of the extent of this tyrannical prejudice, I will as briefly as possible state the evidence, and leave them to judge of it, as their hearts and consciences may dictate.

In the first place, an unjust law exists in this Commonwealth, by which marriages between persons of different color is pronounced illegal.[2] I am perfectly aware of the gross ridicule to which I may subject myself by alluding to this particular; but I have lived too long, and observed too much, to be disturbed by the world's mockery. In the first place, the government ought not to be invested with power to control the affections, any more than the consciences of citizens. A man has at least as good a right to choose his wife, as he has to choose his religion. His taste may not suit his neighbors; but so long as his deportment is correct, they have no right to interfere with his concerns. In the second place, this law is a *useless* disgrace to Massachusetts. Under existing circumstances, none but those whose condition in life is too low to be much affected by public opinion, will form such alliances; and they, when they choose to do so, *will* make such marriages, in spite of the law. I know two or three instances where women of the laboring class have

---

2. A Massachusetts law of 1786 forbade the performance of marriages between "any white person" and "any Negro, Indian or Mulatto" and pronounced such marriages "null and void." Garrison's *Liberator* had launched a campaign against this law on 8 January 1831. It was finally repealed in February 1843.

been united to reputable, industrious colored men. These husbands regularly bring home their wages, and are kind to their families. If by some of the odd chances, which not unfrequently occur in the world, their wives should become heirs to any property, the children may be wronged out of it, because the law pronounces them illegitimate. And while this injustice exists with regard to *honest,* industrious individuals, who are merely guilty of differing from us in a matter of taste, neither the legislation nor customs of slave-holding States exert their influence against *immoral* connexions.

In one portion of our country this fact is shown in a very peculiar and striking manner. There is a numerous class at New Orleans, called Quate-roons, or Quadroons, because their colored blood has for several successive generations been intermingled with the white. The women are much distin-guished for personal beauty and gracefulness of motion; and their parents frequently send them to France for the advantages of an elegant education. White gentlemen of the first rank are desirous of being invited to their parties, and often become seriously in love with these fascinating but unfor-tunate beings. Prejudice forbids matrimony, but universal custom sanctions temporary connexions, to which a certain degree of respectability is allowed, on account of the peculiar situation of the parties. These attachments often continue for years—sometimes for life—and instances are not unfrequent of exemplary constancy and great propriety of deportment.

What eloquent vituperations we should pour forth, if the contending claims of nature and pride produced such a tissue of contradictions in some other country, and not in our own!

There is another Massachusetts law, which an enlightened community would not probably suffer to be carried into execution under any circum-stances; but it still remains to disgrace the statutes of this Commonwealth.— It is as follows:

"No African or Negro, other than a subject of the Emperor of Morocco, or a citizen of the United States, (proved so by a certificate of the Secretary of the State of which he is a citizen,) shall tarry within this Commonwealth longer than two months; and on complaint a justice shall order him to depart in ten days; and if he do not then, the justice may commit such African or Negro to the House of Correction, there to be kept at hard labor; and at the next term of the Court of C. P., he shall be tried, and if convicted of remaining as aforesaid, shall be whipped not exceeding ten lashes; and if he or she shall not *then* depart such process shall be repeated and punishment inflicted *toties quoties.*" Stat. 1788, Ch. 54.

An honorable Haytian or Brazilian, who visited this country for business or information, might come under this law, unless public opinion rendered it a mere dead letter.

There is among the colored people an increasing desire for information, and a laudable ambition to be respectable in manners and appearance. Are we not foolish as well as sinful, in trying to repress a tendency so salutary to themselves, and so beneficial to the community? Several individuals of this class are very desirous to have persons of their own color qualified to teach something more than mere reading and writing. But in the public schools, colored children are subject to many discouragements and difficulties; and into the private schools they cannot gain admission. A very sensible and well-informed colored woman in a neighboring town, whose family have been brought up in a manner that excited universal remark and approbation, has been extremely desirous to obtain for her eldest daughter the advantages of a private school; but she has been resolutely repulsed, on account of her complexion. The girl is a very light mulatto, with great modesty and propriety of manners; perhaps no young person in the Commonwealth was less likely to have a bad influence on her associates. The clergyman respected the family, and he remonstrated with the instructer; but while the latter admitted the injustice of the thing, he excused himself by saying such a step would occasion the loss of all his white scholars.

In a town adjoining Boston, a well-behaved colored boy was kept out of the public school more than a year, by vote of the trustees. His mother, having some information herself, knew the importance of knowledge, and was anxious to obtain it for her family. She wrote repeatedly and urgently; and the school-master himself told me that the correctness of her spelling, and the neatness of her hand-writing formed a curious contrast with the notes he received from many white parents. At last, this spirited woman appeared before the committee, and reminded them that her husband, having for many years paid taxes as a citizen, had a right to the privileges of a citizen; and if her claim were refused, or longer postponed, she declared her determination to seek justice from a higher source. The trustees were, of course, obliged to yield to the equality of the laws, with the best grace they could. The boy was admitted, and made good progress in his studies. Had his mother been too ignorant to know her rights, or too abject to demand them, the lad would have had a fair chance to get a living out of the State as the occupant of a workhouse, or penitentiary.

The attempt to establish a school for African girls at Canterbury, Connecticut, has made too much noise to need a detailed account in this volume.[3] I do not know the lady who first formed the project, but I am told that she is a benevolent and religious woman. It certainly is difficult to imagine any other motives than good ones, for an undertaking so arduous and unpopular. Yet had the Pope himself attempted to establish his supremacy over that commonwealth, he could hardly have been repelled with more determined and angry resistance.—Town meetings were held, the records of which are not highly creditable to the parties concerned. Petitions were sent to the Legislature, beseeching that no African school might be allowed to admit individuals not residing in the town where said school was established; and strange to relate, this law, which makes it impossible to collect a sufficient number of pupils, was sanctioned by the State. A colored girl, who availed herself of this opportunity to gain instruction, was warned out of town, and fined for not complying; and the instructress was imprisoned for persevering in her benevolent plan.

It is said, in excuse, that Canterbury will be inundated with vicious characters, who will corrupt the morals of the young men; that such a school will break down the distinctions between black and white; and that marriages between people of different colors will be the probable result. Yet they seem to assume the ground that colored people *must* always be an inferior and degraded class—that the prejudice against them *must* be eternal; being deeply founded in the laws of God and nature.—Finally, they endeavored to represent the school as one of the *incendiary* proceedings of the Anti-Slavery Society; and they appeal to the Colonization Society, as an aggrieved child is wont to appeal to its parent.

The objection with regard to the introduction of vicious characters into a village, certainly has some force; but are such persons likely to leave cities for a quiet country town, in search of moral and intellectual improvement? Is it not obvious that the *best* portion of the colored class are the very ones to prize such an opportunity for instruction? Grant that a large proportion of these unfortunate people *are* vicious—is it not our duty, and of course our wisest policy, to try to make them otherwise? And what will so effectually

3. The Quaker teacher Prudence Crandall (1803–90) first admitted an African American child into the girls' school she had founded in Canterbury, Connecticut, in 1831, and then, when white parents withdrew their daughters, converted it into a school for "young ladies and little misses of color." The citizens of the town poisoned Crandall's well, organized a boycott against her and her students, had Crandall imprisoned for one night, took her to court, and finally burned the school down in 1834.

elevate their character and condition, as knowledge? I beseech you, my countrymen, think of these things wisely, and in season.

As for intermarriages, if there be such a repugnance between the two races, founded in the laws of *nature,* methinks there is small reason to dread their frequency.

The breaking down of distinctions in society, by means of extended information, is an objection which appropriately belongs to the Emperor of Austria, or the Sultan of Egypt.[4]

I do not know how the affair at Canterbury is *generally* considered; but I have heard individuals of all parties and all opinions speak of it—and never without merriment or indignation. Fifty years hence, the *black* laws of Connecticut will be a greater source of amusement to the antiquarian, than her famous *blue* laws.

A similar, though less violent opposition arose in consequence of the attempt to establish a college for colored people at New Haven. A young colored man, who tried to obtain education at the Wesleyan college in Middletown, was obliged to relinquish the attempt on account of the persecution of his fellow students. Some collegians from the South objected to a colored associate in their recitations; and those from New England promptly and zealously joined in the hue and cry. A small but firm party were in favor of giving the colored man a chance to pursue his studies without insult or interruption; and I am told that this manly and disinterested band were all Southerners. As for those individuals, who exerted their influence to exclude an unoffending fellow-citizen from privileges which ought to be equally open to all, it is to be hoped that age will make them wiser—and that they will learn, before they die, to be ashamed of a step attended with more important results than usually belong to youthful follies.

It happens that these experiments have all been made in Connecticut; but it is no more than justice to that State to remark that a similar spirit would probably have been manifested in Massachusetts, under like circumstances. At our debating clubs and other places of public discussion, the demon of prejudice girds himself for the battle, the moment negro colleges and high schools are alluded to. Alas, while we carry on our lips that religion which teaches us to "love our neighbor as ourselves," how little do we cherish its

---

4. Child's point is that laws against interracial marriage smack of despotic regimes like those of the Austro-Hungarian empire and the sultanate of Egypt; hence they are inappropriate in a democratic republic.

blessed influence within our hearts! How much republicanism we have to *speak of,* and how little do we practise!

Let us seriously consider what injury a negro college could possibly do us. It is certainly a fair presumption that the scholars would be from the better portion of the colored population; and it is an equally fair presumption that knowledge would improve their characters. There are already many hundreds of colored people in the city of Boston.—In the street they generally appear neat and respectable; and in our houses they do not "come between the wind and our nobility."[5] Would the addition of one or two hundred more even be perceived? As for giving offence to the Southerners by allowing such establishments—they have no right to interfere with our internal concerns, any more than we have with theirs.—Why should they not give up slavery to please us, by the same rule that we must refrain from educating the negroes to please them? If they are at liberty to do wrong, we certainly ought to be at liberty to do right. They may talk and publish as much about us as they please; and we ask for no other influence over them.

It is a fact not generally known that the brave Kosciusko[6] left a fund for the establishment of a negro college in the United States. Little did he think he had been fighting for a people, who would not grant one rood of their vast territory for the benevolent purpose!

According to present appearances, a college for colored persons will be established in Canada; and thus, by means of our foolish and wicked pride, the credit of this philanthropic enterprise will be transferred to our mother country.

The preceding chapters show that it has been no uncommon thing for colored men to be educated at English, German, Portuguese and Spanish Universities.

In Boston there is an Infant School, three Primary Schools, and a Grammar School. The two last, are I believe supported by the public; and this fact is highly creditable. [A building for the colored Grammar School is not supplied by the city, though such provision is always made for similar institutions for white boys.—The apartment is close and uncomfortable, and many pupils stay away, who would gladly attend under more convenient circumstances. There ought likewise to be a colored teacher instead of a white one.

5. From *Henry IV,* pt. 1, 1.3.43–45: "He called them untaught knaves, unmannerly, / To bring a slovenly unhandsome corse / Betwixt the wind and his nobility."

6. The Polish patriot Tadeusz Kosciusko (1746–1817) joined the American Revolutionary army in 1777; his name was almost as well known as Lafayette's.

Under the dominion of existing prejudices, it is difficult to find a white man, well qualified to teach such a school, who feels the interest he ought to feel, in these Pariahs[7] of our republic. The parents would repose more confidence in a colored instructer; and he, both from sympathy and pride, would be better fitted for his task.

It is peculiarly incumbent on the city authorities to supply a commodious building for the colored grammar school, because public prejudice excludes these oppressed people from all lucrative employments, and they cannot therefore be supposed to have ample funds of their own.][8]

I was much pleased with the late resolution awarding Franklin medals to the colored pupils of the grammar school; and I was still more pleased with the laudable project, originated by Josiah Holbrook, Esq. for the establishment of a colored Lyceum.[9] Surely a better spirit *is* beginning to work in this cause; and when once begun, the good sense and good feeling of the community will bid it go on and prosper. How much this spirit will have to contend with is illustrated by the following fact. When President Jackson[10] entered this city, the white children of all the schools were sent out in uniform, to do him honor. A member of the Committee proposed that the pupils of the African schools should be invited likewise; but he was the only one who voted for it. He then proposed that the yeas and nays should be recorded; upon which, most of the gentlemen walked off, to prevent the question from being taken. Perhaps they felt an awkward consciousness of the incongeniality of such proceedings with our republican institutions. By order of the Committee the vacation of the African schools did not commence until the day after the procession of the white pupils; and a note to the instructer intimated that the pupils were not expected to appear on the Common. The reason given was because "their numbers were so few;" but in private conversation, fears were expressed lest their sable faces should give offence to our slave-holding President. In all probability the sight of the colored children would have been agreeable to General Jackson, and seemed more like home, than anything he witnessed.

---

7. The Pariahs are the lowest and most degraded caste in Hindostan. The laws prevent them from ever rising in their condition, or mingling with other castes. [LMC's note]

8. Bracketed passage omitted from the 1836 edition. [Ed. Patricia G. Holland]

9. Josiah Holbrook (1788–1854) founded the first American lyceum in 1826. Intended to educate the public through lectures and exhibitions, lyceums spread throughout the United States.

10. Andrew Jackson (1767–1845), seventh president of the United States.

In the theatre, it is not possible for respectable colored people to obtain a decent seat. They must either be excluded, or herd with the vicious.

A fierce excitement prevailed, not long since, because a colored man had bought a pew in one of our churches. I heard a very kind-hearted and zealous democrat declare his opinion that "the fellow ought to be turned out by constables, if he dared to occupy the pew he had purchased." Even at the communion-table, the mockery of human pride is mingled with the worship of Jehovah. Again and again have I seen a solitary negro come up to the altar, meekly and timidly, after all the white communicants had retired. One Episcopal clergyman of this city, forms an honorable exception to this remark. When there is room at the altar, Mr—— often makes a signal to the colored members of his church to kneel beside their white brethren; and once, when two white infants and one colored one were to be baptized, and the parents of the latter bashfully lingered far behind the others, he silently rebuked the unchristian spirit of pride, by first administering the holy ordinance to the little dark-skinned child of God.

An instance of prejudice lately occurred, which I should find it hard to believe, did I not positively know it to be a fact. A gallery pew was purchased in one of our churches for two hundred dollars. A few Sabbaths after, an address was delivered at that church, in favor of the Africans. Some colored people, who very naturally wished to hear the discourse, went into the gallery; probably because they thought they should be deemed less intrusive there than elsewhere. The man who had recently bought a pew, found it occupied by colored people, and indignantly retired with his family. The next day, he purchased a pew in another meeting-house, protesting that nothing would tempt him again to make use of seats, that had been occupied by negroes.

A well known country representative, who makes a very loud noise about his democracy, once attended the Catholic church. A pious negro requested him to take off his hat, while he stood in the presence of the Virgin Mary. The white man rudely shoved him aside, saying, "You son of an Ethiopian, do you dare to speak to me!" I more than once heard the hero repeat this story; and he seemed to take peculiar satisfaction in telling it. Had he been less ignorant, he would not have chosen "son of an *Ethiopian*" as an *ignoble* epithet; to have called the African his own equal would have been abundantly more sarcastic. The same republican dismissed a strong, industrious colored man, who had been employed on the farm during his absence. "I am too great a democrat," quoth he, "to have any body in my house, who don't sit at my table; and I'll be hanged, if I ever eat with the son of an Ethiopian."

Men whose education leaves them less excuse for such illiberality, are yet vulgar enough to join in this ridiculous prejudice. The colored woman, whose daughter has been mentioned as excluded from a private school, was once smuggled into a stage, upon the supposition that she was a white woman, with a sallow complexion. Her manners were modest and prepossessing, and the gentlemen were very polite to her. But when she stopped at her own door, and was handed out by her curly-headed husband, they were at once surprised and angry to find they had been riding with a mulatto—and had, in their ignorance, been really civil to her!

A worthy colored woman, belonging to an adjoining town, wished to come into Boston to attend upon a son, who was ill. She had a trunk with her, and was too feeble to walk. She begged permission to ride in the stage. But the passengers with *noble* indignation, declared they would get out, if she were allowed to get in. After much entreaty, the driver suffered her to sit by him upon the box. When he entered the city, his comrades began to point and sneer. Not having sufficient moral courage to endure this, he left the poor woman, with her trunk, in the middle of the street, far from the place of her destination; telling her, with an oath, that he would not carry her a step further.

A friend of mine lately wished to have a colored girl admitted into the stage with her, to take care of her babe. The girl was very lightly tinged with the sable hue, had handsome Indian features, and very pleasing manners. It was, however, evident that she was not white; and therefore the passengers objected to her company. This of course, produced a good deal of inconvenience on one side, and mortification on the other. My friend repeated the circumstance to a lady, who, as the daughter and wife of a clergyman, might be supposed to have imbibed some liberality. The lady seemed to think the experiment was very preposterous; but when my friend alluded to the mixed parentage of the girl, she exclaimed, with generous enthusiasm, "Oh, that alters the case, *Indians* certainly *have* their rights."

Every year a colored gentleman and scholar is becoming less and less of a rarity—thanks to the existence of the Haytian Republic, and the increasing liberality of the world! Yet if a person of refinement from Hayti, Brazil, or other countries, which we deem less enlightened than our own, should visit us, the very boys of this republic would dog his footsteps with the vulgar outcry of "Nigger! Nigger!" I have known this to be done, from no other provocation than the sight of a colored man with the dress and deportment of a gentleman. Were it not that republicanism, like Christianity, is often perverted from its true spirit by the bad passions of mankind, such things as these would make every honest mind disgusted with the very name of republics.

I am acquainted with a gentleman from Brazil who is shrewd, enterprising, noble-spirited, and highly respectable in character and manners; yet he has experienced almost every species of indignity on account of his color. Not long since, it became necessary for him to visit the southern shores of Massachusetts, to settle certain accounts connected with his business. His wife was in a feeble state of health, and the physicians had recommended a voyage. For this reason, he took passage for her with himself in the steam-boat; and the captain, as it appears, made no objection to a colored gentleman's money. After remaining on deck some time, Mrs —— attempted to pass into the cabin; but the captain prevented her; saying, "You must go down forward."— The Brazilian urged that he had paid the customary price, and therefore his wife and infant had a right to a place in the ladies' cabin. The captain answered, "Your wife a'n't a lady; she is a nigger." The forward cabin was occupied by sailors; was entirely without accommodations for women, and admitted the seawater, so that a person could not sit in it comfortably without keeping the feet raised in a chair. The husband stated that his wife's health would not admit of such exposure; to which the captain still replied, "I don't allow any niggers in my cabin." With natural and honest indignation, the Brazilian exclaimed, "You Americans talk about the Poles! You are a great deal more Russian than the Russians."[11] The affair was concluded by placing the colored gentleman and his invalid wife on the shore, and leaving them to provide for themselves as they could. Had the cabin been full, there would have been some excuse; but it was occupied only by two sailors' wives. The same individual sent for a relative in a distant town on account of illness in his family. After staying several weeks, it became necessary for her to return; and he procured a seat for her in the stage. The same ridiculous scene occurred; the passengers were afraid of losing their dignity by riding with a neat, respectable person, whose face was darker than their own. No public vehicle could be obtained, by which a colored citizen could be conveyed to her home; it therefore became absolutely necessary for the gentleman to leave his business and hire a chaise at great expense. Such proceedings are really inexcusable. No authority can be found for them in religion, reason, or the laws.

11. Poland had been fighting for freedom from Russian domination since the uprising led by Kosciusko (see note 6) in 1794; the latest Polish uprising had been brutally suppressed in 1831.

The Bible informs us that "a man of Ethiopia, a eunuch of great authority under Candace, Queen of the Ethiopians, who had charge of all her treasure, came to Jerusalem to worship."[12] Returning in his chariot, he read Esaias, the Prophet; and at his request Philip went up into the chariot and sat with him, explaining the Scriptures. Where should we now find an apostle, who would ride in the same chariot with an Ethiopian!

Will any candid person tell me why respectable colored people should not be allowed to make use of public conveyances, open to all who are able and willing to pay for the privilege? Those who enter a vessel, or a stagecoach, cannot expect to select their companions. If they can afford to take a carriage or boat for themselves, then, and then only, they have a right to be exclusive. I was lately talking with a young gentleman on this subject, who professed to have no prejudice against colored people, except so far as they were ignorant and vulgar; but still he could not tolerate the idea of allowing them to enter stages and steam-boats. "Yet, you allow the same privilege to vulgar and ignorant white men, without a murmur," I replied; "Pray give a good republican reason why a respectable colored citizen should be less favored." For want of a better argument, he said—(pardon me, fastidious reader)—he implied that the presence of colored persons was less agreeable than Otto of Rose, or Eau de Cologne; and this distinction, he urged was made by God himself. I answered, "Whoever takes his chance in a public vehicle, is liable to meet with uncleanly white passengers, whose breath may be redolent with the fumes of American cigars, or American gin. Neither of these articles have a fragrance peculiarly agreeable to nerves of delicate organization. Allowing your argument double the weight it deserves, it is utter nonsense to pretend that the inconvenience in the case I have supposed is not infinitely greater. But what is more to the point, do you dine in a fashionable hotel, do you sail in a fashionable steam-boat, do you sup at a fashionable house, without having negro servants behind your chair. Would they be any more disagreeable, as *passengers* seated in the corner of a stage, or a steam-boat, than as *waiters* in such immediate attendance upon your person?"

Stage-drivers are very much perplexed when they attempt to vindicate the present tyrannical customs; and they usually give up the point, by saying they themselves have no prejudice against colored people—they are merely afraid of the public. But stage-drivers should remember that in a popular govern-

12. The story of how the apostle Philip converted the Ethiopian eunuch appears in Acts 8.26–38.

ment, they, in common with every other citizen, form a part and portion of the dreaded public.

The gold was never coined for which I would barter my individual freedom of acting and thinking upon any subject, or knowingly interfere with the rights of the meanest human being. The only true courage is that which impels us to do right without regard to consequences. To fear a populace is as servile as to fear an emperor. The only salutary restraint is the fear of doing wrong.

Our representatives to Congress have repeatedly rode in a stage with colored servants at the request of their masters. Whether this is because New Englanders are willing to do out of courtesy to a Southern gentleman, what they object to doing from justice to a colored citizen,—or whether those representatives, being educated men, were more than usually divested of this absurd prejudice,—I will not pretend to say.

The state of public feeling not only makes it difficult for the Africans to obtain information, but it prevents them from making profitable use of what knowledge they have. A colored man, however intelligent, is not allowed to pursue any business more lucrative than that of a barber, a shoe-black, or a waiter. These, and all other employments, are truly respectable, whenever the duties connected with them are faithfully performed; but it is unjust that a man should, on account of his complexion, be prevented from performing more elevated uses in society. Every citizen ought to have a fair chance to try his fortune in any line of business, which he thinks he has ability to transact. Why should not colored men be employed in the manufactories of various kinds? If their ignorance is an objection, let them be enlightened, as speedily as possible. If their moral character is not sufficiently pure, remove the pressure of public scorn, and thus supply them with motives for being respectable. All this can be done. It merely requires an earnest wish to overcome a prejudice, which has "grown with our growth and strengthened with our strength," but which is in fact opposed to the spirit of our religion, and contrary to the instinctive good feelings of our nature. When examined by the clear light of reason, it disappears. Prejudices of all kinds have their strongest holds in the minds of the vulgar and the ignorant. In a community so enlightened as our own, they must gradually melt away under the influence of public discussion. There is no want of kind feelings and liberal sentiments in the American people; the simple fact is, they have not *thought* upon this subject.—An active and enterprising community are not apt to concern themselves about laws and customs, which do not obviously inter-

fere with their interests or convenience; and various political and pruden-
tial motives have combined to fetter free inquiry in this direction. Thus we
have gone on, year after year, thoughtlessly sanctioning, by our silence and
indifference, evils which our hearts and consciences are far enough from
approving.

It has been shown that no other people on earth indulge so strong a
prejudice with regard to color, as we do. It is urged that negroes are civilly
treated in England, because their numbers are so few. I could never discover
any great force in this argument. Colored people are certainly not sufficiently
rare in that country to be regarded as a great show, like a giraffe, or a
Sandwich Island king; and on the other hand, it would seem natural that
those who were more accustomed to the sight of dark faces would find their
aversion diminished, rather than increased.

The absence of prejudice in the Portuguese and Spanish settlements is
accounted for, by saying that the white people are very little superior to the
negroes in knowledge and refinement. But Doctor Walsh's book[13] certainly
gives us no reason to think meanly of the Brazilians; and it has been my good
fortune to be acquainted with many highly intelligent South Americans, who
were divested of this prejudice, and much surprised at its existence here.

If the South Americans are really in such a low state as the argument
implies, it is a still greater disgrace to us to be outdone in liberality and
consistent republicanism by men so much less enlightened than ourselves.

Pride will doubtless hold out with strength and adroitness against the
besiegers of its fortress; but it is an obvious truth that the condition of the
world is rapidly improving, and that our laws and customs must change with
it.

Neither ancient nor modern history furnishes a page more glorious than
the last twenty years in England; for at every step, free principles, after a long
and arduous struggle, have conquered selfishness and tyranny. Almost all
great evils are resisted by individuals who directly suffer injustice or inconvenience from them; but it is a peculiar beauty of the abolition cause that its
defenders enter the lists against wealth, and power, and talent, not to defend
their own rights, but to protect weak and injured neighbors, who are not
allowed to speak for themselves.

Those, who become interested in a cause laboring so heavily under the
pressure of present unpopularity, must expect to be assailed by every form of

---

13. *Notices of Brazil in 1828 and 1829* (1831), by Robert Walsh (1772–1852).

bitterness and sophistry. At times, discouraged and heart-sick, they will perhaps begin to doubt whether there are in reality any unalterable principles of right and wrong. But let them cast aside the fear of man, and keep their minds fixed on a few of the simple, unchangeable laws of God, and they will certainly receive strength to contend with the adversary.

Paragraphs in the Southern papers already begin to imply that the United States will not look tamely on, while England emancipates her slaves; and they inform us that the inspection of the naval stations has become a subject of great importance since the recent measures of the British Parliament.[14] A republic declaring war with a monarchy, because she gave freedom to her slaves, would indeed form a beautiful moral picture for the admiration of the world!

Mr Garrison was the first person who dared to edit a newspaper, in which slavery was spoken of as altogether wicked and inexcusable. For this crime the Legislature of Georgia have offered five thousand dollars to any one who will "arrest and prosecute him to conviction *under the laws of that State.*"[15] An association of gentlemen in South Carolina have likewise offered a large reward for the same object. It is, to say the least, a very remarkable step for one State in this Union to promulgate such a law concerning a citizen of another State, merely for publishing his opinions boldly. The disciples of Fanny Wright[16] promulgate the most zealous and virulent attacks upon Christianity, without any hindrance from the civil authorities; and this is done upon the truly rational ground that individual freedom of opinion ought to be respected—that what is false cannot stand, and what is true cannot be overthrown. We leave Christianity to take care of itself; but slavery is a "delicate subject,"—and whoever attacks that must be punished. Mr Garrison is a disinterested, intelligent, and remarkably pure-minded man, whose only fault is that he cannot be moderate on a subject which it is exceedingly difficult for an honest mind to examine with calmness. Many, who highly respect his character, and motives, regret his tendency to use wholesale and unqualified expressions; but it is something to have the truth

14. Parliament had just passed a bill abolishing slavery in Britain's West Indian colonies, to go into effect on 1 August 1834.

15. William Lloyd Garrison (1805–79) began publication of the *Liberator* on 1 January 1831. The state legislature of Georgia did indeed set a price on his head.

16. The English-born feminist reformer Frances Wright (1795–1852) preached the free-thinking doctrines of the British socialist Robert Owen in her 1829 lecture tour of U.S. cities. To many, Fanny Wrightism became synonymous with atheism and free love.

told, even if it be not in the most judicious way. Where an evil is powerfully supported by the self-interest and prejudice of the community, none but an ardent individual will venture to meddle with it. Luther was deemed indiscreet even by those who liked him best; yet a more prudent man would never have given an impetus sufficiently powerful to heave the great mass of corruption under which the church was buried. Mr Garrison has certainly the merit of having first called public attention to a neglected and very important subject.[17] I believe whoever fairly and dispassionately examines the question, will be more than disposed to forgive the occasional faults of an ardent temperament, in consideration of the difficulty of the undertaking, and the violence with which it has been opposed.

The palliator of slavery assures the abolitionists that their benevolence is perfectly quixotic—that the negroes are happy and contented, and have no desire to change their lot. An answer to this may, as I have already said, be found in the Judicial Reports of slave-holding States, in the vigilance of their laws, in advertisements for runaway slaves, and in the details of their own newspapers. The West India planters make the same protestations concerning the happiness of their slaves; yet the cruelties proved by undoubted and unanswerable testimony are enough to break a compassionate heart. It is said that slavery is a great deal worse in the West Indies than in the United States; but I believe precisely the reverse of this proposition has been true within late years; for the English government have been earnestly trying to atone for their guilt, by the introduction of laws expressly framed to guard the weak and defenceless. A gentleman who has been a great deal among the planters of both countries, and who is by no means favorable to anti-slavery, gives it as his decided opinion that the slaves are better off in the West Indies, than they are in the United States. It is true we *hear* a great deal more about West Indian cruelty than we do about our own.—English books and periodicals are continually full of the subject; and even in the colonies, newspapers openly denounce the hateful system, and take every opportunity to prove the amount of wretchedness it produces. In this country, we have not, until very recently, dared to publish anything upon the subject. Our books, our reviews, our newspapers, our almanacs, have all been silent, or exerted their influence

17. This remark is not intended to indicate want of respect for the early exertions of the Friends, in their numerous manumission societies; or for the efforts of that staunch, fearless, self-sacrificing friend of freedom—Benjamin Lundy; but Mr. Garrison was the first that boldly attacked slavery as a sin, and Colonization as its twin sister. [Note by LMC added to 1836 edition.—Ed. Patricia G. Holland]

on the wrong side. The negro's crimes are repeated, but his sufferings are never told. Even in our geographies it is taught that the colored race *must* always be degraded. Now and then anecdotes of cruelties committed in the slave-holding States are told by individuals who witnessed them; but they are almost always afraid to give their names to the public, because the Southerners will call them "a disgrace to the soil," and the Northerners will echo the sentiment.—The promptitude and earnestness with which New England has aided the slave-holders in repressing all discussions which they were desirous to avoid, has called forth many expressions of gratitude in their public speeches, and private conversation; and truly we have well earned Randolph's favorite appellation, "the white slaves of the North,"[18] by our tameness and servility with regard to a subject where good feeling and good principle alike demanded a firm and independent spirit.

We are told that the Southerners will of themselves do away slavery, and they alone understand how to do it.—But it is an obvious fact that all their measures have tended to perpetuate the system; and even if we have the fullest faith that they mean to do their duty, the belief by no means absolves us from doing ours. The evil is gigantic; and its removal requires every heart and head in the community.

It is said that our sympathies ought to be given to the masters, who are abundantly more to be pitied than the slaves. If this be the case, the planters are singularly disinterested not to change places with their bondmen. Our sympathies *have* been given to the masters—and to those masters who seemed most desirous to remain forever in their pitiable condition. There are hearts at the South sincerely desirous of doing right in this cause; but their generous impulses are checked by the laws of their respective States, and the strong disapprobation of their neighbors. I know a lady in Georgia, who would, I believe, make any personal sacrifice to instruct her slaves, and give them freedom; but if she were found guilty of teaching the alphabet, or manumitting her slaves, fines and imprisonment would be the consequence; if she sold them, they would be likely to fall into hands less merciful than her own. Of such slave-owners we cannot speak with too much respect and tenderness. They are comparatively few in number, and stand in a most perplexing situation; it is a duty to give all our sympathy to *them*. It is mere mockery to say, what is so often said, that the Southerners, as a body, really

18. Virginia congressman John Randolph of Roanoke (1773–1833) was known for his caustic tongue and his ardent support of southern interests.

wish to abolish slavery. If they wished it, they certainly would make the attempt. When the majority heartily desire a change, it is effected, be the difficulties what they may. The Americans are peculiarly responsible for the example they give; for in no other country does the unchecked voice of the people constitute the whole of government.

We must not be induced to excuse slavery by the plausible argument that England introduced it among us.—The wickedness of beginning such a work unquestionably belongs to her; the sin of continuing it is certainly our own. It is true that Virginia, while a province, did petition the British government to check the introduction of slaves into the colonies; and their refusal to do so was afterward enumerated among the public reasons for separating from the mother country: but it is equally true that when we became independent, the Southern States stipulated that the slave trade should not be abolished by law until 1808.

The strongest and best reason that can be given for our supineness on the subject of slavery, is the fear of dissolving the Union. The Constitution of the United States demands our highest reverence. Those who approve, and those who disapprove of particular portions, are equally bound to yield implicit obedience to its authority. But we must not forget that the Constitution provides for any change that may be required for the general good. The great machine is constructed with a safety valve, by which any rapidly increasing evil may be expelled whenever the people desire it.

If the Southern politicians are determined to make a Siamese question of this also—if they insist that the Union shall not exist without slavery—it can only be said that they join two things, which have no affinity with each other, and which cannot permanently exist together.—They chain the living and vigorous to the diseased and dying; and the former will assuredly perish in the infected neighborhood.

The universal introduction of free labor is the surest way to consolidate the Union, and enable us to live together in harmony and peace. If a history is ever written entitled "The Decay and Dissolution of the North American Republic," its author will distinctly trace our downfall to the existence of slavery among us.

There is hardly anything bad, in politics or religion, that has not been sanctioned or tolerated by a suffering community, because certain powerful individuals were able to identify the evil with some other principle long consecrated to the hearts and consciences of men.

Under all circumstances, there is but one honest course; and that is to do right, and trust the consequences to Divine Providence. "Duties are ours; events are God's." Policy, with all her cunning, can devise no rule so safe, salutary, and effective, as this simple maxim.

We cannot too cautiously examine arguments and excuses brought forward by those whose interest or convenience is connected with keeping their fellow creatures in a state of ignorance and brutality; and such we shall find in abundance, at the North as well as the South. I have heard the abolition of slavery condemned on the ground that New England vessels would not be employed to export the produce of the South, if they had free laborers of their own. This objection is so utterly bad in its spirit, that it hardly deserves an answer. Assuredly it is a righteous plan to retard the progress of liberal principles, and "keep human nature forever in the stocks" that some individuals may make a few hundred dollars more per annum! Besides, the experience of the world abundantly proves that all such forced expedients are unwise. The increased prosperity of one country, or of one section of a country, always contributes, in some form or other, to the prosperity of other states.—To "love our neighbor as ourselves" is, after all, the shrewdest way of doing business.

In England, the abolition of the *traffic* was long and stoutly resisted, in the same spirit, and by the same arguments, that characterize the defence of the *system* here; but it would now be difficult to find a man so reckless, that he would not be ashamed of being called a slave dealer. Public opinion has nearly conquered one evil, and if rightly directed, it will ultimately subdue the other.

Is it asked what can be done? I answer, much, very much, can be effected, if each individual will try to deserve the commendation bestowed by our Saviour on the woman of old—"She hath done what she could."

The Friends,—always remarkable for fearless obedience to the inward light of conscience,—early gave an example worthy of being followed. At their annual meeting in Pennsylvania, in 1688, many individuals urged the incompatibility of slavery and Christianity; and their zeal continued until, in 1776, all Quakers who bought or sold a slave, or refused to emancipate those they already owned, were excluded from communion with the society. Had it not been for the early exertions of these excellent people, the fair and flourishing State of Pennsylvania might now, perchance, be withering under the effects of slavery. To this day, the Society of Friends, both in England and America, omit no opportunity, public or private, of discountenancing this bad system; and the Methodists (at least in England) have earnestly labored in the same glorious cause.

The famous Anthony Benezet,[19] a Quaker in Philadelphia, has left us a noble example of what may be done for conscience' sake. Being a teacher, he took effectual care that his scholars should have ample knowledge and christian impressions concerning the nature of slavery; he caused articles to be inserted in the almanacs likely to arrest public attention upon the subject; he talked about it, and wrote letters about it; he published and distributed tracts at his own expense; if any person was going a journey, his first thought was how he could make him instrumental in favor of his benevolent purposes; he addressed a petition to the Queen for the suppression of the slave-trade; and another to the good Countess of Huntingdon[20] beseeching that the rice and indigo plantations belonging to the orphan-house, which she had endowed near Savannah, in Georgia, might not be cultivated by those who encouraged the slave trade; he took care to increase the comforts and elevate the character of the colored people within his influence; he zealously promoted the establishment of an African school, and devoted much of the two last years of his life to personal attendance upon his pupils. By fifty years of constant industry he had amassed a small fortune; and this was left, after the decease of his widow, to the support of the African school.

Similar exertions, though on a less extensive scale, were made by the late excellent John Kenrick,[21] of Newton, Mass. For more than thirty years the constant object of his thoughts, and the chief purpose of his life, was the abolition of slavery. His earnest conversation aroused many other minds to think and act upon the subject. He wrote letters, inserted articles in the newspapers, gave liberal donations, and circulated pamphlets at his own expense.

Cowper contributed much to the cause when he wrote the "Negro's Complaint,"[22] and thus excited the compassion of his numerous readers. Wedgewood aided the work, when he caused cameos to be struck, representing a kneeling African in chains, and thus made even capricious fashion an avenue

19. Anthony Benezet (1713–84) played a key role in the early antislavery movement.

20. Selina Hastings, countess of Huntingdon (1707–91), was a strong supporter of the evangelical preacher George Whitefield, the founder of the orphanage she had endowed in Georgia. Her evangelical faith also led her to sympathize with the antislavery cause and to sponsor the publication of the African American Phillis Wheatley's first book of poems.

21. John Kenrick (1755–1833) published *Horrors of Slavery* (1817) and served as one of the first presidents of the New England Anti-Slavery Society.

22. The British poet William Cowper (1731–1800) was beloved by abolitionists for his antislavery verses. "The Negro's Complaint" (1788) protests against slavery and the slave trade from the point of view of a kidnapped African: "Fleecy locks, and black complexion / Cannot forfeit nature's claim; / Skins may differ, but affection / Dwells in white and black the same."

to the heart.[23] Clarkson assisted by patient investigation of evidence; and Fox and Wilberforce by eloquent speeches.[24] Mungo Park gave his powerful influence by the kind and liberal manner in which he always represented the Africans.[25] The Duchess of Devonshire wrote verses and caused them to be set to music; and wherever those lines were sung, some hearts were touched in favor of the oppressed. This fascinating woman made even her far-famed beauty serve in the cause of benevolence. Fox was returned for Parliament through her influence, and she is said to have procured more than one vote, by allowing the yeomanry of England to kiss her beautiful cheek.

All are not able to do so much as Anthony Benezet and John Kenrick have done; but we can all do something. We can speak kindly and respectfully of colored people upon all occasions; we can repeat to our children such traits as are honorable in their character and history; we can avoid making odious caricatures of negroes; we can teach boys that it is unmanly and contemptible to insult an unfortunate class of people by the vulgar outcry of "Nigger!—Nigger!"—Even Mahmoud of Turkey rivals us in liberality—for he long ago ordered a fine to be levied upon those who called a Christian a dog; and in his dominions the *prejudice* is so great that a Christian must be a degraded being. A residence in Turkey might be profitable to those Christians who patronize the eternity of prejudice; it would afford an opportunity of testing the goodness of the rule, by showing how it works both ways.

If we are not able to contribute to African schools, or do not choose to do so, we can at least refrain from opposing them. If it be disagreeable to allow colored people the same rights and privileges as other citizens, we can do with our prejudice, what most of us often do with better feelings—we can conceal it.

23. The cameo of a kneeling slave designed in 1787 by Josiah Wedgwood (1730–95), founder of the Wedgwood pottery business and a member of the British Committee to Abolish the Slave Trade, was reproduced in many media over the caption "Am I Not a Man and a Brother?"

24. Thomas Clarkson (1760–1846) and William Wilberforce (1759–1833) were the two most famous leaders of the British antislavery movement. Clarkson's two-volume *History of the Rise, Progress, and Accomplishment of the Abolition of the African Slave-Trade* (1808) was one of Child's principal sources for her chapter on the slave trade. Wilberforce led the movement in Parliament to its successful culmination in 1807 with the support of Foreign Secretary Charles James Fox (1749–1806).

25. The Scottish explorer Mungo Park (1771–1806), whose *Travels in the Interior Districts of Africa* (1799) was an important source for the *Appeal*, did not advocate the abolition of the slave trade, but he did portray African cultures sympathetically and unstereotypically. In a famous passage describing African women's hospitality toward him, he quotes a song they improvised about him, which Georgiana Cavendish, duchess of Devonshire (1757–1806), rendered in eighteenth-century-style verse.

Our almanacs and newspapers can fairly show both sides of the question; and if they lean to either party, let it not be to the strongest. Our preachers can speak of slavery, as they do of other evils. Our poets can find in this subject abundant room for sentiment and pathos. Our orators (provided they do not want office) may venture an allusion to our *in*-"glorious institutions."

The union of individual influence produces a vast amount of moral force, which is not the less powerful because it is often unperceived. A mere change in the *direction* of our efforts, without any increased exertion, would in the course of a few years, produce an entire revolution of public feeling. This slow but sure way of doing good is almost the only means by which benevolence can effect its purpose.

Sixty thousand petitions have been addressed to the English parliament on the subject of slavery, and a large number of them were signed by women. The same steps here would be, with one exception, useless and injudicious; because the general government has no control over the legislatures of individual States. But the District of Columbia forms an exception to this rule.— *There* the United States have power to abolish slavery; and it is the duty of the citizens to petition year after year, until a reformation is effected. But who will present remonstrances against slavery? The Hon. John Q. Adams[26] was intrusted with fifteen petitions for the abolition of slavery in the District of Columbia; yet, clearly as that gentleman sees and defines the pernicious effects of the system, he offered the petitions only to protest against them! Another petition to the same effect, intrusted to another Massachusetts representative, was never noticed at all. "Brutus is an honorable man:—So are they all—all honorable men."[27] Nevertheless, there is, in this popular government, a subject on which it is *impossible* for the people to make themselves heard.

By publishing this book I have put my mite into the treasury. The expectation of displeasing all classes has not been unaccompanied with pain. But it has been strongly impressed upon my mind that it was a duty to fulfil this task; and earthly considerations should never stifle the voice of conscience.

---

26. John Quincy Adams (1767–1848), sixth president of the United States, joined the House of Representatives in 1830 as a Massachusetts congressman after he failed to win a second presidential term. Though not an abolitionist, he presented his constituents' antislavery petitions in Congress.

27. *Julius Caesar*, 3.2.87–88.

The Black Saxons

Tyrants are but the spawn of ignorance,
Begotten by the slaves they trample on;
Who, could they win a glimmer of the light,
And see that tyranny is *always* weakness,
Or fear with its own bosom ill at ease,
Would laugh away in scorn the sand-wove chain,
Which their own blindness feigned for adamant.
Wrong ever builds on quicksands; but the Right
To the firm centre lays its moveless base.
—J. R. Lowell[1]

Mr. Duncan was sitting alone in his elegantly furnished parlour, in the vicinity of Charleston, South Carolina. Before him lay an open volume, Thierry's History of the Norman Conquest.[2] From the natural kindliness of his character, and democratic theories deeply imbibed in childhood, his thoughts dwelt more with a nation prostrated and kept in base subjection by the strong arm of violence, than with the renowned robbers, who seized their rich possessions, and haughtily trampled on their dearest rights.

"And so that bold and beautiful race became slaves!" thought he. "The brave and free-souled Harolds, strong of heart and strong of arm; the fair-haired Ediths, in their queenly beauty, noble in soul as well as ancestry; these all sank to the condition of slaves. They tamely submitted to their lot, till their free, bright beauty passed under the heavy cloud of animal dullness, and the contemptuous Norman epithet of 'base Saxon churls' was but too significantly true. Yet not without efforts did they thus sink. How often renewed, or how bravely sustained, we know not; for Troubadours rarely sing of the defeated, and conquerors write their own History. That they did not relin-

Liberty Bell (1841); reprinted in *Fact and Fiction: A Collection of Stories* (1846), pp. 190–204.

1. From "Prometheus" (1843), by James Russell Lowell (1819–91). Child added this epigraph to the story when she reprinted it in *Fact and Fiction: A Collection of Stories* (1846). The italics are hers.

2. Jacques Nicolas Augustin Thierry (1795–1856), *History of the Conquest of England by the Normans* (1825). Child refers in the next paragraph to Thierry's accounts of Harold II (1022?–1066), the last Saxon king of England before the Norman Conquest of 1066; his sister Edith, famous for her beauty; and the legendary outlaw Robin Hood, leader of a Saxon bandit troop.

quish freedom without a struggle, is proved by Robin Hood and his bold followers, floating in dim and shadowy glory on the outskirts of history; brave outlaws of the free forest, and the wild mountain-passes, taking back, in the very teeth of danger, a precarious subsistence from the rich possessions that were once their own; and therefore styled thieves and traitors by the robbers who had beggared them. Doubtless they had minstrels of their own; unknown in princely halls, untrumpeted by fame, yet singing of their exploits in spirit-stirring tones, to hearts burning with a sense of wrong. Troubled must be the sleep of those who rule a conquered nation!"

These thoughts were passing through his mind, when a dark mulatto opened the door, and making a servile reverence, said, in wheedling tones, "Would massa be so good as gib a pass to go to Methodist meeting?"

Mr. Duncan was a proverbially indulgent master; and he at once replied, "Yes, Jack, you may have a pass; but you must mind and not stay out all night."

"Oh, no, massa. Tom neber preach more than two hours."

Scarcely was the pass written, before another servant appeared with a similar request; and presently another; and yet another. When these interruptions ceased, Mr. Duncan resumed his book, and quietly read of the oppressed Saxons, until the wish for a glass of water induced him to ring the bell. No servant obeyed the summons. With an impatient jerk of the rope, he rang a second time, muttering to himself, "What a curse it is to be waited upon by slaves! If I were dying, the lazy loons would take their own time, and come dragging their heavy heels along, an hour after I was in the world of spirits. My neighbours tell me it is because I never flog them. I believe they are in the right. It is a hard case, too, to force a man to be a tyrant, whether he will or no."

A third time he rang the bell more loudly; but waited in vain for the sound of coming footsteps. Then it occurred to him that he had given every one of his slaves a pass to go to the Methodist meeting. This was instantly followed by the remembrance, that the same thing had happened a few days before.

We were then at war with Great Britain;[3] and though Mr. Duncan often boasted the attachment of his slaves, and declared them to be the most contented and happy labourers in the world, who would not take their freedom if they could, yet, by some coincidence of thought, the frequency of

3. The War of 1812 (see note 6, below).

Methodist meetings immediately suggested the common report that British troops were near the coast, and about to land in Charleston. Simultaneously came the remembrance of Big-boned Dick, who many months before had absconded from a neighbouring planter, and was suspected of holding a rendezvous for runaways, in the swampy depths of some dark forest. The existence of such a gang was indicated by the rapid disappearance of young corn, sweet potatoes, fat hogs, &c., from the plantations for many miles round.

"The black rascal!" exclaimed he: "If my boys *are* in league with him"—

The coming threat was arrested by a voice within, which, like a chorus from some invisible choir, all at once struck up the lively ballad of Robin Hood; and thus brought Big-boned Dick, like Banquo's Ghost,[4] unbidden and unwelcome, into incongruous association with his spontaneous sympathy for Saxon serfs, his contempt of "base Saxon churls," who tamely submitted to their fate, and his admiration of the bold outlaws, who lived by plunder in the wild freedom of Saxon forests.

His republican sympathies, and the "system entailed upon him by his ancestors," were obviously out of joint with each other; and the skilfullest soldering of casuistry could by no means make them adhere together. Clear as the tones of a cathedral bell above the hacks and drays of a city, the voice of Reason rose above all the pretexts of selfishness, and the apologies of sophistry, and loudly proclaimed that his sympathies were right, and his practice wrong. Had there been at his elbow some honest John Woolman,[5] or fearless Elias Hicks, that hour might perhaps have seen *him* a freeman, in giving freedom to his serfs. But he was alone; and the prejudices of education, and the habits of his whole life, conjured up a fearful array of lions in his path; and he wist not that they were phantoms. The admonitions of awakened conscience gradually gave place to considerations of personal safety, and plans for ascertaining the real extent of his danger.

The next morning he asked his slaves, with assumed nonchalance, whether they had a good meeting.

---

4. In Shakespeare's *Macbeth*, the ghost of the murdered Banquo repeatedly reappears before the guilty Macbeth.

5. John Woolman (1720–72) and Elias Hicks (1748–1830) were Quaker preachers fervently committed to following the promptings of the Inner Light and testifying against slavery. Woolman's "Some Considerations on the Keeping of Negroes" (1754) exerted a great influence on the early Quaker antislavery movement. Hicks reignited the spirit of antislavery activism and the belief in the Inner Light among nineteenth-century Quakers. His followers (Hicksites) separated from orthodox Quakers in 1828.

"Oh, yes, massa; bery good meeting."

"Where did you meet?"

"In the woods behind Birch Grove, massa."

The newspaper was brought, and found to contain a renewal of the report that British troops were prowling about the coast. Mr. Duncan slowly paced the room for some time, apparently studying the figures of the carpet, yet utterly unconscious whether he trod on canvass or the greensward. At length, he ordered his horse and drove to the next plantation. Seeing a gang at work in the fields, he stopped; and after some questions concerning the crop, he said to one of the most intelligent, "So you had a fine meeting last night?"

"Oh, yes, massa, bery nice meeting."

"Where was it?"

The slave pointed far *east* of Birch Grove. The white man's eye followed the direction of the bondman's finger, and a deeper cloud gathered on his brow. Without comment he rode on in another direction, and with apparent indifference made similar inquiries of another gang of labourers. They pointed *north* of Birch Grove, and replied, "In the Hugonot woods, massa."

With increasing disquietude, he slowly turned his horse toward the city. He endeavoured to conceal anxiety under a cheerful brow; for he was afraid to ask counsel, even of his most familiar friends, in a community so prone to be blinded by insane fury under the excitement of such suspicions. Having purchased a complete suit of negro clothes, and a black mask well fitted to his face, he returned home, and awaited the next request for passes to a Methodist meeting.

In a few days, the sable faces again appeared before him, one after another, asking permission to hear Tom preach. The passes were promptly given, accompanied by the cool observation, "It seems to me, boys, that you are all growing wonderfully religious of late."

To which they eagerly replied, "Ah, if massa could hear Tom preach, it make his hair stand up. Tom make ebery body tink weder he hab a soul."

When the last one had departed, the master hastily assumed his disguise, and hurried after them. Keeping them within sight, he followed over field and meadow, through woods and swamps. As he went on, the number of dark figures, all tending toward the same point, continually increased. Now and then, some one spoke to him; but he answered briefly, and with an effort to disguise his voice. At last, they arrived at one of those swamp islands, so common at the South, insulated by a broad, deep belt of water, and effectually screened from the main-land by a luxuriant growth of forest trees, matted together by a rich entanglement of vines and underwood. A large tree had been felled for a bridge; and over this dusky forms were swarming, like ants into their new-made nest.

Mr. Duncan had a large share of that animal instinct called physical courage; but his heart throbbed almost audibly, as he followed that dark multitude.

At the end of a rough and intricate passage, there opened before him a scene of picturesque and imposing grandeur. A level space, like a vast saloon, was enclosed by majestic trees, uniting their boughs over it, in fantastic resemblance to some Gothic cathedral. Spanish moss formed a thick matted roof, and floated in funereal streamers. From the points of arches hung wild vines in luxuriant profusion, some in heavy festoons, others lightly and gracefully leaping upward. The blaze of pine torches threw some into bold relief, and cast others into a shadowy background. And here, in this lone sanctuary of Nature, were assembled many hundreds of swart figures, some seated in thoughtful attitudes, others scattered in moving groups, eagerly talking together. As they glanced about, now sinking into dense shadow, and now emerging into lurid light, they seemed to the slaveholder's excited imagination like demons from the pit, come to claim guilty souls. He had, however, sufficient presence of mind to observe that each one, as he entered, prostrated himself, till his forehead touched the ground, and rising, placed his finger on his mouth. Imitating this signal, he passed in with the throng, and seated himself behind the glare of the torches. For some time, he could make out no connected meaning amid the confused buzz of voices, and half-suppressed snatches of songs. But, at last, a tall man mounted the stump of a decayed tree, nearly in the centre of the area, and requested silence.

"When we had our last meeting," said he, "I suppose most all of you know, that we all concluded it was best for to join the British, if so be we could get a good chance.[6] But we didn't all agree about our masters. Some thought we should never be able to keep our freedom, without we killed our masters, in the first place; others didn't like the thoughts of that; so we agreed to have another meeting to talk about it. And now, boys, if the British land here in Caroliny, what shall we do with our masters?"

---

6. A British army landed on the shores of the Chesapeake in August 1814. In chapter 3 of *An Appeal in Favor of That Class of Americans Called Africans*, Child mentions that 774 slaves escaped to the British during the War of 1812 and were resettled in Trinidad as free laborers. According to historian Frank A. Cassell, the number of Virginia and Maryland slaves who escaped to the British during the War of 1812 was as high as 3,000–5,000. The British had previously carried off and freed thousands of slaves during the American Revolution.

He sat down, and a tall, sinewy mulatto stepped into his place, exclaiming, with fierce gestures, "Ravish wives and daughters before their eyes, as they have done to *us!* Hunt them with hounds, as they have hunted *us!* Shoot them down with rifles, as they have shot *us!* Throw their carcasses to the crows, they have fattened on *our* bones; and then let the Devil take them where they never rake up fire o' nights. Who talks of *mercy* to our masters?"

"I do," said an aged black man, who rose up before the fiery youth, tottering as he leaned both hands on an oaken staff. "I do;—because the blessed Jesus always talked of mercy. I know we have been fed like hogs, and shot at like wild beasts. Myself found the body of my likeliest boy under the tree where buckra[7] rifles reached him. But thanks to the blessed Jesus, I feel it in my poor old heart to forgive them. I have been member of a Methodist church these thirty years; and I've heard many preachers, white and black; and they all tell me Jesus said, Do good to them that do evil to you, and pray for them that spite you. Now I say, let us love our enemies; let us pray for them; and when our masters flog us, and sell our piccaninnies, let us break out singing:

"You may beat upon my body,
But you cannot harm my soul;
I shall join the forty thousand by and by.

"You may sell my children to Georgy,
But you cannot harm their soul;
They will join the forty thousand by and bye.

"Come, slave-trader, come in too;
The Lord's got a pardon here for you;
You shall join the forty thousand by and bye.

"Come, poor nigger, come in too;
The Lord's got a pardon here for you;
You shall join the forty thousand by and bye.

"My skin is black, but my soul is white;
And when we get to Heaven we'll all be alike;
We shall join the forty thousand by and bye.

That's the way to glorify the Lord."

Scarcely had the cracked voice ceased the tremulous chant in which these words were uttered, when a loud altercation commenced; some crying out

7. Buckra is the negro term for white man. [LMC's note]

vehemently for the blood of the white men, others maintaining that the old man's doctrine was right. The aged black remained leaning on his staff, and mildly replied to every outburst of fury, "But Jesus said, do good for evil." Loud rose the din of excited voices; and the disguised slaveholder shrank deeper into the shadow.

In the midst of the confusion, an athletic, gracefully-proportioned young man sprang upon the stump, and throwing off his coarse cotton garments, slowly turned round and round, before the assembled multitude. Immediately all was hushed; for the light of a dozen torches, eagerly held up by fierce revengeful comrades, showed his back and shoulders deeply gashed by the whip, and still oozing with blood. In the midst of that deep silence, he stopped abruptly, and with stern brevity exclaimed, "Boys! *shall* we not murder our masters?"

"Would you murder *all?*" inquired a timid voice at his right hand. "They don't all cruellize their slaves."

"There's Mr. Campbell," pleaded another; "he never had one of his boys flogged in his life. You wouldn't murder *him,* would you?"

"Oh, no, no, no," shouted many voices; "we wouldn't murder Mr. Campbell. He's always good to coloured folks."

"And I wouldn't murder *my* master," said one of Mr. Duncan's slaves; "and I'd fight anybody that set out to murder him. I an't a going to work for him for nothing any longer, if I can help it; but he shan't be murdered; for he's a good master."

"Call him a good master, if ye like!" said the bleeding youth, with a bitter sneer in his look and tone. "I curse the word. The white men tell us God made them our masters; I say it was the Devil. When they don't cut up the backs that bear their burdens; when they throw us enough of the grain we have raised, to keep us strong for another harvest; when they forbear to shoot the limbs, that toil to make *them* rich; there *are* fools who call them good masters. Why should *they* sleep on soft beds, under silken curtains, while *we,* whose labour bought it all, lie on the floor at the threshold, or miserably coiled up in the dirt of our own cabins? Why should I clothe my master in broadcloth and fine linen, when he knows, and I know, that he is my own brother? and I, meanwhile, have only this coarse rag to cover my aching shoulders?" He kicked the garment scornfully, and added, "Down on your knees, if ye like, and thank them that ye are not flogged and shot. Of *me* they'll learn another lesson!"

Mr. Duncan recognised in the speaker, the reputed son of one of his friends, lately deceased; one of that numerous class, which southern vice is thoughtlessly raising up, to be its future scourge and terror.

The high, bold forehead, and flashing eye, indicated an intellect too active and daring for servitude; while his fluent speech and appropriate language betrayed the fact that his highly educated parent, from some remains of instinctive feeling, had kept him near his own person, during his lifetime, and thus formed his conversation on another model than the rude jargon of slaves.

His poor, ignorant listeners stood spell-bound by the magic of superior mind; and at first it seemed as if he might carry the whole meeting in favour of his views. But the aged man, leaning on his oaken staff, still mildly spoke of the meek and blessed Jesus; and the docility of African temperament responded to his gentle words.

Then rose a man of middle age, short of stature, with a quick roguish eye, and a spirit of knowing drollery lurking about his mouth. Rubbing his head in uncouth fashion, he began: "I don't know how to speak like Bob; for I never had no chance. He says the Devil made white men our masters. Now dat's a ting I've thought on a heap. Many a time I've axed myself how pon arth it was, that jist as sure as white man and black man come togeder, de white man sure to git he foot on de black man. Sometimes I tink one ting, den I tink anoder ting; and dey all be jumbled up in my head, jest like seed in de cotton afore he put in de gin. At last, I find it all out. White man *always* git he foot on de black man; no mistake in *dat*. But how he do it? I'll show you how!"

Thrusting his hand into his pocket, he took out a crumpled piece of printed paper, and smoothing it carefully on the palm of his hand, he struck it significantly with his finger, and exclaimed triumphantly, "Dat's de way dey do it! Dey got de *knowledge!* Now, it'll do no more good to rise agin our masters, dan put de head in de fire and pull him out agin; and may be you can't pull him out agin. When I was a boy, I hear an old conjuring woman say she could conjure de Divil out of anybody. I ask her why she don't conjure her massa, den; and she tell me, 'Oh, nigger neber conjure buckra—can't do't.' But I say nigger *can* conjure buckra. How he do it? Get de knowledge! Dat de way. We make de sleeve wide, and fill full of de tea and de sugar, ebery time we get in missis' closet. If we take half so much pains to get de knowledge, de white man take he foot off de black man. Maybe de British land, and maybe de British no land; but tell you sons to marry de free woman, dat know how to read and write; and tell you gals to marry de free man, dat know how to read and write; and den, by'm bye, you be de British *yourselves!* You want to know how I manage to get de knowledge? I tell you. I want right bad to larn to read. My old boss is the most begrudgfullest massa, and I know he won't let me larn. So, when I see leetle massa wid he book, (he about six year old,) I say to him, What you call dat? He tell me dat is A. Oh, dat is A! So I take old newspaper, and I ax missis, may I hab dis to rub my brasses? She say yes. I put it in my pocket, and by'm by, I look to see I find A; and I look at him till I know him bery well. Den I ask my young massa, What you call dat? He say, dat is B. So I find him on my paper, and look at him, till I know him bery well. Den I ask my young massa what C A T spell? He tell me cat. Den, after great long time, I can read de newspaper. And what you tink I *find* dere? I read British going to land! Den I tell all de boys British going to land; and I say what you *do,* s'pose British land? When I stand behind massa's chair, I hear him talk, and I tell all de boys what he say. Den Bob say must hab Methodist meeting, and tell massa, Tom going to preach in de woods. But what you tink I did toder day? You know Jim, massa Gubernor's boy? Well, I want mighty bad to let Jim know British going to land. But he lib ten mile off, and old boss no let me go. Well, massa Gubernor he come dine my massa's house; and I bring he horse to de gate; and I make my bow, and say, massa Gubernor, how Jim do? He tell me Jim bery well. Den I ax him, be Jim good boy? He say yes. Den I tell him Jim and I leetle boy togeder; and I want mighty bad send Jim someting. He tell me Jim hab enough of ebery ting. Oh, yes, massa Gubernor, I know you bery good massa, and Jim hab ebery ting he want; but when leetle boy togeder, dere is always someting *here* (laying his hand on his heart). I want to send a leetle backy to Jim. I know he hab much backy he want; but Jim and I leetle boy togeder, and I want to send Jim someting. Massa Gubernor say, bery well, Jack. So I gib him de backy, done up in de bery bit o' newspaper dat tell British going to land! And massa Gubernor *himself* carry it! And massa Gubernor *himself* carry it!!"

He clapped his hands, kicked up his heels, and turned somersets like a harlequin. These demonstrations were received with loud shouts of merriment; and it was sometime before sufficient order was restored to proceed with the question under discussion.

After various scenes of fiery indignation, gentle expostulation, and boisterous mirth, it was finally decided, by a considerable majority, that in case the British landed, they would take their freedom *without* murdering their masters; not a few, however, went away in wrathful mood, muttering curses deep.

With thankfulness to Heaven, Mr. Duncan again found himself in the open field, alone with the stars. Their glorious beauty seemed to him, that night, clothed in new and awful power. Groups of shrubbery took to themselves startling forms; and the sound of the wind among the trees was like the unsheathing of swords. Again he recurred to Saxon history, and remembered how he had thought that troubled must be the sleep of those who rule a conquered people. A new significance seemed given to Wat Tyler's address to the insurgent labourers of *his* day;[8] an emphatic, and most unwelcome application of *his* indignant question why serfs should toil unpaid, in wind and sun, that lords might sleep on down, and embroider their garments with pearl.

"And these Robin Hoods, and Wat Tylers, were my Saxon ancestors," thought he. "Who shall so balance effects and causes, as to decide what portion of my present freedom sprung from their seemingly defeated efforts? Was the place I saw to-night, in such wild and fearful beauty, like the haunts of the *Saxon* Robin Hoods? Was not the spirit that gleamed forth as brave as *theirs?* And who shall calculate what even such hopeless endeavours may do for the future freedom of this down-trodden race?"

These cogitations did not, so far as I ever heard, lead to the emancipation of his bondmen; but they did prevent his revealing a secret, which would have brought hundreds to an immediate and violent death. After a painful conflict between contending feelings and duties, he contented himself with advising the magistrates to forbid all meetings whatsoever among the coloured people until the war was ended.

He visited Boston several years after, and told the story to a gentleman, who often repeated it in the circle of his friends. In brief outline it reached my ears. I have told it truly, with some filling up by imagination, some additional garniture of language, and the adoption of fictitious names, because I have forgotten the real ones.

---

8. Wat Tyler (d. 1381) led a peasants' rebellion in 1381 and articulated their demands: that the goods of the church be divided among the parishioners and that villeage be abolished and all Britons made free and "of one condition."

To Abolitionists

Were you an abolitionist in the good old days of persecution from without, and of cordial, heart-filling sympathy from our little world within? Oh, the brave old days!—When sects were fused together by the heat of a holy zeal! It was worth living for, to have been thus raised above worldly considerations, selfish aims, and the circumscribed vision of creeds, into the open sunlight of universal love, the bracing atmosphere of free opinion!

Were you an abolitionist *then,* and are you disappointed that duty and this high joy no longer go together?

Had our earnestness in the work given us time to pause and prophesy, we could have foreseen that divisions must necessarily come; that the everlasting duality in man's soul always had, and always must, split men into two parties, on every new application of old principles to existing institutions, or modes of thought. The "conservative" and the "reform," the "stop there," and the "go ahead" spirit straightway manifests itself, as soon as human minds are brought into combined action by the attractive power of one great Idea, which they hold in common.

Perhaps the universal brotherhood of mankind may, more justly than any other, be defined as the central Idea of the Christian reform. In that reform, Paul conspicuously belonged to the "go ahead" school; and he found it to be his duty publicly to reprove Peter, concerning the application of this Idea to the custom of not eating with the Gentiles. Mark, probably from want of sufficient faith or zeal, fell back from the first mission he undertook with Paul and Barnabas. After this, Barnabas was willing to unite with him again, but Paul dared not trust his lukewarmness; and scripture informs us "the contention was so sharp between them, that they departed asunder one from the other."[1]

It is pleasant to remember that Mark did not abjure Christianity; neither did he seek to injure the persecuted sect with either Jews or Gentiles; but making the only good use of Paul's indignation, he cast aside the lukewarmness and irresolution which occasioned it, and became a very zealous preacher.

Years after these events, we find more extensive division among the early

Editorial, *National Anti-Slavery Standard,* 20 May 1841, p. 198.

1. On Paul's differences with Barnabas, Mark, and Peter over whether Gentile converts to Christianity should be required to observe Jewish dietary and circumcision practices and whether Jewish and Gentile converts should eat together, see Acts 15 and Galatians 2.11–14.

Christians, concerning the application of their central Idea to the custom of circumcision; which was closely interwoven with the prejudices of the Jews, having ever been the distinguishing sign between them and the heathen nations. Here again, Peter was on the conservative side, and Paul on the reforming. The *latter* tells us of "false brethren, unawares brought in, who came in privily to spy out our *liberty,* which we have in Christ Jesus, that they might bring us into bondage: To whom we gave place by subjection, no, not for an hour; that the truth of the gospel might continue with you."—He complains of those who "*seemed* to be somewhat," who were of no service, "but contrariwise, when they saw that the gospel of uncircumcision was committed unto him as the gospel of circumcision was unto Peter." And he adds, "For he that wrought effectually in *Peter* to the apostleship of the circumcision, the same was mighty in *me* toward the Gentiles."[2] In modern phrase this would be equivalent to saying, "The idea which binds Peter and me together in one discipleship, appears to *me,* in its full application, to overturn customs and prejudices, which *he* continues to hold sacred. I ought to be true to the voice of God in *my* soul, and he to *his.*"

These, and other similar passages in the early Christian history, appear to be forgotten by people, who ask the abolitionists, "Why can't you carry on your work of benevolence without division, as the apostles did?"

The central Idea of the Protestant reform was individual freedom in the examination of matters of faith. Its attractive power brought together men of all nations and character; but conservatism and reform soon occasioned divisions and secessions without number. Controversies concerning the ordaining of ministers led to the total abjuration, in some minds, of any such order as a ministry; and the freedom of laymen to examine and interpret for themselves the revelations made to holy men of old, came out in the unexpected form of a belief that immediate revelations were still continued to every individual soul. The "stop there" party, as usual, were shocked at the utter recklessness of the "go ahead;" and renewed the old, anxious question, "Where is this to end?" To those who thought Episcopacy a sufficient reform of Roman Catholic abuses, the Calvinist might well seem a daring and dangerous innovator; and, naturally enough, the Calvinist could not perceive that the Quaker was a legitimate result of his own Idea of Individual Freedom, so sturdily maintained.[3] And the warfare still goes on, splitting the split;

2. Galatians 2.4–8.

3. Child is referring to the range of sects that contested the Catholic church's hegemony during the Protestant Reformation in the name of combating corruption, restoring Chris-

dividing Episcopacy into High and Low, Presbyterianism into Old and New, Quaker into Orthodox and Hicksite, &c. &c. Each new party deems that it has settled certain points for all coming time; and, like Hannah More,[4] "cannot abide those who wish to reform the Reformation." But man's history, is eternal progression. There is no "stop there," howsoever earnestly we may desire it, for the sake of quiet.—Every principle of truth, from the most common and obvious, to the most abstract and incomprehensible, will be more extensively applied by some minds than others; and every new application will create fresh ferment.

Thus in the Anti-Slavery Reform, the central Idea was, that one man had no right to make property of another man. "Stop there" minds applied it only to negro chattels; "go ahead" minds saw it in various collateral bearings. In England, behind the image of the chained slave, arose the debased Hindoo, and the fiery Chartist,[5] fiercely asking, "Am *I* too not a chattel? Be true to your principle, and cut the cords that fetter *me*, body and soul."

In America, women heard it announced, and repeated, that every human soul had a right to full and free opportunities for the development of all their powers; and that any laws or customs, which obstructed this, were odious forms of that open violence by which the fighting barons of old held men in brutal vassalage. Some asked themselves, "How does this principle apply to *my* condition? Do laws and customs leave *me* the free exercise of all my powers?" This half-defined sentiment might not have taken a distinct form, had not the rising question been answered by husbands, forbidding wives to sign anti-slavery petitions, and brothers, seeking to control the spontaneous gushings of a sister's sympathy, on the ground that the subject was a political

---

tianity to its primitive simplicity, and providing believers with more direct access to God and the Bible. The Episcopalians eliminated the pope and substituted English services for the Latin Mass; the Calvinists eliminated church ritual and the Book of Common Prayer; and the Quakers eliminated ordained ministers, formal church services, and doctrines.

4. Hannah More (1745–1833), English bluestocking and religious writer of the evangelical school, was notorious for her conservatism.

5. Child refers to parallel movements against the abuses of British colonial rule in India, which was impoverishing and oppressing the Indian people, and in favor of working-class rights in England. Anticolonial ferment in India would explode in the brutally suppressed Mutiny of 1857. Many British abolitionists and liberals were calling for reforms in India, though not independence. The Chartist movement, originating among artisans thrown out of work by the new industrial technology, took its name from its founding document, the People's Charter of 1838, which demanded universal male suffrage and the abolition of property qualifications preventing workers from serving in Parliament and thus representing their own interests.

one, and women had no right to take part therein. Under the action of these circumstances, (the results of which no abolitionist had calculated or foreseen,) the nucleus of a new and agitating Idea took to itself shape, as rapidly as the blossom bursts from its sheath.—A large and stirring class of minds asked, "*Why* has woman nothing to do with politics? Is she not bought, and sold, and brutalized, by laws which politicians make and sustain?" While they paused for a satisfactory answer, Angelina Grimke[6] and her sister came among them; commanding respect by their superior intelligence, their quiet modesty, and still more, by the conscientious discharge of what they deemed a duty. Their course was more than tolerated by abolitionists; nearly every layman, and many clergymen, viewed it with enthusiastic approbation. Some minds, tending to conservatism on this point, yet unwilling to repress their own spontaneous impulses, apologized by saying, "It is a common thing for *Quaker* women to speak in public." To which another class of minds replied, "What does *that* signify, except that the Quakers have fought a moral battle with the world, and won the victory? a thing which others too may surely do."

Curiosity, combined with better motives, brought crowds to hear the Carolinian sisters; and it became necessary to ask the use of churches to accommodate them. With many clergymen this became really a troublesome question of conscience; and many were willing to use it as such, to veil their hostility to anti-slavery. "Stop there"! minds looked back anxiously to St. Paul to arrest the progress of this innovation. Some, who were reforming on this point, and conservative on others, found a conflict within themselves, and strove to prove that St. Paul had in reality uttered no gospel on this subject, any more than he had upon the counterfeiting of bank-bills. This did not satisfy a class of minds more entirely of the "go-ahead" cast; they boldly asked, "What if I do differ from St. Paul? So he differed from Peter on some points. Why should I wear Jewish garments? I was never measured for them, and they do not fit."

This shocks conservative minds so much, that many think all investiga-

---

6. Angelina E. Grimké (1805–79) and her sister, Sarah Moore Grimké (1792–1873), grew up in a prominent slaveholding family of Charleston, South Carolina. After converting to Quakerism and moving to Philadelphia, they joined the abolitionist movement in 1835 and began lecturing against slavery in 1836, at first to women's groups and then to audiences that included both sexes. Opposition by conservatives to women's public speaking caused dissension among abolitionists, climaxing in 1840 with a schism between Garrisonian and evangelical abolitionists. Child is quoting from the sisters' testimony in *American Slavery As It Is: Testimony of a Thousand Witnesses* (1839), the tract they joined Theodore Dwight Weld in compiling (22, 52–54).

tion of truth had better stop at once; and that it would have been wiser for Christendom to have remained under the spiritual guardianship of the Romish church, than thus to swing loose from all outward restraint. They forget the simple fact that the world *could* not so remain. Were not the spectacle somewhat of the saddest, one might smile to see how man, from the beginning, has fretted away his strength, and wasted his activity, in vain efforts to fence the infinite.

In the early days of anti-slavery, nothing was more frequently repeated than a denial of the charge, so often brought, that abolitionists wished to excite insurrection.—Warmly they took the ground that slaves *ought* to wait quietly for their emancipation to be effected by the exertion of moral power; that to murder their masters would be contrary to the gospel of Christ. All classes of minds united in this; for all shuddered at being the cause, however remotely, of a civil war. But minds of a conservative cast, with their usual passivity, saw just so much as applied to negro slaves, and no more. The activity of reform was busy, meanwhile, in fresh applications. The question arose, "Then what right had *we* to fight at Bunker Hill? What right had we to promote insurrection among the *Poles*, by sending them standards and flaming addresses?"[7] The opposite class of minds had no answer ready; and the newly stimulated thought fed upon itself, and daily gathered strength from its observation of men and things. There was no escape from one of two alternatives; the principle, if true, made all war a violation of the gospel; if not, it should no longer be repeated to screen abolitionists from a painful accusation; nay, if it were not true, might it not some day become a *duty* to send swords and standards to *black* Poles? A very few boldly and honestly took this ground. Many more, as honestly and boldly, accepted the other alternative, wheresoever it might lead them. Another large class, not so bold or frank, simply wished to give the subject the go-by. Thus, beneath the swift stream of anti-slavery was forming a powerful under current; both rising in the same spring, both tending to the same ocean. Then came the news of Lovejoy's[8] death, to be received by minds thus previously stirred to active inquiry. Some

7. Radical abolitionists argued against applying a double standard to revolutionary violence by blacks and whites. Anyone who celebrated the exploits of Massachusetts soldiers at the Battle of Bunker Hill (1775) or supported aiding Polish revolutionaries to overthrow their Russian overlords ought to defend the slaves' right to revolt, Child suggests; conversely, anyone who condemns slave violence must also condemn Americans' revolutionary fathers and urge pacifism on Polish as well as African American rebels.

8. Elijah Parish Lovejoy (1802–37), abolitionist editor of the *Alton Observer*, had three presses destroyed by antiabolitionist mobs before being killed defending his fourth in Alton, Illinois.

called him a martyr; others said "No; had he been killed without arms in his hands, he *would* have been a martyr." Some were shocked that a minister of Christ should have died thus; others asked, "Is not that which is wrong in a minister, wrong in any man? Ought we not *all* to be ministers of Christ?" Here was a glimpse of a new collateral bearing, destined to disturb the peace. Some said, "Though a minister, he did right to resist, for he had the mayor's permission to do so." Others asked, "Do the orders of a magistrate, or the laws of a government, make that right which is in itself wrong? Could all the penalties of government force you to deliver up a fugitive slave?"

Verily, the boundary of this question seemed like the horizon line, which stretches beyond and beyond, if you pursue it to the end of the world. Why should they who dare not pursue it, quarrel with those who do? Let Peter and Paul fulfill their respective missions.

The position of the old anti-slavery *societies,* as I understand it, is simply this: Every truth is infinite in its relations; and this is a law of the universe, which they cannot help, if they would. Earnestly pleading for one great truth, they, by reason of this law, and quite unconsciously to themselves, roused into action many other truths involved therein. These are received or rejected, praised or scorned, according to the temperament and character of various individuals. Some love them, some hate them, but more fear them, as they do a path through an intricate forest, to which there seems no end. Some embrace them with enlightened faith, others confuse distinctions between the true and the false. The *Society* simply says, "We will not be umpire in any of these controversies. We have no right to do it; and beside that, the thing is obviously impossible. All we ask of our members, is, 'Do you sincerely wish to abolish *slavery;* and will you use for that purpose all such means as conscience allows you to use for other purposes near to your heart' "?

"Can two walk together, except they be agreed?" said a Calvinist to George Bradburn,[9] as they walked arm in arm through Washington street, arguing as they went; "Certainly," replied Mr. Bradburn, "if they agree to *walk* together." This is the mere A.B.C. of combined action, making no infringement on individual freedom. When will men learn it? They can act upon it, while building houses and ships, and electing magistrates, and a thousand other things; why can they not thus abolish slavery?

Looked at with calm observation, there is nothing alarming in the duallistic tendency, I have attempted to define, though there is much that is trouble-

---

9. George Bradburn (1806–80) was an antislavery Whig member of the Massachusetts House of Representatives. He would join the Liberty party in 1844.

some. The two extremes, and the vibrations between them, are as necessary to preserve a balance in the moral world, as the centripetal and centrifugal force are to keep the planets in their places.

All conservative minds are not necessarily narrow and base, nor all reforming minds honest and true. The anxious "stop there!" may arise from an innocent timidity of temperament; from a sensitive conscientiousness; from a long cherished reverence for forms which once embodied sacred truths, and which are now perceived to embody them no longer; it may arise from a want of faith or zeal in the principle professed; or from a selfish love of ease and popularity; or simple inability to perceive the bearings of a truth; or the instinctive dogmatism of ignorance; or the rancor of sectarian prejudice.

The "go ahead!" may be a bold and conscientious seeking for truth, at all hazards; or it may be a restless desire for notoriety. Even when most honest, it may sometimes lead into the paths of error, in a too eager chase after truth. Why should we trouble ourselves to adjust the balance of motives? It can never be done save by Him who knows the secrets of all hearts.

Honestly follow your own convictions, and thus fulfil *your* mission, be it centripetal or centrifugal; but for your own soul's sake, see that you do it honestly. Eschew all sophistry, all evasion, all false pretences. If the very devil seem to you better than he is represented, say it of him, but call him by his name.

Minds cannot be chained, year after year, to one application of one idea; it will inevitably be looked at in its collateral, as well as its lineal relations.

What matters it to you, whether your neighbor sees only the foot of a mountain, while you see a large plain beyond, and a new circle of hills rising in the misty distance? Let him walk according to his sight; if he does not travel far, he will, if in earnest, travel well; if not in earnest, let him stop.

Finally, these divisions among us have not in reality altered our line of duty. The slave still stands in chains, counting the time of his redemption by minutes, while we count it by years. The blighting influences, which must eventually destroy institutions making the nearest approach to freedom of any in the known world, are actively doing their evil work. The well-being of nations and of races are at stake, and in constant peril; and the cure for all this lies in the exertion of moral influence, in such ways as conscience points out to each individual.

We have the same work as at the beginning; bravely begun, and needing to be bravely ended. The same efficient tools lie all around us, ready for the using. These tools are thy written and spoken word, thy daily, hourly deeds.

Shrink from no principle, and no application of a principle which seems to yourself true. Leaving others in freedom, and such peace as their consciences permit, do thou dare simply to "live as a life that which is apprehended as truth." But be careful not to "yield unto others by subjection, no, not for an hour;" lest they "bring you under bondage" to their prejudices. It is necessary to be watchful and brave in this, "that the truth may *continue* with you."[10] Any degree of peace obtained by an opposite course, must necessarily be very brief, because it must be merely apparent, not real.

If a few thousands, nay a few hundreds, through the length and breadth of this land, would resolutely do thus, the work of emancipation would soon be completed, though earth and hell are both arrayed against it.

Fear nothing, but be strong, and of good cheer. The planets will keep their places. Not one will fly out of its sphere, or be swallowed by the sun.—L.M.C.

10. Child quotes freely from Galatians 2.4–5 and an unidentified source.

Annette Gray

> "He bought me—somewhat high—
> For with me came a heart he couldn't buy."
> —Byron's *Corsair*[1]

The following story I tell as it was told to me, by one of the most intelligent slaves I ever met. I am aware of making myself liable to the charge of indelicacy; but the pure-minded will take no offense. There is an awful amount of facts in connection with the licentiousness of slavery, which are continually suppressed, from the difficulty of giving them utterance without disgusting modest ears. Those which I relate are not of this coarse, revolting kind; but to people of reflecting minds they will imply more than they reveal.

Annette Gray (I give her a fictitious name, because we of the free States are *not* free;)[2] was born and educated on the frontiers of slavery. Her master and mistress were English people, very kind to their slaves, and remarkably scrupulous concerning the modesty of their deportment. They never allowed any of the temporary connexions so universal among slaves; and the master observed as much propriety toward his female servants, as toward his own daughters. The lady, too, inculcated many lessons to prove how sinful, and how disgraceful, were the profligate connexions so common between masters and their slaves. Annette's mother being a religious woman, and many years a servant in this well-ordered family, frequently and earnestly repeated such lessons; so that the young girl grew up with a degree of purity and self-respect very unusual among her wretched class.

Was it a regard for the rights of an injured race, that led this English family to pursue a course so honorable? No; it was merely pride of their own respectability.—Their slaves might have said, with the poor mourners in the Bride of Lammermoor,[3] "Their gifts are dealt for nae love for *us*—nor for respect whether *we* feed or starve. They wad gie us whinstones for loaves, if it

Editorial, *National Anti-Slavery Standard*, 22 July 1841, pp. 26–27.

1. George Gordon, Lord Byron (1788–1824), *The Corsair* (1814), canto 3, stanza 8: 4, lines 18–19. The lines are spoken by the harem slave Gulnare, who repudiates her status as a favorite slave and reacts with disgust to her master's caresses, much as "Annette Gray" does.

2. Child is referring to the Fugitive Slave Law of 1793, which not only authorized the pursuit and recapture of slaves who fled to free states, but imposed a $500 fine on any citizen who knowingly harbored a fugitive slave.

3. From *The Bride of Lammermoor* (1819), novel by Sir Walter Scott (1771–1832), chap. 34; the speaker is the witch Ailsie Gourlay.

would serve their ain vanity; and yet they expect us to be gratefu', as they ca' it, as if they served us for true love and liking."

Facts justify this seemingly harsh conclusion. When Annette was about fifteen years old, her master became heir to a valuable estate in England, and concluded to remove thither. His American property was all sold: and with the carriage-horses, and "sundry old candle-boxes," was sold Annette. Young, motherless, sensitively modest, and with an unusual share of personal comeliness, she was sold to the highest bidder—the most notorious old profligate in the city!

His ostensible purpose was to purchase her as a waiting-maid for his wife. When she first entered the family, he had a favorite mistress among the slaves, and for the time being took very little notice of other individuals.—Annette became a favorite with the lady. Being intelligent and tasteful, the expense of learning three distinct trades was incurred, with a view to make her services more valuable; and, in process of time, she could dress hair in the most approved French style, fit dresses neatly, and give to caps and bonnets the true Parisian air. This brought her into frequent contact with the fashionable friends of her wealthy mistress, and she acquired a gentility of manner, and correctness of pronunciation, indicating any thing but slavery.

Meanwhile the favorite mistress, for some whim or other, was discarded and sold, and her master was casting his eye around in search of a new Sultana. Well might Mr. Preston tell Harriet Martineau that "the progress of southern society was continually toward orientalism!"[4]

Annette, young, fresh, and innocent, naturally attracted his attention; but experience had made him refined in his vices, and he sought excitement by self-imposed restraint. No coarse ribaldry, no personal rudeness, startled the modesty of his helpless slave; but his smiles were frequent and most gracious, his flattery most insidious, his presents abundant. By degrees, as he met her on the stairs, or in the passage-ways, he would playfully touch her under the chin, or twine his fingers in her glossy black ringlets, and then smile to see her blush. One day, he suddenly entered the room where she usually sat sewing for her mistress, and when she timidly rose to depart, he forbade her to leave the room. Perceiving her terror, he said to her, "You foolish child, what is there to be afraid of? Don't I always treat you well? And since your room is

---

4. The British writer Harriet Martineau (1802–76) described her impressions of the United States in *Society in America* (3 vols., 1837). The chapter "Morals of Slavery" reports many conversations with slaveholders, but not with a Mr. Preston. Possible candidates are Virginia state legislator William Ballard Preston (1805–62) and South Carolina senator William Campbell Preston (1794–1860).

cooler than my own, why should you object to my coming here when I choose?" She did object, however, and sought to avoid him; but he forbade her to keep the door closed, and she was afraid to inform her mistress. She showed me some very pretty specimens of carved whale-bone and ivory, which he had cut during these lounging hours in her apartment; and all this while, the most cunning flattery was poured into her ear. Among other things, he said, "Do you remember, about six years ago, when you were a little girl, meeting a gentleman in——Square, riding on a white horse? Do you remember how the horse caricoled and reared, as you crossed the street? And do you remember how the gentleman turned the horse round, looked after you, and nodded at you?"

Annette said that she recollected it very well, for she thought it strange the gentleman should take so much notice of her.

"I was that gentleman," said he; "and from that moment I resolved that, sooner or later, I would have you. I inquired, then, to whom you belonged, and kept my eye on you ever after."

Where a man has irresponsible power over his victim, reserve is of course banished as soon as it suits his convenience. The master became more explicit in his language, but still sought to gain her affections. She remonstrated; begging him to choose another, among the many slaves who would be proud of his addresses; for herself, she had been educated to consider such connexions sinful and degrading. At first he laughed, and then he swore.

He had made no perceptible progress in her good graces, when a journey to Sulphur Springs in Virginia, was agreed upon. Annette and one man-servant were the only slaves they took with them. In describing this journey to me, I was much struck with the vividness of her description. As nearly as I can remember, it was as follows:

"When I asked for a bed at the hotel, they laughed in my face. 'Give a nigger a bed!'—said they. 'We never heard of such a thing.' However, my mistress interceded for me, and I had a bed. In general, the female slaves slept on the floor, or on the skins that covered the travelling trunks; and the men slept in the carriages. If any of them got angry with another, they would often run the carriage into the river while he was asleep, and leave it there.

["]The hotel had a piazza round it. All about were scattered huts for travellers, some single, some in rows, some in Gothic style, and some very light and airy; well wooded hills closed it in all round, and a pond sparkled at a little distance. One day, as I stood on the piazza, I saw a great many slaves at the pond, washing clothes and spreading them out on the grass. They danced and capered about in such a strange manner, that I went down to ask what could be the matter. 'Oh,' said they, in their slave gibberish. 'Don't you know? Van June's coming.' 'Who is Van June?' 'Oh, don't you know Van June, one big buckra man from the North; and Missis gib me new apron and new handkercher, because Van June's coming!'

"The 'big buckra man' was Van Buren, the President.[5] They made a great ball for him. The hotel and all the travellers' huts were illuminated; and the trees on the sides of the hills were all hung with lamps. It was a beautiful sight to see couples dancing on the green, and the ladies dressed in white, glancing in and out among the shadows. Here and there, slaves were coming out from between the trees into the broad light, looking like Devils. Van Buren brought a mulatto servant with him, named Charles Ingram. Sometimes he said he was free, and sometimes he said he was a slave. I think he was a slave, because Williams, who superintended the President's affairs, flogged him one day for not putting away the harness.

"The slaves at the Springs made a ball, and gave a dinner to Charles Ingram; and I danced with him. They called him 'the black President.' Van Buren came in to see us dance. He shook hands with us all round, and told us to be obedient to our masters, and they would be good to us; that the Bible said we ought to obey our masters."

Among the songs on this grand occasion, she repeated the following:

"Come, broders, let us leave
Dis buckra land for Hayti—
An' der we be receive
As gran as Lafayettee.

Der we make a mighty show,
As grannus as you see—
I shall be all the go,
An' you like Governor Shootsy.

No more the barrow wheel,
An' that's a mighty jerkus;
No more we 'bliged to steal,
An' then be sent to work-hus.

5. Martin Van Buren (1782–1862), eighth president of the United States (1837–41).

An' dance us in a hall,
Hold a half a million—
There we dance the great big jig,
The white man call cotillion.

Lead your partners out—
Forward two and backee,
Wheel and turn about,
And then go home in hackey."

At Sulphur Springs her master first employed coercion, in the form of a threat. He soon surrounded himself with a convivial club, who drank with him all night, and slept or gambled through the day. Some of these men were ferocious in their tempers, and far more indecent in their manners than himself. They assailed poor Annette with all sorts of obscene jests, and the more she was confused, the more they enjoyed their manly sport.

To a Mississippian, one of the most violent and despicable of these men, her master threatened to sell her, unless she proved obedient to his wishes. This terrified her exceedingly. She knew that she should have to encounter the same sort of persecution, probably in a more odious form, and perhaps coupled with cruel punishments, which she had never yet experienced. Then came the sickening thought of being so far separated from home and friends, without hope of ever seeing them again. Still she begged him to seek some other object, and leave her in peace. At last, he lost all patience, and said, "If you dare to fasten your door to-night, or to make any complaint to your mistress, I will sell you to the Mississippian to-morrow; and a grand exchange you will make of it, I can tell you."

The door was not fastened; and the poor girl, shrinking from the degradation of her fate, became her master's paramour; a situation to which most of her degraded class would have been proud to attain.

When the family returned home, she again made an effort to free herself from the disagreeable thraldom; urging her oppressive sense of shame, and the scruples in which she had been educated. "I have often thought," said Annette to me, "how lucky it was that my master was not young and handsome, and that he so often disgusted me by his beastly intoxication. He was so kind to me, that I might have been tempted to love him; it would have been natural, you know. Slave mistresses do sometimes love their masters; and it almost kills them when they are turned away for somebody else. I cannot be thankful enough that my master was not young and handsome; for it would have been a sin to love him.—As it was, though I could not help myself, and would gladly have done so if I could, yet I could not look my mistress in the eye. My chamber was directly over hers. She heard his footsteps and his voice there; and when I came into her room in the morning, and left him in my own, I never could help hanging my head for shame. She never spoke to me about it; but sometimes, when I came to dress her, she was violently cross, and scolded me for every thing; then, in a few minutes, she would speak kindly, and try to make up by giving me some present.—I imagined I could read her thoughts. I suppose she said to herself, 'Poor, young creature, it is no fault of hers. How can she help herself?' I think so, because she never used to treat me so capriciously before we went to Sulphur Springs.

"They were a wretched couple, rich as they were.—The house was superbly furnished—full length mirrors, marble tables, and carpets from garret to basement, so thick and soft that you could not hear a foot fall. Many a time, when the bell has summoned me to the drawing-room have I found my mistress at one end of the apartment behind the heavily-fringed damask curtains, her eyes red with weeping; and at the other end my master dozing on the rich sofa, drunk with champagne. Perhaps they had not spoken to each other for days. When I entered, both would give me orders at once; and if I obeyed my mistress, my master would sometimes seize a book, or a shoe, or anything within his reach, and throw it at my head, cursing me for not minding him first; yet I did not dare to do otherwise than wait upon my mistress first for I was bought for her waiting maid; besides, I pitied her, and felt ashamed before her.

"Some of the slaves were very impudent to him, especially when they saw him intoxicated. He had a French mulatto coachman, who said all manner of saucy things, and seldom got punished for it. I never knew how it was that he would bear so much from that mulatto. The other slaves said he knew something, that made his master afraid of him. One day he called to the groom, 'Bring out the horses! Massa and me go to Hell today.' This made a great laughing and joking, and he was ordered to be whipped for it; but he made Mr. —— believe that he meant to say he was going to Summer *Hill,* only he was French, and did not know how to speak the word.

"One day, some garden rakes had been left in the path, and Mr. —— ordered the coachman to pick them up, and put them out of his way. 'Where shall I carry them?' 'To Hell, for all I care.' 'Massa, that be right *in* your way.' The other slaves that heard it looked at each other, and showed all their white teeth; but the Frenchman was not even scolded at.

"I grew very unhappy. My master was disagreeable to me; and I could never forget what my mother used to say about the sin and shame of such connexions. Sometimes I wished, since I was so entirely in his power, that I could love him; and then I was shocked at myself for such a wicked thought. I was made more uncomfortable by the suspicion that I might become a mother; and from the first day I belonged to this man, I had heard the servants tell that he always sold his own children soon after they were born, in order to keep them out of his wife's way. This thought haunted me from morning till night. I could not bear to think that such would be the fate of my child.

"Again I tried to break my shameful bonds; and threatened to appeal to my mistress for protection, begging her to sell me to a man of better character. This made my master very angry. He told me 'I need not feel so safe because I was at home. He knew how to punish me. He had only to write a letter to Mississippi, and send me off by the next slave ship.'

"After that threat, I had no peace. I fancied he showed me less kindness, and that this was a sign he was about to sell me. My mind turned towards the Free States and I listened eagerly to everything that was said about them. I heard of a colored man, who had helped off some slaves. I went to him and asked him if he could help me. He said he would; but advised me not to leave, except when the house was full of company. It was easy to find such a time; for our house was thronged with visiters; but I waited for a chance to leave on Saturday—knowing that they could not advertise me in the papers until Monday. A celebrated beauty and heiress from the North, (a lady well known to the editor,) was passing through the city; and as her stay was short, my mistress made a Ball for her on Saturday. The slaves were all of a hoity toity; for they take great pride in their master's having famous guests, and making grand entertainments. All of them were talking about the rich Miss ——, the beautiful Miss ——. I, of course, was one to receive the ladies, as they came; and my curiosity was great to see the Northern belle. Among the crowd, one particularly attracted my attention by the extreme simplicity of her dress. She wore plain white muslin, with a satin sash, without ornament of any kind, save a single band of pearl around her head. When I rested on one knee to arrange her shoe-lacing, she thanked me, with a very sweet smile, and said she preferred to do it herself. What was my surprise to discover that this was the famous belle! When I told it to the servants, they seemed to have no opinion of her at all.—'She can be no great things,' said they, 'if she ties her own shoes. She's never been used to be waited upon, that's plain enough.'

"I wondered within myself whether she was a sample of the ladies in the Free States. I had already told my colored friend what evening I had chosen to escape; and he told me I should find walking to and fro, in front of his house, a white man in Quaker dress. If I spoke to him, and he answered, 'Thy name is Jane Neal,' it would be a sign I had found the right person. My heart throbbed with the hopes of escape and the fear of failure. What money and trinkets I had were sewed within the clothes I wore. I was afraid to take any bundle, lest the other servants might notice it as something singular.—While planning how I should slip out unperceived, I was told to go and order some fresh ice-creams from the confectioner's. The party may be waiting for the ice-creams to this day, for ought I know. I had other business on hand. With great difficulty, I found, in the obscurity of evening, the house where I had agreed to meet the stranger. I soon saw a man in Quaker dress, walking to and fro. He gave me the signal agreed upon, and said, 'Follow me, friend.' He had a wagon and horses in readiness, and he carried me thirty miles that night to the house of another friend, who carried me fifty miles further on; and at last I found myself in Philadelphia. At one place, I staid three days at the rail-road depot; for the man who had the management of it told me there were advertisements posted up describing such a person as I was, and he advised me to hide myself. I was concealed in a chamber in his house; and peeping from the windows I saw two constables, whom I knew to be in my master's employ, go on in the cars, and on the third day go back. I had little doubt they were searching for me; for I was told two men from the South had been making very close inquiries for a runaway slave. I eluded them, however, and came safely to New York."

Annette remained some time in New York, and would not have left it, had she not met in the streets so many gentleman and ladies, whom she had seen as guests at her master's hospitable mansion. Thinking Boston would be the safer place, she took passage thither. In that city her babe was born. Some of the colored people, who knew her history, advised her to put the child in the almshouse; but she replied, "No, I will never desert it. I wish it had died when it was born; but since it is here, it is my duty to take care of it; if the child is ruined, he shall never have occasion to reproach my neglect as the cause.["]

This virtuous resolution she carried into effect. Finding it impossible to pursue her trade, of mantua-making, with the constant care of her babe, she went out to service, and devoted nearly all her wages to pay for its being nursed. In the streets, she sometimes met those who had visited at her master's; but as none recognized her, she grew bold in a feeling of security, and not only went into the streets, but ventured to meeting on Sunday. One day, turning a corner suddenly, she came upon a whole family of travellers, near neighbors of her master. "How do you do? Jeannette," said they: "We did not know you were here. Where does your mistress put up?"—"At the Tremont," was the ready reply. "What number?" "Twenty-eight." "Tell her I shall call to see her immediately. I had no idea she was in the city."

With a palpitating heart, Annette hastened home, resolving to show her face no more in the street, till the travelling season was over. But the news of her whereabout was probably conveyed by writing; for, about six weeks after, a genteel-looking young man came to the back door of the house where she lived, under pretence of inquiring for the master. She was startled, for she thought she had seen him when she was a slave; and she was perfectly sure that the cane he carried was one of a number her master had made from the ruins of some old Fort, as convenient presents for his friends. This gave her an air of embarrassment, much increased by his scrutinizing gaze, and his questions concerning her name, birth-place, &c. That same evening, a message was brought, purporting to be from a colored woman of her acquaintance, in Southack St., who wished to see her at eight o'clock, alone, on particular business. This changed suspicion into alarm. She was put into a carriage, and brought to the house of a friend of mine; and there I heard her story.

We deemed it best for her to leave Boston. Her present prospects are good; I would mention them, if we, of the nominally free States, were really free.

The *men* of New England may bear this state of things with silent submission, and call their criminal acquiescence patriotism; but a thousand times has my pulse beat high with indignation, to find that I, too, a free-born woman of Massachusetts, was a bond slave of the South; obliged to suppress my best impulses, and obey the dictates of my conscience by stealth. The slaveholder's whip has a long lash, that reaches from Georgia far beyond Mason and Dixon's line.

"Oh, what a precious name is Liberty, to scare, or cheat, the simple into slaves."—L.M.C.

Letters from New-York, Number 12

I propose to fill this letter with an account of some remarkable individuals among the colored population. In the days of thoughtless romance, I might have smiled at such an idea, or have introduced it with some playful apology; such as the fact in natural history, that lions are black in Africa, and that she has her black swans also. But I have thought too deeply of this people's wrongs, and have discovered in them capabilities too high, to admit of merriment.

Among these lions, the brave Cinquez,[1] and his thirty-four associates, are of course most prominent. Through the friendly thoughtfulness of Lewis Tappan, I received notice of a farewell meeting of the Mendians, at Zion's church, last week; and there I heard them for the first and last time.

I shall not give you a detailed account of the highly interesting services; for they were similar to those so often repeated in the newspapers; but I will glance at a few things which stand in most distinct relief on the tablet of my memory. Mr. A. T. Williams,[2] their teacher, to whom they seemed warmly attached, opened the meeting, by giving a brief account of them. His introductory remarks jarred slightly on my feelings; for they *seemed* like ministering to an unjust public sentiment, though I do not think they were so *intended*. He said he wished to do away two errors, which had crept into the popular mind concerning these people. In the first place, they were not cannibals in their native country. In the next place, they did not rise against their masters, for cruel treatment; but in consequence of being tormented by the cook, who told them they would be cut up and salted for sale, as soon as

National Anti-Slavery Standard, 2 December 1841, p. 103; reprinted in *CC* 12/293.

1. Cinquez, or Singbe, led the slave revolt on board the Spanish slave-trading schooner *Amistad* in 1839. The fifty-three illegally kidnapped Africans from Mende mutinied on the *Amistad* near Cuba, killed the captain and two crew members, and demanded that their Spanish owner, a former sea captain, navigate them back to Africa. He sailed the ship into a Long Island port instead. While awaiting a verdict on their legal status, the captives were imprisoned in Hartford. The evangelical abolitionist Lewis Tappan (1788–1873) organized a defense team headed by John Quincy Adams to sue for the captives' freedom, and the U.S. Supreme Court ruled in their favor. Public sympathy shifted toward the Mendians during the long trial. After the trial, they toured the Northeast with their abolitionist and missionary benefactors to raise funds for their transportation back to their homeland.

2. A. F. Williams, an abolitionist from Farmington, Connecticut, hosted the Mendians on his farm until their departure for Africa in November 1841. Their teacher, however, was not Williams, but Professor George E. Day.

they arrived in port. I would rather not have had the motive presented to my mind in such an unheroic form. It knocked in the head all my *romantic* associations with Cinquez, as a brave soul, preferring death to slavery. I thought of his speech, which, had it been uttered by an ancient hero, Plutarch would have recorded as a gem. To a soul that could utter itself thus, it appeared to me that being sold salted must have appeared far preferable to being sold alive.—However, I am not disposed to quarrel with fact, because it is not romance. But when it was explained, as if in apology, that they did not rise against their masters, I felt disturbed. I was strongly moved to ask, "By what standard are these strangers to be tried? By the gospel standard, of which they had then never heard? Or by the same standard that the world judges of Washington, Kosciusko, and William Tell?["]³ The latter was the standard, not *professed* merely, (like the gospel) but *practically* acknowledged by nearly all of every American audience. Why, then, should an assembly with such sentiments be assured, in tones of apology, that Cinquez had not done what Washington and Kosciusko would assuredly have done under similar circumstances? If any people on earth have a right to fight in self-defense, the captured and enslaved negro has most peculiarly that right; and the advocates of defensive war are neither consistent nor magnanimous in refusing to make this admission. I, of course, cannot make it; because I believe all war to be a violation of the gospel.

Mr. Williams bore testimony to the very scrupulous honesty of these Mendians, and to their remarkable adherence to truth; which they had never been known to violate, in a single instance, though there had sometimes been very strong temptation to do it, to escape from blame. This quality was conspicuous in the artlessness of their remarks, and their unwillingness to say anything that was not really *within* them. Hence, there was a very observable difference between their manner of answering questions connected with their own experience and knowledge, and those relating merely to speculative faith.

All these interesting strangers carried their heads as freemen are wont to do, and several of them had very expressive countenances. Next to Cinquez, the youthful Kinna appeared most intelligent and interesting. Alluding to the progress in their education, he said, "When in Hartford, good gentleman

3. Child is comparing Cinquez and the *Amistad* rebels to America's Revolutionary War heroes George Washington and Tadeusz Kosciusko (1746–1817), known as the Polish Lafayette, and to the fourteenth-century Swiss patriot William Tell, who, according to legend, helped win his country's independence from Austria.

bring us book—we no care much about. We say what good? Maybe to-morrow we die. But when we go to Farmington, and they tell us we no die, then we read—like much. We will tell Mendi people all whites no bad. We think all whites be same. But we find there be darkness-white, him you call Spaniard—that be evil white. But the snow-white—the 'Meriky-white, that be much good."

Being asked if he could love his enemies, he replied, with a strong foreign accent, "Yes I love *him*. Can pray to God forgive *him*." "If Ruiz should come to Mendi, and you should meet him alone in the bushes, what would you do?" "I let him *go*, I no touch *him*. But if him catch our children—him see what he catch!"

A loud shout of laughter and applause, from the crowded audience, here announced the universality of the instinct of retaliation; nor could I refrain from smiling at the *naive* earnestness of the reply.

Some one asked him when he experienced a change of heart; to which he answered, with most refreshing simplicity: "In prison, at Hartford, I think much of wrong things I do. I remember many wrong thing. I no want to do no more wrong thing. I pray to God he forgive me, I no do no more wrong thing. Good man say Christ die for me. I thank Christ because he pray his Father to come die for me."

"How do you know the Bible is the word of God?" Kinna looked perplexed at this question, as if it conveyed no definite idea to his mind. After listening intently, as it was a second time repeated, he said: "In prison, I think I die. I no die. Good man say God take me out of jaws of my enemy. I thank God. Bible tell 'bout God. Like read much."

"How will you *prove* to the Mendi people that the Bible is the word of God?"

Here was a poser, that might have perplexed deeper theologians than the untutored African. He seemed puzzled; but after a little thought, answered with the unpretending honesty of a little child: "I ask Mendi people, 'You ever know Mendi to come back to father and mother, when darkness-white man catch him?' They say, 'No, never came back. We never no more see him.' I say, '*We* come back to Mendi. God put it in the hearts of good 'Meriky people. Bible tell 'bout God. You read Bible, you know 'bout God, that send us back to Mendi.'"

I thought these honest creatures would be vexatious materials, should any theological drill serjeant try to substitute a routine of catechisms and creeds for the indwelling life. Spiritual murderers are all such—men who smother human souls—to whatever sect they may belong. May none such tarnish the truthful simplicity of these poor children of the sun.

James Covey,[4] the interpreter, after describing in his broken language, his introduction to the captives, and how he discovered that they spoke the same language as his father and mother, repeated some little incidents, one of which pleased me much. "One Sunday, when I go to prison, Cinquez hear the bell ring. He say 'what for bell ring?' I tell him when 'Meriky people go pray to God, they ring bell. He say, 'These people be fool. When want pray to God, what for ring bell?'"

Three or four of the company read quite tolerably; and the boy, Kali, spelled entire sentences of Scripture with great correctness. Five of them united in singing, "When I can read my title clear," to the tune of "Auld lang syne." Two songs were then sung in their native dialect; both decidedly pleasant to my ear, but the last particularly so. The first strongly resembled a German catch, which I have somewhere heard. The last was soft, melodious, and friendly in its sound; consisting of question and response, plainly marked in the emphasis and cadence of the tones.

I imagined it must be very like the Italian gondoliers, replying to each other in music across the Venetian waters. Their teacher explained that it was an African welcome to newly-arrived guests; the constantly-recurring chorus, which sounded like "Come—O? Come—O?" signified "Will you stay? Will you stay?" The answer, as often repeated, "I love you, and will stay with you."

Wm. W. Anderson, formerly Solicitor-General for Jamaica, made some interesting statements concerning the missionary spirit excited among the emancipated of that island, and gave a very satisfactory account of their rapid improvement in knowledge, morality, and religion.

Through all the services, Cinquez had remained seated among his brethren, in a quiet, unpretending manner, yet evidently the great man of the evening. Several of them whispered to him; to which he replied with a dignified bend of the head, not even turning his eyes. Toward the close of the evening he gave an account, in his native tongue, of taking the Amistad from their Spanish masters. His style of eloquence was perfectly electrifying. He

---

4. Born in Mende, James Covey learned English in Sierra Leone. After being kidnapped into slavery and rescued by a British cruiser that captured the slaver transporting him to Havana, he enlisted as a sailor on the British man-of-war *Buzzard*. The *Buzzard* happened to be in New York while the *Amistad* captives' abolitionist defenders were searching for an interpreter for Cinquez. Covey interpreted for them throughout the trial and subsequently sailed with them for Sierra Leone.

moved rapidly about the pulpit, his eyes flashed, his tones were vehement, his motions graceful, and his gestures, though taught by nature, were in the highest style of dramatic art. He seemed to hold the hearts of his companions chained to the magic of his voice. During his narrative, they ever and anon broke forth into spontaneous responses, with the greatest animation. He illustrates perfectly the description given by Lander,[5] and other travellers, of the eloquent and exciting *palavers* of Africa.

Theodore Wright,[6] pastor of the African Presbyterian church, spoke very feelingly of the Mendian mission, as one that rejoiced the hearts of the colored people. It was the first one in which they had been able to unite with their whole souls. All other missions had been in partnership with colonization, that worst enemy of their persecuted race; or they had joined hands with the slaveholder, by consenting to accept from his treasury the price of African blood. But he thanked God the skirts of *this* mission were pure. Not a cent from those who bought or sold human beings would ever be allowed to pollute its funds.

There is beautiful propriety in the fact, that these interesting strangers, so wonderfully rescued from slavery, are the first occasion of *such* a mission. May it be wisely conducted, and abundantly blessed!

Above all people in the world, the African race are probably most susceptible of religious feeling, and have the strongest tendency to devotion. Swedenborg[7] speaks of them as being nearer to Christians in the spiritual world than any other heathen; by reason of their docility and reverence. He moreover makes the remarkable statement that the only church on earth, acknowledged by the angels as a true church, is in the centre of Africa, unvisited and unknown to the rest of the world; and if I recollect aright, he implies that, by simplicity and obedience, they have preserved that visible intercourse with spiritual beings, which is recorded of the most ancient church.

Whether this be true or not, the world will probably find out some time

5. Child refers repeatedly to the popular travel accounts by the British explorer Richard Lander (1804–34): *Journal of a Second expedition into the Interior of Africa, from the bight of Benin to Soccatoo. By the late Commander Clapperton. . . . To which is added, the Journal of Richard Lander from Kano to the Sea-coast . . .* (1829); *R. Lander's Records of Captain Clapperton's Last Expedition* (1830); and *R. and J. Lander's Journal of an Expedition to Explore the Course and Termination of the Niger* (1832).

6. The abolitionist minister Theodore Sedgwick Wright (1797–1847) was the first African American to graduate from a U.S. theological seminary (Princeton, 1828). A founder of the American Anti-Slavery Society (1833), he sided with evangelical abolitionists in the 1840 schism.

7. Emanuel Swedenborg (1688–1772), a Swedish scientist turned mystic, wrote many volumes of visionary works. Child had joined the Swedenborgian New Church in 1822.

or other; but of one thing I have long been assured—that a very prominent place among the nations must be assigned to the African race, whenever the age of Moral Sentiment arrives. Creatures of affection and of faith, everything marks them peculiarly appropriate to represent a religious age, as the Anglo-Saxons were to represent an intellectual one.

Every idea that one has in these days, if they do not make great haste to utter it, is sure to come to them from a hundred other sources. Thus I found the thought so long familiar to my mind echoed by Kinmont, in his Lectures on Man.[8] Speaking of the civilization of Africa, he says: "It will be—indeed it must be—civilization of a peculiar stamp; perhaps we might venture to conjecture, not so much distinguished by *art* as a certain beautiful *nature;* not so marked or adorned by *science,* as exalted and refined by a new and lovely *theology;* a reflection of the light of heaven, more perfect and endearing than that which the intellects of the Caucasian race have ever yet exhibited. There is more of the *child,* of unsophisticated *nature,* in the negro race than in the European." And again: "The sweeter graces of the Christian religion appear almost too tropical and tender plants to grow in the soil of the Caucasian mind. They require a character of human nature, of which you can see the rude lineaments in the Ethiopian, to be implanted in and grow naturally and beautifully withal."

Dr. Channing[9] says, "A short residence among the negroes of the West Indies impressed me with their capacity of improvement. On all sides I heard of their religious tendencies, the noblest in human nature."—Speaking of British emancipation, he says: "History contains no record more touching than the account of the religious, tender thankfulness which this vast boon awakened in the negro breast."

A few evenings since, I went to Asbury-street church to hear a blind Methodist preacher, who had once been a slave. His countenance was good, but he had not that frank, noble bearing of the Haitian, or the African, fresh from his native deserts. This no man can attain to in a community that treats him as an inferior. His voice, like that of most Methodist preachers, sounded like a rasp going over hard wood; the result of their loud style of speaking,

---

8. *Twelve Lectures on the Natural History of Man, and the Rise and Progress of Philosophy* (1839), by Alexander Kinmont (1799–1838), was widely cited by abolitionists. Child is quoting from Lectures 7 and 8, "On the Origin and Perpetuation of Natural Races of Mankind" and "On the Unity in Variety of the Human Race."

9. The influential Unitarian minister William Ellery Channing (1780–1842) was converted to abolitionism by Child's *Appeal.* Child is quoting from his book *Emancipation* (1840).

continued for an astonishing length of time without cadence or intonation. But there was a charm in his earnest, and evidently sincere feeling; and touches of real eloquence were interspersed here and there, like stars in a cloudy sky. He spoke of "Brother Paul," with a familiarity well suited to this most democratic of all sects. The picture he drew of Paul and Silas in prison, showed great vividness of imagination. Speaking of the chains, he placed his hand upon his heart, and exclaimed, "But they couldn't chain him *here!* They might gag his mouth; but every whisper of his soul God would hear in Heaven."

This William Harden has the acute senses and strong memory common to the totally blind. Though he was never able to read, he can repeat the Bible from one end to the other, and give out any hymn in the book, from memory. In this interesting man I probably had a good sample of some of the slave preachers, addressing their fellow slaves from a stump in the forest, and often attracting the planters and their families by their untutored eloquence.

It is invidious to single out a few individuals, where many deserve commendation; but as I lately met with Hester Lane, I cannot forbear giving her a passing notice. Diligent, capable, and laborious, she has earned a great deal of money by washing and ironing. With these hard earnings she has purchased ten out of the house of bondage; in some cases receiving her pay by small instalments, in others receiving nothing. The heart of a king may dwell in a pedlar's breast, and right regal may be the soul of a washerwoman. I have another heroine to describe, but must reserve her for my next letter.—L.M.C.

The Iron Shroud

Several years ago, we read, in some English periodical, a very exciting article bearing the above title.[1] It was the story of a prisoner of State, placed in a large dungeon, with iron walls, lighted from the top by fourteen long, narrow windows. The second day of his imprisonment, he could count but thirteen windows; the next day, but twelve; and so on, until he became aware of the awful fact, that the walls of his prison were every day closing in upon him, and must finally crush him in their iron embrace. Again, and again, have we thought of this thrilling story in connection with slavery; and never so much as within the last two years. It becomes more and more obvious that the walls *are* closing in upon the foul system, and that it must inevitably be crushed. Not only is there an immense force of moral influence brought to bear upon it from the whole civilized world, but *events* are closing upon it with tremendous power. Slavery is not merely fighting with a few thousands of abolitionists, or even with the moral convictions of the age; I speak reverently, when I say God himself has visibly entered the lists against her.

How wonderfully has the anti-slavery flame been kindled and fed, through all manner of clouds and tempests! Again, and again, has slavery sent up a triumphant shout that its light had gone out in a fog;—but lo! the fog rolled up, like a curtain, and there, on the mountain-top, blazed the beacon-fire, higher and brighter, kindling hill-sides and valleys with its glow!

My mind is filled with wonder, when I look back upon the rise and progress of this cause, to reflect how, from *every* class of life, and for *every* species of work, there was a laborer raised up, at precisely the moment he was needed. Half a century of silent acquiescence, and of almost unconscious partnership in the guilt of slavery, had wonderfully stupified the moral sense of the people. To speak in the language of metaphor, there was an immense gulf formed, from which issued pestilential vapors, fatal to the nation's health; and it could not, like the famous Roman abyss, be closed by the voluntary sacrifice of one victim.[2] It was necessary for hundreds and thou-

Editorial, *National Anti-Slavery Standard*, 3 March 1842, pp. 154–55.

1. Child reprinted "The Iron Shroud. A Tale of Italy" in the *National Anti-Slavery Standard* 8 and 15 Dec. 1842, 108, 112.

2. Child is comparing the moral "gulf" of the American nation's acquiescence in slavery to the legendary chasm that opened in the middle of the Roman forum in 362 B.C. When soothsayers prophesied that the abyss could be closed only by the sacrifice of Rome's most

sands of the brave and disinterested to throw themselves in, and thus form a safe bridge for the timid and the time-serving to pass over. How nobly they came up to the work—eager to be trampled on! We had, indeed, no Curtius, with horse and armor; for we had no need of the *soldier's* aid. But the merchant came with his wealth; the author with his popularity; woman with her social influence; the scholar, and the rich man's son, surrendering all that gave them name or place; the slaveholder relinquishing his slaves; the bigot throwing away his prejudices; yeoman and mechanic, with the whole of their free, honest hearts; and hardest of all, the clergyman giving up parish popularity, and the good opinion of his brotherhood. All were needed, all came, and all were sacrificed. Of all may it be said, "the places that once knew them, know them no more."[3] Rank and popularity are gone; and those who look on the surface of things, say that they have lost all social influence also. What matter?—They have formed the bridge, and the people are pouring over it *en masse.*

And all along our course, *events,* which we could neither forsee nor control, have aided us with miraculous power. It is curious now to imagine what might have been the present state of things, if Garrison had never been imprisoned at Baltimore for publishing an article against a slavetrading yankee, and if the kind heart of Arthur Tappan [had] not been stirred thereby to pay his fine of a thousand dollars.[4]

In our small beginnings, the Faculty of Lane Seminary,[5] did us most important service. For the sake of securing southern patronage, they made a

---

precious asset, the soldier Marcus Curtius leaped into it on horseback, proclaiming that nothing could be worth more than a Roman citizen.

3. Quoted freely from Job 7.10: "He shall return no more to his house, neither shall his place know him any more."

4. As coeditor of the *Genius of Universal Emancipation* in Baltimore, William Lloyd Garrison (1805–79) accused the Newburyport, Massachusetts, merchant Francis Todd of engaging in slave trading. Though the charge was justified, Todd had Garrison fined $100 (not $1,000, as Child alleges) and jailed for libel in 1830. The wealthy New York merchant Arthur Tappan (1786–1865), a financial mainstay of both evangelical causes and the abolitionist movement, paid Garrison's fine and thus secured his release. Further radicalized by this experience, Garrison went on to found his famous newspaper, *The Liberator,* on 1 January 1831.

5. In 1834 the students of the newly founded Lane Theological Seminary in Cincinnati, Ohio, many of them sons of slaveholders, held an eighteen-day debate over the relative merits of immediate abolition and colonization as means of ending slavery. Led by Theodore Dwight Weld (1803–95), the debate culminated in the conversion to abolition of all but one student. When the trustees, faculty, and president of Lane, Lyman Beecher (1775–1863), the father of Harriet Beecher Stowe, forbade the students to continue their antislavery activism, which included literacy work among Cincinnati's African American community, the students deserted Lane and went on to become antislavery lecturers.

strong effort to suppress the utterance of free thought; and thus they sent forth the flower of the institution to become anti-slavery lectures, at a time when they were most needed. In the words of George Thompson, "these young men were firebrands, which Dr. Beecher, finding too hot for his hands to manage, threw from him, and scattered all over the land."[6]

The outrage on the United States mail, the murder of Lovejoy, the Boston and New York mobs, the burning of Pennsylvania Hall, and innumerable other incidents of the same character, all conspired to do our work, in a manner perceptible enough to *us*, though not to the world.[7] Slaveholders and their abettors have been our most powerful agents from the beginning; and they will be so unto the end. They cannot help it, let them resolve as much discretion as they may; their free-will is evermore girt round by the iron ring of necessity, forged by the circumstance of their own false position.—Would it have been safe for their system to have Congress receive petitions for its abolition, and allow free discussion thereon? Most manifestly not. So they made war upon the right of petition, and thus compelled the North, grievously against her will, to calculate the value of the Union.

And how strange it is that a man should have been educated and trained, as it were, for thirty years, on purpose to do our work in Congress. John Quincy Adams[8] has long been behind the scenes, in the great game of poli-

6. For an account of the British abolitionist George Thompson (1804–78), see "Letters from New-York," number 33, reprinted in this volume.

7. Child is referring to some of the most notorious incidents of antiabolitionist violence: the July 1835 attack on the U.S. post office in Charleston, South Carolina, where a mob ransacked the mail for abolitionist publications, threw them into a bonfire, and burned effigies of prominent abolitionist leaders in a mock lynching; the 1837 mob murder of the abolitionist editor Elijah Lovejoy; the attempted lynching of Garrison by a mob that disrupted a meeting of the Boston Female Anti-Slavery Society and vandalized the Massachusetts Anti-Slavery Society's office in October 1835; the July 1834 riot in New York that targeted African American neighborhoods as well as the homes of wealthy white abolitionists; and the burning down of Pennsylvania Hall in Philadelphia, newly erected with abolitionist funds, during a mob attack on the Convention of Anti-Slavery Women in May 1838.

8. Beginning in 1836, abolitionists tried to inundate Congress with petitions against those aspects of slavery over which the federal government had jurisdiction, such as the interstate slave trade, the legality of slavery and the slave trade in the District of Columbia, and the threatened annexation of Texas. In response, Congress passed a "gag rule" automatically tabling all petitions relating to slavery without discussion or mention in the written record. The gag rule remained in effect from 1836 till 1844. After his defeat for a second term in 1828, ex-president John Quincy Adams (1767–1848) won election to the House of Representatives, where he defended the right of petition and attempted to present his Massachusetts constituents' antislavery petitions despite the ban.

tics. He knows all the dirty bell-ropes, phosphoric lightning, and tin-kettle thunder. He knows too much to be afraid, and far too much not to be feared. He has been President of the United States, and, like his father, thrown out of office by the slaveholding power. If this has not embittered his feelings, it has at least made him keenly observing of southern trickery and usurpation.— Thus has the South, in no small degree, prepared *him* for the arduous task, which he performs like a brave old giant. Long may his mortal frame be kept strong enough to do the work of mind and heart!

But of all events having an important bearing on our cause, there is none so remarkable as the case of the Amistad.[9] That those Africans should have been cast upon *our* shores, of all the shores of this wide earth; that they should have entered a *northern,* instead of a southern port; that public opinion should have been wrought up, by preceding events, to just the right pitch to make the proper moral *improvement* of these incidents; that the slaveholding influence in the Supreme Court should have been diminished by the sudden death of a Judge; truly these things are wonderful!

Not less wonderful is the fact, that the Amistad case should have prepared the way for the Creole.[10] A few years ago, Madison Washington would have been dismissed by the American press as a "base wretch," "a cut-throat," &c. Now the press of the free States, with few exceptions, utters no condemnation, while very many pour forth expressions of sympathy, not unmingled with admiration. The spontaneous gushings of the popular heart in favor of the Amistad captives doubtless performed a large share of this work.

The South itself is in a state of intense fermentation. In Kentucky is a strong party in favor of getting rid of slavery. Western Virginia can scarcely repress her murmurings against the foul system; but lately, they were uttered in a petition to Congress for abolition.[11] Virginia is moreover in an angry

9. See Child's account of the *Amistad* captives in "Letters from New-York," number 12, 2 Dec. 1841, reprinted in this volume.

10. On 7 November 1841, 135 slaves aboard the *Creole,* an American slave-trading vessel en route from Hampton Roads, Virginia, to New Orleans, overpowered the crew, killed one white man, and forced the officers to sail to the British port of Nassau in the Bahamas, where they were freed. Madison Washington was the leader of the *Creole* revolt.

11. West Virginia, which would secede from Virginia during the Civil War and pass a state constitution abolishing slavery, had a majority population of nonslaveholders but was underrepresented in the Virginia legislature as a result of apportionment laws that favored slaveholders in the eastern part of the state. The smoldering conflict between western and eastern Virginia flared up after the 1840 census revealed that the western white population outnumbered the eastern by more than two thousand. Westerners unsuccessfully demanded a constitu-

snarl with New York, whose free-law loco-motive ran against her baggage car, called "Peculiar Institution," on the high-way of State intercourse.[12] This gives birth to lively discussion between proprietors and passengers of the two cars, of which the results will prove most significant. Maryland, in distress for her runaway "property," strives to hold a convention to secure it. Ashamed of her own secrets, she imprisons a peaceable northern reporter, and all the free States hiss thereat, to her great annoyance; and to increase her troubles, the more religious portion of her own citizens rise to rebuke her doings.[13] South Carolina is in a fury with Great Britain about her shipwrecked slaves;[14] yet can she in no wise refrain from making common cause with Virginia in her battle with New York. Louisiana terrified at the increasing population and wealth of the free blacks, at the vicinity of the British West Indies, and the

---

tional convention to address their grievances. In the *Standard* of 10 February 1842, p. 143, Child had reported under the "Congressional" column that on 29 January a petition for the abolition of slavery in the District of Columbia, signed by ninety-three men in Lewis County, Virginia, a region settled by nonslaveholding migrants from Pennsylvania, had been received by Congressman J. M. Botts of Virginia, who had refused to present it.

12. Child is referring to the ongoing dispute between the two states over New York governor William H. Seward's refusal to comply with Virginia's demand that several African American citizens of New York, charged with abetting the escape of fugitive slaves, be extradited to stand trial in Virginia. New York also allowed apprehended fugitive slaves a jury trial—a right southern states were seeking to abolish. Through her train metaphor, Child is evoking the Underground Railroad and comparing the law of freedom, which treats human beings as agents with the right of unrestricted locomotion, to the law of slavery, which treats human beings as "baggage" or property.

13. In response to increasing numbers of slave escapes, blamed on the state's large population of free African Americans, Maryland slaveholders held a convention in Annapolis in January 1842, at which they proposed draconian laws to tighten restrictions on manumissions, impose more severe penalties for aiding runaways, and strip free African Americans of rights they had hitherto exercised, forcing them to choose between emigration and quasi slavery. The *Standard* of 24 Feb., p. 151, reported a protest by Baltimore Quakers against the proposed measures, which were ultimately defeated by nonslaveholders who depended on free black labor. The Massachusetts abolitionist Charles T. Torrey was arrested and jailed when he attended the slaveholders' convention to report on it for the *Emancipator*.

14. Besides supporting Virginia in the dispute with New York (see note 12 above), South Carolina and Georgia were engaged in disputes with Maine, Massachusetts, and England over the Negro Seamen Acts, under which black sailors on board ships touching at southern ports, or shipwrecked on southern shores, were imprisoned at the ships' expense and threatened with sale as slaves unless their captains paid their jail costs. Georgia and Virginia called for the quarantining of ships from Maine and New York; Maine, on the other hand, complained that southern domination of Congress had resulted in curtailing New England states' once profitable trade with the British West Indies because the South feared the influence of the West Indies' newly emancipated slaves. Child may also be referring to Britain's role in liberating the slave rebels of the *Creole* (see note 10 above).

exertion of English influence in Cuba, finds time likewise to join hands with Virginia and South Carolina in this crusade.[15] Georgia does the same, though her old slave controversy with Maine is still unsettled. All combine together, and in their far-sighted wisdom, pass non-intercourse and inspection laws, which clash with the Constitution. Thus again does the southern whip drive the North to calculate the value of the Union. Mississippi is groaning aloud under her State debts, incurred in part for the purchase of slaves, and involving suits in the Supreme Court of the United States destined to have a very important bearing on the issue between slavery and freedom.

Then comes the heavy unpaid *debts* of the South, moving northern merchants, manufacturers, and mechanics, to execrations altogether irreverent toward the sacred Union;[16] and in the midst of the curses, not a few are brought to see and acknowledge that it can in no degree be profitable for communities to eat their own laborers. To this the South replies that the laborers eat their masters; the North responds that she grows daily more dubious whether a partnership in such victualling establishment can be in any wise advantageous.

Then come ship-loads of East India cotton,[17] and the phantoms of thousands more, across the already choked-up path of the "peculiar institution;" whereat statesmen utter a chorus of howls, which avail nothing.

It were well for the South to pause, and ask herself with whom she is playing her desperate game, when she finds herself thus check-mated at every turn.

On one side is all Europe, combined with South America, and even Texas,

15. The *Liberator* of 24 December 1841, p. 206, had reprinted an article from the *New Orleans Bee,* reporting that the British consul in Cuba was seeking to secure the emancipation of slaves transferred from Jamaica to Cuba by their owner. The 1834 abolition of slavery in the British West Indies and an 1820 treaty with Spain outlawing the slave trade in Cuba and other Spanish colonies made such exportation doubly illegal. Child refers in the last paragraph of her editorial to international efforts to suppress the slave trade.

16. In the wake of the Panic of 1837, cotton prices were low, and southern planters squeezed for cash were unable to repay their debts to northern merchants and manufacturers. The *Liberator* had reported on such complaints in an article titled "Trade with the South," 29 Oct. 1841, p. 174. In the *Standard* of 24 February 1842, p. 149, Child reprinted an article from the *Pittsburgh Gazette,* "Cause of Hard Times," which estimated northern losses at over three hundred million dollars and referred to "the universal bankruptcy of northern dealers in southern trade."

17. In the *Standard* of 14 October 1841, Child had reprinted a long article from *Hunt's Merchant Magazine* citing figures to show that Britain would soon find it cheaper to substitute cotton, sugar, and rice produced by "free" labor in India for the raw materials produced by slave labor in the South. Abolitionists hoped that such economic forces would help bring about emancipation.

for the suppression of the slave trade. On the other, is the United States separated from the civilized world, trying to stretch her starry flag over the foul enormity. Between the two lies war with England. For the back-ground of that battle piece, see the British West Indies, swarming with black troops, who well remember what slavery is; Haiti, with its vivid recollections, and active sympathies, all arrayed against slavery; Mexico, with abundant cause to hate the United States, particularly the southern portion of it; and the Indians, swarming on our borders, with long arrears of wrong to settle, after their fashion, with tomahawk and scalping knife. These wrongs, too, are linked with slavery; for what is our "Great Florida Negro Hunt," but a war for the right of kidnapping Indian babes, by mothers once held as slaves?[18] To crown all, the focus around which these inflammable materials are collecting, is the gathering-place for slaves of the worst description. Does a slave commit a crime? He is sold to the southwest. Is he so intelligent, or so violent, as to be considered dangerous? He is sold to the southwest. Is he suspected of plotting insurrection? He is sold to the southwest; there to be goaded into fury by severity greater than that from which he escapes.

Surely the walls *are* closing around slavery.—L.M.C.

18. American settlers in Texas had won independence from Mexico in 1836, but the state remained too sparsely populated to be economically viable; hence Texans were weighing the advantages of annexation by the United States versus development assistance by England (on condition that Texas remain independent and agree to abolish slavery). It was feared that an American attempt to annex Texas might lead to war with both Mexico and England. Child suggests that in such a war, the newly emancipated slaves of the British West Indies, the Haitians who had overthrown slavery and founded a black republic in 1804, and the Indians driven off their land by proslavery expansionists would unite with Mexico and England against the United States. The "Great Florida Negro Hunt" was the Seminole War of 1835–42, one of whose pretexts was that slaves were escaping into Florida and living among the Seminole Indians. When the United States finally defeated the combined Seminole and African American forces, slaveholders claimed as their property not only fugitive slaves who had intermarried with the Seminole, but their offspring as well.

Talk about Political Party

 A. I wish you would explain to me the position of the American Society with regard to political action.

B. In good truth, I am weary of explaining what appears to my own mind so perfectly clear, that I cannot easily imagine how it can seem obscure to any one. The American Society stands on precisely the same principles that it did the first year of its formation. Its object was to change public opinion on the subject of slavery, by the persevering utterance of truth. This change they expected would show itself in a thousand different forms;—such as conflict and separation in churches; new arrangements in colleges and schools; new customs in stages and cars;[1] and new modifications of policy in the political parties of the day. The business of anti-slavery was, and is, to purify the *fountain,* whence all these streams flow; if it turns aside to take charge of any *one* of the streams, however important, it is obvious enough that the whole work must retrograde; for, if the fountain be not kept pure, no one of the streams will flow with clear water. But just so sure as the fountain is taken proper care of, the character of all the streams *must* be influenced thereby. We might form ourselves into a railroad society, to furnish cars with the same conveniences for all complexions; but we feel that we are doing a far more effectual work, so to change popular opinion, that there will be no *need* of a separate train of cars. We might expend all our funds and energies in establishing abolition colleges; but we feel sure, that we have the power in our hands to abolitionize *all* colleges. With this reliance on the might of moral influence, the American Society started; and her faith in it is undiminished. Many have faltered by the way, on account of sectarian attachments, or an honest fear of being implicated in the advancement of other things which they did not approve, or from impatience to do up the arduous work by a quicker method. Some of these have misunderstood us, others have intentionally misrepresented; but through all forms of mistake and calumny, the American Society stands on precisely the same basis it did at the outset.

A. I cannot myself tell in what particular it has changed; but I know it is

National Anti-Slavery Standard, 7 July 1842, pp. 18–19.

1. On the discrimination African Americans faced in educational and transportation facilities, see chapter 8 of *An Appeal in Favor of That Class of Americans Called Africans,* reprinted in this volume. In 1842 abolitionists were vigorously protesting against segregated railway cars, a campaign in which Frederick Douglass was playing a leading role.

very common to hear people say, that they have no choice except between Non-resistance and Liberty party.[2]

B. As it is a very common *ruse* for whigs and democrats to stigmatize each other as abolitionists, for the purpose of exciting popular odium, so is it a common devise of the third party to stigmatize all abolitionists, who do not co-operate with them, as non-resistants. Political trickery is alike in its character, under all forms. If "Liberty party" writers and editors are not aware of the fact that the American Society no more endorses non-resistance, than it does baptism, or Unitarianism, or Calvinism, or homeopathy, it certainly is not for the want of means of information. Probably not ten in a thousand of the American Society are non-resistants; but when it was demanded by some that these ten *should* vote, or else be turned out of the society, a very large number arrayed themselves against it; because such a proceeding would violate the very principles of freedom, on which our platform rests.[3] Had any one proposed that abolitionists should *not* be allowed to vote, a majority would have stood equally strong to protect freedom on *that* side. Had the Quaker demanded that those should be turned out of the society who endeavored to advance the cause by stated prayer, every liberal mind would have resisted the test, as a violation of freedom; and if the Calvinist had made an opposite demand, the feeling would have been the same.

A. But you advise people not to vote for pro-slavery candidates, and not to join the liberty party; if this isn't non-resistance in practice, I don't know what is.

B. The difficulty in your mind arises, I think, from want of faith in the efficiency of moral influence. You cannot see that you act on politics *at all,* unless you join the caucus, and assist in electioneering for certain individuals; whereas you may, in point of fact, refuse co-operation, and thereby exert a

2. The doctrine of non-resistance, held by Garrison and a minority of his followers, condemned any recourse to physical force and refused allegiance to human government as by definition coercive; consequently, non-resistants did not vote, although they did not require other abolitionists to abstain from voting. Evangelical abolitionists denounced the doctrine on both religious and political grounds. The Liberty party was founded by political abolitionists in 1840 as an alternative to the Whig and Democratic parties, on the one hand, and non-resistance, on the other. The former Kentucky slaveholder James G. Birney served as the party's first presidential candidate in the elections of 1840 and 1844. The party won only a few votes in these elections, but siphoned off antislavery voters from the major parties, especially the Whigs.

3. In 1839, political abolitionists attempted to force non-resistants out of the movement by proposing a resolution that all abolitionists who had the right to vote must exercise it. Garrisonian abolitionists defeated the measure and defined a broad platform leaving all abolitionists free to act against slavery in whatever ways their consciences dictated.

tenfold influence on the destiny of parties. In Massachusetts, for instance, before the formation of a distinct abolition political party, both parties were afraid of the abolitionists; both wanted their votes; and therefore members of both parties in the legislature were disposed to grant their requests. All, who take note of such things, can remember how the legislature seemed to be abolitionized, as it were, by miracle. "The anti-slavery folks are coming strong this session," said a member to a leading democrat; "they want a hearing on five or six subjects, at least." "Give 'em *all* they ask," replied the leader; "we can't afford to offend them." When a similar remark was made to a whig leader, the same session, his answer was, "Concede everything; it wont do to throw them into the arms of the democrats." Now, there is a third party in Massachusetts, the two great parties have much less motive to please the abolitionists. Last year, the legislature of that State seemed to have gone back on anti-slavery, as fast as it once went forward. In Vermont, the system of refusing co-operation produced the effect of inducing both whigs and democrats to put up an abolition candidate, in order to secure abolition votes; neither party was willing to give its opponent the advantage that might be gained by pleasing this troublesome class. Had we never turned aside from this plan, I believe the political influence of anti-slavery would have been an hundred fold greater than it now is.

A. But after all, these legislators that you speak of, were not made genuine abolitionists, or else they would not slip back so easily. I want to see the Statehouse filled with true anti-slavery men.

B. Those men, let me tell you, did the *work* of sound anti-slavery; and *in* doing it, got imbued more or less with anti-slavery sentiment, in spite of themselves. The machinery of a third political party may send into Congress, or the halls of State legislation, a few individuals, who are anti-slavery to the back-bone. But could *one* Alvan Stuart do as much for our cause in Congress, as *twenty* of Joshua R. Giddings?[4] Fifty men who have a strong motive for obliging the abolitionists, could surely *do* more for our cause, in such a position, than merely two or three radical abolitionists. I too want to see *all* our legislators anti-slavery; but when that time comes, there will most ob-

4. Alvan Stewart (1790–1849), a leading political abolitionist, helped found the Liberty party. Congressman Joshua Giddings of Ohio (1795–1864) represented his antislavery constituency in the Western Reserve as a Whig from 1838 on and joined John Quincy Adams in defending the right of petition. Child's point is that even if Giddings may have been politically less radical than Stewart, he acted more effectively in favor of the abolitionist cause as a member of a major political party. She also argues that larger numbers of antislavery representatives could be elected to Congress under the aegis of the major parties than as members of a small fringe party.

viously be no *need* of a distinct abolition party; and in order to bring about that time, we must diligently exert *moral influence* to sway *all* parties; so we move round in a circle, and come back to where we started from. As for purity of *motive,* in those who aid anti-slavery politically, do you think the "Liberty party" runs the chance of more thorough and disinterested recruits? Look around you, in every part of the country, and see how many belong to that party, who were never before heard of as abolitionists! how many, that up to the date of their joining, even opposed abolition! In one county, you see democrats joining with "liberty party," pro tem. to defeat the election of a whig, which they could not accomplish by their own unaided strength; in another county, you will see a transient accession of whigs to defeat a demo-cratic candidate. Are these elements any purer to work with, or any more to be relied on, than the legislators of Massachusetts, who were willing to give the abolitionists everything they asked? I never doubted that large numbers of the third party were influenced by perfectly honest motives, and were sincere abolitionists; but I do say, that by the natural laws of attraction, their party will draw around them the selfish and the ambitious; and this they will find to their cost, much as they may scorn the prediction now.

A. But if party machinery does as much mischief to moral influence as you think, how can you work with whigs or democrats? You talked just now of making them *both* set up candidates that would be afraid to go wrong on this question.

B. By adhering closely to moral influence, we work *through* both parties, but not *with* them. They do *our* work; we do not *their's.* We are simply the atmosphere that makes the quicksilver rise or fall.

A. But you say by your plan, men will eventually have more freedom to vote as conscience dictates on other subjects, without being false to anti-slavery principles. If politics are so polluting as non-resistants suppose, how can they do this?

B. Into the question of non-resistance, I do not enter; not from disrespect, or to avoid odium; but simply because it does not belong to the anti-slavery enterprise. Long and long before non-resistants were heard of, religious men, of all denominations, took note of the polluting tendency of political par-tisanship. Thus John Newton[5] says: "From poison and politics, good Lord deliver us. The *crooked* things I would leave to Him who alone can make them

---

5. After undergoing a conversion experience, the former British slave trader John Newton (1725–1807) repented and became a leading antislavery advocate, as well as an evangelical preacher. The quotation remains unidentified.

straight. Politics is a pit, which will swallow up the life and spirit, if not the form of religion." My own observation abundantly confirms the truth of this. I decide for no man, whether he ought to vote, or not; that lies between his own conscience and his God. An overwhelming majority of the American Society consider it both a privilege and a duty. It is obvious enough that the debasing tendency of caucusing, and party management, and party strife, need not reach the quiet citizen, who simply deposits his vote for what he deems good men and measures.

A. But if you believe many liberty party men to be honest and sincere, why need you quarrel with them[?]

B. I do not quarrel with them; and most earnestly do I wish they could understand me as speaking my own convictions, without any admixture of partisan jealousy, or personal unkindness. I believe that the tendency of their scheme is to weaken our cause; I believe it has greatly retarded its progress, and will retard it more; I believe that it is of vast importance to keep alive the old-fashioned anti-slavery, whose work it was to purify the *fountain* of public opinion, and thence affect the streams, political and ecclesiastical. Therefore I deem it absolutely necessary to warn our agents, and others, against *admixture* with this policy. I do not ask them to make war; I only beseech them to keep clear of it.

A. I think you must admit that the South dread anti-slavery at the *ballot-box,* more than anywhere else?

B. Again you return to your idea that the ballot-box cannot be affected, except by a distinct abolition *party.* I never doubted that political action would be a powerful engine for the overthrow of slavery. The only question between you and the American Society seems to be, whether the speediest and most extensive political effect would be produced by the *old* scheme of holding the balance between the two parties, or the *new* scheme of forming a distinct party. I apprehend what the slaveholders would like least of all things, would be to see *both* the great political parties consider it for their interest to nominate abolitionists; and this *would* be the case if anti-slavery voters would only be consistent and firm.

A. Ah, there is the pinch! They will *not* be consistent and firm. Under the old scheme, they were always coaxed aside to their favorite party banners; one voting for Harrison, and another for Van Buren.[6]

---

6. William Henry Harrison (1773–1841) and incumbent President Martin Van Buren (1782–1862) were the Whig and Democratic candidates in the 1840 presidential election, which Harrison won.

B. And by what superior magic does the "liberty party" expect to keep its allies more closely rallied around *her,* in time of tempting emergency? Will the two-thirds abolitionized democrat, who has joined them to defeat a whig, stand by them when his vote is greatly needed to secure a triumph to his own party, at the polls? Will the half-abolitionized whig, who has been drawn into their ranks, pass safe through the fire of a similar temptation? I trow not.

Men of strong party predilections, favorably inclined to anti-slavery, might be induced to act openly in its favor, if they had the two-fold object of obeying their own consciences, and of gaining all the strength of the abolition voters who were inclined to the same party. But when a distinct abolition party is formed, this stimulus is taken away. In acting with such a party, a man must not only take upon himself the unpopularity of abolition, but must relinquish action upon all other subjects which may seem to him important; such as national bank, tariff, &c. Politicians may be induced to do this for a while; but it is not according to human nature that it should last.— Should the "liberty party" obtain sufficient power to sway the legislation of State or nation, that moment one man will demand action for the tariff, and another against the tariff; they will split, and be swallowed by the great parties from which they seceded; of course, their strength, as a party, will be broken the very moment it could be brought to act.

A. Perhaps legislators would be conscientious enough to sacrifice all minor considerations to anti-slavery.

B. Then their constituents would say their interests on *other* subjects had not been attended to; and they would not vote for them again. A democratic district would not re-elect a man who sustained a national bank, because a majority of the abolition party chose to do it; they could not do so with a clear conscience; and so, vice versa. In the nature of things, abolition cannot be the whole of Church and State; but it can be a moral atmosphere modifying the whole. This difficulty is seen at the outset, in the attempt to form a *church* on anti-slavery grounds. It proposes to include only *evangelical* sects; for the simple reason that these could not conscientiously co-operate with Unitarians, Quakers, Universalists, &c. If they can compromise on minor matters, such as baptism, church discipline, &c. so as to remain united for any considerable length of time, they will work wonders. But in the meantime, an influence is needed to move both orthodox and liberal sects, on this plain question of humanity and justice. Again we have gone round the circle, and come back to *moral influence,* as the legitimate work of anti-slavery.

A. But while people are working for liberty party, they are at the same time exerting moral influence.

B. With sadly diminished power, let me assure you—Their motives are distrusted; suspicion enters the mind, that they may care more for offices than for truth; and they themselves gradually get accustomed to trust more to party machinery, than they do to the potency of truth. The advocates of "liberty party" show a most glaring want of faith in moral influence. Some of them, who used to talk and write as if it could regenerate the world, now speak of it with contumely and scorn.

A. But since the liberty party *is* started, if they set up candidates who are good men and thorough abolitionists, ought we not to vote for them?

B. I believe that is the bait that has hooked half their numbers. Men who consider the third party a hindrance to the cause, yet co-operate with it, because it is started, and its existence cannot be helped. The consequences of this are more important than appears on the surface. One of these elements *destroys the other. Moral* influence dies under *party* action. If you do not see this now, you will see it. Many honest minds will try the experiment, with perfect sincerity of purpose; they will gradually become disgusted with the management and crooked devices, that always spring up in political encounters, and which are sure to increase in proportion as a party gains power; they will lose their confidence in men, if not in principles; they will cease to attend anti-slavery meetings, and will feel disheartened in their efforts for the cause. To some extent, this is already the case. I hope those who think of voting for a "liberty-party" candidate, because they believe him to be a good man, will reflect well whether the limited good they may effect thereby, will not be overbalanced by the harm they will inevitably do in sustaining a fallacious and mischievous scheme.

A. But what am I to do if they really become powerful enough to choose their own candidates, and men of whom I approve?

B. Wait till that time comes, and decide your duty then.—L.M.C.

Letters from New-York, Number 33

It is curious how a single note in the great hymn of Nature sometimes recalls the memories of years—opens whole galleries of soul-painting, stretching far off into the remote perspective of the past. Rambling on the Brooklyn side of the ferry the other evening, I heard the note of a Katy-did.[1] Instantly it flashed upon my recollection, under what impressive circumstances I, for the first time in my life, heard the singular note of that handsome insect. Six years ago, George Thompson[2] accompanied us to New-York. It was August; a month which the persecuted abolitionists were wont to observe brought out a multitude of snakes and southerners. The comparison was made with no sectional hostility, but in reference to the effects such visiters produced on the comfort and safety of ourselves and the colored population. When southern merchants and travellers abound in our cities, the chance is, mobs and kidnappers will abound also.

Times have changed since 1835. Thanks to the despised agency of anti-slavery societies, the abolition sentiment has now spread widely, and taken a firm hold of the sympathies of the people. Moreover, southern trade is in less esteem than it was then; and they who have made us "a nation of bankrupts," have now less to expend for eggs and brick-bats, or to hire the hands that throw them.[3] In 1835, they were in the full tide of successful experiment, and the whole North trembled before them; with the exception of one small but undaunted phalanx. The steamboat, which brought us to New-York,

National Anti-Slavery Standard, 18 August 1842, p. 43; reprinted in *CC* 15/399.

1. katydid: a large grasshopper that produces a loud, shrill sound.

2. George Thompson (1804–78), the British abolitionist whose eloquence was credited with hastening Parliament's passage of the act emancipating the slaves in the British West Indies, toured the United States in 1834–35. Although his speeches electrified antislavery audiences, he encountered so much harassment and violence from proslavery mobs like the one Child describes here that he had to cut short his tour and flee Boston in an open boat. On this occasion the Childs were accompanying him to New York to hide him with antislavery sympathizers there until Boston mobs lost track of him. On revisiting the United States during the Civil War, Thompson received accolades and addressed the U.S. Congress.

3. "nation of bankrupts": the panic of 1837 was widely blamed on unbridled speculation in cotton. Northern merchants and manufacturers involved in the cotton textile industry, who viewed agitation of the slavery question as a threat to their economic partnership with southern cotton growers, joined with the latter in trying to suppress the abolitionist movement; they played an active role in financing, fomenting, and sometimes even leading mob attacks against abolitionists.

was filled with our masters. We saw one after another pointing out George Thompson; and never has it been my fortune to witness such fierce manifestations of hatred written on the human countenance. Men, who a few moments before seemed like polished gentlemen, were suddenly transformed into demons.—They followed close behind us, as we walked the deck, with clenched fists, and uttering the most fearful imprecations. One man, from Georgia, drew a sword from his cane, and swore he would kill whoever dared to say a word against slavery. It was our intention to stop at Newport, to visit a relative; and I was glad that it so happened; for had we gone on, the boat would have arrived in New-York just at dark; and I, for one, had no inclination to land at that hour, with such a set of ferocious characters, to whom our persons were well known, and whom we had observed in whispered consultation, ominous of mischief. We pursued our route the next day, without attracting attention; and fearing that George Thompson would bring ruin to the dwelling of any acquaintance we might visit in the city, we crossed over to Brooklyn, to the house of a friend who had known and loved him in Europe. The katydids were then in full concert; and their name was legion. It was the first time I had ever heard them; and my mind was in that excited state, which made all sounds discordant. We were most hospitably received; yet it was evident that our host had much rather we had staid at home.—He told us that the news of George Thompson's approach had preceded us, and that the most awful excitement prevailed in the city; it was as much as his house was worth, to have it known that the roof covered him.—For his sake, we kept within doors, and avoided the front windows. The next day, he brought over from the city a placard which was posted up on posts, and at street-corners, throughout New-York. I have it now; and never look at it without seeing images of the French revolution. It ran thus:

"That notorious English swindler and vagabond, George Thompson, is now in the city, and supposed to be at the house of Lewis Tappan, No. 40 Rose street. I hereby order my trusty followers to bring him before me, without delay. JUDGE LYNCH."[4]

Mr. Thompson seemed, as he did on all similar occasions, very little disturbed concerning his own danger; but our host was so obviously anxious, that it imparted a degree of uneasiness to us all. That night, I started at every

4. Judge Lynch: a call for lynching Thompson, issued in the name of the eighteenth-century American justice of the peace whose kangaroo courts directed against Tories gave rise to the term. Lewis Tappan (1788–1873) and his brother Arthur (1786–1865) were prominent New York merchants and evangelical abolitionists.

sound; and when the harsh and unusual notes of that army of katydids met my ear, I was again and again deceived by the impression that they were the shouts of a mob in the distance. I shall never be able to get rid of the image thus engraved; to my mind the katydid will forever speak of mobs. I am sorry for it; for it is a pretty creature, and meant me no such harm. The next day, Thompson returned to Boston by a 4 o'clock morning boat. We afterward learned that extensive preparations had been made to mob Lewis Tappan's house, in obedience to the commands of "Judge Lynch." A few southerners, probably those who came in the boat with us, had hired their "trusty followers" to have a ladder in readiness in rear of the building, and proceed in any way most likely to secure Thompson. Luckily, the agents of the intended mischief mentioned it to a political comrade, who had become somewhat infected with abolition himself. He gave information of names, dates, and places; upon which the mayor addressed letters to several gentlemen, warning them of the liabilities they would incur, by this mode of sustaining the "patriarchal institution." Finding their names were known to the authorities, they relinquished their design. Our host was by no means quite reassured, even when Thompson and my husband had both left. I was not of sufficient consequence to endanger anybody; but should I be recognized, it might naturally be reported that Thompson was in the same house. Resolving that no one should incur risk on my account, and being utterly without friends in New-York, I went to a hotel at Bath, and staid there alone. Never, before or since, have I experienced such utter desolation, as I did the few days I remained there. It seemed to me as if anti-slavery had cut me off from all the sympathies of my kind. As I sat there alone, watching the surging sea, I wrote the following lines, for George Thompson's magnificent album. They have been several times printed; but as my reminiscences are busy with him, I will repeat them:

> I've heard thee when thy powerful words
>   Were like the cataract's roar—
> Or like the ocean's mighty waves
>   Resounding on the shore.
>
> But even in reproof of sin,
>   Love brooded over all—
> As the mild rainbow's heavenly arch
> Rests on the waterfall.
>
> I've heard thee in the hour of prayer,
>   When dangers were around:

Thy voice was like the royal harp,
   That breathed a charmed sound.

The evil spirit felt its power,
   And howling turned away;
And some, perchance, "who came to scoff,
   Remained with thee to pray."[5]

I've seen thee, too, in playful mood,
   When words of magic spell
Dropped from thy lips like fairy gems,
   That sparkled as they fell.

Still great and good in every change!
   Magnificent and mild!
As if a seraph's god-like power
   Dwelt in a little child.

Among the various exciting recollections with which Thompson is associated, no one is impressed so deeply on my mind as the 1st of August, 1835. It was the first anniversary of emancipation in the British West Indies; and the abolitionists of Boston proposed to hold a meeting in commemoration of that glorious event. The Tremont House was swarming with southerners; and they swore that George Thompson should not be allowed to speak. The meeting was, however, held at Julian Hall. Few people were there, and I had a chance to observe them all. Near the stairs, was a line of men in fine broadcloth, whom I saw at a glance were slaveholders; the fact was plainly enough written in the clenched fist, the fiercely compressed lip, and the haughty carriage of the head. In front of them were a dozen or more stout truckmen,[6] in shirt sleeves, with faces red enough to make a rain-drop sizzle, if it should chance to fall upon them. Various nods and glances were exchanged between fine broadcloth and shirt sleeves; there seemed to be an understanding between them; they were in fact "the glorious Union." Near the front seats, in the midst of the abolitionists, was an ill-looking fellow, whose bloated countenance, so furious and so sensual, seemed a perfect embodiment of the

5. From the lines describing the village pastor in *The Deserted Village* (1770), by Oliver Goldsmith (1728–74): "Truth from his lips prevail'd with double sway, / And fools, who came to scoff, remain'd to pray" (1. 179–80).

6. truckmen: members of a fire department unit that operates a hook-and-ladder truck; volunteer fire companies were bastions of the Democratic party's working-class constituency, tightly allied with its other main constituency, southern planters. The groups that sought to suppress agitation against slavery claimed to be acting to preserve the Union.

French revolution. A genteel-looking young man, with nice gloves, and white fur hat, held frequent whispered consultations with this vile-looking personage. It seemed to me a strange alliance. I inquired who the white hat was, and was told that it was Mr. Stetson, bar-keeper of the Tremont. I mentioned this fact to my husband, who saw in it the same significance that I did.

Thompson came in late, while S. J. May[7] was speaking. Fine broadcloth pointed thumbs at him significantly, shirt sleeves nodded, and white hat whispered to M. Guillotine.[8] My heart throbbed violently; I saw that there were well-managed preparations for a savage mob. Thompson could not have been unconscious of this, even if violent threats had not reached him before he came. Yet he was perfectly self-collected; and such burning torrents of eloquence as he poured forth, I never before listened to! There was nothing vulgar or vindictive, but it scorched like the lightning. The southerners writhed under it; the truckmen were amazed. He described what the foul system *was* that had been destroyed in the British West Indies; what it was, and must be, in all countries, and under all governments.—He told of the negroes' gratitude, and of their midnight chorus of prayer and praise. Then, in tones deep and solemn, like an old cathedral bell, he added, slowly, "It is the death-knell of American slavery!"

Excited by the powerful eloquence, and goaded with rage, the southerners rose in a body, and with loud stamping, left the hall. The truckmen went tearing down stairs after them, like so many furies. When the noise subsided, Thompson, half smiling, said, "Since the gentlemen for whose especial benefit I have been speaking have withdrawn, I will soon finish my remarks." Their allies had not all withdrawn, however; for well do I remember the dark and threatening scowls that followed this cool declaration.

When the meeting closed, the heart of every abolitionist beat with a quickened pulse, for Thompson's safety. From time to time, the fierce, impatient faces of the truckmen, were seen above the staircase; their courage evidently reinforced by fresh supplies of rum, paid for by southern generosity. Abolitionists, who left the meeting, came back to tell that the stairway and entry were lined with desperate-looking fellows, brandishing clubs and

7. Samuel J. May (1797–1871), a Unitarian minister, was one of Garrison's earliest abolitionist converts.

8. Continuing the analogy between the rule of proslavery mobs in the United States and the Reign of Terror that followed the French Revolution, during which large numbers of citizens suspected of counterrevolutionary sympathies were executed at the guillotine, Child calls the leader of the anti-Thompson mob "M. Guillotine."

cart-whips; and that a carriage, with the steps down, stood close to the door. I did not then know that a train was laid by our friends for Thompson's escape. All I could do, was to join with the women, who formed a dense circle around him; a species of troops in much requisition at that period, and well known by the name of "Quaker militia."[9] My husband, in the meantime, being acquainted with the bar-keeper of the Tremont, entered into conversation with him, and held him by the coat-button, to his most visible annoyance. Near the platform where the speakers had stood, was a private door, leading, by a flight of back stairs, into a store-room, that opened into another street than the front entrance. The mob were either ignorant of this entrance, or forgetful; but our friends were neither. One of our number held the key; a second had engaged a carriage, with swift horses, and a colored driver; a third made a signal from a window, for the carriage to approach the store communicating with the back passage. Holding Thompson in friendly chat, the women, as it were quite accidentally, approached the private door. The circle opened—the door opened—a volley of oaths from the truckmen, and a deafening rush down the front stairs—but where was *he?*

For a few agonizing moments, we who remained in the hall could not answer. But presently, S. J. May came to us, with a face like Carara marble, and breathed, rather than uttered, the welcome words, "Thank God! he's safe!"

Their carriage was in readiness, to convey him to a southern vessel, and an ignominious death; but he entered *our* carriage, and was off like the wind; though the mob turned the corner of the building quick enough to clutch at the wheels, as they started.

Much as southerners hated George Thompson, he was the very man they would have peculiarly admired, had any other subject than slavery been the theme of his eloquence. His bold frankness, his earnest enthusiasm, his rapid changes from the thrilling to the comic—the spontaneous heartiness of his whole character and manner, were all well calculated to please southern taste. Mr. Kingsley,[10] of Florida, fully concurred in this sentiment. "I've heard many

9. Because mobs did not dare to assault white "ladies," women frequently acted as bodyguards for male abolitionists in the manner Child describes. The term *Quaker militia* refers ironically to the Quakers' well known pacifism.

10. In "Letters from New-York," number 30, which appeared in the *Standard* on 7 July 1842, Child had described the eccentric Florida slaveholder Z. Kinsley (Zephaniah Kingsley, 1765–1843), author of "a very odd pamphlet" titled *A Treatise on the Patriarchal, or Co-operative System of Society as It Exists in Some Governments, and Colonies in America, and in the United*

public speakers in my life-time," said he, "but I never but once heard elo-quence to be compared to George Thompson. His only equal, in my estima-tion, was Sheridan, an emancipated slave, sent out to Africa, by the coloniza-tion society. The planters used to ride miles and miles to hear him; and all agreed that they never heard so great a natural orator. I used to tell them, 'Hear George Thompson, and he'll captivate you, in spite of your teeth.'"

No effort of Thompson's ever *surprised* me more than his discussion with R. R. Gurley,[11] in Boston. No one who had lived here from the first concep-tion of the colonization society, could have brought a greater amount of in-formation to bear on that treacherous scheme. It was a beautiful sight, to see his manly directness and eloquent sincerity, in contrast with Mr. Gurley's je-suitical evasions, hair-splitting subtlety, and cunning appeals to popular prej-udice. I shall never forget the expressive beauty of his countenance, and the gracefulness of his unstudied attitude, as he stood with his cloak folded about him, like some fine old statue, and answered Mr. Gurley's reiterated sneers at England: "I rejoice to hear the guilt charged upon England. Yes, heap it upon erring, sinning England! Mountains on mountains, till it reaches to the skies! So much the more need that I, a humble representative of England, should strive to *atone* for the mischief she has done. As you have copied England in her *sin,* copy her in her *repentance!*"

This devoted friend of humanity is now exerting his admirable powers to the utmost, for the repeal of the corn laws, and the oppressed in the East Indies.[12] The respect and love of thousands of England's best and noblest spirits follow him wherever he goes. The proscribed of America is the idol of Great Britain. Yet he writes to me, "I long, impatiently and painfully, again to tread the shores of America; not merely to grasp those I love by the hand, but to share again the labors and sufferings of the devoted ones who are still striving to sustain the standard of freedom and equality—to endure the *extra*

States under the Name of Slavery, with Its Necessity and Advantages (1829). Taking the unusual view that "the free people of colour . . . ought to be made eligible to all offices and means of wealth," Kingsley lived openly with an African wife. His admiration of Thompson was no doubt equally atypical for a proslavery southerner.

11. Ralph Randolph Gurley (1797–1872) served as agent, secretary, vice president, and life director of the American Colonization Society, whose program for repatriating African Ameri-cans to Africa was strongly opposed by abolitionists.

12. The corn laws levied taxes on imported grain, driving up food prices for the poor. As a member of the Anti–Corn Law League (founded in 1838) and the British India Association (1839–43), George Thompson worked to revoke the corn laws (a goal accomplished in 1849) and to promote land reform and improved living and working conditions for the Indian poor.

persecution which would be awarded to me, the most obnoxious and hated being that ever stood on American soil. But my work is here; and I must not permit inclination to be my guide. Never, for a moment, think my zeal in your cause has abated. The links that bind me to you are as bright and strong as ever; and if God permits, I hope yet to realize the cherished wish of my heart, and see you again, though it be but for a short time. Oh, how distinct are the scenes we have passed through together. Your attendance at my lectures; the Gurley debate; those trying scenes at Brooklyn; the farewell, when Judge Lynch was announced at New York. Oh, how vivid are all these memories, though seven years have rolled away! God bless you both, and those who labor with you to advance the best of causes."

I never saw George Thompson again, after that hurried farewell at morning twilight, when "Judge Lynch" was lying in wait for him. He left the country a few months after.—L.M.C.

Slavery's Pleasant Homes

A FAITHFUL SKETCH

> 'Thy treasures of gold
> Are dim with the blood of the hearts thou hast sold;
> Thy home may be lovely, but round it I hear
> The crack of the whip, and the footsteps of fear.'[1]

When Frederic Dalcho brought his young bride from New-Orleans to her Georgian home, there were great demonstrations of joy among the slaves of the establishment,—dancing, shouting, clapping of hands, and eager invocations of blessing on the heads of 'massa and missis'; for well they knew that he who manifested most zeal was likely to get the largest coin, or the brightest handkerchief.

The bride had been nurtured in seclusion, almost as deep as that of the oriental harem.[2] She was a pretty little waxen plaything, as fragile and as delicate as the white Petunia blossom. She brought with her two slaves. Mars, a stalwart mulatto, of good figure, but a cunning and disagreeable expression of countenance. Rosa, a young girl, elegantly formed, and beautiful as a dark velvet carnation. The blush, so easily excited, shone through the transparent brown of her smooth cheek, like claret through a bottle in the sunshine. It was a beautiful contrast to see her beside her mistress, like a glittering star in attendance upon the pale and almost vanishing moonsickle. They had grown up from infancy together; for the mother of Rosa was foster-mother of Marion; and soon as the little white lady could speak, she learned to call Rosa *her* slave. As they grew older, the wealthy planter's daughter took pride in her servant's beauty, and loved to decorate her with jewels. 'You shall wear my

---

The Liberty Bell (1843), pp. 147–160.

1. From "The Yankee Girl" (1835), an antislavery poem by John Greenleaf Whittier (1807–92). Perhaps because she considered the story too radical for a general audience, Child did not include "Slavery's Pleasant Homes" in her 1846 collection, *Fact and Fiction*. See Carolyn L. Karcher, *The First Woman in the Republic: A Cultural Biography of Lydia Maria Child*, for a discussion of the story and its sources.

2. Child is drawing an analogy between the southern plantation household and the Islamic harem, in which the wives and concubines of wealthy men lived hidden from the public gaze. The analogy suggests both the sexual license of the slaveholder and the slavelike status of the southern white woman.

golden ornaments whenever you ask for them,' said she; 'they contrast so well with the soft, brown satin of your neck and arms. I will wear pearls and amethysts; but gold needs the dark complexion to show its richness. Besides, you are a handsome creature, Rosa, and gold is none too good for you.'

Her coachman, Mars, was of the same opinion: but the little petted coquette tossed her graceful head at him, and paid small heed to his flattering words. Not so with George, the handsome quadroon brother of Frederic Dalcho, and his favorite slave; but the master and mistress were too much absorbed with their own honey-moon, to observe them. Low talks among the rose-bushes, and stolen meetings by moonlight, passed unnoticed, save by the evil eyes of Mars. Thus it passed on for months. The young slaves had uttered the marriage vow to each other, in the silent presence of the stars.

It chanced, one day, that Rosa was summoned to the parlor to attend her mistress, while George stood respectfully, hat in hand, waiting for a note, which his master was writing. She wore about her neck a small heart and cross of gold, which her lover had given her the night before. He smiled archly, as he glanced at it, and the answer from her large, dark eyes was full of joyful tenderness. Unfortunately, the master looked up at that moment, and at once comprehended the significance of that beaming expression. He saw that it spoke whole volumes of mutual, happy love; and it kindled in him an unholy fire. He has never before realized that the girl was so very handsome. He watched her, as she pursued her work, until she felt uneasy beneath his look. From time to time, he glanced at his young wife. She, too, was certainly very lovely; but the rich, mantling beauty of the slave had the charm of novelty. The next day, he gave her a gay dress; and when he met her among the garden shrubbery, he turned her glossy ringlets over his finger, and called her a pretty darling. Poor Rosa hastened away, filled with terror. She wanted to tell her mistress all this, and claim her protection; but she dared not. As for George, he was of a proud and fiery nature, and she dreaded the storm it would raise in his breast. Her sleeping apartment adjoined that of her mistress, and she was now called to bring water to her master at a much later hour than had been usual with him. One night, no answer was given to the summons. Rosa was not in her room. When questioned in the morning, she stammered out an incoherent excuse, and burst into tears. She was ordered, somewhat sternly, to be very careful not to be again absent when called for.

Marion took an early opportunity to plead her favorite's cause. 'I have suspected, for some time,' said she, 'that George and Rosa are courting; and for my part, I should like very well to have them married.' Her husband made no reply, but abruptly left the room. His conduct towards George became singularly capricious and severe. Rosa wept much in secret, and became shy as a startled fawn. Her mistress supposed it was because Mr. Dalcho objected to her marriage, and suspected nothing more. She tried to remonstrate with him, and learn the nature of his objections; but he answered sharply, and left her in tears.

One night, Marion was awakened by the closing of the door, and found that Frederic was absent. She heard voices in Rosa's apartment, and the painful truth flashed upon her. Poor young wife, what a bitter hour was that!

In the morning, Rosa came to dress her, as usual, but she avoided looking in her face, and kept her eyes fixed on the ground. As she knelt to tie the satin shoe, Marion spoke angrily of her awkwardness, and gave her a blow. It was the first time she had ever struck her; for they really loved each other. The beautiful slave looked up with an expression of surprise, which was answered by a strange, wild stare. Rosa fell at her feet, and sobbed out, 'Oh, mistress, I am not to blame. Indeed, indeed, I am very wretched.' Marion's fierce glance melted into tears. 'Poor child,' said she, 'I ought not to have struck you; but, oh, Rosa, I am wretched, too.' The foster-sisters embraced each other, and wept long and bitterly; but neither sought any further to learn the other's secrets.

At breakfast, George was in attendance, but he would not look at Rosa, though she watched for a glance with anxious love. When she found an opportunity to see him alone, he was sullen, and rejected her proffered kiss. 'Rosa, where were you last night?' said he, hastily. The poor girl blushed deeply, and strove to take his hand; but he flung her from him, with so much force that she reeled against the wall. 'Oh, George,' said she, with bitter anguish, 'what *can* I do? I am his *slave*.' The justice of her plea, and the pathos of her tones, softened his heart. He placed her head on his shoulder, and said more kindly, 'Keep out of his way, dear Rosa; keep out of his way.'

Rosa made strong efforts to follow this injunction; and dearly did she rue it. George was sent away from the house, to work on the plantation, and they were forbidden to see each other, under penalty of severe punishment. His rival, Mars, watched them, and gave information of every attempt to transgress this cruel edict. But love was more omnipotent than fear of punishment, and the lovers did sometimes catch a stolen interview. The recurrence of this disobedience exasperated their master beyond endurance. He swore he would overcome her obstinacy, or kill her; and one severe flogging succeeded another, till the tenderly-nurtured slave fainted under the cruel infliction, which was rendered doubly dangerous by the delicate state of her health. Maternal pains came on prematurely, and she died a few hours after.

George wandered into the woods, and avoided the sight of his reckless master, who, on his part, seemed willing to avoid an interview. Four days had passed since Rosa's death, and the bereaved one had scarcely tasted food enough to sustain his wretched life. He stood beside the new-made grave, which he himself had dug. 'Oh, Father in Heaven!' he exclaimed, 'what would I give, if I had not flung her from me! Poor girl, *she* was not to blame.' He leaned his head against a tree, and looked mournfully up to the moon struggling through clouds. Cypresses reared their black forms against the sky, and the moss hung from bough to bough, in thick, funereal festoons. But a few months ago, how beautiful and bright was Nature—and now, how inexpressibly gloomy. The injustice of the past, and the hopelessness of the future, came before him with dreary distinctness. 'He is my brother,' thought he, 'we grew up side by side, children of the same father; but I am his slave. Handsomer, stronger, and more intelligent than he; yet I am his *slave*. And now he will sell me, because the murdered one will forever come up between us.'

He thought of Rosa as he first saw her, so happy, and so beautiful; of all her gushing tenderness; of her agonized farewell, when they last met; of her graceful form bleeding under the lash, and now lying cold and dead beneath his feet.

He looked toward his master's house. 'Shall I escape now and forever?' said he; 'or shall I first'—he paused, threw his arms widely upward, gnashed his teeth, and groaned aloud, 'God, pity me! He murdered my poor Rosa.'

On that night, Marion's sleep was disturbed and fitful. The memory of her foster-sister mingled darkly with all her dreams. Was that a shriek she heard? It was fearfully shrill in the night-silence! Half sleeping and half waking, she called wildly, 'Rosa! Rosa!' But a moment after, she remembered that Rosa's light step would never again come at her call. At last a drowsy slave answered the loud summons of her bell. 'I left your master reading in the room below,' said she; 'go and see if he is ill.' The girl came back, pallid and frightened. 'Oh, mistress, he is dead!' she exclaimed; 'there is a dagger through his heart.'

Neighbors were hastily summoned, and the slaves secured. Among them was George, who, with a fierce and haggard look, still lingered around Rosa's grave.

The dagger found in Frederic Dalcho's heart was the one he had himself been accustomed to wear. He lay upon the sofa, with an open book beside him, as if he had fallen asleep reading. A desk in the room was broken open, and a sum of money gone. Near it, was dropped a ragged handkerchief, known to belong to Mars. Suspicion hovered between him and George. Both denied the deed. Mars tried hard to fix the guilt on his hated rival, and swore to many falsehoods. But as some of these falsehoods were detected, and the stolen money was found hidden in his bed, the balance turned against him. After the brief, stern trial awarded to slaves, with slave-holders for judges and jurors, Mars was condemned to be hung. George thought of his relentless persecutions, and for a moment triumphed over the cunning enemy, who had so often dogged poor Rosa's steps; but his soul was too generous to retain this feeling.

The fatal hour came. Planters rode miles to witness the execution, and stood glaring at their trembling victim, with the fierceness of tigers. The slaves from miles around were assembled, to take warning by his awful punishment. The rope was adjusted on the strong bough of a tree. Mars shook like a leaf in the wind. The countenance of George was very pale and haggard, and his breast was heaving with tumultuous thoughts. 'He is my enemy,' said he to himself; ''tis an awful thing to die thus. The *theft* I did not commit; but if I take all the blame, they can do no more than hang me.'

They led the shivering wretch towards the tree, and were about to fasten the fatal noose. But George rushed forward with a countenance ghastly pale, and exclaimed, 'Mars is innocent. I murdered him—for he killed my wife, and hell was in my bosom.'

No voice praised him for the generous confession. They kicked and cursed him; and hung up, like a dog or a wolf, a man of nobler soul than any of them all.

The Georgian papers thus announced the deed: '*Fiend-like Murder.* Frederic Dalcho, one of our most wealthy and respected citizens, was robbed and murdered last week, by one of his slaves. The black demon was caught and hung; and hanging was too good for him.'

The Northern papers copied this version; merely adding, 'These are the black-hearted monsters, which abolition philanthropy would let loose upon our brethren of the South.'

Not one was found to tell how the slave's young wife had been torn from him by his own brother, and murdered with slow tortures. Not one recorded the heroism that would not purchase life by another's death, though the victim was his enemy. His very *name* was left unmentioned; he was only Mr. Dalcho's *slave!*

Reply of Mrs. Child [to Mrs. Mason]

WAYLAND, Mass., Dec. 17th, 1859.

Prolonged absence from home has prevented my answering your letter so soon as I intended. I have no disposition to retort upon you the "two-fold damnation," to which you consign me.[1] On the contrary, I sincerely wish you well, both in this world and the next. If the anathema proved a safety valve to your own boiling spirit, it did some good to you, while it fell harmless upon me. Fortunately for all of us, the Heavenly Father rules His universe by laws, which the passions or the prejudices of mortals have no power to change.

As for John Brown, his reputation may be safely trusted to the impartial pen of History; and his motives will be righteously judged by Him who knoweth the secrets of all hearts. Men, however great they may be, are of small consequence in comparison with principles; and the principle for which John Brown died is the question at issue between us.

You refer me to the Bible, from which you quote the favorite text of slaveholders:—

"Servants, be subject to your masters with all fear; not only to the good and gentle, but also to the froward."—1 Peter, 2:18.

Abolitionists also have favorite texts, to some of which I would call your attention:—

"Remember those that are in bonds as bound with them."—Heb. 13:3.

"Hide the outcasts. Bewray not him that wandereth. Let mine outcasts dwell with thee. Be thou a covert to them from the face of the spoiler."—Isa. 16:3, 4.

"Thou shalt not deliver unto his master the servant which is escaped from his master unto thee. He shall dwell with thee where it liketh him best. Thou shalt not oppress him."—Deut. 23:15, 16.

"Open thy mouth for the dumb, in the cause of all such as are appointed to destruction. Open thy mouth, judge righteously, and plead the cause of the poor and needy."—Prov. 29:8, 9.

Correspondence between Lydia Maria Child and Gov. Wise and Mrs. Mason, of Virginia (1860), pp. 18–28.

1. Mrs. Mason's letter of 11 November opens: "Do you read your Bible, Mrs. Child? If you do, read there, 'Woe unto you, hypocrites,' and take to yourself with two-fold damnation that terrible sentence."

"Cry aloud, spare not, lift up thy voice like a trumpet, and show my people their transgression, and the house of Jacob their sins."—Isa. 58:1.

I would especially commend to slaveholders the following portions of that volume, wherein you say God has revealed the duty of masters:—

"Masters, give unto your servants that which is just and equal, knowing that ye also have a Master in heaven."—Col. 4:1.

"Neither be ye called masters; for one is your master, even Christ; and all ye are brethren."—Matt. 23:8, 10.

"Whatsoever ye would that men should do unto you, do ye even so unto them."—Matt. 7:12.

"Is not this the fast that I have chosen, to loose the bands of wickedness, to undo the heavy burdens, and to let the oppressed go free, and that ye break every yoke?"—Isa. 58:6.

"They have given a boy for a harlot, and sold a girl for wine, that they might drink."—Joel 3:3.

"He that oppresseth the poor, reproacheth his Maker."—Prov. 14:31.

"Rob not the poor, because he is poor; neither oppress the afflicted. For the Lord will plead their cause, and spoil the soul of those who spoiled them."—Prov. 22:22, 23.

"Woe unto him that useth his neighbor's service without wages, and giveth him not for his work."—Jer. 22:13.

"Let him that stole, steal no more, but rather let him labor, working with his hands."—Eph. 4:28.

"Woe unto them that decree unrighteous decrees, and that write grievousness which they have prescribed; to turn aside the needy from judgment, and to take away the right from the poor, that widows may be their prey, and that they may rob the fatherless."—Isa. 10:1, 2.

"If I did despise the cause of my man-servant or of my maid-servant, when they contend with me, what then shall I do when God riseth up? and when he visiteth, what shall I answer Him?"—Job 31:13, 14.

"Thou hast sent widows away empty, and the arms of the fatherless have been broken. Therefore snares are round about thee, and sudden fear troubleth thee; and darkness, that thou canst not see."—Job 22:9, 10, 11.

"Behold, the hire of your laborers, who have reaped down your fields, which is of you kept back by fraud, crieth; and the cries of them which have reaped are entered into the ears of the Lord of sabaoth. Ye have lived in pleasure on the earth, and been wanton; ye have nourished your hearts as in a day of slaughter; ye have condemned and killed the just."—James 5:4.

If the appropriateness of these texts is not apparent, I will try to make it so, by evidence drawn entirely from *Southern* sources. The Abolitionists are not such an ignorant set of fanatics as you suppose. They *know* whereof they affirm. They are familiar with the laws of the Slave States, which are alone sufficient to inspire abhorrence in any humane heart or reflecting mind not perverted by the prejudices of education and custom. I might fill many letters with significant extracts from your statute-books; but I have space only to glance at a few, which indicate the *leading* features of the system you cherish so tenaciously.

The universal rule of the slave State is, that "the child follows the condition of its *mother.*" This is an index to many things. Marriages between white and colored people are forbidden by law; yet a very large number of the slaves are brown or yellow. When Lafayette visited this country in his old age, he said he was very much struck by the great change in the colored population of Virginia; that in the time of the Revolution, nearly all the household slaves were black, but when he returned to America, he found very few of them black. The advertisements in Southern newspapers often describe runaway slaves that "pass themselves for white men." Sometimes they are described as having "straight, light hair, blue eyes, and clear complexion." This could not be, unless their fathers, grandfathers, and great-grandfathers had been white men. But as their *mothers* were slaves, the law pronounces *them* slaves, subject to be sold on the auction-block whenever the necessities or convenience of their masters or mistresses require it. The sale of one's own children, brothers, or sisters, has an ugly aspect to those who are unaccustomed to it; and, obviously, it cannot have a good moral influence, that law and custom should render licentiousness a *profitable* vice.

Throughout the Slave States, the testimony of no colored person, bond or free, can be received against a white man. You have some laws, which, on the face of them, would seem to restrain inhuman men from murdering or mutilating slaves; but they are rendered nearly null by the law I have cited. Any drunken master, overseer, or patrol, may go into the negro cabins, and commit what outrages he pleases, with perfect impunity, if no white person is present who chooses to witness against him. North Carolina and Georgia leave a large loophole for escape, even if white persons are present, when murder is committed. A law to punish persons for "maliciously killing a slave" has this remarkable qualification: "Always provided that this act shall not extend to any slave dying of moderate correction." We at the North find it difficult to understand how *moderate* punishment can cause *death.* I have read several of your law-books attentively, and I find no cases of punishment for the murder of a slave, except by fines paid to the *owner,* to indemnify him for the loss of his *property:* the same as if his horse or cow had been killed. In the South Carolina Reports is a case where the State had indicted Guy Raines for the murder of a slave named Isaac. It was proved that William Gray, the owner of Isaac, had given him *a thousand lashes.* The poor creature made his escape, but was caught, and delivered to the custody of Raines, to be carried to the county jail. Because he refused to go, Raines gave him five hundred lashes, and he died soon after. The counsel for Raines proposed that he should be allowed to acquit himself by his *own oath.* The Court decided against it, because *white witnesses* had testified; but the Court of Appeals afterward decided he *ought* to have been exculpated by his own oath, and he was *acquitted.* Small indeed is the chance for justice to a slave, when his own color are not allowed to testify, if they see him maimed or his children murdered; when he has slaveholders for Judges and Jurors; when the murderer can exculpate himself by his own oath; and when the law provides that it is no murder to kill a slave by "moderate correction"!

Your laws uniformly declare that "a slave shall be deemed a chattel personal in the hands of his owner, to all intents, constructions, and purposes whatsoever." This, of course, involves the right to sell his children, as if they were pigs; also, to take his wife from him "for any intent or purpose whatsoever." Your laws also make it death for him to resist a white man, however brutally he may be treated, or however much his family may be outraged before his eyes. If he attempts to run away, your laws allow any man to shoot him.

By your laws, all a slave's earnings belong to his master. He can neither receive donations nor transmit property. If his master allows him some hours to work for himself, and by great energy and perseverance he earns enough to buy his own bones and sinews, his master may make him pay two or three times over, and he has no redress. Three such cases have come within my own knowledge. Even a written promise from his master has no legal value, because a slave can make no contracts.

Your laws also systematically aim at keeping the minds of the colored people in the most abject state of ignorance. If white people attempt to teach them to read or write, they are punished by imprisonment or fines; if they attempt to teach others, they are punished with from twenty to thirty-nine lashes each. It cannot be said that the anti-slavery agitation produced such laws, for they date much further back; many of them when we were Provinces. They are the *necessities* of the system, which, being itself an outrage upon human nature, can be sustained only by perpetual outrages.

The next reliable source of information is the advertisements in the Southern papers. In the North Carolina (Raleigh) *Standard*, Mr. Micajah Ricks advertises, "Runaway, a negro woman and her two children. A few days before she went off, I burned her with a hot iron on the left side of her face. I tried to make the letter M." In the Natchez *Courier*, Mr. J. P. Ashford advertises a runaway negro girl, with "a good many teeth missing, and the letter A branded on her cheek and forehead." In the Lexington (Ky.) *Observer*, Mr. William Overstreet advertises a runaway negro with "his left eye out, scars from a dirk on his left arm, and much scarred with the whip." I might quote from hundreds of such advertisements, offering rewards for runaways, "dead or alive," and describing them with "ears cut off," "jaws broken," "scarred by rifle-balls," &c.

Another source of information is afforded by your "Fugitives from Injustice," with many of whom I have conversed freely. I have seen scars of the whip and marks of the branding-iron, and I have listened to their heart-breaking sobs, while they told of "piccaninnies" torn from their arms and sold.

Another source of information is furnished by emancipated slaveholders. Sarah M. Grimke, daughter of the late Judge Grimke, of the Supreme Court of South Carolina, testifies as follows: "As I left my native State on account of Slavery, and deserted the home of my fathers to escape the sound of the lash and the shrieks of tortured victims, I would gladly bury in oblivion the recollection of those scenes with which I have been familiar. But this cannot be. They come over my memory like gory spectres, and implore me, with resistless power, in the name of a God of mercy, in the name of a crucified Saviour, in the name of humanity, for the sake of the slaveholder, as well as the slave, to bear witness to the horrors of the Southern prison-house." She proceeds to describe dreadful tragedies, the actors in which she says were "men and women of the first families in South Carolina;" and that their cruelties did not, in the slightest degree, affect their standing in society. Her sister, Angelina Grimke, declared: "While I live, and Slavery lives, I *must* testify against it. Not merely for the sake of my poor brothers and sisters in bonds; for even were Slavery no curse to its victims, the exercise of arbitrary power works such fearful ruin upon the hearts of slaveholders, that I should feel impelled to labor and pray for its overthrow with my latest breath." Among the horrible barbarities she enumerates is the case of a girl thirteen years old, who was flogged to death by her master. She says: "I asked a prominent lawyer, who belonged to one of the first families in the State, whether the murderer of this helpless child could not be indicted, and he coolly replied that the slave was Mr. ——'s property, and if he chose to suffer the *loss,* no one else had anything to do with it." She proceeds to say: "I felt there could be for me no rest in the midst of such outrages and pollutions. Yet I saw nothing of Slavery in its most vulgar and repulsive forms. I saw it in the city, among the fashionable and the honorable, where it was garnished by refinement and decked out for show. It is my deep, solemn, deliberate conviction that this is a cause worth dying for. I say so from what I have seen, and heard, and known, in a land of Slavery, whereon rest the darkness of Egypt and the sin of Sodom." I once asked Miss Angelina if she thought Abolitionists exaggerated the horrors of Slavery. She replied, with earnest emphasis: "They *cannot* be exaggerated. It is impossible for imagination to go beyond the facts." To a lady who observed that the time had not yet come for agitating the subject, she answered: "I apprehend if thou wert a *slave,* toiling in the fields of Carolina, thou wouldst think the time had *fully* come."

Mr. Thome,[2] of Kentucky, in the course of his eloquent lectures on this subject, said: "I breathed my first breath in an atmosphere of Slavery. But though I am heir to a slave inheritance, I am bold to denounce the whole system as an outrage, a complication of crimes, and wrongs, and cruelties, that make angels weep."

"Mr. Allen, of Alabama, in a discussion with the students at Lane Seminary, in 1834, told of a slave who was tied up and beaten all day, with a paddle full of holes. At night his flesh was literally pounded to a jelly. The punishment was inflicted within hearing of the Academy and the Public Green. But no one took any notice of it. No one thought any wrong was done. At our house, it is so common to hear screams from a neighboring plantation, that we think nothing of it. Lest any one should think that the slaves are *generally* well treated, and that the cases I have mentioned are exceptions, let me be distinctly understood that cruelty is the *rule,* and kindness is the exception."

2. James A. Thome (1809–73) and William T. Allan (d. 1882), mentioned in the next paragraph, were southern students at Lane Theological Seminary who became convinced of the sinfulness of slavery and converted to abolitionism during the 1834 debate there prompted by Theodore Dwight Weld, later the husband of Angelina Grimké. Child quotes freely from p. 7 of *Debate at the Lane Seminary, Cincinnati. Speech of James A. Thome, of Kentucky, Delivered at the Annual Meeting of the American Anti-Slavery Society, May 6, 1834 . . .* (1834) and from unidentified sources.

In the same discussion, a student from Virginia, after relating cases of great cruelty, said: "Such things are common all over Virginia; at least, so far as I am acquainted. But the planters generally avoid punishing their slaves before *strangers.*"

Miss Mattie Griffith,[3] of Kentucky, whose entire property consisted in slaves, emancipated them all. The noble-hearted girl wrote to me: "I shall go forth into the world penniless; but I shall work with a light heart, and, best of all, I shall live with an easy conscience." Previous to this generous resolution, she had never read any Abolition document, and entertained the common Southern prejudice against them. But her own observation so deeply impressed her with the enormities of Slavery, that she was impelled to publish a book, called "The Autobiography of a Female Slave." I read it with thrilling interest; but some of the scenes made my nerves quiver so painfully, that I told her I hoped they were too highly colored. She shook her head sadly, and replied: "I am sorry to say that every incident in the book has come within my own knowledge."

St. George Tucker,[4] Judge and Professor of Law in Virginia, speaking of the legalized murder of runaways, said: "Such are the cruelties to which a state of Slavery gives birth—such the horrors to which the human mind is capable of being reconciled by its adoption." Alluding to our struggle in '76, he said: "While we proclaim our resolution to live free or die, we imposed on our fellow-men, of different complexion, a Slavery ten thousand times worse than the utmost extremity of the oppressions of which we complained."

Governor Giles,[5] in a Message to the Legislature of Virginia, referring to the custom of selling free colored people into Slavery, as a punishment for offences not capital, said: "Slavery must be admitted to be a *punishment of the highest order;* and, according to the just rule for the apportionment of punishment to crimes, it ought to be applied only to *crimes of the highest order.* The most distressing reflection in the application of this punishment to female offenders is, that it extends to their offspring; and the innocent are thus

---

3. After emancipating her slaves, Martha (Mattie) Griffith (ca. 1838–1906) published the fictional *Autobiography of a Female Slave* (1857) to support herself and expose the horrors of slavery.

4. Child is quoting freely from *A Dissertation on Slavery: with a Proposal for the Gradual Abolition of It, in the State of Virginia* (1796), by St. George Tucker (1752–1827), professor of law at the College of William and Mary. The quotations are from pp. 10 and 54.

5. William Branch Giles (1762–1830), Democrat, served as governor of Virginia from 1827 to ca. 1830.

punished with the guilty." Yet one hundred and twenty thousand innocent babes in this country are annually subjected to a punishment which your Governor declared "ought to be applied only to crimes of the highest order."

Jefferson said: "One *day* of American Slavery is worse than a *thousand years* of that which we rose in arms to oppose." Alluding to insurrections, he said: "The Almighty has no attribute that can take side with us in such a contest."[6]

John Randolph[7] declared: "Every planter is a sentinel at his own door. Every Southern mother, when she hears an alarm of fire in the night, instinctively presses her infant closer to her bosom."

Looking at the system of slavery in the light of all this evidence, do you candidly think we deserve "two-fold damnation" for detesting it? Can you not believe that we may hate the system, and yet be truly your friends? I make allowance for the excited state of your mind, and for the prejudices induced by education. I do not care to change your opinion of me; but I do wish you could be persuaded to examine this subject dispassionately, for the sake of the prosperity of Virginia, and the welfare of unborn generations, both white and colored. For thirty years, Abolitionists have been trying to reason with slaveholders, through the press, and in the halls of Congress. Their efforts, though directed to the *masters only,* have been met with violence and abuse almost equal to that poured on the head of John Brown. Yet surely we, as a portion of the Union, involved in the expense, the degeneracy, the danger, and the disgrace, of this iniquitous and fatal system, have a *right* to speak about it, and a right to be *heard* also. At the North, we willingly publish pro-slavery arguments, and ask only a fair field and no favor for the other side. But you will not even allow your own citizens a chance to examine this important subject. Your letter to me is published in Northern papers, as well as Southern; but my reply will not be allowed to appear in any Southern paper. The despotic measures you take to silence investigation, and shut out the light from your own white population, prove how little reliance you have on the strength of your cause. In this enlightened age, all despotisms *ought* to

---

6. Child is quoting from Jefferson's *Notes on the State of Virginia* (1785), Query 18, and from his letter to Jean Nicolas Démeunier of 26 June 1786 (Julian P. Boyd, ed., *The Papers of Thomas Jefferson* [Princeton: Princeton UP, 1954], 10:63). While abolitionists frequently cited Query 18, proslavery apologists as frequently cited Query 14, in which Jefferson postulates that Africans are biologically inferior to whites in body and mind.

7. Though a strong defender of states' rights, southern interests, and control of government by a propertied elite, Virginia slaveholder John Randolph (1773–1833) regarded slavery as a curse and freed his slaves on his death. Child may be quoting from one of his congressional speeches.

come to an end by the agency of moral and rational means. But if they resist such agencies, it is in the order of Providence that they *must* come to an end by violence. History is full of such lessons.

Would that the veil of prejudice could be removed from your eyes. If you would candidly examine the statements of Governor Hincks[8] of the British West Indies, and of the Rev. Mr. Bleby, long time a Missionary in those Islands, both before and after emancipation, you could not fail to be convinced that Cash is a more powerful incentive to labor than the Lash, and far safer also. One fact in relation to those Islands is very significant. While the working people were slaves, it was always necessary to order out the military during the Christmas holidays; but, since emancipation, not a soldier is to be seen. A hundred John Browns might land there, without exciting the slightest alarm.

To the personal questions you ask me,[9] I will reply in the name of all the women of New England. It would be extremely difficult to find any woman in our villages who does *not* sew for the poor, and watch with the sick, whenever occasion requires. We pay our domestics generous wages, with which they can purchase as many Christmas gowns as they please; a process far better for their characters, as well as our own, than to receive their clothing as a charity, after being deprived of just payment for their labor. I have never known an instance where the "pangs of maternity" did not meet with requisite assistance; and here at the North, after we have helped the mothers, *we do not sell the babies.*

I readily believe what you state concerning the kindness of many Virginia matrons. It is creditable to their hearts: but after all, the best that can be done in that way is a poor equivalent for the perpetual wrong done to the slaves, and the terrible liabilities to which they are always subject. Kind masters and mistresses among you are merely lucky accidents. If any one *chooses* to be a brutal despot, your laws and customs give him complete power to do so. And

---

8. Sir Francis Hincks (1807–85), governor of Barbados and the Windward Islands from 1855 to 1862, asserted that the value of Barbadian property had been increased by abolition because free labor was cheaper than slave labor. Henry Bleby (d. 1878) served as a Methodist minister in the West Indies for forty-six years. Child may be quoting from his book, *Death Struggle of Slavery.*

9. Mrs. Mason had asked Child: "[W]ould *you* stand by the bedside of an old negro, dying of a hopeless disease, to alleviate his sufferings as far as human aid could? Have *you* ever watched the last, lingering illness of a consumptive, to soothe, as far as in you lay, the inevitable fate? Do *you* soften the pangs of maternity in those around you by all the care and comfort you can give? . . . Did *you* ever sit up until the 'wee hours' to complete a dress for a motherless child?"

the lot of those slaves who have the kindest masters is exceedingly precarious. In case of death, or pecuniary difficulties, or marriages in the family, they may at any time be suddenly transferred from protection and indulgence to personal degradation, or extreme severity; and if they should try to escape from such sufferings, anybody is authorized to shoot them down like dogs.

With regard to your declaration that "no Southerner ought henceforth to read a line of my composition," I reply that I have great satisfaction in the consciousness of having nothing to lose in that quarter. Twenty-seven years ago, I published a book called "An Appeal in behalf of that class of Americans called Africans." It influenced the minds of several young men, afterward conspicuous in public life, through whose agency the cause was better served than it could have been by me. From that time to this, I have labored too earnestly for the slave to be agreeable to slaveholders. Literary popularity was never a paramount object with me, even in my youth; and, now that I am old, I am utterly indifferent to it. But, if I cared for the exclusion you threaten, I should at least have the consolation of being exiled with honorable company. Dr. Channing's[10] writings, mild and candid as they are, breathe what you would call arrant treason. William C. Bryant,[11] in his capacity of editor, is openly on our side. The inspired muse of Whittier[12] has incessantly sounded the trumpet for moral warfare with your iniquitous institution; and his stirring tones have been answered, more or less loudly, by Pierpont, Lowell, and Longfellow.[13] Emerson, the Plato of America, leaves the scholastic seclusion he loves so well, and, disliking noise with all his poetic soul, bravely takes his stand among the trumpeters.[14] George W. Curtis,[15] the brilliant writer,

10. William Ellery Channing (1780–1842) was a Unitarian minister whose tracts *Slavery* (1835) and *Emancipation* (1840) represented moderate antislavery opinion.

11. The poet William Cullen Bryant (1794–1878) edited the *New York Evening Post,* a Democratic newspaper.

12. John Greenleaf Whittier (1807–92) was the unofficial poet laureate of the abolitionist movement.

13. The Unitarian minister John Pierpont (1785–1866) and his more famous literary contemporaries James Russell Lowell (1819–91) and Henry Wadsworth Longfellow (1807–82) all wrote antislavery poetry.

14. The individualist philosophy and contemplative tastes of the transcendentalist Ralph Waldo Emerson (1803–82) had kept him aloof from the abolitionist cause until 1844, but after the passage of the 1850 Fugitive Slave Law, he lectured frequently against slavery. Child had previously criticized his silence on the issue.

15. George William Curtis (1824–92), who would become influential as the editor of *Harper's Weekly* (1863–92), had recently begun lecturing against slavery. He married the sister of Robert Gould Shaw (see Child's tribute to Shaw, reprinted in this volume).

the eloquent lecturer, the elegant man of the world, lays the wealth of his talent on the altar of Freedom, and makes common cause with rough-shod reformers.

The genius of Mrs. Stowe carried the outworks of your institution at one dash, and left the citadel open to besiegers, who are pouring in amain. In the church, on the ultra-liberal side, it is assailed by the powerful battering-ram of Theodore Parker's[16] eloquence. On the extreme orthodox side is set a huge fire, kindled by the burning words of Dr. Cheever.[17] Between them is Henry Ward Beecher,[18] sending a shower of keen arrows into your entrenchments; and with him ride a troop of sharp-shooters from all sects. If you turn to the literature of England or France, you will find your institution treated with as little favor. The fact is, the whole civilized world proclaims Slavery an outlaw, and the best intellect of the age is active in hunting it down.

L. Maria Child

16. The theological radicalism of the Unitarian minister Theodore Parker (1810–60) had led to his ostracism. An ardent abolitionist, he was among the Secret Six who provided John Brown with financial backing.

17. The Calvinist minister George B. Cheever (1807–90), known as a fiery speaker, was a zealous advocate of abolition and temperance.

18. The liberal Congregationalist Henry Ward Beecher (1813–87), brother of Harriet Beecher Stowe (1811–96), to whose novel *Uncle Tom's Cabin* (1852) Child refers above, delivered eloquent antislavery sermons and occupied a middle position between the religious liberalism of Parker and the orthodoxy of Cheever. Child is arguing that ministers representing the entire range of theological opinion have united in condemning slavery.

Mrs. L. Maria Child to the President
of the United States[1]

It may seem a violation of propriety for a woman to address the Chief Magistrate of the nation at a crisis so momentous as this. But if the Romans, ages ago, accorded to Hortensia[2] the right of addressing the Senate on the subject of a tax unjustly levied on the wealthy ladies of Rome, surely an American woman of the nineteenth century need not apologize for pleading with the rulers of her country in behalf of the poor, the wronged, the cruelly oppressed. Surely the women of America have a right to inquire, nay, demand, whether their husbands, sons, and brothers are to be buried by thousands in Southern swamps, without obtaining thereby "indemnity for the past and security for the future."

In your Appeal to the Border States, you have declared slavery to be "that without which the war could never have been," and you speak of emancipation as "the step which at once shortens the war."[3] I would respectfully ask how much longer the nation is to wait for the decision of the Border States, paying, meanwhile $2,000,000 a day, and sending thousands of its best and bravest to be stabbed, shot, and hung by the rebels, whose property they are employed to guard. How much longer will pro-slavery officers be permitted to refuse obedience to the laws of Congress, saying, "We shall continue to

National Republican; reprinted in the *National Anti-Slavery Standard,* 6 September 1862, and in *CC* 53/1426.

1. Prominently featured on p. 1 of the *National Republican* of 22 August 1862, and reprinted in the *Liberator* of 29 August and the *National Anti-Slavery Standard* of 6 September, this letter was one of many urging Lincoln to issue an emancipation proclamation. See also *New York Tribune* editor Horace Greeley's "The Prayer of Twenty Millions" (20 Aug. 1862) and Harriet Beecher Stowe's "Prayer" (*Independent* 28 Aug. 1862).

2. Hortensia, daughter of the Roman orator Quintus Hortensius, protested to the Roman Senate in 43 B.C. when Mark Anthony, Octavian, and Lepidus sought to raise money for a civil war against the assassins of Julius Caesar by taxing the property of 1,400 wealthy women. Arguing that women should not be taxed to support a war they had not voted to approve, she succeeded in reducing the number of women taxed to 400 and in having a similar tax levied on men.

3. Child is referring to a presidential message of 6 March 1862 in which Lincoln asked Congress to pass a joint resolution offering financial aid to "any state which may adopt a gradual abolishment of slavery"—a proposition he urged slaveholders in the border states to consider. Child had greeted this message with jubilation and had been disappointed when nothing came of it.

send back fugitives to their masters until we receive orders from the *President* to the contrary."[4] What fatal spell is cast over your honest mind, that you hesitate so long to give such orders? Be not deceived; God is not mocked. Neither nations nor individuals sin against His laws with impunity. Hear the old Hebrew Prophet, whose words seem as if spoken for *us:* "Thou should'st not have stood in the crossway to cut off those that did escape; neither should'st thou have delivered up those that did remain in the day of distress. For thy violence against thy brother, shame shall cover thee, and thou shalt be cut off forever. The pride of thine heart hath deceived thee, saying, who shall bring *me* down to the ground? Though thou exalt thyself as the *eagle,* and though thou set thy nest among the *stars,* thence will I bring thee down, saith the Lord."[5]

The American people have manifested almost miraculous patience, forbearance, and confidence in their rulers. They have given incontrovertible proof that their intelligence, their love of country, may be trusted to any extent. They are willing to sacrifice their fortunes and their lives, but they very reasonably wish to know what they are sacrificing them for. Men, even the bravest, do not go resolutely and cheerfully to death in the name of diplomacy and strategy. The human soul, under such circumstances, needs to be lifted up and sustained by great ideas of Justice and Freedom.

President Lincoln, it is an awful responsibility before God to quench the moral enthusiasm of a generous people. It wastes thousands of precious lives, causes an unutterable amount of slow, consuming agony, and tarnishes our record on the pages of history. Again I respectfully ask, how much longer we are to wait for the Border States, at such tremendous cost and with such a fearful risk? When a criminal is on trial, it is not deemed prudent to try by a jury who are interested in the crime. Slavery is on trial, and the verdict is left to slaveholders in the Border States. The report of their majority shows them to be slaveholders in heart and spirit. The process of reasoning and entreaty has been very properly tried with them, and the people of the free States have waited long and patiently for some obvious good result. They are getting

---

4. At the beginning of the war, anxious not to alienate slaveholders loyal to the Union, Lincoln instructed military officers to send all fugitive slaves who fled to Union army camps back to their masters—a policy that outraged Child and other abolitionists. On 10 March 1862, Congress enacted an article of war forbidding officers to return fugitive slaves to their masters, on the grounds that it would shorten the war to deprive Confederates of their labor force and to employ those laborers on the Union side.

5. Child quotes, in order, from Obadiah 1.14, 1.10, 1.3, and 1.4.

restive; very restive. Everywhere I hear men saying: "Our President is an honest, able man, but he appears to have no firmness of purpose. He is letting the country drift to ruin for want of earnest action and a consistent policy." This is not the utterance of any one class or party. It may be heard everywhere; by the wayside, in the cars, and at the depots. Nor can I deny that some speak with less moderation. Shall I tell you what I said when cold water was thrown on the spark of enthusiasm kindled by the brave, large-hearted Gen. Hunter?[6] I exclaimed, with a groan, "Oh, what a misfortune it is to have an extinguisher instead of a Drummond[7] Light in our watchtower, when the Ship of State is reeling under such a violent storm, in the midst of sunken rocks, with swarms of unprincipled wreckers everywhere calculating on the profit they may derive from her destruction." The crew are working at the pumps with manly vigor and almost superhuman endurance. They look out upon a prospect veiled by dense fog, and their cry is, "Oh! God, let us know whither we are driving. Give us a clear, steady light to guide us through the darkness of the storm."

I trust you will not deem me wanting in respect for yourself or your high position, if I say frankly that you seem to trust too much to diplomatic and selfish politicians, and far too little to the heart of the people. You do them wrong, irreparable wrong, by stifling their generous instincts, and putting an extinguisher on every scintillation of moral enthusiasm. Are you not aware that moral enthusiasm is the mightiest of all forces? It is the fire which produces the steam of energy and courage, and the motion of all the long train of crowded cars depends on its expansive power. In the name of our suffering country, for the sake of a world that needs enfranchisement, I beseech you not to check the popular enthusiasm for freedom! Would that you could realize what a mighty power there is in the *heart* of a free people! No proclamations, no speeches, have stirred it to its depths, as did the heroic and kindly Gen. Banks, when he gave the weary little slave girl a ride upon his cannon.[8] I hail the omen of that suffering little one riding

6. On 9 May 1862 General David Hunter (1802–86), acting as head of the Department of the South, declared all the slaves in his jurisdiction free. Lincoln promptly revoked the proclamation on the grounds that Hunter had no authority to issue it.

7. The Drummond light, named after its 1825 inventor, was a limelight.

8. Nathaniel P. Banks (1816–94), legislator and governor of Massachusetts (1858–60), served as a Union general in the Civil War. The *Liberator* of 18 July 1862, p. 115, reprinted a letter from General Banks, replying to the charge that "persons of color were allowed Government transportation" on his retreat from Strasburg, "while white people, including sick and wounded

to freedom on the cannon of the United States. It is impossible to estimate the benign, far-reaching influences of such an action. They cannot be arranged in statistics, and will therefore be neglected by political economists. They cannot be bought up for electioneering purposes, and therefore men called statesmen attach no importance to them. But they will run through all the patterns of our future, though history will be unable to trace to their origin in the web those golden threads that here glow in the heart of a flower, and there light up the eye of a bird. Gen. Banks was not aware of the magnetism in that simple act of humanity. It owed its magnetic power to the fact that "what within is good and true, he saw it with his *heart*." And so it wakened a responsive thrill in other kindly, generous hearts, who all remembered the words, "Inasmuch as ye did it unto the least of these, ye did it unto me."⁹ Such potency was there in it, that it proved an Ithuriel's¹⁰ spear to disguised forms of selfishness and treason. When it touched the toads, they started up devils.

In thus entreating you to trust to the impulses of the people, I by no means overlook the extreme difficulties of your position. I know that the proslavery spirit of the land is a mighty giant, characterized by unscrupulous selfishness and exceeding obstinacy. But I also know that all the enthusiasm is on the side of freedom. Despotism has its ugly Caliban¹¹ of obstinate pride always at work for mischief. But enthusiasm is the swift and radiant Ariel,

---

soldiers, were compelled to walk." Banks pleaded innocent, "with one exception": "a little girl, about eight years of age, who was toddling over the stones by the wayside." Learning that she had been walking all the way from Winchester, Banks acknowledged: "I requested the cannoneers to give her a lift, and the gallant men . . . answered with alacrity." He went on to say that no one had attempted to "ascertain her complexion, but it is not impossible that she belonged to the class referred to in the resolution, and that her little limbs had been strengthened by some vague dream of liberty, to be lost or won in that hurried night march."

9. In Matthew 25.40, Jesus addresses these words to the righteous, who will earn their heavenly reward for having treated the humblest and neediest of humankind as they would have treated Jesus himself.

10. Ithuriel is one of the angels sent by Gabriel to guard Adam and Eve in *Paradise Lost*, 4.809–13. Finding Satan "Squat like a Toad, close at the ear of Eve" (799), "Ithuriel with his Spear / Touch'd lightly; for no falsehood can endure / Touch of Celestial temper, but returns / Of force to its own likeness: up he starts / Discover'd and surpris'd."

11. Child refers to the paired characters who serve the magician Prospero in Shakespeare's *The Tempest*. Caliban (now commonly identified as a representation of the dark peoples seeking to resist European colonization) is depicted in the play as an evil and bestial savage. Ariel, an airy spirit who had been imprisoned by Caliban's mother, the witch Sycorax, shows his gratitude to Prospero for releasing him by serving him willingly. Child identifies Caliban with the slaves of despotism (proslavery forces) and Ariel with the servants of freedom (abolitionists).

always prompt in the service of freedom. These two agents are in active competition. Choose which of them you will trust.

That you sincerely wish to save the republic the people do not doubt for a moment; and your scruples about constitutional obligations have commanded their respect. But events have educated them rapidly, and they now deny that any constitutional obligation exists toward rebels who have thrown off the Constitution, spit upon it, and trampled it under their feet. If you entered into partnership with a man who robbed you of your funds, set your house on fire, and seized you by the throat with intent to strangle you, should you consider yourself still legally bound by the articles of partnership? I trow not. But it is urged that some slaveholders are loyal. I apprehend that their name is not legion, nor their loyalty always of a kind that will stand much wear and tear. The course that some of them have pursued recalls to my mind the words of the same old Hebrew prophet: "The men of the Confederacy have brought thee even to the border. The men that were at peace with thee have deceived thee. They that eat thy bread have laid a wound under thee."[12]

Much has been said concerning the inhumanity of arming the blacks. All war is necessarily inhuman. But I cannot perceive why there is more inhumanity in a black man fighting for his freedom than in a white man fighting for the same cause. Doubtless long years of oppression has [*sic*] brutalized many of the slaves, and darkened their moral sense almost as much as it has that of the slaveholders. If, wearied out with their long waiting in vain for help, and goaded by the increase of their sufferings, they should resort to insurrection, indiscriminate cruelty might be the result. But this danger would be averted by organizing them under the instruction and guidance of officers who would secure their confidence by just treatment. They are by nature docile, and have been trained to habits of obedience. There seems no reason to apprehend that their passage through any district would be accompanied with more devastation than that of other troops. As for bravery, they would be stimulated to it by the most powerful motives that can act on human nature; the prospect of freedom on the one hand, and the fear of falling into their masters' power on the other.

I need not speak of emancipation as a measure of policy. Enough has been said and written to prove that enlightened self-interest requires it at our hands. But there is one aspect of the question which seems to me very

12. Obadiah 1.7.

important, though generally overlooked. I mean the importance of securing the *confidence* of the slaves, of making them feel *secure* of their freedom, if they serve the United States. One of the "contrabands"[13] at Fortress Monroe said: "We *want* to work for the United States; but we can't work with *heart,* because we feel anxious about what the United States means to do with us when the war is over." I often see suggestions about impressing the negroes and compelling them to work for us. Last night's paper states that orders have been given to employ them in some of the camps, and to pay wages to those of them who are *free*. In the name of justice, what right have we to force *slaves* to work without wages? What right have we to recognize *slaves* in persons working for the United States? Have we gone so far in this struggle, without learning yet that *heart*-labor is of infinitely more value than compulsory labor? [I]t is our duty, as well as our best policy, to deal justly and kindly by the poor fugitives who toil for us, and to stimulate their energies by making them feel *secure* of their freedom. *Your* word, officially spoken, can alone do this. So long as you delay to utter it, one officer will scourge them and send them to their masters to be again scourged, while another will protect them. The poor creatures, whose minds are darkened by ignorance and perplexed by their masters' falsehoods about the Yankees, become completely bewildered, and know not whom to trust. Their simple declaration, "We *want* to work for the United States, but we can't work with heart," seemed to me very significant and pathetic. Is not the *heart*-service of these loyal thousands too valuable to be thrown away? If their masters, in desperation, should promise them freedom as the reward for fighting *against* us, they would doubtless accept the offer as the best bargain they could make; because, alas, they have been unable to find out what the United States means to do with them. What candid person could blame them for such a course? Should not we do the same under similar circumstances?

Oh, President Lincoln, God has placed you as a father over these poor oppressed millions. Remember their forlorn condition! Think how they have been for generations deprived of the light of knowledge and the hope of freedom! Think of the cruel lashes inflicted on them for trying to learn to read the Word of God! Think of their wives polluted, and their children

---

13. Fugitive slaves who escaped to Union lines were called "contrabands." The term originated with General Benjamin Butler, who justified treating these runaways as "contraband of war"—"goods . . . directly auxiliary to military operations" and hence properly subject to confiscation from the enemy. Butler applied this policy at Fort Monroe, Virginia, where some nine hundred "contrabands" had gathered by late July 1861.

sold, without any means of redress for such foul and cruel wrongs! Imagine them stealing through midnight swamps, infested with snakes and alligators, guided toward freedom by the North Star, and then hurled back into bondage by Northern bloodhounds in the employ of the United States[!] Think how long their groans and prayers for deliverance have gone up before God, from the hidden recesses of Southern forests! Listen to the refrain of their plaintive hymn, "Let my people go!" Above all, think of their present woeful uncertainty, scourged and driven from one to another, not knowing whom to trust! We are told that uncounted prayers go up from their bruised hearts, in the secrecy of their rude little cabins, that "God would bress Massa Lincoln." Is there nothing that touches your heart in the simple trust of these poor, benighted suffering souls? In view of it, can you still allow the officers of the United States to lash them at their pleasure and send them back to their masters, on the plea that the *President* has given no orders on the subject? Shall *such* officers go unrebuked, while Gen. Hunter is checked in his wise and humane policy, and when the great, honest soul of Gen. Phelps[14] is driven to the alternative of disobeying the convictions of his own conscience, or quitting the service of his country? If you *can* thus stifle the moral enthusiasm of noble souls; if you *can* thus disappoint the hopes of poor, helpless wretches, who trust in you as the appointed agent of their deliverance, may God forgive you! It will require *infinite* mercy to do it.

I can imagine, in some degree, the embarrassments of your position, and I compassionate you for the heavy weight of responsibility that rests upon your shoulders. I know that you are surrounded by devils that have squeezed themselves into the disguise of toads. I pray you to lose no more time in counting these toads and calculating how big a devil each may contain. Look upward instead of downward. Place your reliance on *principles* rather than on men. God has placed you at the head of a great nation at a crisis when its free institutions are in extreme peril from enemies within and without. Lay your right arm on the buckler of the Almighty, and march fearlessly forward to universal freedom in the name of the Lord!

Pardon me if, in my earnestness, I have said aught that seems disrespectful. I have not so intended. I have been impelled to write this because night and day the plaintive song of the bondmen resounds in my ears:

14. General John Wolcott Phelps (1813–85), an abolitionist from Vermont, resigned his commission on 21 August 1862 when his superior, General Benjamin Butler, refused to allow him to recruit "contrabands" as soldiers and ordered him to set them at chopping wood instead.

"Go down, Moses, go down to Egypt's land,
And say to Pharaoh: 'Let my people go.' "[15]

That you may be guided by Him who has said: "First righteousness; and then peace," is the earnest prayer of

Yours, respectfully,
L. MARIA CHILD

15. The spiritual "Go Down, Moses" was first transcribed and published in 1861 by the Reverend Lewis C. Lockwood, a missionary organizing relief work among the "contrabands" of Fort Monroe. He sent Child a copy of it, which she refers to as "The Song of the Contrabands"; see LMC to Mary Stearns, 15 Dec. 1861, *SL* 400. In the next sentence Child paraphrases Isaiah 32.17 ("The work of righteousness shall be peace") and James 3.18 ("And the fruit of righteousness is sown in peace of them that make peace").

A Letter from L. Maria Child:

Emancipation and Amalgamation[1]

To the Editor of the N.Y. Tribune.

Sir: A gentleman in Maryland, to whom I sent my Tract on West India Emancipation, entitled "The Right Way the Safe Way,"[2] replied:

"On the wisdom of emancipation, and as proving that the right way is the safe way, I think your pamphlet is unanswerable. But here other things than wisdom are to be met. One of the most foolish and yet most potent assertions is that negroes and whites will amalgamate if the slaves are freed. My own belief, founded on very sufficient reasons, is that slavery, and not freedom, is the fruitful source of amalgamation; but I have no figures or evidence of any kind to prove this, other than what I see around me. If you have any statistics on this subject, which you think would be useful to the cause of Emancipation, you would much oblige me by forwarding them."

In reply, I wrote as follows:

"I am not aware that any statistics are on record concerning the subject of your inquiry. The outcry about future amalgamation is merely one of the artful dodges by which slaveholders and their allies seek to evade the main question. Of course, anybody who knows anything about slavery is well aware that amalgamation is the universal and inevitable result of that system. Gen. Lafayette, during his last visit to this country, remarked upon the *great change of complexion* that had taken place among the slaves since the period of our Revolution. I could furnish you with innumerable advertisements

New York Daily Tribune, 3 September; reprinted in the *National Anti-Slavery Standard,* 13 September 1862; and in *CC* 53/1423.

1. By sending this letter first to the *Tribune,* the leading Republican newspaper, Child was trying to reach a broad, mainstream audience.

2. In 1862, with the aim of fostering emancipationist sentiment in the border states, Child issued a second, updated edition of her tract *The Right Way the Safe Way, Proved by Emancipation in the British West Indies, and Elsewhere.* Addressed to a southern audience, the tract presents a mere "*business-*view" of the economic and social benefits that have resulted from emancipation in other countries. Child personally mailed copies to all state legislators in Maryland and Delaware and to hundreds of people in Virginia. Her tract reportedly won many converts in West Virginia, which broke away from Virginia and provided for gradual emancipation as of July 1863. The letter from this Maryland correspondent suggests that *The Right Way the Safe Way* may have exerted some influence there, too; Maryland abolished slavery in 1864.

from Southern papers describing runaway slaves with 'sandy hair,' 'blue eyes,' 'ruddy complexion,' 'easily passing for a white man,' etc., to say nothing of 'yellow boys' and 'light mulattoes.' But this is unnecessary; for your letter admits that slavery is a fruitful source of amalgamation."

Whether amalgamation would take place *legally*, as it now does *illegally*, if the slaves were freed, is not a question susceptible of *proof*. It must of course, remain a matter of *opinion* till experience furnishes evidence. But it seems to me quite superfluous to trouble ourselves about it. If there *is* an instinctive antipathy between the races, it will take care of itself, as natural antipathies and attractions are always sure to do. If there is *not* any natural antipathy, then the horror of amalgamation has no rational foundation. My own opinion is that there is *not* a natural antipathy between white and colored people. My reason for thinking so is that wherever the two classes have been brought into vicinity they have invariably mixed extensively; and, in view of their relative positions, it must be admitted that the mixture has been sought by the *whites*.

My own belief also is that prejudice against complexion is entirely founded upon pride, and grows out of the debased and degraded condition in which our laws and customs keep the colored people. This is sufficiently proved by the fact that slaveholders have the utmost horror of *legalized* amalgamation, while they have none at all of *illegal*. They would consider their families disgraced forever if a son should *marry* the most beautiful and intelligent of quadroons, but are quite undisturbed by his brood of illegitimate mulatto children, owning some "Coal-black Rose"[3] for their mother.

From all the information I can obtain, I should judge that there is much *less* mixture of white and colored in the British West Indies than there was before emancipation. The bad habits formed in slavery still cling to them in a considerable degree; for generations must be educated under better influences before the corrupt effects of a system so thoroughly unclean can be washed out of the character of a people. But the colored inhabitants of those islands are gradually acquiring habits of self-respect, and they more and more discountenance neglect of the marriage ceremony. Marriages have occurred between white and colored, and in some cases they have been persons of high position. Some judges and lawyers of distinction in the West Indies have married handsome, intelligent and well-educated mulatto ladies, and nothing has occurred to make them ashamed of their choice; for their wives

3. "Coal-black Rose" was a popular minstrel song.

preside over their households in a manner so graceful and dignified as to command respect even from *American* guests. But such cases are exceptional. Prejudices wear out slowly, and finally disappear, without violent collisions with the changing state of things. Carlyle[4] said, very wisely: "Be not dismayed. The old skin never falls off till a new skin has formed under it." We may safely trust to this law of nature. Legalized amalgamation can never become common so long as there is a prevailing prejudice against color; and when that "phantom dynasty" passes away with the centuries, its disappearance will harm no one, and posterity will wonder at the power it once exercised, as we now marvel at the terror our ancestors had of witchcraft. It is the duty of our day to obey the plain dictates of justice and humanity, which are also the dictates of enlightened policy. God will not fail in his promise that "the effects of righteousness shall be peace."[5]

This outcry about amalgamation, as the result of emancipation, is simply ridiculous, in view of the swarms of mulattoes, quadroons and octoroons, produced by slavery; but in view of the momentous issues now at stake in this country, it is worse than ridiculous, it is heartless, wicked trifling with the destinies of a great nation.

Candid, reflecting, disinterested men, all over the civilized world, agree that slavery is a bad system, injurious to *all* parties connected with it. Statistics abundantly prove that agriculture, commerce, manufactures, morals, education and internal improvements of all sorts, are rapidly advanced by free institutions. There is ample evidence of this in the comparative progress of different States in this country. Virginia furnishes one of these instructive illustrations. She surpasses other States in richness of soil, attractions of scenery and climate, wealth of mineral resources, noble rivers, and commodious harbors. At the time of the Revolution, her commerce was four times that of New-York; but in 1853 the imports into New York were valued at $180,000,000, while those of Virginia were less than $400,000. "Lands in Virginia, capable of producing from 25 to 30 bushels of wheat to the acre, and only 24 hours by rail from New York, are to be had for one-fortieth the price

---

4. Child is quoting freely from the chapter "Organic Filaments" in *Sartor Resartus* (1833–34), by the Scottish essayist and social critic Thomas Carlyle (1795–1881). The actual quotation reads: " 'In the living subject,' says [Professor Teufelsdröckh], 'change is wont to be gradual: thus, while the serpent sheds its old skin, the new is already formed beneath.' " " 'Said I not, Before the old skin was shed, the new had formed itself beneath it?' "

5. Isaiah 32.17: "And the work of righteousness shall be peace; and the effect of righteousness quietness and assurance for ever."

of similar land in New York itself." Such was the comparative value of land in those two States in 1856.

The prosperity of any State depends very largely on an intelligent, thriving *middle class*. Where slavery exists, society inevitably arranges itself into two classes, very widely separated from each other, and mutually deteriorated in character by the pernicious system which gives them no interests in common. The masters are unenterprising and indolent, from pride and inertia produced by the habit of living on another's earnings; while the slaves are lazy and shiftless, because they have no hope of bettering their condition by exertion. Slavery endangers our republican institutions by rendering impossible that enlightened middle class, which forms the solid foundation of republics. Freedom of speech, freedom of the press and free extension of knowledge, are the bulwarks of liberty; but slavery annuls them all, because their exercise is incompatible with its own safety. The phrase, "irrepressible conflict,"[6] merely expresses the *moral* antagonism, which *must*, in the very nature of things, exist between slavery and freedom. Slavery cannot preserve its own existence without undermining and eventually destroying that on which the very life of free institutions depends. On the other hand, free institutions cannot carry out the principles on which they are founded, without bringing the permanence of slavery into peril, even where there is no such intention. The principles of slavery, or the principles of freedom, *must* inevitably rule in this country. Is there anything so lovely, so beneficial or so reputable in slavery, that men should be willing to sacrifice this republic for the sake of preserving it?

It was formerly asserted that emancipation would produce massacres, fires, and all sorts of horrors. But England, France, the Dutch, the Swedes and the Danes successively emancipated their slaves, and not a throat was cut, or a building fired, in consequence.[7] That pretext being taken away, slaveholders now say: "The two races cannot live together in freedom. If we emancipate, universal amalgamation will be the consequence." What a laughable contradiction there is between the two propositions! If there is such imminent *danger* of mixture, what becomes of the alleged *natural antipathy* of the races?

I presume you are aware that slavery has forced even the United States census into its service; making use of *compulsory* labor, as usual. In order to

6. "The Irrepressible Conflict" was the title of a famous 1858 speech by Republican William Henry Seward (1801–72), Lincoln's secretary of state.

7. Child demonstrates this in *The Right Way the Safe Way.*

prove that freedom produces insanity in colored people, it returns an extraordinary number of colored lunatics in the free States; but, as often happens to dealers in falsehood, a hole is left in the bag, through which the cat's head and claws peep out; for some places represented as encumbered with colored lunatics had not a single colored resident. Mr. De Bow,[8] the unscrupulous champion of slavery, gives no particular statistics of amalgamation; but in his Compendium of the United States Census for 1850 he makes a remark apparently intended to show that where the colored people are free, amalgamation increases. He says: "While nearly half of the colored population in the non-slaveholding States are mulatto, only about one-ninth in the slaveholding States are mulatto." His own tables, in the same census, show that less than one-third of the colored population of the free States are mulattoes. If you carefully cipher out these tables, you will find that in the free States there is a considerable fraction less than *one* mulatto to every two hundred whites; while in the slave States there are more than *eleven* mulattoes to every two hundred whites. A careful computation of the proportions shows thirteen times more amalgamation at the South than in the North; but in making this estimate an important fact is kept out of view, viz: that very many of our colored citizens originated in the South, and a large proportion came to us already bleached to various shades of brown or yellow, by plantation processes. This is meagre information in answer to your request for statistics on the subject, but it is all I can furnish.

With the hope that Maryland will ere long be blessed with free institutions,

I am respectfully yours,

L. Maria Child.

8. James Dunwoody Brownson De Bow (1820–67) founded and edited the proslavery journal *De Bow's Commercial Review*. He directed the census bureau in Louisiana from 1850 to 1853 and was appointed superintendent of the U.S. census in 1853.

A Tribute to Col. Robert G. Shaw

My heart is full of sorrow and sympathy, which seek expression. From the beginning of the war I have watched the course of Col. Robert G. Shaw with intense and peculiar interest; for I knew his character abounded in those noble and excellent qualities of which the country and the times stand so much in need; and always I have feared that he might be cut off in the morning of his beautiful life.

Then that Fifty-fourth regiment, offering their lives with such cheerful bravery, to achieve the freedom of their cruelly oppressed race! If only their lives had been sacrificed, we should have been sad, but exultant withal; for this existence is brief at best, and self-sacrifice is holy and immortal. But to think of those brave, devoted men, after their exhaustion by hunger, fatigue and the hard labors of battle, sent to Charleston, to be insulted and tortured by ferocious tyrants, and then sold into slavery! Father of Mercies! how this thought agonizes just and humane souls!

As for the mean, vindictive answer to the request for the body of their brave young Colonel, it will produce the effect that all such manifestations do. It will impress more deeply than ever upon the minds of the people how infernal the spirit of slavery is. To the pure and heroic soul, which had just parted from that beautiful body, it could do no harm; and his immediate family have principles that will lift them above the possibility of feeling degraded by suffering with, and dying with, and being buried with God's despised and persecuted poor. They will not forget the words, "Inasmuch as ye did it unto the least of these my brethren, ye did it unto me."[1]

I was thinking this as I walked homeward, after reading the daily news. I reflected how every inch of freedom had been won for the human race by the sacrifice of thousands of precious lives. There passed before me a long procession of men,

> "For God, for Truth, for Freedom's sake,
> Content the bitter cup to take,

New York Evening Post; reprinted in the *National Anti-Slavery Standard,* 15 August 1863; and in *CC* 56/1498.

1. In Matthew 25.40, Jesus addresses these words to the righteous, who will earn their heavenly reward for having treated the humblest and neediest of humankind as they would have treated Jesus himself.

> And silently, in fearless faith,
> Bowing their noble souls to death."

I remembered how despotism had always delighted to make their martyrdom look mean, and in how many signal instances the effort had failed. When priests and centurions crucified Jesus between thieves, they satisfied the arrogance and prejudice of his day, and thought they had effectually disgraced him. But instead thereof they handed themselves down to everlasting disgrace; while the cross, which they regarded with such proud contempt, floats through the world's history transfigured with holy life.

I was pondering these thoughts so deeply that I started involuntarily as my eyes turned toward the setting sun. A dark cloud rested on the horizon, and downward through it meandered a narrow line of intensely brilliant sunlight, precisely in the form of an S. When we are overwhelmed with some great sorrow I suppose, we are all more or less inclined to be superstitious; for at such moments the soul, in its utter helplessness, looks tremblingly beyond this dark vale of shadows, and implores some light from Heaven. The splendid vision was soon wavering and sinking behind a veil of mist. But while it lasted it lifted my soul out of its deep despondency; for it seemed as if the dark gate through which that lovely young soul had passed had been transiently left ajar, and I had caught a glimpse of the immortal glory into which he had entered.

My state of feeling will not seem to you exaggerated, for you are probably aware how much the cause of Freedom owes to several members of the Shaw family; and that, too, at a time when anti-slavery was not beginning to be respectable as it now is, but when no wealth or standing could protect its advocates from the neglect and sarcasm of society. The money they gave so liberally was the smallest portion of the aid they afforded. With moral courage beyond all praise, they stood side by side with a despised band of reformers against the world of wealth and fashion to which they by position belonged; and the crowning beauty of all was that it was done simply and naturally, without the slightest indication of conscious merit.

The capacity to do this, I think, they derived, by the blessing of God, from the founder of the family, Robert G. Shaw, the best of the "merchant princes" of Boston. When I say that he was a thoroughly honest man, I do not mean to limit the significance of the term to its relation with dollars and cents. He had an honest moral sense, which pervaded all he did and thought. He never espoused the anti-slavery cause, perhaps from habitual prudence, perhaps because he was getting too old to throw himself into new agitations. But it needed no great insight to conjecture what such a man thought of a system that robbed poor laborers of their wages, and added thereto the blasphemy of calling itself an ordination of Providence. A short time before his death he said to Col. Shaw, and another grandson who was present, then mere lads, "My children, I am leaving the stage of action, and you are entering upon it. I exhort you to use your example and influence against intemperance and slavery." As the last great change approached, he seemed dreamily to pass into a land of vision, and his lips murmured words of recognition to departed friends and relatives, as if he already saw them in the spirit world. One of these murmured recognitions indicated the kindly sympathies of his great, good heart. "Ah," said he, "here is an old negro just come into this world. He has been a slave. Poor fellow! how much he has suffered."

If some of his children inherited from him the qualities which prompted them to espouse an unpopular cause, and to stand by it steadfastly, for righteousness' sake, it is likely that he, on his part, had his own honest convictions deepened by their open and uniform testimony. Doubtless the state of mind revealed in these last hours may be partly traced to the influence of a noble son and two noble daughters. I have before me now a vision of one of those sisters, which I hope to find in my gallery of choicest pictures when I exchange this world of false shows for the higher world of realities. She was presiding over a table at one of our annual anti-slavery fairs, according to her usual custom. On her right hand was the table of a very intelligent, lady-like person, whose complexion was brown. It was a rainy day, and few purchasers came. She remarked to me that she seemed to be of no use, for one could easily tend several tables. I replied, "But you are of great use. For a person of your position to be merely seen here, in close proximity with one of a race that is socially proscribed, is of incalculable moral use." "Is it?" said she, in her quiet, unaffected way. "Do let me move nearer to her, then." And, after some show of arranging things on her table, she moved her chair farther to the right. It was to the right in more senses than one. How I loved and reverenced her! As she uttered those simple, unpretending words it seemed to me that her countenance was irradiated with moral beauty. I looked at them both, as they sat side by side, and the picture was inwardly daguerreotyped, which I hope to see outwardly in my gallery above. It was a charming picture; for they were fine specimens of different types of the human family. She of the fairest Anglo-Saxon type, the other with the warmly-tinted complexion and large, lustrous dark eyes of the Anglo-African.

Young Col. Shaw had many healthy influences to shield him from the corrupting and weakening effects of worldly prosperity. He inherited from his excellent grandfather that innate honesty of character which is far more valuable than bank shares and broad acres; and instead of being diminished by transmission through his parents, they confirmed and developed it by the largest and wisest moral culture.

At the outbreak of this war he stood on the threshold of life, with the fairest and happiest prospects spread before him. An only son, dearly and deservedly beloved by his parents and by a group of sympathizing sisters, a favorite with a numerous band of relatives and friends, to whom he was endeared by his gentle, refined and conscientious nature, no person who saw him before the war could have imagined that it would be his destiny to die, sword in hand, storming a fort, amid flashes of lightning and roar of artillery. But when the free institutions of the country he loved were brought into peril by traitors he did not pause to dally with the allurements of life. He marched at once, with the New York Seventh, to the protection of the Capital. As a soldier his bravery and firmness were only equalled by his kindness. He took the gentlest care of wounded comrades, and evinced a woman's thoughtful tenderness in cutting locks of hair from the dead to solace the bleeding hearts of distant relatives.

When the raising of colored troops was proposed, his well-known character caused him to be at once singled out as a desirable officer. When the great moral influence he could thus exert was urged upon him, he did, as his noble-hearted aunt had done when a similar suggestion was made to her, he moved to the right immediately. His parents were well aware of the terrible risks he would incur, but they conquered all personal considerations, and cheerfully advised him to follow the promptings of his own conscience. There was a tie of peculiar tenderness which bound him to this life. I allude to his young bride only to show how much he sacrificed to a sense of duty. But this is sacred ground; and with reverent sympathy I throw a veil over the unspeakable agony of that separation. Whether the parting exhortation of his honored grandfather recurred to his mind, and helped him to form his decision with such solemn, self-sacrificing heroism, I know not. But he took the dangerous post without any other hesitation than that which arose from a modest distrust of his own experience and ability. In what manner of spirit he undertook this great responsibility may be inferred from the following little incident: While the Fifty-fourth were being drilled at Readville, many people visited the encampment. Among them were two intelligent, well-bred colored strangers, who brought letters of introduction to the Colonel. When he invited them to dine with him, they thanked him, but respectfully declined. Being urged, they said: "You are aware, Colonel Shaw, that there is a prejudice against our complexion." "All gentlemen are the same to me," he replied, "whatever their complexion may be." He seated them at his table, and treated them with the same unpatronizing courtesy with which he would have treated the Duke of Argyle. His letters to friends at that time were filled with expressions of pleasure at the number of intelligent colored people with whom he was brought into contact. He seemed to rejoice over all indications of their progress, as a generous heart does over the good luck of a brother who has been kept down by misfortune. The good character the regiment obtained in the neighborhood of the encampment was a source of great gratification to him, and in a letter from James's Island, received almost simultaneously with the tidings of his death, he expressed delight at the high terms in which everybody spoke of the bravery of the Fifty-fourth.

I have said that three of the immediate descendants of Robert G. Shaw fought the moral battle against slavery with quiet but steadfast heroism for many years, and the two grandsons, who received his parting injunction, have followed their courageous example in the sterner warfare that is now waging. One of them, a worthy son of her who moved so promptly to the right side, is battling manfully in the ranks of Freedom. God grant that his life may be spared to see the existence of this republic secured on the only safe and permanent basis—the utter extinction of slavery.

There was another cousin of Colonel Shaw's, by the mother's side, who, like him, passed away in the storm of battle from a world which had great attractions for him. I remember Theodore Parkman when he was a vision of infant beauty. His exquisitely fair complexion, blue eyes, and shower of golden ringlets at once brought to mind the words of Pope Gregory, *"Non Angli, sed Angeli."*[2] Afterward, I heard of him as a gentle, refined, highly cultured young man, just returned from Europe, with qualifications to render him an ornament to any path of life his taste might suggest. But the trump of war had sounded, and like his noble-hearted cousins he left the flowery paths of life without a murmur, and relinquished all his high aspirations and tender associations, to serve his suffering country in her hour of

2. "Not Angles but Angels," traditionally quoted as the words of Pope Gregory I (540–604) when he saw two English slaves (Angles) in the market.

need. His body lies in North Carolina under a tree on which a comrade hastily carved his initials.

> "Eyes of light and lips of roses,
>   Such as Hylas wore,
> Over all that curtain closes
>   Which shall rise no more!
> Who shall offer youth and beauty
>   On the wasting shrine
> Of a stern and lofty duty,
>   With a faith like thine?"

When I gazed on that remarkable sunset, which seemed like a gleam of eternal glory beyond the dark curtain, I felt that the young hero for whom my tears were falling was not a lonely stranger in that realm of light. I seemed to see the kindly grandfather placing his hand in benediction on his head, and gentle cousin Theodore greeting him with love. Many of the Fifty-fourth had followed their brave leader through the dark gate, and among them the poor old negro who, years ago, had been seen in vision, recognized also his kindred and descendants. They all smiled on each other, and when memory glanced backward to the loved ones in the world they had left so suddenly, the genial patriarch said: "Be not disturbed; the separation is but for a moment, they will follow."

Meanwhile, the voices of mourners on earth struggled with tears while they sang:

> "Peace be with thee, O our brother,
>   In the spirit-land!
> Vainly look we for another
>   In thy place to stand.
> Unto Truth and Freedom giving
>   All thy early powers,
> Be thy virtues with the living,
>   And thy spirit ours!"
> —L.M.C.

Advice from an Old Friend

For many years I have felt great sympathy for you, my brethren and sisters, and I have tried to do what I could to help you to freedom. And now that you have at last received the long-desired blessing, I most earnestly wish that you should make the best possible use of it. I have made this book to encourage you to exertion by examples of what colored people are capable of doing. Such men and women as Toussaint l'Ouverture, Benjamin Banneker, Phillis Wheatley, Frederick Douglass, and William and Ellen Crafts,[1] prove that the power of *character* can overcome all external disadvantages, even that most crushing of all disadvantages, Slavery. Perhaps few of you will be able to stir the hearts of large assemblies by such eloquent appeals as those of Frederick Douglass, or be able to describe what you have seen and heard so gracefully as Charlotte L. Forten does.[2] Probably none of you will be called to govern a state as Toussaint l'Ouverture did; for such a remarkable career as his does not happen once in hundreds of years. But the Bible says, "He that ruleth his own spirit is greater than he that ruleth a kingdom";[3] and such a ruler every man and woman can become, by the help and blessing of God. It is not the *greatness* of the thing a man does which makes him worthy of respect; it is the doing *well* whatsoever he hath to do. In many respects, your opportunities for usefulness are more limited than those of others; but you

The Freedmen's Book (1865), pp. 269–276.

1. Toussaint L'Ouverture (ca. 1743–1803) led the slave uprising in Santo Domingo that culminated in the founding of Haiti. Benjamin Banneker (1731–1806), born of free African American parents, published the first almanac in the United States and won respect as a mathematician and astronomer. Phillis Wheatley (ca. 1753–84), kidnapped into slavery as a child, published the first book by an African American, *Poems on Various Subjects, Religious and Moral* (1773). Frederick Douglass (1818–95) became the best known African American in abolitionist ranks after his escape from slavery; he published several autobiographies and edited his own newspaper. William (1824–1900) and Ellen (1826–91) Craft were famous for their daring escape from slavery, Ellen disguised as a white man and William as her slave, recounted in their narrative *Running a Thousand Miles for Freedom* (1860). Child included biographies of these and many other African American role models in *The Freedmen's Book*.

2. Charlotte Forten Grimké (1837–1914), born into Philadelphia's most prominent African American family, joined Boston-area abolitionist circles in the 1850s and went to Port Royal, South Carolina, during the Civil War to teach the newly emancipated slaves. A long extract from her two-part *Atlantic Monthly* article on her experiences, "Life on the Sea Islands" (1864), appears in *The Freedmen's Book*.

3. Child is paraphrasing Proverbs 16.32: "He that is slow to anger is better than the mighty; and he that ruleth his spirit than he that taketh a city."

have one great opportunity peculiar to yourselves. You can do a vast amount of good to people in various parts of the world, and through successive generations, by simply being sober, industrious, and honest. There are still many slaves in Brazil and in the Spanish possessions. If you are vicious, lazy, and careless, their masters will excuse themselves for continuing to hold them in bondage, by saying: "Look at the freedmen of the United States! What idle vagabonds they are! How dirty their cabins are! How slovenly their dress! That proves that negroes cannot take care of themselves, that they are not fit to be free." But if your houses look neat, and your clothes are clean and whole, and your gardens well weeded, and your work faithfully done, whether for yourselves or others, then all the world will cry out, "You see that negroes *can* take care of themselves; and it is a sin and a shame to keep such men in Slavery." Thus, while you are serving your own interests, you will be helping on the emancipation of poor weary slaves in other parts of the world. It is a great privilege to have a chance to do extensive good by such simple means, and your Heavenly Father will hold you responsible for the use you make of your influence.

Your manners will have a great effect in producing an impression to your advantage or disadvantage. Be always respectful and polite toward your associates, and toward those who have been in the habit of considering you an inferior race. It is one of the best ways to prove that you are not inferior. Never allow yourselves to say or do anything in the presence of women of your own color which it would be improper for you to say or do in the presence of the most refined white ladies. Such a course will be an education for them as well as for yourselves. When you appoint committees about your schools and other public affairs, it would be wise to have both men and women on the committees. The habit of thinking and talking about serious and important matters makes women more sensible and discreet. Such consultations together are in fact a practical school both for you and them; and the more modest and intelligent women are, the better will children be brought up.

Personal appearance is another important thing. It is not necessary to be rich in order to dress in a becoming manner. A pretty dress for festival occasions will last a long while, if well taken care of; and a few wild-flowers, or bright berries, will ornament young girls more tastefully than jewels. Working-clothes that are clean and nicely patched always look respectable; and they make a very favorable impression, because they indicate that the wearer is neat and economical. And here let me say, that it is a very great saving to mend garments well, and before the rents get large. We thrifty Yankees have a saying that "a stitch in time saves nine"; and you will find by experience that neglected mending will require more than nine stitches instead of one, and will not look so well when it is done.

The appearance of your villages will do much to produce a favorable opinion concerning your characters and capabilities. Whitewash is not expensive; and it takes but little time to transplant a cherokee rose, a jessamine, or other wild shrubs and vines, that make the poorest cabin look beautiful; and, once planted, they will be growing while you are working or sleeping. It is a public benefit to remove everything dirty or unsightly, and to surround homes with verdure and flowers; for a succession of pretty cottages makes the whole road pleasant, and cheers all passers by; while they are at the same time an advertisement, easily read by all men, that the people who live there are not lazy, slovenly, or vulgar. The rich pay a great deal of money for pictures to ornament their walls, but a whitewashed cabin, with flowering-shrubs and vines clustering round it, is a pretty picture freely exhibited to all men. It is a public benefaction.

But even if you are as yet too poor to have a house and garden of your own, it is still in your power to be a credit and an example to your race: by working for others as faithfully as you would work for yourself; by taking as good care of their tools as you would if they were your own; by always keeping your promises, however inconvenient it may be; by being strictly honest in all your dealings; by being temperate in your habits, and never speaking a profane or indecent word,—by pursuing such a course you will be consoled with an inward consciousness of doing right in the sight of God, and be a public benefactor by your example, while at the same time you will secure respect and prosperity for yourself by establishing a good character. A man whose conduct inspires confidence is in a fair way to have house and land of his own, even if he starts in the world without a single cent.

Be careful of your earnings, and as saving in your expenses as is consistent with health and comfort; but never allow yourselves to be stingy. Avarice is a mean vice, which eats all the heart out of a man. Money is a good thing, and you ought to want to earn it, as a means of improving the condition of yourselves and families. But it will do good to your character, and increase your happiness, if you impart a portion of your earnings to others who are in need. Help as much as you conveniently can in building churches and school-houses for the good of all, and in providing for the sick and the aged. If your former masters and mistresses are in trouble, show them every kindness in your power, whether they have treated you kindly or not. Remember the words of the blessed Jesus: "Do good to them that hate you, and pray for them which despitefully use you and persecute you."[4]

There is one subject on which I wish to guard you against disappointment. Do not be discouraged if freedom brings you more cares and fewer advantages than you expected. Such a great change as it is from Slavery to Freedom cannot be completed all at once. By being brought up as slaves, you have formed some bad habits, which it will take time to correct. Those who were formerly your masters have acquired still worse habits by being brought up as slaveholders; and they cannot be expected to change all at once. Both of you will gradually improve under the teaching of new circumstances. For a good while it will provoke many of them to see those who were once their slaves acting like freemen. They will doubtless do many things to vex and discourage you, just as the slaveholders in Jamaica did after emancipation there.[5] They seemed to want to drive their emancipated bondmen to insurrection, that they might have a pretext for saying: "You see what a bad effect freedom has on negroes! We told you it would be so!" But the colored people of Jamaica behaved better than their former masters wished them to do. They left the plantations where they were badly treated, or poorly paid, but they worked diligently elsewhere. Their women and children raised vegetables and fowls and carried them to market; and, by their united industry and economy, they soon had comfortable little homes of their own.

I think it would generally be well for you to work for your former masters, if they treat you well, and pay you as much as you could earn elsewhere. But if they show a disposition to oppress you, quit their service, and work for somebody who will treat you like freemen. If they use violent language to you, never use impudent language to them. If they cheat you, scorn to cheat them in return. If they break their promises, never break yours. If they propose to women such connections as used to be common under the bad system of Slavery, teach them that freedwomen not only have the legal power

4. Matthew 5.44.

5. *The Freedmen's Book* includes a long article on "The Beginning and Progress of Emancipation in the British West Indies" in which Child stresses the success of the former slaves in acquiring land and establishing schools, churches, and mutual aid societies. In her tract *The Right Way the Safe Way*, however, she also acknowledges that the transition from slavery to freedom had been rougher in Jamaica than elsewhere because Jamaican planters fiercely resisted emancipation and tried to replace slavery with an equally exploitative system of peonage. Taking a leaf from the Jamaican example, southern slaveholders enforced such peonage by preventing African Americans from buying land.

to protect themselves from such degradation, but also that they have pride of character. If in fits of passion, they abuse your children as they formerly did, never revenge it by any injury to them or their property. It is an immense advantage to any man always to keep the right on his side. If you pursue this course you will always be superior, however rich or elegant may be the man or woman who wrongs you.

I do not mean by this that you ought to submit tamely to insult or oppression. Stand up for your rights, but do it in a manly way. Quit working for a man who speaks to you contemptuously, or who tries to take a mean advantage of you, when you are doing your duty faithfully by him. If it becomes necessary, apply to magistrates to protect you and redress your wrongs. If you are so unlucky as to live where the men in authority, whether civil or military, are still disposed to treat the colored people as slaves, let the most intelligent among you draw up a statement of your grievances and send it to some of your firm friends in Congress, such as the Hon. Charles Sumner, the Hon. Henry Wilson, and the Hon. George W. Julian.[6]

A good government seeks to make laws that will equally protect and restrain all men. Heretofore you had no reason to respect the laws of this country, because they punished you for crime, in many cases more severely than white men were punished, while they did nothing to protect your rights. But now that good President Lincoln has made you free, you will be legally protected in your rights and restrained from doing wrong, just as other men are protected and restrained. It is one of the noblest privileges of freemen to be able to respect the law, and to rely upon it always for redress of grievances, instead of revenging one wrong by another wrong.

You will have much to put up with before the new order of things can become settled on a permanent foundation. I am grieved to read in the newspapers how wickedly you are still treated in some places; but I am not surprised, for I knew that Slavery was a powerful snake, that would try to do mischief with its tail after its head was crushed. But, whatever wrongs you may endure, comfort yourselves with two reflections: first, that there is the

6. Child names three of the most committed Radical Republicans in Congress: Massa-chusetts senator Charles Sumner (1811–74), who not only shaped the Fourteenth and Fifteenth Amendments giving African American men citizenship and the vote, but campaigned for a civil rights amendment; Massachusetts senator Henry Wilson (1812–75), later vice president under Ulysses S. Grant; and Indiana congressman George Washington Julian (1817–99), who called for confiscating the estates of former Confederates and parcelling them out among emancipated slaves and poor whites.

beginning of a better state of things, from which your children will derive much more benefit than you can; secondly, that a great majority of the American people are sincerely determined that you shall be protected in your rights as freemen. Year by year your condition will improve. Year by year, if you respect yourselves, you will be more and more respected by white men. Wonderful changes have taken place in your favor during the last thirty years, and the changes are still going on. The Abolitionists did a great deal for you, by their continual writing and preaching against Slavery. Then this war enabled thousands of people to see for themselves what a bad institution Slavery was; and the uniform kindness with which you treated the Yankee soldiers raised you up multitudes of friends. There are still many pro-slavery people in the Northern States, who, from aristocratic pride or low vulgarity, still call colored people "niggers," and treat them as such. But the good leaven is now fairly worked into public sentiment, and these people, let them do what they will, cannot get it out.

The providence of God has opened for you an upward path. Walk ye in it, without being discouraged by the brambles and stones at the outset. Those who come after you will clear them away, and will place in their stead strong, smooth rails for the steam-car called Progress of the Colored Race.

Through the Red Sea into the Wilderness

To The Editor of the Independent:

I cannot look out upon the world, even for a few hours, without being struck by the marvelous changes that have taken place since I first began to think seriously on the destiny and dangers of this country. It seems but yesterday that the South called Massachusetts to account for allowing the publication of a newspaper that expressed sympathy for the slaves; and the Hon. Harrison Gray Otis,[1] a representative man of the Boston respectables, courteously assured our masters that there was no cause for alarm, he having examined the premises of said newspaper, and found therein "only one poor printer and a negro boy." If I had at that time prepared a book to encourage the black men of the South, and to diminish prejudice against color at the North, I could have only got it before a very small public, by means of "one poor printer and a negro boy." Now, my "Freedmen's Book" is printed at the best press in the country, and issued from the elegant store of Ticknor & Fields, without exciting, so far as I can observe, any distaste in the numerous clerks. I do not exult for myself over the stylish company in which my book appears; but over its significance with regard to my abused brother Sambo I do exult mightily.

I remember, as a dream of last night, how I saw the supplicating figure of the slave standing behind the minister in his pulpit, the judge upon the bench, the writer at his desk, and senators and presidents taking their oath of office. Always and everywhere the dark, sad shadow rose before me, and it grieved me that so few others could see it. Now, the black man is introduced to me in every form of art and literature. In music stores I find him "marching on" with John Brown to the "year of jubilo." If I go to Williams & Everett's, the first that attracts my attention, among the admirable statu- ettes by Rogers, is a stalwart negro guiding a wounded soldier through the swamp.[2] With what brotherly tenderness he holds the fainting Yankee in his

Independent, 21 December 1865, p. 1.

1. Harrison Gray Otis (1765–1848) was the mayor of Boston when William Lloyd Garrison began publishing the *Liberator,* to which Child refers here. She is implicitly contrasting the friendly reception of *The Freedmen's Book* with the hostile reception of her *Appeal in Favor of That Class of Americans Called Africans* thirty-two years before.

2. Child is describing *The Wounded Scout: A Friend in the Swamp* (1864), one of the best known and most successful of the Civil War groups produced by the Massachusetts sculptor

arms, and how confidingly the wounded man leans upon him! It brings moisture to my eyes to look upon it; for there is more in that expressive group than the kind negro and the helpless white, put on an equality by danger and suffering; it is a significant lesson of human brotherhood for all the coming ages.

Artistically considered, it seems to me that the best of all these excellent statuettes by Rogers is the one entitled "Taking the Oath, and Asking for Rations."[3] The lady, a dainty specimen of Southern beauty, averts her head while she places her hand on the book, and looks down compassionately on her hungry little boy, as if he were her excuse for professing loyalty. The United States officer, who administers the oath, is a noble specimen of modern knighthood. Raising his cap reverently and gracefully, in the presence of God and beauty, he looks upon the lady with a mingled expression of gallantry and pity. Of course, the scene would be incomplete without Sambo; and he is introduced in the form of a ragged negro lad, leaning on an old basket, that is to be filled with rations from the United States. He watches "missis" very earnestly, being obviously curious to see what wry faces she will make while swallowing the bitter pill; but she knows it is only a *bread* pill, and she takes it very calmly. The pretty hand that rests on the Bible looks too delicate to handle a whip; but we know that very lady-like looking hands *have* done such things, and will do them again, if the power remains.

Among the beautiful works of art always on exhibition at the store of Childs & Jenks, my attention was soon attracted by Bellows' fine picture called "The Echo."[4] One returning soldier is wakening echo with his bugle, while in another part of the boat a pale and wounded comrade is lying down with his head in his mother's lap. At the stern, the inevitable Sambo is taking care of the ample folds of a U.S. flag.

John Rogers (1829–1904), an abolitionist sympathizer known for his naturalistic narrative approach. The original is in bronze, but Rogers mass-produced his statuettes as plaster casts. The scene refers to the vital assistance that southern slaves gave to Union soldiers during the war, when a reverse Underground Railroad run by African Americans helped whites to escape from Confederate captors and prisons.

3. Another of John Rogers's Civil War sculptures. With many plantations devastated by Union troops or lying idle after the mass flight of former slaves, hunger stalked the conquered South. To be eligible for U.S. government rations, southern whites had to take a loyalty oath.

4. Probably Albert Fitch Bellows (1829–83), Massachusetts painter. Although "The Echo" remains unidentified, the scene depicted again alludes to the role of African Americans in guarding the U.S. flag during the war, both literally in battles such as the assault on Fort Wagner and symbolically by helping to defeat the Confederacy and save the Union.

Ah, thought I, everybody sees him now. Passing into the street, I saw two good-looking colored men in a carriage, whose dress indicated that they were officers of the U.S. A white driver was saying to them, respectfully, "Where shall I drive?" It was gratifying to me to see that patriotism had so far conquered prejudice that he could respect men who had served the country, whatever might be their complexion. I felt as if that sight repaid me for thirty years of conflict. All through the progress of the war I longed for that great glow of the heart which would have been kindled by the sight of a nation truly repentant and eager to make atonement for a great wrong. We early Abolitionists, you know, dreamed of great miracles to be wrought by moral influence. We greeted Birney, and Thome, and the Grimkes, as forerunners of a regenerated South.[5] We were mistaken in that. A little leaven will, indeed, leaven the whole lump, provided you can get it in; but despotism guarded itself so strictly at the South that the leaven of freedom could be worked in only by the sword. Yet our arduous mission was far enough from being in vain; for when the inevitable time for the sword came, would Northern sentiment have been in any readiness to meet the grand emergency had it not been for truths previously scattered broadcast through the land by the warnings, exhortations, and rebukes of the early Abolitionists? I trow not. Proslavery remained strong at the North, in spite of all our efforts; but the truths we uttered did so far leaven the whole cold mass of public sentiment that the Free States were prepared to resist the further encroachments of slavery into the territories. This seemed to us a small result for so much zeal and labor; but behold what has come of it! Slavery is abolished and cast out of the Constitution.

An old Rip Van Winkle,[6] whose long conservative nap was disturbed by the anti-slavery excitement, said: "I wonder what ails the people. It seems as if there was something going about in the air to make them crazy." And there is indeed something marvelous in the moral electricity which flashes through all classes when the hour of great reformations is approaching. It is doubtless evolved by spiritual laws, as invisible in their preparation and as certain in

5. James Gillespie Birney (1792–1857), James A. Thome (1809–73), and Sarah and Angelina Grimké (1792–1873, 1805–79) were all converts to abolition from southern slaveholding ranks who joined the movement in 1834–35.

6. Rip Van Winkle, the title character of Washington Irving's famous story, sleeps through the American Revolution and is taken by the townspeople for a Tory when he describes himself as a good subject of King George III. Child is implying that the Civil War has been a second American Revolution through which proslavery aristocrats have slept.

their effects as are the natural laws which produce thunder and lightning when the atmosphere needs purification.

The electricity of anti-slavery was attracted toward heroic natures, and its touch made them more heroic. Would that the record of the brave unknown could have been preserved! It would be a noble monument to the courage, self-sacrifice, and liberality of the working-classes of the Free States. One incident, which made a lively impression on me at the time, recurs to my mind. When the Ladies' Anti-Slavery Society was driven from their room in Boston, Francis Jackson offered them the use of his house for another meeting.[7] When warned that it might be demolished by a mob, he calmly replied: "Then I will build another, where you can meet." Among those notified to attend the meetings was a worthy woman at the North End of the city—one of the honorable few who believe in labor, and prove their faith by their works. She was busy at the wash-tub when told that there was to be a meeting at Mr. Jackson's, and that the ladies expected to be mobbed again. She wiped the suds from her arms, and, resting them a-kimbo on her sides, she said, slowly and emphatically, with an air that might have defied armies: "So you expect a mob, do you? I'll *certainly* be there." The Hon. Harrison Gray Otis would have ranked the words of that woman at the wash-tub with the labors of the "poor printer and the negro boy," as things of no account to the Southern aristocracy. But such agents constitute the foundation of society; and when society heaves at its foundations, strong castles are destined to fall.

We have traveled far since those days. We have passed through the Red Sea, and here we are in the Wilderness, with multitudes ready to bow down and worship the golden calf of trade, and a doubtful sort of Moses, who seems to occupy himself more earnestly with striving to save the drowning host of Pharaoh than he does with leading Israel into the promised land.[8]

---

7. In October 1835, a mob broke up the meeting of the Boston Female Anti-Slavery Society, at which George Thompson was rumored to be speaking. Thompson had already been spirited out of Boston by the Childs, but the mob vandalized the Massachusetts Anti-Slavery Society office and abducted Garrison, driving him through the streets with a rope around his body until he was rescued by a sympathizer and lodged in jail for his own protection. The wealthy Bostonian Francis Jackson (1789–1861) was a strong supporter of the abolitionist cause and served many years as president of the Massachusetts Anti-Slavery Society.

8. Child is drawing an analogy between the American people's passage from slavery to freedom and the biblical story of the Exodus. When Moses led the children of Israel out of slavery in Egypt, the armies of Pharoah pursued them up to the Red Sea, but God enabled Moses to divide the sea, allowing the children of Israel to pass through it and drowning Pharoah's army in the waters. In a subsequent episode, Moses' brother Aaron induces the

On this point the President's Message does not reassure me very strongly.[9] It contains good-sounding generalities. But I like not the promise that the freedmen shall be "protected in their rights *as laborers.*" It seems to imply a distinction between the rights of *men* and the rights of *laborers.* Such a promise would be deemed an insult to Yankee working-men, or Irish laborers. The assumption that there is no difference between loyal states and states that remained disloyal till rebellion was outwardly put down by force leads to conclusions that seem very illogical. The President says that, if the U.S. Government regulates suffrage in the rebellious states, it is bound to do the same in the loyal states. Is he then bound to appoint provisional governors for New York and Massachusetts because he has appointed them in Carolina, Mississippi, etc.? When an individual commits a breach of the peace he forfeits his civil rights, and puts himself out of the protection of the government. Should it not be the same with states that have committed such an awful breach of the peace? The President seems bent upon carrying out his hazardous plan of reconstruction, if he possibly can; and if he can't, he won't. Let us hope that he can't. The opening of Congress promises well. The Republican members stand in solid phalanx, facing in the right direction. May Heaven preserve them from the old chronic disease of Congress—weakness of the spine!

---

children of Israel to build and worship a golden calf while Moses is away. As a result of this transgression, God condemned them to wander in the wilderness for forty years before reaching the promised land of Canaan. Lincoln had been hailed by many as a Moses to African Americans; after Lincoln's assassination, Johnson made a speech promising African Americans that he would be their new Moses.

9. Child is referring to President Andrew Johnson's annual message to Congress of 4 December 1865. One of the key points at issue between Johnson and his conservative supporters, on the one hand, and Radical Republicans, on the other, was the question of whether or not the former Confederate states had forfeited the rights they had previously exercised under the Constitution. Radical Republicans held that these states should be treated either as conquered provinces or as territories, subject to the authority of Congress. Democrats and conservative Republicans wanted to avoid undermining states' rights to control their own internal affairs, which meant restoring the former Confederate states as quickly as possible to their prewar legal status.

Homesteads

In the March number of the *American Missionary* is a very interesting account of Moses Fisher. Taking advantage of the confusion of wartime, he absconded from his master's premises, and started with his family for the United States camp. They travelled forty miles through the deepest recesses of the woods, careful to keep in solitary places, lest they should be seized and dragged back into slavery. The parents carried on their heads their little stock of rags, dishes, and kettles, and the children trudged after, leading their blind old grandmother. How many such groups the stars looked down upon, while the armies of the North were fighting for one idea and slowly finding another![1] At last, the weary fugitives came in sight of the United States flag, and under cover of the night crept into the camp. There they poured forth their grateful hearts in thanks to God for the freedom they had gained, and there they remained to render willing and faithful service for the protection they received. A Bible was wrapped up in the rags they "toted" on their heads. None of them could read a word of it; but Moses felt assured he had a treasure shut up there, that some time or other would be unlocked for him. All through the war, he guarded it carefully, sleeping with it under his head, and hiding it in safe places in time of danger.

When the war was over, Moses, with thousands of his brothers, were left without resources, to wander among a people who hated them for their loyalty to the United States. There were thousands of acres of wild land in the South, but none for the homeless freedmen. A timid Congress "dawdled" away its opportunities, and the President busied himself with restoring plantations to rebel masters. They were all too much occupied with conciliating the Democratic Party, to think of providing the black soldiers and servants of the United States army with a patch of ground whereon to raise food for their families.

But no discouragements could dishearten Moses Fisher. He had nothing but his wife and children, his rags and kettles. But he made a bargain with a white man to clear up an almost impenetrable swamp, for the privilege of cultivating for three years such land as he could subdue. There the whole family toiled at ditching and grubbing the soil, with such rude implements as

National Anti-Slavery Standard, 28 March 1869, p. 2.
1. Child refers to the war's initial goal of saving the Union and its eventual displacement by the later goal of abolishing slavery.

they could contrive. In summer, the mother and children picked berries and carried them to market; at other times, they made up bundles of light-wood, which they carried on their backs in search of purchasers. In one season, the mother and her little girl picked and sold forty-three dollars worth of berries; and the father and his little boy tapped and dipped two hundred and sixty dollars worth of turpentine; but of this sum he was obliged to give half to the owner of the soil. Undismayed by the formidable obstacles they had to contend with, this brave family toiled on, month after month, cutting away thick under-brush, grubbing up tangled roots, and planting corn and potatoes. With the logs they hewed they made themselves a comfortable shelter, and a few rude articles of furniture. Before their harvest was ripe, a log-barn was erected wherein to store it. In a shattered box brought from the army was stored the precious Bible, which as yet none of them could read. But at last some of the noble army of Northern teachers penetrated into that region. The nearest school was five miles off. But for two years the little boy and girl trudged thither in the morning and back again in the afternoon, scarcely ever missing a day. From their little tongues the patient and trusting father at last heard the contents of the Bible he had treasured so long. One day the Northern teacher walked home with these bright, industrious children, and was warmly welcomed by the grateful parents. They showed with great satisfaction the hundred bushels of corn which they had stored in their little barn. The Bible was brought from its box and its history related. "All the while I was toting it about," said Moses, "I knowed there was a heap o' good inside of it, and I had faith that some time or other it would come out of it to me; and now my little children are teaching me the heavenly message."

This simple story of persevering faith and patience affected me deeply; and it made it harder than ever to forgive Congress for not having provided these poor outcasts of slavery with small homesteads of their own, at moderate prices. Poor Moses, after wearing out his muscles with incessant toil for three years, will not own one rood of the land he has cleared. He will still be landless and homeless, and compelled for daily food to submit to the hard terms of grasping, unpitying masters, who are accustomed to consider his race fore-ordained to toil without wages. If it had been made easy for the freedmen to become owners of land, how much their industry would have been stimulated and the wealth of the nation increased! Nothing improves the characters of human beings like having a home of their own; and a country has no element of prosperity so certain as that of laborers who own the soil they cultivate.

Philanthropists have given large sums of money to Lee's College in Virginia, where the Traitor Chief "teaches the young idea how to shoot" at the United States Flag, when another opportunity offers.[2] If the money thus bestowed had been formed into a fund to purchase tracts of land, and sell it at low prices to the homeless freedmen, what a vast amount of good might have been accomplished!

The murderous delays in the prosecution of the war, the deferring of justice till it became a necessity, the "dawdling" of Congress while the golden sands of opportunity were running through the hour-glass, were very trying to honest and earnest souls; but that which has since assumed the name of magnanimity, because it not only forgives crime but rewards it, is perhaps the most trying of all. After all the contempt and violence we have received at the hands of our former masters, the slaveholders, it seems as if we were still too much dazzled by their assumption of lordly superiority, to be able to judge Gen. Lee of Arlington House precisely as we should judge one of his black servants, if guilty of the same enormous crimes.

Certainly, I rejoice that we did not imitate the barbarisms of England toward her Scottish rebels, or toward her Hindoo rebels of more recent date.[3] But taking land from industrious, loyal freedmen who were cultivating it, and giving it back to proud and lazy rebels, who had forfeited it, does not seem to me either magnanimous in principle, or wise as policy. Travelling to Virginia to congratulate Jeff Davis and be responsible for his Honor's honor, talking of "the brave Gen. Lee," and loading him with donations to endow a college of young rebels, while Wurtz,[4] the poor, ignorant tool of those bad men, was ignominiously hung, seems to me outrageous injustice, and calculated to produce in the minds of the people utter confusion of ideas concerning right and wrong; a confusion which in future emergencies may do much to hinder a great uprising for the right.

But though I complain that forbearance toward a guilty party has been

2. After the Civil War, Confederate General Robert E. Lee assumed the presidency of Washington and Lee University in Lexington, Virginia, which he held until 1870. Formerly Washington College, the university was renamed in his honor.

3. Child probably refers to Britain's brutal suppression of rebellions by Scottish Jacobites in 1746 and Indian soldiers in 1857–59. George, duke of Cumberland, the British leader who defeated the Scots at Culloden, came to be known as "butcher"; draconian legislation completed the work of subjugating the Scots. In India, reprisals against the rebels took the form of floggings and summary executions.

4. Henry Wirz (1823–65), commandant of the notorious Confederate prison camp at Andersonville, where 13,000 of the 45,000 soldier inmates died of disease, exposure, or malnutrition, was the only Confederate to be tried and executed for war crimes after the war.

carried to excess, involving, as it has done, injustice toward an innocent party, and unsettling the foundations of right and wrong, still, I never for one moment wished that any class or condition of men at the South should be without homesteads and the means of obtaining an independent living by their own industry and enterprise. To the "poor whites" who fought against us in the blindness of their ignorance, I would offer every facility for obtaining as much land as they would cultivate, and I would try to raise them up to the idea that honest labor is honorable above all things. And though my sympathies do not flow out so readily to the slaveholders as to their victims, white and black, I do not forget that they also were the victims of a bad institution, and that we, if we had been brought up under the influences of slavery, should have formed the same bad habits and the same false principles. Their sons will mature into truer manhood, under a better order of things. And I should be sorry to see the generation that is passing away deprived of homesteads and a sufficiency of land. Incurably violent and arrogant as they are, I would not impoverish them if I could. But I *would* so manage affairs, by confiscation, fines, or sale for taxes, that one rebel master should not hold in his exclusive possession from one thousand to twenty thousand acres, while his loyal laborers cannot own ground enough for a potato patch. In some way or other, this great evil *can* be remedied, and the good of all classes in the country requires that it *should* be remedied, as soon as possible.

L. Maria Child

William Lloyd Garrison

Since the death of the Hon. Charles Sumner,[1] no event has so stirred the popular heart as the decease of William Lloyd Garrison. In the highest signification of the term, he was preëminently a fortunate man: fortunate in the circumstances of his life, even when they seemed most adverse; and especially was he blessed to fall asleep in the arms of domestic affection, honored by the wise and good, and blessed with the grateful benediction of the poor. All the events of his career seemed to curve naturally toward the completion of a circle; and this because habitual unselfishness was the pivot around which they revolved.

He was fortunate in being early subjected to the rigid discipline of poverty, which developed his energies and strengthened his will, as the muscles of a blacksmith have their power increased by the weight of his hammer and the hardness of the material on which he works. It is not easy to overestimate the blessed results of early self-denial and the necessity to labor. "The good Goddess of Poverty teaches her children the secret of God, of which she knows more than all the doctors and all the bishops. She is their robust nurse, their church militant."

It was another piece of rare good fortune that Mr. Garrison, at an early period, devoted his life to a distinct purpose,—a purpose which exercised his faculties, and at the same time consecrated them to high uses. Intellectually, he was by no means a remarkable man. He had not the profoundness of Emerson, the brilliancy of Phillips, or Whittier's visions of truth draped in poetic beauty. He simply had strong, practical good sense; but this was combined with intense moral earnestness, and the hammer and the fire together molded the hardest materials into the shape he willed.

It was a common charge against him that he used harsh and abusive language; and he undoubtedly had a predilection for strong epithets, which I think was partly owing to his being very thoroughly imbued with the phraseology of the Bible. Believing that the constitution of the United States had deliberately made a compromise with slavery, he called it "a covenant with death." The statement was true, but not considered sufficiently respectful

Atlantic Monthly (August 1879): 234–238.
    1. Sumner had died in March 1874, and as in the case of Garrison, Child had taken heart from the outpouring of public tributes indicating that even in a period of reaction, his ideals were still being honored.

toward the framers of that instrument. It was sometimes said of him that he needed to be prayed for after the fashion of a Massachusetts minister in the olden time, who thus petitioned the throne of grace in behalf of a brother clergyman: "We pray thee to teach him more moderation in his speech; for thou knowest, O Lord, that he will take a beetle to brush a fly from a man's face, when a feather would do as well." This was not, however, strictly applicable to Mr. Garrison; for he was dealing with something more formidable than flies, and weapons stronger than feathers were needed. He roused his audiences as no coiner of smooth and elegant phrases could possibly have done. Samuel J. May, whom he always stirred to the depths of his gentle nature, after listening to the vehement outpourings of his righteous indignation, exclaimed, "Why, Brother Garrison, you are all on fire!" To which Mr. Garrison replied, with characteristic solemnity of voice and manner, "Brother May, I have *need* to be all on fire, for I have mountains of ice around me to melt." Margaret Fuller, in answer to the charge of hard language, on the part of Mr. Garrison, said, "It is no wonder that he speaks loud, when he has so long been calling to deaf people."

His character, had, undoubtedly, a strong stamp of Puritanism, partly in his organization, and partly the result of being reared in an atmosphere of Calvinism. But, though he was always stern and uncompromising in the rebuke of wrong, those who knew him well were aware of an undertone of deep tenderness in his feelings. It was, in fact, a genuine love for his fellow-men that rendered him so severe in his denunciations of oppression. Any contemptuous estimate of human beings, whether they were women, negroes, or Chinese,[2] kindled his indignation, and he never paused to measure the fashion of its utterance. But when he encountered a reasonable, manly antagonist, no one could be more courteous in debate than he. While traveling on a steamboat, he accidentally fell into conversation with a stranger, who proved to be a South Carolinian. The subject of slavery was almost immediately introduced, for in those days Southerners were even more alert to vindicate their "peculiar institution" than the abolitionists were to attack it. Mr. Garrison, in reply to the statements of his companion, frankly avowed that he was himself an ultra-abolitionist; and he went on to explain why he thought the abolition of so bad a system would prove equally beneficial to the white

---

2. Child refers to Garrison's early support of women's rights and to his denunciation, shortly before his death, of the latest congressional attempt to ban Chinese immigration. The first federal Chinese exclusion law would be passed in 1882.

race and the colored. The Southern gentleman listened with apparent interest, and prolonged the conversation till the steamboat landed. At parting, he said, "I am pleased to have met you. If all the abolitionists were like you, they would not be such disturbers of the peace; but as for that violent fellow, Garrison, who is trying to instigate the slaves to cut their masters' throats, that fellow ought to be silenced." Mr. May, who stood near, now came forward with a bow and a smile, and said, "This is Mr. Garrison."

Our great reformer was not what is termed a cultured man. He had merely shared the common inheritance of good New England schooling. But it was, perhaps, a part of his good fortune that the native freedom and vigor of his soul had never been cramped by the elaborate drilling of what is called a finished education. The highest type of what is styled self-culture fell to his lot. His wide-awake mind gleaned knowledge everywhere, and made it a living power by converting it to immediate use. And he derived constant and healthy mental stimulus from richly endowed minds, whose scholarly advantages had been superior to his own, and who had been drawn into intimate relations with him by the magnetism of his earnest convictions of duty. He was slandered and persecuted for his persistent efforts to right a great wrong; and even his life was sometimes in imminent peril. But, in compensation for all this abuse and danger, his unflinching moral courage commanded the respect of a high order of minds, and gained for him a social position more advantageous than he would otherwise have occupied. This result would not have taken place if he had worked for that end. It is an old saying that "ghosts follow those who look for them;" but it is otherwise with the respect and admiration of mankind. The self-conscious may easily obtain present notoriety, but fame follows him who thinks not of it in his eager pursuit of a noble aim.

Moral directness was the most striking trait in Mr. Garrison's character. It was literally impossible for him to pursue a truth by any crooked or circuitous route. Without reasoning that "a straight line is always the shortest, in morals as in mathematics," the necessity was upon him to steer directly for any point he had in view. In this respect there was a strong resemblance between him and the Hon. Charles Sumner. A gentleman who was arguing with the senator remarked, "All men do not look upon slavery as you do; they view it from another side." "Sir," replied Mr. Sumner, "on a question like this there *is* no other side."

Merchants might talk of cotton as the mainspring of commerce, and contend that slavery was essential to the production of cotton. Office lovers might urge that discussion angered the South, in whose hands were the reins of political power. Sumner and Garrison scornfully denied that such pleas were the other side of a great moral question. They sturdily maintained that such reasons for silence had no affinity whatever with *any* principle. They saw in slavery a violation of divine law, a criminal infringement of human rights, a shameful contradiction of the professed principles of our religion and our government, and to their minds it had no other side. It was precisely this inflexible moral directness and rectitude which made both of those men such plagues to politicians, and such towers of strength to the popular conscience.

Doubtless minds thus constituted are in danger of becoming dictatorial and exclusive; of being as obstinately tenacious of mere opinions as they are in their adherence to eternal and universal principles. Mr. Garrison, with his Cromwellian temperament and his Calvinistic training, might perhaps have become a bigot, had not his zeal as a reformer brought him into close contact with honest, conscientious people, holding all sorts of opinions concerning theology; in all of them he saw that moral principle had but one side, while opinion had many.

It was impossible to keep theology out of the antislavery conflict. Many were zealous to maintain that the Bible sanctioned slavery. Mr. Garrison denied it; but, with his usual directness, he said, "If you can prove that the Bible sanctions slavery, so much the worse for the Bible." The pathway thus opened proved wider and longer than was at first perceived. To many minds this statement seemed to be a plain admission that the Bible was amenable to the moral consciousness of man, and that its contents were to be received or rejected according as they stood that test. Mr. Garrison knew the venerable volume by heart, from beginning to end. It was an arsenal full of weapons for the defense of the poor and the oppressed, and no man could parry and thrust with them more skillfully than he. He had appropriate quotations ready for all occasions, and his felicitous application of them often imparted to his utterance a singular degree of beauty and power.

But, as a mere matter of controversy, the Bible question, as it was called, became the *bête noir* of conventions. It was unspeakably tedious at the time, and the apparent results were small. It seemed like traveling over a stony road with a lame horse to hear men declare that the curse upon Canaan was divine authority for negro slavery, and in proof thereof proceed to trace the genealogy of Africans from the dim historical spectre of Ham, who was doomed to be the servant of Japheth. But this controversy, so wearisome at the time, and apparently useless, was imperceptibly loosening other rivets than those which fastened the chains of negro chattels; and, without diminishing the reverential tendency of Mr. Garrison's mind, it helped to bring him out upon the high and broad plane of unqualified freedom of thought on all questions of religion. In the later years of his life, his sympathies embraced all the religions of the world.

Indeed, nothing proves the unity of truth so forcibly as the effort to controvert any one truth. It is impossible to present a single ray of light without producing a rainbow,—a bow forever reappearing in the clouds, a signal that God will keep his covenant with the earth, and never allow it to be overwhelmed with a deluge of error.

Carlyle says, "Any road will lead to the end of the world, if you do but follow it;"[3] and antislavery, in its straightforward progress through the traditions and prejudices of men, perhaps illustrated the truth of this saying even more forcibly than the reformation by Luther.

As the right to discuss slavery unavoidably introduced questions of religious freedom, it also inevitably involved equality between the sexes. Orthodox clergymen were shocked when Abby Kelly,[4] a modest, sensible young Quakeress, rose to make a remark upon the subject under debate. It was pleaded, in excuse for her, that women had always been accustomed to speak in Quaker meetings; but Garrison rejected any such plea. He maintained that whoever had anything to say had a right to say it, and needed not the apology of Quaker custom. This paved the way for Angelina Grimke,[5] a noble-hearted

3. Child is quoting freely from the chapter "Idyllic," book 2, chap. 2, of *Sartor Resartus* (1833–34), by Thomas Carlyle (1795–1881).

4. Abigail (Abby) Kelley Foster (1810–87), Quaker-born abolitionist and women's rights advocate, made her first public speech to a mixed audience of men and women at the 1838 Convention of Anti-Slavery Women, held in Philadelphia. The incident to which Child refers occurred a few weeks later at the New England Anti-Slavery Convention of May 1838, where Kelley was appointed along with two men to a committee to draft an address to the ecclesiastical bodies of New England, urging them to speak out against slavery. Conservative clergymen asked her to withdraw and protested against admitting women as official participants in the convention, but they were outvoted and Kelley remained. At the New England convention of 1839, the conservatives walked out and formed a rival organization, the Massachusetts Abolition Society. The final split in the movement occurred at the American Anti-Slavery Society's 1840 annual meeting in New York. There Abby Kelley's nomination to the business committee of the national organization precipitated a walkout by some three hundred conservatives, who proceeded to form the American and Foreign Anti-Slavery Society. Child's chronology seems to be somewhat confused, however. Kelley's public speaking career was influenced by Angelina Grimké's, and not the reverse.

5. Angelina Grimké addressed the Massachusetts legislature on 21 February 1838 (some three months before Abby Kelley's first speech) to testify against slavery and defend the propriety of northern antislavery agitation.

woman from South Carolina, herself the inheritor of slaves, to make an eloquent protest against the system before the legislature of Massachusetts. The native largeness of soul which led Mr. Garrison instinctively to step over all limitations of color or race, sex or creed, induced him to refuse to take a seat in the World's Antislavery Convention, at London, because English conservatism excluded Lucretia Mott,[6] who was sent from Philadelphia as a delegate. His manner towards women habitually indicated a frank, respectful, fraternal affection and confidence; and this was, indeed, the prevailing characteristic of most of the earliest abolitionists. It had no tinge of that odious thing called gallantry, distasteful to sensible women, because it is obviously a mere veil for condescension and often for profligacy. Mr. Garrison and his comrades simply acted with entire unconsciousness of any question of relative superiority. They consulted with antislavery women, and listened to their suggestions with the same respectful interest that they listened to each other.

The value of this as a means of education for the minds and consciences of women cannot be overestimated. I have seen a picture of the funeral of a German poet, whose pall-bearers were women, in token of gratitude for the respect for women manifested in his writings. If Mr. Garrison had received a similar tribute it would have been well deserved; for he was a veritable Bayard[7] in the cause of women from the beginning to the end of his career.

Again I cannot but repeat what a fortunate man he was! It is not often the lot of mortals to witness the realization of reformatory ideas on which they have expended the energies of their youth. He lived to see negro slavery abolished beyond all chance of restoration, and colored men chosen as members of the legislature of Massachusetts, and the Congress of the United States. He lived to see Jews and Buddhists citizens of the United States, with the legal right to worship God in their own way. In the same community where Abby Kelly's right to make a remark in meeting had been vehemently

6. Lucretia Coffin Mott (1793–1880), Quaker abolitionist and women's rights advocate, founded the Philadelphia Female Anti-Slavery Society in 1833 and was one of three Quaker women to participate in the founding meeting of the American Anti-Slavery Society that December, where she intervened in the discussion several times. When the American Anti-Slavery Society sent Mott, along with several other women delegates, to represent it at the 1840 World's Anti-Slavery Convention in London, the British organizers refused to seat the women and relegated them to the position of silent spectators in the gallery. In protest, Garrison and the African American abolitionist Charles Lenox Remond joined the women in the gallery.

7. Child may be referring to Pierre du Terrail, Chevalier de Bayard (1476–1524), known as the knight "sans peur et sans reproche" (without fear and without reproach).

disputed, he lived to see Mrs. Livermore[8] receive more invitations into pulpits than time would allow her to accept. And when the end came, death was to him merely passing from one room into another, both filled with friends; for his faith in reunion with those he loved was so strong that he called it knowledge.

In the very city where he had been dragged to prison to save his life from a mob, and where his effigy had been hung on a gallows before his own door, the flags were placed at half-mast to announce his decease, and the universal tributes of respect to his memory almost amounted to an apotheosis.

And blessed above all is he in the long train of influences he leaves behind him. Time will never diminish the impulses he gave to human freedom in various directions, because all the orbs of his thought revolved round a centre of fixed principle. Those who hereafter seek to redress human wrongs will derive strength from the proofs he has given that all obstacles must yield to the power of self-forgetful moral earnestness. And those who long to keep their faith in the upward and onward tendencies of the human race will be cheered by the fact that such wonderful revolutions in public sentiment were produced within the memory of one generation by the exercise of clear-sighted conscience and indomitable will.

The models men venerate indicate the measure of their own aspirations, and the possibility of their realization. Therefore, I look upon the spontaneous ovations to the memory of such men as Charles Sumner and William Lloyd Garrison as among the best guarantees for the stability of this republic.

8. The abolitionist and woman suffragist Mary Ashton Rice Livermore (1820–1905) was currently editing the *Woman's Journal* and touring the country as a lecturer.

Part Four

Journalism and Social

Critique

Introduction

"At one time Mrs. Child was almost at the head of journalism in America, as we now understand it,—for she had that independence of character and that general cultivation of mind which are now recognized, though they were not then, as the indispensable and distinguishing traits of a good journalist." An obituary tribute by the Boston correspondent of the *Springfield Republican*,[1] this acknowledgment of Child's role in pioneering the field of nineteenth-century American journalism strikingly testifies to the stature she achieved in the profession. Although Child led the entry of women into journalism, preceding Margaret Fuller, Grace Greenwood, Fanny Fern, and Gail Hamilton, her memorialist did not limit her contribution to founding a feminine school, but credited her with having set new standards of integrity and literary quality for the craft as a whole. Nearly forty years had elapsed since she had made history by assuming the editorship of the *National Anti-Slavery Standard* in May 1841, yet her fellow journalist still remembered "what an admirable paper it was" and what a "hit" her famous column for the *Standard*, "Letters from New-York," had been.

Prior to taking on this challenging assignment, Child had served a three-year apprenticeship on her husband's newspaper, the *Massachusetts Journal* (1828–31). Under the cover of anonymity, she had written reviews and cultural criticism for the paper and launched a column titled "Original Miscellany, For the *Massachusetts Journal*," featuring essays, sketches, and social commentary much like her "Letters from New-York" of the 1840s. She had also helped turn a dry, partisan organ into a family newspaper that could appeal to female as well as male household members and attract subscribers seeking literary and intellectual as well as political fare.

These were precisely the innovations Child introduced into the *Standard;* she wooed readers to the antislavery cause "with the garland of imagination and taste," as she later spelled out.[2] She succeeded so well that during her two-year tenure the subscription list of the *Standard* doubled from 2,500 to 5,000—a record for an antislavery newspaper at a time when the movement was still contending with widespread hostility.

Of all the feature items with which Child enhanced the *Standard*, none

---

1. "L. Maria Child," *Springfield Republican*, rpt. *Woman's Journal*, 6 Nov. 1880, pp. 354–55.
2. See her "Farewell" editorial, *Standard* 4 May 1843, pp. 190–91.

drew more readers than her column "Letters from New-York," placed strategically right next to her editorials. These freewheeling journalistic sketches described the sights, institutions, and inhabitants of the nation's largest metropolis, sliding from the material into the moral and spiritual realms, from pictorial representation into social criticism and philosophical speculation. Often overlapping in content with Child's editorials, the letters integrated abolitionism into a comprehensive philanthropy that connected slavery with other social problems: urban poverty, an unjust prison system, capital punishment, the oppression of women, prostitution, alcoholism, and prejudice against Jews, Catholics, Irish, and Indians. Indeed, the diversity of humanitarian causes championed in "Letters from New-York" and the sympathy the column promoted for the white derelicts roaming the streets and incarcerated in the jails of northern cities gives the lie to caricatures of abolitionists transmitted to posterity by their detractors. Contrary to the allegations of Nathaniel Hawthorne and Ralph Waldo Emerson, for example, Child and her fellow abolitionists were hardly people of "one idea" or hypocrites who wept over the imaginary wrongs of "black folk a thousand miles off" but turned a blind eye to the sufferings of their white neighbors.[3]

Child's broad social criticism was not what endeared "Letters from New-York" to the public, however. Instead, the column owed its popularity to Child's ability to give readers the illusion that she was speaking personally to each of them, that she was guiding them into the recesses of a world beyond their horizons, that she was articulating their anxieties about the rapid changes taking place in their society—the mushrooming of cities, the influx of immigrants, the increase of crime—even while she was teaching them to embrace rather than fear the new polyglot, multiracial America.

Readers of "Letters from New-York" appreciated the column's literary style as well. "[I]t is a perfect encyclopedia of anecdotes and interesting realities, in endless variety. . . . [T]here is a quickness, a brilliancy in her comparisons and analogies," wrote Thomas Wentworth Higginson in an 1843 review.[4] Higginson also recognized Child's affinities with the transcendentalists. Like her transcendentalist peers Emerson, Henry David Thoreau, Margaret Fuller, and Walt Whitman, Child espoused an aesthetic of spontaneity

3. Nathaniel Hawthorne, "The Hall of Fantasy," *The Pioneer* 1 (Feb. 1843): 53; Ralph Waldo Emerson, "Self-Reliance," Stephen E. Whicher, ed., *Selections from Ralph Waldo Emerson* (Boston: Houghton Mifflin, 1957) 150.

4. "H" [Thomas Wentworth Higginson], "Mrs. Child's Letters from New York," *The Present* 1 (15 Nov. 1843): 135.

that elevated the unconscious over the conscious mind, the intuitive over the rational, the natural over the contrived. Carrying this aesthetic to new heights, she perfected a style of free association that anticipated stream of consciousness. "I seldom can write a letter without making myself liable to the Vagrant Act," she commented on her literary practice. "My pen . . . paces or whirls, bounds or waltzes, steps in the slow minuet, or capers in the fantastic fandango, according to the tune within." "Flibbertigibbet himself never moved with more unexpected and incoherent variety."[5]

Whatever stylistic proclivities she shared with them, Child differed from Emerson and Thoreau (and resembled Whitman) in shifting the scene of her transcendentalist explorations from rural nature to urban streets and slums. Unlike Emerson's *Nature* (1836) and Thoreau's *Walden* (1854), "Letters from New-York" celebrated not the lone individual, but the community, not "Life in the Woods," but life in the city. The transcendental ideal of "the Beautiful," as Higginson put it, "does not exist for her only in the moonlight trembling on the quiet water . . . ; she finds it equally in the dark gray city, where beats the sorrowing, striving heart of man."[6]

An audience far wider than the *Standard*'s subscribers reveled in "Letters from New-York," and organs as diverse as the *New York Tribune, Graham's Magazine,* and the *Democratic Review* urged Child to collect and reissue her newspaper sketches in book form. Thus, when she decided to quit the paper and resume her literary career, she set about adapting the letters to the tastes of the general public. This entailed dropping three of the most radical anti-slavery letters (among them number 12, about the *Amistad* captives, and number 33, about the mob attack on George Thompson, reprinted in part 3), cutting disdainful remarks about Congress and the government, eliminating passages addressed to an in-group of comrades-in-arms, substituting the word *reformers* for *abolitionists,* and deleting the names of prominent figures in the movement. Still, at least nine of the forty letters Child reprinted from the fifty-four that had constituted the original series in the *Standard* offer some antislavery commentary, a prime example being number 11 on "the eloquent coloured preacher," included here.

Child's self-censorship did not satisfy the press that had solicited the manuscript, however. The Langley brothers, publishers of the *Democratic*

---

5. Quotations are from Lydia Maria Child, *Letters from New York. Second Series* (New York: C. S. Francis, 1845) number 28: 257; and *Letters from New York [First Series]* (1843; Freeport, N.Y.: Books for Libraries P, 1970) number 10: 69.

6. *The Present* 1 (15 Nov. 1843): 135.

Review, were closely associated with the Democratic party, which combined advocacy on behalf of white wage laborers and Irish immigrants with unconditional support of slavery and white supremacy. They no doubt hoped to capitalize on the appeal that Child's sketches of urban poverty would exert for the Democrats' northern constituents. At the same time, they could not afford to alienate their patrons by seeming to endorse antislavery views incompatible with the party's platform. Hence, telling Child that "it would injure their business very much if any expression in a book they published should prove offensive to the South," they demanded a complete expurgation of the antislavery material.[7] Other commercial presses proved equally squeamish, and Child ended up having the book published (intact) at her own expense by the firm of a distant cousin, C. S. Francis.

To the mutual astonishment of Child and her publisher, *Letters from New York* (1843) garnered excellent reviews, even in most of the conservative journals, sold out its first print run of 1,500 copies within four months, and went through ten more printings in seven years. Its popular success earned Child an invitation to start a second "Letters from New-York" column in the *Boston Courier,* a mainstream newspaper, which dramatically increased her readership. *Courier* subscribers greeted the letters with the same excitement that had once prompted children to sit on their doorsteps waiting for the *Juvenile Miscellany.* "The counting-room of the *Courier* was filled by an eager crowd, half an hour before the proper time," on the days when the column was expected, recalled the abolitionist-feminist Caroline Healey Dall: "The paper came damp from the press, and many a delicate glove bore traces of the fervor with which the owner had grasped the sheet. Men read it as they walked slowly up School Street. Young women ran into Munroe and Francis' bookstore for their first glimpse. These letters were read aloud at the tea-table, and the next day everybody passed their bright sayings along."[8]

Child collected a year's worth of her *Courier* column, too, into a book: *Letters from New York. Second Series* (1845). Equally well received by reviewers and beloved by the public, it nonetheless lacks the freshness and vitality of its predecessor. It also lacks the first series's reformist edge, reflecting Child's withdrawal from political activism into mysticism and the arts.

After a hiatus of almost two decades, journalism again became Child's

---

7. LMC to Louisa Loring, 29 May 1841, *CC* 17/496.

8. Caroline Healey Dall, "Lydia Maria Child and Mary Russell Mitford," *Unitarian Review* 19 (June 1883): 526.

principal avenue of political expression during the Civil War and Reconstruction. Like her editorials of the 1840s, many of her articles of the 1860s reveal her literary bent and penchant for narrative, metaphor, and allegory (see especially "Through the Red Sea into the Wilderness" and "Homesteads," in part 3). In two articles for the *Independent,* Child returned to the mode of her old "Letters from New-York."

The selections reprinted here represent a sampling of the social issues Child addresses in the first *Letters from New York,* illustrate her style of free association, and give a taste of her late journalism. Number 1 introduces many of the themes that run through the volume: the glaring disparities between rich and poor; the complicity of the North in slavery; the "common bond of brotherhood" linking classes, races, and nations; the attractions of cultural diversity; the conflict between the Practical and the Ideal. Number 11, portraying the black Methodist preacher Julia Pell, exemplifies Child's manner of weaving protest against slavery and racial prejudice into the book. The second of three letters describing the religious services of New York's different communities (the first and the third being accounts of Child's visits to a Jewish synagogue and a Catholic cathedral), it also furthers the breakdown of "sectarian walls"—another of the book's major themes. Its vindication of a woman's right to preach connects this letter as well to number 34, on women's rights (reprinted in part 5). Number 14 is one of several that hauntingly evoke poverty and homelessness in New York, mourn the burial of immigrants' dreams under city pavements, and remind readers of the divine potentiality hidden within even the most degraded human beings. Number 29 takes readers on a tour of the institutions designed to segregate the poor from the rich and to punish any transgression of boundaries: prisons, insane asylums, almshouses, and orphanages. In the process it questions the moral distinctions between the inmates of these institutions and the respectable men and women who look down on them from their comfortable social sanctums. The cure for crime, Child argues, is not to build more prisons, but to abolish poverty. "A High-Flying Letter," published in the *Independent* a quarter century later (28 June 1866), decries the aping of Europe's elites by post–Civil War Americans and calls for a rededication to republican ideals of equality.

Letters from New York, Number 1

You ask what is now my opinion of this great Babylon; and playfully remind me of former philippics,[1] and a long string of vituperative alliterations, such as magnificence and mud, finery and filth, diamonds and dirt, bullion and brass-tape, &c. &c. Nor do you forget my first impression of the city, when we arrived at early dawn, amid fog and drizzling rain, the expiring lamps adding their smoke to the impure air, and close beside us a boat called the 'Fairy Queen,' laden with dead hogs.

Well, Babylon remains the same as then. The din of crowded life, and the eager chase for gain, still run through its streets, like the perpetual murmur of a hive. Wealth dozes on French couches, thrice piled, and canopied with damask, while Poverty camps on the dirty pavement, or sleeps off its wretchedness in the watch-house. There, amid the splendour of Broadway, sits the blind negro beggar, with horny hand and tattered garments, while opposite to him stands the stately mansion of the slave trader, still plying his bloody trade, and laughing to scorn the cobweb laws, through which the strong can break so easily.

In Wall-street, and elsewhere, Mammon, as usual, coolly calculates his chance of extracting a penny from war, pestilence, and famine; and Commerce, with her loaded drays, and jaded skeletons of horses, is busy as ever fulfilling the 'World's contract with the Devil.' The noisy discord of the street-cries gives the ear no rest; and the weak voice of weary childhood often makes the heart ache for the poor little wanderer, prolonging his task far into the hours of night. Sometimes, the harsh sounds are pleasantly varied by some feminine voice, proclaiming in musical cadence, 'Hot corn! hot corn!' with the poetic addition of 'Lily white corn! Buy my lily white corn!' When this sweet, wandering voice salutes my ear, my heart replies—

> 'Tis a glancing gleam o' the gift of song—
> And the soul that speaks hath suffered wrong.

There *was* a time when all these things would have passed by me like the flitting figures of the magic lantern, or the changing scenery of a theatre, sufficient for the amusement of an hour. But now, I have lost the power of

National Anti-Slavery Standard, 19 August 1841; reprinted in *Letters from New York* (1843), pp. 13–17.
1. philippics: tirades.

looking merely on the surface. Every thing seems to me to come from the Infinite, to be filled with the Infinite, to be tending toward the Infinite. Do I see crowds of men hastening to extinguish a fire? I see not merely uncouth garbs, and fantastic flickering lights of lurid hue, like a tramping troop of gnomes,—but straightway my mind is filled with thoughts about mutual helpfulness, human sympathy, the common bond of brotherhood, and the mysteriously deep foundations on which society rests; or rather, on which it now reels and totters.

But I am cutting the lines deep, when I meant only to give you an airy, unfinished sketch. I will answer your question, by saying, that though New-York remains the same, I like it better. This is partly because I am like the Lady's Delight,[2] ever prone to take root, and look up with a smile, in whatever soil you place it; and partly because bloated disease, and black gutters, and pigs uglier than their ugly kind, no longer constitute the foreground in my picture of New-York. I have become more familiar with the pretty parks, dotted about here and there; with the shaded alcoves of the various public gardens; with blooming nooks, and 'sunny spots of greenery.' I am fast inclining to the belief, that the Battery rivals our beautiful Boston Common. The fine old trees are indeed wanting; but the newly-planted groves offer the light, flexile gracefulness of youth, to compete with their matured majesty of age. In extent, and variety of surface, this noble promenade is greatly inferior to ours; but there is

> The sea, the sea, the open sea;
> The fresh, the bright, the ever free.[3]

Most fitting symbol of the Infinite, this trackless pathway of a world! heaving and stretching to meet the sky it never reaches—like the eager, unsatisfied aspirations of the human soul. The most beautiful landscape is imperfect without this feature. In the eloquent language of Lamartine[4]—'The sea is to the scenes of nature what the eye is to a fine countenance; it illuminates them, it imparts to them that radiant physiognomy, which makes them live, speak, enchant, and fascinate the attention of those who contemplate them.'

If you deem me heretical in preferring the Battery to the Common, conse-

2. Lady's Delight: pansy.

3. From "The Sea," by English poet Bryan Waller Procter (1787–1874); Child slightly misquotes the second line.

4. Alphonse de Lamartine (1790–1869), French Romantic poet; the quotation remains unidentified.

crated by so many pleasant associations of my youth, I know you will forgive me, if you will go there in the silence of midnight, to meet the breeze on your cheek, like the kiss of a friend; to hear the continual plashing of the sea, like the cool sound of oriental fountains; to see the moon look lovingly on the sea-nymphs, and throw down wealth of jewels on their shining hair; to look on the ships in their dim and distant beauty, each containing within itself, a little world of human thought, and human passion. Or go, when 'night, with her thousand eyes, looks down into the heart, making it also great'—when she floats above us, dark and solemn, and scarcely sees her image in the black mirror of the ocean. The city lamps surround you, like a shining belt of descended constellations, fit for the zone of Urania; while the pure bright stars peep through the dancing foliage, and speak to the soul of thoughtful shepherds on the ancient plains of Chaldea. And there, like mimic Fancy, playing fantastic freaks in the very presence of heavenly Imagination, stands Castle Garden—with its gay perspective of coloured lamps, like a fairy grotto, where imprisoned fire-spirits send up sparkling wreaths, or rockets laden with glittering ear-drops, caught by the floating sea-nymphs, as they fall.

But if you would see the Battery in *all* its glory, look at it when, through the misty mantle of retreating dawn, is seen the golden light of the rising sun! Look at the horizon, where earth, sea, and sky, kiss each other, in robes of reflected glory! The ships stretch their sails to the coming breeze, and glide majestically along—fit and graceful emblems of the Past; steered by Necessity; the Will constrained by outward Force. Quick as a flash, the steamboat passes them by—its rapidly revolving wheel made golden by the sunlight, and dropping diamonds to the laughing Nereides, profusely as pearls from Prince Esterhazy's embroidered coat.[5] In that steamer, see you not an appropriate type of the busy, powerful, self-conscious Present? Of man's Will conquering outward Force; and thus making the elements his servants?

From this southern extremity of the city, anciently called 'The Wall of the Half-Moon,' you may, if you like, pass along the Bowery to Bloomingdale, on the north. What a combination of flowery sounds to take captive the imagination! It is a pleasant road, much used for fashionable drives; but the lovely names scarcely keep the promise they give the ear; especially to one accustomed to the beautiful environs of Boston.

5. The Nereides, beautiful nymphs who lived at the bottom of the sea with their father, Nereus, watched over sailors. Prince Esterhazy, Nicholas IV (1765–1833) of Hungary, was notorious for his extravagance; in "Letter from an Old Woman, on Her Birthday," reprinted in part 2, Child refers to him as dropping seed-pearls from his embroidered coat.

During your ramble, you may meet wandering musicians. Perhaps a poor Tyrolese with his street-organ, or a Scotch lad, with shrill bag-pipe, decorated with tartan ribbons. Let them who will, despise their humble calling. Small skill, indeed, is needed to grind forth that machinery of sounds; but my heart salutes them with its benison, in common with all things that cheer this weary world. I have little sympathy with the severe morality that drove these tuneful idlers from the streets of Boston. They are to the drudging city, what Spring birds are to the country. This world has passed from its youthful, Troubadour Age, into the thinking, toiling Age of Reform. This we may not regret, because it needs must be. But welcome, most welcome, all that brings back reminiscences of its childhood, in the cheering voice of poetry and song.

Therefore blame me not, if I turn wearily aside from the dusty road of reforming duty, to gather flowers in sheltered nooks, or play with gems in hidden grottoes. The Practical has striven hard to suffocate the Ideal within me; but it is immortal, and cannot die. It needs but a glance of Beauty from earth or sky, and it starts into blooming life, like the aloe touched by fairy wand.

Letters from New York, Number 11

A friend passing by the Methodist church in Elizabeth street, heard such loud and earnest noises issuing therefrom, that he stepped in to ascertain the cause. A coloured woman was preaching to a full audience, and in a manner so remarkable that his attention was at once rivetted. The account he gave excited my curiosity, and I sought an interview with the woman, whom I ascertained to be Julia Pell, of Philadelphia. I learned from her that her father was one of the innumerable tribe of fugitives from slavery, assisted by that indefatigable friend of the oppressed, Isaac T. Hopper.[1] This was quite a pleasant surprise to the benevolent old gentleman, for he was not aware that any of Zeek's descendants were living; and it was highly interesting to him to find one of them in the person of this female Whitfield.[2] Julia never knew her father by the name of Zeek; for that was his appellation in slavery, and she had known him only as a freeman. Zeek, it seems, had been 'sold running,' as the term is; that is, a purchaser had given a very small part of his original value, taking the risk of not catching him. In Philadelphia a coloured man, named Samuel Johnson, heard a gentleman making inquiries concerning a slave called Zeek, whom he had 'bought running.' 'I know him very well,' said Samuel; 'as well as I do myself; he's a good-for-nothing chap; and you'll be better without him than with him.' 'Do you think so?' 'Yes; if you gave what you say for him, it was a bite—that's all. He's a lazy, good-for-nothing dog; and you'd better sell your right in him the first chance you get.' After some further talk, Samuel acknowledged that Zeek was his brother. The gentleman advised him to buy him; but Samuel protested that he was such a lazy, vicious dog, that he wanted nothing to do with him. The gentleman began to have so bad an opinion of his bargain, that he offered to sell the fugitive for sixty dollars. Samuel, with great apparent indifference, accepted the terms, and the necessary papers were drawn. Isaac T. Hopper was in the

National Anti-Slavery Standard, 9 December 1841; reprinted in *Letters from New York* (1843), pp. 73–82.

1. The Quaker abolitionist and prison reformer Isaac T. Hopper (1771–1852), best known for his Underground Railroad activities, was Child's host for most of her nine-year stay in New York. See her biography of him, *Isaac T. Hopper: A True Life* (1853).

2. The Anglican clergyman George Whitefield (1714–70) was famous for his rousing evangelical preaching, which helped ignite the Great Awakening of 1740 during his tour of the American colonies.

room during the whole transaction; and the coloured man requested him to examine the papers to see that all was right. Being assured that every thing was in due form, he inquired, 'And is Zeek now free?' 'Yes, entirely free.' 'Suppose I was Zeek, and that was the man that bought me; couldn't he take me?' 'Not any more than he could take me,' said Isaac. As soon as Samuel received this assurance, he made a low bow to the gentleman, and, with additional fun in a face always roguish, said, 'Your servant, sir; I am Zeek!' The roguishness characteristic of her father is reflected in some degree in Julia's intelligent face; but imagination, uncultivated, yet highly poetic, is her leading characteristic.

Some have the idea that our destiny is prophesied in early presentiments: thus, Hannah More,[3] when a little child, used to play, 'Go up to London and see the bishops'—an object for which she afterwards sacrificed a large portion of her own moral independence and freedom of thought. In Julia Pell's case, 'coming events cast their shadows before.'[4] I asked her when she thought she first 'experienced religion.' She replied, 'When I was a little girl, father and mother used to go away to meetings on Sundays, and leave me and my brothers at home all day. So, I thought I'd hold class-meetings as the Methodists did. The children all round in the neighbourhood used to come to hear me preach. The neighbours complained that we made such a noise, shouting and singing; and every Monday father gave us a whipping. At last, he said to mother, "I'm tired of beating these poor children every week to satisfy our neighbours. I'll send for my sister to come, and she will stay at home on Sundays, and keep them out of mischief." So my aunt was brought to take care of us; and the next Sunday, when the children came thronging to hear me preach, they were greatly disappointed indeed to hear me say, in a mournful way, "We can't have any more meetings now; because aunt's come, and she won't let us." When my aunt heard this, she seemed to pity me and the children; and she said if we would get through before the folks came home, we might hold a meeting; for she should like to see for herself what it was we did, that made such a fuss among the neighbours. Then we had a grand

3. Hannah More (1745–1833) was an English bluestocking and conservative religious writer. The anecdote is authentic. Child may be referring either to More's criticism of Mary Wollstonecraft or to her disavowal of her own *Strictures on the Modern System of Education* (1799) when it was criticized by her friend Archdeacon Daubeny. Implicitly, Child is contrasting More's outwardly directed piety, driven by the desire to placate religious authorities, with Pell's inwardly derived spirituality, which remains true to her own convictions.

4. From "Lochiel's Warning" (1802), by the Scottish poet Thomas Campbell (1777–1844).

meeting. My aunt's heart was taken hold of that very day; and when we all began to sing, "Come to the Saviour, poor sinner, come!" she cried, and I cried; and when we had done crying, the whole of us broke out singing "Come to the Saviour." That very instant I felt my heart leap up, as if a great load had been taken right off of it! That was the beginning of my getting religion; and for many years after that, I saw all the time a blue smoke rising before my eyes—the whole time a blue smoke rising, rising.' As she spoke, she imitated the ascent of smoke, by a graceful, undulating motion of her hand.

'What do you suppose was the meaning of the blue smoke?' said I.

'I don't know, indeed, ma'am; but I always supposed it was my sins rising before me, from the bottomless pit.'

She told me that when her mother died, some years after, she called her to her bed-side, and said, 'Julia, the work of grace is only begun in you. You haven't got religion yet. When you can freely forgive all your enemies, and love to do them good, then you may know that the true work is completed within you.' I thought the wisest schools of theology could not have established a better test.

I asked Julia, if she had ever tried to learn to read. She replied, 'Yes, ma'am, I tried once; because I thought it would be such a convenience, if I could read the Bible for myself. I made good progress, and in a short time could spell B-a-k-e-r, as well as anybody. But it dragged my mind *down*. It dragged it *down*. When I tried to think, every thing scattered away like smoke, and I could do nothing but spell. Once I got up in an evening meeting to speak; and when I wanted to say, "Behold the days come," I began "B-a—.' I was dreadfully ashamed, and concluded I'd give up trying to learn to read.'

These, and several other particulars I learned of Julia, at the house of Isaac T. Hopper. When about to leave us, she said she felt moved to pray. Accordingly, we all remained in silence, while she poured forth a brief, but very impressive prayer for her venerable host; of whom she spoke as 'that good old man, whom thou, O Lord, hast raised up to do such a blessed work for my down-trodden people.'

Julia's quiet, dignified, and even lady-like deportment in the parlour, did not seem at all in keeping with what I had been told of her in the pulpit, with a voice like a sailor at mast-head, and muscular action like Garrick in Mad Tom.[5] On the Sunday following, I went to hear her for myself; and in good

---

5. The famous English actor David Garrick (1717–79), manager of the Drury Lane Theater, played a great variety of roles. Eric Partridge's *Routledge Dictionary of Historical Slang* identifies

truth, I consider the event as an era in my life never to be forgotten. Such an odd jumbling together of all sorts of things in Scripture, such wild fancies, beautiful, sublime, or grotesque, such vehemence of gesture, such dramatic attitudes, I never before heard and witnessed. I verily thought she would have leaped over the pulpit; and if she had, I was almost prepared to have seen her poise herself on unseen wings, above the wondering congregation.

I know not whether her dress was of her own choosing; but it was tastefully appropriate. A black silk gown, with plain, white cuffs; a white muslin kerchief, folded neatly over the breast, and crossed by a broad black scarf, like that which bishops wear over the surplice.

She began with great moderation, gradually rising in her tones, until she arrived at the shouting pitch, common with Methodists. This she sustained for an incredible time, without taking breath, and with a huskiness of effort, that produced a painful sympathy in my own lungs. Imagine the following, thus uttered: that is, spoken without punctuation: 'Silence in Heaven! The Lord said to Gabriel, bid all the angels keep silence. Go up into the third heavens, and tell the archangels to hush their golden harps. Let the mountains be filled with silence. Let the sea stop its roaring, and the earth be still. What's the matter now? Why, man has sinned, and who shall save him? Let there be silence, while God makes search for a Messiah. Go down to the earth; make haste, Gabriel, and inquire if any there are worthy; and Gabriel returned and said, No, not one. Go search among the angels, Gabriel, and inquire if any are worthy; make haste, Gabriel; and Gabriel returned and said, No, not one. But don't be discouraged. Don't be discouraged, fellow-sinners. God arose in his majesty, and he pointed to his own right hand, and said to Gabriel, Behold the Lion of the tribe of Judah; he alone is worthy. He shall redeem my people.'

You will observe it was purely her own idea, that silence reigned on earth and in heaven, while search was made for a Messiah. It was a beautifully poetic conception not unworthy of Milton.

Her description of the resurrection and the day of judgment, must have been terrific to most of her audience, and was highly exciting even to me, whose religious sympathies could never be roused by fear. Her figure looked strangely fantastic, and even supernatural, as she loomed up above the pulpit, to represent the spirits rising from their graves. So powerful was her rude

---

"Mad Tom" as "a rogue who counterfeits madness"; no specific character or play by that title has turned up.

eloquence, that it continually impressed me with grandeur, and once only excited a smile; that was when she described a saint striving to rise, 'buried perhaps twenty feet deep, with three or four sinners a top of him.'

This reminded me of a verse in Dr. Nettleton's Village Hymns:[6]

'Oh how the resurrection light
Will *clarify* believers' sight,
How joyful will the saints arise,
And *rub the dust* from off their eyes.'

With a power of imagination singularly strong and vivid, she described the resurrection of a young girl, who had died a sinner. Her body came from the grave, and her soul from the pit, where it had been tormented for many years. 'The guilty spirit came up with the flames all around it—rolling—rolling—rolling.' She suited the action to the word, as Siddons[7] herself might have done. Then she described the body wailing and shrieking, 'O Lord! must I take that ghost again? Must I be tormented with that burning ghost for ever?'

Luckily for the excited feelings of her audience, she changed the scene, and brought before us the gospel ship, laden with saints, and bound for the heavenly shore. The majestic motion of a vessel on the heaving sea, and the fluttering of its pennon in the breeze, was imitated with wild gracefulness by the motion of her hands. 'It touched the strand. Oh! it was a pretty morning! and at the first tap of Heaven's bell, the angels came crowding round, to bid them welcome. There you and I shall meet, my beloved fellow-travellers. Farewell—Farewell—I have it in my temporal feelings that I shall never set foot in this New-York again. Farewell on earth, but I shall meet you there,' pointing reverently upward. 'May we all be aboard that blessed ship!' Shouts throughout the audience, 'We will! We will!' Stirred by such responses, Julia broke out with redoubled fervour. 'Farewell—farewell. Let the world say what they will of me, I shall surely meet you in Heaven's broad bay. Hell clutched me, but it hadn't energy enough to hold me. Farewell on earth. I shall meet you in the morning.' Again and again she tossed her arms abroad, and uttered her wild 'farewell;' responded to by the loud farewell of a whole congregation, like the shouts of an excited populace. Her last words were the poetic phrase, '*I shall meet you in the morning!*'

Her audience were wrought up to the highest pitch of enthusiasm I ever

6. *Village Hymns for Social Worship, Selected and Original* (1824), by the American Congregational evangelist Asahel Nettleton (1783–1844).

7. Sarah Siddons (1755–1831) was a famous British actress.

witnessed. 'That's God's truth!' 'Glory!' 'Amen!' 'Hallelujah!' resounded throughout the crowded house. Emotion vented itself in murmuring, stamping, shouting, singing, and wailing. It was like the uproar of a sea lashed by the winds.

You know that religion has always come to me in stillness; and that the machinery of theological excitement has ever been as powerless over my soul, as would be the exorcisms of a wizard. You are likewise aware of my tendency to *generalize;* to look at truth as *universal,* not merely in its particular relations; to observe human nature as a *whole,* and not in fragments. This propensity, greatly strengthened by the education of circumstances, has taught me to look calmly on all forms of religious opinion—not with the indifference, or the scorn, of unbelief; but with a friendly wish to discover everywhere the great central ideas common to all religious souls, though often reappearing in the strangest disguises, and lisping or jabbering in the most untranslated tones.

Yet combined as my religious character is, of quiet mysticism, and the coolest rationality, will you believe me, I could scarcely refrain from shouting Hurrah for that heaven-bound ship! and the tears rolled down my cheeks, as that dusky priestess of eloquence reiterated her wild and solemn farewell.

If she gained such power over my spirit, there is no cause to marvel at the tremendous excitement throughout an audience so ignorant, and so keenly susceptible to outward impressions. I knew not how the high-wrought enthusiasm would be let down in safety. The shouts died away, and returned in shrill fragments of echoes, like the trembling vibrations of a harp, swept with a strong hand, to the powerful music of a war-song. Had I remembered a lively Methodist tune, as well as I recollected the words, I should have broke forth:

> 'The gospel ship is sailing by!
> The Ark of safety now is nigh;
> Come, sinners, unto Jesus fly,
> Improve the day of grace.
> Oh, there'll be glory, hallelujah,
> When we all arrive at home!'

The same instinct that guided me, impelled the audience to seek rest in music, for their panting spirits and quivering nerves. All joined spontaneously in singing an old familiar tune, more quiet than the bounding, billowy tones of my favourite Gospel Ship. Blessings on music! Like a gurgling brook to feverish lips are sweet sounds to the heated and weary soul.

Everybody round me could sing; and the tones were soft and melodious. The gift of song is universal with Africans; and the fact is a prophetic one. Sculpture blossomed into its fullest perfection in a Physical Age, on which dawned the intellectual; Painting blossomed in an Intellectual Age, warmed by the rising sun of moral sentiment; and now Music goes forward to its culmination in the coming Spiritual Age. Now is the time that Ethiopia begins 'to stretch forth her hands.'[8] Her soul, so long silenced, will yet utter itself in music's highest harmony.

When the audience paused, Mr. Matthews, their pastor, rose to address them. He is a religious-minded man, to whose good influence Julia owes, under God, her present state of mind. She always calls him 'father,' and speaks of him with the most affectionate and grateful reverence. At one period of her life, it seems that she was led astray by temptations, which peculiarly infest the path of coloured women in large cities; but ever since her 'conversion to God,' she has been strictly exemplary in her walk and conversation. In her own expressive language, 'Hell clutched her, but hadn't energy enough to hold her.' The missteps of her youth are now eagerly recalled by those who love to stir polluted waters; and they are brought forward as reasons why she ought not to be allowed to preach. I was surprised to learn that to this prejudice was added another, against women's preaching. This seemed a strange idea for Methodists, some of whose brightest ornaments have been women preachers. As far back as Adam Clarke's[9] time, his objections were met by the answer, 'If an *ass* reproved Balaam, and a *barn-door fowl* reproved Peter, why shouldn't a *woman* reprove sin?'

This classification with donkeys and fowls is certainly not very complimentary. The first comparison I heard most wittily replied to, by a coloured woman who had once been a slave. 'Maybe a speaking woman *is* like an Ass,' said she; 'but I can tell you one thing—the Ass saw the angel, when Balaam didn't.'[10]

---

8. Psalm 68.31, "Ethiopia shall soon stretch out her hands unto God," was frequently cited by abolitionists and interpreted as prophesying Africa's redemption from oppression.

9. Adam Clarke (ca. 1760–1832) was an Irish-born Wesleyan preacher and theologian. The anecdote remains unverified, but it refers to Numbers 22.21–35 and Mark 14.66–72. In the first, the ass carrying the false prophet Balaam repeatedly balks when an angel of God blocks the path; when Balaam, who does not see the angel, beats the animal, it protests; in the end, God reveals himself to Balaam and rebukes him. In the second biblical passage, Peter denies Christ three times before the cock crows twice, but the cock does not actually reprove Peter.

10. In her article "*The Liberator* and Its Work," *Independent* 28 Dec. 1865, *CC* 64/1698, Child attributes this witticism to the antislavery and women's rights speaker and evangelist Sojourner Truth (ca. 1797–1883).

Father Matthews, after apologizing for various misquotations of Scripture, on the ground of Julia's inability to read, added:—'But the Lord has evidently called this woman to a great work. He has made her mighty to the salvation of many souls, as a cloud of witnesses can testify. Some say she ought not to preach, because she is a woman. But I say, "Let the Lord send by whom he *will* send." Let everybody that has a message, deliver it—whether man or woman, white or coloured! Some say women mustn't preach, because they were first in the transgression; but it seems to me hard that if they helped us *into* sin, they shouldn't be suffered to help us *out*. I say, "Let the Lord send by whom he *will* send;" and my pulpit shall be always open.'

Thus did the good man instil a free principle into those uneducated minds, like gleams of light through chinks in a prison-wall. Who can foretell its manifold and ever-increasing results in the history of that long-crippled race? Verily great is the Advent of a true Idea, made manifest to men; and great are the miracles of works—making the blind to see, and the lame to walk.

Letters from New York, Number 14

I was always eager for the spring-time, but never so much as now!

Patience yet a little longer! and I shall find delicate bells of the trailing arbutus, fragrant as an infant's breath, hidden deep, under their coverlid of autumn leaves, like modest worth in this pretending world. My spirit is weary for rural rambles. It is sad walking in the city. The streets shut out the sky, even as commerce comes between the soul and heaven. The busy throng, passing and repassing, fetter freedom, while they offer no sympathy. The loneliness of the soul is deeper, and far more restless, than in the solitude of the mighty forest. Wherever are woods and fields I find a home; each tinted leaf and shining pebble is to me a friend; and wherever I spy a wild flower, I am ready to leap up, clap my hands, and exclaim, 'Cocatoo! he know me very well!' as did the poor New Zealander, when he recognised a bird of his native clime, in the menageries of London.

But amid these magnificent masses of sparkling marble, hewn *in prison*, I am alone. For eight weary months, I have met in the crowded streets but two faces I had ever seen before. Of some, I would I could say that I should never see them again; but they haunt me in my sleep, and come between me and the morning. Beseeching looks, begging the comfort and the hope I have no power to give. Hungry eyes, that look as if they had pleaded long for sympathy, and at last gone mute in still despair. Through what woful, what frightful masks, does the human soul look forth, leering, peeping, and defying, in this thoroughfare of nations. Yet in each and all lie the capacities of an archangel; as the majestic oak lies enfolded in the acorn that we tread carelessly under foot, and which decays, perchance, for want of soil to root in.

The other day, I went forth for exercise merely, without other hope of enjoyment than a farewell to the setting sun, on the now deserted Battery, and a fresh kiss from the breezes of the sea, ere they passed through the polluted city, bearing healing on their wings. I had not gone far, when I met a little ragged urchin, about four years old, with a heap of newspapers, 'more big as he could carry,' under his little arm, and another clenched in his small, red fist. The sweet voice of childhood was prematurely cracked into shrillness, by screaming street cries, at the top of his lungs; and he looked blue, cold, and

National Anti-Slavery Standard, 17 February 1842; reprinted in *Letters from New York* (1843), pp. 94–100.

disconsolate. May the angels guard him! How I wanted to warm him in my heart. I stood looking after him, as he went shivering along. Imagination followed him to the miserable cellar where he probably slept on dirty straw; I saw him flogged, after his day of cheerless toil, because he had failed to bring home pence enough for his parents' grog; I saw wicked ones come muttering and beckoning between his young soul and heaven; they tempted him to steal to avoid the dreaded beating. I saw him, years after, bewildered and frightened, in the police-office, surrounded by hard faces. Their law-jargon conveyed no meaning to his ear, awakened no slumbering moral sense, taught him no clear distinction between right and wrong; but from their cold, harsh tones, and heartless merriment, he drew the inference that they were enemies; and, as such, he hated them. At that moment, one tone like a mother's voice might have wholly changed his earthly destiny; one kind word of friendly counsel might have saved him—as if an angel, standing in the genial sunlight, had thrown to him one end of a garland, and gently diminishing the distance between them, had drawn him safely out of the deep and tangled labyrinth, where false echoes and winding paths conspired to make him lose his way.

But watchmen and constables were around him, and they have small fellowship with angels. The strong impulses that might have become overwhelming love for his race, are perverted to the bitterest hatred. He tries the universal resort of weakness against force; if they are too strong for *him*, he will be too cunning for *them*. *Their* cunning is roused to detect *his* cunning: and thus the gallows-game is played, with interludes of damnable merriment from police reports, whereat the heedless multitude laugh; while angels weep over the slow murder of a human soul.

When, O when, will men learn that society makes and cherishes the very crimes it so fiercely punishes, and *in* punishing reproduces?

> 'The key of knowledge first ye take away,
> And then, because ye've robbed him, ye enslave;
> Ye shut out from him the sweet light of day,
> And then, because he's in the dark, ye pave
> The road, that leads him to his wished-for grave,
> With stones of stumbling: then, if he but tread
> Darkling and slow, ye call him "fool" and "knave";—
> Doom him to toil, and yet deny him bread:
> Chains round his limbs ye throw, and curses on his head.'

God grant the little shivering carrier-boy a brighter destiny than I have foreseen for him.

A little further on, I encountered two young boys fighting furiously for some coppers, that had been given them and had fallen on the pavement. They had matted black hair, large, lustrous eyes, and an olive complexion. They were evidently foreign children, from the sunny clime of Italy or Spain, and nature had made them subjects for an artist's dream. Near by on the cold stone steps, sat a ragged, emaciated woman, whom I conjectured, from the resemblance of her large dark eyes, might be their mother; but she looked on their fight with languid indifference, as if seeing, she saw it not. I spoke to her, and she shook her head in a mournful way, that told me she did not understand my language. Poor, forlorn wanderer! would I could place thee and thy beautiful boys under shelter of sun-ripened vines, surrounded by the music of thy mother-land! Pence I will give thee, though political economy reprove the deed. They can but appease the hunger of the body; they cannot soothe the hunger of thy heart; that I obey the kindly impulse may make the world none the better—perchance some iota the worse; yet I must needs follow it—I cannot otherwise.

I raised my eyes above the woman's weather-beaten head, and saw, behind the window of clear, plate glass, large vases of gold and silver, curiously wrought. They spoke significantly of the sad contrasts in this disordered world; and excited in my mind whole volumes, not of political, but of angelic economy. 'Truly,' said I, 'if the Law of Love prevailed, vases of gold and silver might even more abound—but no homeless outcast would sit shivering beneath their glittering mockery. All would be richer, and no man the poorer. When will the world learn its best wisdom? When will the mighty discord come into heavenly harmony?' I looked at the huge stone structures of commercial wealth, and they gave an answer that chilled my heart. Weary of city walks, I would have turned homeward; but nature, ever true and harmonious, beckoned to me from the Battery, and the glowing twilight gave me friendly welcome. It seemed as if the dancing Spring Hours had thrown their rosy mantles on old silvery winter in the lavishness of youthful love.

I opened my heart to the gladsome influence, and forgot that earth was not a mirror of the heavens. It was but for a moment; for there, under the leafless trees, lay two ragged little boys, asleep in each other's arms. I remembered having read in the police reports, the day before, that two little children, thus found, had been taken up as vagabonds. They told, with simple pathos, how both their mothers had been dead for months; how they had formed an intimate friendship, had begged together, ate together, hungered together, and together slept uncovered beneath the steel-cold stars.

The twilight seemed no longer warm; and brushing away a tear, I walked hastily homeward. As I turned into the street where God has provided me with a friendly shelter, something lay across my path. It was a woman, apparently dead; with garments all draggled in New-York gutters, blacker than waves of the infernal rivers. Those who gathered around, said she had fallen in intoxication, and was rendered senseless by the force of the blow. They carried her to the watch-house, and the doctor promised she should be well attended. But, alas, for watch-house charities to a breaking heart! I could not bring myself to think otherwise than that hers *was* a breaking heart! Could she but give a full revelation of early emotions checked in their full and kindly flow, of affections repressed, of hopes blighted, and energies misemployed through ignorance, the heart would kindle and melt, as it does when genius stirs its deepest recesses.

It seemed as if the voice of human wo was destined to follow me through the whole of that unblest day. Late in the night I heard the sound of voices in the street, and raising the window, saw a poor, staggering woman in the hands of a watchman. My ear caught the words, 'Thank you kindly, sir. I should *like* to go home.' The sad and humble accents in which the simple phrase was uttered, the dreary image of the watch-house, which that poor wretch dreamed was her *home*, proved too much for my overloaded sympathies. I hid my face in the pillow, and wept; for 'my heart was almost breaking with the misery of my kind.'

I thought, then, that I would walk no more abroad, till the fields were green. But my mind and body grow alike impatient of being inclosed within walls; both ask for the free breeze, and the wide, blue dome that overarches and embraces *all.* Again I rambled forth under the February sun, as mild and genial as the breath of June. Heart, mind, and frame grew glad and strong, as we wandered on, past the old Stuyvesant church, which a few years agone was surrounded by fields and Dutch farm-houses, but now stands in the midst of peopled streets;—and past the trim, new houses, with their green verandahs, in the airy suburbs. Following the railroad, which lay far beneath our feet, as we wound our way over the hills, we came to the burying-ground of the poor. Weeds and brambles grew along the sides, and the stubble of last year's grass waved over it, like dreary memories of the past; but the sun smiled on it, like God's love on the desolate soul. It was inexpressibly touching to see the frail memorials of affection, placed there by hearts crushed under the weight of poverty. In one place was a small rude cross of wood, with the initials J. S. cut with a penknife, and apparently filled with ink. In another a small hoop had been bent into the form of a heart, painted green, and nailed on a stick at the head of the grave. On one upright shingle was painted only 'MUTTER'; the German word for MOTHER. On another was scrawled, as if with charcoal, '*So ruhe wohl, du unser liebes kind.*' (Rest well, our beloved child.) One recorded life's brief history thus: 'H. G. born in Bavaria; died in New-York.' Another short epitaph, in French, told that the sleeper came from the banks of the Seine.

The predominance of foreign epitaphs affected me deeply. Who could now tell with what high hopes those departed ones had left the heart-homes of Germany, the sunny hills of Spain, the laughing skies of Italy, or the wild beauty of Switzerland? Would not the friends they had left in their child-hood's home, weep scalding tears to find them in a pauper's grave, with their initials rudely carved on a fragile shingle? Some had not even these frail memorials. It seemed there was none to care whether they lived or died. A wide, deep trench was open; and there I could see piles of unpainted coffins heaped one upon the other, left uncovered with earth, till the yawning cavity was filled with its hundred tenants.

Returning homeward, we passed a Catholic burying-ground. It belonged to the upper classes, and was filled with marble monuments, covered with long inscriptions. But none of them touched my heart like that rude shingle, with the simple word 'Mutter' inscribed thereon. The gate was open, and hundreds of Irish, in their best Sunday clothes, were stepping reverently among the graves, and kissing the very sods. Tenderness for the dead is one of the loveliest features of their nation and their church.

The evening was closing in, as we returned, thoughtful, but not gloomy. Bright lights shone through crimson, blue, and green, in the apothecaries' windows, and were reflected in prismatic beauty from the dirty pools in the street. It was like poetic thoughts in the minds of the poor and ignorant; like the memory of pure aspirations in the vicious; like a rainbow of promise, that God's spirit never leaves even the most degraded soul. I smiled, as my spirit gratefully accepted this love-token from the outward; and I thanked our heavenly Father for a world beyond this.

Letters from New York, Number 29

I went last week to Blackwell's Island, in the East River, between the city and Long Island. The environs of the city are unusually beautiful, considering how far Autumn has advanced upon us. Frequent rains have coaxed vegetation into abundance, and preserved it in verdant beauty. The trees are hung with a profusion of vines, the rocks are dressed in nature's green velvet of moss, and from every little cleft peeps the rich foliage of some wind-scattered seed. The island itself presents a quiet loveliness of scenery, unsurpassed by anything I have ever witnessed; though Nature and I are old friends, and she has shown me many of her choicest pictures, in a light let in only from above. No form of gracefulness can compare with the bend of flowing waters all round and round a verdant island. The circle typifies Love; and they who read the spiritual alphabet, will see that a circle of *waters* must needs be very beautiful. Beautiful it *is*, even when the language it speaks is an unknown tongue. Then the green hills beyond look so very pleasant in the sunshine, with *homes* nestling among them, like dimples on a smiling face. The island itself abounds with charming nooks—open wells in shady places, screened by large weeping willows; gardens and arbours running down to the river's edge, to look at themselves in the waters; and pretty boats, like white-winged birds, chased by their shadows, and breaking the waves into gems.

But man has profaned this charming retreat. He has brought the screech-owl, the bat, and the vulture, into the holy temple of Nature. The island belongs to government; and the only buildings on it are penitentiary, mad-house, and hospital; with a few dwellings occupied by people connected with those institutions. The discord between man and nature never before struck me so painfully; yet it is wise and kind to place the erring and the diseased in the midst of such calm, bright influences. Man may curse, but Nature for ever blesses. The guiltiest of her wandering children she would fain enfold within her arms to the friendly heart-warmth of a mother's bosom. She speaks to them ever in the soft, low tones of earnest love: but they, alas, tossed on the roaring, stunning surge of society, forget the quiet language.

As I looked up at the massive walls of the prison, it did my heart good to see doves nestling within the shelter of the deep, narrow, grated windows. I

National Anti-Slavery Standard, 6 October 1842; reprinted in *Letters from New York* (1843), pp. 199–212.

thought what blessed little messengers of heaven they would appear to me, if I were in prison; but instantly a shadow passed over the sunshine of my thought. Alas, doves do not speak to *their* souls, as they would to *mine;* for they have lost their love for child-like, and gentle things. *How* have they lost it? Society, with its unequal distribution, its perverted education, its manifold injustice, its cold neglect, its biting mockery, has taken from them the gifts of God. They are placed here, in the midst of green hills, and flowing streams, and cooing doves, after the heart is petrified against the genial influence of all such sights and sounds.

As usual, the organ of justice (which phrenologists[1] say is unusually developed in my head) was roused into great activity by the sight of prisoners. 'Would you have them prey on society?' said one of my companions. I answered, 'I am troubled that society has preyed upon *them.* I will not enter into an argument about the right of society to punish these sinners; but I say she *made* them sinners. How much I have done toward it, by yielding to popular prejudices, obeying false customs, and suppressing vital truths, I know not; but doubtless I have done, and am doing, my share. God forgive me. If He dealt with us, as we deal with our brother, who could stand before him?'

While I was there, they brought in the editors of the Flash, the Libertine, and the Weekly Rake. My very soul loathes such polluted publications; yet a sense of justice again made me refractory. These men were perhaps trained to such service by all the social influences they had ever known. They dared to *publish* what nine-tenths of all around them *lived* unreproved. Why should they be imprisoned, while —— —— flourished in the full tide of editorial success, circulating a paper as immoral, and perhaps more dangerous, because its indecency is slightly veiled? Why should the Weekly Rake be shut up, when daily rakes walk Broadway in fine broadcloth and silk velvet?

Many more than half the inmates of the penitentiary were women; and of course a large proportion of them were taken up as 'street-walkers.' The men who made them such, who, perchance, caused the love of a human heart to be its ruin, and changed tenderness into sensuality and crime—these men live

---

1. The popular pseudoscience of phrenology originated with Franz-Josef Gall and Johann Gaspar Spurzheim, whose tour of the United States in 1832 sparked a phrenology mania. Their American disciples Orson and Lorenzo Fowler established a Phrenological Cabinet in New York where many celebrities, including Child, had their skulls examined. Phrenologists claimed to be able to read a person's character from the bumps on his or her skull, which supposedly registered the development of different "organs" of the brain.

in the 'ceiled houses' of Broadway, and sit in council in the City Hall, and pass 'regulations' to clear the streets they have filled with sin. And do you suppose their poor victims do not *feel* the injustice of society thus regulated? Think you they respect the *laws?* Vicious they are, and they may be both ignorant and foolish; but, nevertheless, they are too wise to respect such laws. Their whole being cries out that it is a mockery; all their experience proves that society is a game of chance, where the cunning slip through, and the strong leap over. The criminal *feels* this, even when incapable of *reasoning* upon it. The laws do not secure his reverence, because he sees that their operation is unjust. The secrets of prisons, so far as they are revealed, all tend to show that the prevailing feeling of criminals, of all grades, is that they are *wronged.* What we call *justice,* they regard as an unlucky *chance;* and whosoever looks calmly and wisely into the foundations on which society rolls and tumbles, (I cannot say on which it *rests,* for its foundations heave like the sea,) will perceive that they *are* victims of chance.

For instance, everything in school-books, social remarks, domestic conversation, literature, public festivals, legislative proceedings, and popular honours, all teach the young soul that it is noble to retaliate, mean to forgive an insult, and unmanly not to resent a wrong. Animal instincts, instead of being brought into subjection to the higher powers of the soul, are thus cherished into more than natural activity. Of three men thus educated, one enters the army, kills a hundred Indians, hangs their scalps on a tree, is made major general, and considered a fitting candidate for the presidency. The second goes to the Southwest to reside; some 'roarer' calls him a rascal—a phrase not misapplied, perhaps, but necessary to be resented; he agrees to settle the question of honour at ten paces, shoots his insulter through the heart, and is hailed by society as a brave man. The third lives in New-York; a man enters his office, and, true, or untrue, calls him a knave. He fights, kills his adversary, is tried by the laws of the land, and hung. These three men indulged the same passion, acted from the same motives, and illustrated the same education: yet how different their fate!

With regard to dishonesty, too—the maxims of trade, the customs of society, and the general unreflecting tone of public conversation, all tend to promote it. The man who has made 'good bargains,' is wealthy and honoured; yet the details of those bargains few would dare to pronounce good. Of two young men nurtured under such influences, one becomes a successful merchant; five thousand dollars are borrowed of him; he takes a mortgage on a house worth twenty thousand dollars; in the absence of the owner, when sales are very dull, he offers the house for sale, to pay his mortgage; he bids it in himself, for four thousand dollars; and afterwards persecutes and imprisons his debtor for the remaining thousand. Society calls him a shrewd business man, and pronounces his dinners excellent; the chance is, he will be a magistrate before he dies. The other young man is unsuccessful; his necessities are great; he borrows some money from his employer's drawer, perhaps resolving to restore the same; the loss is discovered before he has a chance to refund it; and society sends him to Blackwell's island, to hammer stone with highway robbers. Society made both these men thieves; but punished the one, while she rewarded the other. That criminals so universally *feel* themselves victims of injustice, is one strong proof that it is true; for impressions entirely without foundation are not apt to become universal. If society does make its own criminals, how shall she cease to do it? It can be done only by a change in the structure of society, that will diminish the temptations to vice, and increase the encouragements to virtue. If we can abolish *poverty,* we shall have taken the greatest step towards the abolition of *crime;* and this will be the final triumph of the gospel of Christ. Diversities of gifts will doubtless always exist; for the law written on spirit, as well as matter, is infinite variety. But when the kingdom of God comes 'on earth as it is in heaven,' there will not be found in any corner of it that poverty which hardens the heart under the severe pressure of physical suffering, and stultifies the intellect with toil for mere animal wants. When public opinion regards wealth as a *means,* and not as an *end,* men will no longer deem penitentiaries a necessary evil; for society will then cease to be a great school for crime. In the meantime, do penitentiaries and prisons increase or diminish the evils they are intended to remedy?

The superintendent at Blackwell told me, unasked, that ten years' experience had convinced him that the whole system tended to *increase* crime. He said of the lads who came there, a large proportion had already been in the house of refuge; and a large proportion of those who left, afterward went to Sing Sing. 'It is as regular a succession as the classes in a college,' said he, 'from the house of refuge to the penitentiary, and from the penitentiary to the State prison.' I remarked that coercion tended to rouse all the bad passions in man's nature, and if long continued, hardened the whole character. 'I know that,' said he, 'from my own experience; all the devil there is in me rises up when a man attempts to compel me. But what can I do? I am *obliged* to be very strict. When my feelings tempt me to unusual indulgence, a bad use is almost always made of it. I see that the system fails to produce the effect intended; but I cannot change the result.'

I felt that his words were true. He could not change the influence of the system while he discharged the duties of his office; for the same reason that a man cannot be at once slave-driver and missionary on a plantation. I allude to the necessities of the office, and do not mean to imply that the character of the individual was severe. On the contrary, the prisoners seemed to be made as comfortable as was compatible with their situation. There were watch-towers, with loaded guns, to prevent escape from the island; but they conversed freely with each other as they worked in the sunshine, and very few of them looked wretched. Among those who were sent under guard to row us back to the city, was one who jested on his own situation, in a manner which showed plainly enough that he looked on the whole thing as a game of chance, in which he *happened* to be the loser. Indulgence cannot benefit such characters. What is wanted is, that no human being should grow up without deep and friendly interest from the society round him; and that none should feel himself the victim of injustice, because society punishes the very sins which it teaches, nay drives men to commit. The world would be in a happier condition if legislators spent half as much time and labour to *prevent* crime, as they do to *punish* it. The poor need houses of *encouragement*; and society gives them houses of *correction*. Benevolent institutions and reformatory societies perform but a limited and temporary use. They do not reach the groundwork of evil; and it is reproduced too rapidly for them to keep even the surface healed. The natural spontaneous influences of society should be such as to supply men with healthy motives, and give full, free play to the affections, and the faculties. It is horrible to see our young men goaded on by the fierce, speculating spirit of the age, from the contagion of which it is almost impossible to escape, and then see them tortured into madness, or driven to crime, by fluctuating changes of the money-market. The young soul is, as it were, entangled in the great merciless machine of a falsely-constructed society; the steam he had no hand in raising, whirls him hither and thither, and it is altogether a lottery-chance whether it crushes or propels him.

Many, who are mourning over the too obvious diseases of the world, will smile contemptuously at the idea of *reconstruction*. But let them reflect a moment upon the immense changes that have already come over society. In the middle ages, both noble and peasant would have laughed loud and long at the prophecy of such a state of society as now exists in the free States of America; yet here we are!

I by no means underrate modern improvements in the discipline of prisons, or progressive meliorations in the criminal code. I rejoice in these things as facts, and still more as prophecy. Strong as my faith is that the time will come when war and prisons will both cease from the face of the earth, I am by no means blind to the great difficulties in the way of those who are honestly striving to make the best of things as they *are*. Violations of right, continued generation after generation, and interwoven into the whole structure of action and opinion, will continue troublesome and injurious, even for a long time after they are outwardly removed. Legislators and philanthropists may well be puzzled to know what to do with those who have become hardened in crime; meanwhile, the highest wisdom should busy itself with the more important questions, How did these men *become* criminals? Are not social influences largely at fault? If society is the criminal, were it not well to reform society?

It is common to treat the inmates of penitentiaries and prisons as if they were altogether unlike ourselves—as if they belonged to another race; but this indicates superficial thought and feeling. The passions which carried those men to prison, exist in your own bosom, and have been gratified, only in a less degree: perchance, if you look inward, with enlightened self-knowledge, you will perceive that there have been periods in your own life when a hair's-breadth further in the wrong would have rendered you amenable to human laws; and that you were prevented from moving over that hair's-breadth boundary by outward circumstances, for which you deserve no credit.

If reflections like these make you think lightly of sin, you pervert them to a very bad use. They *should* teach you that every criminal has a human heart, which *can* be reached and softened by the same means that will reach and soften your own. In all, even the most hardened, love lies folded up, perchance buried; and the voice of love calls it forth, and makes it gleam like living coals through ashes. This influence, if applied in season, would assuredly *prevent* the hardness, which it has so much power to soften.

That most tender-spirited and beautiful book, entitled 'My Prisons, by Sylvio Pellico,'[2] abounds with incidents to prove the omnipotence of kindness. He was a gentle and a noble soul, imprisoned merely for reasons of state, being suspected of republican notions. Robbers and banditti, confined in the same building, saluted him with respect as they passed him in the court; and he always returned their salutations with brotherly cordiality. He says, 'One of them once said to me, "Your greeting, signore, does me good.

---

2. *My Prisons* (1832), by the Italian patriot Silvio Pellico (1789–1854), tells of his sufferings as a political prisoner.

Perhaps you see something in my face that is not very bad? An unhappy passion led me to commit a crime; but oh, signore, I am not, indeed I am not a villain." And he burst into tears. I held out my hand to him, but he could not take it. My guards, not from bad feelings, but in obedience to orders, repulsed him.'

In the sight of God, perchance their repulse was a heavier crime than that for which the poor fellow was imprisoned; perhaps it *made* him a 'villain,' when the genial influence of Sylvio Pellico might have restored him a blessing to the human family. If these things *are* so, for what a frightful amount of crime are the coercing and repelling influences of society responsible!

I have not been happy since that visit to Blackwell's Island. There is something painful, yea, terrific, in feeling myself involved in the great wheel of society, which goes whirling on, crushing thousands at every turn. This relation of the individual to the mass is the sternest and most frightful of all the conflicts between necessity and free will. Yet here, too, conflict *should* be harmony, and *will* be so. Put far away from thy soul all desire of retaliation, all angry thoughts, all disposition to overcome or humiliate an adversary, and be assured thou hast done much to abolish gallows, chains, and prisons, though thou hast never written or spoken a word on the criminal code.

God and good angels alone know the vast, the incalculable influence that goes out into the universe of spirit, and thence flows into the universe of matter, from the conquered evil, and the voiceless prayer of one solitary soul. Wouldst thou bring the world unto God? Then live near to him thyself. If divine life pervade thine own soul, every thing that touches thee will receive the electric spark, though thou mayest be unconscious of being charged therewith. This surely would be the highest, to strive to keep near the holy, not for the sake of our own reward here or hereafter, but that through love to God we might bless our neighbour. The human soul can perceive this, and yet the beauty of the earth is everywhere defaced with jails and gibbets! Angelic natures can never deride, else were there loud laughter in heaven at the discord between man's perceptions and his practice.

At Long Island Farms I found six hundred children, supported by the public. It gives them wholesome food, comfortable clothing, and the common rudiments of education. For this it deserves praise. But the aliment which the spirit craves, the *public* has not to give. The young heart asks for *love,* yearns for love—but its own echo returns to it through empty halls, instead of answer.

The institution is much lauded by visiters, and not without reason; for everything looks clean and comfortable, and the children appear happy. The drawbacks are such as inevitably belong to their situation, as children of the public. The oppressive feeling is, that there are no *mothers* there. Everything moves by machinery, as it always must with masses of children, never sub-divided into families. In one place, I saw a stack of small wooden guns, and was informed that the boys were daily drilled to military exercises, as a useful means of forming habits of order, as well as fitting them for the future service of the state. Their infant school evolutions partook of the same drill charac-ter; and as for their religion, I was informed that it was 'beautiful to see them pray; for at the first tip of the whistle, they all dropped on their knees.' Alas, poor childhood, thus doth 'church and state' provide for thee! The state arms thee with wooden guns, to play the future murderer, and the church teaches thee to pray in platoons, 'at the first tip of the whistle.' Luckily they cannot drive the angels from thee, or most assuredly they would do it, *pro bono publico.*

The sleeping-rooms were clean as a Shaker's apron. When I saw the long rows of nice little beds, ranged side by side, I inquired whether there was not a merry buzz in the morning. 'They are not permitted to speak at all in the sleeping apartments,' replied the superintendent. The answer sent a chill through my heart. I acknowledged that in such large establishments the most exact method was necessary, and I knew that the children had abundant opportunity for fun and frolic in the sunshine and the open fields, in the after part of the day; but it is so natural for all young things to crow and sing when they open their eyes to the morning light, that I could not bear to have the cheerful instinct perpetually repressed.

The hospital for these children is on the neighbouring island of Blackwell. This establishment, though clean and well supplied with outward comforts, was the most painful sight I ever witnessed. About one hundred and fifty children were there, mostly orphans, inheriting every variety of disease from vicious and sickly parents. In beds all of a row, or rolling by dozens over clean matting on the floor, the poor little pale, shrivelled, and blinded creatures were waiting for death to come and release them. Here the absence of a mother's love was most agonizing; not even the patience and gentleness of a saint could supply its place; and saints are rarely hired by the public. There was a sort of resignation expressed in the countenances of some of the little ones, which would have been beautiful in maturer years, but in childhood it spoke mournfully of a withered soul. It was pleasant to think that a large proportion of them would soon be received by the angels, who will doubtless let them sing in the morning.

That the law of Love may cheer and bless even *public* establishments, has been proved by the example of the Society of Friends. They formerly had an establishment for their own poor, in the city of Philadelphia, on a plan so simple and so beautiful, that one cannot but mourn to think it has given place to more common and less brotherly modes of relief. A nest of small households enclosed, on three sides, an open space devoted to gardens, in which each had a share. Here each poor family lived in separate rooms, and were assisted by the Society according to its needs. Sometimes a widow could support herself, with the exception of rent; and in that case, merely rooms were furnished gratis. An aged couple could perhaps subsist very comfortably, if supplied with house and fuel; and the friendly assistance was according to their wants. Some needed entire support; and to such it was ungrudgingly given. These paupers were oftentimes ministers and elders, took the highest seats in the meeting-house, and had as much influence as any in the affairs of the Society. Everything conspired to make them retain undiminished self-respect. The manner in which they evinced this would be considered impudence in the tenets of our modern alms-houses. One old lady being supplied with a load of wood at her free lodgings, refused to take it, saying, that it did not suit her; she wanted dry, small wood. 'But,' remonstrated the man, 'I was ordered to bring it here.' 'I can't help that. Tell 'em the best wood is the best economy. I do not want such wood as that.' Her orders were obeyed, and the old lady's wishes were gratified. Another, who took great pride and pleasure in the neatness of her little garden, employed a carpenter to make a trellis for her vines. Some objection was made to paying this bill, it being considered a mere superfluity. But the old lady maintained that it was necessary for her comfort; and at meetings and all public places, she never failed to rebuke the elders. 'O *you* profess to do unto others as you would be done by, and you have never paid that carpenter his bill.' Worn out by her perseverance, they paid the bill, and she kept her trellis of vines. It probably was more necessary to her comfort than many things *they* would have considered as not superfluous.

The poor of this establishment did not feel like dependents, and were never regarded as a burden. They considered themselves as members of a family, receiving from brethren the assistance they would have gladly bestowed under a reverse of circumstances. This approaches the gospel standard. Since the dawn of Christianity, no class of people have furnished an example so replete with a most wise tenderness, as the Society of Friends, in the days of its purity. Thank God, nothing good or true ever dies. The lifeless form falls from it, and it lives elsewhere.

A High-Flying Letter

I see that your city is undertaking to pioneer the way in the navigation of the air.[1] It cannot seem more impracticable than the proposed substitution of steam for horses did less than half a century ago. In view of the wonders man works with fire and water, it is not difficult to believe that he may attain to mastery over all the elements. Having put those powerful giants in harness, and made them as obedient to his will as the gentlest carriage-horses; having trained lightning to do his errands, and induced the sun to picture all creation for him in three leaps of a hare; what can he now do that will seem very surprising?

Many years ago, Dr. Channing[2] told me he thought the time would come when electricity would supersede steam, and when men would navigate the air as skillfully as they did the water. When I read of your aeronaut's sanguine hopes of being able to steer his ship whithersoever he would, I gave ready credence to the possibility of such a thing, and imagination began to play with it as a new and pleasing toy. I thought how entertaining it would be if the balloon could be anchored somewhere, or hitched to something, so that it could remain stationary at a hight sufficiently near the world to see it revolving beneath. But I reflected that banks of cloud were too flighty to hold an anchor, and that the horns of the moon had the double disadvantage of being inaccessible and subject to motion. "Pooh! pooh!" said imagination to reason; "haven't you wit enough to surmount *that* difficulty? You know that the earth rolls toward the east in its diurnal course. All you have to do is to steer your ship westward through the air, and then you'll see what you'll see!" Sure enough! instead of being laboriously wheeled over the world to look upon its wonders, the world, in the pursuit of its usual business, would wheel past *us* and we might sit in our easy-chair while the varied panorama of an entire zone revolved beneath our delighted vision. We might see shepherds tending their flocks in the primitive little republic of Andorra, hidden among the

Independent, 28 June 1866; reprinted in *CC* 65/1727

1. Balloon flights began in France in 1783 and occurred in New York throughout the nineteenth century. The *New York Times* reported a trapeze stunt from a balloon at the New Bowery Theater on 6 July 1866 (p. 8, col. 2), but nothing in the weeks before Child's letter. Her imaginary voyage around the world in a balloon follows the French science fiction writer Jules Verne's *Five Weeks in a Balloon* (1863), but precedes his *Around the World in Eighty Days* (1873).

2. William Ellery Channing (1780–1842) was a Unitarian minister.

snow-capped mountains of the Pyrenees. We might look down on the dancing peasantry of Provence, the harvest-homes of grape-bearing Italy, the leaning tower of Pisa, the gliding gondolas of Venice, the crescent-crowned mosques of Turkey, the rich caravans of Persia, the crowded lamaseries of Tibet, the Tartars racing over desert plains, in wildest costume and on wildest steeds, the bamboo cities of Japan, and the ships of all the world crossing and recrossing the Pacific. Then Oregon would present itself with its picturesque scenery of mountains and cañons; and great Salt Lake, with its sad company of concubines;[3] and wide prairies, where feather-crowned Pawnees scatter herds of buffalo with their swift arrows; and the great city of Chicago, that grew up as if by touch of an enchanter's wand; and the waving harvests of Ohio; and the flaming oil-wells of Pennsylvania; and so home again to the great reservoir of New York. What a voyage would that be, my countrymen! The English and American line of steamers would advertise in vain for passengers; for the tour of Europe would become in comparison as tedious as a twice-told tale. The victualing for such an excursion need not amount to much, since the world moves round in twenty-four hours; and we might descend before dark, unless we chose to remain to overlook the gas-lighted cities of the Western hemisphere, or the many-colored lanterns of the Eastern. Moreover, modern enterprise would consider it a mere trifle to take up a ready-furnished hotel along with the balloon. The young, who are fond of castles in the air, would be sure to patronize it largely; and, if they should get up a ball, it would be a charming novelty to have the building dance with the dancers, at a height far higher than any ever attempt on slack rope or tight rope.

If all this should be realized, we might, for awhile, look up in wonderment at such unwonted fleets floating over our heads; but they would soon attract no more attention than flocks of wild-geese. Perhaps they would now and then drop something inconveniently heavy upon our heads; but the fishes have long been subject to such accidents, when our anchors go rattling down among them. Now and then a wrecked balloon might tumble into a corn-field, and make sad havoc, just as sea-gardens have been crushed by the sudden descent of our iron steamers.

In a moral point of view, perhaps this mode of seeing Europe might, in some respects, be less disadvantageous than traveling through it. So far as I have had an opportunity to observe, people generally come back from a

3. An allusion to the polygamy practiced by the Mormons of Utah.

prolonged sojourn in the Old World with diminished faith in republican institutions and increased belief in the necessity of strong demarcation of ranks in society. They are apt to become indifferent to public affairs in their own country, and to avoid participation therein. To do homage to the "porcelain clay" of society, and gracefully describe the elegant pier-glasses[4] wherein its gauze and diamonds were reflected, formed a very prominent feature in the results of N. P. Willis's[5] European travel. Yet God has endowed him with genius capable of much higher things. He voted for the first time in 1856—many years after his return to his native country; and so unaware was he of the seething volcano, then beginning visibly to heave the nation from its foundation with its violent throes, that he was completely astounded by the effect his vote produced on "the porcelain clay" of the South. One of our Boston young gentlemen, returning from a long sojourn in Europe, was in the habit of shrinking so daintily from plebeian contact that he was pro-verbially called "the duke." I lately heard of a very intelligent and highly respectable nurse, who, being weary with night-watching, seated herself for a few minutes while she answered the inquiries of a young lady concerning the symptoms of the invalid under her care. She was rebuked by the observation, "It is proper for you to stand while you are speaking to *me.*" The young lady had recently returned from England, where she had apparently been bathed in "British fluid."

That this country is growing prematurely old in vice and crime, by rea-son of the vagrants and convicts which Europe continually pours upon our shores, is known and lamented by all reflecting people; but they take less note of the subtle, insidious, undermining influences continually filtering into the national mind through foreign education and foreign travel. Yet I am some-times tempted to think that these latter influences are the most dangerous of the two.

A young lady who had made the fashionable tour, and who considered herself "porcelain clay," said to a friend of mine, "You will, of course, send your children to Europe to be educated. Everybody agrees that a suitable education cannot be obtained in America." I am sorry to observe that this

---

4. pier glass: a large, high mirror, especially one designed to occupy the wall space between windows.

5. Nathaniel Parker Willis (1806–67), best known today as Harriet Jacobs's employer in New York and as Fanny Fern's brother, courted Child in her youth. She refers frequently to his aristo-cratic tastes, social snobbery, dandyism, and political conservatism. His myriad travel books focus on high society and *Famous Persons and Places,* as the title of an 1854 work indicates.

view is becoming more and more fashionable. Thorough intellectual training is undoubtedly very desirable; but there are other considerations still more important. Young people educated abroad may have opportunities to make greater proficiency in various sciences and in elegant accomplishments; but, while acquiring these, they are almost unavoidably influenced by habits and opinions which are the outgrowth of institutions older and narrower than our own. Imbued with these, they return a foreign shape into their own country. Surely, instead of sending our sons to Europe to study the classics and the sciences, accompanied by gratuitous teaching of aristocracy, it would be a wiser plan to raise our own universities and schools to the highest level. Men who are to assume the immense responsibilities and perform the sublime duties of American citizens should be educated in America, under the influence of our republican institutions, breathing an atmosphere of equal rights, and habitually feeling themselves, to all intents and purposes, a portion of the people.

No one can be blind to the fact that for the last half century the feeling has been growing in this country that labor is disreputable. The sons of farmers and mechanics are rarely willing to follow the useful and honorable occupations of their fathers. It is difficult to obtain good mechanical work, while there is everywhere a superabundance of merchants, doctors, lawyers, and clergymen; many of whom were evidently not intended by nature for the vocations they have adopted. I attribute the prevailing contempt for labor to three causes. First, the existence of slavery in a portion of the country; second, the inundation of Irish peasantry, who, by the influence of their previous circumstances, came to us too rude and ignorant to be agreeable associates for intelligent American laborers; and, third, the increasing tendency to travel in Europe and educate our children there. Slavery has received its death-blow, though the monster will doubtless be long in dying. The second generation of Irish, thanks to our free schools, become sufficiently enlightened to reflect credit on their occupations. But the influences arising from social intercourse with Europe continue and increase. Some of its effects are doubtless very salutary. After principles are formed, and reason sufficiently matured to distinguish right from wrong, it enlarges the mind to learn by observation and experience that good as well as evil is the growth of all soils. Nations, as well as individuals, think better of each other, and feel more kindly toward each other, if they are in the habit of meeting frequently. It is mutual give-and-take between those who tend to opposite extremes. America, with her go-ahead tendencies, might be in danger of flying out of her appointed orbit, were it not for the centripetal attraction of the old institutions, habits, and opinions of Europe; and certainly the slow Old World would have fallen to the sun, and been consumed, if the fast New World had not kept her in motion. It was a delightful programme, that of being poised above the earth, and seeing it roll by, merely for our entertainment; but I admit it was rather a selfish one.

Part Five

Sexuality and

the Woman Question

Introduction

✽ Feminist consciousness dawned in Child at a young age, though she did not give it coherent political expression until the 1840s. Well before her twelfth year, she learned that a passion for books aroused pride when exhibited by a son and alarm when betrayed by a daughter. Like her older brother Convers, who encouraged her intellectual curiosity, Child grew up with a hunger for education and a longing to exchange the incessant drudgery of their father's bakeshop for a more stimulating cultural milieu. Yet while Convers fulfilled his dream of going to Harvard, Child languished for a year in a girls' finishing school, after which she was dispatched to her sister Mary's household in Norridgewock, Maine, for tutelage in the domestic arts.

Even so, Child's six-year sojourn in Maine (1815–21) contributed to the development of her feminist consciousness by enabling her to observe the vastly different lives of nearby Penobscot and Abenaki women. If these women could accompany their tribes on "long tramps" through the snow with their children strapped on their backs, carry heavy loads on their shoulders, and get up from childbirth to wash their newborn babies in icy rivers, then physical frailty could not be an innate female trait, and the stultifying feminine ideal her own society upheld could not be rooted in nature, Child concluded, as she later spelled out in her articles "Concerning Women" (*Independent* 15 July and 21 Oct. 1869, reprinted here) and "Physical Strength of Women" (*Woman's Journal* 15 Mar. 1873).

Such perceptions no doubt remained inchoate in her youth, but they seem to have inspired the plot of her first novel, *Hobomok, a Tale of Early Times* (1824), which liberates its heroine, Mary Conant, from the misogyny of Puritan New England by marrying her off to an Indian and settling her in a wigwam for three years. Whether or not Child fantasized such an escape for herself, she projected her revolt against woman's lot not only onto Mary Conant and Sally Oldham of *Hobomok,* but onto the female characters of her second novel, *The Rebels, or Boston before the Revolution* (1825).

Child also acted out her desire for a life beyond the bounds of conventional femininity by marrying a man who admired her intellect, recognized her flair for political writing, and needed the income she earned as a literary woman. Yet her marriage to David Lee Child in October 1828 prompted a retreat from her early feminism. Almost immediately, she began to publish articles in her husband's newspaper, the *Massachusetts Journal,* measuring the

"Comparative Strength of Male and Female Intellect" to the disadvantage of women and disavowing the doctrines of sexual equality promulgated by the radical feminist Frances Wright.[1] It hardly seems coincidental that Child was simultaneously helping her husband to edit his paper and diverting her literary talents into domestic advice books and other profit-making endeavors for the sake of paying the debts he incurred through mismanagement. Though already suffering the consequences of nineteenth-century marriage law, under which all her earnings and the copyrights to her books belonged to her husband (and to his creditors), she was no longer willing to probe her culture's gender hierarchies.

If in theory Child now repudiated feminism, in practice she followed the course described in her *National Anti-Slavery Standard* editorial "Speaking in the Church" (15 July 1841, reprinted here): "I prefer, as quietly and unobtrusively as possible, to *take* my freedom without disputing about my claim to it." Thus, when her conscience impelled her to fight against slavery, she simply ignored strictures against women's engagement in political controversy. By publishing *An Appeal in Favor of That Class of Americans Called Africans* (1833) and by attending antislavery meetings with her husband, Child set precedents for other women. Still, she conformed to the rules interdicting women's public speaking, always enlisting male mouthpieces to transmit her views to the assembly. At the same time, she preferred such male-dominated forums to separate female organizations, which seemed to her "like half a pair of scissors."[2]

Child expressed her conflicted attitude toward the "woman question" in a work that supplied her sisters in the antislavery movement with ammunition for challenging the doctrine of "woman's sphere" but that avoided formulating such a challenge. Her two-volume *History of the Condition of Women, in Various Ages and Nations* (1835) anticipates today's multicultural approach to Women's Studies by exploring commonalities and differences in the status of women across the globe, from ancient times to the mid-nineteenth century, from the remotest tribes of Siberia, Africa, and the Pacific islands to the nations of Europe and the Americas. Most remarkable is the eighty-page chapter devoted to African women (partially reprinted in part 5), which situates them in complex cultures and depicts them as practicing many ar-

1. "Comparative Strength of Male and Female Intellect," *Massachusetts Journal* (weekly ed.) 4 Mar. 1829, p. 2; "Letter from a Lady, concerning Miss Wright," *Massachusetts Journal* (weekly ed.) 14 Aug. 1829, p. 3.
2. LMC to Lucretia Mott, 5 Mar. 1839, *SL* 106.

tisanal crafts, accompanying their labor with songs, performing elaborate dances, and participating in political palavers, hunts, and battles. Child judges the "condition of women" in a given society by examining an array of indicators: marriage customs reflecting the valuation of women as drudges, sexual objects, reproducers, child rearers, or simply property; laws regulating virginity, adultery, concubinage, polygamy, prostitution, and divorce—and the differential application of such laws to men and women; patrilineal versus matrilineal reckoning of descent, paternal versus maternal custody of children, and the extent of discrimination between males and females when disposing of surplus children through infanticide or sale; women's occupations in relation to men's; their access to education, moneymaking activities, political power, the priesthood, and other avenues to prestige; and the degree of personal freedom or confinement they experienced.

Child's encyclopedic research clearly points toward the conclusions she refrains from drawing: that no monolithic concept of womanhood can accommodate the overwhelming diversity of the world's gender and sexual arrangements, and that nurture rather than nature determines women's roles. Within less than a decade two major works of feminist theory written by her friends—Sarah Grimké's *Letters on the Equality of the Sexes, and the Condition of Woman* (1838) and Margaret Fuller's *Woman in the Nineteenth Century* (1845)—explicitly advanced the arguments for women's emancipation that Child had left unstated. Both mined her *History of the Condition of Women* for evidence supporting their feminist theses.

Child's *History* appeared at a particularly timely juncture in the antislavery movement. As her "Letters from New-York," number 33, on the mobbing of George Thompson (reprinted in part 3) indicates, by 1835 antiabolitionist violence was propelling women into unaccustomed stances. Because rioters did not dare attack white "ladies," abolitionist women began acting as bodyguards for targeted men. In October 1835 a mob in pursuit of George Thompson and William Lloyd Garrison even threatened a meeting of the Boston Female Anti-Slavery Society (BFASS). Emboldened by their success at facing down male assailants, women were starting to demand a greater share in the antislavery movement, and they eagerly seized on the implications of Child's wide-ranging cross-cultural study.

The radicalization of abolitionist women accelerated when Angelina and Sarah Grimké, daughters of a prominent South Carolina slaveholder and recent converts to the antislavery cause, set out in the summer of 1837 on a lecture tour of New England sponsored by the BFASS. Initially confined to women's groups, their audience quickly crossed gender boundaries as men, too, flocked to hear the sisters' powerful testimony on the atrocities they had witnessed in the slaveholding households of Charleston's elite. "Speaking in the Church" captures the dilemma that the Grimkés' unorthodox lectures to "promiscuous" (sexually mixed) audiences posed for the Calvinist clergy in abolitionist ranks. Clerical bemusement quickly gave way to outright opposition when the General Association of Massachusetts Congregational Clergy, controlled by antiabolitionist conservatives, issued a pastoral letter condemning public speaking by women as a violation of Scripture. The Grimkés and their supporters responded by defending women's right to contribute to the cause in any manner their consciences dictated (Sarah Grimké wrote her *Letters on the Equality of the Sexes* specifically for this purpose). By 1838 the dispute over the "woman question" had polarized the antislavery movement between Garrisonian radicals (who favored allowing women full participation in the meetings, committees, and governance of antislavery societies) and religious conservatives, who began organizing rival societies barred to women—a schism that culminated in May 1840.

Throughout the dispute Child warmly championed the Grimkés. Yet, characteristically, she also urged them "not to *talk* about our right, but simply [to] go forward and *do* whatsoever we deem a duty." She herself, meanwhile, turned down invitations to follow the Grimkés to the podium, despite the secret hankering that made her lament to an abolitionist friend: "Oh, if I was a man, how I *would* lecture! But I am a woman, and so I sit in the corner and knit socks."[3]

Indeed, just as the Grimkés were opening up new opportunities for abolitionist women, Child was again retreating into wifely self-abnegation. After the collapse of the *Massachusetts Journal* and the failure of his law practice, David Child decided to move to Northampton, Massachusetts, with the aim of growing sugar beets—a project he hoped would undercut the slave system by furnishing an alternative to slave-grown cane sugar. For two terrible years in 1838–39 and 1840–41, Child gave up her literary vocation and buried herself in farm work. (She spent the intervening year in Boston, joining her Garrisonian comrades in the antislavery schisms and attending her friend Margaret Fuller's feminist Conversations.) What finally rescued her from this quagmire was an urgent appeal to save the fragmented abolitionist move-

---

3. "Letter from Mrs. Child, on the Present State of the Anti-Slavery Cause," *Liberator* 6 Sept. 1839, *SL* 119–24, quotation on 123; LMC to Louisa Loring, [March? 1837] 64.

ment by taking on the editorship of the *National Anti-Slavery Standard* in New York.

As editor, Child initially resisted her feminist friends' urgings to "come out concerning the Rights of Women."[4] Except for "Speaking in the Church" and a brief reference in her first editorial, "To Abolitionists," she maintained a conspicuous silence on the "vexed question." Not until February 1843 did she finally endorse the women's rights cause in two of her last "Letters from New-York" for the *Standard* (numbers 50 and 51, 16 and 23 Feb., amalgamated and renumbered 34 in the book version, which is included here). Tellingly, this "coming out" coincided with a more formal separation from her husband that would last until 1849. The new departure it signified for Child is reflected in the language of her letter, which explodes with anger against men. Accusing men of having systematically kept women in subjection through methods ranging from "physical force" and verbal ridicule to "gallantry" and intellectual condescension, Child forcefully advocates a single standard for the sexes in all departments of life.

It was in the department of sexual mores that a single standard came to seem most pressing to Child during her separation from her husband. While in New York, Child took refuge from her wrecked marriage in platonic relationships, forming deep attachments to two younger men: the Quaker lawyer John Hopper, to whom she dedicated *Letters from New York,* and the Norwegian violinist Ole Bull, whose concerts she reviewed in the *Boston Courier.* Apparently her sense of indulging in illicit passion led her to empathize strongly with the "fallen women" she encountered so frequently in the streets and prisons of New York. Her writings of the mid-1840s—represented here by her uncollected letter from New York on the Amelia Norman case (*Boston Courier* 6 Feb. 1844) and her story "Hilda Silfverling" (Oct. 1845, rpt. *Fact and Fiction*)—focus obsessively on women's victimization by a repressive moral code that denies them the right to their own sexuality and condemns them to prostitution, imprisonment, or death if they lapse from virtue. Child's affirmation of sexual desire as natural rather than depraved distinguished her from the evangelical and Quaker moral reformers then seeking to rehabilitate prostitutes. At the same time, it linked her with Margaret Fuller, who not only offered a parallel critique of the sexual double

---

4. Child refers to her friends' demands that she "come out" on women's rights in the opening paragraph of "Letters from New-York," number 50, *National Anti-Slavery Standard* 16 Feb. 1843. She deleted this paragraph and the one that follows from the book version.

standard in *Woman in the Nineteenth Century*, but praised Child for championing the cause of an "injured sister," Amelia Norman, "undeterred by custom or cavil."[5]

In publicly defending Norman, a young workingwoman indicted for having tried to murder the gentleman rake who had seduced and abandoned her, Child risked scurrilous attacks on her own character. Yet she went to extraordinary lengths for Norman. Not content with speaking out on her behalf, helping her find a lawyer, and contributing to winning her acquittal, Child took the young woman home with her and eventually placed her with a sympathetic employer. In her letter from New York about Norman, Child blames men for forcing women into prostitution and then hypocritically sitting in judgment on them. She reiterates the charge even more strongly in a fictionalized version of Norman's saga, "Rosenglory" (Oct. 1846), where the very magistrate who sends the fallen heroine to prison later propositions her. Commenting on her heroine's puzzlement over the contradiction, Child writes: "She had never read or heard anything about 'Woman's Rights;' otherwise it might have occurred to her that it was because men made all the laws, and elected all the magistrates."[6]

Through journalism and realistic fiction, Child redirected public censure from fallen women to the male-dominated social system responsible for their plight. She also turned to literary forms that permitted greater license, as she sought to imagine a world in which sexuality might enjoy free play. "Hilda Silfverling" swerves away from the conventional fallen woman narrative ending in death. Instead, Child endows her fallen heroine with a second chance for happiness by drawing on two genres that feminist writers have found exceptionally conducive to reenvisioning gender roles and sexual practice: science fiction and the trickster tale. The science fiction device of having Hilda's body frozen in a laboratory for a century enables Child to let her heroine live down her disgrace and begin anew. The portrayal of Hilda's lover, Alerik, as a trickster—a folk character who outwits death, violates

5. *Woman in the Nineteenth Century* (1845), rpt. Mary Kelley, ed., *The Portable Margaret Fuller* (New York: Viking Penguin, 1994) 312–13. On evangelical and Quaker moral reformers, see Carroll Smith-Rosenberg, *Disorderly Conduct: Visions of Gender in Victorian America* (New York: Oxford UP, 1985) 109–28; and Estelle B. Freedman, *Their Sisters' Keepers: Women's Prison Reform in America, 1830–1930* (Ann Arbor: U of Michigan P, 1981) chap. 2.

6. Published in the *Columbian Lady's and Gentleman's Magazine*, "Rosenglory" is reprinted in *Fact and Fiction: A Collection of Stories* (New York: C. S. Francis, 1846) 241–60, quotation on 255.

taboos, defies authority, switches gender, and embodies unbridled libido—creates an ideal vehicle for liberating the sexuality of women and men alike from social constraints. Remarkable for its bawdy celebration of sexuality as well as for its use of science fiction to emancipate rather than destroy a woman character subjected to a male experiment, "Hilda Silfverling" invites comparison with Hawthorne's "The Birth-mark" (1843), "Rappaccini's Daughter" (1844), and *The Scarlet Letter* (1850).

Three years after Child published "Hilda Silfverling," her friends Lucretia Mott and Elizabeth Cady Stanton organized the first Woman's Rights Convention at Seneca Falls, New York, in July 1848. An outgrowth of the previous decade's agitation on the woman question, the convention had been gestating in Mott's and Stanton's minds since 1840, when women were denied seats as official delegates to the World's Anti-Slavery Convention in London. The Seneca Falls Declaration of Sentiments, modeled on the Declaration of Independence, charged men with "repeated injuries and usurpations" aimed at instituting "absolute tyranny" over women. The most radical demand presented at the convention was that women be granted the right to vote.

Distrustful of electoral politics,[7] Child at first seems to have taken little notice of the campaign for woman suffrage. By 1856, however, when she shifted from criticizing political abolitionism to backing the Republican party's first presidential candidate, John C. Frémont, she enthusiastically embraced the new feminist goal. "What a shame that *women* can't vote!" she exclaimed to an abolitionist correspondent.[8] She pictures women as active political agents in her story "The Kansas Emigrants," published in the *New York Tribune* on the eve of the 1856 election.

Still, Child did not begin publicly advocating woman suffrage until after the Civil War, when abolitionists were trying to secure the vote for African American men. Her article "Woman and Suffrage" (*Independent* 17 Jan. 1867, reprinted here), the second half of a two-part response to the conservative cleric Tayler Lewis, calls for granting voting rights to women as well as to African American men. While acknowledging that political conditions in the South make suffrage a more "imperious necessity" for the latter group, Child refutes claims that enfranchising women will unsex them or imperil the unity of the family. The analogy she draws between freedom of conscience in

7. See "Talk about Political Party," reprinted in part 3.
8. LMC to Sarah Shaw, 3 Aug. 1856, *SL* 291. For more on Child's political views, see the introduction to part 3.

religion and in politics is tailored shrewdly to the evangelical readership of the *Independent*.

Unlike Child and most other abolitionist women, Elizabeth Cady Stanton and her coworker Susan B. Anthony did not agree that black suffrage deserved higher priority than woman suffrage. Angered by Republican leaders' refusal to support woman suffrage, in 1867 Stanton and Anthony turned to the Democrats, despite the Democratic party's consistent antiblack record. By 1869 they were courting southern white women as well as Democrats and openly pandering to the racism of their new allies. In her passionate rebuke, "Women and the Freedmen" (*Standard* 28 Aug. 1869), Child argues that human beings always pay a heavy price in the long run for sacrificing principles to obtain short-run advantages. She also reminds white women of the debt they owe the ex-slaves for having so often saved the lives of Union soldiers during the war. To oppose black suffrage, she implies, is to deliver the freedpeople into the hands of the Ku Klux Klan.[9]

The bitter split in feminist ranks over whether to support a suffrage amendment that did not include women has often been described as pitting the "radicals" of the Stanton-Anthony faction against the "conservatives" of the abolitionist camp for whom Child spoke. Conversely, Stanton and Anthony's capitulation to racism has sometimes been seen as discrediting the entire woman suffrage movement. Child's critique provides a lens through which to reexamine this controversial episode of women's history.

However dismayed that "female politicians" should "so *soon* begin to follow the crooked ways" of their male predecessors, Child remained a staunch advocate of woman suffrage. The penultimate article included in part 5, "Concerning Women" (*Independent* 15 July and 21 Oct. 1869), takes a long historical view of the debate over how political enfranchisement would affect women. It also revisits the terrain of Child's 1835 *History of the Condition of Women, in Various Ages and Nations*. This time, however, Child supplies the feminist analysis she had earlier eschewed. As she measures the distance women have traveled since ancient times, assesses the narrowing gap between the sexes, and compares women's roles in different societies, she also fittingly sums up the evolution her thinking on the "woman question" has undergone over three and a half decades.

---

9. For more details on the Klan's activities in the postwar South, see the introduction to part 3; also Eric Foner, *Reconstruction: America's Unfinished Revolution, 1863–1877* (New York: Harper and Row, 1988) 425–44.

Extracts from "African Women"

The dwellings of negroes are generally huts made of the branches of trees and thatched with palmetto. The king's residence usually consists of a number of these huts surrounded by a clay wall. Each wife has a separate building, sometimes divided from the apartments of the men by a slight bamboo fence. Some of the African huts are very prettily painted, or stained, and the walls adorned with curious straw work. The Ashantees display a considerable degree of taste and even elegance in their architecture. Their houses and door-posts are elaborately carved with representations of warlike processions, and serpents seizing their prey. . . .

The African women wear two long strips of cotton cloth, either blue or white. One is tied round the waist and falls below the knees; the other is worn over the shoulders like a mantle. The latter garment is generally thrown aside when they are at work. The upper part of the person is almost universally exposed. The wealthy sometimes wear a kind of robe without sleeves, under their *pagnes,* or mantles. Mungo Park[1] speaks of seeing women in Bondou, who wore a thin kind of gauze, called *byqui,* which displayed their shape to the utmost advantage. Sandals are sometimes worn, but they more frequently go barefoot. Women of the island of St. Louis, who are generally handsome, and many of them fair, by frequent intermarriages with Europeans, wear a long garment of striped cotton fastened at the waist, with another four or five yards in length thrown over the shoulders in the antique style. Striped cloth is twisted round the head, so as to form a high turban. Their slippers are usually of red, yellow, or green morocco, and they are seldom without golden ear-rings, necklaces, and bracelets.

The Kaffer women wear a cloak made of leopard or calf skins, dressed in such a manner as to be exceedingly soft and pliant. This garment, which is worn over the shoulders, and conceals all the upper part of the person, is never laid aside except in the very hottest weather. They wear no other clothing but a small apron. It is a singular fact that the Kaffer men care much more about ornaments than the women. Almost every individual wears necklaces of beads, or polished bone, with several ivory bracelets about his

The History of the Condition of Women, in Various Ages and Nations (1835), 1:245–285.

1. The Scottish explorer Mungo Park (1771–1806), author of *Travels in the Interior Districts of Africa* (1799). Child refers to a passage in Chap. 4.

arms and ankles. Those who can afford it have wreaths of copper beads around their heads, from which brass chains are suspended. The women, on the contrary, seldom wear any other ornament than a row of beads, or small shells, around the edges of their aprons. Females of the royal family sometimes have a few brass buttons on their cloaks, and beads or shells on the skin caps they wear in cold weather. The other African women are very fond of ornaments. They decorate their heads with coral beads, sea-shells, and grains of gold and silver. Sometimes a small plate of gold is worn in the middle of the forehead. The gold dust, which they collect, is kept in quills, stopped with cotton; and these are frequently displayed in the hair. Sometimes strips of linen are stretched upon a stick, so as to form a turban in the shape of a sugar loaf, the top of which is covered with a colored handkerchief. In some places the hair is raised high by means of a pad, and decorated with an expensive species of coral brought from the Red sea. Among some tribes the women twist their woolly locks around straws greased with butter; and when the straws are drawn out, the hair remains curled in small tufts. This process requires a whole day. A more neat and simple style, is to braid the hair in several tresses, made to meet on the top of the head. Almost all the Africans grease their heads and anoint their bodies; a custom said to be necessary to prevent cutaneous diseases, and the attacks of insects, in warm climates. Tattooing is very common, and almost every tribe has a style peculiarly its own. The gold ornaments worn in Africa are generally very massive. The heavy ear-rings sometimes lacerate the ear, to avoid which they are often supported by a band of red leather, passing over the head from one ear to the other. The necklaces and bracelets are sometimes of gold fillagree work, very ingeniously wrought. Daughters of rich families wear a necklace of coral, intermixed with gold and silver beads, which crosses below the breast, and is fastened behind, under the shoulders. The skins of sharks, or strings of beads as large as a pigeon's egg, are sometimes worn around the waist, and smaller beads decorate the ankles. In Bornou, they frequently wear a piece of coral, ivory, or polished oyster-shell thrust through the nose. African teeth are universally very white and regular. They are continually rubbed with a small stick of tamarind-wood, which they hold between their lips like a toothpick. Some tribes on the banks of the Gambia file their teeth to a sharp point. Mollien[2] is, I believe, the only writer who speaks of veils worn by any except

---

2. The French explorer Count Gaspard Theodore Mollien (1796–1872), author of *Travels in the Interior of Africa, to the Sources of the Senegal and Gambia . . . in 1818* (trans. 1820). Child quotes freely from Chap. 4, entry of March 3d.

the Moorish ladies. He thus describes the sister and niece of a *marabout,*[3] who was his guide: "They had oval faces, fine features, elegant figures, and a skin as black as jet. I was charmed with the modesty of these women; whenever I looked at them they cast down their eyes, and covered their faces with their muslin veils."

The inhabitants of Madagascar are tall, well proportioned, and of a very dark olive complexion. The women wear long robes reaching to the feet, over which is a straight tunic, that covers the upper part of the person.

The African women make butter by stirring the cream violently in a large calabash, or shaking it in skins, after the Arab fashion. In the forests of Bambarra is a tree called *shea,* from the kernel of which, when boiled in water, a species of vegetable butter is produced. The women put it down in earthen pots, and preserve it for a long time. Mungo Park says: "Besides the advantage of keeping a whole year without salt, it is whiter, firmer, and to my palate of a richer flavor, than the best butter I ever tasted made of cow's milk."

Cheese is never made in the interior of Africa. They give as a reason for it, the heat of the climate, and the great scarcity of salt.

When the planting season arrives, women dig small holes in the ground, into each of which they drop three grains of millet, and cover it with their feet. This simple process is sufficient in a country where the soil yields almost spontaneously. When the grain is nearly ripe, they erect tall platforms on poles, where the women and children are stationed by turns to frighten away the birds, by uttering loud cries. If the birds become so much accustomed to the noise as to disregard it, they bind a handful of leaves or straw around each ear of millet, to prevent their depredations.

Grain, instead of being threshed, is pounded in a mortar, and the chaff blown away. Mortars are used to prepare it for cooking, except in Abyssinia, where a daily supply of corn is ground in small hand-mills.

The African women separate the seeds from cotton by rolling it with a thick iron spindle; and instead of carding it, beat it violently on a close mat. In spinning, they use the distaff in preference to the wheel. Throughout the country they may be seen seated on a mat in front of their huts, engaged in this old-fashioned employment. Weaving is generally done by men. The women make nets and sails for their husbands, and cut and sew their garments with needles of native manufacture. They likewise dye cloth of a rich and permanent blue, with a fine purple gloss; these cloths are beautifully glazed. In the manufacture of common earthen vessels for domestic use, the

---

3. *marabout:* A black Mohammedan priest. [LMC's note.]

women are as skilful as the men. A good deal of care is required to prepare the manioc, which forms a great article of food. This root is ground in a mill, and dried in small furnaces, before it can be used as flour. Mats, both for the table and for seats, are woven very firmly and neatly; hats and baskets are likewise very tastefully made of rushes stained with different colors; and the gourds from which they drink are often prettily ornamented with a sort of bamboo work, dyed in a similar manner.

The Kaffer women make baskets of a strong reedy grass, the workmanship of which is so clever that they will contain water. At Sackatoo, Mr. Clapperton[4] met a troop of African girls drawing water from the gushing rocks. He says: "I asked them for drink. Bending gracefully on one knee, and displaying at the same time teeth of pearly whiteness, and eyes of the blackest lustre, they presented a gourd, and appeared highly delighted when I thanked them for their civility; remarking to one another, 'Did you hear the white man thank me?' "

Here, as in Asia, the women generally act as porters, carrying large burdens on the head. Sometimes they may be seen sitting on mats by the roadside, selling potatoes, beans, and small bits of roasted meat, to travellers.

Men and women are both employed in digging and washing gold for the Moorish markets. Small shells, called *cowries,* constitute the general currency of Africa. All payments from the king's household are made in branches containing two thousand cowries each. The women pierce and string these, deducting one-fortieth part as their own perquisite. Four hundred and eighty of these shells are equivalent to a shilling. The Africans are said to manifest a most extraordinary facility in reckoning the large sums exchanged for articles of merchandise. Europeans have been much surprised at this, being themselves unable to calculate so rapidly without the use of figures.

The wives of the king of Dahomey, generally to the number of three thousand, are formed into a regiment, part of which act as his body-guard, equipped with bows, arrows, drums, and sometimes muskets. They are regularly trained to the use of arms, and go through their evolutions with as much expertness as any other of his majesty's soldiers.

---

4. The English explorer Hugh Clapperton (1788–1827), author of *Narrative of Travels and Discoveries in Northern and Central Africa, in the years 1822, 1823, and 1824 by Major [Dixon] Denham, Captain Clapperton, and the Late Dr. Oudney* (1826) and *Journal of a Second Expedition into the Interior of Africa, from the Bight of Benin to Soccatoo. By the Late Commander Clapperton . . . To which is Added, the Journal of Richard Lander from Kano to the Sea-coast* (1829). The quotations remain unidentified.

Captain Clapperton thus describes a visit he received from the king of Kiama: "Six young girls, without any apparel, except a fillet on the forehead, and a string of beads round the waist, carrying each three light spears, ran by the side of his horse, keeping pace with it at full gallop. Their light forms, the vivacity of their eyes, and the ease with which they seemed to fly over the ground, made them appear something more than mortal. On the king's entrance they laid down their spears, wrapped themselves in blue mantles, and attended on his majesty. On his taking leave, they discarded their attire; he mounted his horse, and away went the most extraordinary cavalcade I ever saw in my life."

In time of battle the African women encourage the troops, supply them with fresh arrows, and hurl stones at their enemies. In some tribes it is common for them to unite with the men in hunting the lion and the leopard.

Mr. Campbell[5] attended a palaver, or council, in Southern Africa. He says, "The speeches were replete with frankness, courage, often with good sense, and even with a rude species of eloquence. The women stood behind and took an eager interest in the debate—cheering those whose sentiments they approved, or bursting into loud laughter at any thing they considered ridiculous."

If the king of Congo dies without sons, his daughter, if she be marriageable, becomes absolute mistress of the kingdom. She visits various towns and villages, where she causes the men to appear before her, that she may select a husband from among them. When her choice is made, she resigns all authority into his hands, and he becomes the king.

Every great man has bands of minstrels, of both sexes, who sing his praises in extempore poetry, while they play upon drums, or guitars with three strings.

Some of these *guiriots*, or minstrels, travel about the country with their families, dancing and singing at every village where their services are required. The Africans are so partial to these wandering musicians, that they often make them quite rich by their liberality. The female singers are covered with various colored beads, and not unfrequently with ornaments of the precious metals. But though the *guiriots* are always welcome at weddings and festivals, though their songs kindle the soldier's courage as he goes to battle, and enliven the dreariness of journeys through the desert, yet they are re-

5. The Scottish missionary and traveler John Campbell (1766–1840) published *Travels in South Africa* (1814). The quotation remains unidentified.

garded with even more contempt than falls upon similar classes in other parts of the world. Not even a slave would consent to marry into a family that had followed this profession; and when they die, their bodies are placed in hollow trees, from the idea that crops of millet would certainly fail if they were buried in the earth. The *guiriots* dance in the same immodest style that characterizes the Asiatic performers. Their dances are always accompanied by drums and other musical instruments. Among the Wolofs none but public singers play on any instrument, it being considered disrespectable for others to practise this amusement.

The African women are so passionately fond of dancing, that wherever the itinerant minstrels appear, they flock around them, and encourage them by songs, while they beat time by clapping their hands. Indeed with this mirth-loving race every thing furnishes occasion for festivity and frolic. Their marriages and funerals conclude with dances; all their festivals are commemorated with songs and dances; every moonlight night the men and women meet in great numbers to enjoy this favorite exercise; and if the moon be wanting, they dance by the light of large fires. The young girls often unite together to buy palm wine, and after an entertainment at the hut of one of their companions, they go together through the village, singing in chorus a variety of charming airs, marking time by clapping their hands; these strains, though simple, and often repeated, are by no means monotonous. The Fulah songs are said to have a melancholy sweetness which is exceedingly captivating; and some of the Wolof airs are gracefully pathetic, while the measures in which they are composed indicates skill in music somewhat remarkable in a people so little civilized. On the banks of rivers and on the sea-coast, the inhabitants of villages one or two miles distant may be heard singing the same song, and alternately answering each other. Drums are their most common musical instruments; beside which they have a guitar of three strings, made of half a calabash covered with leather; a species of castanets, made of small gourd shells, filled with pebbles, or Guinea peas, which the dancers shake in a lively manner; and an instrument resembling a spinnet, called the *balafo,* in which the notes are struck by small sticks, terminated by knobs covered with leather. These instruments are generally of rude construction, and produce dull, heavy tones; but the voices of the people are peculiarly soft and melodious, and they are said to keep time with great exactness. Music is never mute in Africa. Whether the inhabitants are weaving at their doors, laboring in the fields, rowing their boats, or wandering in the desert, songs may be heard resounding through the air. Even the poor slaves dragged to distant markets, suffering with hunger, and thirst, and cruel laceration, will begin to sing as soon as they have a few moments rest; particularly if the assurance is given them that after they pass a certain boundary, they shall be free and dressed in red. Thus does the God of love console his guileless children even under circumstances of the greatest external misery! and man, in the wantonness of his pride, makes this blessed influence of Divine Providence an excuse for continued cruelty!

The Africans at their convivial meetings are extremely fond of listening to stories of wild and ludicrous adventures, and the wonderful effects of magic and enchantments. They have likewise a species of pantomime or puppet-shows. The women are extravagantly fond of a game called *ouri*, which they learned from the Arabs. A box with twelve square holes contains a quantity of round seeds, generally from the baobab tree. Each player has twenty-one seeds to dispose of; they play alternately, and draw lots who shall begin. The combinations are said to be more numerous and complicated than those of chess; yet girls of ten or twelve years old may often be seen sitting under the shade of a tree intently studying this difficult game.

Some of the African tribes have become Mohammedans in consequence of their connection with the Moors; but in general they are pagans. The belief in one Supreme Being and a future state of rewards and punishments is, however, universal, and without exception; they likewise believe that the Almighty has intrusted the government of the world to subordinate spirits, with whom they suppose certain magical ceremonies have great influence. When questioned upon these subjects, they always endeavor to wave the conversation, by answering reverently that such matters are far above the understanding of man. At the return of the new moon, (which they suppose to be each time newly created,) every individual offers a short whispered prayer of thanksgiving; but they pray at no other time; saying it is presumptuous for mortals to ask the Deity to change decrees of unerring wisdom. When asked why they observe a festival at the new moon, they simply answer that their fathers did so before them. . . .

An annual festival, called the *tampcara*, is distinguished by a strange superstitious custom. At this period a personage appears on the banks of the Gambia, to whom they give the name of Tampcara. The natives believe him to be a demon, and bestow without resistance whatever he pleases to demand. He appears only in the night, but his door is at all hours open to the women. Husbands dare not betray the slightest symptoms of jealousy, for fear of incurring the awful displeasure of Tampcara.

There is another pretended demon, called Mumbo Jumbo, whose mysteries are celebrated in the night-time. Several nights previous to his arrival, a great noise is heard in the adjoining woods. The men go out to meet him, and find him with a stick in his hand, decorated in a hideous and fantastic manner with the bark of trees. Preceded by a band of music, he approaches the village, where the women ranged in a circle fearfully await his arrival. Songs accompany the instruments, and Mumbo Jumbo himself sings an air peculiar to the occasion. The most profound silence follows. After a pause, Mumbo Jumbo points out those women who have behaved improperly during the year. They are immediately seized, tied to a post, and whipped by the mysterious visiter, with more or less severity, according to the nature of their offence. All the assembly join in shouts of derision, and the women are quite as ready to take part against their sisters in disgrace as they are accused of being in more civilized countries. When African wives are refractory, it is a common threat to remind them of the annual visit of Mumbo Jumbo, who will assuredly find out their faults and punish them accordingly. The dress in which he usually appears is often kept hung upon the trees, by way of admonition. This dreaded personage no doubt receives his information from the husband or father of the culprit; but the secret of the institution is so carefully preserved, that a king, whose young wife had coaxed him to tell it, was afterward persuaded to put all his wives to death to prevent discovery. . . .

The African laws are simple and rude, like their habits; but it appears from the accounts of travellers that widows retain peaceable possession of their property, and are able to transact business with perfect security. This implies a degree of good order in society, which one would not expect to find in uncivilized states.

In most of the tribes on the southern and western coast of Africa, women do not inherit the property of their fathers, either real or personal.

Among the Wolofs when a young man wishes to marry, he signifies it to the parents of the girl, who meet him at some public place in the village. When the young couple are surrounded by a circle of relatives, the man offers as much gold or merchandise, oxen or slaves, as he can afford to pay. The girl's consent is not necessary for the completion of the bargain; but if she refuses to fulfil the promise of her parents, she can never marry another; should she attempt to do so, the first lover can claim her as his slave. As soon as the parties have agreed upon the price, the young man pays the required sum; and the same evening the bride is conveyed to the bridegroom's hut, by a troop of relations and friends. On these occasions she always wears a white veil of her own weaving. The rejoicings continue for eight days, during which the guests are abundantly supplied with palm wine and other liquors.

Among the Sereres, when a lover has formally obtained the consent of relations, he summons his friends to assist him in carrying off the object of his choice. The bride shuts herself up in a hut with her companions, where they maintain an obstinate siege before they surrender to the assailants.

In Bambuk, the bride is escorted to the hut of her future husband. When she arrives at the door, she takes off her sandals, and a calabash of water is placed in her hand. She knocks, and the door is opened by the relations of the bridegroom, who remains seated in the midst of the hut. The bride kneels before him, pours the water over his feet, and wipes them with her mantle, in token of submission.

Mr. Park speaks of seeing a betrothed girl at Baniseribe, who knelt before her lover, and presenting a calabash of water, desired him to wash his hands; when he had done so, she drank the water, apparently with delight; this being considered a great proof of fidelity and love. In Madagascar, wives salute their husbands just returned from war, by passing the tongue over his feet, in the most respectful manner.

Among the Mandingoes, when the lover has settled the bargain with the girl's parents, she is covered with the bridal veil of white cotton, and seated on a mat, with all the elderly women of the neighborhood ranged in a circle round her. They give her sage instructions concerning the performance of her duties and the propriety of her deportment as a matron. A band of female *guiriots* come in and disturb their serious lessons with music, singing, and dancing. The bridegroom in the mean time entertains his friends without doors. A plentiful supper is provided, and the evening is devoted to mirth. Before midnight the bride is privately conducted by her female relatives to the hut which is to be her future residence. The bridal party generally continue dancing and singing until broad daylight. . . .

The pagan Africans are formally married but to one wife; but they take as many mistresses as they can maintain, and send them away when they please. The lawful wife, provided she has children, has authority over all the female members of the household, and her children enjoy privileges superior to the rest; but if she is so unfortunate as not to be a mother, she is not considered as the head of the establishment.

The women belonging to one household generally live very peaceably. Each one takes her turn in cooking and other domestic avocations; and the husband is expected to be equally kind, generous, and attentive to all.

A *slatee,* with whom Mr. Park entered Kamalia, brought with him a young girl as his fourth wife, for whom he had given her parents three slaves. His other wives received her at the door very kindly, and conducted her into one of the best huts, which they had caused to be swept and whitewashed on purpose for her reception.

Dissensions, it is said, do sometimes occur, and the husband finds it necessary to administer a little chastisement before tranquillity is restored.

Unfaithfulness to the marriage vow is said to be very rare among the Mandingoes and the Kaffers. Throughout Africa this crime in a woman is punished by being sold into slavery; but the punishment cannot be arbitrarily and immediately inflicted by the husband, as is the case in many Asiatic countries; it is necessary to call a public palaver, or discussion, upon the subject. The price of a woman condemned for this vice is divided between the king and his grandees; it is therefore probable that they keep rather a strict watch upon the morality of their female subjects. Sometimes the paramour is likewise sentenced to be sold into slavery; sometimes he receives a severe flogging, amid the shouts and laughter of the multitude; and not unfrequently he is murdered by the abused husband. In this latter case, unless the murderer can buy a pardon from his prince, he is obliged to seek refuge in some other kingdom, where he falls at the feet of some rich person, and voluntarily acknowledges himself a slave; but he can never be sold, and is in fact regarded as one of the family. It frequently happens that the whole family of the culprit are obliged to flee their country, to avoid being sold into slavery for the crime of their relative. . . .

Infants of a few hours old are washed in cold water and laid on a mat, with no other covering than a cotton cloth thrown loosely over them.

In twelve or fifteen days the mothers carry them about, suspended at their backs, by means of the *pagne* or mantle, which they fasten around the hips, and over one shoulder. Infants are kept in this situation nearly the whole day, while the women are busy at their various avocations. They are nursed until they are able to walk; sometimes until three years old. A few tumbles, or similar trifling accidents, are not considered worthy of much anxiety or commiseration. Till ten or twelve years old, children wear no clothing, and do nothing but run about and sport on the sands. Those who live near the sea-shore, are continually plunging into the water; in consequence of which scarcely any disease appears among them, except the small-pox. A child receives its name when it is eight days old. A sort of paste, called *dega,* is prepared for the occasion, and the priest recites prayers over it. He takes the babe in his arms, invokes the blessing of heaven upon it, whispers a few words in its ear, spits three times in its face, pronounces aloud the name that is given to it, and returns it to the mother. He then divides the consecrated *dega* among the guests, and if any person be sick, he sends them some of it. A similar custom prevails in the Barbary states.

The moment an African ceases to breathe, his wife runs out of the hut, beating her breast, tearing her hair, and summoning her neighbors by loud cries. Friends and relatives soon assemble in the hut, and join in her lamentations, continually repeating, "Woe is me!"

When the marabouts have rubbed the corpse with oil and covered it with cloths, each person goes up and addresses it, as if still living. In a few minutes they go away, saying, "He is dead;" the lamentations are renewed, and continue till the next day, when the burial takes place. Major Denham speaks of hearing the Dugganah women singing funeral dirges all night long in honor of their husbands, who had fallen in battle. These dirges were prepared for the occasion, and were so solemn and plaintive, that they could not be listened to without the deepest sympathy.

The body is conveyed to the grave in straw mats. Women hired for the occasion follow it with loud shrieks, and the most extravagant demonstrations of sorrow. They return howling to the hut, where they pronounce an eulogium on the deceased. If they perform their parts well, they are complimented by relations, and are treated with palm wine, or other spirituous liquors. For eight days in succession these women go to the grave at sunrise and sunset, and renew their lamentations, saying, "Hadst thou not wives, and arms, and horses, and pipes, and tobacco? Wherefore then didst thou leave us?"

The relations and friends of the deceased remain in seclusion with his widow eight days, to console her grief.

The Abyssinian women wound their faces while they lament for the dead. In Congo, the relatives shave their heads, anoint their bodies, and rub them with dust, during the eight days of mourning. They consider it very indecorous for a widow to join in any festivity for the space of one year after her husband's death.

Speaking in the Church

Abolitionists have not forgotten, and will not soon forget, the enthusiasm that prevailed when Angelina Grimke and her sister were lecturing in New England.[1] The force of their influence and example did more than all other causes put together, to give prominence to what is called the "Woman question." The clergy were every where roused by the innovation; and women who most gladly would have avoided discussion on the subject of their own rights, were often reluctantly drawn into controversy, by their generous wish to shield those conscientious and intelligent strangers.

To me this "vexed question" has ever been distasteful. 1st. Because, if I must, at the bidding of conscience, enter the arena and struggle for human rights, I prefer they should be the rights of others, rather than my own. 2d. Because I prefer, as quietly and unobtrusively as possible, to *take* my freedom without disputing about my claim to it; and this is easily done by illustrating Bonaparte's favorite maxim: "The tools to those who can use them." 3d. Because I have ever considered duties and rights as reverse sides of the same thing; and to me duty presents the lovelier aspect. Wherever rights are infringed, duties have been previously violated; and the honest discharge of duties is the surest way to recover rights.

But, in common with others, I was sometimes forced from my neutrality in defence of the Grimkes. I record the following, not to throw down the gauntlet of controversy, or to sustain the argument pro or con; but simply as an amusing incident, the recollection of which sometimes makes me smile. What vote the American Society,[2] or even the Executive Committee, would take upon its insertion in the Standard, I know not; for I never asked them, and probably never shall.

Angelina had been invited to lecture at N——, a small, and rather obscure town in the interior of Massachusetts. One day, when I returned a call from

National Anti-Slavery Standard 15 July 1841, p. 22.

1. Angelina Emily Grimké (1805–79) and her sister Sarah Moore Grimké (1792–1873) lectured throughout New England from June to December 1837. Incidents similar to the one Child describes below took place in many villages and towns, among them Worcester. The village of N—— mentioned in the next paragraph may be South Natick, where Child was staying with her father.

2. Child refers to the American Anti-Slavery Society and its executive committee, which could exercise control over the contents of its organ, the *National Anti-Slavery Standard*.

the Calvinistic clergyman of that place, he immediately entered into conversation on this point, and seemed much pleased at the prospect of hearing that distinguished southern woman and repentant slaveholder. He said all his people, whether abolitionists or not, were eager to hear her, and he presumed nearly every individual of his parish would attend.

"Do you think the meeting-house will be large enough to accommodate the audience?" said I.

"The meeting-house!" he exclaimed, abruptly. "Do you suppose she intends to speak in the *meeting-house!*"

"I really know nothing about it; but I supposed the school-house was of course too small to contain half who wish to hear her."

He looked on the figures of the carpet for awhile, before he said, slowly, as if to himself, "The school-house *is* too small. I wonder I did not think of that." Then looking up, he inquired, with anxious emphasis, "Does she speak in the *pulpit?*"

"I believe she speaks wherever it is most convenient for the audience to hear; and in many cases the pulpit has been selected, as best answering this purpose."

He paused again, before he answered, in a troubled voice, "I am sorry that I did not think of this."

"The lecture can be easily set aside, if you wish.—The pressure of their engagements is such, that they will doubtless be glad to be released from one."

"But I wish very much to hear them; and my people wish very much to hear them; and I think they can do a great deal of good by coming. If there were only a suitable place provided, there would be no difficulty. But I cannot overcome my religious scruples. I consider the injunction of Scripture binding upon us in all particulars; and you know St. Paul says, "I suffer not a woman to speak in the Church."[3]

"You told me, did you not, that all your people would go to hear her? If the Church are assembled in the school-house, will she not, to all intents and purposes, speak in the Church? I presume you do not consider the plank and boards, which compose a building, the Church?"

He did not answer these questions; but replied, "You are doubtless aware that such proceedings are contrary to the discipline of Calvinistic churches."

"I am aware of it; but I supposed you had settled that matter in your own

3. 1 Timothy 2.12. See also 1 Corinthians 14.34: "Let your women keep silence in the churches: for it is not permitted unto them to speak."

mind or you would not have invited Miss Grimke to address your people. However, I think it may easily be arranged by applying to the Methodist minister for the use of his meeting-house. He is in favor of anti-slavery, you know, and the discipline of his church differs from yours."

"I thank you for that suggestion, Mrs. Child. That will be just the thing. I have no doubt he and his people will both be perfectly willing to have their house used. It is common for women to speak in the Methodist church."

I could not forbear looking in his face with a roguish expression, as I asked, "But what will you do with St. Paul, whose every injunction is binding upon us in all particulars?"

He seemed confused; and forbearing to continue an argument by which neither of us would have been convinced, I said, laughingly, "Ah, Mr. ——, you have set in motion machinery that you cannot stop. The sects called evangelical, were the first agitators of the woman question."

"Pray how do you make that out?"

"In the good old days, when Mrs. Hutchinson was tried as a heresiarch, synods declared that 'A *few* women might meet together, to pray and edify one another, yet a set assembly, where sixty or more did meet every week, and one woman took upon her the whole exercise, (in a prophetical way, by expounding scripture and resolving questions of doctrine,) was agreed to be disorderly and without rule.'[4] In modern times, the evangelical sects have highly approved of female prayer meetings. In the cause of missions and the dissemination of tracts, they have eloquently urged upon women their pro-digious influence, and consequent responsibility, in the great work of re-generating a world lying in wickedness. Under the influence of these stirring appeals, women have sacrificed personal ornaments, home, kindred, and friends, for the sake of conveying the gospel to the heathen. They have gone out as missionaries; and, in the absence of their husbands, very arduous responsibilities of teaching have often devolved on them. Their sympathies and thoughts, thus made active, and enlarged far beyond the bounds of the

4. The English-born Puritan midwife Anne Hutchinson (1591–1643) sparked what became known as the Antinomian Controversy when she started holding religious meetings in her home, first for women, then for men as well. In 1637 a synod of church leaders passed the resolution Child quotes. One of them also told Hutchinson: "You have stept out of your place, *you have rather bine a Husband than a Wife and a preacher than a Hearer; and a Magistrate than a Subject.*" Child's sources are probably "The Examination of Mrs. Anne Hutchinson at the Court at Newtown," "Trial of Anne Hutchinson before Boston church," and the *Journal of John Winthrop.*

hearth and the nursery, naturally enough refuse limitation, and enter upon various good works with the zeal and strength of newly-exercised freedom. Those who set the wheel in motion, seeing it take unexpected directions, wish to stop it; but in vain."

This reminds me of the story of the German wizard.[5] By certain incantations he could cause a broom to become a man, and rapidly bring buckets of water from a neighboring river; and when the required work was completed, another spell transformed him to a broom again.—The wizard's apprentice, being one day left with a charge to wash the shop and tools very thoroughly, thought he, too, would avail himself of the service of the broom.—He succeeded in repeating the first spell correctly; and to his great joy, saw arms and feet start forth to do his bidding. With supernatural activity, the bewitched household utensil brought water, water, water, till tubs were filled, the floor overflowed, the furniture deluged. "Stop! stop!" cried the terrified apprentice: "We shall all be drowned, if you don't stop!" But, unfortunately, he had forgotten the backward spell, and the animated tool went on with frightful diligence.

Thus it is with those who urged women to become missionaries, and form tract societies. They have changed the household utensil to a living, energetic being; and they have no spell to turn it into a broom again.

5. Child refers to the tale popularly known as "The Sorcerer's Apprentice," narrated in the ballad "Der Zauberlehrling" (1797), by Johann Wolfgang von Goethe (1749–1832).

Letters from New York, Number 34

You ask what are my opinions about 'Women's Rights.' I confess, a strong distaste to the subject, as it has been generally treated. On no other theme probably has there been uttered so much of false, mawkish sentiment, shallow philosophy, and sputtering, farthing-candle wit. If the style of its advocates has often been offensive to taste, and unacceptable to reason, assuredly that of its opponents have been still more so. College boys have amused themselves with writing dreams, in which they saw women in hotels, with their feet hoisted, and chairs tilted back, or growling and bickering at each other in legislative halls, or fighting at the polls, with eyes blackened by fisticuffs. But it never seems to have occurred to these facetious writers, that the proceedings which appear so ludicrous and improper in *women*, are also ridiculous and disgraceful in *men*. It were well that *men* should learn not to hoist their feet above their heads, and tilt their chairs backward, nor to growl and snap in the halls of legislation, nor give each other black eyes at the polls.

Maria Edgeworth says, 'We are disgusted when we see a woman's mind overwhelmed with a torrent of learning: that the tide of literature has passed over it should be betrayed only by its fertility.'[1] This is beautiful and true; but is it not likewise applicable to man? The truly great never seek to display themselves. If they carry their heads high above the crowd, it is only made manifest to others by accidental revelations of their extended vision. 'Human duties and proprieties do not lie so very far apart,' said Harriet Martineau; 'if they did, there would be two gospels and two teachers, one for man and another for woman.'[2]

National Anti-Slavery Standard, 16 and 23 February 1843; reprinted in *Letters from New York* (1843), pp. 245–252.

1. The British writer Maria Edgeworth (1767–1849) actually defends education for women in her *Letters for Literary Ladies* (1795) and *Practical Education* (1798). Child may be (mis)quoting from memory Edgeworth's "Answer to the Preceding Letter" (by a gentleman hostile to women's education), in *Letters,* in which she says: "When you say that men of superior understanding dislike the appearance of extraordinary strength of mind in the fair sex, you probably mean that the display of that strength is disgusting." Edgeworth goes on to make an argument very similar to Child's.

2. Child seems to be quoting from memory from the chapter "Woman" in *Society in America* (3 vols., 1837), by the British writer Harriet Martineau (a chapter that also refers to Child and some of her abolitionist friends, though not by name). Martineau's actual words are:

It would seem indeed, as if men were willing to give women the exclusive benefit of gospel-teaching. '*Women* should be gentle,' say the advocates of subordination; but when Christ said, 'Blessed are the meek,' did he preach to women only? '*Girls* should be modest,' is the language of common teaching, continually uttered in words and customs. Would it not be an improvement for men also to be scrupulously pure in manners, conversation and life? Books addressed to young married people abound with advice to the *wife*, to control her temper, and never to utter wearisome complaints, or vexatious words when the husband comes home fretful and unreasonable from his out-of-door conflicts with the world. Would not the advice be as excellent and appropriate, if the husband were advised to conquer *his* fretfulness, and forbear *his* complaints, in consideration of his wife's ill-health, fatiguing cares, and the thousand disheartening influences of domestic routine? In short, whatsoever can be named as loveliest, best, and most graceful in woman, would likewise be good and graceful in man. You will perhaps remind me of courage. If you use the word in its highest signification, I answer, that woman, above others, has abundant need of it in her pilgrimage: and the true woman wears it with a quiet grace. If you mean mere animal courage, *that* is not mentioned in the Sermon on the Mount, among those qualities which enable us to inherit the earth, or become the children of God. That the feminine ideal approaches much nearer to the gospel standard, than the prevalent idea of manhood, is shown by the universal tendency to represent the Saviour and his most beloved disciple with mild, meek expression, and feminine beauty. None speak of the bravery, the might, or the intellect of Jesus; but the devil is always imagined as a being of acute intellect, political cunning, and the fiercest courage. These universal and instinctive tendencies of the human mind reveal much.

That the present position of women in society is the result of physical force, is obvious enough; whosoever doubts it, let her reflect why she is afraid to go out in the evening without the protection of a man. What constitutes the danger of aggression? Superior physical strength, uncontrolled by the moral sentiments. If physical strength were in complete subjection to moral influence, there would be no need of outward protection. That animal in-

---

"How fearfully the morals of woman are crushed, appears from the prevalent persuasion that there are virtues which are peculiarly masculine, and others which are peculiarly feminine. . . . [If this were true], instead of the character of Christ being the meeting point of all virtues, there would have been a separate gospel for women, and a second company of agents for its diffusion" (3:115).

stinct and brute force now govern the world, is painfully apparent in the condition of women everywhere; from the Morduan Tartars,[3] whose ceremony of marriage consists in placing the bride on a mat, and consigning her to the bridegroom, with the words, 'Here, wolf, take thy lamb,'—to the German remark, that 'stiff ale, stinging tobacco, and a girl in her smart dress, are the best things.' The same thing, softened by the refinements of civilization, peeps out in Stephens's remark, that 'woman never looks so interesting, as when leaning on the arm of a soldier;' and in Hazlitt's complaint that 'it is not easy to keep up a conversation with women in company. It is thought a piece of rudeness to differ from them; it is not quite fair to ask them a *reason* for what they say.'[4]

This sort of politeness to women is what men call gallantry; an odious word to every sensible woman, because she sees that it is merely the flimsy veil which foppery throws over sensuality, to conceal its grossness. So far is it from indicating sincere esteem and affection for women, that the profligacy of a nation may, in general, be fairly measured by its gallantry. This taking away *rights,* and *condescending* to grant *privileges,* is an old trick of the physical-force principle; and with the immense majority, who only look on the surface of things, this mask effectually disguises an ugliness, which would otherwise be abhorred. The most inveterate slave-holders are probably those who take most pride in dressing their household servants handsomely, and who would be most ashamed to have the name of being *unnecessarily* cruel. And profligates, who form the lowest and most sensual estimate of women, are the very ones to treat them with an excess of outward deference.

There are few books which I can read through, without feeling insulted as a woman; but this insult is almost universally conveyed through that which

3. Probably a corruption of *Mordvinian* Tartars; Mordvinia, also called Mordovia, in the middle of the Volga River basin, was invaded by the Tartars of central Asia, who influenced the culture. One of the customs practiced among them was to pretend to kidnap brides in the face of mock resistance.

4. The New Jersey–born writer John Lloyd Stephens (1805–52) published several travel books, but this quotation remains unidentified. The English journalist and literary critic William Hazlitt (1778–1830) is best known for his *Table Talk* (1821). Child may be quoting from memory from essay 8, "On the Ignorance of the Learned," in which Hazlitt writes: "Women have often more of what is called *good sense* than men. They have fewer pretensions; are less implicated in theories; and judge . . . more truly and naturally. They cannot reason wrong; for they do not reason at all. They do not think or speak by rule; and they have in general more eloquence and wit, as well as sense, on that account. By their wit, sense, and eloquence together, they generally contrive to govern their husbands."

was intended for praise. Just imagine, for a moment, what impression it would make on men, if women authors should write about *their* 'rosy lips,' and 'melting eyes,' and 'voluptuous forms,' as they write about *us!* That women in general do not feel this kind of flattery to be an insult, I readily admit; for, in the first place, they do not perceive the gross chattel-principle, of which it is the utterance; moreover, they have, from long habit, become accustomed to consider themselves as household conveniences, or gilded toys. Hence, they consider it feminine and pretty to abjure all such use of their faculties, as would make them co-workers with man in the advancement of those great principles, on which the progress of society depends. 'There is perhaps no *animal*,' says Hannah More, 'so much indebted to subordination, for its good behaviour, as woman.'[5] Alas, for the animal age, in which such utterance could be tolerated by public sentiment!

Martha More, sister of Hannah, describing a very impressive scene at the funeral of one of her Charity School teachers, says: 'The spirit within seemed struggling to speak, and I was in a sort of agony; but I recollected that I had heard, somewhere, a woman must not speak in the *church*. Oh, had she been buried in the church-*yard*, a messenger from Mr. Pitt[6] himself should not have restrained me; for I seemed to have received a message from a higher Master within.'

This application of theological teaching carries its own commentary.

I have said enough to show that I consider prevalent opinions and customs highly unfavourable to the moral and intellectual development of women: and I need not say, that, in proportion to their true culture, women will be more useful and happy, and domestic life more perfected. True culture, in them, as in men, consists in the full and free development of individual character, regulated by their *own* perceptions of what is true, and their *own* love of what is good.

This individual responsibility is rarely acknowledged, even by the most refined, as necessary to the spiritual progress of women. I once heard a very

5. Hannah More (1745–1833), English bluestocking and conservative religious writer. Martha More (d. 1819), mentioned in the next paragraph, was her elder sister. Both quotations are from letters reprinted in William Roberts, *Memoirs of the Life and Correspondence of Mrs. Hannah More* (4 vols., 1834). The first is in a famous 1793 letter from Hannah More to the Earl of Orford, in which she says that she is "invincibly resolved not to" read Mary Wollstonecraft's *A Vindication of the Rights of Woman* (1792) because the very title is "absurd" and the subject is "ridiculous" (2:371); the second is in a letter from Martha More to Hannah of 18 Aug. 1795 (2:443).

6. The reference is to William Pitt the Younger (1759–1806), then Prime Minister.

beautiful lecture from R. W. Emerson, on Being and Seeming.[7] In the course of many remarks, as true as they were graceful, he urged women to *be,* rather than *seem.* He told them that all their laboured education of forms, strict observance of genteel etiquette, tasteful arrangement of the toilette, &c., all this *seeming* would not *gain hearts* like *being* truly what God made them; that earnest simplicity, the sincerity of nature, would kindle the eye, light up the countenance, and give an inexpressible charm to the plainest features.

The advice was excellent, but the motive, by which it was urged, brought a flush of indignation over my face. *Men* were exhorted to *be,* rather than to *seem,* that they might fulfil the sacred mission for which their souls were embodied; that they might, in God's freedom, grow up into the full stature of spiritual manhood; but *women* were urged to simplicity and truthfulness, that they might become more *pleasing.*

Are we not all immortal beings? Is not each one responsible for himself and herself? There is no measuring the mischief done by the prevailing tendency to teach women to be virtuous as a duty to *man* rather than to *God*—for the sake of pleasing the creature, rather than the Creator. '*God* is thy law, *thou* mine,' said Eve to Adam.[8] May Milton be forgiven for sending that thought 'out into everlasting time' in such a jewelled setting. What weakness, vanity, frivolity, infirmity of moral purpose, sinful flexibility of principle—in a word, what soul-stifling, has been the result of thus putting man in the place of God!

But while I see plainly that society is on a false foundation, and that prevailing views concerning women indicate the want of wisdom and purity, which they serve to perpetuate—still, I must acknowledge that much of the talk about Women's Rights offends both my reason and my taste. I am not of

7. "Being and Seeming" was part of the Course of Lectures on Human Culture delivered by Ralph Waldo Emerson (1803–82) in the winter of 1837–38. Emerson's message to men is: "Trust *being* and let us seem no longer. . . . If a man know that he can do any thing; that he can do it better than any one else; he has a perfect assurance before him of an acknowledgment of that fact by all persons, as surely as his shadow follows his body." In the case of women, Emerson decries relying on Appearance rather than on Being: "Let [women] know that whatever they think they have seen to the contrary it is not the form or the face, much less the skill of dress that conquers opinion and hearts, but that faces are urns into which they may infuse an inexpressible loveliness, and that everything they do, every noble choice they make, every forbearance, every virtue, beautifies them with a charm to all beholders." See *Early Lectures of Ralph Waldo Emerson,* ed. Stephen E. Whicher et al., 2:301–2.

8. From *Paradise Lost* 4.635–38: "My Author and Disposer, what thou biddst / Unargu'd I obey; so God ordains, / God is thy law, thou mine: to know no more / Is woman's happiest knowledge and her praise." Child quotes this passage in a letter to her brother Convers, written at age fifteen, where she objects that "Milton asserts the superiority of his own sex in rather too lordly a manner" (*CC* 1/1).

those who maintain there is no sex in souls; nor do I like the results deducible from that doctrine. Kinmont, in his admirable book, called the Natural History of Man,[9] speaking of the warlike courage of the ancient German women, and of their being respectfully consulted on important public affairs, says: 'You ask me if I consider all this right, and deserving of approbation? or that women were here engaged in their appropriate tasks? I answer, yes; it is just *as* right that they should take this interest in the honour of their country, as the other sex. Of course, I do not think that women were *made* for war and battle; neither do I believe that *men* were. But since the fashion of the times had made it so, and settled it that war was a necessary element of greatness, and that no safety was to be procured without it, I argue that it shows a healthful state of feeling in other respects, that the feelings of both sexes were *equally* enlisted in the cause: that there was no *division* in the house, or the state; and that the serious pursuits and objects of the one were also the serious pursuits and objects of the other.'

The nearer society approaches to divine order, the less separation will there be in the characters, duties, and pursuits of men and women. Women will not become less gentle and graceful, but men will become more so. Women will not neglect the care and educasion of their children, but men will find themselves ennobled and refined by sharing those duties with them; and will receive, in return, co-operation and sympathy in the discharge of various other duties, now deemed inappropriate to women. The more women become rational companions, partners in business and in thought, as well as in affection and amusement, the more highly will men appreciate *home*—that blessed word, which opens to the human heart the most perfect glimpse of Heaven, and helps to carry it thither, as on an angel's wings.

> 'Domestic bliss,
> That can, the world eluding, be itself
> A world enjoyed; that wants no witnesses
> But its own sharers and approving heaven;
> That, like a flower deep hid in rocky cleft,
> Smiles, though 'tis looking only at the sky.'

Alas, for these days of Astor houses and Tremonts, and Albions![10] where families exchange comfort for costliness, fireside retirement for flirtation and

9. Child quotes from lecture 9, "On the Character of the Ancient Germans," in *Twelve Lectures on the Natural History of Man* (1839), by Alexander Kinmont (1799–1838).

10. All three were luxury hotels, the Astor House on Broadway in New York, the Albion and Tremont House on Tremont Street in Boston.

flaunting, and the simple, healthful, cozy meal, for gravies and gout, dainties and dyspepsia. There is no characteristic of my countrymen, which I regret so deeply as their slight degree of adhesiveness to home. Closely intertwined with this instinct, is the religion of a nation. The Home and the Church bear a near relation to each other. The French have no such word as home in their language, and I believe they are the least reverential and religious of all the Christian nations. A Frenchman had been in the habit of visiting a lady constantly for several years, and being alarmed at a report that she was sought in marriage, he was asked why he did not marry her himself. '*Marry* her!' exclaimed he,—'Good heavens! *where should I spend my evenings?*' The idea of domestic happiness was altogether a foreign idea to his soul, like a word that conveyed no meaning. Religious sentiment in France leads the same roving life as the domestic affections; breakfasting at one restaurateur's and supping at another's. When some wag in Boston reported that Louis Philippe had sent over for Dr. Channing[11] to manufacture a religion for the French people, the witty significance of the joke was generally appreciated.

There is a deep spiritual reason why all that relates to the domestic affections should ever be found in close proximity with religious faith. The age of chivalry was likewise one of unquestioning veneration, which led to the crusade for the holy sepulchre. The French revolution, which tore down churches, and voted that there was no God, likewise annulled marriage; and the doctrine, that there is no sex in souls, has usually been urged by those of infidel tendencies. Carlyle says, 'But what feeling it was in the ancient, devout, deep soul, which of marriage made a *sacrament*, this, of all things in the world, is what Diderot will think of for aeons without discovering; unless perhaps it were to increase the *vestry fees.*'[12]

The conviction that woman's present position in society is a false one, and therefore re-acts disastrously on the happiness and improvement of man, is pressing by slow degrees on the common consciousness, through all the obstacles of bigotry, sensuality, and selfishness. As man approaches to the truest life, he will perceive more and more that there is no separation or discord in their mutual duties. They will be one; but it will be as affection and thought are one; the treble and bass of the same harmonious tune.

---

11. Louis-Philippe (1773–1850) was king of France from 1830 to 1848. The Unitarian clergyman William Ellery Channing (1780–1842) was Boston's most famous preacher and moralist.

12. Child quotes from Carlyle's essay "Diderot" (1833), published in vol. 3 of his *Critical and Miscellaneous Essays* (1839). Denis Diderot (1713–84) was a French Enlightenment philosophe.

Uncollected Letter from New-York

Unusual excitement has prevailed in this city for a fortnight past, concerning the trial of Amelia Norman for an assault on Henry S. Ballard, with intent to kill. That the prosecutor is a Bostonian by birth, is a fact I would gladly suppress, for the credit of my native city, and for the sake of his worthy and highly respectable parents.

There was a host of witnesses, many of them of the highest respectability, ready to prove that this was a case of deliberate seduction and base desertion. That the poor girl had been subjected to wrongs and insults, enough to drive her mad. At the period of her arrest, she was living at the house of a respectable and kind-hearted German, by the name of Behren. He supposed her to be a widow, and hired her to iron shirts for his clothing-store; an employment she would not have been likely to seek, if she had been the abandoned creature Ballard chooses to represent her. The German testified that for several days previous to her arrest, he and his family considered her insane; that she acted in the wildest way, and was evidently quite unconscious what she was doing; that at times, her anguish seemed intolerable, and vented itself in sobs and tears; then she would laugh, by the half hour together, with a mad laughter. Whether she was an accountable being at the moment she committed the desperate deed, and how far she was in a state to be capable of deliberate intent, passes the wisdom of mortals to decide. She herself says: "God alone can judge me, for he alone knows to what a dreadful state of agony and desperation I was driven."

In prison, her despair was most painful to witness. The physician, as he passed and repassed her cell, in the course of his professional duties, often saw her for hours together, lying on the stone floor, sobbing and groaning in mortal agony. I shall never forget her pale and haggard looks, and the utter hopelessness of her tones, when I first saw her in that tomb-like apartment. May I be forgiven, if, at times, I hated law, so unequal in its operation, so crushing in its power. The kind-hearted physician made the most touching representations concerning the state of her health, and his continual fear of suicide. The bail demanded for her temporary release, was $5,000. Efforts were made to reduce this sum; but Ballard's counsel, aware that her situation

Boston Courier, 6 February 1844; reprinted in the *National Anti-Slavery Standard,* 22 February; and in *CC* 19/536.

excited commiseration, spared no pains to prevent it. Exertions were made to obtain affidavits that she still continued to say she would kill her seducer, if ever she could get at him. But the sympathies of all who approached her were excited in her favor, and the worst thing they could report of her was, that in one of her bitter moods, she said, "she sometimes thought turn about was fair play." Two-thirds of the community, nurtured and trained as they are in the law of violence, needed to summon all *their* respect for law and order, to keep from openly expressing sympathy with this opinion. Let them ask themselves what they would have said and done, if they had been situated like her; with all those terrible wrongs eating into her heart and brain, like fire. May this consideration lead no one to excuse or palliate the dreadful crime of murder, but may it teach them to reflect well on the false structure of society.

William Thom, the Beggar Poet of England,[1] says, with impetuous eloquence:

Here let me speak out—and be heard, too, while I tell it—that the world does not at all times know how unsafely it sits; when Despair has loosed honor's last hold upon the heart—when transcendent wretchedness lays weeping Reason in the dust—when every unsympathizing on looker is deemed an enemy—who THEN can limit the consequences? For my own part, I confess that, ever since that dreadful night, I can never hear of an extraordinary criminal, without the wish to pierce through the mere judicial views of his career, under which, I am persuaded, there would often be found to exist an unseen impulse—a chain with one end fixed in nature's holiest ground, that drew him on to his destiny.

The trial was to have commenced on Monday, the 15th. On the preceding Saturday afternoon, the prisoner's counsel announced the necessity of withdrawing his services, in order to attend to another important case, which came on the same day. The idea of transferring her case to a stranger, without time to examine into its merits, proved the drop too much for a spirit that had so long been under the pressure of extreme despondency. The unfortunate girl made preparations for suicide, by braiding a rope from her bedclothes. In twenty minutes more, she would have passed beyond the power of human tribunals; but the keeper chanced at that moment to enter her gallery, to summon another prisoner, and discovered her preparations.

Ballard's counsel was extremely desirous to push the case through on

---

1. The Scottish poet and weaver William Thom (1798?–1848) gained attention through his poem "The Blind Boy's Pranks" (1841). His *Rhymes and Recollections* came out in 1844.

Monday. He seemed to calculate that it would be an easy matter to thrust aside this "vile prostitute," as he termed her, and by adroit management of legal technicalities, screen his client from public exposure. But, thank God, human sympathies are warm and active, even amid the malaria of cities. The young friend to whom I dedicated my volume of New-York Letters,[2] whose kindness of heart is only equalled by his energy of purpose, gained the ear of the judges, and earnestly entreated for postponement. He took upon himself the expenses of the trial, trusting Providence for aid. A noble-souled, warm-hearted stranger, a Mr. Carney, of Boston, though a man of limited means, offered fifty dollars, and went with him to procure the services of David Graham,[3] esq. one of the ablest lawyers in our criminal courts. The sum was of course much smaller than his usual fee, but he was influenced by higher motives than pecuniary recompense. When he entered upon the case, he was surprised at the amount of respectable testimony in favor of the girl's character, previous to her acquaintance with Ballard. His heart was touched by the story of her wrongs, confirmed as it was by a multitude of witnesses. On the second day of the trial, he wrote me a noble letter, returning the money, for the prisoner's benefit, declaring that this trial involved considerations higher and holier than the relations of lawyer and client. The blessing of God be with him! During four weary days, he exerted himself with watchful vigilance and untiring zeal. His appeal in behalf of outraged womanhood, was a noble burst of heartfelt eloquence, which I shall forever remember with gratitude and admiration.

The case was likewise conducted with great ability on the part of Mr. Sandford,[4] counsel for the prosecution, and a personal friend of Ballard's; but it was a kind of ability from which my open-hearted nature shrinks, as it would from the cunning of the fox, and the subtlety of the serpent. He could not have managed the case as he did, if he had ever had a sister or daughter thus betrayed. This consideration abated the indignation which sometimes kindled in my soul, at witnessing so much power exerted against a poor human being, already so crushed and desolate. Moreover, I pitied him for obvious ill-health, for having the management of so bad a cause, and for the almost total want of sympathy to sustain him in his trying position.

2. Child refers to the Quaker lawyer John Hopper (1815–64), the son of her host in New York.

3. David Graham (1808–52) was a well-known New York criminal lawyer.

4. Possibly Charles W. Sanford (1796–1878), listed in *Appleton's Cyclopaedia of American Biography* as a well-known member of the New York bar.

In opening the case, he assured the jury that Amelia Norman was a woman of the town, before Ballard became acquainted with her; that she had decoyed him to her lodgings, and had followed him up with a series of annoying persecutions, to obtain money, according to the custom of prostitutes with their poor victims. That on one occasion, she had even gone to his store with an infamous companion, and beat him with their parasols. He did not, however, mention that this companion was another victim of his treacherous client. Having thus blackened the character of the unfortunate prisoner, he contended that no evidence concerning her character or Ballard's should be admitted; that the testimony must be strictly confined to the evening when the stabbing took place. The judge sustained him; and for two days, there was a perpetual fighting with witnesses, to keep the truth out of court. Sandford contended that the jury were to decide solely upon the fact whether the woman assaulted Ballard with intent to kill; and that they had nothing to do with the prior or subsequent history of either of the parties. Graham, on the other hand, urged that it was necessary to prove the wrongs she had suffered, and her consequent state of mind and health, in order to decide upon her intent. There was keen sparring between the lawyers, and the witnesses were sometimes bewildered which to answer. This suppression of evidence, after defaming the character of the girl in such wholesale terms, doubtless produced its effect on the mind of the jury, and somewhat influenced their verdict.

But though Mr. Sandford sprung every way, to stop up any crevice through which the impertinent light might enter, enough did get before the jury, to satisfy them that Amelia Norman had been a virtuous, discreet, amiable, and quiet girl, before her acquaintance with Ballard; and that the history of her wrongs was no fiction of romance.

The counsel for the prisoner, on his part, described her seducer's character and conduct in terms that must have been anything but soothing or agreeable to his ear.[5] Mr. Sandford reminded the jury that one lawyer's word

---

5. He stated that a deliberate pla[n] of seduction had been laid, that Ballard had lived with the prisoner at various respectable boarding-houses, calling her his wife, assuming the name of Mr. and Mrs. Brown, Mr. and Mrs. Williams, &c. That he had afterward left her at a house of prostitution, pretending it was a respectable boarding-house, and had gone to Europe without her knowledge, leaving her without money. That she left the house as soon as she discovered its character, and strove to earn her living by honest industry. That when he returned from Europe, she remonstrated with him for deserting her, and he answered, "Damn you, go and get your living, as other prostitutes do." [LMC's note]

was just as much to be believed as another; that it was their duty to be guided only by the evidence. Mr. Graham retorted, "But where is *your* evidence? There stand *our* thirty witnesses, ready to prove every word we have stated, and a good deal more, if the court will only allow them to be heard." And then he distinctly named the witnesses, their occupations, places of residence, &c. with what they *would* testify if opportunity were given.

It was an adroit game; as exciting to watch, as a skillful game of chess. I never before felt so much intellectual respect, and so much moral aversion, for the legal profession.

Mr. Sandford's Biblical arguments evinced much less acuteness than his legal distinctions. While portraying the horrors of murder, he urged the usual plea, that the Divine abhorrence of it was evinced by the requisition of "blood for blood," and he sustained this position, by the mark which God set upon Cain.[6] He apparently forgot that the mark was set upon Cain in order that men should *not* slay him. Unfortunately for the advocates of capital punishment, this is the only case on record, where the direct agency of God was interposed in a case of murder.

Mr. Sandford likewise found the first seducer in the Bible, in the person of our mother Eve, and said the serpent had been busy with the sex ever since. He drew a lively picture of poor innocent men tempted, betrayed, and persecuted by women. This was putting the saddle on the wrong horse, with a vengeance! And he himself afterward implied as much; for he reminded the jury that there were twelve thousand prostitutes in New-York, supported by money that came from our citizens; and added, that *all these prostitutes had the same wrongs to revenge upon somebody.* He asked the jury whether it would be worse to have the virtue of their daughters ruined, or their young and generous sons brought home stabbed by the hands of prostitutes. If this precedent were established, he feared that strangers visiting New-York would stumble over the dead bodies of citizens, at the very thresholds of their own doors.

I had no doubt that if all deeply injured women were to undertake to redress their wrongs in this bad way, there would be a huge pile of dead citizens. (I even thought it not impossible that some of the honorable court themselves might be among the missing.) I was aware that ribs all around the

6. In the biblical story of Cain and Abel, Cain murders his brother, Abel. God condemns Cain to be "a fugitive and a vagabond," but sets a mark upon him "lest any finding him should kill him" (Gen. 4.14–15).

room felt unsafe in view of the picture the pleader had drawn. It unquestionably was an argument that came home to men's business and bosoms. Yet I felt no very active pity for their terror. I indignantly asked what had been done to the twelve thousand men, who made these poor creatures prostitutes? I remembered that strangers visiting our city continually stumbled upon something worse than dead bodies, viz: degraded, ruined souls, in the forms of those twelve thousand prostitutes; and I asked, what do "law and order" do for *them?* Mr. Sandford declared that women could take care of themselves as well as men. Perhaps so; but his twelve thousand facts show that women do *not* take care of themselves; and he urged that "generous youths" were continually led astray by this band of prostitutes, though of course, the temptation must be merely animal, unmingled with the seductive influence of the affections, which so often leads woman to ruin, through the agency of her best impulses.

But to return to the trial; Mr. Graham dwelt strongly on the point that unless the jury deemed there was sufficient evidence of deliberate intent, to constitute murder in case the man had died, they were bound to acquit. The jury were doubtless in a state to go through any legal loophole, that might be opened. The frantic state of the prisoner's mind, so clearly shown in the evidence, seemed to them too nearly akin to insanity to be easily distinguished. The inequality of the laws roused their sense of justice, and probably made them feel that a verdict of guilty would be like tying down the stones and letting the mad dogs loose. They felt little anxiety to protect Ballard, by sending his victim to Sing Sing, that he might feel safe to prowl about after other daughters and sisters of honest families. The popular indignation, which was with difficulty suppressed by a strong constabulary force, showed plainly enough that the public would like to say to them—

> "I beseech you,
> Wrest once the law to your authority;
> To do a great right do a little wrong;
> And curb this cruel devil of his will."[7]

I believe they strove to resist this magnetic influence, and to return such a verdict as they honestly believed the testimony in the case rendered lawful. When the foreman pronounced the words "Not Guilty!" the building shook

---

7. From *The Merchant of Venice*, 4.1.214–17: in the Court of Justice in Venice, Bassanio is asking the Duke to bend the law to curb Shylock.

with such a thunder of applause as I never before heard. Some of the very officers appointed to keep order, involuntarily let their tip-staffs fall on the floor, and clapped with the multitude. It was the surging of long repressed sympathies coming in like a roaring sea.

I am by no means deaf to the plea for the preservation of law and order. My compassion for the prisoner's wrongs has never for a moment blinded me to the guilt of revenge. But legislators may rest assured that law will yield, like a rope of sand before the influence of humane sentiments, in cases of this kind, until the laws are better regulated. Seduction is going on by wholesale, with a systematic arrangement, and a number and variety of agents, which would astonish those who have never looked beneath the hypocritical surface of things. In our cities, almost every girl, in the humbler classes of life, walks among snares and pitfalls at every step, unconscious of their presence, until she finds herself fallen, and entangled in a frightful net-work, from which she sees no escape. Life and property are protected, but what protection is there for pure hearts, confiding souls, and youthful innocence?

During the first two days of the trial, Ballard was brought into court, by subpoena from the prisoner's counsel, and they took mischievous satisfaction in calling him forward when the court opened. But forward he would *not* come. He hid behind stove pipes, and skulked in corners. This was, perhaps, a prudent measure, for the populace were in that excited state, that it might have been unsafe for him to have been generally recognized. As he passed out of court, the citizens around the door would call out, "Don't come too near us! It is as much as we can do to keep our canes and umbrellas off your shoulders." The expressions were rude, but the sentiment which dictated them was noble. I hope I have not spoken too harshly of this individual. I certainly wish him nothing worse than he has brought upon himself. What can be more pitiful than the old age of a seducer, going unmourned to his grave, with the remembered curses of his victims? What more painful than the consciousness of such a return to all a mother's love, and a mother's prayers? What penalty more severe than the loss of those pure domestic affections, which he has so wantonly desecrated? What punishment equal to the recollections of his dying bed? God pity him! For him, too, there is a return path to our Father's mansion; would that he might be persuaded to enter it.

The conduct of the prisoner, during the trial, was marked by a beautiful propriety. Sad and subdued, she made no artificial appeals to sympathy, and showed no disposition to consider herself a heroine of romance. When the verdict was given, she became very faint and dizzy, and for some time after, seemed stunned and bewildered. Her health is much shattered by physical suffering and mental excitement; but her constitution is naturally good, and under the influence of care and kindness, the process of renovation goes rapidly on. She is evidently a girl of strong feelings, but quiet, reserved, and docile to the influence of those she loves. A proper education would have made of her a noble woman. I sometimes fear that, like poor Fleur de Marie, she will never be able to wash from her mind the "stern inexorable past." I shall never forget the mournful smile with which she said, "I don't know as it is worth while to try to make anything of me. I am nothing but a wreck." "Nay, Amelia," replied I, "noble vessels may be built from the timbers of a wreck."

The public sympathy manifested in this case, has cheered my hopes, and increased my respect for human nature. When the poor girl returned to her cell, after her acquittal, some of the judges, several of the jury, her lawyers, and the officers of the prison, all gathered round her to express congratulation and sympathy. There was something beautiful in the compassionate respect with which they treated this erring sister, because she was unfortunate and wretched. I trust that no changes of politics will ever dismiss Dr. Macready, the physician of the Tombs,[8] or Mr. Falloo, the keeper. I shall always bless them; not merely for their kindness to this poor girl, but for the tenderness of heart, which leads them to treat all the prisoners under their care with as much gentleness as possible. May the foul, moral atmosphere of the place never stifle their kind impulses.

The hours I spent in that hateful building, awaiting the opening of this case, were very sad to me. It was exceedingly painful to see poor ragged beggars summarily dismissed to the penitentiary, for petty larcenies; having the strong conviction, ever present in my mind, that all society is carrying on a great system of fraud and theft, and that these poor wretches merely lacked the knowledge and cunning necessary to keep theirs under legal protection.

The Egyptian architecture, with its monotonous recurrence of the straight line and the square, its heavy pillars, its cavernous dome of massive rings, its general expression of overpowering strength, is well suited to a building for such a purpose. But the graceful palm leaves, intertwined with

---

8. New York's Halls of Justice and House of Detention was known as the Tombs because its design was inspired by a photograph of an Egyptian tomb. Hence Child's reference below to the building's Egyptian architecture.

lotus blossoms, spoke soothingly to me of the occasional triumph of the moral sentiments over legal technicalities, and of beautiful bursts of eloquence from the heart. Moreover, I remembered that time had wrought such changes in opinion, that thousands of convents had been converted into manufactories and primary schools; and I joyfully prophesied the day when regenerated society would have no more need of prisons.[9] The Tombs, with its style of architecture too subterranean for picture galleries or concert rooms, may then be reserved for fossil remains and mineralogical cabinets.

9. Like most Protestants, Child viewed Catholic convents as relics of a superstitious age analogous to prisons. Convents were converted into schools both during the Protestant Reformation in England and during the French Revolution.

Hilda Silfverling

A FANTASY

> "Thou hast nor youth nor age;
> But, as it were, an after dinner's sleep,
> Dreaming on both."
> —*Measure for Measure*[1]

Hilda Gyllenlof was the daughter of a poor Swedish clergyman. Her mother died before she had counted five summers. The good father did his best to supply the loss of maternal tenderness; nor were kind neighbors wanting, with friendly words, and many a small gift for the pretty little one. But at the age of thirteen, Hilda lost her father also, just as she was receiving rapidly from his affectionate teachings as much culture as his own education and means afforded. The unfortunate girl had no other resource than to go to distant relatives, who were poor, and could not well conceal that the destitute orphan was a burden. At the end of a year, Hilda, in sadness and weariness of spirit, went to Stockholm, to avail herself of an opportunity to earn her living by her needle, and some light services about the house.

She was then in the first blush of maidenhood, with a clear innocent look, and exceedingly fair complexion. Her beauty soon attracted the attention of Magnus Andersen, mate of a Danish vessel then lying at the wharves of Stockholm. He could not be otherwise than fascinated with her budding loveliness; and alone as she was in the world, she was naturally prone to listen to the first words of warm affection she had heard since her father's death. What followed is the old story, which will continue to be told as long as there are human passions and human laws. To do the young man justice, though selfish, he was not deliberately unkind; for he did not mean to be treacherous to the friendless young creature who trusted him. He sailed from Sweden with the honest intention to return and make her his wife; but he was lost in a storm at sea, and the earth saw him no more.

Columbian Lady's and Gentleman's Magazine (1845); reprinted in *Fact and Fiction: A Collection of Stories* (1846), pp. 205–40.

1. Lines spoken to Claudio in prison by the Duke (disguised as a friar); like Hilda, Claudio has been condemned to death, and the ostensible friar tells him that death is no more to be feared than sleep (3.1.32–34).

Hilda never heard the sad tidings; but, for another cause, her heart was soon oppressed with shame and sorrow. If she had had a mother's bosom on which to lean her aching head, and confess all her faults and all her grief, much misery might have been saved. But there was none to whom she dared to speak of her anxiety and shame. Her extreme melancholy attracted the attention of a poor old woman, to whom she sometimes carried clothes for washing. The good Virika, after manifesting her sympathy in various ways, at last ventured to ask outright why one so young was so very sad. The poor child threw herself on the friendly bosom, and confessed all her wretchedness. After that, they had frequent confidential conversations; and the kind-hearted peasant did her utmost to console and cheer the desolate orphan. She said she must soon return to her native village in the Norwegian valley of Westfjordalen; and as she was alone in the world, and wanted something to love, she would gladly take the babe, and adopt it for her own.

Poor Hilda, thankful for any chance to keep her disgrace a secret, gratefully accepted the offer. When the babe was ten days old, she allowed the good Virika to carry it away; though not without bitter tears, and the oft-repeated promise that her little one might be reclaimed, whenever Magnus returned and fulfilled his promise of marriage.

But though these arrangements were managed with great caution, the young mother did not escape suspicion. It chanced, very unfortunately, that soon after Virika's departure, an infant was found in the water, strangled with a sash very like one Hilda had been accustomed to wear. A train of circumstantial evidence seemed to connect the child with her, and she was arrested. For some time, she contented herself with assertions of innocence, and obstinately refused to tell anything more. But at last, having the fear of death before her eyes, she acknowledged that she had given birth to a daughter, which had been carried away by Virika Gjetter, to her native place, in the parish of Tind, in the Valley of Westfjordalen. Inquiries were accordingly made in Norway, but the answer obtained was that Virika had not been heard of in her native valley, for many years. Through weary months, Hilda lingered in prison, waiting in vain for favourable testimony; and at last, on strong circumstantial evidence, she was condemned to die.

It chanced there was at that time a very learned chemist in Stockholm; a man whose thoughts were all gas, and his hours marked only by combinations and explosions. He had discovered a process of artificial cold, by which he could suspend animation in living creatures, and restore it at any prescribed time. He had in one apartment of his laboratory a bear that had been in a torpid state five years, a wolf two years, and so on. This of course excited a good deal of attention in the scientific world. A metaphysician suggested how extremely interesting it would be to put a human being asleep thus, and watch the reunion of soul and body, after the lapse of a hundred years. The chemist was half wild with the magnificence of this idea; and he forthwith petitioned that Hilda, instead of being beheaded, might be delivered to him, to be frozen for a century. He urged that her extreme youth demanded pity; that his mode of execution would be a very gentle one, and, being so strictly private, would be far less painful to the poor young creature than exposure to the public gaze.

His request, being seconded by several men of science, was granted by the government; for no one suggested a doubt of its divine right to freeze human hearts, instead of chopping off human heads, or choking human lungs.[2] This change in the mode of death was much lauded as an act of clemency, and poor Hilda tried to be as grateful as she was told she ought to be.

On the day of execution, the chaplain came to pray with her, but found himself rather embarrassed in using the customary form. He could not well allude to her going in a few hours to meet her final judge; for the chemist said she would come back in a hundred years, and where her soul would be meantime was more than theology could teach. Under these novel circumstances, the old nursery prayer seemed to be the only appropriate one for her to repeat:

> "Now I lay me down to sleep,
> I pray the Lord my soul to keep:
> If I should die before I wake,
> I pray the Lord my soul to take."

The subject of this curious experiment was conveyed in a close carriage from the prison to the laboratory. A shudder ran through soul and body, as she entered the apartment assigned her. It was built entirely of stone, and rendered intensely cold by an artificial process. The light was dim and spectral, being admitted from above through a small circle of blue glass. Around the sides of the room, were tiers of massive stone shelves, on which reposed various objects in a torpid state. A huge bear lay on his back, with paws crossed on his breast, as devoutly as some pious knight of the fourteenth century. There

---

2. Child had earlier protested against capital punishment in letter 31 of *Letters from New York*.

was in fact no inconsiderable resemblance in the proceedings by which both these characters gained their worldly possessions; they were equally based on the maxim that "might makes right." It is true, the Christian obtained a better name, inasmuch as he paid a tithe of his gettings to the holy church, which the bear never had the grace to do. But then it must be remembered that the bear had no soul to save, and the Christian knight would have been very unlikely to pay fees to the ferryman, if he likewise had had nothing to send over.

The two public functionaries, who had attended the prisoner, to make sure that justice was not defrauded of its due, soon begged leave to retire, complaining of the unearthly cold. The pale face of the maiden became still paler, as she saw them depart. She seized the arm of the old chemist, and said, imploringly, "You will not go away, too, and leave me with these dreadful creatures?"

He replied, not without some touch of compassion in his tones, "You will be sound asleep, my dear, and will not know whether I am here or not. Drink this; it will soon make you drowsy."

"But what if that great bear should wake up?" asked she, trembling.

"Never fear. He cannot wake up," was the brief reply.

"And what if I should wake up, all alone here?"

"Don't disturb yourself," said he, "I tell you that you will not wake up. Come, my dear, drink quick; for I am getting chilly myself."

The poor girl cast another despairing glance round the tomb-like apartment, and did as she was requested. "And now," said the chemist, "let us shake hands, and say farewell; for you will never see me again."

"Why, wont you come to wake me up?" inquired the prisoner; not reflecting on all the peculiar circumstances of her condition.

"My great-grandson may," replied he, with a smile. "Adieu, my dear. It is a great deal pleasanter than being beheaded. You will fall asleep as easily as a babe in his cradle."

She gazed in his face, with a bewildered drowsy look, and big tears rolled down her cheeks. "Just step up here, my poor child," said he; and he offered her his hand.

"Oh, don't lay me so near the crocodile!" she exclaimed. "If he *should* wake up!"

"You wouldn't know it, if he did," rejoined the patient chemist; "but never mind. Step up to this other shelf, if you like it better."

He handed her up very politely, gathered her garments about her feet, crossed her arms below her breast, and told her to be perfectly still. He then covered his face with a mask, let some gasses escape from an apparatus in the centre of the room, and immediately went out, locking the door after him.

The next day, the public functionaries looked in, and expressed themselves well satisfied to find the maiden lying as rigid and motionless as the bear, the wolf, and the snake. On the edge of the shelf where she lay was pasted an inscription: "Put to sleep for infanticide, Feb. 10, 1740, by order of the king. To be wakened Feb. 10, 1840."

The earth whirled round on its axis, carrying with it the Alps and the Andes, the bear, the crocodile, and the maiden. Summer and winter came and went; America took place among the nations; Bonaparte played out his great game, with kingdoms for pawns; and still the Swedish damsel slept on her stone shelf with the bear and the crocodile.

When ninety-five years had passed, the bear, having fulfilled his prescribed century, was waked according to agreement. The curious flocked round him, to see him eat, and hear whether he could growl as well as other bears. Not liking such close observation, he broke his chain one night, and made off for the hills. How he seemed to his comrades, and what mistakes he made in his recollections, there were never any means of ascertaining. But bears, being more strictly conservative than men, happily escape the influence of French revolutions, German philosophy, Fourier theories,[3] and reforms of all sorts; therefore Bruin doubtless found less change in *his* fellow citizens, than an old knight or viking might have done, had he chanced to sleep so long.

At last, came the maiden's turn to be resuscitated. The populace had forgotten her and her story long ago; but a select scientific few were present at the ceremony, by special invitation. The old chemist and his children all "slept the sleep that knows no waking." But carefully written orders had been transmitted from generation to generation; and the duty finally devolved on a great grandson, himself a chemist of no mean reputation.

Life returned very slowly; at first by almost imperceptible degrees, then by a visible shivering through the nerves. When the eyes opened, it was as if by

3. The French utopian socialist theorist François-Marie-Charles Fourier (1772–1837) articulated a far-ranging critique of capitalism and bourgeois society and advocated reconstructing society on the basis of "phalanxes," or communal associations. Transplanted to the United States after his death, Fourier's ideas inspired a utopian socialist movement that reached its height in the mid-1840s, leading to the founding of many utopian communities, including Brook Farm (1841–46). Child read Fourier attentively, referred to him often in her "Letters from New-York," and took great interest in Brook Farm, where she had several close friends.

the movement of pulleys, and there was something painfully strange in their marble gaze. But the lamp within the inner shrine lighted up, and gradually shone through them, giving assurance of the presence of a soul. As consciousness returned, she looked in the faces round her, as if seeking for some one; for her first dim recollection was of the old chemist. For several days, there was a general sluggishness of soul and body; an overpowering inertia, which made all exertion difficult, and prevented memory from rushing back in too tumultuous a tide.

For some time, she was very quiet and patient; but the numbers who came to look at her, their perpetual questions how things seemed to her, what was the state of her appetite and her memory, made her restless and irritable. Still worse was it when she went into the street. Her numerous visitors pointed her out to others, who ran to doors and windows to stare at her, and this soon attracted the attention of boys and lads. To escape such annoyances, she one day walked into a little shop, bearing the name of a woman she had formerly known. It was now kept by her grand-daughter, an aged woman, who was evidently as afraid of Hilda, as if she had been a witch or a ghost.

This state of things became perfectly unendurable. After a few weeks, the forlorn being made her escape from the city, at dawn of day, and with money which had been given her by charitable people, she obtained a passage to her native village, under the new name of Hilda Silfverling. But to stand, in the bloom of sixteen, among well-remembered hills and streams, and not recognise a single human face, or know a single human voice, this was the most mournful of all; far worse than loneliness in a foreign land; sadder than sunshine on a ruined city. And all these suffocating emotions must be crowded back on her own heart; for if she revealed them to any one, she would assuredly be considered insane or bewitched.

As the thought became familiar to her that even the little children she had known were all dead long ago, her eyes assumed an indescribably perplexed and mournful expression, which gave them an appearance of supernatural depth. She was seized with an inexpressible longing to go where no one had ever heard of her, and among scenes she had never looked upon. Her thoughts often reverted fondly to old Virika Gjetter, and the babe for whose sake she had suffered so much; and her heart yearned for Norway. But then she was chilled by the remembrance that even if her child had lived to the usual age of mortals, she must have been long since dead; and if she had left descendants, what would they know of *her*? Overwhelmed by the complete desolation of her lot on earth, she wept bitterly. But she was never utterly hopeless; for in the midst of her anguish, something prophetic seemed to beckon through the clouds, and call her into Norway.

In Stockholm, there was a white-haired old clergyman, who had been peculiarly kind, when he came to see her, after her centennial slumber. She resolved to go to him, to tell him how oppressively dreary was her restored existence, and how earnestly she desired to go, under a new name, to some secluded village in Norway, where none would be likely to learn her history, and where there would be nothing to remind her of the gloomy past. The good old man entered at once into her feelings, and approved her plan. He had been in that country himself, and had staid a few days at the house of a kind old man, named Eystein Hansen. He furnished Hilda with means for the journey, and gave her an affectionate letter of introduction, in which he described her as a Swedish orphan, who had suffered much, and would be glad to earn her living in any honest way that could be pointed out to her.

It was the middle of June when Hilda arrived at the house of Eystein Hansen. He was a stout, clumsy, red-visaged old man, with wide mouth, and big nose, hooked like an eagle's beak; but there was a right friendly expression in his large eyes, and when he had read the letter, he greeted the young stranger with such cordiality, she felt at once that she had found a father. She must come in his boat, he said, and he would take her at once to his island-home, where his good woman would give her a hearty welcome. She always loved the friendless; and especially would she love the Swedish orphan, because her last and youngest daughter had died the year before. On his way to the boat, the worthy man introduced her to several people, and when he told her story, old men and young maidens took her by the hand, and spoke as if they thought Heaven had sent them a daughter and a sister. The good Brenda received her with open arms, as her husband had said she would. She was an old weather-beaten woman, but there was a whole heart full of sunshine in her honest eyes.

And this new home looked so pleasant under the light of the summer sky! The house was embowered in the shrubbery of a small island, in the midst of a fiord, the steep shores of which were thickly covered with pine, fir, and juniper, down to the water's edge. The fiord went twisting and turning about, from promontory to promontory, as if the Nereides,[4] dancing up from the sea, had sportively chased each other into nooks and corners, now hiding

---

4. Nereides were saltwater nymphs—beautiful naked women living at the bottom of the sea with their father, Nereus. They watched over sailors and occasionally surfaced to mate with humans.

away behind some bold projection of rock, and now peeping out suddenly, with a broad sunny smile. Directly in front of the island, the fiord expanded into a broad bay, on the shores of which was a little primitive romantic-looking village. Here and there a sloop was at anchor, and picturesque little boats tacked off and on from cape to cape, their white sails glancing in the sun. A range of lofty blue mountains closed in the distance. One giant, higher than all the rest, went up perpendicularly into the clouds, wearing a perpetual crown of glittering snow. As the maiden gazed on this sublime and beautiful scenery, a new and warmer tide seemed to flow through her stagnant heart. Ah, how happy might life be here among these mountain homes, with a people of such patriarchal simplicity, so brave and free, so hospitable, frank and hearty!

The house of Eystein Hansen was built of pine logs, neatly white-washed. The roof was covered with grass, and bore a crop of large bushes. A vine, tangled among these, fell in heavy festoons that waved at every touch of the wind. The door was painted with flowers in gay colours, and surmounted with fantastic carving. The interior of the dwelling was ornamented with many little grotesque images, boxes, bowls, ladles, &c., curiously carved in the close-grained and beautifully white wood of the Norwegian fir. This was a common amusement with the peasantry, and Eystein being a great favourite among them, received many such presents during his frequent visits in the surrounding parishes.

But nothing so much attracted Hilda's attention as a kind of long trumpet, made of two hollow half cylinders of wood, bound tightly together with birch bark. The only instrument of the kind she had ever seen was in the possession of Virika Gjetter, who called it a *luhr,* and said it was used to call the cows home in her native village, in Upper Tellemarken. She showed how it was used, and Hilda, having a quick ear, soon learned to play upon it with considerable facility.

And here in her new home, this rude instrument reappeared; forming the only visible link between her present life and that dreamy past! With strange feelings, she took up the pipe, and began to play one of the old tunes. At first, the tones flitted like phantoms in and out of her brain; but at last, they all came back, and took their places rank and file. Old Brenda said it was a pleasant tune, and asked her to play it again; but to Hilda it seemed awfully solemn, like a voice warbling from the grave. She would learn other tunes to please the good mother, she said; but this she would play no more; it made her too sad, for she had heard it in her youth.

"Thy youth!" said Brenda, smiling. "One sees well that must have been a long time ago. To hear thee talk, one might suppose thou wert an old autumn leaf, just ready to drop from the bough, like myself."

Hilda blushed, and said she felt old, because she had had much trouble.

"Poor child," responded the good Brenda: "I hope thou hast had thy share."

"I feel as if nothing could trouble me here," replied Hilda, with a grateful smile; "all seems so kind and peaceful." She breathed a few notes through the *luhr*, as she laid it away on the shelf where she had found it. "But, my good mother," said she, "how clear and soft are these tones! The pipe I used to hear was far more harsh."

"The wood is very old," rejoined Brenda: "They say it is more than a hundred years. Alerik Thorild gave it to me, to call my good man when he is out in the boat. Ah, he was such a Berserker[5] of a boy! and in truth he was not much more sober when he was here three years ago. But no matter what he did; one could never help loving him."

"And who is Alerik?" asked the maiden.

Brenda pointed to an old house, seen in the distance, on the declivity of one of the opposite hills. It overlooked the broad bright bay, with its picturesque little islands, and was sheltered in the rear by a noble pine forest. A water-fall came down from the hill-side, glancing in and out among the trees; and when the sun kissed it as he went away, it lighted up with a smile of rainbows.

"That house," said Brenda, "was built by Alerik's grandfather. He was the richest man in the village. But his only son was away among the wars for a long time, and the old place has been going to decay. But they say Alerik is coming back to live among us; and he will soon give it a different look. He has been away to Germany and Paris, and other outlandish parts, for a long time. Ah! the rogue! there was no mischief he didn't think of. He was always tying cats together under the windows, and barking in the middle of the night, till he set all the dogs in the neighbourhood a howling. But as long as it was Alerik that did it, it was all well enough: for everybody loved him, and he always made one believe just what he liked. If he wanted to make thee think thy hair was as black as Noeck's[6] mane, he *would* make thee think so."

Hilda smiled as she glanced at her flaxen hair, with here and there a gleam

5. A warrior famous in the Northern Sagas for his stormy and untamable character. [LMC's note]

6. An elfish spirit, which, according to popular tradition in Norway, appears in the form of a coal black horse. [LMC's note]

of pale gold, where the sun touched it. "I think it would be hard to prove *this* was black," said she.

"Nevertheless," rejoined Brenda, "if Alerik undertook it, he would do it. He always has his say, and does what he will. One may as well give in to him first as last."

This account of the unknown youth carried with it that species of fascination, which the idea of uncommon power always has over the human heart. The secluded maiden seldom touched the *luhr* without thinking of the giver; and not unfrequently she found herself conjecturing when this wonderful Alerik would come home.

Meanwhile, constant but not excessive labour, the mountain air, the quiet life, and the kindly hearts around her, restored to Hilda more than her original loveliness. In her large blue eyes, the inward-looking sadness of experience now mingled in strange beauty with the out-looking clearness of youth. Her fair complexion was tinged with the glow of health, and her motions had the airy buoyancy of the mountain breeze. When she went to the mainland, to attend church, or rustic festival, the hearts of young and old greeted her like a May blossom. Thus with calm cheerfulness her hours went by, making no noise in their flight, and leaving no impress. But here was an unsatisfied want! She sighed for hours that did leave a mark behind them. She thought of the Danish youth, who had first spoken to her of love; and plaintively came the tones from her *luhr,* as she gazed on the opposite hills, and wondered whether the Alerik they talked of so much, was indeed so very superior to other young men.

Father Hansen often came home at twilight with a boat full of juniper boughs, to be strewed over the floors, that they might diffuse a balmy odour, inviting to sleep. One evening, when Hilda saw him coming with his verdant load, she hastened down to the water's edge to take an armful of the fragrant boughs. She had scarcely appeared in sight, before he called out, "I do believe Alerik has come! I heard the organ up in the old house. Somebody was playing on it like a Northeast storm; and surely, said I, that must be Alerik."

"Is there an organ there?" asked the damsel, in surprise.

"Yes. He built it himself, when he was here three years ago. He can make anything he chooses. An organ, or a basket cut from a cherry stone, is all one to him.

When Hilda returned to the cottage, she of course repeated the news to Brenda, who exclaimed joyfully, "Ah, then we shall see him soon! If he does not come before, we shall certainly see him at the weddings in the church to-morrow."

"And plenty of tricks we shall have now," said Father Hansen, shaking his head with a good-natured smile. "There will be no telling which end of the world is uppermost, while he is here."

"Oh yes, there will, my friend," answered Brenda, laughing; "for it will certainly be whichever end Alerik stands on. The handsome little Berserker! How I should like to see him!"

The next day there was a sound of lively music on the waters; for two young couples from neighbouring islands were coming up the fiord, to be married at the church in the opposite village. Their boats were ornamented with gay little banners, friends and neighbours accompanied them, playing on musical instruments, and the rowers had their hats decorated with garlands. As the rustic band floated thus gayly over the bright waters, they were joined by Father Hansen, with Brenda and Hilda in his boat.

Friendly villagers had already decked the simple little church with evergreens and flowers, in honour of the bridal train. As they entered, Father Hansen observed that two young men stood at the door with clarinets in their hands. But he thought no more of it, till, according to immemorial custom, he, as clergy man's assistant, began to sing the first lines of the hymn that was given out. The very first note he sounded, up struck the clarinets at the door. The louder they played, the louder the old man bawled; but the instruments gained the victory. When he essayed to give out the lines of the next verse, the merciless clarinets brayed louder than before. His stentorian voice had become vociferous and rough, from thirty years of halloing across the water, and singing of psalms in four village churches. He exerted it to the utmost, till the perspiration poured down his rubicund visage; but it was of no use. His rivals had strong lungs, and they played on clarinets in F. If the whole village had screamed fire, to the shrill accompaniment of rail-road whistles, they would have over-topped them all.

Father Hansen was vexed at heart, and it was plain enough that he was so. The congregation held down their heads with suppressed laughter; all except one tall vigorous young man, who sat up very serious and dignified, as if he were reverently listening to some new manifestation of musical genius. When the people left church, Hilda saw this young stranger approaching toward them, as fast as numerous hand-shakings by the way would permit. She had time to observe him closely. His noble figure, his vigorous agile motions, his expressive countenance, hazel eyes with strongly marked brows, and abundant brown hair, tossed aside with a careless grace, left no doubt in her mind that this was the famous Alerik Thorild; but what made her heart beat more wildly was his strong resemblance to Magnus the Dane. He went up to Brenda and kissed her, and threw his arms about Father Hansen's neck, with expressions of joyful recognition. The kind old man, vexed as he was, received these affectionate demonstrations with great friendliness. "Ah, Alerik," said he, after the first salutations were over, "that was not kind of thee."

"Me! What!" exclaimed the young man, with well-feigned astonishment.

"To put up those confounded clarinets to drown my voice," rejoined he bluntly. "When a man has led the singing thirty years in four parishes, I can assure thee it is not a pleasant joke to be treated in that style. I know the young men are tired of my voice, and think they could do things in better fashion, as young fools always do; but I may thank thee for putting it into their heads to bring those cursed clarinets."

"Oh, dear Father Hansen," replied the young man, in the most coaxing tones, and with the most caressing manner, "you *couldn't* think I would do such a thing!"

"On the contrary, it is just the thing I think thou couldst do," answered the old man: "Thou need not think to cheat me out of my eye-teeth, this time. Thou hast often enough made me believe the moon was made of green cheese. But I know thy tricks. I shall be on my guard now; and mind thee, I am not going to be bamboozled by thee again."

Alerik smiled mischievously; for he, in common with all the villagers, knew it was the easiest thing in the world to gull the simple-hearted old man. "Well, come, Father Hansen," said he, "shake hands and be friends. When you come over to the village, tomorrow, we will drink a mug of ale together, at the Wolf's Head."

"Oh yes, and be played some trick for his pains," said Brenda.

"No, no," answered Alerik, with great gravity; "he is on his guard now, and I cannot bamboozle him again." With a friendly nod and smile, he bounded off, to greet some one whom he recognised. Hilda had stepped back to hide herself from observation. She was a little afraid of the handsome Berserker; and his resemblance to the Magnus of her youthful recollections made her sad.

The next afternoon, Alerik met his old friend, and reminded him of the agreement to drink ale at the Wolf's head. On the way, he invited several young companions. The ale was excellent, and Alerik told stories and sang songs, which filled the little tavern with roars of laughter. In one of the intervals of merriment, he turned suddenly to the honest old man, and said, "Father Hansen, among the many things I have learned and done in foreign countries, did I ever tell you I had made a league with the devil, and am shot-proof?"

"One might easily believe thou hadst made a league with the devil, before thou wert born," replied Eystein, with a grin at his own wit; "but as for being shot-proof, that is another affair."

"Try and see," rejoined Alerik. "These friends are witnesses that I tell you it is perfectly safe to try. Come, I will stand here; fire your pistol, and you will soon see that the Evil One will keep the bargain he made with me."

"Be done with thy nonsense, Alerik," rejoined his old friend.

"Ah, I see how it is," replied Alerik, turning towards the young men. "Father Hansen used to be a famous shot. Nobody was more expert in the bear or the wolf-hunt than he; but old eyes grow dim, and old hands will tremble. No wonder he does not like to have us see how much he fails."

This was attacking honest Eystein Hansen on his weak side. He was proud of his strength and skill in shooting, and he did not like to admit that he was growing old. "I not hit a mark!" exclaimed he, with indignation: "When did I ever miss a thing I aimed at?"

"Never, when you were young," answered one of the company; "but it is no wonder you are afraid to try now."

"Afraid!" exclaimed the old hunter, impatiently. "Who the devil said I was afraid?"

Alerik shrugged his shoulders, and replied carelessly, "It is natural enough that these young men should think so, when they see you refuse to aim at me, though I assure you that I am shot-proof, and that I will stand perfectly still."

"But art thou really shot-proof?" inquired the guileless old man. "The devil has helped thee to do so many strange things, that one never knows what he will help thee to do next."

"Really, Father Hansen, I speak in earnest. Take up your pistol and try, and you will soon see with your own eyes that I am shot-proof."

Eystein looked round upon the company like one perplexed. His wits, never very bright, were somewhat muddled by the ale. "What shall I do with this wild fellow?" inquired he. "You see he *will* be shot."

"Try him, try him," was the general response. "He has assured you he is shot-proof; what more do you need?"

The old man hesitated awhile, but after some further parley, took up his pistol and examined it. "Before we proceed to business," said Alerik, "let me tell you that if you do *not* shoot me, you shall have a gallon of the best ale you ever drank in your life. Come and taste it, Father Hansen, and satisfy yourself that it is good."

While they were discussing the merits of the ale, one of the young men took the ball from the pistol. "I am ready now," said Alerik: "Here I stand. Now don't lose your name for a good marksman."

The old man fired, and Alerik fell back with a deadly groan. Poor Eystein stood like a stone image of terror. His arms adhered rigidly to his sides, his jaw dropped, and his great eyes seemed starting from their sockets. "Oh, Father Hansen, how *could* you do it!" exclaimed the young men.

The poor horrified dupe stared at them wildly, and gasping and stammering replied, "Why he said he was shot-proof; and you all told me to do it."

"Oh yes," said they; "but we supposed you would have sense enough to know it was all in fun. But don't take it too much to heart. You will probably forfeit your life; for the government will of course consider it a poor excuse, when you tell them that you fired at a man merely to oblige him, and because he said he was shot-proof. But don't be too much cast down, Father Hansen. We must all meet death in some way; and if worst comes to worst, it will be a great comfort to you and your good Brenda that you did not intend to commit murder."

The poor old man gazed at them with an expression of such extreme suffering, that they became alarmed, and said, "Cheer up, cheer up. Come, you must drink something to make you feel better." They took him by the shoulders, but as they led him out, he continued to look back wistfully on the body.

The instant he left the apartment, Alerik sprang up and darted out of the opposite door; and when Father Hansen entered the other room, there he sat, as composedly as possible, reading a paper, and smoking his pipe.

"There he is!" shrieked the old man, turning paler than ever.

"Who is there?" inquired the young men.

"Don't you see Alerik Thorild?" exclaimed he, pointing, with an expression of intense horror.

They turned to the landlord, and remarked, in a compassionate tone, "Poor Father Hansen has shot Alerik Thorild, whom he loved so well; and the dreadful accident has so affected his brain, that he imagines he sees him."

The old man pressed his broad hand hard against his forehead, and again groaned out, "Oh, don't you see him?"

The tones indicated such agony, that Alerik had not the heart to prolong the scene. He sprang on his feet, and exclaimed, "Now for your gallon of ale, Father Hansen! You see the devil did keep his bargain with me."

"And *are* you alive?" shouted the old man.

The mischievous fellow soon convinced him of that, by a slap on the shoulder, that made his bones ache.

Eystein Hansen capered like a dancing bear. He hugged Alerik, and jumped about, and clapped his hands, and was altogether beside himself. He drank unknown quantities of ale, and this time sang loud enough to drown a brace of clarinets in F.

The night was far advanced when he went on board his boat to return to his island home. He pulled the oars vigorously, and the boat shot swiftly across the moon-lighted waters. But on arriving at the customary landing, he could discover no vestige of his white-washed cottage. Not knowing that Alerik, in the full tide of his mischief, had sent men to paint the house with a dark brown wash, he thought he must have made a mistake in the landing; so he rowed round to the other side of the island, but with no better success. Ashamed to return to the mainland, to inquire for a house that had absconded, and a little suspicious that the ale had hung some cobwebs in his brain, he continued to row hither and thither, till his strong muscular arms fairly ached with exertion. But the moon was going down, and all the landscape settling into darkness; and he at last reluctantly concluded that it was best to go back to the village inn.

Alerik, who had expected this result much sooner, had waited there to receive him. When he had kept him knocking a sufficient time, he put his head out of the window, and inquired who was there.

"Eystein Hansen," was the disconsolate reply. "For the love of mercy let me come in and get a few minutes sleep, before morning. I have been rowing about the bay these four hours, and I can't find my house any where."

"This is a very bad sign," replied Alerik, solemnly. "Houses don't run away, except from drunken men. Ah, Father Hansen! Father Hansen! what *will* the minister say?"

He did not have a chance to persecute the weary old man much longer; for scarcely had he come under the shelter of the house, before he was snoring in a profound sleep.

Early the next day, Alerik sought his old friends in their brown-washed cottage. He found it not so easy to conciliate them as usual. They were really grieved; and Brenda even said she believed he wanted to be the death of her old man. But he had brought them presents, which he knew they would like particularly well; and he kissed their hands, and talked over his boyish days, till at last he made them laugh. "Ah now," said he, "you have forgiven me, my dear old friends. And you see, father, it was all your own fault. You put the mischief into me, by boasting before all those young men that I could never bamboozle you again."

"Ah thou incorrigible rogue!" answered the old man. "I believe thou hast indeed made a league with the devil; and he gives thee the power to make every body love thee, do what thou wilt."

Alerik's smile seemed to express that he always had a pleasant conscious-ness of such power. The *luhr* lay on the table beside him, and as he took it up, he asked, "Who plays on this? Yesterday, when I was out in my boat, I heard very wild pretty little variations on some of my old favourite airs."

Brenda, instead of answering, called, "Hilda! Hilda!" and the young girl came from the next room, blushing as she entered. Alerik looked at her with evident surprise. "Surely, this is not your Gunilda?" said he.

"No," replied Brenda, "She is a Swedish orphan, whom the all-kind Father sent to take the place of our Gunilda, when she was called hence."

After some words of friendly greeting, the visitor asked Hilda if it was she who played so sweetly on the *luhr*. She answered timidly, without looking up. Her heart was throbbing; for the tones of his voice were like Magnus the Dane.

The acquaintance thus begun, was not likely to languish on the part of such an admirer of beauty as was Alerik Thorild. The more he saw of Hilda, during the long evenings of the following winter, the more he was charmed with her natural refinement of look, voice, and manner. There was, as we have said, a peculiarity in her beauty, which gave it a higher character than mere rustic loveliness. A deep, mystic, plaintive expression in her eyes; a sort of graceful bewilderment in her countenance, and at times in the carriage of her head, and the motions of her body; as if her spirit had lost its way, and was listening intently. It was not strange that he was charmed by her spiritual beauty, her simple untutored modesty. No wonder she was delighted with his frank strong exterior, his cordial caressing manner, his expressive eyes, now tender and earnest, and now sparkling with merriment, and his "smile most musical," because always so in harmony with the inward feeling, whether of sadness, fun, or tenderness. Then his moods were so bewitchingly various. Now powerful as the organ, now bright as the flute, now *naive* as the oboe. Brenda said every thing he did seemed to be alive. He carved a wolf's head on her old man's cane, and she was always afraid it would bite her.

Brenda, in her simplicity, perhaps gave as good a description of genius as *could* be given, when she said everything it did seemed to be alive. Hilda thought it certainly was so with Alerik's music. Sometimes all went madly with it, as if fairies danced on the grass, and ugly gnomes came and made faces at them, and shrieked, and clutched at their garments; the fairies pelted them off with flowers, and then all died away to sleep in the moonlight. Sometimes, when he played on flute, or violin, the sounds came mournfully as the midnight wind through ruined towers; and they stirred up such sorrowful memories of the past, that Hilda pressed her hand upon her swelling heart, and said, "Oh, not such strains as that, dear Alerik." But when his soul overflowed with love and happiness, oh, then how the music gushed and nestled!

> "The lark could scarce get out his notes for joy,
> But shook his song together, as he neared
> His happy home, the ground."

The old *luhr* was a great favourite with Alerik; not for its musical capabilities, but because it was entwined with the earliest recollections of his childhood. "Until I heard thee play upon it," said he, "I half repented having given it to the good Brenda. It has been in our family for several generations, and my nurse used to play upon it when I was in my cradle. They tell me my grandmother was a foundling. She was brought to my great-grandfather's house by an old peasant woman, on her way to the valley of Westfjordalen. She died there, leaving the babe and the *luhr* in my great-grandmother's keeping. They could never find out to whom the babe belonged; but she grew up very beautiful, and my grandfather married her."

"What was the old woman's name?" asked Hilda; and her voice was so deep and suppressed, that it made Alerik start.

"Virika Gjetter, they have always told me," he replied. "But my dearest one, what *is* the matter?"

Hilda, pale and fainting, made no answer. But when he placed her head upon his bosom, and kissed her forehead, and spoke soothingly, her glazed eyes softened, and she burst into tears. All his entreaties, however, could obtain no information at that time. "Go home now," she said, in tones of deep despondency. "To-morrow I will tell thee all. I have had many unhappy hours; for I have long felt that I ought to tell thee all my past history; but I was afraid to do it, for I thought thou wouldst not love me any more; and that would be worse than death. But come tomorrow, and I will tell thee all."

"Well, dearest Hilda, I will wait," replied Alerik; "but what my grand-mother, who died long before I was born, can have to do with my love for thee, is more than I can imagine."

The next day, when Hilda saw Alerik coming to claim the fulfilment of her promise, it seemed almost like her death-warrant. "He will not love me any more," thought she, "he will never again look at me so tenderly; and then what can I do, but die?"

With much embarrassment, and many delays, she at last began her strange story. He listened to the first part very attentively, and with a gather-ing frown; but as she went on, the muscles of his face relaxed into a smile; and when she ended by saying, with the most melancholy seriousness, "So thou seest, dear Alerik, we cannot be married; because it is very likely that I am thy great-grandmother"—he burst into immoderate peals of laughter.

When his mirth had somewhat subsided, he replied, "Likely as not thou art my great-grandmother, dear Hilda; and just as likely I was thy grand-father, in the first place. A great German scholar[7] teaches that our souls keep coming back again and again into new bodies. An old Greek philosopher is said to have come back for the fourth time, under the name of Pythagoras.[8] If these things are so, how the deuce is a man ever to tell whether he marries his grandmother or not?"

"But, dearest Alerik, I am not jesting," rejoined she. "What I have told thee is really true. They did put me to sleep for a hundred years."

"Oh, yes," answered he, laughing, "I remember reading about it in the Swedish papers; and I thought it a capital joke. I will tell thee how it is with thee, my precious one. The elves sometimes seize people, to carry them down into their subterranean caves; but if the mortals run away from them, they, out of spite, forever after fill their heads with gloomy insane notions. A man in Drontheim ran away from them, and they made him believe he was an earthen coffee-pot. He sat curled up in a corner all the time, for fear some-body would break his nose off."

"Nay, now thou art joking, Alerik; but really"—

"No, I tell thee, as thou hast told me, it was no joke at all," he replied. "The man himself told me he was a coffee-pot."

7. Lessing [LMC's note, referring to Gotthold Ephraim Lessing (1729–81)].

8. The sixth-century B.C. philosopher and mathematician Pythagoras preached the doc-trine of reincarnation that Child attributes above to Lessing. In *The Progress of Religious Ideas, through Successive Ages,* Child speculates that Pythagoras derived this doctrine from the ancient Egyptians. Alerik summarizes the Egyptian doctrine of reincarnation on p. 392, below.

"But be serious, Alerik," said she, "and tell me, dost thou not believe that some learned men can put people to sleep for a hundred years?"

"I don't doubt some of my college professors could," rejoined he; "provided their tongues could hold out so long."

"But, Alerik, dost thou not think it possible that people may be alive, and yet not alive?"

"Of course I do," he replied; "the greater part of the world are in that condition."

"Oh, Alerik, what a tease thou art! I mean, is it not possible that there are people now living, or staying somewhere, who were moving about on this earth ages ago?"

"Nothing more likely," answered he; "for instance, who knows what people there may be under the ice-sea of Folgefond? They say the cocks are heard crowing down there, to this day. How a fowl of any feather got there is a curious question; and what kind of atmosphere he has to crow in, is another puzzle. Perhaps they are poor ghosts, without sense of shame, crowing over the recollections of sins committed in the human body. The ancient Egyptians thought the soul was obliged to live three thousand years, in a succession of different animals, before it could attain to the regions of the blest. I am pretty sure I have already been a lion and a nightingale. What I shall be next, the Egyptians know as well as I do. One of their sculptors made a stone image, half woman and half lioness. Doubtless his mother had been a lioness, and had transmitted to him some dim recollection of it. But I am glad, dearest, they sent thee back in the form of a lovely maiden; for if thou hadst come as a wolf, I might have shot thee; and I shouldn't like to shoot my— great-grandmother. Or if thou hadst come as a red herring, Father Hansen might have eaten thee in his soup; and then I should have had no Hilda Silfverling."

Hilda smiled, as she said, half reproachfully, "I see well that thou dost not believe one word I say."

"Oh yes, I do, dearest," rejoined he, very seriously. "I have no doubt the fairies carried thee off some summer's night and made thee verily believe thou hadst slept for a hundred years. They do the strangest things. Sometimes they change babies in the cradle; leave an imp, and carry off the human to the metal mines, where he hears only clink! clink! Then the fairies bring him back, and put him in some other cradle. When he grows up, how he does hurry skurry after the silver! He is obliged to work all his life, as if the devil drove him. The poor miser never knows what is the matter with him; but it is all because the gnomes brought him up in the mines, and he could never get the clink out of his head. A more poetic kind of fairies sometimes carry a babe to Aeolian caves, full of wild dreamy sounds; and when he is brought back to upper earth, ghosts of sweet echoes keep beating time in some corner of his brain, to something which *they* hear, but which nobody else is the wiser for. I know that is true; for I was brought up in those caves myself."

Hilda remained silent for a few minutes, as he sat looking in her face with comic gravity. "Thou wilt do nothing but make fun of me," at last she said. "I do wish I could persuade thee to be serious. What I told thee was no fairy story. It really happened. I remember it as distinctly as I do our sail round the islands yesterday. I seem to see that great bear now, with his paws folded up, on the shelf opposite to me."

"He must have been a great bear to have staid there," replied Alerik, with eyes full of roguery. "If I had been in his skin, may I be shot if all the drugs and gasses in the world would have kept *me* there, with my paws folded on my breast."

Seeing a slight blush pass over her cheek, he added, more seriously, "After all, I ought to thank that wicked elf, whoever he was, for turning thee into a stone image; for otherwise thou wouldst have been in the world a hundred years too soon for me, and so I should have missed my life's best blossom."

Feeling her tears on his hand, he again started off into a vein of merriment. "Thy case was not so very peculiar," said he. "There was a Greek lady, named Niobe, who was changed to stone.[9] The Greek gods changed women into trees, and fountains, and all manner of things. A man couldn't chop a walking-stick in those days, without danger of cutting off some lady's finger. The tree might be—his great-grandmother; and she of course would take it very unkindly of him."

"All these things are like the stories about Odin and Frigga,"[10] rejoined Hilda. "They are not true, like the Christian religion. When I tell thee a true story, why dost thou always meet me with fairies and fictions?"

"But tell me, best Hilda," said he, "what the Christian religion has to do with penning up young maidens with bears and crocodiles? In its marriage ceremonies, I grant that it sometimes does things not very unlike that, only omitting the important part of freezing the maiden's heart. But since thou

9. Niobe's twelve children were killed by the gods to punish her for boasting. She wept inconsolably until Zeus turned her into a stone.

10. In Norse mythology, Odin was the hero of warriors and god of the dead, of cunning, of poetry, and of wisdom. His wife, Frigga, was goddess of marriage and fertility.

hast mentioned the Christian religion, I may as well give thee a bit of consolation from that quarter. I have read in my mother's big Bible, that a man must not marry his grandmother; but I do not remember that it said a single word against his marrying his *great*-grandmother."

Hilda laughed, in spite of herself. But after a pause, she looked at him earnestly, and said, "Dost thou indeed think there would be no harm in marrying, under these circumstances, if I were really thy great-grandmother? Is it thy earnest? Do be serious for once, dear Alerik!"

"Certainly there would be no harm," answered he. "Physicians have agreed that the body changes entirely once in seven years. That must be because the soul outgrows its clothes; which proves that the soul changes every seven years, also. Therefore, in the course of one hundred years, thou must have had fourteen complete changes of soul and body. It is therefore as plain as daylight, that if thou wert my great-grandmother when thou fell asleep, thou couldst not have been my great-grandmother when they waked thee up."

"Ah, Alerik," she replied, "it is as the good Brenda says, there is no use in talking with thee. One might as well try to twist a string that is not fastened at either end."

He looked up merrily in her face. The wind was playing with her ringlets, and freshened the colour on her cheeks. "I only wish I had a mirror to hold before thee," said he; "that thou couldst see how very like thou art to a— great-grandmother."

"Laugh at me as thou wilt," answered she; "but I assure thee I have strange thoughts about myself sometimes. Dost thou know," added she, almost in a whisper, "I am not always quite certain that I have not died, and am now in heaven?"

A ringing shout of laughter burst from the light-hearted lover. "Oh, I like that! I like that!" exclaimed he. "That is good! That a Swede coming to Norway does not know certainly whether she is in heaven or not."

"Do be serious, Alerik," said she imploringly. "Don't carry thy jests too far."

"Serious? I am serious. If Norway is not heaven, one sees plainly enough that it must have been the scaling place, where the old giants got up to heaven; for they have left their ladders standing. Where else wilt thou find clusters of mountains running up perpendicularly thousands of feet right into the sky? If thou wast to see some of them, thou couldst tell whether Norway is a good climbing place into heaven."

"Ah, dearest Alerik, thou hast taught me that already," she replied, with a glance full of affection; "so a truce with thy joking. Truly one never knows how to take thee. Thy talk sets everything *in* the world, and *above* it, and *below* it, dancing together in the strangest fashion."

"Because they all do dance together," rejoined the perverse man.

"Oh, be done! be done, Alerik!" she said, putting her hand playfully over his mouth. "Thou wilt tie my poor brain all up into knots."

He seized her hand and kissed it, then busied himself with braiding the wild spring flowers into a garland for her fair hair. As she gazed on him earnestly, her eyes beaming with love and happiness, he drew her to his breast, and exclaimed fervently, "Oh, thou art beautiful as an angel; and here or elsewhere, with thee by my side, it seemeth heaven."

They spoke no more for a long time. The birds now and then serenaded the silent lovers with little twittering gushes of song. The setting sun, as he went away over the hills, threw diamonds on the bay, and a rainbow ribbon across the distant waterfall. Their hearts were in harmony with the peaceful beauty of Nature. As he kissed her drowsy eyes, she murmured, "Oh, it was well worth a hundred years with bears and crocodiles, to fall asleep thus on thy heart."

The next autumn, a year and a half after Hilda's arrival in Norway, there was another procession of boats, with banners, music and garlands. The little church was again decorated with evergreens; but no clarinet players stood at the door to annoy good Father Hansen. The worthy man had in fact taken the hint, though somewhat reluctantly, and had good-naturedly ceased to disturb modern ears with his clamorous vociferation of the hymns. He and his kind-hearted Brenda were happy beyond measure at Hilda's good fortune. But when she told her husband anything he did not choose to believe, they could never rightly make out what he meant by looking at her so slily, and saying, "Pooh! Pooh! tell that to my—great-grandmother."

Woman and Suffrage

To Theodore Tilton   [Before 17 January 1867]

Professor Lewis says, very truly, that the questions of black *men's* voting and of white *women's* voting are not analogous.[1] And I confess to a
reluctance to urge the question of female suffrage upon Congress at this time,
when they have so many other difficult problems to solve. That the loyal
blacks of the South should vote is a present and very imperious necessity—
not only for their own protection, but also for the safety of the small minority
of whites who are true to the Government: This is another of those remarkable leadings of Divine Providence which have been so conspicuous throughout the war, whereby the people have been compelled to do justly for the sake
of their own interest.

I will say, in passing, that there is a fallacy in the phrase "impartial suffrage," as used by many friends of the colored people. They propose that the
elective franchise should not be taken away from any who have heretofore
exercised it; but that hereafter only those should vote who can read and write.
Thus thousands of foreigners, who cannot write their own names, or read
their own votes, would be allowed to influence the elections of the country,
while numerous native citizens, who are ignorant because our own laws have
hitherto prevented them from obtaining the rudiments of learning, would
be excluded from the polls. This is *not* impartial suffrage. Either *all* voters
should be required to have some degree of education, or *none* should be
subject to such limitations.

I have always thought that suffrage ought to rest on an educational basis.
There is no hardship in such an arrangement, in a country where the means
of obtaining the requisite qualification are offered to every one at the public
expense. As a stimulus to education, it would be valuable beyond measure.

Independent, 17 January 1867; reprinted in *Lydia Maria Child: Selected Letters, 1817–1880,*
pp. 468–472.

1. This is the second installment of a two-part article on "Woman and Suffrage" addressed
to Theodore Tilton, editor of the *Independent.* The first installment (10 Jan.) begins: "You ask
what are my opinions concerning suffrage." Child replies here to a two-part article titled
"Household Suffrage," which had appeared in the *Independent* on 6 and 20 Dec. 1866. Its
author, Tayler Lewis (1802–77), Professor of Greek at the University of the City of New York,
was a conservative evangelical abolitionist, who supported suffrage for African American men,
but not for women. He argued that the patriarchal family was divinely sanctioned and that the
husband's sovereignty authorized him to vote for his wife and unmarried daughters.

Probably no motive would operate so strongly on the "poor whites" of the South; and their enlightenment is greatly needed as a check to that arrogant class who led them blindfold into a worse than needless war—a class whose patriarchal tendencies make them the natural enemies of a republic, and whose boast it has been that society among them was becoming "more and more oriental." This patriarchal element would, of course, ultimately destroy our free institutions, if unimpeded in its operations. It is important for the salvation of the nation that it should be kept in check until it disappears before the advances of a higher degree of civilization; and that can only be done by the moral and intellectual improvement of the people, black and white.

The suffrage of woman can better afford to wait than that of the colored people; and they speak truly who say that a majority of women would negative the claim, if left to their decision. In a recent debate in Congress several senators declared themselves ready to grant suffrage to women whenever a considerable number of them asked for it. I smiled at this adroit way of handing over a perplexing question to their sons or grandsons. But this state of mind in women proves nothing, except that human beings are creatures of habit. If a Chinese woman should let the feet of her infant daughter grow to the natural size, and furnish her with suitable shoes to walk in the street, would she not be regarded by her own sex as a shameless innovator? That Chinese men should regard such a proceeding as threatening the disintegration of patriarchal society would be a matter of course. Yet it would be a great improvement in the condition of China if the women were allowed to let their feet grow, and were at liberty to walk with them. When Frederick the Great emancipated the serfs, many of them petitioned to be exempted from the operation of his decree. He persisted in freeing them, for their own good; and at this day Prussia is all the stronger for it.[2] One of the teachers of freedmen at the South informs us that both parents and children complain because there is no whipping in schools. "I really think I should behave better if you would whip me," said one of the boys. He had been brought up under "the patriarchal system," and could not easily get rid of the habits thus acquired.

In my former letter, I showed how women were gradually becoming accustomed to many pursuits that once seemed to them strange and inappropriate. It would be the same with their exercise of the rights of citizenship.

2. Frederick II (1712–86), King of Prussia (1740–86) did not actually abolish serfdom, but passed measures to reform its abuses.

Very few would vote at first; but year by year the number of those interested in public affairs would increase. They would doubtless make mistakes, as all beginners do. Some of them would be easily duped, and some would be over-conceited with a little superficial information. The present enlargement of woman's sphere of action is not without such results; and the same is true of the colored people. But I think candid observers would admit that the general gain to character is much greater than the loss.

It is the theory of our government that the people govern. Women constitute half of the people. It has been legally decided that they are citizens; and, as citizens, constituting so large a portion of the people, I think they plainly have a right to vote. I believe it would be good for them to exercise the right, because all human souls grow stronger in proportion to the increase of their responsibilities, and the high employment of their faculties. For ten or twelve years I lived in the midst of Quakers; and I could not but observe that their women were superior to women in general in habits of reflection and independent modes of thinking. I remember a Quaker cobbler who was much addicted to talking, not very wisely, about public affairs. His wife would look up from her knitting, now and then, and quietly remark, "I do not agree with thee, Reuben. Thee has not got on the right principle there, Reuben." If she had voted, it certainly would have been in a manner very different from him; but I don't think there would ever have been any nearer approach to a quarrel than that frequently expressed in her calm dissent from his opinions. This staid and self-relying character in Quaker women I attribute to the fact that they share equally with men in the management of all the business of the society. Frivolous pursuits make frivolous characters. Society has done grievous wrong to the souls of women by fencing them within such narrow enclosures. And then it adds insult to injury by mocking at the meanness it has made. The literature of all nations abounds with jibes, and jeers, and degrading comparisons concerning women. This is so common that men in general probably pass it by unnoticed; but to sensible women it is a perpetual offense. "More than a thousand women is one man worthy to see the light of life," says Euripides. "Stiff ale, stinging tobacco, and a girl in a smart dress are the best things," says the tradesman in Goethe's Faust.[3] "There are exceedingly good points about the Turks; chibouks, coffee,

---

3. Child quotes accurately from line 830 of *Faust* (1808, 1832), by Johann Wolfgang von Goethe. The quotation from the Greek playwright Euripides (ca. 484–406 B.C.) remains unidentified.

and as many wives as they please. Under their system women become as gentle, as docile, and as tractable as any domestic animal," says Stephens, in his "Incidents of Travel."[4] "Such a thing may happen as that the woman, not the man, may be in the right, (I mean when both are godly); but ordinarily it is otherwise," says John Bunyan.[5] . . . And all this comes upon us in consequence of our having been systematically excluded from the professions, the trades, the arts, the sciences, the halls of legislation; in a word, from all the pursuits that are best calculated to enlarge the mind, to occupy it profitably, and to raise it above mean and petty subjects of thought. Professor Lewis asks whether, if wives and daughters voted, their influence would be as potent and healthy as it now is. I do not think the mere act of voting would make any difference, one way or the other; but I do think the education they would gradually acquire by taking a part in public affairs would make them more instructive and more interesting as household companions. I believe the domestic bond will never reach its possible hight of perfection till women occupy their thoughts and feelings with all that occupies the thoughts and feelings of men. The astronomer and the chemist would find home more satisfactory with wives who could understand their investigations and feel interested in their discoveries. The architect would find himself both enlivened and aided by a companion who had an eye for form and color, and a talent for inventing conveniences. If mothers, wives, and daughters were more generally interested in the ethics of politics, our statesmen would not so often waste their abilities on games of compromise, risking the interests of freedom on the hazard of their play.

How many such struggles we have witnessed as this concerning admitting Colorado and Nebraska into a free republic with a deep taint of despotism in their constitutions! And how very rare are legislators like Charles Sumner, who can never be induced, by any amount of reproach or persuasion, to sacrifice eternal principles to temporary expediency! What a stainless record he is leaving for history!

There is an obvious fallacy in Professor Lewis's statement that women *do* vote in the same way that all our people vote for President: that is, they choose their elector to vote *for* them. The circumstances of the times are

4. Child quotes from *Incidents of Travel in Greece, Turkey, Russia and Poland* (2 vols., 1838) by the New Jersey–born travel writer John Lloyd Stephens (1805–52); the passages occur in Vol. 1, Chap. 8, where he comments on "Turkish ladies" and the "Sight of a Harem."

5. John Bunyan (1628–88) wrote the popular Christian allegory *The Pilgrim's Progress* (1678–79). The quotation remains unidentified.

always changing, requiring new men and new measures, and when men vote for electors to choose a President, they vote for such electors as are suited to the present emergency. But, admitting that, when a woman marries, and thus becomes "dead in the law,"[6] she chooses an elector to vote for her; what manifold changes may take place in affairs, and in his character, if they live together twenty or thirty years! How many chances there are that he will cease to represent her views, even if he does not vote for measures that she entirely disapproves. The Professor again observes: "Women choose their electors, or he is *provided* for them by one of the most precious ordinances of God and Nature." If a husband or a father should become an atheist or an infidel, while his wife and daughters of mature age wished to give their influence and a share of their earnings to the support of evangelical churches, would the Professor decide that the husband and father was their divinely-appointed representative, and that they ought to act only through him? In large portions of Christendom people believe that heads of the Church are divinely appointed to prescribe the faith of other men. I once asked an acquaintance how he came to turn Roman Catholic; and he replied, "It is so convenient to have a bishop to think *for* me." A young lady once told me that she went to all the churches in Boston by turns, because she did not want to decide till she knew what would be the religion of the man she married. Some time afterward she married a Roman Catholic; and, having chosen him to do her believing, she joined his church. What vitality can there be in a religion assumed under such circumstances? The fact is all conclusions are fallacious based on the hypothesis that one human soul can be merged in another soul. No human being can possibly think for me, or believe for me, any more that he can eat for me, or drink for me, or breathe for me. The family is a very sacred thing; but it appears to me that in a family of true order each one would think, feel, and act, as an individual, with respectful regard to the freedom of the other members, and a conscientious feeling of duty concerning the influence exerted on their characters and happiness. I do not see why difference in voting should necessarily produce dissension between husband and wife, any more than the mere difference of opinion which so frequently exists without such result. Nor do I see why the mere circumstance of depositing a vote need to make women boisterous, or expose them to rudeness.

---

6. Under English common law a married woman was "*feme covert*," meaning that her legal status was "covered" by her husband's and her legal existence merged into his, defining her as dead in the eyes of the law. Married women consequently could not own property in their own name, sign contracts, or lay claim to their own earnings.

They are accustomed to press through crowds to go to theaters and operas, and meetings at Faneuil Hall; they go with the throng to hear orators and statesmen, and nobody treats them uncivilly, or considers their presence an unbecoming intrusion. Their appearance at the polls would soon cease to be a novelty, and the depositing of a vote might be done as easily and as quietly as leaving a card at a hotel.

I respect the fears of kind and conscientious conservatives, like Professor Lewis, although I do not share them. There is one abiding consolation for all that class of thinkers. God has so wisely arranged the laws of the universe that great changes *cannot* come till the way is prepared for them. History plainly shows his hand continually preparing the way for the complete individualizing of the masses. Paul spoke for a much larger audience than the churches of Galatia, when he said, "There is neither Jew nor Greek, there is neither bond nor free, there is neither male nor female: for ye are all one in Christ Jesus."[7] With increasing knowledge the work goes on with accelerated speed; but the world is far enough yet from the great festival of ALL SOULS.

7. Galatians 3.28.

Concerning Women

Part 1

Looking out from "the loopholes of retreat,"[1] upon the movements of this rapidly progressive age, I watch for nothing with more interest than for indications of enlargement and elevation in the views of women. My interest in this question has not, however, been unmixed with some degree of anxiety. We all know that, if the pressure of the atmosphere were removed, men could not stand upon their feet; but all would go topsy-turvy. And the truth is that the *social* atmosphere has pressed so heavily upon women, from the beginning of time, that full development of their faculties and feelings has been impossible. They have almost universally been as unconscious of this pervading, pressure on their souls as we all are of the immense pressure of the material atmosphere upon our bodies; but, accustomed to it as they always have been, I have sometimes queried whether, if this unrecognized pressure were removed, they would stand steadily upon their feet. That they would do so eventually I never doubted; because this social atmosphere is merely the result of human prejudices and habits, and, therefore, not essential to our well-being, like the regulations of the Creator. I believe that perfect equality of the sexes in all the departments of life would be merely the development of the original plan of Divine Providence for the ultimate perfection of the human race. We have proof of this in the fact that the best standard for the measurement of true civilization is universally acknowledged to be the estimation in which women are held, and the degree to which their sphere of action is enlarged. The world has been gradually moving onward in this respect; but every step of progress has been hindered by conventional prejudices. The apostles exhorted female converts not to appear in public without veils,[2] obviously because such an innovation would bring discredit on the

Independent, 15 July 1869, p. 1; 21 October 1869, p. 1.

1. From "The Task" (1785), by the British antislavery poet William Cowper (1731–1800): " 'Tis pleasant, through the loopholes of retreat, / To peep at such a world,—to see the stir / Of the great Babel, and not feel the crowd" (4.88–90).

2. In 1 Corinthians 11.5 and 11.13, Paul calls it unseemly for a woman to "pray unto God uncovered." In some translations "covered" is rendered as "veiled." According to the *Anchor Bible Dictionary,* however, veils were worn during worship but were not generally required in public (2:237). Child's source for her assertion remains unidentified.

name of Christians at a period when public opinion stamped a woman as impudently immodest if she uncovered her face in an assembly of men. Certainly it was a discomfort to half the human race to be excluded from open vision and free air; but at that time the enjoyment of such a natural right was deemed a departure from woman's appropriate sphere, and to this day it would be hard to convince Asiatics that the world would not go to wreck and ruin if women were permitted to walk the streets unveiled. The ancient Grecians, refined and cultivated as they were, excluded women from their social gatherings. The French claim the honor of having introduced the feminine element into conversation by mingling men and women in their parties. *Now,* to dispense with the conversation of intelligent and cultivated women would be deemed as absurd as to leave soprano out of music. When I was a young girl, the aged Hannah Adams was pointed out as a great curiosity, because she had written a short History of the Jews.[3] Innumerable stories were told to show how she had unsexed herself by her learning. She was said not only to be unconscious of a hole in her stocking, but to be absolutely unable to recognize her own face in the glass; and if *that* was not being unfeminine, pray tell me what *could* be. When I published my first book, I was gravely warned by some of my female acquaintances that no woman could expect to be regarded as a *lady* after she had written a book. Now every tenth woman writes a book. This partnership in literature has become a recognized institution, and women are none the less feminine. There was a still stronger prejudice against women's speaking in public; but that also has ceased to be a novelty or a discredit. Quite as easily will the world become accustomed to women's voting and holding civil offices; and it will be seen that, in the long run, good will come of it, rather than harm. Great changes do not come over society till antecedent influences have prepared the way for them; or, as Carlyle expresses it, "The old skin never falls off till a new one has formed under it."[4]

Therefore, I never hesitate for a moment in my conviction that unlimited freedom for the development of woman's faculties, and the consequent equality of the sexes in every department of life, will prove both safe and salutary. But I confess that the conservative element is sufficiently strong in

3. Hannah Adams (1755–1831), author of *The History of the Jews from the Destruction of Jerusalem to the Nineteenth Century* (1812), among other works, was said to be the first American woman to support herself as a professional writer.

4. From the chapter "Organic Filaments" in *Sartor Resartus* (1833–34), by the Scottish essayist and social critic Thomas Carlyle (1795–1881).

me to make me a little anxious about women's doing any discredit to their good cause in the transition period from the old state of things to the new. The best constructed ship will make a poor voyage if she puts out to sea without ballast enough for her sails. And all individuals, races, or classes who have been unaccustomed to wide freedom and grave responsibilities are liable to carry more sail than ballast when they start on a voyage of experiment. This, I think, has already been the case, to some degree, in the management of "the woman question." But, on the whole, women seem to me to have managed the discussion with a remarkable degree of womanly dignity and sound common sense. Such a goodly ship as the Mrs. Livermore,[5] steering straight to port, with all sails spread, yet carrying ballast enough for safety, is a cheering omen. I should have no misgivings concerning the speedy elevation and enlargement of character in women if it were not for their extravagant passion for dress—a passion the gratification of which necessarily absorbs a great portion of their time and attention. The desire to look pretty is natural, and there is nothing blamable in it. The invention of beautiful costume is one of the fine arts; and, like other pleasures of the eye, should receive a due share of cultivation. But Beauty is one thing, and Fashion is another. Nine times out of ten there is no beauty in a new fashion, and there is often positive ugliness. It is laughable to see how thousands of people put themselves to great expense and inconvenience to follow some fashion which originated in the personal defect of some distinguished individual. . . .

I might fill several columns with descriptions of the splendid, costly costumes worn by men. I have not introduced the subject for the purpose of retorting upon men the charge of personal vanity—the few facts I have stated tend to prove that there is about as much human nature in men as in women; but I have brought them forward merely to derive encouragement from the fact that a striking change has taken place in the costume of men. There has been an increasing tendency to simple colors and convenient forms, until at the present time their dress is universally unostentatious and useful. This is doubtless owing to nearer and nearer approaches to equality among mankind. Privileged classes, who lived on the toil of others, are disappearing. The complicated toggery worn by the old nobility would be too inconvenient for merchants, manufacturers, mechanics, and others who have work to do in the world. Men now pride themselves upon spending their wealth on col-

5. The abolitionist and woman suffragist Mary Ashton Rice Livermore (1820–1905) was currently editing the *Woman's Journal*, the weekly founded by Lucy Stone.

leges, railroads, steamers, and other public improvements, rather than upon personal decorations. Finery is considered decidedly unmanly.

And, as women become invested with larger responsibilities, and become conscious of living for more extensive usefulness, will they not shake off the tyranny of fashion, and learn to combine gracefulness with simplicity and convenience in their costume? I believe so; for there is the same human nature in men and women, and similar influences will produce similar results in both.

Part 2

. . . I have always thought that some writers assume too much with regard to the moral superiority of women. It seems to me that the average of women are better than the average of men, in some respects, simply because the relative situation of the sexes places one in the midst of more temptations than the other; while, on the other hand, the average of women are more defective in some points of character than the average of men, because the laws and customs of society have always tended to stunt the growth of such qualities in the souls of women. There is more *petitesse* among women as a class than there is among men as a class. How can we expect largeness in souls that have never had room to grow? There is less intellectual strength among women than among men. How can it be otherwise, with minds always occupied with trivial things? Would the arms of blacksmiths and gold-beaters be so sinewy if they had always used them to make whip-syllabubs and tatten?[6] There is more moral weakness among women than among men. How can it be otherwise, when all the influences around them, from their cradle upward, have impressed them with the idea that it is their crowning grace always to take their tone from society, and never to form opinions for themselves?

There is doubtless a spiritual difference between masculine and feminine natures; but it is the same tune starting from a different key-note. There is the same human nature for a common basis, and unimpeded growth would bring forth similar fruits in both. In some respects the influence of women would tend to purify politics. They would help to make wiser regulations concerning licentiousness and intemperance, for instance; because they are

---

6. whip syllabubs: a dessert of sweetened milk or cream beaten to a froth and flavored with wine or liquor; tatten: tatting, a delicate handmade lace.

prodigious sufferers by those vices. On the other hand, many of them would be liable to become the tools of flattering and selfish politicians, and would seek the attainment of good ends by indirect and dishonest means, just as men have done. Place men and women on a perfect equality in all the departments of art, science, literature, politics, professions, and trades, and the result would be a great number of individuals among both sexes who would prove their capability of doing all sorts of things well.

Some men will exclaim, "That is the very thing we predict and deprecate. We have no taste for women who can stand alone. It is a duty for them to lean upon us, and it is our pride and pleasure to protect and support them. Man is the strong, majestic oak; and woman should be the graceful, clinging vine." I could point out many families where women are the oaks and men are the vines. But our conservative brethren need feel no alarm at the progress of "woman's rights." They, and their sons, and their sons' sons, will find plenty of clinging vines. So long as the article is in demand, the market will be abundantly supplied with women who have been trained to consider it unfeminine to think, unladylike to work, and who spend their days in decorating their persons to catch the eye of purchasers. Meanwhile, be assured, my brethren, that you, as well as we, are losers by the present unequal arrangements. The harems of Asia afford no companionship for men; and, poorly as those great doll-houses compare with European homes, the households of the future will have a still greater superiority over the households of the present.

The reference to Asia is not inappropriate; for many of our customs and opinions are mere modifications of traditions derived from the East, and dating back to the infancy of society. The plain, undisguised truth is that women are everywhere tacitly recognized as articles of merchandise; and everywhere they, more or less, "accept the situation." The fact is so covered with an embroidered veil that they are generally unconscious of its presence while acting under its influence. Many avenues are open to the ambition of men; but marriage has been the only avenue open for women, and it is still the principal one. Consequently, by a law of human nature, mothers seek to form wealthy connections for their daughters; and girls, indirectly, if not directly, trained to consider this the great object in life, use their time and faculties in decorating their persons to please men. And, while men in all ages have expended jests and sarcasms upon the vanity and extravagance of women, they have always practically encouraged those faults. Do men show a preference for economical, industrious, plainly-dressed women? By no means. The dashing, extravagant woman has prodigiously the advantage over sensible, unpretending women in securing what the world calls "a good match."

I do not believe that women have by nature more personal vanity than men. They are more vain because society puts a premium upon their vanity. Like all human beings, they seek to make their fortunes by pleasing those who have the power to dispense them. Why did the men of Queen Elizabeth's time go so flauntingly in rich velvets and satins, embroidery and ermines, ribbons and ruffles, feathers and furbelows? Because the Queen was proud to have a splendidly dressed court, and to please the Queen was the surest way to obtain honor and emolument. Nor was this weakness peculiar to queens. Louis the 14th, who was considered the greatest monarch in Christendom, deemed it essential that his court should be more magnificently dressed than any other in the world. All the new fashions invented by tailors, mantua-makers, and milliners were exhibited before him and subjected to his decision. Not till the aged king was about to pass away from the vanities of this world did he consent to relinquish his sovereignty over silks and laces, head-gear and shoe-ties. He had become very feeble when he informed a fashion committee, who waited upon him, that the ladies of his court might make such changes in their costume as they pleased; showing, however, a flicker of the old flame by reminding them that he never liked aprons. Look at pictures of the French gentlemen of that period! See their bright-colored velvet coats embroidered with gold, their rich laces dangling from wrist and knee, the feathers floating from their caps, the high red heels, and the great silken butterfly bows appended to their shoes! Why did personal vanity manifest itself so much more in the dress of men of that period than it does in this age of "self-made men"? Simply because the king had a passion for extravagant dressing, and to please the king was the readiest way to fortune. For the same reason do women now dress to please King Homo, who has the monopoly of wealth and honors, and can confer them on his favorites.

Even in physical strength, I doubt whether there is so much difference between men and women as has been generally assumed. Female slaves did as much and as hard work upon the plantations as the male slaves. In the long tramps of the Indian tribes, the women carry all the heavy burdens, in addition to their children, strapped upon their backs. Many years ago, I was visiting in Maine, about four miles from an encampment of Penobscot Indians. One cold winter's day, when a deep snow had fallen and remained almost unbroken, one of their women came to the house where I was, to beg.

The salt-fish she asked for was readily given; and she went ploughing her way back through four miles of snow-drift. The next day she brought a bag to be filled with potatoes; and strapped on her shoulders was a babe, born since we had last seen her, and which she told us she had washed in the river, having first broken a hole in the ice. Sea-captains who first visited the colony at Pitcairn's Island inform us that there seemed to be little or no difference of strength between the men and the women; that either of them would lift a cask of water to their shoulders, and carry it with apparent ease up the steep and rocky shores of the island. Travelers tell us of peasant women yoked to plows in France, and paving the streets in Russia. These things indicate physical strength in the natural constitutions of women; but they are sad to look upon, because they are done in obedience to task-masters—not voluntarily, and with improving effects upon their own characters and condition.

I return to the proposition that the radical difficulty at the basis of this whole subject is that women are considered as *belonging* to men. In Africa and Asia girls are openly sold to husbands for a stipulated sum. It was a very ancient custom in Asia for the seller to throw a shoe to the buyer, in token that their bargain was completed; hence, a shoe was thrown after bridegroom and bride, to signify that the girl was no longer owned by her father, but had become the property of her husband. The custom is sometimes playfully observed among us, without thought or knowledge of its origin. But, in reality, it has not entirely lost its original significance with us; for highly-civilized people do sell their daughters to the highest bidders, though the transaction is gracefully covered with veil and flowers.

Women and the Freedmen

For more than a year past, I have observed in the writings of some advocates of women's suffrage, sentiments, more or less openly expressed, which have excited a fear in my mind that rotten timbers were getting introduced into the foundation of our cause. In allusions to the freedmen's right to vote I have occasionally noticed something of the sneering tone habitually assumed by slaveholders and their copperhead[1] allies. Complaints that negroes were allowed to vote, while women were excluded from the polls, have been followed by a very obvious readiness on the part of some to set aside the rights of the colored people for the advancement of the woman cause.

Mrs. Stanton, in a letter of invitation to a Convention of Women, last Spring, expressed her surprise and gratification at the number of sympathizing letters she received from Southern women.[2] I probably should have been surprised also, if my mind had not previously been excited to watchfulness by the symptoms to which I have just alluded. If the Pope should join the Free Religious Association in Boston, I should at once query with myself how he was calculating to use the Association for the benefit of Rome;[3] and the singular spectacle of Southerners, especially of Southern women, in love with progress, at once gave rise to similar questions. I could not but observe that while *they* were said to be zealous for women's voting, the freedmen were charged with being opposed to it. Years ago, I used to say that negroes were anti-slavery, as naturally as hens were anti-hawk; and I asked myself, Are their

National Anti-Slavery Standard, 28 August 1869, p. 2; reprinted in *The Woman's Advocate*.

1. copperhead: the term applied to Northerners who sympathized with the Confederacy or sabotaged the Union government's policies during the Civil War (derived from the venomous copperhead snake).

2. Child may be referring to the formation of the National Woman Suffrage Association by Elizabeth Cady Stanton and Susan B. Anthony, announced in their newspaper, the *Revolution*, on 20 May 1869. At the meeting of the American Equal Rights Association the preceding week, Stanton and Anthony had argued against the Fifteenth Amendment, using language of the kind Child cites. They decided to form the NWSA when the majority of the American Equal Rights Association voted to support the Fifteenth Amendment and to call for a separate Sixteenth Amendment enfranchising women.

3. The Free Religious Association was founded by progressive Unitarians in 1867 and invited representatives of all faiths, including non-Christian religions and agnostics, to "come together as equal brothers." From her liberal Protestant standpoint, Child views the pope as embodying the dogmatism and bigotry the Free Religious Association opposed.

instincts true in this matter also? Do they "feel it in their bones" that Southern women will be certain to aid Southern men in their determined efforts to deprive them of the right to vote? We all know how proofs of that unrelenting determination are piled up mountain-high in the accounts of elections at the South. It requires no great acuteness to perceive what an advantage will be gained by the enemies of the United States if they can secure the elective franchise for rebel women, and take it away from loyal blacks. In the days of slave-holding supremacy, the aristocracy of the South always had a party of male politicians at the North, who, while they talked loudly about human rights, were ever ready to rivet more firmly the chains of the slave, for the sake of securing Southern patronage in carrying out their own personal and party plans. And now, when Southern women manifest a tendency to enter the political arena, we see a party of female politicians at the North ready to sacrifice the rights of colored men in order to secure the co-operation of Southern ladies in their efforts for the enfranchisement of women. What an argument is this to put into the mouths of those who deny that the suffrage of women would tend to purify politics!

I was glad to see, in THE WOMAN'S ADVOCATE, an article from Wendell Phillips rebuking these women for their faithlessness to principle; and glad to notice also that Mr. Smalley, in one of his Letters to the *Tribune*, expresses his disapprobation of such a course.[4] For myself, I find it requires a good deal of restraining grace to speak in moderate terms of a compromise so utterly wrong in principle, so shamefully mean and selfish in its spirit. God forbid that women should ever consent to take one iota from the rights of others for the sake of advancing their own! Will human beings never learn that no good thing can ever be firmly established on a basis of violated principle? There may seem to be some present advantages gained by such a course, but, in some form or other, the wrong is sure to return and plague the doer. Grant that women might be allowed to vote a few years sooner in consequence of exerting their influence against the freedmen's right of suffrage, what would be the consequence? They would have obtained an external good at the price of a great internal injury to themselves. They would show that the conscience of woman was in the auction-room, for hackneyed politicians to bid upon its price. They would prove themselves unworthy to vote, unfit to discharge the

---

4. Wendell Phillips (1811–84) emerged as the American Anti-Slavery Society's most prominent and radical leader after 1865. George Washburn Smalley (1833–1916) was a staff writer and foreign correspondent for the *New York Tribune* after the war.

responsible duties of citizenship; and by so doing they would hinder the real progress of women more than any legal disabilities could possibly do.

I am glad to know that many women view this subject as I do. They see, as I do, that when a thing is radically wrong, no array of possible advantages can make it right. As American citizens, we profess to believe that every human being has a right to a voice in the laws by which he is governed; and if we do not believe this, our professions of freedom are hollow brass. The people born with dark complexions have this right in common with all human beings; and, in addition to this universal right, they have an especial claim upon our gratitude, as well as our sense of justice. They hid our hunted soldiers, they fed the famishing, they tended the sick, they guided our wanderers to places of safety. Many a wife and mother among us owes the return of dear ones to their loyalty, intelligence, and tender care. And shall we allow ourselves to become accomplices of their oppressors? Shall our influence go to strengthen the murderous hands of the Ku-Klux-Klan? If we think *our* rights would be more perfectly secured if we were allowed to vote, how much more true is it of *them*, who are living in the midst of cunning and malignant enemies! I regard it as a shame to womanhood that any one should think of bartering away their rights for the sake of more promptly securing her own.

I have never been so sanguine as many concerning the great purification that would be wrought in politics by the admission of women to the polls; and therefore I am not much disappointed at this proof that they have the same human nature as men; I am only a little surprised that they should so *soon* begin to follow the crooked ways of politicians. It does not, however, in the least change my conviction that women ought to vote, and that, their voting would, on the whole, have a beneficial effect upon themselves and the community. In the first place, we are human beings; and I regard it as an eternal principle of right that every human being should have a voice in the laws that govern him. In the next place, the exercise of that right involves large responsibilities, and necessarily ennobles character, in proportion as those responsibilities are understood and appreciated; and we can understand them and appreciate them only by incurring them. Lastly there are several subjects on which it is obviously for the interest of women to vote wisely. The cause of temperance, for instance, would doubtless find powerful allies in them. Some of them will exhibit a talent for politics, which practically means indirectness and compromise; but that class I think will always be a small minority, and will do no more harm than the corresponding class of men do.

Part Six

Religion

Introduction

✾ "I wish I could find some religion in which my heart and understanding could unite," Child wrote at age eighteen to her brother Convers Francis, a Unitarian minister.[1] Although she never succeeded in finding such a religion, her lifelong quest for it impelled her to read widely in the world's sacred literatures, ranging far beyond the bounds of Christianity. It also inspired her passionate commitment to breaking down sectarian walls and fostering religious tolerance—another aspect of the impulse to unify the family of humankind that she expressed through the trope of interracial marriage.

Brought up a Calvinist, Child rebelled very early against her parents' "fierce theology," with its ever present threat of damnation. "Strictly and truly, it is 'Devil Worship,'" she later explained; "for the God which Calvin made in his own image has all the worst attributes ascribed to the Devil. Who but the Prince of Fiends could create beings and fore-ordain them to eternal torment?"[2] At the opposite extreme, the "cold intellectual respectability" of her brother's Unitarianism did not satisfy her emotional hunger;[3] nor did it satisfy the visionary, mystical inclinations that she shared with future transcendentalists such as Ralph Waldo Emerson and Margaret Fuller. This penchant for mysticism initially attracted Child (as it did Emerson) to the teachings of the Swedish seer Emanuel Swedenborg. His theory that an intricate system of "correspondences" linked the realms of matter and spirit "seemed a golden key to unlock the massive gate between the external and the spiritual worlds," Child wrote in retrospect.[4] Thus she joined the Swedenborgian New Church in 1822.

Child's preoccupation with religion pervades her early novels. Debates between Calvinist bigots and religious liberals punctuate *Hobomok, A Tale of Early Times* (1824) and *The Rebels, or Boston before the Revolution* (1825). In both novels, Child highlights the virulent misogyny of her Calvinist spokesmen. *Hobomok* also reveals Child's affinities with the transcendentalists and foreshadows her research into non-Christian religions. The "creation . . . is God's library—the first Bible he ever wrote," proclaims the heroine's mother, Mrs. Conant (76), anticipating the credo of Emerson's *Nature* (1836). The

1. LMC to Convers Francis, 31 May 1820, *SL* 2.
2. LMC to [Lucy Osgood?], 17 Dec. 1870, *CC* 74/1966.
3. LMC to Lucy Osgood, 28 June 1846, *SL* 226.
4. LMC to Parke Godwin, 20 Jan. 1856, *SL* 275.

heroine herself, Mary Conant, appropriately relies on the evidence of nature to refute her father's belief that only a "small . . . remnant . . . are pleasing in the sight of God." The evening star, she notes, "smile[s] on distant mosques and temples" as well as on Calvinist churches (47–48).

Following the logic of this observation, Child shifts the scene from Christian churches to pagan temples in her third novel, *Philothea* (1836), set in ancient Greece. There Plato delights the heroine with an exposition of his mystical philosophy, which parallels Swedenborgianism in celebrating the "everlasting harmony between the soul of man and the visible forms of creation" (40). By then, Child was already looking beyond Swedenborg for spiritual nourishment; however much the doctrine of correspondences appealed to her imagination, the New Church did not long sustain either her heart or her understanding. When Child publicly embraced the antislavery cause in 1833, she discovered to her dismay that her Swedenborgian congregation and pastor were "bitterly proslavery . . . and intensely bigotted." The church's doctrine, moreover, turned out to be as narrow and exclusive as Calvinism, merely substituting Swedenborg's authority for Saint Paul's.[5]

Just as involvement in antislavery activism alienated her from Swedenborgianism, so the schisms that caused her withdrawal from the movement temporarily propelled her back into the New Church.[6] In a pattern she would repeat in the 1870s, Child transposed her crusade for human brotherhood from the temporal to the religious sphere. Her renewed quest for religious faith prompted her to visit a variety of churches, including a Catholic cathedral and a Jewish synagogue, but none fulfilled her spiritual needs. The initial phase of this quest is reflected in her two volumes of newspaper sketches, *Letters from New York* (1843, 1845). While promoting religious tolerance along with social reform, they also expound the doctrine of correspondences and embark on flights of mysticism.

The most ambitious product of Child's quest is her three-volume comparative study, *The Progress of Religious Ideas, Through Successive Ages* (1855), which took her eight years to finish. Encompassing all the major religions of the ancient world—Hinduism, Buddhism, Jainism, Confucianism, Taoism, and Zoroastrianism; Egyptian, Chaldaic, Greco-Roman, and Celtic myths and cults; Judaism, Christianity, and Islam—the book seeks to exhibit each "in its own light; that is, as it appeared to those who sincerely believed it to be

5. LMC to Gerrit Smith, 4 Apr. 1864, *SL* 441; LMC to Lucy Osgood, 28 June 1846, *SL* 226.
6. For details on the antislavery schisms, see the introductions to parts 3 and 5.

of divine origin"; to illustrate "the beauties and the blemishes" of every religion through quotations from its own sacred scriptures; and to preserve "complete impartiality" (viii–ix). It was the first work that digested for the general public the findings of orientalist and biblical scholars, who were then undermining the status of Christianity as revealed truth by exploring the striking similarities between the story of Jesus and the myths of Krishna, Osiris, and other ancient deities. Not surprisingly, Child's reviewers accused her of "too great partiality for Paganism, and too great prejudice against the sacred Books of Christians."[7] In personal letters and obituary tributes to Child, however, many readers credited *The Progress of Religious Ideas* with liberating their minds from the stranglehold of dogma and guiding them toward a spirituality that transcended sectarian disputes. The warmest praise came from Elizabeth Cady Stanton, who went on to build her feminist re-write of Scripture, *The Woman's Bible* (1895), on Child's research.

After publishing her magnum opus, Child plunged back into antislavery activism, which engrossed her attention until the passage of the black suffrage amendment in 1870. What apparently rekindled her interest in religion was a series of articles in the *Atlantic Monthly* by the Unitarian scholar James Freeman Clarke, collected and reprinted in his *Ten Great Religions* (1871). Clarke compared Christianity with other religions only to establish its superiority; no other religion, he argued, was better suited for universal adoption or more capable of "keeping abreast with the advancing civilization of the world" (29–30). In a letter to a friend, Child commented that the universality Clarke attributed to Christianity was due to all the "accretions" it had received from earlier religions[8]—a debt he failed to recognize. She set out to demonstrate this in two articles of her own for the *Atlantic,* "Resemblances between the Buddhist and the Roman Catholic Religions" (Dec. 1870) and "The Intermingling of Religions" (Oct. 1871). Updating and condensing the information presented in *The Progress of Religious Ideas,* they take issue not only with Clarke but with other apologists of Christianity.

Christian theologians had attempted to explain away parallels between the Bible and the much older sacred texts of Hindus and Buddhists—which seemed to indicate Christian borrowings from those sources—by claiming that early missionaries had introduced elements of Christian doctrine into

---

7. Review of *The Progress of Religious Ideas, New Englander* 54 (May 1856): 321. See also the reviews in the *New-York Evangelist* 6 Dec. 1855, p. 194; and the *New-York Observer* 15 Nov. 1855, p. 366.

8. LMC to Lucy Osgood, 28 Mar. 1869, *CC* 71/1893.

Hinduism and Buddhism. Child refutes such claims. Instead, she suggests, Christianity took root in regions teeming with cultural influences from all over Asia, which it absorbed along with the creeds, festivals, and even the deities of the peoples it converted. Child also contests Clarke's assertions that Christianity spread by peaceful proselytism rather than by conquest and that its universalism contrasts with the "ethnic" character of Buddhism. Far from attempting to elevate Jesus over Buddha, she retorts, "those who look upon all mankind as brethren" ought to rejoice in learning of another prophet who preached a religion dedicated to "sweeping away the ancient barriers that had separated classes and peoples."

Child's emphasis on the commonalities that link Buddhism to Christianity, and particularly to Catholicism, also serves an ulterior purpose, hinted at in her article's reference to "John Chinaman and Patrick O'Dublin." In 1871 Irish Catholics were leading a campaign to ban Chinese immigration that would culminate in the Chinese Exclusion Bill of 1882. Child counters their stereotypes of the Chinese as unassimilable aliens both by underscoring the similarities between the two peoples' religions and by describing Christianity itself as a religion that has assimilated an entire panoply of Asian elements. Symbolically, the Eclectic Church of the Future, which she offers as a model of religious and political unity, takes the form of a Catholic cathedral but preserves the beauties of "all ages and nations."

At the end of her life, Child sought to speed the advent of the "Eclectic Church" she envisioned by producing an "Eclectic Bible." Titled *Aspirations of the World. A Chain of Opals* (1878), it culls "the *best* portions" (3) of the world's sacred books and arranges them in chronological order under such headings as "Benevolence," "Brotherhood," and "Fraternity of Religions." Revealing how far she had traveled from the religion of her youth, quotations from Greco-Roman, Buddhist, Persian, Hindu, and Chinese sacred scriptures (in decreasing order of frequency) far outnumber extracts from the Old and New Testaments.

In our secular age, the religious tolerance Child advocated may no longer sound radical, and much of her scholarship has been superseded by advances in the field of comparative religion. Nevertheless, developments of the late twentieth century—the worldwide resurgence of fundamentalism and religious warfare, the rise of the Christian right, and the revival of calls to define the United States as a Christian country—suggest that the countervision Child holds out in "The Intermingling of Religions" remains timely and relevant.

The Intermingling of Religions

In the November number of the Atlantic for 1870 some striking resemblances were pointed out between the Buddhist and Roman Catholic religions. This similarity, which has long been recognized, can be accounted for only in two ways: either Roman Catholics must have borrowed from Buddhists or Buddhists must have borrowed from them. The latter supposition has been generally adopted; the coincidences being traced to the teaching of Nestorian missionaries in India. Some say the Apostle Thomas carried Christianity into India, and that the resemblances are the fruits of his preaching. But there are many reasons why both these conclusions seem improbable.

Early in the fifth century Christians began to call Mary the "Mother of God." Nestorius,[1] Patriarch of Constantinople, objected to the phrase, saying she had never been so considered by the Apostles, and that such a title was calculated to remind people of the genealogy of the heathen gods. This brought him into a very warm controversy; and he, being a devout believer in the divinity of Jesus, though opposed to the adoration of Mary, took the ground that Jesus had two natures, one human, the other divine, and that Mary was mother only of the human portion. A Council of Bishops was called at Chalcedon to settle the disputed question, and they decided that Mary was the Mother of God. Nestorius and his followers maintained the ground they had taken, and were so hotly persecuted as heretics, that they fled to countries beyond the jurisdiction of the Christian Church. Many of them settled on the coast of Malabar, where over two hundred thousand of their descendants still remain, and are called Nazarenes by the Hindoos. One sect of them is known by the name of Christians of Saint Thomas, which probably gave rise to the idea that they were founded by the Apostle Thomas. Some have stated that his tomb is to be seen there; but many scholars say that the inscription indicates the burial-place of a Nestorian missionary named Thomas. But whoever was the original teacher of this ancient sect, there is certainly nothing in their customs or worship to remind one of the elaborate ceremonials of the Buddhist or of the Catholic Church. Living isolated from the Christian world, they have not been affected by the immense changes that

Atlantic Monthly 28 (October 1871): 385–95.

1. The Syrian ecclesiastic Nestorius (d. A.D. 451) was banished to Petra in Arabia after the Council at Ephesus in 431. Small communities of Nestorian Christians still live in Kurdistan and Iraq, as well as in India.

have passed over Christianity in an interval of time certainly embracing more than a thousand years. They retain the primitive habits of the early centuries. They still celebrate the Love Feasts, called Agapae, said to have been introduced in the time of the Apostles. There are no monasteries among them, and their priests are allowed to marry. With regard to the administration of the Lord's Supper, they incline to the ideas of Protestants. The cross is the only symbol in their churches, and they have an extreme hostility to pictures and images. When some Jesuit missionaries offered them an image of the Virgin Mary, they replied, "We are Christians, not idolaters."

If the Apostle Thomas ever travelled into India, it is difficult to imagine what could have induced him to teach the people to prostrate themselves before images, to establish monasteries, to say their prayers on rosaries, and believe in miracle-working relics. The Jews, among whom Thomas was educated, were accustomed to none of these things. They formed no part of the teaching of Jesus, in which we find none of the characteristic features of Oriental asceticism. His enemies reproached him that he "came eating and drinking," and that he did not impose frequent fasts upon his disciples. He sanctioned a wedding with his presence, and said nothing to indicate that celibacy was essential to holiness. We have no means of knowing whether his disciples were generally married men; but that Peter had a wife is implied by the Scripture, which informs us that her mother "lay sick of a fever."[2]

It also seems unlikely that Nestorians, of any sect, should have introduced monasteries, rosaries, etc., into India, for they were separated from the Christian Church early in the fifth century, and the first monastery in Christendom was established by Saint Benedict full a hundred years later; and this was followed by the introduction of rosaries to facilitate the recitation of prayers. In brief, these and many other customs of the Catholic Church cannot be historically traced to the Jews, or to Jesus, or to the Apostles, or to the Christian churches in the first centuries, or to Nestorius, who was cut off from the Christian Church because he objected to the worship of the Virgin.

But in ancient Hindostan, ages before the birth of Jesus, we do find models for these things. Their earliest Sacred Books teach that the soul of man, by entering a mortal body, had become separated from the Supreme Soul of the Universe, and that the only way to become one with God again was to mortify and abuse the body, and keep the soul constantly occupied

---

2. Mark 1.30: "But Simon's wife's mother lay sick of a fever." See also parallel passages in Matthew 8.14 and Luke 4.38.

with the contemplation of divine things. Some of the Hindoo devotees stood for years on one foot; others lived sunk up to their chins in deep narrow holes of the ground, dependent upon charity for the food that kept them alive. Simeon Stylites, the Christian devotee, made his body about as uncomfortable, by living thirty-seven years on the top of a high pillar that afforded merely room enough to stand upon.[3] Long before our era there were communities of Hindoo hermits who took vows of celibacy, fasted to extremity, and spent their lives repeating prayers on strings of beads. Some of them were vowed to perpetual silence, and kept skulls constantly before them, to remind them of the emancipation of the soul by the dissolution of the body. They had very close imitators in the Catholic monks of La Trappe,[4] who daily dug their own graves, and never spoke, except to salute each other, as they passed, with the words, "We must die."

An historical glance backward will help to explain many things that might otherwise seem unaccountable. At the time that Christianity began to assume the form of a distinct religion the world was in an unprecedented state of activity, intercommunication, and change. The conquests of Julius Caesar and Alexander the Great had brought remote nations into contact. The pathway of commerce was immensely extended, and philosophers and devotees from all points of the compass followed in her train. Two new forces were beginning to agitate the world, both of them animated by the zeal which characterizes reformers before their ideas become established. Buddha had striven to teach his countrymen that their religious ideas were too narrow and exclusive; that the road to holiness was open to all classes and conditions; to women as well as men, to foreign nations as well as to Hindoos.[5] Expelled from Hindostan by reason of these doctrines, his disciples had spread over various Asiatic countries, and eighty thousand of their missionaries were perambulating the world. Among the Jews, who considered them-

3. The Syrian hermit Simeon Stylites (ca. 390–459), sometimes called Simeon the Elder to distinguish him from a sixth-century stylite by the same name.

4. The Trappist order was founded in 1662 by the courtier Armand de Rancé (1626–1700), a convert who had governed the Cistercian Abbey of La Trappe. Trappists practiced extreme austerity and maintained absolute silence.

5. The Indian prince Siddhartha Gautama, who became known as the Buddha, or "the enlightened," lived ca. 566–486 B.C. He left his court for a life of wandering asceticism at about the age of thirty, and began preaching six years later, after attaining enlightenment. The core of Buddhism is the Eightfold Path through which believers avoid suffering by renouncing desire. Before being expelled from India, Buddhism was adopted as the state religion by King Ashoka (ca. 270–230 B.C.).

selves the chosen people of Jehovah, in whose sight all other nations were unclean, had arisen a great reformer, who held communication with despised Samaritans and publicans, and taught that all men were brethren. His disciples were also driven from their native land, and spread into the neighboring kingdoms of Asia, among the Grecians in Europe, and throughout the Roman Empire, where their countrymen were already more numerous than in Palestine. And wherever these missionaries went they proclaimed the doctrine that God was equally the Father of all; that in his sight there was "neither Jew nor Gentile, bond or free, men or women; but all were one in Christ Jesus."[6] To those who look upon all mankind as brethren, there is something beautiful in both these great tides of reform, enlarging the scope of human sympathies, and sweeping away the ancient barriers that had separated classes and peoples.

Antioch, where the first church of Christians was gathered in Gentile lands, was on the high road between Europe and Asia. Ephesus, one of the earliest head-quarters of the Christians, was always swarming with foreigners, especially with Orientals. Rome, where a Christian church was very early gathered, was full of the spoils of many conquered nations, and of their theories also. Alexander the Great had built the new Egyptian city of Alexandria, to which he was very desirous to attract the learning and commerce of the world. For that purpose he encouraged the greatest freedom of discussion, and unbounded toleration of opinions. Thither flocked zealots and philosophers from all quarters, eager for controversy. Such a seething caldron of doctrines the world had never witnessed. Dion Chrysostom, who wrote in the beginning of the second century, informs us that Greeks and Romans, Syrians, Ethiopians, Arabians, Persians, and travellers from India were always to be found in that cosmopolitan city. In this focus of diverse ideas the Christians early planted a church.[7] Jewish converts to Christianity were for a long time extremely tenacious of their old Hebrew traditions and customs; while Gentile converts, from various nations, manifested a great tendency to amalgamate the teaching of Jesus with the old ideas and ceremonies in which they had been educated. In the conflict of sects arising from this state of things it was almost inevitable that the teaching of Jesus and his Apostles should become more or less largely interfused with ideas from various reli-

---

6. Galatians 3.28; Child substitutes "Gentile" for Paul's "Greek." See also 1 Corinthians 12.13, a similar passage in which Paul does use the word *Gentile.*

7. Dion Chrysostom (ca. 40–112 A.D.) was a Greek rhetorician and philosopher. Child may have read an English edition of the *Select Essays of Dion Chrysostom* (1800).

gions; especially with those from Hindostan and Persia, which prevailed so extensively at that period.

These Oriental ideas have had such a very important influence, not only on the faith, but on the social conditions of men, that it is worth while to trace them briefly to their abstract source. Orientals conceived of the Supreme as the Central Source of Being, dwelling in passionless repose in regions of resplendent light. He did not create anything; but all spirits radiated from him, in successive series of emanations, from the highest seraphs down to the souls of men. Coeternal with him was an antagonistic principle called Matter; a dark, inert mass, which gave birth to the Devil and all forms of evil. When some of the lower series of Spirits of Light approached the region of Matter, the Spirits of Darkness were attracted by their splendor and sought to draw them down among themselves. They succeeded; and thus mankind came into existence, with ethereal souls derived from God and material bodies derived from the Devil. The only way for these Spirits of Light, imprisoned in Matter, to get back to the Divine Source whence they emanated was to subdue the body by all sorts of abstinence and tormenting penance, while the soul was kept in steadfast contemplation on spiritual things.

The Jews had quite a different theory of creation. They conceived of God as an active Being, who made the body of man with his own hands and then breathed a soul into it. Thus regarding the body as divine workmanship, they had no contempt for it and did not consider its senses sinful.

When these different ideas, coming from afar, met front to front in the Christian churches, they gave rise to a motley amalgamation of doctrines. The most conspicuous specimen of this is to be found in the numerous sects classed under the general denomination of Gnostics. The name is derived from the Greek word "Gnosis," signifying wisdom; and it was bestowed on them because, however they might differ on other points, they all believed that by subjugation of the senses human souls might be restored to their original oneness with God, and thus become recipients of intuitive wisdom directly emanating from him. With few exceptions, all these Gnostics were of Gentile origin, and their doctrines bear the obvious stamp of Hindostan and Persia; though it is likely that they derived them from various intermediate sources. Many of their leaders were men of uncommon talent and learning, wedded to ancient theories, but sincerely attracted by the teaching of Jesus. They troubled the Christian churches as early as the time of Paul, who alludes to them as "seducing spirits, forbidding to marry and commanding to abstain from meats."[8] Their theories proved very attractive, especially to scholars prone to abstract speculations. The celebrated Saint Augustine[9] was for several years a Gnostic, and Christian converts were not unfrequently drawn aside into their erratic paths. They increased with such rapidity, that at one time their flood of Oriental ideas threatened to sweep away the Jewish foundations of Christianity. In the middle of the fifth century, the Bishop of Cyprus records that he found a million of them in his diocese, and succeeded in bringing them all within the fold of his church. How much it was necessary to compromise with their ideas in order to accomplish that object he does not inform us.

The different elements that were jostled into contact during this transition state of the world gave rise to much controversy that sounds odd enough to modern ears. The Jews were such an exclusive people, that Gentile nations had very little opportunity to become acquainted with their religious views, till they met together on the common ground of reverence for Jesus. Jehovah was to them an altogether foreign God; and having no traditional reverence for his name, they discussed his character as freely as we do that of Jupiter. It was a revolting idea to them that the Supreme Being could have formed anything out of Matter, which in their minds was associated with everything evil and unclean. And believing that all Spirits were evolved, without effort, from the Central Source, by the mere necessity of outflowing, they ridiculed the idea that God worked six days to make the world, and then had to rest from his labors. They declared that if Jehovah confined his care to one people, and was jealous when they gave glory to other gods, if his anger waxed hot when they disobeyed him, if he commanded them to slaughter their enemies, and promised them mere earthly rewards for obedience to his laws, he could not possibly be the Supreme Being, for he was altogether free from passion. Some of the Gnostics admitted that Jehovah might belong to one of the inferior orders of Spirits, evolved from the Source of Light; others maintained that he must be an Evil Spirit, and that the Scriptures said to be inspired by him were obviously the work of the Devil. They all believed Jesus to be one of the Spirits of Light; but their ideas concerning the inherent wickedness of Matter led them to reject the idea that he could be born of a woman. They said he merely appeared to have a body, for the purpose of

8. Child partially quotes 1 Timothy 4.1 and 4.3.

9. The Carthaginian bishop of Hippo, Saint Augustine (354–430 A.D.), describes his Manichaean phase in books 3–5 of his *Confessions* (397). As Child implies in her reference to Mani below, Manichaeanism was a late form of Gnosticism.

performing on earth the benevolent mission of helping Spirits out of the prison-house of Matter, and restoring them to their original oneness with God. Paul probably aimed a shaft at this doctrine, when he said, "Every spirit that confesseth not that Jesus is Christ come in the *flesh* is not of God."[10] Asceticism, in a greater or less degree, characterized all the Gnostic sects. They despised all luxuries, ornaments, shows, and amusements; everything, in fact, which contributed to the pleasure of the senses. They abstained from wine and animal food, and ate merely sufficient to sustain life. They all regarded matrimony as incompatible with holiness; and some thought it a great sin, inasmuch as the reproduction of human bodies was entering into a league with Spirits of Darkness to help them to incarcerate Spirits of Light in the prison-house of Matter.

These ascetic ideas, so conspicuous in very ancient Hindoo writings, were, in one form or another, afloat almost everywhere at the time the Christian Church was in the process of formation out of a great variety of nations. By early emigration, or otherwise, they had come to prevail extensively in Egypt, where the deserts swarmed with hermits vowed to celibacy and severe mortification of the senses. In Grecian mythology, copied by the Romans, there was no antagonism between Spirit and Matter. Those nations had never been taught that their bodies came from the Devil, and consequently they had no contempt for the senses. They revelled in physical enjoyment, and ascribed the same tendencies to their gods. Bacchus was their jovial companion, and Venus adored as the beautifier of life. But though the people were on such gay and sociable terms with their deities, philosophers had introduced from Egypt the sombre ideas of the Orient. Plato taught that Matter was the original Source of Evil, antagonistic to the Principle of Good.[11] Plotinus,[12] the most celebrated of his later followers, was ashamed of his body, though it is said to have been a remarkably beautiful one. He blushed for his parents that they had given birth to it, and any allusion to physical instincts or necessities was deeply mortifying to him. While Egyptian zealots and Grecian philosophers were strewing abroad the seed of ancient asceticism, Buddhist missionaries were also industriously propagating it. We are told that travellers from India were always in Alexandria, which was

10. The quotation is actually from 1 John 4.3, not from Paul.

11. The idea that matter is the original source of evil is more implicit than explicit in Plato, though commentators have inferred it from his writings.

12. The Roman philosopher Plotinus (205–70 A.D.) is regarded as the founder of Neoplatonism.

the great focus of Gnostic sects. Bardesanes, one of the leaders of the Gnostics in the second century, wrote an account of religious communities in India,[13] the members of which merely endured life as an inevitable bondage, and sought, by devout contemplation and severe mortification of the senses, to rise above the prison-house of the body. Mani, who lived in the third century, and was perhaps the most remarkable of all the Gnostics, studied a book called "The Treasury of Mysteries, by Buddha, said to have been born of a Virgin."[14] And it was a common doctrine with these sects that Zoroaster, Buddha, and Jesus were the same Spirit of Light appearing on earth in different places and forms, for the benevolent purpose of bringing back to oneness with God those stray Spirits which had become separated from him by being shut up in material bodies. These sects, standing between the old religions and the new, were hotly persecuted by both. They finally vanished from the scene; but for several centuries their theories, under various modifications, reappeared to trouble the churches.

Every one knows that the Roman Catholic Church abounds in ceremonies and traditions of which no trace can be found in the Old Testament or the New. The teachers of that church say they are derived from the Christian Fathers, whose authority they deem sacred. The prominent preachers of Christianity during the first three centuries, called Fathers of the Church, were, almost without exception, converts from the Gentile religions, mostly Greek and Roman. The rejection of foreign customs had been religiously inculcated upon Jews; and those of them who accepted Jesus as their promised Messiah retained that extreme aversion to innovation which characterized them as a people. But Gentile converts, who were far more numerous, had received quite a different training. Grecians easily adopted the festivals and the gods of other nations; and Romans manifested still greater facility in that respect. They never attempted to convert the numerous nations they conquered. If they found among them religious festivals which seemed useful or agreeable, they adopted them; and if they took a liking to

13. Bardesanes, or Bar Daisan (154–222 A.D.), was a leading exponent of Syrian Gnosticism and an early Christian missionary in Syria. Child may be referring to his work, *The Dialogue of Destiny, or The Book of the Laws of the Countries,* which was recorded by his disciple Philip.

14. Mani, also known as Manes or Manichaeus (216–274? A.D.), was the Iranian founder of Manichaeanism, a dualistic religion that viewed matter as evil and taught asceticism as the means of releasing the spirit from its imprisonment in matter. He made converts in India and regarded the Indian Buddha as one of his precursors.

any of their deities, they placed their images in the Pantheon with their own gods.

These elastic habits of mind may have had considerable influence in producing that system of politic adaptation to circumstances observable in the Christian Church, especially after Constantine had made Christianity the established religion of the state.[15] I believe it is Mosheim, who, in allusion to this process of adaptation to the customs of converted nations, says: "It is difficult to determine whether the heathen were most Christianized, or Christians most heathenized."[16]

The Emperor Constantine was for forty years a worshipper of Apollo, God of the Sun, whom he regarded as his tutelary deity, his own especial guardian and benefactor. Many things show that this long habit of trust and reverence was never quite obliterated from his mind. One of the earliest acts of his reign was to require the universal observance of the Sun's Day; for which purpose he issued a proclamation: "Let all the people rest on the venerated Day of the Sun." Saturday, the seventh day of the week, was the Sabbath of the Jews, and converts from Judaism to Christianity long continued to observe that as their holy day; but Christians were accustomed to meet together on the first day of the week, in memory of the resurrection of Jesus; and as that harmonized with the proclamation of the Emperor, and with an old custom in Grecian and Roman worship, the Sabbath of the Apostles was superseded by Sun-Day.

Festivals that were universally observed, and endeared to the populace by long habit and as occasions for social gatherings, were generally retained by the Christian Church, though the old forms were consecrated to new ideas. Almost all the ancient nations hailed the return of the sun from the winter solstice by a great festival on the 25th of December, during which they performed religious ceremonies in honor of the sun, feasted each other, and interchanged gifts. To have abolished this day would have been as unpopular among the masses of Gentile proselytes as the abolition of Thanksgiving day would be in New England. It was accordingly retained as the birthday of the "Sun of Righteousness," concerning whose real birthday history leaves us entirely in the dark.

The ancient Germans observed in the early spring a festival in honor of

15. Constantine I (280–337 A.D.), emperor of Rome, converted to Christianity in 312, extended toleration to Christians in 313, and made Christianity the state religion in 324.

16. The German Lutheran theologian Johann Lorenz von Mosheim (1694–1755) founded a new school of church history that insisted on objective, critical treatment of original sources.

Ostera, who was probably their Goddess of Nature, or of the Earth. Scholars derive her name from Oster, which signifies rising. The festival was to hail the rising of Nature from her winter sleep. Oster-fires were kindled in honor of the returning warmth, and Oster-eggs were exchanged; the egg being an ancient and very common symbol of fecundity, or germinating life. Teutonic converts to Christianity were allowed to keep up their old festival, but they were taught to do it in honor of the rising of Jesus, instead of the rising of Nature. Easter-fires are still kindled, and Easter-eggs, variously ornamented, are still exchanged in several Catholic countries. Almost all ancient nations had a great festival in the spring. The Jewish Passover occurred at that season. Converts from all nations were well satisfied to keep up their old holiday and accept its new significance.

Religious ceremonies in honor of departed ancestors were universal in the ancient world. Beside the prayers and offerings at tombs by private families, the Roman annually set apart a day for religious ceremonies in memory of all their deceased ancestors. This custom was perpetuated by the Catholic Church under the name of All Souls' day. The day kept by Romans in honor of their departed heroes and benefactors was transferred to the honor of the Christian martyrs under the name of All Saints' day.

Mortals, finding themselves surrounded by solemn mysteries, feeling the need of constant protection, and unable to comprehend the Infinite Being from whom existence is derived, have always manifested a strong tendency to bring God nearer to themselves by means of intermediate spiritual agents. Almost every ancient nation had some Mother Goddess, whose favor they sought to propitiate by prayers and offerings. As Osiris and Isis were believed to take especial care of Egypt, so other countries had each some spiritual protector especially devoted to its interests. It was the same with cities; each was presided over by some deity, as Athens was by Pallas. Trades and individuals had each a tutelary deity, on whose care they especially relied, as the Emperor Constantine did on the God of the Sun. To us these ideas have become mere poetic imagery, mere playthings of the fancy; but it was quite otherwise with our brethren of the ancient world. They verily believed that Naiads did take care of the rivers, and Oreads of the mountains; that Neptune did regulate the waves and storms of the ocean; that Apollo did inspire poets and orators; that Bacchus did fill the grapes with exhilarating juice; that Pan did watch over shepherds and their flocks. To propitiate these numerous Guardian Spirits they placed their images and altars in temples and houses, vineyards and fields, and sought to secure their favor by sacrifices, oblations, and prayers. Gratitude for benefits received was expressed by offerings suited to the occasions. Warriors who had conquered in battle dedicated to Pallas or Bellona[17] spears and shields made of brass or gold. Those who escaped from shipwreck placed in the temple of Neptune oars and models of ships made of wood, ivory, or gold. Beautiful drinking-vessels were dedicated to Bacchus, as thank-offerings for productive vineyards. Successful poets and orators adorned the temples of Apollo and the Muses with crowns and harps of ivory inlaid with gold. Individuals commemorated the birth of children, or recovery from sickness, or escape from danger, by offerings to their tutelary deities, more or less costly according to their wealth, such as garlands, cups of gold or silver, sculptured images, embroidered mantles, and other rich garments. Every five years the people of Athens expressed their gratitude to Pallas for protecting their city by carrying to her temple, in grand procession, a white robe embroidered all over with gold. Pictures were often hung in the temples representing some scene or event which excited peculiar thankfulness to the gods. When people changed their employments or modes of life, it was customary to dedicate implements or articles of furniture to some appropriate deity. When beautiful women grew old, they placed their mirrors in the temple of Venus. Shepherds dedicated to Pan the pipes with which they had been accustomed to call their flocks, and fishermen offered their nets to the Nereids.[18] The particular occasion which induced the offering was sometimes inscribed on the article; and where that was not convenient, the story was written on a tablet and hung up with it. The pillars and walls of the temples were covered with these votive tablets.

When Christianity superseded the old religions, the ancient ideas and forms took new names. By a gradual process of substitution, the Saints of the Catholic Church glided into the place of the old guardian deities. Nations that had been accustomed to worship the Goddess of Nature as a Mother Goddess easily transferred their offerings and prayers to the Virgin Mary, their Spiritual Mother. Every country had its own tutelary Saint, as Saint George of England, Saint Denis of France, Saint James of Spain, and Saint Patrick of Ireland. Each city also had its chosen protector, as Saint Genevieve of Paris, Saint Mark of Venice, and Saint Ambrose of Milan. Every class and trade was under the care of some Saint. Saint Nicholas, whose name has been shortened to Santa Claus, took care of children and of the helpless gener-

17. Bellona was the Roman goddess of war.
18. The Nereids were saltwater nymphs who watched over sailors.

ally; Saint Martha, of cooks and housekeepers; Saint Eloy, of goldsmiths and workers in metals; Saint Crispin, of shoemakers; Saint Blaise, of wool-combers; Saint Jerome, of scholars and learned men; Saint Ursula, of schools and teachers; Saint Magdalen, of frail and penitent women; and Saint Martin, of penitent drunkards. Families and individuals were also under special guardianship. The Medici family were under the protection of Saint Cosmo and Saint Damian. Children in Catholic countries generally receive the name of the Saint on whose Festival-Day they are born; and that Saint is ever after honored by them as their especial protector through life.

The walls and pillars of Catholic churches are as much covered with votive offerings and tablets as were the ancient temples. The jewels and rich garments thus dedicated could not be easily counted. Ferdinand, king of Spain, embroidered a petticoat for the Virgin with his own royal hands; and so elaborately was it ornamented, that it occupied him several years. Wealthy people who wish to propitiate this "Queen of Heaven," or to thank her for some benefit received, often present her with robes and mantles of silk or velvet, richly embroidered, and sometimes adorned with precious gems. But the most common gifts are dresses glittering with tinsel and spangles; while the poorest peasants bring her their simple offerings of ribbons and garlands. Some images of the Virgin are all ablaze with the offerings of her wealthy worshippers, such as golden coronets, diamond rings, costly necklaces and bracelets, and jewelled belts.

Pictures are a common form of votive offerings. In these paintings the donor is usually represented as kneeling before the Virgin, with his own Patron Saint near him, while other Saints, appropriate to the occasion, introduce him to her notice. Pictures intended to express thanks for military success are dedicated to the Madonna under her title of "Our Lady of Victory"; and the kneeling worshipper is introduced to her notice by Saint Michael, Saint George, and Saint Maurice, who are the Patron Saints of soldiers. Pictures to avert epidemic diseases are dedicated to the Madonna under her title of "Our Lady of Mercy." In such cases the suppliant is introduced by Saint Sebastian and Saint Roch, they being protectors against pestilence, and guardians of hospitals. In chapels dedicated to prayers for the dead are many votive pictures representing angels pleading with the Virgin for mercy to the deceased, while lower down are seen other angels drawing liberated souls out of purgatory.

The numerous deities of Greece and Rome were distinguished by symbols, signifying their characters or achievements. Jupiter was represented with a thunderbolt, Neptune with a trident, Minerva with an owl, Apollo with a lyre, and Mercury with a rod twined with serpents. The host of Christian Saints are also distinguished by emblems indicating well-known traditions. Saint Peter is represented with two keys, Saint Agnes with a lamb, Saint John with a sacramental cup, Saint Catherine with a wheel, Saint Lucia with a lamp. Some of these Saints are of universal popularity, others are local favorites. In various subordinate degrees they share the honors paid to the Virgin. Churches and chapels are dedicated to them, adorned with their pictures and symbols, and with their images in marble or ivory, clay or chalk. The walls are hung with votive tablets, written or printed, describing their miraculous intervention to avert dangers or cure diseases. If a cripple has had the use of a limb restored, he hangs up in the church of some Saint a written record of the miracle, often accompanied by an image of an arm or a leg, made of marble, ivory, or wax. Saint Agnes, who is the guardian of youth and innocence, has her altars covered with votive garlands and images of lambs. Saint Margaret, who presides over birth, shares with the Madonna many votive offerings of baby-dolls, more or less richly dressed.

Thus is human life in all its phases presented to the notice and protection of tutelary saints, as it formerly was to tutelary deities. It is curious to trace the manner in which the multifarious traditions of these saints have grown up.

Professor Max Müller,[19] in one of his lectures, describes a singular migration from the records of Eastern Saints into those of the Western. Johannes Damascenus, who was a famous Christian theologian a thousand years ago, had passed his youth in the court of the Caliph Almanzor, where his father held a position of trust. There he stored his mind with Asiatic lore, and the Life of Buddha was among the books he read. His imagination was captivated by the account of that prince, whose tenderness of heart had led him to renounce his rank and devote himself to prayers for his fellow-creatures and to the alleviation of their misery. Damascenus wove the main points of the story into a religious novel entitled "Balaam and Josaphat." A later age accepted it as the veritable history of a Christian Saint; and thus Buddha became regularly canonized under the name of Saint Josaphat, whose festival is observed by the Greek Church on the 16th of August, and by the Roman Catholic Church on the 27th of November.

Whether there was the same facility in adopting widely extended and deeply rooted doctrines, that was manifested in the adoption of old customs

19. The German orientalist Max Müller (1823–1900) taught modern languages and comparative philology at Oxford and edited *The Sacred Books of the East* (51 vols., 1879–1904). Child may have read his essay "Comparative Mythology" (*Oxford Essays*, 1856).

and legends, is an open question. In ambitious minds, a desire to extend the power and increase the wealth of the Church would prove a very strong temptation to compromise with the preconceived ideas of influential converts; and even devout, unselfish men might be drawn into it by a benevolent wish to bring peoples into a better form of religion by such processes as were readiest at hand. Paul, whose life was spent in Gentile lands, seems to have lost much of Jewish exclusiveness, and to have acquired something of Grecian and Roman facility of adaptation to circumstances. To the church at Corinth he wrote: "Unto the Jews I became as a Jew, that I might gain the Jews; to them that are without the Law [of Moses] as without the Law, that I might gain them that are without the Law. To the weak became I as weak, that I might gain the weak: I am made all things to all men, that I might by all means save some."

Such intermingling of various elements is by no means peculiar to the Christian Church. It is according to the laws of human nature. The same mosaic of patterns and colors can be found throughout the world's history, in all changes of Church or State, by whomsoever seeks the separate stones that form the picture. The modern theory that nothing is created entirely new, but that every form of being is the development of some antecedent form, may or may not be true in natural science, but it is certainly true of all spiritual progress.

When mortals find a kernel of truth, they seek to appropriate it as exclusively their own; and whatsoever kernel is picked up by others is declared to be a stone, from which no bread of life can ever be produced. But the great harvest-field of the world is managed on different principles by the Father of All. While men are planting in narrow enclosures, he sends forth seed upon the winds; he scatters them on great floods, whose waters subside and leave them in rich alluvial soil; and birds of the air, unconscious of anything but their own subsistence, are his agents to scatter them abroad all over the earth. And when we think we have the harvest all to ourselves, lo! we find the same grain waving in far-off fields.

Undeniably there *is* a strong resemblance between the Buddhist and Roman Catholic churches; and whether India is the borrower or the lender does not affect the assertion that John Chinaman and Patrick O'Dublin have an equal right to the free exercise of their religion under our impartial laws.[20] All

20. "John Chinaman" and "Patrick O'Dublin" were stock names for Chinese and Irishmen. Child is responding to both Protestant persecution of Irish Catholics and Irish-led efforts to ban Chinese immigration.

we have to do, in either case, is to spread abroad as much light as possible, that all men may have a chance to distinguish between the true and the spurious. Having done this duty, we must leave the result to time.

Enlightened travellers would doubtless find in Buddhist countries a vast deal that seemed like very puerile and absurd superstitions and gross immorality under the garb of religion; but a similar impression would be produced on their minds by a sojourn in Italy or Spain. The Catholic Church abounds in holy sayings and examples, and because it is a Christian church they do not excite our surprise; but when we find similar things among the Buddhists, we ask with astonishment whence they could possibly have come; forgetful that "God is the Father of *all*," and that "*every* good gift cometh from him." The Commandments of the Buddhists are very similar to our own. There are commands not to kill, not to steal, not to lie, not to be licentious, and not to utter slanders; and to these are added, "Thou shalt not drink wine, nor any intoxicating liquors." "Thou shalt not excite quarrels by repeating the words of others." "Thou shalt not speak of injuries." The following are among the maxims of Buddhist Saints: "Glory not in thyself, but rather in thy neighbor." "Be lowly in thy heart, that thou mayest be lowly in thy acts." "Judge not thy neighbor." "Be equally kind to all men." "Use no perfumes but the sweetness of thy thoughts." In some respects Buddhism can show a cleaner record than Christianity. It has had no such institution as the Inquisition, and has never put men to death for heretical opinions. They treat with reverence whatsoever is deemed holy by other men. When the king of Siam was told that an image in his court was Saint Peter, he immediately said to his little boy, "Do obeisance to it, my son; it is one of the holy men." When the Jesuit missionaries Huc and Gabet explained to one of the Lamas that they were from France, he replied: "What matter where you are from? All men are brothers. Men of prayer belong to all countries. They are strangers nowhere. Such is the doctrine taught by our Holy Books." He took up their breviary; and when they informed him what it was, he raised it reverentially to his forehead, saying, "It is your book of prayer. We ought always to honor and respect prayer."

Though the Founder of Christianity preached a Gospel of Peace, the religion that took his name was far from being peaceful in its progress, after the first three centuries.[21] Into Armenia, Norway, and Germany Christianity was introduced at the point of the sword. Conquered armies had no alterna-

---

21. Child is replying here to James Freeman Clarke's claim that Christianity spread peacefully, in contrast to other religions (see his *Ten Great Religions* 18–19).

tive but baptism or slaughter. And the number of Jews, Romans, and heretics who were slain to bring about the unity of the Christian Church is too large for calculation. Though Buddhism spread through many countries, I have found no record that it was in a single instance established by force.

The fact is, the more we know of our brethren in the East, the more the conviction grows upon us that Buddha was a great reformer and a benevolent, holy man. The present state of the world is in some respects similar to its condition at the commencement of our era. Electricity and steam bring remote countries into acquaintance with each other. Old traditions are everywhere relaxing their hold upon the minds of men. From all parts of the world come increasing manifestations of a tendency toward eclecticism. Men find there are gems hidden among all sorts of rubbish. These will be selected and combined in that Church of the Future now in the process of formation. We shall not live to see it; but we may be certain that, according to the laws of spiritual growth, it will retain a likeness to all the present, as the present does to all the past. But it will stand on a higher plane, be larger in its proportions, and more harmonious in its beauty. Milan Cathedral, lifting its thousand snow-white images of saints into the clear blue of heaven, is typical of that Eclectic Church, which shall gather forms of holy aspiration from all ages and nations, and set them on high in their immortal beauty, with the sunlight of heaven to glorify them all.

Suggestions for Further Reading

1. Selected Works of Lydia Maria Child (Listed Chronologically)

Hobomok, A Tale of Early Times. By An American. Boston: Cummings, Hilliard, 1824. *HOBOMOK and Other Writings on Indians.* Ed. Carolyn L. Karcher. New Brunswick: Rutgers UP, 1986. 1–150.

Evenings in New England. Intended for Juvenile Amusement and Instruction. By An American Lady. Boston: Cummings, Hilliard, 1824.

The Rebels, or Boston before the Revolution. By the author of *Hobomok.* Boston: Cummings, Hilliard, 1825.

"Adventure in the Woods." *Juvenile Miscellany* 1 (Sept. 1826): 5–13.

"The Adventures of a Bell." *Juvenile Miscellany* 2 (Mar. 1827): 24–30.

"The Indian Boy." *Juvenile Miscellany* 2 (May 1827): 28–31.

The First Settlers of New-England: or, Conquest of the Pequods, Narragansets and Pokanokets: As Related by a Mother to Her Children, and Designed for the Instruction of Youth. By a Lady of Massachusetts. Boston: Munroe & Francis/New York: Charles S. Francis, [1829].

The Frugal Housewife. Boston: Marsh & Capen, and Carter & Hendee, 1829.

The Mother's Book. Boston: Carter, Hendee & Babcock/Baltimore: Charles Carter, 1831.

The Coronal. A Collection of Miscellaneous Pieces, Written at Various Times. Boston: Carter & Hendee, 1832.

An Appeal in Favor of That Class of Americans Called Africans. Boston: Allen and Ticknor, 1833. Ed. Carolyn L. Karcher. Amherst: U of Massachusetts P, 1996.

"Mary French and Susan Easton." *Juvenile Miscellany* 3rd ser. 6 (May 1834): 186–202.

The Oasis (edited, with contributions by Child, including "Malem-Boo. The Brazilian Slave"). Boston: Allen and Ticknor, 1834.

The History of the Condition of Women, in Various Ages and Nations. Vols. 4 and 5 of *Ladies' Family Library.* Boston: John Allen, 1835.

Anti-Slavery Catechism. Newburyport, Mass.: Charles Whipple, 1836.

Philothea. A Romance. Boston: Otis, Broaders/New York: George Dearborn, 1836.

Letters from New-York [First Series]. New York: Charles S. Francis/Boston: James Munroe, 1843; London: Bentley, 1843.

Flowers for Children. I. (For Children Eight or Nine Years Old). New York: C. S. Francis/Boston: J. H. Francis, 1844.

Flowers for Children. II. (For Children from Four to Six Year Old). New York: C. S. Francis, 1845.

Letters from New York. Second Series. New York: C. S. Francis/Boston: J. H. Francis, 1845.

Fact and Fiction: A Collection of Stories. New York: C. S. Francis/Boston: J. H. Francis, 1846.

Flowers for Children. III. (For Children of Eleven and Twelve Years of Age). New York: C. S. Francis/Boston: J. H. Francis, 1847.

Isaac T. Hopper: A True Life. Boston: John P. Jewett/Cleveland: Jewett, Proctor & Worthington/London: Sampson Low, 1853.

The Progress of Religious Ideas, Through Successive Ages. 3 vols. New York: C. S. Francis/London: S. Low, 1855.

A New Flower for Children. New York: C. S. Francis, 1856.

Autumnal Leaves: Tales and Sketches in Prose and Rhyme. New York: C. S. Francis, 1857.

"Loo Loo. A Few Scenes from a True History." *Atlantic Monthly* 1 (May 1858): 801–12; (June 1858): 32–42.

Correspondence between Lydia Maria Child and Gov. Wise and Mrs. Mason, of Virginia. Boston: American Anti-Slavery Society, 1860.

The Right Way the Safe Way, Proved by Emancipation in the British West Indies, and Elsewhere. New York: 5 Beekman Street, 1860.

The Patriarchal Institution, As Described by Members of Its Own Family. Ed. Lydia Maria Child. New York: American Anti-Slavery Society, 1860.

The Duty of Disobedience to the Fugitive Slave Act: An Appeal to the Legislators of Massachusetts. Boston: American Anti-Slavery Society, 1860.

Jacobs, Harriet A. *Incidents in the Life of a Slave Girl*. Ed. Lydia Maria Child. Boston: privately published, 1861. Ed. Jean Fagan Yellin. Cambridge: Harvard UP, 1987.

Looking toward Sunset. From Sources Old and New, Original and Selected (edited, with contributions by Child). Boston: Ticknor and Fields, 1865.

The Freedmen's Book (edited, with contributions by Child). Boston: Ticknor and Fields, 1865.

A Romance of the Republic. Boston: Ticknor and Fields, 1867.

"Letter from L. Maria Child" [on the labor question]. *National Standard* 17 Sept. 1870: 5. CC 74/1959a.

"Resemblances between the Buddhist and the Roman Catholic Religions." *Atlantic Monthly* 26 (Dec. 1870): 660–65.

"Economy and Work." *National Standard* 5 Aug. 1871: 4–5.

Aspirations of the World. A Chain of Opals (edited with an introductory essay by Child). Boston: Roberts Brothers, 1878.

Letters of Lydia Maria Child with a Biographical Introduction by John Greenleaf Whittier and an Appendix by Wendell Phillips. [Ed. Harriet Winslow Sewall]. Boston: Houghton Mifflin, 1882.

The Collected Correspondence of Lydia Maria Child, 1817–1880 (abbreviated as *CC*). Ed. Patricia G. Holland, Milton Meltzer, and Francine Krasno. Millwood, N.Y.: Kraus Microform, 1980.

Lydia Maria Child: Selected Letters, 1817–1880 (abbreviated as *SL*). Ed. Milton Meltzer, Patricia G. Holland, and Francine Krasno. Amherst: U of Massachusetts P, 1982.

2. Works about Lydia Maria Child

Abzug, Robert H. *Cosmos Crumbling: American Reform and the Religious Imagination*. New York: Oxford UP, 1994. 193–202.

Arch, Stephen Carl. "Romancing the Puritans: American Historical Fiction in the 1820s." *ESQ: A Journal of the American Renaissance* 39 (2nd and 3rd Quarters 1993): 107–32.

Baer, Helene G. *The Heart Is Like Heaven: The Life of Lydia Maria Child.* Philadelphia: U of Pennsylvania P, 1964.

Baym, Nina. *American Women Writers and the Work of History, 1790–1860.* New Brunswick: Rutgers UP, 1995.

——. *Feminism and American Literary History.* New Brunswick: Rutgers UP, 1992. 22–25.

Clifford, Deborah Pickman. *Crusader for Freedom: A Life of Lydia Maria Child.* Boston: Beacon, 1992.

Conrad, Susan Phinney. *Perish the Thought: Intellectual Women in Romantic America, 1830–1860.* New York: Oxford UP, 1976.

Dall, Caroline Healey. "Lydia Maria Child and Mary Russell Mitford." *Unitarian Review* 19 (June 1883): 519–34.

Fetterley, Judith, ed. *Provisions: A Reader from 19th-Century American Women.* Bloomington: Indiana UP, 1985. 159–67.

Finkelman, Paul. "Manufacturing Martyrdom: The Antislavery Response to John Brown's Raid." *His Soul Goes Marching On: Responses to John Brown and the Harpers Ferry Raid.* Ed. Paul Finkelman. Charlottesville: UP of Virginia, 1995. 41–66.

Hallowell, Anna D. "Lydia Maria Child." *Medford Historical Register* 3 (July 1900): 95–117.

Higginson, Thomas Wentworth. "Lydia Maria Child." *Contemporaries.* Vol. 2 of *Writings of Thomas Wentworth Higginson.* Boston: Houghton Mifflin, 1900. 108–41.

Holland, Patricia G. "Lydia Maria Child As a Nineteenth-Century Professional Author." *Studies in the American Renaissance* 1981: 157–67.

Holland, Patricia G., Milton Meltzer, and Francine Krasno. *The Collected Correspondence of Lydia Maria Child, 1817–1880. Guide and Index to the Microfiche Edition.* Millwood, N.Y.: Kraus Microform, 1980.

Jeffrey, Kirk. "Marriage, Career, and Feminine Ideology in Nineteenth-Century America: Reconstructing the Marital Experience of Lydia Maria Child, 1828–1874." *Feminist Studies* 2 (No. 2/3, 1975): 113–30.

Karcher, Carolyn L. *The First Woman in the Republic: A Cultural Biography of Lydia Maria Child.* Durham: Duke UP, 1994.

Kerber, Linda K. "The Abolitionist Perception of the Indian." *Journal of American History* 62 (Sept. 1975): 271–95.

Maddox, Lucy. *Removals: Nineteenth-Century American Literature and the Politics of Indian Affairs.* New York: Oxford UP, 1991. 92–103.

Marshall, Ian. "Heteroglossia in Lydia Maria Child's *Hobomok.*" *Legacy: A Journal of American Women Writers* 10 (No. 1, 1993): 1–16.

Meltzer, Milton. *Tongue of Flame: The Life of Lydia Maria Child.* New York: Crowell, 1965.

Mills, Bruce. *Cultural Reformations: Lydia Maria Child and the Literature of Reform.* Athens: U of Georgia P, 1994.

Nelson, Dana D. *The Word in Black and White: Reading "Race" in American Literature, 1638–1867.* New York: Oxford UP, 1992. 78–89.

Osborne, William S. *Lydia Maria Child.* Boston: Twayne, 1980.

Person, Leland S., Jr. "The American Eve: Miscegenation and a Feminist Frontier Fiction."
American Quarterly 37 (Winter 1985): 668–85.

Samuels, Shirley. *The Culture of Sentiment: Race, Gender, and Sentimentality in
Nineteenth-Century America.* New York: Oxford UP, 1992. 157–71.

Sánchez-Eppler, Karen. *Touching Liberty: Abolition, Feminism, and the Politics of the Body.*
Berkeley: U of California P, 1993. 14–49.

Smith, Stephanie A. *Conceived by Liberty: Maternal Figures and Nineteenth-Century American Literature.* Ithaca: Cornell UP, 1994. 31–68.

Streeter, Robert E. "Mrs. Child's 'Philothea'—a Transcendental Novel?" *New England
Quarterly* 16 (Dec. 1943): 648–54.

Venet, Wendy Hamand. " 'Cry Aloud and Spare Not': Northern Antislavery Women and
John Brown's Raid." *His Soul Goes Marching On: Responses to John Brown and the
Harpers Ferry Raid.* Ed. Paul Finkelman. Charlottesville: UP of Virginia, 1995. 98–115.

Yellin, Jean Fagan. *Women and Sisters: The Antislavery Feminists in American Culture.* New
Haven: Yale UP, 1989. 53–76.

3. The Indian Question

Berkhofer, Robert F. Jr. *The White Man's Indian: Images of the American Indian from
Columbus to the Present.* 1978. New York: Vintage-Random, 1979.

Brown, Dee. *Bury My Heart at Wounded Knee: An Indian History of the American West.*
New York: Holt, 1970.

Dippie, Brian W. *The Vanishing American: White Attitudes and U.S. Indian Policy.* Middletown: Wesleyan UP, 1982.

Drinnon, Richard. *Facing West: The Metaphysics of Indian-Hating and Empire-Building.*
New York: New American Library, 1980.

Eckstorm, Fannie Hardy. "The Attack on Norridgewock, 1724." *New England Quarterly* 7
(Sept. 1934): 541–78.

Francis, Convers. "Life of Sebastian Rale, Missionary to the Indians." *Lives of John Ribault,
Sebastian Rale, and William Palfrey.* Boston: Little, Brown, 1845. 159–333. Vol. 17 of
Library of American Biography. Ed. Jared Sparks.

Kerber, Linda K. "The Abolitionist Perception of the Indian." *Journal of American History*
62 (Sept. 1975): 271–95.

Kolodny, Annette. *The Land Before Her: Fantasy and Experience of the American Frontiers,
1630–1860.* Chapel Hill: U of North Carolina P, 1984.

Maddox, Lucy. *Removals: Nineteenth-Century American Literature and the Politics of Indian Affairs.* New York: Oxford UP, 1991.

Mardock, Robert W. *Reformers and the American Indian.* Columbia: U of Missouri P, 1971.

Pearce, Roy Harvey. *The Savages of America: A Study of the Indian and the Idea of Civilization.* Rev. ed. Baltimore: Johns Hopkins UP, 1965.

Perdue, Theda, and Michael D. Green, eds. *The Cherokee Removal: A Brief History with
Documents.* New York: Bedford-St. Martin's, 1995.

Slotkin, Richard. *The Fatal Environment: The Myth of the Frontier in the Age of Industrialization, 1800–1890.* 1985. Middletown: Wesleyan UP, 1986.

——. *Regeneration through Violence: The Mythology of the American Frontier, 1600–1860.* Middletown: Wesleyan UP, 1973.

United States. Cong. House. *Annual Report of the Commissioner on Indian Affairs.* 40th Cong., 3rd Sess. 1868. "Report to the President by the Indian Peace Commission, January 7, 1868." House Executive Document 1: 486–510.

4. Children's Literature and Domestic Advice

Ariès, Philippe. *Centuries of Childhood: A Social History of Family Life.* Trans. Robert K. Baldic. New York: Random-Vintage, 1962.

Beecher, Catharine. *Treatise on Domestic Economy, for the Use of Young Ladies at Home, and at School.* 1841. Rev. ed. New York: Harper and Brothers, 1845.

Brodhead, Richard H. "Sparing the Rod: Discipline and Fiction in Antebellum America." *Representations* 21 (Winter 1988): 67–96.

Cole, Thomas R. *The Journey of Life: A Cultural History of Aging in America.* Cambridge: Cambridge UP, 1992.

Degler, Carl N. *At Odds: Women and the Family in America from the Revolution to the Present.* New York: Oxford UP, 1980.

Elbert, Sarah. *A Hunger for Home: Louisa May Alcott's Place in American Culture.* New Brunswick: Rutgers UP, 1987.

Fischer, David Hackett. *Growing Old in America.* Rev. ed. New York: Oxford UP, 1978.

Kelly, R. Gordon, ed. *Children's Periodicals of the United States.* Westport: Greenwood, 1984.

——. *Mother Was a Lady: Self and Society in Selected American Children's Periodicals, 1865–1890.* Westport: Greenwood, 1974.

Kerber, Linda K. *Women of the Republic: Intellect and Ideology in Revolutionary America.* Chapel Hill: U of North Carolina P, 1980.

Kramnick, Isaac. "Children's Literature and Bourgeois Ideology: Observations on Culture and Industrial Capitalism in the Later Eighteenth Century." *Culture and Politics: From Puritanism to the Enlightenment.* Ed. Perez Zagorin. Berkeley: U of California P, 1980.

Kuhn, Anne L. *The Mother's Role in Childhood Education: New England Concepts, 1830–1860.* New Haven: Yale UP, 1947.

MacLeod, Anne Scott. *A Moral Tale: Children's Fiction and American Culture, 1820–1860.* Hamden, Conn.: Archon, 1975.

Reinier, Jacqueline S. "Rearing the Republican Child: Attitudes and Practices in Post-Revolutionary Philadelphia." *William and Mary Quarterly* 39 (Jan. 1982): 150–63.

Ryan, Mary P. *Cradle of the Middle Class: The Family in Oneida County, New York, 1790–1865.* New York: Cambridge UP, 1981.

——. *The Empire of the Mother: American Writing about Domesticity, 1830–1860.* New York: Haworth, 1982.

Sigourney, Lydia Huntley. *Letters to Mothers.* New York: Harper and Brothers, 1838.

Sklar, Kathryn Kish. *Catharine Beecher: A Study in American Domesticity.* 1973. New York: Norton, 1976.

5. Slavery, Race, and Reconstruction

Aptheker, Herbert. *Abolitionism: A Revolutionary Movement.* Boston: Twayne-Hall, 1989.
——. *American Negro Slave Revolts.* 1943. New York: International Publishers, 1952.
Berlin, Ira. *Slaves without Masters: The Free Negro in the Antebellum South.* 1974. New York: Vintage-Random, 1976.
Bernstein, Iver. *The New York City Draft Riots: Their Significance for American Society and Politics in the Age of the Civil War.* New York: Oxford UP, 1990.
Blassingame, John W. *The Slave Community: Plantation Life in the Antebellum South.* New York: Oxford UP, 1972.
Blight, David W. *Frederick Douglass' Civil War: Keeping Faith in Jubilee.* Baton Rouge: Louisiana State UP, 1989.
Cain, William E., ed. *William Lloyd Garrison and the Fight against Slavery: Selections from* The Liberator. Boston: Bedford-St. Martin's, 1995.
Davis, David Brion. *The Problem of Slavery in the Age of Revolution, 1770–1823.* Ithaca: Cornell UP, 1975.
Delany, Martin R. *Blake; or, The Huts of America.* 1859. Ed. Floyd J. Miller. Boston: Beacon P, 1970.
——. *The Condition, Elevation, Emigration and Destiny of the Colored People of the United States.* 1852. Baltimore: Black Classic, 1993.
Dillon, Merton L. *The Abolitionists: The Growth of a Dissenting Minority.* De Kalb: Northern Illinois UP, 1974.
Douglass, Frederick. *Life and Times of Frederick Douglass.* 1892. New York: Collier-Macmillan, 1962.
——. *My Bondage and My Freedom.* 1855. New York: Dover, 1969.
——. *Narrative of the Life of Frederick Douglass, an American Slave. Written by Himself.* 1845. *The Oxford Frederick Douglass Reader.* Ed. William L. Andrews. New York: Oxford UP, 1996. 21–97.
Du Bois, W. E. B. *Black Reconstruction in America, 1860–1880.* 1935. New York: Atheneum, 1977.
Duncan, Russell, ed. *Blue-Eyed Child of Fortune: The Civil War Letters of Colonel Robert Gould Shaw.* Athens: U of Georgia P, 1992.
Filler, Louis. *The Crusade against Slavery, 1830–1860.* New York: Harper, 1960.
Finkelman, Paul, ed. *His Soul Goes Marching On: Responses to John Brown and the Harpers Ferry Raid.* Charlottesville: UP of Virginia, 1995.
Foner, Eric. *Free Soil, Free Labor, Free Men: The Ideology of the Republican Party before the Civil War.* New York: Oxford UP, 1970.
——. *Politics and Ideology in the Age of the Civil War.* New York: Oxford UP, 1980.

——. *Reconstruction: America's Unfinished Revolution, 1863–1877.* New York: Harper, 1988.

Foster, Frances Smith, ed. *A Brighter Coming Day: A Frances Ellen Watkins Harper Reader.* New York: Feminist, 1990.

Fredrickson, George M. *The Black Image in the White Mind: The Debate on Afro-American Character and Destiny, 1817–1914.* New York: Harper, 1971.

——. *The Inner Civil War: Northern Intellectuals and the Crisis of the Union.* 1965. New York: Harper, 1968.

Friedman, Lawrence J. *Gregarious Saints: Self and Community in American Abolitionism, 1830–1870.* New York: Cambridge UP, 1982.

Garrison, William Lloyd. *The Letters of William Lloyd Garrison,* ed. Walter M. Merrill and Louis Ruchames. 6 vols. Cambridge: Belnap-Harvard UP, 1971–81.

Genovese, Eugene D. *Roll, Jordan, Roll: The World the Slaves Made.* New York: Pantheon, 1974.

Grimké, Angelina. *Appeal to the Christian Women of the South.* 1836. Reprint, New York: Arno P and *New York Times,* 1969.

Harding, Vincent. *There Is a River: The Black Struggle for Freedom in America.* 1981. New York: Vintage-Random, 1983.

Jacobs, Harriet A. *Incidents in the Life of a Slave Girl. Written by Herself.* Ed. Lydia Maria Child. 1861. Ed. Jean Fagan Yellin. Cambridge: Harvard UP, 1987.

Kraditor, Aileen S. *Means and Ends in American Abolitionism: Garrison and His Critics on Strategy and Tactics, 1834–1850.* New York: Pantheon, 1969.

Litwack, Leonard L. *North of Slavery: The Negro in the Free States, 1790–1860.* Chicago: U of Chicago P, 1961.

Masur, Louis P. *"The Real War Will Never Get in the Books": Selections from Writers During the Civil War.* New York: Oxford UP, 1993.

McPherson, James M. *Battle Cry of Freedom: The Civil War Era.* 1988. New York: Ballantine, 1989.

——. *The Struggle for Equality: Abolitionists and the Negro in the Civil War and Reconstruction.* Princeton: Princeton UP, 1964.

Nye, Russel B. *Fettered Freedom: Civil Liberties and the Slavery Controversy, 1830–1860.* 1963. Urbana: U of Illinois P, 1972.

Pease, Jane H., and William H. Pease. *Bound with Them in Chains: A Biographical History of the Antislavery Movement.* Westport: Greenwood, 1972.

Perry, Lewis. *Radical Abolitionism: Anarchy and the Government of God in Antislavery Thought.* Ithaca: Cornell UP, 1973.

Perry, Lewis, and Michael Fellman. *Antislavery Reconsidered: New Perspectives on the Abolitionists.* Baton Rouge: Louisiana State UP, 1979.

[Putnam, Mary Lowell]. *Record of an Obscure Man.* Boston: Ticknor and Fields, 1861.

Quarles, Benjamin. *Black Abolitionists.* New York: Oxford UP, 1969.

Rawick, George P. *From Sundown to Sunup: The Making of the Black Community.* Westport: Greenwood, 1972.

Richards, Leonard L. *"Gentlemen of Property and Standing": Anti-Abolition Mobs in Jacksonian America.* New York: Oxford UP, 1970.

Ripley, C. Peter. et al., eds. *Witness for Freedom: African American Voices on Race, Slavery, and Emancipation.* Chapel Hill: U of North Carolina P, 1993.

Ruchames, Louis, ed. *The Abolitionists: A Collection of Their Writings.* New York: Putnam, 1963.

——, ed. *A John Brown Reader: The Story of John Brown in His Own Words, in the Words of Those Who Knew Him, and in the Poetry and Prose of the Literary Heritage.* New York: Abelard-Schuman, 1959.

Stampp, Kenneth M. *The Peculiar Institution: Slavery in the Ante-Bellum South.* New York: Knopf, 1956.

Sterling, Dorothy. *Ahead of Her Time: Abby Kelley and the Politics of Antislavery.* New York: Norton, 1991.

Stewart, James Brewer. *Holy Warriors: The Abolitionists and American Slavery.* New York: Hill and Wang, 1976.

Stuckey, Sterling. *Going through the Storm: The Influence of African American Art in History.* New York: Oxford UP, 1994.

——. *Slave Culture: Nationalist Theory and the Foundations of Black America.* New York: Oxford UP, 1987.

Venet, Wendy Hamand. *Neither Ballots Nor Bullets: Women Abolitionists and the Civil War.* Charlottesville: UP of Virginia, 1991.

Walker, David. *Appeal to the Coloured Citizens of the World, but in particular, and very expressly, to those of the United States of America.* 1829. Ed. Charles M. Wiltse. New York: Hill and Wang, 1965.

Walters, Ronald G. *The Antislavery Appeal: American Abolitionism After 1830.* Baltimore: Johns Hopkins UP, 1976.

[Weld, Theodore Dwight, Angelina Grimké Weld, and Sarah Grimké]. *American Slavery As It Is. Testimony of a Thousand Witnesses.* 1839. Arno P and *New York Times*, 1969.

White, Deborah Gray. *Ar'n't I a Woman? Female Slaves in the Plantation South.* New York: Norton, 1985.

Yellin, Jean Fagan. *Women and Sisters: The Antislavery Feminists in American Culture.* New Haven: Yale UP, 1989.

Yellin, Jean Fagan, and John C. Van Horne, eds. *The Abolitionist Sisterhood: Women's Political Culture in Antebellum America.* Ithaca: Cornell UP, 1994.

6. Journalism and Social Critique

Fern, Fanny. *RUTH HALL and Other Writings.* Ed. Joyce W. Warren. New Brunswick: Rutgers UP, 1986.

Freedman, Estelle B. *Their Sisters' Keepers: Women's Prison Reform in America, 1830–1930.* Ann Arbor: U of Michigan P, 1981.

Fuller, Margaret. *The Portable Margaret Fuller.* Ed. Mary Kelley. New York: Penguin, 1994.

——. *"These Sad but Glorious Days": Dispatches from Europe, 1846–1850.* Ed. Larry J. Reynolds and Susan Belasco Smith. New Haven: Yale UP, 1991.

Rothman, David J. *The Discovery of the Asylum: Social Order and Disorder in the New Republic.* 1971. Rev. ed. Boston: Little, 1990.

Stansell, Christine. *City of Women: Sex and Class in New York, 1789–1860.* 1982. Urbana: U of Illinois P, 1987.

7. The Woman Question

Abzug, Robert H. *Cosmos Crumbling: American Reform and the Religious Imagination.* New York: Oxford UP, 1994. 183–229.

Boydston, Jeanne, Mary Kelley, and Anne Margolis. *The Limits of Sisterhood: The Beecher Sisters on Women's Rights and Woman's Sphere.* Chapel Hill: U of North Carolina P, 1988.

Braude, Ann. *Radical Spirits: Spiritualism and Women's Rights in Nineteenth-Century America.* Boston: Beacon, 1989.

Carby, Hazel. *Reconstructing Womanhood: The Emergence of the Afro-American Woman Novelist.* New York: Oxford UP, 1987.

Cott, Nancy F. *The Bonds of Womanhood: "Woman's Sphere" in New England, 1790–1835.* New Haven: Yale UP, 1977.

DuBois, Ellen Carol. *Feminism and Suffrage: The Emergence of an Independent Woman's Movement in America, 1848–1869.* New York: Columbia UP, 1978.

Flexner, Eleanor. *Century of Struggle: The Woman's Rights Movement in the United States.* 1959. New York: Atheneum, 1973.

Foster, Frances Smith, ed. *A Brighter Coming Day: A Frances Ellen Watkins Harper Reader.* New York: Feminist, 1990.

——. *Written by Herself: Literary Production by African American Women, 1746–1892.* Bloomington: Indiana UP, 1993.

Fuller, Margaret. *Woman in the Nineteenth Century.* 1845. *The Portable Margaret Fuller.* Ed. Mary Kelley. New York: Viking-Penguin, 1994. 228–62.

Griffith, Elisabeth. *In Her Own Right: The Life of Elizabeth Cady Stanton.* New York: Oxford UP, 1984.

Grimké, Sarah Moore. *Letters on the Equality of the Sexes, and the Condition of Woman. Addressed to Mary S. Parker, President of the Boston Female Anti-Slavery Society.* 1838. New York: Source Book, 1970.

Hersh, Blanche Glassman. *The Slavery of Sex: Feminist-Abolitionists in America.* Urbana: U of Illinois P, 1978.

Hewitt, Nancy A. *Women's Activism and Social Change: Rochester, New York, 1822–1872.* Ithaca: Cornell UP, 1984.

Kerr, Andrea Moore. *Lucy Stone: Speaking Out for Equality.* New Brunswick: Rutgers UP, 1992.

Lerner, Gerda. *The Grimké Sisters from South Carolina: Rebels against Slavery.* Boston: Houghton, 1967.

——. *The Majority Finds Its Past: Placing Women in History.* New York: Oxford UP, 1979.

Melder, Keith E. *Beginnings of Sisterhood: The American Woman's Rights Movement, 1800–1850.* New York: Schocken, 1977.

Peterson, Carla L. *"Doers of the Word": African-American Women Speakers and Writers in the North, 1830–1880.* New York: Oxford UP, 1995.

Smith-Rosenberg, Carroll. *Disorderly Conduct: Visions of Gender in Victorian America.* New York: Oxford UP, 1985.

Stanton, Elizabeth Cady, with Susan B. Anthony, Matilda Joslyn Gage, Ida Husted Harper, and others. *History of Woman Suffrage.* 6 vols. New York: Fowler and Wells, 1881–1922.

Sterling, Dorothy. *Ahead of Her Time: Abby Kelley and the Politics of Antislavery.* New York: Norton, 1991.

Yellin, Jean Fagan. *Women and Sisters: The Antislavery Feminists in American Culture.* New Haven: Yale UP, 1989.

Yellin, Jean Fagan and John C. Van Horne, eds. *The Abolitionist Sisterhood: Women's Political Culture in Antebellum America.* Ithaca: Cornell UP, 1994.

8. Religion

Abzug, Robert H. *Cosmos Crumbling: American Reform and the Religious Imagination.* New York: Oxford UP, 1994.

Ahlstrom, Sydney E. *A Religious History of the American People.* New Haven: Yale UP, 1972.

Christy, Arthur. *The Orient in American Transcendentalism: A Study of Emerson, Thoreau, and Alcott.* 1932. New York: Octagon, 1963.

Clarke, James Freeman. *Ten Great Religions: An Essay in Comparative Theology.* Boston: James R. Osgood, 1871.

Higginson, Thomas Wentworth. *The Sympathy of Religions.* Boston: Free Religious Association, 1876.

Howe, Daniel Walker. *The Unitarian Conscience: Harvard Moral Philosophy, 1805–1861.* Cambridge: Harvard UP, 1970.

Miller, Perry, ed. *The Transcendentalists: An Anthology.* Cambridge: Harvard UP, 1950.

Muller, Friedrich Max. *Comparative Mythology.* New York: Arno, 1977.

Persons, Stow. *Free Religion: An American Faith.* New Haven: Yale UP, 1947.

Reynolds, David S. *Faith in Fiction: The Emergence of Religious Literature in America.* Cambridge: Harvard UP, 1981.

Robinson, David. *The Unitarians and Universalists.* Westport: Greenwood, 1985.

Sharpe, Eric J. *Comparative Religion: A History.* London: Duckworth, 1975.

Stanton, Elizabeth Cady. *The Woman's Bible.* 1895. Boston: Northeastern UP, 1993.

Index

Grateful acknowledgment is made to the Boston Athenaeum for permission to use the 1865 carte-de-visite photograph of Child by John Adams Whipple that appears on the cover; the Massachusetts Historical Society for permission to quote from Child's uncollected and unpublished letters of 28 Aug. [1827] and 31 May 1834 to Catharine Maria Sedgwick in the Catharine Maria Sedgwick Papers, Part III, and from Mary T. Peabody to Miss Rawlins Pickman, 16 Apr. 1826, in the Horace Mann II Papers; Rutgers University Press for permission to reprint "The Church in the Wilderness," "Willie Wharton," and *An Appeal for the Indians*, and the accompanying annotations, from *HOBOMOK and Other Writings on Indians* (New Brunswick: Rutgers UP, 1986, 1995); and the University of Massachusetts Press for permission to reprint Chapter 8 from *An Appeal in Favor of That Class of Americans Called Africans* (Amherst: U of Massachusetts P, 1996), with the accompanying textual notes by Patricia G. Holland.

Carolyn L. Karcher is Professor of English, American Studies, and Women's Studies at Temple University. She is author of *Shadow over the Promised Land: Slavery, Race, and Violence in Melville's America* and *The First Woman in the Republic: A Cultural Biography of Lydia Maria Child*, and editor of *HOBOMOK and Other Writings on Indians* and *An Appeal in Favor of That Class of Americans Called Africans* by Lydia Maria Child.

Library of Congress Cataloging-in-Publication Data

Child, Lydia Maria Francis, 1802-1880.
A Lydia Maria Child reader / Carolyn L. Karcher, editor.
p. cm. — (New Americanists)
Includes bibliographical references.
ISBN 0-8223-1954-3 (cloth : alk. paper). — ISBN 0-8223-1949-7 (pbk. : alk. paper)
1. United States—Social conditions—Literary collections.
2. United States—Social conditions—1865–1918. 3. United States—Social conditions—To 1865. 4. Social problems—Literary collections. I. Karcher, Carolyn L., 1945– . II. Series.
PS1293.A6 1997
818'.309—dc20   96-35357
CIP